Lecture Notes in Computer Science   1616

Edited by G. Goos, J. Hartmanis and J. van Leeuwen

Springer

*Berlin
Heidelberg
New York
Barcelona
Hong Kong
London
Milan
Paris
Singapore
Tokyo*

Pierre Cointe (Ed.)

Meta-Level Architectures and Reflection

Second International Conference, Reflection'99
Saint-Malo, France, July 19-21, 1999
Proceedings

 Springer

Series Editors

Gerhard Goos, Karlsruhe University, Germany
Juris Hartmanis, Cornell University, NY, USA
Jan van Leeuwen, Utrecht University, The Netherlands

Volume Editor

Pierre Cointe
Ecole des Mines de Nantes, Computer Science Department
La Chantrerie, 4, rue Alfred Kastler, BP 20722
F-44307 Nantes Cedex 03, France
E-mail: Pierre.Cointe@emn.fr

Cataloging-in-Publication data applied for

Die Deutsche Bibliothek - CIP-Einheitsaufnahme

Meta level architectures and reflection : second international
conference, reflection '99, Saint-Malo, France, July 19 - 21, 1999 /
Pierre Cointe (ed.). - Berlin ; Heidelberg ; New York ; Barcelona ;
Hong Kong ; London ; Milan ; Paris ; Singapore ; Tokyo : Springer,
1999
   (Lecture notes in computer science ; Vol. 1616)
   ISBN 3-540-66280-4

CR Subject Classification (1998): D.2, D.3, F.3, D.1

ISSN 0302-9743
ISBN 3-540-66280-4 Springer-Verlag Berlin Heidelberg New York

© Springer-Verlag Berlin Heidelberg 1999
Printed in Germany

Typesetting: Camera-ready by author
SPIN: 10705212   06/3142 – 5 4 3 2 1 0   Printed on acid-free paper

Preface

This volume constitutes the proceedings of the second conference on Meta-Level Architectures and Reflection (Reflection'99), which will take place in Saint-Malo, France, from 19-21 July 1999.

Upon Reflection'96 held in San Francisco, several workshops organized in cooperation with OOPSLA, ECOOP and IJCAI, the IMSA'92 conference in Tokyo and the founding workshop in Alghero (1986), this year's conference intends to provide a new opportunity for researchers with a broad range of interests to discuss recent developments in the field. Our main goal is to address the issues arising in the definition and construction of reflective systems and to demonstrate their practical applications.

The Reflection'99 programme committee had the hard task of selecting 13 full papers (both research and experiential reports) and 6 short papers out of 44 submissions from all over the world. The selection of papers was carried out during a 1-day meeting at Xerox PARC. The only selection criteria were the quality and originality of the papers themselves. These papers, of both practical and more theoretical bent, cover a wide range of topics including programming languages, systems and applications, software engineering and foundations.
Apart from the presentation of the selected papers, the conference also welcomes John Stankovic, Jean-Bernard Stefani and Yasuhiko Yokote as three keynote speakers.

The success of such an international conference is due to the dedication of many people. I would like to thank the authors for submitting a sufficient number of papers, and the programme committee members and the additional referees for reviewing and selecting the papers contained herein. I would also like to thank Tina Silva and Christine Violeau for organizing the programme committee. Special appreciation goes to Jacques Malenfant, the conference chair, and to Mario Südholt, who was in charge of the electronic paper submissions.

The programme committee members also wish to thank their employers and sponsors for support of these conference activities. Finally, we would like to thank AITO and ACM Sigplan for having provided essential support in organizing Reflection'99.

Ultimately, the success of any conference is measured by the number of attendees who feel they spent their time well. So enjoy the conference and help us to disseminate the idea of open architectures in the software industry.

May 1999   P. Cointe
                                          Reflection'99 Programme Chair

Organization

Reflection'99 is organized by the Université de Bretagne Sud and École des Mines de Nantes under the auspices of AITO (Association Internationale pour les Technologies Objets).

Executive Committee

Conference Chair: Jacques Malenfant (U. de Bretagne Sud, F)
Programme Chair: Pierre Cointe (École des Mines de Nantes, F)
US Coordinator: Gregor Kiczales (Xerox PARC, USA)
Asian Coordinator: Satoschi Matsuoka (Tokyo Institute of Techology, J)

Programme Committee

Gordon Blair (Lancaster University, UK)
Gilad Bracha (Sun Microsystems, USA)
Vinny Cahill (Trinity College, IRL)
Shigeru Chiba (University of Tsukuba, J)
Pierre Cointe (EMNantes, F) Chair
Charles Consel (Irisa, F)
Jean-Charles Fabre (Laas, F)
Jacques Ferber (Lirm, F)
Dan Friedman (Indiana University, USA)
Lee Gasser (University of Illinois, USA)
Rachid Guerraoui (EPFL, CH)
Yutuka Ishikawa (Tsukuba ResearchLab, J)
Gregor Kiczales (Xerox PARC, USA)
John Lamping (Xerox PARC, USA)
Ole Lehrmann Madsen (Aarhus Uinversity, DK)
Jacques Malenfant (Université de Bretagne sud, F)
Satoshi Matsuoka (Tokyo Institute of Techonlogy, J)
José Meseguer (SRI International, USA)
Wolfgang Pree (University of Constance, D)
Jim des Rivières (OTI Inc., CDN)
John A. Stankovic (University of Virginia, USA)
Patrick Steyaert (MediaGeniX, B)
Robert J. Stroud (University of Newcastle, UK)
Carolyn Talcott (Stanford University, USA)
Yasuhiko Yokote (Sony Corporation, J)

Additional Referees

Jim Dowling	Steven E Ganz	Mayer Goldberg
Julia Lawall	Shinn-Der Lee	Eric Maarsden
Anurag Mendhekar	Gilles Muller	Christian Queinnec
Barry Redmond	Jonathan Rossie	Juan Carlos Ruiz-Garcia
Tilman Schaefer	Kris Van Marcke	Johan Vanwelkenhuysen.
Wilfried Verachtert		

Cooperating Institutions of Reflection'99

AITO (Association Internationale pour les Technologies Objets)
http://www.aito.org/

ACM SIGPLAN (Association for Computing Machinery, Special Interest Group in Programming Languages)
http://www.acm.org/sigplan/

Sponsoring Institutions

Conseil Régional de Bretagne
Université de Bretagne Sud
École des Mines de Nantes

Contents

Middleware/Multi Media

Work in Progress (Short Papers)

Invited Talk 3

Applications (Experience Papers)

Meta-Programming

Invited Talk 1
Reflection in Real Time System

John A. Stankovic
Department of Computer Science, University of Virginia
Charlottesville, VA 22903.
E-mail : stankovic@cs.virginia.ed

Reflection was introduced as a main principle in real-time systems in the Spring real-time kernel. Its use coincided with and complemented the notions of admission control and planning-based scheduling for real-time systems. Taken together, these three principles establish a new paradigm for real-time systems. Recently, admission control is being used for soft real-time systems such as distributed multimedia and distributed real-time databases. Once again, reflection can be used as a central organizing and fundamental principle of these system.

This talk first discusses how reflection is used in the more classical real-time systems using examples from the Spring kernel and agile manufacturing. In particular, the synergistic properties that emerge from combining reflection, admission control (for guarantees), and planning will be stressed. I will also discuss how reflection helps resolve a key real-time systems dilemma: the need for abstraction to deal with the complexity versus the need for very specific, low level details to deal with the real-time requirements.

The second part of the talk discusses the more recent use of these principles in global, multimedia real-time databases using examples from the BeeHive system being built at the University of Virginia. In this system, objects are enhance to contain significant amounts of reflective information and algorithms and protocols are developed to make use of this reflective information to improve the performance of the systems along real-time, fault tolerance, security, and quality of service for audio and video dimensions.

Professor John A. Stankovic is the BP America Professor and Chair of the Computer Science Department at the University of Virginia. He is a Fellow of the IEEE and a Fellow of the ACM. Professor Stankovic also serves on the Board of Directors of the Computer Research Association. Before joining the University of Virginia, Professor Stankovic taught at the University of Massachusetts. He has also held visiting positions in the Computer Science Department at Carnegie-Mellon University, at INRIA in France, and Scuola Superiore S. Anna in Pisa, Italy. He has served as the Chair of the IEEE Technical Committee on Real-Time Systems. Prof. Stankovic has also served as an IEEE Computer Society Distinguished Visitor, has given Distinguished Lectures at various Universities, and has been a Keynote Speaker at various conferences. His research interests are in distributed computing, real-time systems, operating systems, distributed multimedia database systems, and global virtual computing.

From *Dalang* to *Kava* - the Evolution of a Reflective Java Extension

Ian Welch and Robert Stroud

University of Newcastle-upon-Tyne, United Kingdom NE1 7RU
{I.S.Welch, R.J.Stroud}@ncl.ac.uk,
WWW home page:http://www.cs.ncl.ac.uk/people/
{I.S.Welch, R.J.Stroud}

Abstract. Current implementations of reflective Java extensions typically either require access to source code, or require a modified Java platform. This makes them unsuitable for applying reflection to Commercial-off-the-Shelf (COTS) systems. In order to address this we developed a prototype Java extension *Dalang* based on class wrapping that worked with compiled code, and was implemented using a standard Java platform. In this paper we evaluate the class wrapper approach, and discuss issues that relate to the transparent application of reflection to COTS systems. This has informed our design of a new version of *Dalang* called *Kava* that implements a metaobject protocol through the application of standard byte code transformations. *Kava* leverages the capabilities of byte code transformation toolkits whilst presenting a high-level abstraction for specifying behavioural changes to Java components.

1 Introduction

We are interested in the problems of applying non-functional requirements to Commercial Off-the-Shelf (COTS) software components. In an environment such as Java components are usually supplied in a compiled form without source code, and can be integrated into a system at runtime.

Metaobject protocols [20] offer a principled way of extending the behaviour of these components. Metaobjects can encapsulate the behavioural adaptations necessary to satisfy desirable non-functional requirements (also referred to as NFRs) such as fault tolerance or application level security [1][30][31] transparently at the metalevel. Ideally we want to apply these metaobjects to compiled code that executes on a standard Java platform.

We reviewed available implementations of reflective Java that could be used to implement these metaobject protocols and found that none of them met our requirements. They either relied upon customised Java platforms or required access to source code. Accordingly we developed a prototype reflective Java extension called *Dalang* based on the standard technique of using class wrappers to intercept method invocation. The advantage of *Dalang* was that it did not require access to source code and was implemented using a standard Java platform.

Our subsequent experiences with *Dalang*[1] have highlighted a number of problems with implementing reflection that arise from the approach of using class wrappers to implement reflection, and more generally with attempting to apply reflection transparently to existing COTS software built from components.

We have applied these lessons to the design of the successor to *Dalang* called *Kava*[2] which is based on wrapping not at the class level, but at the byte code level. *Kava* implements a runtime behavioural metaobject protocol through the application of standard byte code transformations at load time. Metalevel interceptions are implemented using standard byte code transformations, and behavioural adaptation is implemented using Java metaobject classes. Although neither byte code transformation or metaobject protocols are new, what is novel is the implementation of metaobject protocols using byte code transformation in order to provide a higher level view of component adaptation than current byte code transformation toolkits currently provide.

The rest of the paper is organised as follows. In section two we provide a review of different approaches to implementing reflection in Java. Section three gives an overview of the class wrapper approach to implementing reflection. Section four presents an evaluation of the class wrapper approach. Section five discusses some of the problems of applying reflection transparently to existing applications. In section six we discuss the advantages of using byte code transformation to unify class wrappers and wrapped objects. In section seven we outline our design for a new version of *Dalang* called *Kava* that addresses a number of the problems raised in the two previous sections. In section eight we discuss the application of *Kava*. Finally in section nine we present our conclusions.

A prototype implementation of *Dalang* has been completed and is available from *http://www.cs.ncl.ac.uk/people/i.s.welch/home.formal/dalang*. We are currently developing an implementation of *Kava*, for further information see the project page at *http://www.cs.ncl.ac.uk/people/i.s.welch/home.formal/kava*.

2 Review of Reflective Java Implementations

In this section we briefly review a number of reflective Java implementations and attempt to categorise them according to the point in the Java class lifecycle where metalevel interceptions (MLIs)[37] are added. Metalevel interceptions cause the switch during execution from the baselevel to the metalevel thereby bringing the base level object under control of the associated metaobject. Table 1 summarises the features of the different reflective Java implementations.

The Java class lifecycle is as follows. A Java class starts as source code that is compiled into byte code, it is then loaded by a class loader into the Java Virtual Machine (JVM) for execution, where the byte code is further compiled by a Just-in-time compiler into platform specific machine code for efficient execution.

All these implementations have drawbacks that make them unsuitable for use with compiled components or in a standard Java environment. Either they

---

[1] *Dalang* is the puppetmaster in Javanese *wayang kulit* or shadow-puppet plays.
[2] *Kava* is a traditional South Pacific beverage with calming properties.

Table 1. Comparison of Reflective Java Implementations

Point in Lifecycle	Reflective Java	Description	Capabilities	Restrictions
Source Code	Reflective Java [36]	Preprocessor.	Dynamic switching of metaobjects. Intercept method invocations.	Can't make a compiled class reflective, requires access to source code.
Compile Time	OpenJava [32]	Compile-time metaobject protocol.	Can intercept wide range of operations, and extends language syntax.	Requires access to source code.
Byte Code	Bean Extender [17]	Byte code preprocessor.	No need to have access to source code.	Restricted to Java Beans, requires offline preprocessing.
Runtime	MetaXa [14]	Reflective JVM.	Can intercept wide range of operations, Can be dynamically applied.	Custom JVM.
	Rjava [15]	Wrapper based reflection allowing dynamic binding.	Intercepts method invocations, and allows dynamic extension of classes.	Custom JVM - addition of new byte code.
	Guaran [28]	Reflective kernel supported by modified JVM.	Interception of message sends, state access and supports metaobject composition.	Custom JVM.
Just-in-time Compilation	OpenJIT [25]	Compile-time metaobject protocol for compilation to machine language.	Can take advantage of facilities present in the native platform. No need for access to source code. Dynamic adaptation.	Custom Just-in-time compiler.

require access to source code, or they are non-standard because they make use of a modified Java platform. In order to address these drawbacks we implemented a reflective extension called *Dalang* that required only access to compiled classes and use the standard Java platform. It was based upon standard class wrapper approach which we discuss in the next section.

3 Overview of Implementing Reflection Using Wrappers

In this section we give an overview of how class wrappers can be used to implement reflection in statically typed languages such as Java. We use *Dalang* as an example. For a detailed description of *Dalang* refer to [35].

3.1 The Basic Idea

The use of class wrappers or proxy classes in order to implement metalevel interception for method invocation is a common approach for adding reflection into a statically typed language such as C++[5] or Java [15][36]. This approach is similar to the Wrapper or Decorator pattern [13]. Figure 1 shows the collaboration diagram for the general case where a base level object has its method invocations intercepted and handled at a metalevel. Each role in the diagram is detailed below:

BaseObject. The class in this role has the behaviour of method invocations sent to it by a client adapted by the associated Wrapper MetaObject and any Concrete MetaObjects.

MetaObject. This abstract class takes the responsibility of defining the binding between a specific Wrapper MetaObject and the BaseObject, and implementing a general method for invoking methods of the BaseObject.

Wrapper MetaObject. This class extends the behaviour of each public method of the BaseObject class by redefining each method to invoke the respective method in the BaseObject class through a call to the invokeMethod method. Since each invocation is now handled by the invokeMethod method redefining this method will redefine the behaviour of each method invocation sent to the BaseObject.

Concrete MetaObject. There may be any number of Concrete MetaObject classes that are invoked by the Wrapper MetaObject in order to extend the behaviour of the BaseObject class.

The main differences between class wrapper implementations of reflection are the way that class wrappers are generated and how they are substituted for the base object class.

Dalang exploits the reflective hook [22] into the Java class loading mechanism provided by user-defined class loaders. User-defined class loaders can be created by subclassing java.lang.ClassLoader and implementing a custom loadClass() method. Classes are then loaded by the user-defined class loader either explicitly by application code invoking loadClass(), or by the

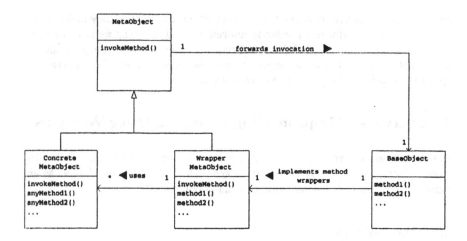

Fig. 1. Class collaboration diagram for class wrapper approach to implementing reflection.

JVM implicitly invoking `loadClass()` to load a class referenced by a class previously loaded by the user-defined class loader. *Dalang* uses a special reflective class loader (`dalang.ReflectiveClassloader`) that transforms classes as they are loaded into the JVM. At load time *Dalang* uses the Java Core Reflection API (JCR) in order to discover the public interface of the *Base Object*. It then generates source code for the `Wrapper MetaObject` which is dynamically compiled. The generated `Wrapper MetaObject` is then switched for the `BaseObject` through class renaming at the byte code level.

Figure 2 shows an overview of the *Dalang* architecture. In this figure the reflective class loader is acting as a bootstrapping class loader. This means that since it loads the root class of the application any class subsequently referred to will also be loaded by the reflective class loader. Therefore all classes are available to be transformed into reflective classes. Note that the metaconfiguration file controls which metaobject class binding to which base level class.

4 Evaluation of Class Wrapper Approach

In this section we evaluate and discuss implementation of reflection using the class wrapper approach. We focus on the following areas:

1. Wrappers
2. Inheritance
3. Security Considerations of applying Metaobjects
4. Class loaders

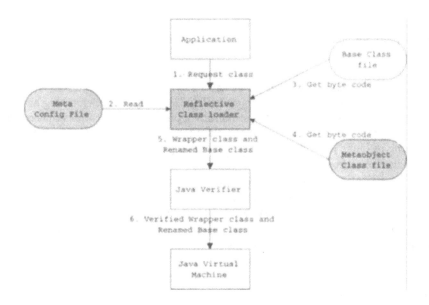

Fig. 2. Overview of Architecture. Shaded parts indicate *Dalang*. Non-shaded parts are the standard Java runtime system.

4.1 Wrappers

In a paper on using class wrappers for adapting independently developed components [16], Holzle makes the point that problems occur when the wrapper object and the object being wrapped are implemented separately as in this approach. He explains that such an approach to wrapping suffers from two major problems: the "self problem", and the encapsulation problem. The identification of these problems is not new but they have not previously been discussed in relation to the implementation of reflective systems. The "self problem" was first described by Lieberman [23]. Lieberman asserts that you cannot use inheritance based languages such as Java to implement delegation. The problem is with the rebinding of the self[3] variable that takes place when the method invocation is delegated. It is possible to work around this by passing the self variable as an additional argument in all method invocations and making all self invocations use this passed variable instead of the default. This requires that the classes follow a particular programming convention. However, since the classes being wrapped were constructed independently of their use with class wrappers it is unlikely that they would support such a convention unless we could transform the compiled classes' methods.

---

[3] In Java the *self* variable is represented by the *this* keyword.

Figure 3 illustrates the problem. In the left hand case where true delegation takes place all method invocations are intercepted by the wrapper for A whilst in the right hand case only the first method invocation is intercepted.

This is a problem for a reflective implementation because all invocations should be intercepted. Whether the semantics of invocation are redefined is being implemented at the metalevel. For example, a metaobject implementing access control might need to redefine the semantics of only those invocations that come from clients of the class not from the class itself whereas a metaobject implementing resource controls would need to intercept and control every invocation regardless of source.

The second problem, an encapsulation problem, is based on the fact that the wrapping implemented above is only a "logical" form of wrapping. The unwrapped class is normally only hidden through a change of name. If the new name is known then it can be used by a programmer and this would allow access to the unwrapped class and new instances of it to be constructed. Another encapsulation problem arises if a method in the new class returns a pointer to the wrapped class. Once a client receives this pointer it can bypass the wrapping by sending method invocations directly to the wrapped class, bypassing the new class that logically wraps it. In order to solve these two problems Holzle proposes removing the separate class that acts as the logical wrapper by unifying the wrapper and object at binary level. If there is no separation then self will refer to the wrapper and the object, and there is no way to break encapsulation. We will discuss how this approach relates to the implementation of reflection in Java in section 6.

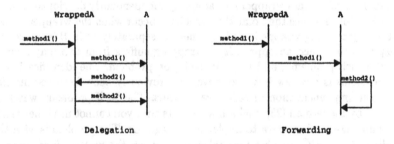

Fig. 3. Interaction diagrams illustrating what happens when a method invocation is sent to *WrapperA*. In the delegation scenario *WrapperA* receives *method1* invocation and invokes *method1* on *A*, *A* then invokes *method2* on itself which as *self* is still bound to *WrapperA* results in the invocation going to *WrapperA* where it is then delegated to *A*. In the forwarding scenario *WrapperA* receives *method1* and forwards the invocations to *A*. *A* then invokes *method2* and since *self* as rebound to *A* it is invoked on *A* directly bypassing *WrapperA*.

4.2 Inheritance

There are two different aspects of inheritance that cause us concern. The first relates to the type hierarchy imposed by the use of a class wrapper, and the second relates to inheritance of metaobject classes. We feel that such implications of inheritance are often neglected in implementations of reflective languages, with the notable exception of *CLOS* [20] and *SOM* [9]. We discuss each problem below. The first problem is that the class wrapper that we create to logically wrap the base class does not share the same type hierarchy as the baselevel class. Instead it extends the metalevel type hierarchy in order to inherit the metaobject implementation. In order that it can be used interchangeably with the baselevel class the interface of the baselevel class (including its superclasses) is replicated in the new class and the class must be tagged as implementing all the interfaces that the baselevel class implemented. Otherwise the new class wrapping the baselevel could not be downcast to any of the interfaces. However, any downcast to one of the supertypes of the baselevel class will fail as, although the interface is present, Java does not see that the class wrapper is a subtype. This could lead to problems with existing client code. Ideally the type hierarchy of the class wrapper should reflect the baselevel application level type hierarchy.

The second problem is the well known meta constraint problem [9]. If a class that is bound to a metaobject class is extended by another class and that class is bound to a different metaobject class then there should be some way of sensibly resolving the effect of both metaobject classes on the resultant class. In *Dalang* the methods inherited from the superclass are controlled by both metaobject classes, whilst those methods introduced by the extending class are only controlled by the later metaclass. In contrast, in SOM a new metaclass would be synthesised that solved the constraints on the two metaobject classes and this new metaclass would control the methods of the extended class. The *Dalang* result appears inconsistent as we would expect on a logical level that if metaobject classes are thought of as adjectives then extending a *red plane* to make a *jetplane* and then applying the adjective *fast* should result in *red* and *fast* being applied to every method of the *jetplane* not just the methods inherited from *plane*. Alternatively only the last applied metaobject class should control the behaviour of the methods of the extended class. An in-between situation seems unsatisfactory.

4.3 Security Considerations of Applying Metaobjects

How do we know that a base class is not bound to a malicious metaobject? This could occur through either the metaobject binding specification being changed, or the metaobject itself being substituted with a malicious version.

In the current *Dalang* security model we assume that both the metaobject classes and the binding specification represented by a metaconfiguration file are trusted. However, if the metaobject has been replaced or corrupted then this introduces a major vulnerability into the system as the malicious metaobject could completely redefine or interfere with the normal operation of the application object it is bound to.

Ideally the JDK1.2 security infrastructure for securing ordinary classes should be also used for metaobject classes. This supports the digital signing of classes using private keys and the checking of the signatures at loadtime by a Secure-ClassLoader. When a class is loaded it has its signature checked automatically and fine-grained controls are placed on its access to system resources. The ReflectiveClassLoader should extend the SecureClassLoader class and throw an exception if the class is not signed with the expected key.

Similarly, some form of protection must be implemented for the metaconfiguration file. Again a digital signature would be appropriate for the integrity check, and the structure of the file should include ownership and change information. If the metaconfiguration file fails its integrity check a runtime exception should be thrown. These two countermeasures will ensure that metaobjects and metaconfiguration file can be trusted (assuming that the Java platform, and *Dalang* implementation have not been corrupted - however, the *Dalang* implementation can also be secured using a SecureClassLoader).

4.4 Class loaders

Several authors [2][8][19] make use of a user-defined class loader to support their extensions to Java as this allows transparent interception and redefinition of class loading. The class loader is used to bootstrap the application which means that the class loader will load all classes referenced in the first class it loads. Therefore it can apply appropriate transformations to all classes. However, if another user-defined class loader is loaded then any class loaded by the new class loader will bypass the bootstrapping class loader[4]. In the case of *Dalang* this means that these classes cannot be made reflective.

This could be avoided if we changed the Java platform either by modifying the standard class loader or by changing the native code that instantiates a class. However, this would reduce the portability of *Dalang* and would not make sense if a change was required for every extension to Java. Arguably the JVM should provide some kind of facility for injecting before and after wrappers around the primordial classloader. As the result of class transformations are always verified by the JVM and don't bypass type checks then this should be a safe approach.

5 Transparency and Reflection

A number of authors, including ourselves, have argued that reflection can be used to transparently implement non-functional requirements (NFRs) such as security [8], fault tolerance [11], distribution [29], atomicity [31], and concurrency [33]. The idea is that components or classes developed independently can be modified

---

[4] There is a related problem with composing class loaders using the JDK1.2 delegation model but there are no current plans to fix it [3]

in a principled way in order to support new properties that are orthogonal to their functionality. The approach provides reusable implementations of NFRs. Our experiences with *Dalang* suggest that there are the following problems with a completely transparent application of reflection:

1. Recursive Reflection
2. Exceptions
3. Composability

The problems discussed in this section are not handled by the current *Dalang* metaobject protocol but have influenced the design of its successor *Kava*.

5.1 Recursive Reflection

In *Dalang* the reflective class loader loads all classes referenced by a reflective class. This means that if necessary these classes can be made reflective. Currently a referenced class will not be made reflective unless specifically bound to a metaobject class in the metaconfiguration file. However, what if the binding is not known ahead of time and the real requirement is that the binding between the initial class and metaclass be recursive in applicability? Thus if the initial reflective class references another class, that class should also be bound to the same metaclass. An example would be persistence, should all classes referenced by a root class be made persistent and a deep copy made when the class is stored? A counterexample might be Java-style serialisation, where it is not appropriate to make a deep copy and a shallow copy only is required. An example of this problem can be seen in the FRIENDS scheme proposal for tracing state changes for checkpointing using reflection [21]. Which changes of state should be tracked is application dependent - in some cases the object referenced by the object being checkpointed should also be checkpointed but in other cases it is a volatile object that should not be checkpointed. There must be some form of application control over recursive reflection at the metalevel either through some policy file such as metaconfiguration file or a metalevel program.

5.2 Exception Handling

Exceptions are an integral part of most modern object-oriented languages. However, it seems to us that they are rarely explicitly addressed by designers of reflective languages with the exceptions of the *Lore* and *Smalltalk* languages [10] where exceptions are implemented reflectively. Recently, our colleagues at York University [4] have argued that using reflection to implement exceptions allows adaptive runtime redefinition of exceptional behaviour. We argue that the behaviour of exception handling should not be redefinable at runtime as it makes validation intractable but nonetheless there is a need to deal with exceptions in the metalevel. Exceptions should be viewed as another possible outcome of a method call. If the behaviour of method calls is reflected upon, then in the same way as the return value of a method call is reified and available to the metalevel, so the raising of an exception by a method should be as well. This need finds expression in two ways. The first is what control and representation is appropriate for exceptions generated at the application level in the metalevel? The second is how do we deal sensibly with exceptions that occur at the metalevel that were never considered when the reflected component was constructed?

Firstly, although we do not want to redefine exception handling there are situations where being able to detect the raising of an exception at the application level, and to switch to the metalevel, is desirable. Consider the intention of taking components and distributing them through the use of reflection. Co-operating components may need to participate in a distributed exception handling routine. This requires the interception of exception raising and switching to the metalevel to propagate the exception to associated distributed components before resuming.

Secondly, when using reflection to add a non-functional characteristic new types of failure become possible that couldn't occur previously. For example, if a component is bound to a client metaobject that allows distributed invocation then a failure such as the loss of a method invocation will generate an exception at the metalevel that the component at the application level was never designed to raise. One approach to this problem would be to modify the application level component on the fly to support the new exception types that can be raised in the metalevel. However, this simply leads to propagation of the problem as any client of the component would also need to be able to handle the new exceptions. Perhaps the only sensible approach is to mask the exception and raise a runtime exception and hope that the existing application handles runtime exceptions in a sensible way. This is not an ideal solution but appears to be a necessary consequence of trying to reuse transparently an independently developed metalayer in a transparent way with an independently developed application layer.

5.3 Composability

In the same way that independently developed metaobject classes are combined with independently developed application components, independently developed metaobject classes may be combined with each other. With wrapper based approaches each object has one statically bound metaobject wrapper. However, this does not mean that only one behaviour can be enforced on an object. This is because chaining can be used to compose metaobjects together at the same metalevel to create a complex meta architecture (similar to the approach described in Mulet et al. [27], or Oliva [28]). We believe that using chaining to achieve composition of metaobjects is more appropriate than using reflection recursively to build a tower of metaobjects (the approach adopted by *FRIENDS* [11]). The advantage of using chaining is that each metaobject may introspect on the baselevel object whereas with a metaobject tower only the base metaobject may introspect on the baselevel object. In addition, with chaining the cost of interception and reification of method calls is only incurred once as we do not have to transform the metaobject classes involved in the tower. The main problem with the tower approach is that it confuses the meta interception mechanism with the metalevel structuring mechanism, which we feel should be kept separate. However, the tower approach is appropriate only when going to a new level of abstraction such as in the *ABCL/R* [24] approach.

6 Byte Code Transformation

In this section we introduce a new metaobject protocol based on byte code transformation that we are implementing as the *Kava* system. As stated in section four the separation of wrapper and wrapped class introduces problems for method call interception, encapsulation and typing. The solution as proposed by Holzle [16] is to unify the wrapper and wrapped class at the binary level. In order to achieve this at load time in Java we need to transform classes at the byte code level using byte code transformation techniques. In this section we discuss the general approach, introduce the two types of standard transformations used to implement MLIs, provide an example of the application of a standard transformation, highlight which aspects of the Java object model can be changed and examine some tricky issues.

6.1 General Approach

Byte code transformation has become an established technique for extending Java both syntactically and behaviourally. For example it has been used to support parametric types [2] and add resource consumption controls to classes [8]. Generic frameworks for transforming byte code such as *JOIE* [7] and *Binary Component Adaptation* [19] have been developed to make coding byte code transformations easier. However, as pointed out by the authors of *JOIE*, most of these frameworks lack a high-level abstraction for describing the behavioural adaptations. This makes coding adaptations difficult as it requires a detailed knowledge of byte code instructions and of the structure of class files. Binary Component Adaptation does support a form of a higher-level abstraction in that it has the concept of *deltaClasses* that describe structural changes to a class file in terms of methods for renaming methods, mixin type methods, etc. However, the purpose of the framework is to support software evolution rather than behavioural adaptation. This means that the focus is on adding, renaming or removing methods and manipulating the type hierarchy in order to adapt ill-fitting components to work together rather than describing behavioural adaptation.

Our contribution is to provide a high-level abstraction for adaptation of component behaviour that specifies the change to behaviour in terms of the Java object model and is implemented using byte code transformation. We exploit the *JOIE* framework to simplify the implementation of this metaobject protocol. The framework frees us from dealing with technical details such as maintaining relative addressing when new byte codes are inserted into a method, or determining the number of arguments a method supports before it has been instantiated as part of a class.

As byte code instructions and the structure of the class file preserve most of the semantics of the source code we can use byte code transformation to implement MLIs for a wide range of aspects of the Java Object model such as caller and receiver method invocation, state access, object finalisation, object initialisation and some aspects of exception handling. Like compile-time reflection we reflect upon the structure of the code in order to implement reflection. However, we work at a level much closer to the Java machine than most compile-time approaches which deal with the higher-level language. Although this means we cannot extend the syntax of the higher-level language it does mean that we can implement some kinds of reflection more easily than in a traditional compile-time MOP. For example, in the application of *OpenC++ version 2* to adding fault tolerance in the form of checkpointing *CORBA* applications [21] data flow analysis is performed on the source code to determine when the state of the object is updated. With *Kava* no such analysis would be necessary; all that would be required is to intercept the update of state of an object by reflecting upon the behaviour of the update field byte code instruction. When an update was done a flag could be set indicating that the current state should be checkpointed.

By transforming the class itself we also address the problems introduced by the separation of baseclass and class wrapper. Instead, standard transformations of byte code are used to wrap individual methods and even bytecode instructions. These micro-wrappers will switch control from the baselevel to metalevel when the methods or byte code instructions are executed at runtime. As with *Dalang* the metalevel will be programmed using standard Java classes. The metalevel will allow the customisation of the Java object model at runtime. The scope of the customisation will be determined by which methods and byte code instructions are wrapped at load time, but the exact nature of the customisation will be adjustable at runtime.

Figure 4 shows the class collaboration diagram for *Kava*. Note that there is no separate class wrapper. This is because wrappers have been applied *within* the base level class. Whenever the `BaseObject` has a method invoked or it performs state access the appropriate method of the bound `Concrete MetaObject` is invoked before and after the operation. For example, when a method invocation is received the associated `Concrete MetaObject`'s method `beforeReceiveMethod()` is called with parameters representing the source, arguments, and method. Subsequently, when the invocation takes place the method `afterReceiveMethod()` is called with a parameter representing the result of the invocation. The `Concrete MetaObject` can cooperate with any number of other `Concrete MetaObjects` to implement the overall behavioural adaptation. All `Concrete MetaObjects` extend the abstract `MetaObject` which defines the default functionality for a `MetaObject`.

6.2 Standard Transformations

There are two types of standard transformation applied by *Kava* to add MLIs to classes.

The first standard transformation makes use of the structure of a class file to identify blocks of byte code representing class methods, initialisation methods, and finalisation methods and then adds wrappers around them. This allows the method invocations sent to the base level to be intercepted and control handed to a metalayer. This is similar to the type of MLIs implemented in *Dalang*. In order to make the metaobject aware of self directed invocations all self invocations in the base level class are rewritten to pass an extra parameter indicating the source of the invocation.

The second standard transformation is applied to byte code instructions such as those dealing with invocation, access to state and wraps these individual instructions. Here fine-grained wrappers are applied around individual instructions. This allows the interception and switch to the metalayer when the class itself makes an invocation or accesses state. These types of interceptions would not be possible if byte code transformation had not been implemented.

In order to safely insert new byte code instructions into a class, some difficult technical issues must be solved. For example, how to handle the effects of inserting instructions on relative branches on other branch instructions and the exception table. Fortunately, we can rely upon the *JOIE* framework to take care of these low-level issues.

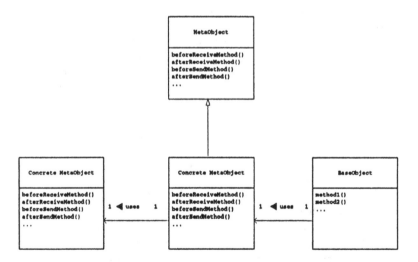

Fig. 4. Class collaboration diagram for *Kava.* Shows the relationship between classes.

6.3 Example

To provide a flavour of this approach we provide an example of the wrapping of access to a field of a base level class. Due to space constraints we present this at a high level using source code instead of byte code. Consider the following field access:

```
helloWorld = "Hello " + name;
```

At the byte code level this is rewritten to:

```
Value fieldValue = Value.newValue("Hello " + name);
meta.beforePutField("helloWorld", fieldValue);
try
{
  helloWorld = (String)fieldValue.getObject();
}
catch (MetaSuppressUpdateException e)
{
}
meta.afterPutField("helloWorld", fieldValue);
```

In this example the first line of code marshalls the value that the field is going to be updated with and then, the beforePutField method of the associated metaobject is invoked with parameters representing the name of the field ("helloWorld"), and the marshalled value.

At the metalevel the value may be modified in order to adjust the final value that is stored in the field. Alternatively the update of field could be suppressed by the throwing of a MetaSuppressUpdateException. This is caught at the base level and causes the update of the base level field not to take place.

The last line calls the afterPutField method of the associated metaobject with the same parameters as the initial call to the metalevel.

6.4 Reflective Aspects of Java Object Model

In this section we highlight the aspects of the Java object model that can be reflected upon by *Kava*.

As object-oriented operations such as object creation, state access and invocation are represented directly as byte codes it is relatively straightforward to identify them within class methods. Once identified the *JOIE* framework can be used to determine the arguments for these operations which in turn allows us to dynamically construct bytecode that marshalls their values. We can then place *before* and *after* calls around the individual operations that can manipulate the arguments and even suppress the operations. We term this *caller side reflection* because it allows us to capture behaviour such as the calling of another method by a class.

As the structure of the class file is known we can easily identify blocks of byte code representing method calls, object initialisation and finalisation methods. Again we can use the *JOIE* framework to determine the arguments for these methods and dynamically generate marshalling code. We can then insert calls to the metaobject's *before* method appropriate to the type of method being instrumented at the beginning of the method's byte code instruction block. Then we insert calls to the metaobject's appropriate *after* method before every return instruction in the method. This allows us to intercept received invocations and represents what we term *receiver side reflection*.

Note that with both *caller side reflection* and *receiver side reflection* we add MLIs into the class' byte code. Each MLI added using byte code transformation switches control from the baselevel to the metalevel which is implemented using metaobject. This means that at runtime we can perform dynamic reflection to adjust the runtime behaviour of the baselevel class by either changing the implementation of the before and after methods of the metaobject associated with the baselevel object or by changing the binding to another metaobject. With such a facility we can easily support per-class instance metaobjects or per-instance metaobjects.

Once a class has been instantiated in the JVM no more MLIs can be added to it. This means that if a MLI has not been added at load time it cannot be exploited at any later stage. For example, if a MLI is not added to a method of a class at load time that method cannot be brought under the control of a metaobject at a later stage. One way of addressing this problem would be to add all possible MLIs by default. However, this would have considerable performance considerations. Ideally we would wish to see some form of lazy reflection taking place with MLIs being switchable on and off once the class is executing in the JVM. There is some lazy evaluation that takes place in a standard JVM where byte codes are replaced at runtime if required and perhaps this could be exploited to provide a form of lazy reflection where a class can be made reflective only as required. Another approach would be to use an *OpenJIT* to add interceptions as required when the Java byte code is compiled to native machine code.

7 Current Work

We are currently implementing the *Kava* system. *Kava* provides the portability benefits of a class wrapper approach without many of the problems. It also provides the opportunity to address some of the more general problems faced by reflective languages. *Kava* will have the following characteristics:

Encapsulation. The MLIs will be non-bypassable as class wrapper and base class are no longer separate. This is important for supporting applications such as security.

Self Problem. It will be possible to specify at the metalayer whether self rebinds or not as this is dependent on the metalevel functionality being provided.

Reflective Capabilities. Unification will allow both reification and reflection upon the receipt of method invocations and also the sending of method invocations. In addition, reification and reflection upon construction and finalisation will be possible. State access will also be under control of the metalayer. There will be some representation of exception handling at the metalayer.

Transparency and Security. We envisage a security model such that a trusted *Kava* kernel exists on the target machine and secure class loaders are used to download application code, metaobject code and the metaobject binding configuration. The use of a secure class loader is necessary so that we can trust the identity of the code and check for tampering. Alternatively where the client machine is totally untrusted we propose that *Kava* be applied before delivery of code to the client either in a web server or through a proxy server.

Inheritance. Due to unification the wrapper and wrapped class will have identical superclasses and the same implementations of application methods. This means that the class wrapper will be indistinguishable from the baselevel wrapped class. Also a subclass of the class wrapper will also inherit any reflective behaviour.

Metaclass constraints. Given that we can construct classes on-the-fly at runtime it will be possible to implement metaclass constraint solving [9].

Recursive Reflection. Like the self problem, whether reflection is applied recursively should be under the control of the metalayer, because the correct behaviour depends on the functionality provided by the metalayer. The recursive class loader should support a metaobject protocol that allows the metalevel programmer to customise its behaviour and devise sophisticated policies for handling recursive reflection.

Metaclass Combination. *Kava* will provide default metaobject classes that support metaclass combination and dynamic rebinding of metaobjects at runtime. We will provide metaobject classes that can be subclassed from that support co-operation between metaobjects, and also the ability to dynamically switch the binding between base and metalevel.

Exception Handling. Although we cannot redefine how the JVM handles the throwing of exceptions we can provide the ability to detect the throwing of exceptions and switch to the metalayer. This should provide the ability to support features such as distributed exception handling.

Visibility of the Metalevel. One aspect that should be configurable by the metalevel programmer is the visibility of the metalevel. Certainly in some cases we want to be able to send method invocations to the metalevel in order to tweak an aspect of the behaviour of the metaobject. For example, we suggest that timeout values of a metaobject that handles distributed communication could be controlled by sending messages to the metalevel.

8   Example Applications of *Kava*

Kava has wide application potential and should prove well suited to the customising the behaviour of COTS applications that are built from dynamically loaded components. As it provides a high-level abstraction for implementing bytecode transformation it could be used to implement behavioural adaptations that have already been implemented through byte code transformation e.g. enforcing resource controls on applications, instrumentation of applications, visualisation support etc. The advantage of using *Kava* would be that these adaptations could be combined as required since they have been built using a common abstraction.

9 Conclusions

Ideally, a reflective extension for Java that is intended to be used to adapt the runtime behaviour of COTS components should not require access to source code, or modifications to the Java platform. Unfortunately, the reflective extensions that we have reviewed do not meet these requirements.

Using class wrappers appears a promising way to implement a reflective extension that does meet the requirements. However, as our experience with *Dalang* has shown there are serious drawbacks to implementing reflection using this general approach. Aside from these problems there are other general issues that must be addressed when attempting to apply reflection transparently to COTS software. Some of the problems identified and discussed were problems associated with inheritance, encapsulation, exception handling etc.

Having identified these problems we discussed how we plan to address a number of these issues by applying reflection to bytecode transformation techniques in a new version of *Dalang* called *Kava*. Although neither reflection or byte code transformation are new concepts, what is new is the implementation of metaobject protocols using byte code transformation in order to provide a high-level abstraction for controlling component adaptation.

We are currently working on the implementation of *Kava*, and intend to use it to implement a reflective security metalayer.

10 Acknowledgements

We would like to thank DERA for their financial support for this work, Brian Randell for helping review an initial version of this paper, and Jim Whitman for his reviewing of the final version of the paper.

References

[1] Benantar M., Blakley B., and Nadain A. J. : Approach to Object Security in Distributed SOM. IBM Systems Journal, Vol35, No.2, (1996).

[2] Agesen, O., Freund S., and Mitchell J. C.: Adding Type Parameterization. In Proceedings of OOPSLA'97, Atlanta,Georgia (1997).

[3] Bracha, Gilad : personal communication (1999).

[4] Burns A., Mitchell S., and Wellings A. J. : Mopping up Exceptions. In ECOOP98 Workshop Reader : Workshop on Reflective Object-Oriented Programming and Systems (1998).

[5] Chiba S and Masuda T. : Designing an Extensible Distributed Language with a Meta-Level Architecture. In proceedings of ECOOP93 (1993).

[6] Chiba S. : A Metaobject Protocol for C++. In proceedings of ECOOP95 (1995).

[7] Cohen, Geoff A., and Chase, Jeffery S. : Automatic Program Transformation with JOIE. Proceedings of USENIX Annual Technical Symposium (1998).

[8] Czaijkowski, Grzegorz and von Eicken, Thorsten. JRes: A Resource Accounting Interface for Java. Proceedings of OOPSLA'98 (1998).

[9] Danforth, S. H. and Forman, I. R. : Reflections on Metaclass Programming in SOM. In proceedings of OOPLSA'94(1994).

[10] Dony, Christophe : Exception Handling and Object Oriented Programming: towards a synthesis. Proceedings ofECOOP/OOPSLA'90. Ottawa, Canada (1990).

[11] Fabre, J.-C. and Perennou, T. : FRIENDS: A Flexible Architecture for Implementing Fault Tolerant and Secure Distributed Applications. Proceedings of the Second European Dependable Computing Conference (EDCC-2) (1996).

[12] Fabre, J.-C. and Nicomette, V. and Perennou, T., Stroud, R. J. and Wu, Z.: Implementing Fault-Tolerant Applications using Reflective Object-Oriented Programming. Proceedings 25th International Symposium on Fault-Tolerant Computing(FTCS-25), (1995).

[13] Gamma E., Helm R., Johnson R., and Vlissides J. : Design Patterns: Elements of Reusable Object-Oriented Software. Reading, Mass.: Addison-Wesley, (1995).

[14] Golm, M. : Design and Implementation of a Meta Architecture for Java. MSc Thesis (1997). University of Erlangen.

[15] Guimares, Jos de Oliveira : Reflection for Statically Typed Languages. Proceedings of ECOOP98 (1998).

[16] Holzle, U. : Integrating Independently-Developed Components in Object-Oriented Languages. Proceedings of ECOOP'93(1993).

[17] IBM. Bean Extender Documentation, version 2.0 (1997).

[18] JavaSoft, Sun Microsystems, Inc. : Reflection, 1997. JDK 1.1 documentation, available athttp://java.sun.com/products/jdk/1.1/docs/guide/reflection.

[19] Keller, R. and Holzle, U. : Binary Component Adaptation. Proceedings of ECOOP'98 (1998).

[20] Kiczales G., des Rivieres J. : The Art of the Metaobject Protocol. MIT Press (1991).

[21] Killijian Marc-Olivier, Fabre Jean-Charles, Ruiz-Garcia Juan-Carlos, and Chiba Shigeru: A Metaobject Protocol for Fault-Tolerant CORBA Applications. Proceedings of SRDS'98 (1998).

[22] Liang, Sheng and Bracha, Gilad : Dynamic Class Loading in the Java(tm) Virtual Machine. Proceedings of OOPSLA'98(1998).

[23] Lieberman, Henry : Using Prototypical Objects to Implement Shared Behaviour in Object-Oriented Systems. Proceedings of OOPSLA'86 (1986).

[24] Masuhara H., Matsuoka S., Watanabe T. and Yonezawa A. : Object-Oriented Concurrent Reflective Languages can be Implemented Efficiently. In proceedings of OOPSLA'92 (1992).

[25] Matsuoka S., Ogawa H., Shimura K., Kimura, Y., and Takagi H. : OpenJIT - A Reflective Java JIT Compiler. Proceedings of Workshop on Reflective Programming in C++ and Java, UTCCP Report 98-4, Center for Computational Physics, University of Tsukuba, Japan ISSN 1344-3135, (1998).

[26] McAffer, J. : Meta-Level Programming with CodA. In proceedings of ECOOP95 (1995).

[27] Mulet, P. and Malenfant, J. and Cointe, P. : Towards a Methodology for Explicit Composition of MetaObjects. Proceedings of OOPSLA'95 (1995).

[28] Oliva, Alexandre; Buzato, Luiz Eduardo; Garcia, Islene Calciolari : The Reflective Architecture of Guaran. Available from: http://www.dcc.unicamp.br/ oliva.

[29] Stroud, Robert : Transparency and Reflection in Distributed Systems. Operating Systems Review 27(2): 99-103 (1993)

[30] Stroud, R. J. and Z. Wu : Using Metaobject Protocols to Satisfy Non-Functional Requirements. Chapter 3 from "Advances in Object-Oriented Metalevel Architectures and Reflection" (1996), ed. Chris Zimmermann. Published by CRC Press.

[31] Stroud, R.J. and Wu, Z. : Using Metaobject Protocols to Implement Atomic Data Types, Proceedings of ECOOP'95(LNCS-925), Aarhus, Denmark, (1995).

[32] Tatsubori, Michiaki and Chiba, Shigeru : Programming Support of Design Patterns with Compile-time Reflection. Proceedings of Workshop on Reflective Programming in C++ and Java, UTCCP Report 98-4, Center for Computational Physics, University of Tsukuba, Japan ISSN 1344-3135, (1998).

[33] Van Oeyen Johan, Bijnens Stijn, Joosen Wouter, Robben Bert, Matthijs Frank and Verbaeten Pierre : A Flexible Object Support System as a Runtime for Concurrent Object-Oriented Languages. Chapter 13 from "Advances in Object-Oriented Metalevel Architectures and Reflection" (1996), ed. Chris Zimmermann. Published by CRC Press.

[34] Welch, Ian and Stroud Robert : Adaptation of Connectors in Software Architectures. ECOOP'98 Workshop on Component-Oriented Programming. Extended abstract published in workshop reader, and full paper published by Turku Centre for Computer Science, (1998).

[35] Welch, Ian and Stroud, Robert : Dalang - A Reflective Extension for Java. Computing Science Technical Report CS-TR-672, University of Newcastle upon Tyne, (1999).

[36] Wu, Z. and Schwiderski, S. : Reflective Java - Making Java Even More Flexible. FTP: Architecture Projects Management Limited (apm@ansa.co.uk), Cambridge, UK (1997).

[37] Zimmerman, Chris : Metalevels, MOPs and What all the Fuzz is All about. Chapter 1 from "Advances in Object-Oriented Metalevel Architectures and Reflection" (1996), ed. Chris Zimmermann. Published by CRC Press.

Jumping to the Meta Level
Behavioral Reflection Can Be Fast and Flexible

Michael Golm, Jürgen Kleinöder

University of Erlangen-Nürnberg
Dept. of Computer Science 4 (Operating Systems)
Martensstr. 1, D-91058 Erlangen, Germany
{golm, kleinoeder}@informatik.uni-erlangen.de

Abstract. Fully reflective systems have the notion of a control transfer from base-level code to meta-level code in order to change the behavior of the base-level system. There exist various opinions on how the programming model of a meta architecture has to look like. A common necessity of all models and systems is the need to intercept messages and operations, such as the creation of objects. We analyze the trade-offs of various message interception mechanisms for Java. We show their impact on the meta-level programming model and performance. We demonstrate that it is beneficial to integrate the interception mechanism with the virtual machine and the just-in-time compiler.

1 Introduction

An important aspect that determines the applicability and performance of a meta architecture is the way the connection between the base-level code and the meta-level code is established and how control and information flows between the two levels.

The modification of the control flow of base-level programs - called *behavioral reflection* - is a very important part of a fully reflective architecture. Most often the meta-level code is hooked into the message passing mechanism. The process of modifying the message passing mechanism is called *reification of message passing*. The importance of this kind of reflection for "real-live problems" can be observed by looking at the huge amount of design patterns whose sole purpose is the interception of messages. The most obvious examples are the proxy and adapter patterns [10].

Although we focus our attention on Java systems, we also consider systems that are based on languages, such as Smalltalk and C++, provided that the features we are interested in are not language-dependent.

This paper is structured as follows. In Section 2 and 3 we evaluate techniques for message interception. In the remaining sections of the paper we describe a technique that requires modifications of the Java Virtual Machine (JVM). Therefore we describe the relevant structures and mechanisms of the JVM in section 4. Section 5 discusses special problems of information transfer between base and meta level. Section 6 describes the changes to the JVM that where necessary to support reflection in our own reflective Java system - *metaXa*. Section 7 describes experiments that we performed to measure the overhead of behavioral reflection when a JIT compiler is used.

2 Implementation of behavioral reflection

There exist several systems with fairly different approaches to reifying message passing. We evaluate message interception techniques, that are used in these systems, according to the criteria *cost*, *functionality*, and *transparency*.

2.1 Costs

The cost for method reification must be paid as an overhead for a certain mechanism or as overhead for the whole system. The cost is paid somewhere between the time the program is developed and the time the mechanism is used. We take a closer look at the following costs:

Virtual method call. The invocation of a (virtual) method is a very frequently executed operation that determines the performance of the whole system. The cost of such a method call in a reflective system should be the same as in a non-reflective system.

Reflective method call. The cost of a reflective method call will naturally be higher than that of a normal method call. However, it should not be too high and it should scale with the complexity of the meta-level interaction. Short and fast meta-level operations should only produce a small call overhead, while complicated operations, that require a lot of information about the base level, could create a larger overhead.

Installation. Installation costs are paid when a method is made reflective. This cost is paid at compile time, load time, or run time.

Memory. Reflective systems consume additional memory for additional classes, an enlarged class structure, enlarged objects, etc.

2.2 Functionality

The implementation technique for the meta-level jump also affects the functionality of the whole meta architecture. We will examine which functionality each of the implementation techniques is able to deliver, according to the following questions:
- Can behavioral reflection be used for single objects or only for object groups, such as all instances of a class?
- What context information is available at the meta-level method? Is it possible to obtain parameters of the intercepted call? Is it possible to obtain information about local variables of the call site?
- Is it possible to build libraries of reusable metaobjects?

2.3 Transparency

As base-level code and meta-level code should be developed and maintained independently from each other, it is essential that the actions of the meta level are transparent to the base-level program. Programmers should not be forced to follow certain coding rules to exploit the services of the meta level. Forcing the programmer to follow certain coding rules would impede resuse of class libraries and applications - one of the most compelling reasons for extending an *existing* systems. If we extend an existing language or runtime system we should take care to guarantee the downward compatibility of the system.

A change in the behavior of a program should be actuated by the meta-level programmer and should not be a side effect of the implementation of the reflective mechanism.

When we consider transparency in the Java environment we must ensure that:

- the identity of objects is preserved (otherwise the locking mechanism would be broken and data inconsistencies can result),
- inheritance relations between classes are not visibly changed (such a change can become visible if the instanceof operator or an invocation of a superclass method or constructor differ from their normal behavior)

3 Implementation techniques

3.1 The preprocessor approach

With the availability of JavaCC [23] and a Java grammar for this compiler generator it seems to be easy to build Java preprocessors. However, we encountered several difficulties while building a preprocessor that inserts code at the begin and end of a method (reification at the callee site) and at each place where a method is called (caller site reification) [2]. While the caller site reification required only an additional try-finally block enclosing the whole method, insertion of code at the caller site was more difficult. If the method has arguments and an expression is passed as argument, this expression has to be evaluated first. This requires introducing new local variables to which the results of these expressions are bound. This must be done confoming to the Java evaluation order.

The preprocessor approach has the disadvantage that the preprocessor must be changed when the base level language is changed. A system that only operates at the bytecode or virtual-machine level must only be modified if the JVM specification is changed. In the past, the Java language was changed more frequently than the JVM specification.

OpenC++ [4] and OpenJava [5] are examples of preprocessors that insert interceptor methods in the base class.

Preprocessor based systems need full information about the used classes at compile time and can not handle dynamic class loading. This can only be done by paying the installation cost at runtime, as done in the classloader and proxy approach.

3.2 The classloader approach

Generating stubs at compile time means that the stub generator has no information about which stubs are really needed, because it is not known which classes are loaded during a program run. To cope with this problem we can move the stub generation from compile time to load time.

The Java system makes the class loading mechanism available to application programs. This reification of class loading is used by systems like JRes [8] and Dalang [25] to modify classes when they are loaded. The original class is renamed and a new class is generated that has the name of the loaded class but contains only stub code to invoke the metaobject. The rest of the program that uses the original class now gets the created class.

By its very nature a classloader approach can only be used for class-based reflection.

Szyperski [24] describes problems that appear when the wrapped object invokes methods at its self reference. The two presented choices are to invoke the method at the wrapper object or at the wrapped object. In our opinion an invocation at the self reference is only a special case of an incoming/outgoing message. So it would be natural not to bypass the wrapper but invoke these methods also at the wrapper object.

3.3 The proxy approach

To overcome the restriction of being class-based, one needs to modify the object code at the time the object is created or even later in the object's life. Therefore the proxy class must be created and compiled at run time. A separate compiler process must be created. This means that there is a high installation cost that has to be paid at runtime.

Identity transparency in the proxy approach means that the proxy and the original object are indistinguishable. This is only ensured if the proxy is the only object that has a reference the original object.

Inheritance transparency can not be accomplished with the proxy approach, because the proxy must be a subclass of the original class [13] . Being a subclass of the wrapped object has the consequence, that all fields of the original object are present in the proxy thus duplicating the memory cost. These problems can only be avoided, if the original object is exclusively used via an interface [22]. Then the proxy implements the same interface as the original class.

The proxy approach is also used in reflective systems that are based on Smalltalk [11], [19]. Smalltalk has a very weak type system which makes it easily possible to replace an object with a proxy. The object and the proxy need not even provide the same interface. The proxy object only defines the "doesNotUnderstand" method, which is called by the Smalltalk runtime if the called method is not implemented by the receiver. Smalltalk systems implement the method invocation mechanism in a way that adds only little overhead when using the "doesNotUnderstand" method.

3.4 The VM approach

Being able to extend the JVM provides complete functionality while preserving transparency.

There are two places where a method call can be intercepted: at the caller or at the callee. At first sight this seems to be no difference at all. But when considering virtual methods one immediately sees the difference. If we want to intercept all methods that are invoked at a specific object X of class C, we have to intercept the method at the callee. Otherwise we are forced to modify every caller site that invokes a method at class C or its superclasses. On the other side, if we are interested in the invocations that are performed by a specific object we have to modify the caller site.

When extending a JVM one has several alternatives to implement the interception mechanism:

New bytecode. All interesting bytecodes (invokevirtual and invokespecial) are replaced by reifying pedants (e.g. invokevirtual_reflective). This is a clean way to create reflective objects but requires an extension of the bytecode set. Replacing the original bytecode by a new one has only a small installation cost. This new bytecode must be understood by the interpreter and the JIT compiler. Additionally, if the system allows the structural reification of a method's bytecodes the new bytecode should not become visible, because this bytecode is only an implementation detail of the message interception mechanism.

Extended bytecode semantics. The interpretation process of interesting bytecodes is extended. Guaraná [21] uses this approach. Creating additional cost for each virtual method invocation degrades the performance of the whole system. Using the kaffee JIT compiler, Oliva et al. [21] measured the invokevirtual overhead on different Pentium and Sparc processors .The overhead they measured on the Pentium Pro (158%) conforms with our measurement on the Pentium 2 (see Section 7.2 and 7.3).

Code injection. Method bytecodes of C.m() are replaced by a stub code which jumps to the meta space. This approach is compatible to JIT compilation. Because normal Java bytecode is inserted, the code can be compiled and optimized by a normal JIT compiler.

Code modification is a powerful technique, that can be used in a variety of ways.

- *Kind of injected code*: The usual way is to execute a virtual method, but we can imagine a static method or just code fragments. Static methods and code fragments can be inlined in the base-level code.
- *Granularity and Location*: Aspect Oriented Programming [14] is such a powerful approach because it provides very fine-graned code injection. This, however, requires to write a complex injection mechanism - called weaver-that can not be generally reused. Furthermore the combination of different aspects, i.e. different code fragments, leads to complex interferences between the injected code sequences.

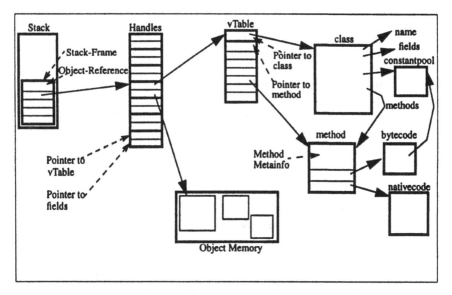

Fig. 1 Classes, Methods, and References in a JVM

Most meta architectures allow the injection of code only at distinct injection points, such as method calls. This makes the job of code injection a lot more easier.

- *Kind of information for the injected code*: This depends on the location of the injected code. Before a method call, the method parameters and local variables of the caller could be interesting; before a new operation, the class of the object is interesting.

4 Java VM implementations

To understand the modifications of the virtual machine that are necessary to enable reification of message passing, one needs a overall understanding of the data structures and mechanisms used inside a JVM. While the JVM specification [16] does not enforce a specific implementation we will base our discussion on the JVM structure outlined in [26]. There exist many JVM implementations that differ from this structure in several aspects [20], [6], [7].

Fig. 1 sketches the relationship between the stack, references, objects, classes, and methods. Local variables are stored in a stack frame. If the local variable has a reference type it contains a pointer to a handle. This handle contains a pointer to the object data and to the virtual method table (vTable). The vTable contains a pointer to the object's class and a list of pointers to the object's methods.

When a virtual method is invoked, the callee reference and all method arguments are pushed on the stack. Then the invokevirtual bytecode is executed. The invokevirtual opcode has three arguments: a class name, a method name and a method signature that are all looked up in the constantpool of the class. The constantpool entry must be resolved to a pointer to a class and an index into the vTable of this class. The method is then looked up using the vTable of the receiver object.

5 Passing information to the meta level

The cost of the meta-level jump itself is proportional to the information that is passed to the meta level. Different metaobjects have different requirements on the kind of information and the way this information is passed. In the following we assume that meta-level code is represented by a virtual method.

Meta interaction is cheapest if the meta level only needs a trigger, just informing the metaobject about the method call but not passing any information to the metaobject.

A bit more expensive is passing control to a meta-level method that has the same signature as the intercepted base-level call [12]. This interception mechanism has the advantage that it is not necessary to copy arguments.

An interaction that is more useful and is commonly used by many meta-level programs in metaXa is the invocation of a generic meta-level method. All arguments of the base-level call are copied into a generic container and this container is passed to the metaobject. The metaobject can then inspect or modify the arguments or pass them through to the original base-level method.

Some sophisticated metaobjects also need information about the broader context where a method was called. Especially the call frame information is needed in addition to the arguments. This information is also packed into a generic container and passed to the metaobject.

While the simple passing strategies are appropriate for situations where the interaction with the meta level has to be fast, some metaobjects need more complex strategies to fulfill their tasks. Thus, we obviously need a mechanism to configure the kind of interaction. Such a configuration can be regarded as a meta-meta level. This meta-meta level is concerned with the kind of code that is provided by the meta level and how this code is injected into the base-level computation. It is also concerned with the way information is passed to the meta level and the kind of this information. The JIT compiler that is described in Section 7 can be considered as such a meta-meta level.

6 How it is done in metaXa

In this section we describe the modifications to the virtual machine necessary to build a system that allows reification of message passing. The modifications allow a level of *transparency* and *functionality* that can not be achieved with the other approaches. In Section 7 we explain how the *cost* can be minimized by using a JIT compiler.

6.1 Shadow classes

Class-based meta architectures associate one metaobject with one base-level class. The reference to the metaobject can be stored in the class structure. Instance-based meta architectures can associate a metaobject with a specific base-level object. The metaobject reference must be stored in an object-specific location. One could store it together with the object fields or in the object handle. Storing it in the handle has the advantage to be reference-specific. Another interesting idea is to generate the slot only when needed, as in MetaBeta with dynamic slots [3]. We have not investigated yet if this mechanism can be implemented efficiently in a JVM. Storing the metaobject reference in the handle means an additional memory consumption in the handle space of 50%. This also applies for VMs where references point directly to the object, without going through a handle. In such an architecture the size of each object must be increased by one word to store the metaobject link.

In metaXa we use a different mechanism to associate the meta object with the base-level object. When a metaobject is attached to an object, a *shadow class* is created and the class link of the object is redirected to this shadow class. The shadow class contains a reference to the associated meta object.

A metaobject can be used to control a number of base-level objects of the same class in a similar manner. It is not necessary to create a shadow class for every object. Shadow classes are thus installed in two steps. In the first step, a shadow class is created. In the second step, the shadow class is installed as the class of the object. Once a shadow class is created, it can be used for several objects.

A shadow class C' is an exact copy of class C with the following properties:

- C and C' are undistinguishable at the base level
- C' is identical to C except for modifications done by a meta-level program
- Static fields and methods are shared between C and C'.

The base-level system can not differentiate between a class and its shadow classes. This makes the shadowing transparent to the base system. Fig. 2 shows, how the object-class relation is modified when a shadow class is created. Objects A and B are instances of class C. A shadow class C' of C is created and installed as class of object B. Base-level applications can not differentiate between the type of A and B, because the type link points to the same class. However, A and B may behave differently. Several problems had to be solved to ensure the transparency of this modification.

Class data consistency. The consistency between C and C' must be maintained. All class-related non-constant data must be shared between C and C', because shadow classes are targeted at changing object-related, not class-related properties. Our virtual machine solves this problem by sharing class data (static fields and methods) between shadow classes and the original class.

Class identity. Whenever the virtual machine compares classes, it uses the original class pointed to by the *type* link (Fig. 2). This class is used for all type checks, for example

- checking assignment compatibility

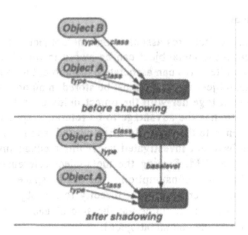

Fig. 2 The creation of a shadow class

- checking if a reference can be cast to another class or interface (checkcast opcode)
- protection checks

Class objects. In Java, classes are first-class objects. Testing the class objects of C and C' for identity must yield true. In the metaXa virtual machine every class structure contains a pointer to the Java object that represents this class. These objects are different for C and C', because the class objects must contain a link back to the class structure. Thus, when comparing objects of type class, the virtual machine actually compares the type links.

Because classes are first class objects it is possible to use them as mutual exclusion lock. This happens when the monitorenter/monitorexit bytecodes are executed or a synchronized static method of the class is called. We stated above that shadowing must be transparent to the base level. Therefore the locks of C and C' must be identical. So, metaXa uses the class object of the class structure pointed to by the type link for locking.

Garbage Collection. Shadow classes must be garbage collected if they are no longer used, i.e. when the metaobject is detached. The garbage collector follows the *baselevel* link (Fig. 2) to mark classes in the tower of shadow classes (tower of metaobjects). Shadowed superclasses are marked as usual following the superclass link in the shadow class.

Code consistency. Some thread may execute in a base-level object of class C when shadowing and modification of the shadow takes place. The system then guarantees that the old code is kept and used as long as the method is executing. If the method returns and is called the next time, the new code is used. This guarantee can be given, because during execution of a method all necessary information, such as the current constantpool or a pointer to the method structure, are kept on the Java stack as part of the execution environment.

Memory consumption. A shadow class C' is a shallow copy of C. Only method blocks are deep copied. A shallow class has a size of 80 bytes. A method has a size of 52 bytes. An entry in the methodtable is a pointer to a method and has a size of 4 bytes. Hence, the cost of shadowing is a memory consumption of about 400 bytes for a shadow class with five methods. The bytecodes of a method are shared with the original class until new bytecodes are installed for this method.

Inheritance. During shadow class creation a shadow of the superclass is created recursively. When the object refers to its superclass with a call to super the shadowed superclass is used. All shadowed classes in the inheritance path use the same metaobject. Fig. 3 shows what happens if a metaobject is attached to a class

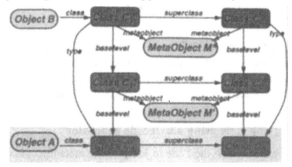

Fig. 3 Metaobjects and inheritance

that has several superclasses. The shaded area marks the original configuration. Object A and B are of class C_1 which is a subclass of C_0. When the metaobject M' is attached to object B, a shadow class C_1' of C_1 is created. Later, the metaobject M" is attached to B. This causes the creation of shadow class C_1".

Original behavior. In addition to the metaobject link a shadow class in metaXa also needs a link baselevel to the original class. It is used when resorting to the original behavior of the class. In all non-shadow classes the baselevel link is null. The base-level link is used to delegate work to the original class of the object.

6.2   Attaching metaobjects to references

In metaXa it is also possible to associate a meta object with a reference to an object. If a metaobject is attached to a reference, method invocations via this *reference* must be intercepted. A reference is a pointer, which is stored on the stack or in objects and points to a handle (Fig. 1). If the reference is copied - because it is passed as a method parameter or written into an object - only the pointer to the handle is copied, still pointing to the same handle as before. To make a reference behave differently, the handle is copied and the class pointer in the handle is changed to point to a shadow class. After copying the handle it is no longer sufficient to compare handles when checking the identity of objects. Instead, the data pointers of the handles are compared. This requires that data pointers are unique, i.e. that every object has at least a size of one byte. The metaXa object store guarantees this. Fig. 4 shows the handle-class relation after a shadow class

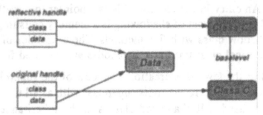

Fig. 4 Attaching to a reference

was installed at a reference. A reference is represented by a handle, which contains a link to the object's data and a link to the object's type (class or method-table). If a shadow class must be attached to the handle (original handle), the handle is cloned (reflective handle) and the class link is set to the shadow class.

6.3   Creating jump code using a bytecode generator

We will now explain how the code to jump to the metaobject is created using a bytecode generator. The problems when directly generating native code are similar. When inserting code into an existing method the jump targets and the exception tables must be corrected. This is done automatically by our very flexible bytecode generator. This generator first translates a method's bytecodes to objects. One can then replace and modify these bytecode objects, and insert new ones. This flexible generator allowed us to easily implement different stub generators but it also leads to high installation costs.

We describe three different mechanisms for which stubs are created:
- a method is sent by the base-level object (*outcall*),
- an object is created by the base-level object (*new*),
- a method is received by the base-level object (*incall*).

outcall. An outgoing messages is caused by the invokevirtual opcode. The other opcodes that invoke methods are invokespecial to call constructors or superclass methods and invokestatic to call class methods. They are not interesting for our current considerations. The invokevirtual opcode has three arguments: a class name, a method name, and a method signature, that are all looked up in the constantpool of the class. The code generator creates the following code and replaces the invokevirtual opcode by a code sequence that performs the following operations:

(1) Create an object that contains information about the method call. This object contains the class name, method name, and signature of the called method. It also contains the arguments of the method call.

(2) At the metaobject invoke a method that is responsible to handle this interception.

new. The new bytecode is replaced by a stub that looks similar to the outcall stub.

incall. While it is rather obvious how the interception code has to look like in the outcall and new interceptions, there are alternatives for the interception of incoming invocations.

- One solution would be to insert calls to the meta level at the beginning of the method. But then it is not possible to avoid the execution of the original method other than throwing an exception. Furthermore, the return from the method can not be controlled by simply replacing the return bytecode. Instead, all exceptions have to be caught by inserting a new entry into the exception table.
- A simpler way of executing code before and after the original method is to completely replace the original method by the stub code that invokes the metaobject. The metaobject then is free to call the original method. This call executes the bytecodes of the original method by doing a lookup in the original class.

7 Integration into the JIT compiler

A central part of metaXa is the bytecode rewriting facility that was explained in the previous section. After we have implemented a just-in-time compiler (JIT) for the metaXa VM [15] it seems more appropriate to directly create instrumented native code instead of instrumented bytecode. Such an integration has several advantages:

- The installation cost is contained in and dominated by the JIT compilation cost, which must be paid even if no meta interaction is required.
- The JIT can inline a call to a meta object, which makes the interaction with meta objects very fast.

Another project that also uses a JIT for meta-level programming is OpenJIT [18]. OpenJIT is a JIT compiler that is designed to be configurable and extensible by metaprograms.

There are other systems that use partial evaluation to remove the overhead of the tower of meta objects, e.g. ABCL/R3 [17]. Because we use the OpenC++ [4] model of method interception, rather than the more general architecture of a meta-circular interpreter, we are faced with a different set of problems.

7.1 Inlining of meta-level methods

The overhead of a meta interaction should grow with the amount of work that has to be done at the meta level. This means especially that simple meta-level operations, such as updating a method invocation counter, should execute with only a minimal overhead. On the other side, it should be possible to perform more complex operations, such as forwarding the method call to a remote machine. In this case a user accepts a larger overhead, because the cost of the meta-level jump is not relevant compared to the cost of the meta-level operation, e.g. a network communication.

The reduce the meta-jump overhead in case of a small meta-level method we use method inlining. Inlining methods results in speedup, because method-call overhead is eliminated and inter-method optimizations can be applied. These optimizations could perform a better register allocation and elimination of unnecessary null-reference tests. A method can be inlined as long as the code that has to be executed is known at compile time. Therefore, one can generally inline only non-virtual (private, static, or final) methods. Fortunately, it is also possible to inline a method call, if the method receiver is known at (JIT-) compile time. When inlining meta-level methods, the metaobject usually already exists and is known to the JIT compiler.

The principle of inlining is very simple. The code of the method call (e.g. invokestatic) is replaced by the method code. The stack frame of the inlined method must be merged into the stack frame of the caller method. The following example illustrates this merging. If a method test() contains the method call a = addInt(a, 2), this call is compiled to

```
aload 0
iload 1
iconst_2
invokenonvirtual addInt(II)I
istore 1
```

The method int addInt(int x, int y) { return x+y; } is compiled to

```
iload 1
iload 2
iadd
ret
```

The merged stack frame has the following layout:

merged stack	stack of test()	stack of addInt()
0	local 0	
1	local 1	
2	operand 0	local 0
3	operand 1	local 1
4	operand 2	local 2
5		operand 0
6		operand 1

The created code would look as follows (bytecodes have stack positions as operands):

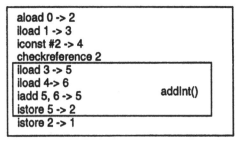

Several optimizations can now be applied to the code. Provided that the method test() only contains the addInt() method call, the code can be transformed using copy propagation and dead code elimination [1] to

```
checkreference 0
iadd 1, #2 -> 5
istore 5 -> 2
istore 5 -> 1
```

Virtual methods can be inlined, if no subclasses override the method. If the JVM loads a subclass that overrides the method, the inlining must be undone. Such code modifications must be done very carefully, because a different thread could be executing this code.

7.2 Experiments

We measured the execution times for the following operations:

ccall and c++call. To have an idea how good or bad the performance of the meta-level interaction actually is, we measured the time for a function call in C and for a virtual method call in C++ (using the gcc compiler with -O2 optimization).

vcall. Invocation of a virtual method through a method table, doing the required null reference check before the method lookup. The called method immediately returns. x instructions are executed on the code path. x memory locations are read.

intercept. A call to a virtual method of a different object is inserted before the original method invocation. The object to be called is known at compile time. This allows inlining of the object reference into the code. It is necessary to register this reference with the garbage collector and unregister the reference if the compiled method is garbage collected. The injected method is called *meta method* in the following. The meta method has the same signature as the original method. The meta method returns immediately.

counter. A very common application for meta methods is counting of base-level method invocations. The meta method increments the counter variable. If this counter reaches a certain value (e.g. 5000), a different method (e.g. action()) is called to perform a meta-level computation, e.g. to make a strategic decision. The bytecode for this meta method is shown below:

```
Method void count()
  0 aload_0
  1 getfield #8 <Field int counter>
  4 sipush 5000
  7 if_icmple 14
 10 aload_0
 11 invokevirtual #7 <Method void action()>
 14 return
```

We measured the times for the following operations:
- not taken: The threshold is never reached and the action method is never called.
- taken1: The threshold is set to 1. This means that the action method is invoked before each invocation of the base-level method.
- taken10 and taken100: The threshold is set to 10 (100). The action method is invoked before every 10th (100th) call of the base-level method.

argobj. The method arguments are copied into a parameter container. This container is then passed to the meta method. The elements of the container are very special because they must contain reference types as well as primitive types, which is not possible when a Java array is used as the container. We rejected the solution to use wrapper classes for the primitive types (the Reflection API does it this way), because this means that additional objects must be created for the primitive parameters. Instead we use a container whose element types can be primitive types and reference types at the same time. As this is not allowed by the Java type system, we have to use native methods to access the container elements. Furthermore, the garbage collector must be changed to cope with this kind of container objects. The test performs the following operations:
- the parameters are read from the stack and written into the container object
- a virtual method is called with this object as parameter
- this method uses a native method to invoke the original method with the original parameters

This test is an optimized version of the metaXa method interception.

inlinedobj. We now instruct the JIT to inline the call. Because the meta method passes the call through to the original method, the result of the inlining should be the original method call.

A requirement for inlining is, that the implementation, that is used to execute the method call, is known at JIT-compile time. Therefore the meta method must either be static, final, or private or the class of the metaobject is known.

The JIT has some further difficulties inlining the method, because the parameter container is accessed using native calls and native methods cannot generally be inlined. So we either have to avoid native methods or enable the JIT to inline them. In the discussion of the argobj test we explained why avoiding the native methods is not possible. In order to inline the native method, the JIT now queries the VM for a native code fragment that can be used as the inlined method. In most cases the VM will not provide such a code segment. For the native methods that access the parameter container such a native code equivalent is provided.

To eliminate the object allocation the JIT must deduce that the parameter container object is only used in this method so that the object can be created on the stack. Our JIT does not do such clever reasoning but it can be implemented using the algorithms described in [9]. In our current implementation we give the JIT a hint that the object is used only locally. Using its copy propagator the JIT can now remove the unnecessary parameter passing through the parameter container.

7.3 Performance results

We were interested in the performance of each of the discussed code injection techniques when using a native code compiler. We did not measure the installation cost (which would include the compilation time) because our JIT compiler is not optimized yet. It operates rather slowly and generates unoptimized code. We used a 350 MHz Pentium 2 with 128 MB main memory and 512 kByte L2 cache. The operating system is Linux 2.0.34. The system was idle.

We first measured the time for an empty loop of 1,000,000 iterations. Then we inserted the operation, that we were interested in, into the loop body and measured again. The difference between the empty loop and the loop that executes the operation is the time needed for 1,000,000 operations. Times for an empty loop of 1,000,000 iterations in C and compiled Java code are 15 milliseconds.

Operation	execution time (in nanoseconds)
ccall	17
c++call	35
vcall	65
vcallchecked	164
intercept	190
counter/not taken	145
counter/taken1	223
counter/taken10	195
counter/taken100	151
argobj	14000
inlinedobj	250

7.4 Analysis

The argobj operation is so extremely slow compared to the other operations, because it is the only operation that jumps into the JVM, executes JVM code, and allocates a new object. All other operations execute only very few JIT-generated machine instructions. However, a general pupose interception mechanism must allow the interceptor to access the method parameters in a uniform way and independent from the method signature. So there seems to be no alternative to using an parameter container. To improve the performance of the interception the compiler must try to eliminate the object allocation overhead, which is possible - as the inlinedobj test shows. We expect that the performance of this operation can be further improved when our JIT generates code that is more optimized.

8 Summary

We have studied several approaches to implement reification of message passing. It became apparent that only a system that integrates the meta architecture with the JVM and the JIT compiler delivers the necessary performance, functionality, and transparency to make behavioral reflection usable. The method interception mechanism can aggressively be optimized by certain techniques, such as inlining of methods and inlining of object allocations. While the JIT compiler can automatically perform such micro-level optimizations it is necessary to have a meta-meta level that controls the configuration of the meta level and selects the appropriate mechanism for the interaction between base level and meta level. For optimal performance this meta-meta level should be part of the just-in-time compiler, or should at least be able to influence the code generation process.

9 References

1. V. A. Aho, R. Sethi, D. J. Ullman: *Compilers: Principles, Techniques, and Tools* , Addison-Wesley 1985

2. M. Bickel: *Realisierung eines Prototyps für die Koordinierungs-Metaarchitektur SMArT in Java. Studienarbeit IMMD 4*, March 1999

3. S. Brandt, R. W. Schmidt: The Design of a Metalevel Architecture for the BETA Language. In *Advances in Object-Oriented Metalevel Architectures and Reflection* , CRC Press, Boca Raton, Florida 1996, pp. 153-179

4. S. Chiba, T. Masuda: Designing an Extensible Distributed Language with a Meta-Level Architecture. In *Proceedings of the European Conference on Object-Oriented Programming '93*, Lecture Notes in Computer Science 707, Springer-Verlag 1993, pp. 482–501

5. S. Chiba, M. Tatsubori: Yet Another java.lang.Class. In *ECOOP'98 Workshop on Reflective Object-Oriented Programming and Systems*, 1998

6. T. Cramer: Compiling Java Just-in-time. In *IEEE Micro* , May 1997

7. R. Crelier: *Interview about the Borland JBuilder JIT Compiler.*

8. G. Czajkowski, T. von Eicken: JRes: A Resource Accounting Interface for Java. In *Proceedings of the Conference on Object-Oriented Programming Systems, Languages, and Applications '98*, ACM Press 1998, pp. 21-35

9. J. Dolby, A. A. Chien: An Evaluation of Object Inline Allocation Techniques. In *Proceedings of the Conference on Object-Oriented Programming Systems, Languages, and Applications '98*, ACM Press 1998, pp. 1-20

10. E. Gamma, R. Helm, Johnson R., J. Vlissides: *Design Patterns: Elements of Reusable Object-Oriented Software* , Addison-Wesley, Reading, MA 1994

11. B. Garbinato, R. Guerraoui, K. Mazouni: Implementation of the GARF Replicated Objects Platform. In *Distributed Systems Engineering Journal* , March 1995

12. J. d. O. Guimaraes: Reflection for Statically Typed Languages. In *Proceedings of the European Conference on Object-Oriented Programming '98*, 1998, pp. 440-461

13. U. Hölzle: Integrating Independently-Developed Components in Object-Oriented Languages. In *Proceedings of the European Conference on Object-Oriented Programming '93*, Lecture Notes in Computer Science 512, July 1993

14. G. Kiczales, J. Lamping, C. Mendhekar, C. Maeda, C. Lopes, J.-M. Loingtier, J. Irwin: Aspect-Oriented Programming. In *Proceedings of the European Conference on Object-Oriented Programming '97*, Lecture Notes in Computer Science 1357, Springer-Verlag, Berlin, Heidelberg, New York, Tokyo 1997

15. H. Kopp: *Design und Implementierung eines maschinenunabhängigen Just-in-time-Compilers für Java. Diplomarbeit (Masters Thesis) IMMD 4*, Sep. 1998

16. T. Lindholm, F. Yellin: *The Java Virtual Machine Specification*. Addison Wesley 1996

17. H. Masuhara, A. Yonezawa: Design and Partial Evaluation of Meta-objects for a Concurrent Reflective Language. In *Proceedings of the European Conference on Object-Oriented Programming '98*, 1998, pp. 418-439

18. S. Matsuoka: OpenJIT - A Reflective Java JIT Compiler. In *OOPSLA '98 Workshop on Reflective Programming in C++ and Java*, UTCCP Report, Center for Computational Physics, University of Tsukuba, Tsukuba, Oct. 1998

19. J. McAffer: Engineering the meta-level. In *Proceedings of Reflection '96*, 1996

20. Microsoft: *Microsoft Web Page. http://www.microsoft.com/java/sdk/20/vm/ Jit_Compiler.htm* 1998

21. A. Oliva, L. E. Buzato: The Design and Implementation of Guaraná. In *COOTS '99*, 1999

22. T. Riechmann, F. J. Hauck, J. Kleinöder: Transitiver Schutz in Java durch Sicherheitsmetaobjekte. In *JIT - Java Informations-Tage 1998*, Nov. 1998

23. SunTest: *JavaCC - A Java Parser Generator,* 1997

24. Z. Szyperski: *Component Software - Beyound Object-Oriented Programming*, ACM Press 1998

25. I. Welch, R. Stroud: Dalang - A Reflective Java Extension. In *OOPSLA '98 Workshop on Reflective Programming in C++ and Java*, UTCCP Report, Center for Computational Physics, University of Tsukuba, Tsukuba, Oct. 1998

26. F. Yellin, T. Lindholm: Java Internals. In *JavaOne '97* 1997

The Oberon-2 Reflection Model and Its Application

Hanspeter Mössenböck, Christoph Steindl

Johannes Kepler University Linz
Institute for Practical Computer Science
Altenbergerstraße 69, A-4040 Linz
{moessenboeck,steindl}@ssw.uni-linz.ac.at

Abstract. We describe the reflection model of Oberon-2, a language in the tradition of Pascal and Modula-2. It provides run-time information about the structure of variables, types and procedures and allows the programmer to manipulate the values of variables. The special aspect of the Oberon-2 reflection model is that metainformation is not obtained via metaclasses. It is rather organized as structured sequences of elements stored on a disk, which can be enumerated by an iterator. This results in a simple and uniform access mechanism and keeps the memory overhead to a minimum. We also show a number of challenging applications that have been implemented with this reflection model.

1. Introduction

Metaprogramming, i.e. the observation and manipulation of running programs, has become an important instrument in the toolbox of today's software engineer. Pioneered by languages such as Lisp and Smalltalk, metaprogramming is now part of many modern programming languages such as Java [ArG96], CLOS [Att89] or Beta [LMN93]. If metaprogramming is not only applied to *other* programs, but also to the program that uses it, it is called *reflection*. A reflective program can obtain and manipulate information about itself.

In this paper we describe the reflection model of Oberon-2 [MöW91], a language in the tradition of Pascal and Modula-2. Oberon-2 is a hybrid object-oriented language. It provides classes with single inheritance that are declared within modules. Oberon [WiG89] is not only a programming language but also a run time environment, providing garbage collection, dynamic module loading, and so-called *commands*, which are procedures that can be invoked interactively from the user interface, thus providing multiple entry points into a system.

Commands and dynamic loading already constitute a kind of metaprogramming. True reflection, however, was added to Oberon-2 by the work of Josef Templ [Tem94]. We adapted and refined his ideas into a reflection model that allows us to answer questions like:

- What are the components of a record type T declared in a module M?
- What procedures are currently active? What are the names, types and values of their local variables?
- Does the caller of the currently executing procedure have a variable named x, and if so, what is its type and value?

Questions like these allow us to do a number of interesting things, which would not be possible with an ordinary programming language. We will show examples of such applications in Section 3 of this paper.

The rest of this paper is organized as follows. In Section 2 we describe the reflection model of Oberon-2 and its general usage. Section 3 shows a number of useful applications that we implemented on top of this reflection model, i.e. a generic output function, an object inspector, an embedded SQL facility, and an exception handling mechanism. In Section 4 we discuss security and performance issues. Section 5 summarizes the results.

2. The Oberon-2 Reflection Model

The reflection model of a programming language is characterized by two aspects:

- What metainformation is available about programs at run time?
- How can this information be accessed in order to observe and manipulate programs?

We will describe these two aspects for Oberon-2. The special thing about our approach is that all metainformation resides on disk instead rather than in main memory and that it is accessed by so-called *riders*, which iterate over the structure and parse it as required. This technique is space-efficient since no metaobjects have to be kept in memory. All access to the metainformation follows the *Iterator* pattern [GHJV95], which guarantees simple and uniform access.

Our reflection mechanism is encapsulated in a library module called *Ref* [StM96]. It defines a *Rider* type for iterating over the metainformation as well as procedures for placing riders on various kinds of metainformation sequences.

In the following sections we will first describe the structure of the metainformation and then explain how to navigate through it.

2.1 Metainformation

As a simple abstraction, a program can be organized as a set of hierarchical sequences. For example, a program consists of a sequence of modules. Every module is a sequence of variables, types and procedures. A procedure, in turn, is a sequence of variables, and so on. Fig. 1 shows an example of such a decomposition.

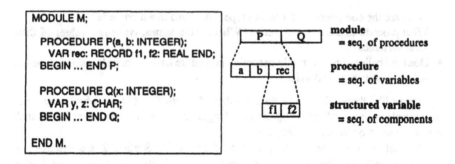

Fig. 1. Metainformation of module *M* in form of hierarchical sequences

Information about such program sequences is called *metainformation* and can be described by the following grammar in EBNF notation (curly brackets denote zero or more repetitions):

```
ProgramStruct = {Module}.
Module        = {Variable} {RecordType} {Procedure}.
RecordType    = {Variable} {Procedure}.
Procedure     = {Variable}.
Variable      = SimpleVar | RecordVar | ArrayVar.
RecordVar     = {Variable}.
ArrayVar      = {Variable}.

ProgramData   = GlobalVars | LocalVars | DynamicVars.
GlobalVars    = {Variable}.
LocalVars     = {Frame}.
Frame         = {Variable}.
DynamicVars   = {HeapObject}.
HeapObject    = {Variable}.
```

The information about the structure of a module is created by the compiler when the module is compiled. It is appended to the module's object file so that it is always copied and moved together with the object file. This avoids inconsistencies between a module and its metainformation.

The structural information is also used to interpret the program's data, which would otherwise be just a sequence of bytes without any interpretation.

2.2 Navigation

The metainformation is accessed by so-called *riders*, which are iterators that allow us to traverse a sequence of elements and to zoom into structured elements. The class *Rider* declared in module *Ref* looks as follows:

```
TYPE
  Rider = RECORD
    name: ARRAY 32 OF CHAR;
    mode: SHORTINT;   (*Var, Type, Proc, …, End*)
    form: SHORTINT;   (*Int, Char, Bool, Record, …*)
    . . .
    PROCEDURE (VAR r: Rider) Next;
    PROCEDURE (VAR r: Rider) Zoom (VAR r1: Rider);
    . . .
  END;
```

When a rider *r* is placed on an element of a sequence, *r.name* holds the name of this element; *r.mode* tells if the element is a variable, a type, a procedure, etc.; *r.form* encodes the type of the element (structured types are denoted by a special code; their components can be inspected by zooming into the element; see below).

Iterating. The following example shows how to traverse the global variables of a module *M* and print their names:

```
Ref.OpenVars("M", r);
WHILE r.mode # Ref.End DO
  Out.String(r.name);
  r.Next
END
```

A rider *r* is opened on the global variables of module *M*. While it is not moved beyond the last variable (*r.mode = Ref.End*) the name of the current variable is printed and the rider is advanced to the next variable by the operation *r.Next*.

Zooming. If a rider is placed on a structured element, it is possible to zoom into this element and to iterate over its components. For example, to access the local variables of the current procedure's caller we can zoom into the second frame on the activation stack, using the following statements:

```
Ref.OpenStack(r);
r.Next;
r.Zoom(r1)
```

Ref.OpenStack(r) opens a rider *r* on the frame of the currently active procedure. *r.Next* moves it to the caller's frame. *r.Zoom(r1)* zooms into that frame and sets a new rider *r1* to the first local variable in that frame. The variables of this frame can then be traversed as above using *r1*.

Placing a rider. Riders can be opened on various kinds of metainformation sequences as shown by the following table:

OpenVars(module, r)	sets *r* to the first global variable of the specified module
OpenStack(r)	sets *r* to the topmost stack frame
OpenPtr(p, r)	sets *r* to the first component of the object pointed to by *p*
OpenProcs(module, r)	sets *r* to the first procedure of the specified module
OpenTypes(module, r)	sets *r* to the first record type of the specified module

If a rider is opened on data (using *OpenVars*, *OpenStack* or *OpenPtr*), and if it is positioned on a non-structured variable, the value of this variable can be read or written using operations such as *r.ReadInt(n)* or *r.WriteInt(n)*. In this case the rider serves as a link between the data (e.g. a stack frame) and the metainformation that is used to interpret that data (Fig.2).

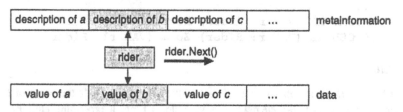

Fig. 2. A rider as a link between data and its metainformation

If a rider is opened on structural information (using *OpenProcs* or *OpenTypes*), there is no data to be read or written. Such riders can only be used to explore the structure of procedures and types.

Details about the *Rider* class, its fields and its operations are described in [StM96]. The difference between our implementation and the one in [Tem94] is mainly that we use a single rider type to iterate over all kinds of metainformation while [Tem94] uses special rider types for variables, procedures, types, etc.

2.3 Examples

The following examples should give you a rough impression of what you can do with the module *Ref* and its riders.

Assume that we want to print the names of all currently active procedures together with the names of their local variables. The following code fragment does the job:

```
VAR r, r1: Ref.Rider;
...
Ref.OpenStack(r);        (*r is on the most recent frame*)
WHILE r.mode # Ref.End DO
  Out.String(r.mod);   (*name of this frame's module*)
  Out.String(".");
  Out.String(r.name); (*name of this frame's proc.*)
  Out.Ln;
  r.Zoom(r1);             (*r1 is on first var. of frame*)
  WHILE r1.mode # Ref.End DO
    Out.String(r1.name); Out.Ln;
    r1.Next
  END;
  r.Next                 (*move to the caller's frame*)
END
```

Of course we could do any processing with the traversed variables or procedures. For example, we could print their values and types (this was actually used for the implementation of the Oberon debugger). We could also look for all occurrences of a certain value within the variable sequence and report them to a client.

The next example looks for a global record variable named *varName* declared in a module named *modName*. Note that the names of the variable and the module need not be statically known. They could have been obtained at run time.

```
VAR
  r: Ref.Rider;
  varName, modName: ARRAY 32 OF CHAR;
. . .
Ref.OpenVars(modName, r);
WHILE (r.mode # Ref.End) & (r.name # varName) DO
  r.Next
END;
IF r.form = Ref.Record THEN (*found*)
  . . .
END
```

3. Applications

In this section we show how the Oberon-2 reflection model can be used to implement a number of interesting system services. In other programming systems, such services are often part of the programming language. Reflection, however, allows us to implement them outside the language in separate library modules so that they don't increase the size and complexity of the compiler. If a user does not need a service, he does not have to pay for it. Reflection also gives the system programmer a chance to adapt these services to special needs.

3.1 A Generic Output Function

In most modern programming languages input/output is not part of the language but is implemented in form of library functions. The problem with this approach is that it requires a separate function for every data type that is to be read or written. A typical output sequence could look as follows:

```
Out.String("Point (");
Out.Int(p.x);
Out.String(", ");
Out.Int(p.y);
Out.String(") is inside the search area");
```

Function overloading alleviates this problem, but still requires multiple function calls to print the above message. It would be nice to have a single generic function which is able to print any sequence of variables of a program with a single call. Reflection allows us to do that.

The following output function takes a string argument with the names of the variables to be printed. For example, the call

```
Put.S("Point (#p.x, #p.y) is inside the search area")
```

prints the argument string, but before printing it, it replaces every variable that is preceded by a # with the value of this variable.

The function *Put.S* is implemented with module *Ref*. It looks up the marked variables of the argument string in various scopes. For example, a variable *rec.arr[i]* is looked up as follows:

- *rec* is first searched in the local scope of the currently active procedure (using *OpenStack*) and—if not found—in the global scope of the current module (using *OpenVars*).

- If *rec* is found and turns out to be a record variable, a rider *r* is positioned on *rec*. *Put.S* zooms into *rec* (using *r.Zoom(r)*) and looks for a field *arr*. If it is found, the rider *r* is positioned on it.

- Since *arr* turns out to be an array, *Put.S* zooms into this array. It starts a new search for the variable *i* (using first *OpenStack*, then *OpenVars* as above). The value of *i* is read, the rider is positioned on the *i*-th element of *arr*, and the value of this element is read. This is the value of *rec.arr[i]*. It is inserted into the output string.

3.2 An Object Inspector

An object inspector is a debugging tool that can be used to inspect the values of the object fields. It can be conveniently implemented with Module *Ref*. To inspect an object that is referenced by a pointer *p*, one opens a rider *r* on the object's fields using *Ref.OpenPtr(p, r)* and iterates over them. Fields with a basic data type are simply shown with their values, whereas structured variables (arrays and records) are first represented in a collapsed form that that can be expanded on demand. When a collapsed variable is expanded, a new rider is placed on the inner elements (using *r.Zoom(r1)*) and is used to traverse the inner sequence.

Fig. 3 shows an example of a variable *head* that points to a list of three nodes. The middle part of the picture shows the list in collapsed state, the right part in expanded state. The triangles are so-called *active text elements* [MöK96] that hide the inner structure of an object. If the user clicks on a filled triangle, the object structure is expanded and shown between hollow triangles. A click on the hollow triangles collapses the structure again.

| TYPE
  Node = POINTER TO
    RECORD
      value: INTEGER;
      next: Node
  END;
VAR head: Node; | head = ^ ▶◀ | head = ^ ▷
  value = 6
  next = ^ ▷
    value = 5
    next = ^ ▷
      value = 4
      next = NIL ◁ ◁ ◁ |

Fig. 3. Object inspector view (collapsed and expanded)

A textual view like the one in Fig.3 is sufficient to represent data structures such as linear lists or trees, but it is less suitable for circular lists or graphs. For such purposes we have implemented a graphical tool that can also show circular data structures. This tool uses the same reflection mechanism as explained above.

3.3 Embedded SQL

SQL (structured query language) is a widely used standard for a database query language. It is normally used interactively from a dialog window. If a programmer wants to issue an SQL query from within a programming language (e.g. C++), however, he has to use an extended form of the language. For C++ there exists such an extension which is called *embedded SQL* [ESQL89]. It adds database query statements that are translated into library calls by a preprocessor.

We used a different implementation for embedded SQL that does not need any language extensions but is based on reflection [Ste96]. SQL queries can be specified as strings, which are passed to a function *Prepare* that analyzes and prepares them for execution. For example, one could write

```
stat := conn.Prepare("CREATE TABLE Persons FOR Person")
```

A prepared SQL statement can be executed with *stat.Execute*. Thus the statement can be executed several times without rebuilding internal data structures every time.

The SQL query can contain names of variables or types, which are then looked up in the calling program and are converted to appropriate data structures of the SQL libraries. For example, *Person* could be a type declared as follows:

```
TYPE
  Person = RECORD
    firstName, lastName: ARRAY 32 OF CHAR;
    age: INTEGER
  END ;
```

Its structure is used by the above SQL statement to create a table with the columns *firstName, lastName* and *age*. To distinguish program variables from database names (e.g. for tables and columns), variables are preceded by a colon in a query. In the following code fragment

```
VAR
  minAge: INTEGER;
  name: ARRAY 32 OF CHAR;
...
stat := conn.Prepare("SELECT firstName FROM Persons
WHERE age > :minAge INTO :name");
```

minAge and *name* are Oberon variables. They are looked up by reflection. The value of *minAge* is used to evaluate the WHERE clause. As a result, the database value *firstName* is transferred to the Oberon variable *name*.

Variables can be either scalar or of a record type. When record variables are specified, they are implicitly expanded to their fields. The statement

```
"SELECT * FROM Persons INTO :person"
```

is therefore equivalent to

```
"SELECT * FROM Persons INTO :person.firstName,
:person.lastName, :person.age".
```

3.4 An Exception Handling Mechanism

Exception handling is often part of a programming language, but it can also be implemented outside of the language, i.e. in a library module [Mil88]. Library-based exception handling is often implemented with the Unix functions *setjmp* and *longjmp*, which save and restore the machine state. We have followed a different approach based on reflection [HMP97]. Our technique has the advantage that it does not slow down programs as long as they do not raise exceptions.

Our exception handling mechanism is based on three concepts: a *guarded block* of statements which is protected against exceptions, one or more *exception handlers*, and a mechanism to *raise* exceptions (Fig. 4).

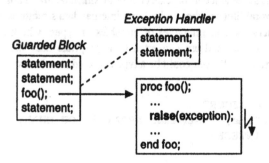

Fig. 4. Exception handling concepts

If an exception is raised in the guarded block or in one of the functions called from it, a suitable exception handler is called. After executing the handler, the program continues with the first statement after the guarded block. Exceptions are classes derived from a common exception class.

In our implementation, the concepts of Fig. 4 are mapped to the Oberon-2 language as follows:

- The guarded block is represented by an arbitrary procedure *P*.
- An exception handler is represented by a local procedure of *P*. It must have a single parameter whose type is a subclass of *Exceptions.Exception*.
- An exception is raised by the call of the library procedure *Exceptions.Raise(e)* where *e* is an object of an exception class.

The following code fragment shows an example (The classes *Overflow* and *Underflow* are subclasses of *Exceptions.Exception*).

```
PROCEDURE GuardedBlock;
  VAR ofl: Overflow; ufl: Underflow;

  PROCEDURE HandleOfl (VAR e: Overflow); …
  END HandleOfl;

  PROCEDURE HandleUfl (VAR e: Underflow); …
  END HandleUfl;

BEGIN
  …
  IF … overflow … THEN
    … fill the ofl object with error information …
    Exceptions.Raise(ofl)
  END;
  …
END GuardedBlock;
```

In this example, *GuardedBlock* raises an exception by calling *Exceptions.Raise(ofl)*. Procedure *Raise* is implemented with reflection. It determines the type of *ofl* and searches through the local procedures of *GuardedBlock* to find a procedure with a matching parameter type. This is the exception handler (in this example *HandleOfl*). If such a handler is found, it is called. Finally, the activation stack is unrolled so that the control is returned to the caller of *GuardedBlock*.

If no matching exception handler is found in *GuardedBlock*, the lookup continues in the caller of *GuardedBlock*. If this caller *P* contains a local procedure *H* with a matching parameter type, *H* is called as an exception handler, and then the program continues with the first statement after *P*.

If no exception handler is found in any of the currently active procedures, the program is aborted with a standard error message. The following pseudocode fragment shows the implementation of *Raise*:

```
PROCEDURE Raise (VAR e: Exceptions.Exception);
  E := dynamic type of e;
  FOR all stack frames in reverse order DO
    P := procedure of this frame;
    FOR all local procedures H of P DO
      IF H has a parameter of type E or a subtype THEN
        Invoke H(e);
        Return to the caller of P
      END
    END
  END
END Raise;
```

Except of the underlined parts, all actions of *Raise* are implemented with the reflection model described in Section 2. In particular, riders are used to traverse the stack frames, the procedures and the parameters to perform the handler lookup. The underlined actions involve stack manipulation. They are implemented using low-level facilities of Oberon-2 and are not show here (see [HMP97]). The dynamic type of an object can be obtained with an Oberon system function.

The exception handling mechanism is encapsulated in a library module with the following simple interface:

```
DEFINITION Exceptions;
  TYPE Exception = RECORD END; (*abstract base class*)
  PROCEDURE Raise (VAR e: Exception);
END Exceptions.
```

4. Discussion

In this section we discuss some consequences and tradeoffs of the Oberon reflection model, namely security and performance issues as well as the interference of reflection with optimizing compilers.

4.1 Security

The Oberon reflection model gives the systems programmer full access to all variables, types and procedures in a program, even to the private objects that are not exported from a module. This of course raises the question of security. The visibility rules of the language can be circumvented by reflection, however, this is necessary to implement system software such as debuggers or inspectors.

Although the whole structure of a program is visible to reflection, it is not possible to access it in an undisciplined way. The Oberon reflection model is strongly typed. All metainformation is read and written according to their types. It is never possible, for example, to access a pointer as an integer or vice versa.

The most critical fact about the Oberon reflection model is that data can not only be read but also written. This is sometimes necessary as for example in the Embedded SQL facility described in Section 3.3. One should use this feature very carefully. According to our experience most reflective applications don't make use of it.

Clearly, reflection allows a programmer to do more than what he could do with an ordinary programming language. But this is exactly its advantage. System programmers need sharper tools than application programmers.

4.2 Interference with Optimizing Compilers

An optimizing compiler may decide to keep variables in registers rather than in memory, to eliminate variables at all, or to introduce auxiliary variables, which are not in the source program. Some of these optimizations are easy to cope with in the reflection model, others are more difficult to handle. The Oberon-2 compiler does not perform aggressive optimizations. In addition to some code modifications (which do not affect the metainformation) the compiler keeps certain variables in registers. For such variables, their register numbers are stored in the metainformation, so that riders can find them. The Oberon-2 compiler does not eliminate, introduce or reorder variables. But even such cases could be handled if the metainformation carried enough information about the optimizations that the compiler performed.

4.3 Performance

The Oberon reflection model leads to small memory overhead at the cost of run time efficiency. The layout of our metainformation is sequential. For example, in order to access the information of the third local variable in the fourth procedure of a module, one has to skip three procedures, zoom into the fourth one and search for the third variable. Table 1 shows the approximate costs for reading (i.e. skipping) various kinds of elements in the metainformation sequence. Of course, the time to skip a procedure or a record type depends on its size.

Table 1. Access times for specific program elements (on a Pentium II with 300 MHz)

Element to be skipped	Cost
Local variable	2 μs
Global variable	2 μs
Record field	2 μs
Record type	9 μs
Procedure	15 μs

The sequential layout of the metainformation as described in Section 2.1 requires us to skip all record types before we get to the first procedure. Furthermore, in our current implementation, the global variables of a module are treated like local variables of the module body, which is considered to be a special procedure. Accessing them requires us to skip to this procedure first. Constraints like these make random access of meta-information elements somewhat inefficient. In practice, however, a typical access pattern involves both random access and sequential access so that the run time was never a serious problem in all the applications described in Section 3. As a task for further research one could try to redesign the metainformation so that it is indexed and random access becomes more efficient.

Our current implementation has the advantage that the metainformation is stored in a very compact form. For example, the metainformation of the whole Oberon compiler (9 modules, 413 procedures, 14 types, 1690 variables and 86 record fields) consumes only 23706 bytes on the disk. When it is accessed it is cached in memory so that it is not necessary to go to the disk for every access. Reading the meta-information of the whole compiler sequentially takes 30 milliseconds.

5. Summary

The fundamental difference between the Oberon-2 reflection model and other models is that the metainformation is not accessed via metaobjects. It is rather parsed on demand from a file (which is usually cached in main memory to avoid file operations). One advantage of this approach is the reduced number of objects needed to represent the metainformation and the reduced memory consumption. For example, when meta-information is used in a post-mortem debugger to produce a readable stack dump, it is important not to waste memory since the reason for the trap might be the lack of memory. A disadvantage of our approach is that the information is parsed again and again. But this is not time-critical as the measurements show.

The Oberon-2 reflection model is currently designed for convenient access to the structure and values of program objects. In the future, we plan to extend it with mechanisms for calling and intercepting methods.

Acknowledgements

The Oberon-2 reflection model was originally designed by Josef Templ [Tem94] in his PhD thesis. We refined his model and adapted it for our purposes. Our colleagues Markus Knasmüller [Kna97], Markus Hof [Hof97], Martin Rammerstorfer and Günter Obiltschnig [Obi98] used the model to implement various applications on top of it. We wish to thank the anonymous referees for their comments that helped us to make the paper more focussed.

References

[ArG96]   Arnold K., Gosling J.: The Java Programming Language. Addison-Wesley, 1996

[Att89]   Attardi G., et al.: Metalevel Programming in CLOS. Proceedings of the ECOOP'89 Conference. Cambridge University Press, 1989

[ESQL89]   Database Language – Embedded SQL (X3.168-1989). American National Standards Institute, Technical Committee X3H2

[GHJV95]   Gamma E., Helm R., Johnson R., Vlissides J.: Design Patterns—Elements of Reusable Object-Oriented Software. Addison-Wesley, 1995

[HMP97]   Hof M., Mössenböck H., Pirkelbauer P.: Zero-Overhead Exception Handling Using Metaprogramming. Proceeding of SOFSEM'97, Lecture Notes in Computer Science 1338, 1997

[Hof97]   Hof M.: Just-In-Time Stub Generation, Proc. Joint Modular Languages Conference '97, Hagenberg, Lecture Notes in Computer Science 1204, Springer-Verlag, 1997

[Kna97]   Knasmüller M.: Oberon-D, On Adding Database Functionality to an Object-Oriented Development Environment, Dissertation, University of Linz, 1997

[LMN93]   Lehrmann-Madsen O., Moller-Pedersen B., Nygaard K.: Object-Oriented Programming in the BETA Programming Language. Addison-Wesley, 1993

[Mil88]   Miller W.M.: Exception Handling without Language Extensions. Proceedings of the USENIX C++ conference, Denver CO, October 1988

[MöK96]   Mössenböck H., Koskimies K.: Active Text for Structuring and Understanding Source Code SOFTWARE - Practice and Experience, 26(7): 833-850, July 1996

[MöW91]   Mössenböck H., Wirth N.: The Programming Language Oberon-2. Structured Programming, 12(4):179-195, 1991

[Obi98]   Obiltschnig G.: An Object-Oriented Interpreter Framework for the Oberon-2 Programming Language, Diploma Thesis, University Linz, 1998

[Ste96]   Steindl Ch.: Accesing ODBC Databases from Oberon Programs. Report 9, University of Linz, Institute for Practical Computer Science, 1996

[StM96]   Steindl Ch., Mössenböck H.: Metaprogramming facilities in Oberon for Windows and Power Macintosh. Report 8, University of Linz, Institute for Practical Computer Science, 1996

[Tem94]   Templ J.: Metaprogramming in Oberon. Dissertation, ETH Zurich, 1994

[WiG89]   Wirth N., Gutknecht J.: The Oberon System. Software—Practice and Experience, 19(9):857-893, 1989

Designing Persistence Libraries in Reflective Models with Intercession Property for a Client-Server Environment

Stéphane Demphlous   Franck Lebastard

CERMICS / INRIA, Database Team
B.P.93, 2004, route des Lucioles, 06902 Sophia Antipolis Cedex, France
Email: {Stephane.Demphlous, Franck.Lebastard} @sophia.inria.fr
URL: http://www.inria.fr/cermics/dbteam/

Abstract. This paper presents an architecture where persistence is added to an object-oriented reflective model in a client-server environment. When the client and the server database management system do not share a common formalism, conversion rules must be set. If the open reflective client has intercession properties and the server does not, for example, when an open reflective language is bound to a relational database management system, we show that the conversion rules may become inadequate when a designer extends the semantics of the client language. An object-oriented reflective system is reified as a metaobject model and intercession is often designed as a metaobject protocol that can be specialized. In this case, we state that the best architecture to bring persistence to a reflective client is to extend the standard metaobject protocol with a fine-grained persistence and conversion protocol. We present such a protocol, and we illustrate it with a binding between Power Classes, an open reflective language, and ObjectDriver, our wrapper to relational databases.

1 Introduction

A key to design modern applications is to use the client-server paradigm. When an application needs to create or to manipulate persistent data, it is a good policy to design a persistent client addressing a server database management system (DBMS).

Now, the reflection, defined in [2] as the ability for a program to manipulate as data something representing its state during its own execution, and the reflection paradigm [3, 7, 19] have become a major issue for system definition. Languages and tools [1, 8, 9] have widened the use of reflection. So client persistent applications may be built using a reflective programming language or be themselves reflective.

Moreover, adding reflective properties to DBMSs appears to be very promising: it helps to adapt the DBMS data model, that is, the formalism in which user data and their definition (metadata) are expressed and controlled. Several studies have shown the interest of such adaptations [14]. The intercession property of many reflective systems, defined in [2] as the ability for a program to modify its own execution state or alter its own interpretation or meaning, can be applied to a DBMS, allowing the user to modify or to extend the data model. Vodak [14] and Tigukat [23] are fully reflective object-oriented DBMSs (OODBMS).

So we believe that, in a near future, there will be growing needs of persistence management in reflective models with intercession properties. Two architectures may arise: the use of a reflective OODBMS, or the reuse of existing DBMSs as servers and the design of reflective persistent clients. However there are few works specifically related to this last problem [22].

Consequently, our aim, in this paper, is to present a way to design persistent clients in a reflective object-oriented system with explicit metaclasses. The respect of the possible intercession property of this system is an important part of our proposals. If a system has this property, a user can modify the system semantics. Therefore it is important to design any part of an open system in a way that allows easy extensions or alterations. Our thesis is that any extension of an open system – including persistent extensions – should be open in the same way than the system itself. We show that this is a very important requirement when the server DBMS is not reflective and/or not object-oriented. We present an implementation example with the language Ilog Power Classes [11] and ObjectDriver our wrapper to relational databases [17].

This paper is divided in five parts. The first one is this introduction. In the second part, we present why the opening property is a key part of a client-server application when only the client is reflective. Moreover, we present why the existing works are not optimal to solve the problems induced by this configuration. In a third part, we present the principles of our proposal, and the need to design a class and metaclass library with a fine-grained metaobject protocol for the persistence management. In the fourth part, we present in a detailed way the persistence and conversion protocols. Finally, we conclude our works.

2 The Opening Property: A Key for Persistence Control

2.1 Homogeneous Client and Server Formalisms

In a client-server architecture where the client and the server share a same object-oriented formalism, the persistence property can be added using a "black box" approach.

In such a configuration, all the standard metaobjects of the client have corresponding standard metaobjects in the server. A user can create, in the client, new persistent objects, instances of standard class metaobjects, and can mark them as persistent. These objects need to be replicated in the server when the transaction in which they have been defined is committed. Their replication is done through a distant instanciation message sending to the server.

For example, let us arbitrarily reduce the scope to metaclass definition and let us imagine that we have a client and a server OODBMS sharing the ObjVLisp model [3]. In this model, a standard class named *object* is the superclass of every classes and *object* is instance of a standard metaclass named *class*, which is instance of itself. Let us note that *class* is subclass of *object*. We consider, to simplify the example, that the class *object* allows its instances to be persistent, that is, to simplify, that a message *save* can be sent to any instance of *object*. Now, we define in the client a new metaclass $(MC)_{client}$, subclass and instance of *class*, a new class $(car)_{client}$, instance of $(MC)_{client}$, and, finally a new object $(myVehicle)_{client}$, instance of the class $(car)_{client}$. If the user wants the objects $(MC)_{client}$, $(car)_{client}$, and $(myVehicle)_{client}$ to be persistent, s/he has to send to each of them the message *save*. Since the server uses the ObjVLisp model, saving the metaclass $(MC)_{client}$ means that an instanciation message is sent to the standard class *class* of the server in order to create there a new metaclass $(MC)_{server}$ associated to the metaclass $(MC)_{client}$. In the same way, saving the $(car)_{client}$ implies the instanciation of $(MC)_{server}$ to create an associated class $(car)_{server}$, and saving $(myVehicle)_{client}$ implies the instanciation of $(car)_{server}$. The figure 1 presents the chain of behaviors invoked in the client and in the server.

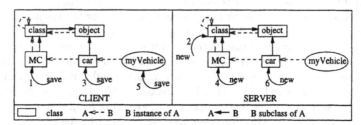

Fig. 1. Homogeneous formalisms between a client and a server: object first saving.

Now, many works have shown that metaclasses can be introduced to extend the semantics of a language [13]. In the previous example, the *MC* metaclass could have been introduced to manage different inheritance rules in its instances, to add them documentation, or to extend the set of legal types for slots. So, the set constituted of the classes *object*, *class* and *MC* fixes a new semantics to the language, different than the standard one. The classes *object* and *class* are common to the client and the server. We have seen that the class *MC* can become persistent and be replicated in the server. It is clear that we can have exactly the same metaobjects in the client and the server, that is, the same language semantics.

In that case, the persistence tool can be provided as a "black box". In a very simplified manner, the persistence tool can be seen as a tool allowing a client to create, in the server, twin objects associated to the client objects. So the server formalism can evolve in the same way than the client formalism. Except for performance or technical reasons, no object or metaobject modeling logically implies to modify the way the saving of objects is done: the only goal is to replicate the objects, or metaobjects, into the server, and this goal is always met.

2.2 Heterogeneous Client and Server Formalisms

In this section, we show that a "black box" approach can raise problems when the client and server formalisms are heterogeneous.

Conversions between Formalisms. This heterogeneity of formalisms can occur, for example, when an object-oriented application must use a relational database. This architecture is very likely to be found since there is a large number of existing relational DBMSs. A DBMS is a key component in a company information system. Many clients may use a relational DBMS through a network, and there is no reason why the choice of an object-oriented technology in some projects in the company should imply the replacement of the existing DBMS server by an object-oriented one.

Now, binding two heterogeneous formalisms implies to realize conversions. These conversions depend on semantic associations between concepts of the two formalisms.

For example, there are many ways to bind an object-oriented application with a relational database. An option is:

- to convert a class by one or several relational tables, which attributes are associated with the slots of the class, and
- to convert objects by tuples of the relational tables associated with their class [18].

Most of the proposed object-relational bindings are associations between a specific object-oriented formalism and the relational one, for example, the C++ language and a relational database [12]. These tools rely on academic works where it is shown that abstract data types can be converted to relational structures [16].

The interesting point to consider at this stage is that, whatever the two heterogeneous formalisms may be, the designer of a two-formalism binding knows that different concepts in different formalisms can be associated, and how to associate them. But, in most of the systems, the conversion paradigm is presented in the documentation but cannot be easily modified.

Need to Keep the System Open. We have seen that a black box approach can be justifiably chosen when the client and the server share a same reflective model. Now, following such a black box approach when conversions must be done, means that the the persistence would not be open, since complex conversion behaviors would be hidden to the designer. This can raise problems.

Let us consider a simple class-based language based on the ObjVLisp model, and enforcing that the slot types are primitive types like integer, float, character, or reference types. A straightforward mapping can be done to relational databases, associating a unique relational table to a class, and an attribute of this relational table to each slot of the class. The attribute type is a primitive type when the slot type is primitive, and it is a foreign key when the slot type is a reference type. With the model of the persistent ObjVLisp of the previous section, we can set a *save* behavior on the class *object* so that these conversions are done. All models and metamodels defined in persistent ObjVLisp are persistent.

However, the set of slot types provided by our small language is obviously too poor. A user would like, for example, to define structured, that is, aggregate, slots in the same manner s/he could do it with the C++ language. A new metaclass *StructuredSlotClass* can be defined so that it allows its instances to declare structured slots. The *StructuredSlotClass* metaclass extends the language semantics. As any class in the system, the classes instances of *StructuredSlotClass* and their own instances are persistent.

Now, the way these objects are stored in the underlying database may not be satisfactory. For example, suppose that we manage a car factory. We can define a class *car* with a structured slot *engine* which has two attributes *power* and *serial number*. The structured values of this slot must be stored in every instance of the class *car*. One solution is to put them linearly in the actual slot value. The *engine* slot value of a vehicle which engine power is *300* and engine serial number is *F1-99* can be "*/power 300 /serialNumber F1-99*". The slot accessors must be redefined so that querying the engine power of a car implies a transparent retrieval of the values stored in the *engine* slot value behind the keyword "*/power*", and querying the engine serial number of a car implies a transparent retrieval of the values stored in the *engine* slot value behind the keyword "*/serialNumber*". The *engine* actual type and the accessors are set by the instanciation protocol defined on *StructuredSlotClass* and its own class. This option is interesting since standard slots can be used: it does not require that a new class of slots is created. Our example is thus simplified.

Now, with the point of view of the persistence protocol, there are only standard slots in the class *car*. So the relational mapping of the class *car* is straightforward: a unique relational table *car* with a primitive attribute *engine*. As a consequence, the *engine* slot value of an object is stored in the database in a straightforward way. For example, the value "*/power 300 /serialNumber F1-99*" will be the *engine* attribute value of a tuple in the relational table *car*. A schema of this configuration can be found in the left of the figure 2.

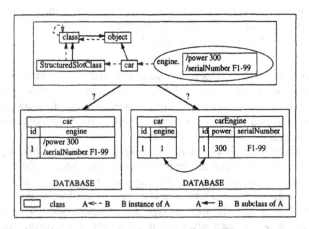

Fig. 2. Inadequate conversions between a client and a server DBMS.

This is not a problem if this client application is the only one to use the underlying database. The objects are saved as described previously, and they are later recreated from relational data without loss of information. If the goal of a binding between an open reflective client and a relational database is to allow the user to extend the language semantics in the client without caring about the way the data are actually stored in the underlying database, there is no need to modify the conversion rules between the client and the server DBMS.

But a DBMS is generally used to share data and schemas. Data can be used by other applications than the ones that created them. So, it is very important, when defining a database, to create clear schemas so that another designer, or a database administrator, can easily understand their semantics.

The relational schema we have described is not clear. It is not obvious that the primitive relational attribute *engine*, in the relational table *car*, represents structured data. Moreover an attribute value like *"/power 300 /serialNumber F1-99"* lacks of expressivity, since it includes keywords like *"/power"* and *"/serialNumber"*: these keywords depend on the implementations of the protocols defined on the class *StructuredSlotClass*. It is almost certain that a designer examining this database would be puzzled and would spend some time to discover its semantics. Moreover it would be difficult to query the power or the serial numbers.

A much better schema would be, for example, to define the *engine* attribute of the relational table *car* as a foreign key to another table *CarEngine* with two attributes *power* and *serialNumber*, as shown on the right of the figure 2.

So we would like to modify the standard conversions so that structured slots are saved in the way we have described. Let us note that we only need to alter slot conversions. The class and the inheritance conversions remain identical.

2.3   Choosing an Architecture

We came to the conclusion that, in a reflective system with intercession properties, the persistence related behaviors can be designed as a black box, with no need to open to the user the mechanisms involved, when:
- there is a same reflective formalism in the client and in the server,
- or the client and the server formalisms are different, but the user does not care about the expressiveness of the stored data, because these data will never be shared.

Since there is a large number of existing DBMSs and since cooperation between applications is increasing, we think that these previous cases are less likely to be found than a third one in which:
- the client and the server do not have a common formalism and
- the data are stored to be shared.

In that last case, whenever the user extends the formalism of the client, he needs to adapt the standard conversions. If he does not, most of the database schemas associated with her/his applications will be hard to reuse. With a triplet composed of a client, a server and the conversion rules between the client and the server, when the client formalism evolves, the server formalism or the conversion rules have to evolve. We study the way to realize the latter conversions. In the persistence domain, this is a new problem which is specific to the binding of reflective systems with intercession properties to existing DBMSs.

2.4   Limits of Related Works

The problems of formalism heterogeneity with a reflective system have been addressed in existing works with two different points of view. A first approach was to use the metamodeling abilities in order to make easier schema conversions between two different formalisms. A second one was to show that the conversions between formalisms can be realized with metaobjects and metaclasses. But, in the first point of view, systems often lack of uniformity, and data, that is, final instances, are not managed. In the second one, easy conversion alterations have not been considered. We develop this subject in the next lines.

Schema Converters. So, a first point of view is to use the metamodeling abilities provided by the reflection paradigm to parameterize schema conversions. This approach has been taken by the TIME [20] and METAGEN [25] systems. The main idea is to let the user describe two formalisms as two object metamodels, and define rules to associate specific data structures of a target metamodel to specific data structures of a origin metamodel.

There are two parts in these tools: a metamodel editor to let the user describe her/his origin and target metamodels, and a rule-based expert system to generate a new schema (model) in the target metamodel from an existing schema in the origin metamodel. Of course, if some metamodels have been already described, they can be used as a pivot metamodel between an origin and a target metamodel in order to reuse existing conversion rules. This point is interesting since it minimizes the work to do when a designer has modified an existing metamodel.

In our previous car factory example, if there are existing rules to link the first version of the object-oriented formalism to the relational formalism, we can define, from scratch, rules to convert slots of the extended object-oriented formalism to the standard one, and be sure that clear relational schemas will be generated.

These tools are very useful to help a designer to create a new object model, or a new database schema, when he needs to migrate an existing application or database, but they do not meet our goals. As a matter of fact,
- they do not take into account the conversions of data and final instances, but only type conversions;
- moreover, they force the designer to understand and use different principles, that is, the object-oriented modeling for metamodel definitions, and a rule-based expert system for conversions between metamodels.

These tools are powerful generic schema converters but can hardly be used in a client-server application.

Bindings Between Object-Oriented Reflective Systems and Relational DBMSs. Several works have been done to bind a reflective object-oriented system with a relational DBMS. However the problem we have shown has never been considered. So, the models involved to realize the binding are not adequate enough to allow easy extensions of conversion rules.

A library has been provided to Vodak to use relational databases [15]. It gives the user means to realize explicit rerouting toward the underlying database by modifying its own source code. For example, the user must define new accessors to reroute slot accesses to the underlying database: these accessor creations are not hidden by the meta level. Moreover, no pre-existing framework helps the designer to realize a complete binding with a relational database.

PCLOS [22] binds the CLOS language with a relational DBMS. But it has not been designed to open to the designer the way the conversions are realized. The only way to modify how objects are saved is to change a type conversion function that binds a CLOS type to a database type. However, these functions were intended to manage primary types, and they discriminate on the type of the saved data. This can lead to confusions. In our car factory example, the structured slot values of final instances are actually strings. We could define a type conversion function dealing with strings but every string in the application would be treated as a structured slot: this is obviously a problem. At the meta level, although another design would be to subclass the class of a standard slot, we could define the structured slots as a standard slot with a string type, assuming that a standard slot belonging to a structured class should be managed in a different way than a standard slot belonging to a standard class. It cannot be, since PCLOS manages every standard slot of the application in a same way. But such a mistake can be done since the persistence algorithms are not presented, so the way the slots are managed is not clear. It appears that PCLOS is not adaptable enough to deal with formalism evolution since it does not offer an open framework for conversion.

The limits of these works, and the need for a new architecture, have been discussed in previous works [4, 5].

3   Designing a Persistence Metaobject Protocol

We believe that an answer to these problems is to provide persistence abilities to a reflective system by a class and metaclass library extending the standard metaobject protocol of the language. This implies that persistence can be added by object-oriented modeling and there is no need of system programming. In a first part, we justify this statement, then in a second part, we present the principles of an open protocol.

3.1   Adding Persistence by Object-Oriented Modeling

Legitimacy. Persistence can be defined as the way to allow entities to survive the application in which they have been created. In an object-oriented reflective system, all the entities are objects. Hence, we need only to consider the persistence of objects.

Let us consider a client-server configuration, and let us assume that we want an object to be persistent. Either the object is persistent when it is created, or it becomes persistent when the user wants it to be so. For example, in the first case, a persistent object could actually be, in the client, when created, a proxy linked to the actual object in a server OODBMS. In the second case, a persistent object could be created on the client side, then be marked as persistent by the user and replicated on the server.

If an object must be persistent when created, we have to manage two kinds of instanciation: a transient one and a persistent one. As usual in metaclass-based system, the instanciation is a message passing to a class metaobject. If an object is transient when created, and then becomes persistent, since the persistence is a property added to the object, we propose that it may be done through a message sending to the object itself.

In any case, the persistent property can be stated by a message passing. Hence, according to the chosen persistence paradigm, persistence can be provided to an object-oriented reflective system, or to an application defined in the system, using a class library or a metaclass library.

In the rest of the paper, we arbitrarily choose that an object is first created transient, and is subsequently marked as persistent and replicated in the server.

Feasibility. We have seen that providing persistence through a class library is legitimate. However, it is important to evaluate its feasibility. According to the persistence paradigm chosen, all of the persistent objects and metaobjects are instances of a common persistence class (in order to be able to be marked as persistent), or have a common persistence metaclass (in order to be able to be created as persistent). Two problems may arise:

The first one is related to the ability to modify standard class metaobjects. If it cannot be, transient metaobjects are considered as any transient object in a standard ODBMS: they are ignored. So, when these metaobjects are needed on the server side to express and control objects, the persistence protocol can, for example, rely on the introspection ability of the language to create twin persistent metaobjects.

A second problem can arise when the language enforces rules to solve the metaclass compatibility problem [10]. For example, the Power Classes language allows explicit metaclasses but enforces that the metaclass of a class C must inherit from the metaclasses of every superclasses of C. In a persistent application, an object o and its class metaobject mo can be both persistent. As a consequence, the class represented by mo and its own class will have both to inherit from a same class. This can lead to metaclass compatibility problems. These problems can be solved enforcing metaclass inheritance rules on the persistence library and on the user classes and metaclasses.

The complete answers to these problems, and their formal presentations, are far beyond the scope of this paper, which purpose is to show an open object-oriented protocol and not to consider the design of persistence library in a general case. They can be found in [6]. Our aim is only to show that the feasibility of our proposals in these cases has been considered, and that models have been proposed. So it legitimates the design of persistence as an open library.

3.2   Designing Persistence as an Open Library

Principles. So we provide a class and metaclass library. Since we want to use heterogeneous databases, we embed the conversion mechanisms in the persistence behaviors related to the saving and retrieval of objects, that are defined on the classes of our persistence library. The goal of the rule-based generic schema converters, that is, minimizing the amount of code needed when a metamodel evolves, and the goal of open reflective OODBMSs, that is, managing metaobjects and final instances, are both legitimate. So, to meet these goals, we use a uniform approach to save objects and metaobjects, we solely rely on object-oriented modeling, and we define conversion behaviors that can easily be parameterized according to the formalism evolution with a minimal amount of code writing.

Our proposal is to embed the conversion mechanisms in the persistence behaviors related with the saving and retrieval of objects, that are defined for the classes of our persistence library. These conversions are structured as a hierarchized protocol.

The main idea is not to offer a unique, "monolithic" conversion message but to propose a whole set of behaviors which is the architecture of the conversion mechanism. So when an object receives a save/convert message, a sequence of message is sent transparently to this object. Each of these messages represents a "semantics stage" of the saving.

For example, to save a class, the system needs to save its superclasses, then its eventual relationships, then to save its slots. So, three messages can be sent to the class. Of course, each of these behaviors could, and should, be divided themselves in several behaviors that may send messages to other metaobjects. If we use a C++ or Java terminology, we can say that the *save* or the *retrieve* behaviors are *"public"* behaviors that invoke several *"protected"* behaviors.

When a designer introduces a new class, s/he can specialize on it one of these behaviors. In our car factory example, the slot conversion protocol is the only part that has to be modified. So only the behaviors managing the conversion of slots have to be specialized on the class metaobjects defined to extend the slot semantics. So, if the protocol is fine-grained the amount of code writing may be minimized.

A metaobject protocol. The protocol approach is not new in the field of object-oriented programming. Most of the object-oriented libraries are built with a protocol approach and visibility choices (private, protected, public). But the use of this approach in a domain where it has not be previously used can be an innovation and can widen the prospects in this domain. So was the definition of the CLOS' documented metaobject protocol [13]. The object-oriented protocol approach applied to metaobjects allows easy language extensions.

We take a similar approach in the persistence field: we design the conversion part as a fine-grained object and metaobject protocol. As far as the authors know, there is no previous attempt to describe the persistence mechanisms at the meta level as a fine-grained object-oriented protocol.

In the car factory example, we have saved and restored metaobjects, like class metaobjects and metaclass metaobjects, and final instances, like the car objects, that represent objects from the real world. The latter ones are not metaobjects. But we use a same user interface for the two kinds of objects, that is, we save and retrieve objects. So, this can bring some confusion: are we really designing a metaobject protocol?

Our aim is to allow the user to provide persistent metaobjects. But we do not want to limit our study to metaobject persistence. So we provide a protocol that can be applied to any object, that is, to final instances and to metaobjects. Any behavior that can be invoked on final instances and that can be invoked, as it stands, on metaobjects, is part of our persistence metaobject protocol. There are behaviors specific to metaobjects, or behaviors that must be specialized on some class of metaobjects. These behaviors are obviously part of the metaobject protocol too. As a consequence, we state that we can rightfully use the term of metaobject protocol: we define the part dedicated to persistence management of an existing metaobject protocol, and subparts of this protocol can be applied to final instances.

Advantages of our architecture. Our architecture has two main advantages. The object-oriented paradigm is the only concept the user has to learn. And a unique methodology is used to extend a language and to adapt the persistence management.

When a user needs to extend the standard semantics of a language, s/he can, for example, define new metaclasses or new classes. First s/he specializes on them the standard metaobject protocol of the language, to give new behaviors to the language. Then s/he specializes on the same class metaobjects the part of the persistence metaobject protocol that has to be adapted, according to the evolution of the language semantics.

4   A Binding between Power Classes and ObjectDriver

We have applied our principles on a real size application binding a reflective object-oriented language with explicit metaclasses to relational DBMSs. In this section, we first shortly present the tools we have used; then we propose an object model; finally we present the protocols.

4.1   An Overview of Involved Tools

Power Classes. We have used Ilog Power Classes [11] as a reflective object-oriented language with intercession properties. It is a commercial version of EuLisp [21] and uses a reflective model, named Telos, close to the one of CLOS. We can note two interesting properties of Power Classes. First, it enforces metaclass compatibility rules: the metaclass of a class C must inherit from, or be equal to, the metaclass of each of the superclass of C. Finally, Power Classes manages multiple inheritance.

ObjectDriver. ObjectDriver [17] is an object wrapper to relational databases which is developed in our team. Its main interest is to propose a powerful Abstract Data Component (ADC) layer that makes possible to reorganize and to access relational data as complex data through complex views. Of course it also allows to make complex data persistent in a relational database. All classical database operations are possible on complex data through the views, that is, inserting, updating, deleting, retrieving and querying with OQL. A convenient interface allows to connect the ADC layer to many object models.

4.2   Object Model

To bind a reflective object-oriented system with a non object-oriented heterogeneous system, we distinguish two important concepts that can be mapped to most of the representation formalisms:

- An object must be converted as data. If we consider the relational formalism, an object should be converted as a tuple in a relation.

- A class must be converted as a data structure. In the relational formalism, a class should be converted as a relation.

Since, in a reflective model, classes are objects, they can also be converted as data in the data structures associated with their own class.

If we consider the ObjVLisp model, we can implement on the class *object* the object conversion protocol associating a tuple to an object, and on the metaclass *class* the class metaobject conversion protocol associating a tuple and relation to a class metaobject.

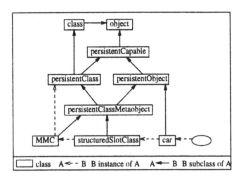

Fig. 3. Object model of our persistence library. The classes with no instanciation link are instance of the class *class*.

Now this model implies that every object in the language is persistent, and, consequently, that the underlying database can describe as many metaschemas as there are meta levels. For example, suppose that a class C_0 is instance of a class metaobject C_1, instance of another class metaobject C_2, ..., instance of C_{n-1} instance of *class*. The class C must be described as a tuple in the relational structure associated with the class C_1 which must be described as a tuple in the relational structure associated with C_2, and so on, until *class* is described as a tuple in its own associated relational structure. We see that n relational tables must be created and that these relational tables define $n-1$ meta-schemas. We have noted that many database administrators do not want such an increase of the number of metaschemas. So we propose to let the user classify its objects and metaobjects in three sets:

- objects that should be converted as data;
- class metaobjects that should be converted as data structures;
- and class metaobjects that should be converted as data and as data structures.

Naturally, these three sets share public persistent behaviors: objects can be marked as persistent, saved, locked, and so on.

So, to express these notions, we define the following classes:

- the abstract class *persistenceCapable* that defines the signature of public persistent behaviors;
- the class *persistentObject*, subclass of *persistenceCapable*, on which is implemented the object conversion protocol;
- the class *persistentClass*, subclass of *persistenceCapable*, on which is implemented the class conversion protocol, generating data structures;

- the class *persistentClassMetaobject* that inherits from *persistentObject* and *persistentClass* and composes their behaviors.

Semantically, the instances of *persistentClass* and *persistentClassMetaobject* are classes. These two classes are metaclasses. As a consequence, we set that *persistentClass* inherits from the class *class*. The figure 3 sums up our object model. Let us note that we have chosen not to modify the language, but to offer a persistence library. So, no persistence protocol is defined on the classes *class* and *object*. We can see that the metaclass compatibility rules of Power Classes are complied.

With this model, the designer can choose the classes that may be handled as objects during the conversions, for example, the classes *car* and *StructuredSlotClass* in the figure 3, and the classes that may not be converted as data in a metaschema, like, for example, the class *MMC* in the same figure.

4.3 Protocols

In this part, we use an intuitive graphical representation to present our protocols. We have chosen to use UML sequence diagrams in an instance form [24] to present representative applications. Such diagrams can be found in the figures 4, 5, 6 and 7. In short, the vertical axis represents the time. The labeled vertical dotted lines represent the cycle of life of an object. Message passing is represented by an horizontal arrow. The arrow head is linked to the receiver object and the arrow bottom is linked to the sender object. The behavior execution is represented by a vertical rectangle. An arrow in the opposite direction to the message passing arrow represents the end of the behavior execution. When choices must be made, for example, according to the return value of a behavior, a fork represents the different choices.

In the following comments, we assume that the underlying heterogeneous database can express data structures, and can associate a key to an elementary set of data (e.g. a tuple or an object) to characterize it. We assume that foreign keys are semantically similar to references in an object world.

Saving objects. In the sequence diagram of the figure 4, we imagine that an object *anObject* refers to a second object *anObject2*. We state that the object *anObject* is instance of a class metaobject *aClass*. Then we consider that the object *anObject* receives a *save* message which semantics is to convert and store the object in the underlying database, when it is not already persistent or saved. We use this example because it is general enough to show two important principles: the reference links and the instanciation links.

We use the persistence root paradigm. It implies that any potentially persistent object referred by any potentially persistent object must be saved when the latter one is saved. It is important to avoid deadlocks when two potentially persistent objects refer to each other, or belong to a cycle. So we define a protocol entry with the message *beingSaved* to check if this object is being saved.

Let us consider that *anObject* is not being saved. First, its own class must be saved, so the *save* message is sent to *aClass*. Then *anObject* can be saved. We must decide if *anObject* must be saved "as a primitive type" or "as an object".

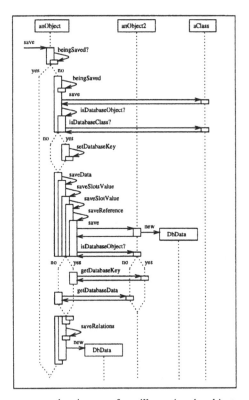

Fig. 4. Diagram sequence in a instance form illustrating the object saving protocol.

This distinction may be puzzling if we forget that the client is an environment where everything is an object, and the server is a environment where there may be data that are not object. For example, in the client, integers, characters, strings may be object, but, in the server, we can imagine that perhaps they cannot be objects, even if it is an object-oriented DBMS. A same problem occurs if we use an underlying relational database. We have chosen to associate at least a relational table to each class and at least a tuple to each object. Now a user can define its own persistent string class *MyOwnString*. A string slot in a class would be typed as a reference to *MyOwnString*. String objects instances of *MyOwnString* must be saved but it is obviously not interesting to define a relational table named *MyOwnString* to store every string defined in the application, and to convert any slot which type is a reference to *MyOwnString* to a foreign key attribute indexing the relational table *MyOwnString*. A much better proposal would be to convert these slots to relational string attributes. So it is interesting to decide if an object must be converted "as a primitive type" or "as an object". So we define a protocol entry, that is a behavior, *isDatabaseObject*. In most of the cases, every instance of a same class should be converted "as objects" or "as data". So the message *isDatabaseClass* is sent to *aClass*. Its semantics is identical to the one of *isDatabaseObject* but it manages the properties of a whole extent of a class.

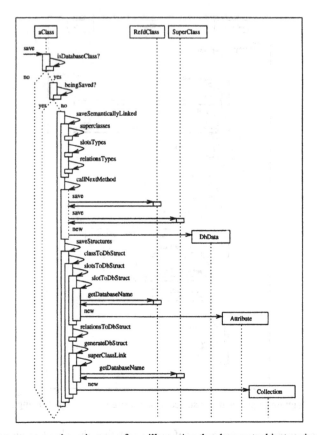

Fig. 5. Diagram sequence in an instance form illustrating the class metaobject saving protocol.

If an object must be saved "as an object", a database key must be associated with it. For example, if we use a relational database, a unique relational key must be set to determine the tuples that represent the object. This is the semantics of the protocol entry *setDatabaseKey*.

Now, the saving of an object is done with two behavior calls: encapsulated data are saved with the behavior *saveSlotsValue* and *saveRelations* saves the objects linked to an object by external relations.

With the behavior *saveSlotValue*, we propose a protocol entry to manage the conversion of slots. If a slot *s* has a primitive type, then primitive conversions are realized. Now, we offer a protocol entry to manage reference slots. If the slot *s* has a reference type then the *saveReference* behavior is invoked. If the referred object *anObject2* that can be reached from *anObject* through *s* must be converted as an object, the *s* slot value of *anObject* has to be converted as a foreign key. So we need to know the database key associated with *anObject2*. This can be done by sending the message *getDatabaseKey* to *anObject2*. But if the referred object *anObject2* must be converted as a literal, we need the whole data representing *anObject2* in order to integrate it in the database structure associated with *s*. So the message *getDatabaseData* is sent.

The behavior *saveRelations* manages the relations between objects that are not modeled by slots in their respective classes. This property can be found in some languages – including Power Classes – where the classes express the internal structures of objects, but not their relations which are expressed outside of the classes and can be added or removed without modifying the class itself. We use the previous conversions and we convert them into foreign keys.

Saving classes. Now we present how a class metaobject can be saved. So we state that the object *anObject* of the previous sequence diagram is instance of a class *aClass* which inherits from another class *superClass*, and that the object *anObject2* is instance of a class *RefdClass*.

Saving a class implies that data structures, in the database, are associated with it. So we define a protocol entry (behavior) *saveStructures* on the class *persistentClass*.

But a class cannot be saved alone. It belongs to a semantic graph of classes. For example, it is necessary to save the superclasses of a class, in order to describe the inherited slots. Moreover, we have seen that reference slots can be described as foreign key relational attributes. In most of the existing relational databases, the only way to define a foreign key attribute is to describe two relational tables and explicitly set an attribute of a table as a foreign key related to the key attribute of the second table. So, if we want to convert a reference slot as a foreign key attribute we need to save the class the slot refers to.

Since classes are objects, semantically related classes should be in most of the cases saved. If we use the object protocol presented in the previous part, whenever a class metaobject *classMO* is saved, every potentially persistent objects referred from it are saved. Superclasses metaobjects are likely to be refered from *classMO* and slot types are likely to be refered from the slot metaobjects, which are themselves referenced from *classMO*. However, there are two problems.

- We want to define a general protocol and we cannot assume that all of the semantics links between classes will be modeled, in every language, by references.
- We have proposed a model so that there may be classes that will not be saved as objects: only structures will be associated to them. These classes are direct instances of *persistentClass* but are not instances of *persistentClassMetaobject*. So we cannot rely on the protocol of *persistentObject* since *persistentClass* does not inherit from *persistentObject*.

So we define a second protocol entry point on *persistentClass* called *saveSemanticallyLinked* that forces semantically linked classes to be saved.

Naturally, the save behavior is specialized on *persistentClassMetaobject* so that either *saveSemanticallyLinked* or the saving by exploration of the reference tree may manage semantically linked classes. With Power Classes, we have arbitrarily chosen to privilege the latter one.

In the figure 5, we show, in a diagram sequence, how the three behaviors *saveSemanticallyLinked*, *save* and *saveStructures* are combined. We assume that *aClass* is instance of *persistentClassMetaobject*. First a class must be saved if it is considered, in the underlying database, as a class, that is, if its instances must be saved as "objects" and not as literals. So, the message *isDatabaseClass* is first sent to *aClass*. Then, the semantically related classes are saved, through a call to *saveSemanticallyLinked*, then the class metaobject is treated as a regular object and, finally, data structures are linked to it.

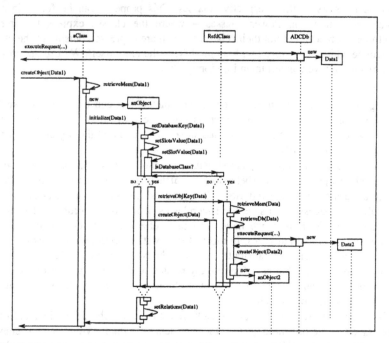

Fig. 6. Diagram sequence in an instance form illustrating the object retrieval protocol.

We distinguish three kinds of class metaobjects that can be semantically linked to a class: its superclasses, the types of some of its slots, and the classes it is linked to by an external relationship. So we define three parts in our protocol: *superClasses*, *slotTypes*, and *relationTypes*. Note that these behaviors are implemented for *persistentClass* and are empty for *persistentClassMetaobject*. As a matter of fact, in our example, the class metaobjects *RefdClass* and *SuperClass* are saved when the implementation of *save* defined on *persistentObject* is invoked.

Retrieving Objects. Binding an object-oriented system to an underlying heterogeneous database implies that, at any moment, queries can be sent to the database, and, consequently, non-object data can be retrieved from it. Retrieving objects means that new objects can be instanciated encapsulating data retrieved from the database. So designing a protocol for object retrieval means designing a protocol for object creation from non-object data.

Now persistent objects to be retrieved can be instances of a persistent class metaobject that must be also retrieved. In the approach we have chosen, it means that it is up to the responsibility of the user to first retrieve the upper instanciation level, that is, the class metaobject, and then retrieve the lower level, that is the instances of these newly created class metaobjects. We do not provide mechanism to transparently retrieve a whole instanciation branch rooted on a existing metaclass, by querying a leaf of this branch: the user has to explicity retrieve each node of the branch.

In this part, we take an example represented by the sequence diagram of the figure 6. We state that a request has been sent to the underlying database and that a data, named *Data1*, has been retrieved. We assume that *Data1* represents an instance of the class *aClass*. So a message *createObject* is sent to *aClass*.

First, it is important to decide if the object represented by *Data1* has been yet retrieved, and is still in memory. We provide the *retrieveMem* entry point to check if there is, in the extent of a class, an object corresponding to the data retrieved from the underlying database. If the object has not been retrieved yet, a new object must be created, so, in the diagram, *anObject* is created, and then initialized when it receives the *initialize* message. It is initialized with the data contained in *Data1*.

The *initialize* protocol is divided into three parts. First, in order to be later retrieved in another application, a database key is associated to the object when the behavior *setDatabaseKey* is invoked. Then the slot values are set with the behavior *setSlotsValue* and finally, the relationships between objects are set.

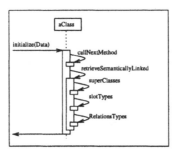

Fig. 7. Diagram sequence in an instance form illustrating the initialization protocol of a class.

Let us consider slot management, with the *setSlotValue* entry point. When the slot type is primitive, basic conversions are done. But a problem may occur when a slot type refers to another class, for example, *RefdClass* in our diagram. The object *anObject* must refer to another object, instance of *RefdClass*. But when it has been previously saved, an object could have been converted "into an object", for example converted into a tuple value in a relational database, or it can be converted "into a literal", for example into an attribute value of a tuple. So, if the instances of *RefdClass* are saved "as objects", *Data1* encapsulates a foreign key representing a link to an instance *anObject2* of *RefdClass*. Now, if the instances of *RefdClass* are saved "as litterals", the whole data corresponding to *anObject2* are encapsulated in *Data1*.

So, when a slot type is a reference type, our protocol tests if the referred class *RefdClass* has been converted "into a class" sending to it the message *isDatabaseClass*. If it does not, a new object instance of *RefdClass* and encapsulating the data corresponding to the referred object that are contained in *Data1* must be created. Hence, a message *createObject* is sent to *RefdClass*. But if it does, the appropriate instance of *RefdClass* has to be found according to the foreign key encapsulated by *Data1*. So the message *retrieveObjKey* is sent to *RefdClass*. The object is first sought in the class extent with the behavior *retrieveMem*. If it is not found, it is retrieved from the underlying database: a message *retrieveDb* is sent to *RefdClass*, a query is generated and sent to the database, and finally a new object *anObject2* is created and initialized.

Retrieving Class Metaobjects: The retrieval protocol of class metaobjects is similar to the one of objects. We just specialize the behavior *initialize* in order to retrieve classes that are not actually linked by the class metaobject but are semantically related to it. This behavior corresponds to the behavior *SaveSemanticallyLinked* in the class metaobject saving protocol. The figure 7 presents a sequence diagram illustrating the initialization of a class *aClass*.

As an example of protocol specialization, in order to manage the factory example of the section 2.2, we only had to specialize the behaviors *saveSlotValue* (object saving protocol), *slotToDbStruct* (class metaobject saving protocol) and *setSlotValue* (object and class metaobject retrieval protocols) since only the slot management had to be modified.

5   Conclusion

In this paper, we have shown that the use of a reflective client with intercession properties coupled with an heterogeneous server can raise problems. Data conversions must be realized between the client and the server. When a user extends the client semantics by introducing new metaobjects, the built-in conversion rules may become inadequate. Adapting the data conversion rules, and the data structures conversion rules with a minimal amount of code to write is necessary.

We propose to bring persistence to a reflective system with a class and metaclass library. We define the persistence protocol, including the conversion protocol as a fine-grained metaobject protocol. This architecture brings three main advantages:

(1) The object-oriented paradigm is the only concept the user must know. We only provide class libraries. For example, there are no external expert system implying to write inference rules in another language than the programming language.

(2) In order to extend the semantics of a language, and to integrate the resulting new language in a persistent environment, the user uses a unique methodology in a unique system. S/he has to extend the standard metaobject protocol to extend the language. To adapt the persistence management s/he needs to extend the part of the metaobject protocol dedicated to persistence. For example, the user can have defined new metaclasses, and have specialized on them the standard metaobject protocol. So s/he will have to specialize on the same metaclasses the persistence protocol.

(3) Finally, this architecture is a convincing example of the interest to define open metaobject protocols. We have seen that persistence can be added in an optimal way extending a standard metaobject protocol. This fact strengthens our thesis. New needs can appear in the persistence field. Since we have designed persistence as a metaobject protocol, we can consider that it could be extended more easily than if it had been designed with another approach.

Moreover we have described a protocol that has been applied to bind the reflective language Ilog Power Classes and relational databases.

73

References

[1] D. Bobrow, L. DeMichiel, R. Gabriel, S. Keene, G. Kiczales and D. Moon, *Common Lisp Object System Specification*, SIGPLAN notices 23 (special issue), 1988

[2] D. Bobrow, R. Gabriel and J. White, *CLOS in Context. In Object-Oriented Programming, the CLOS Perspective*, The MIT Press, chap. 2, pp. 29-61, 1995

[3] P. Cointe, *Metaclasses are First Class: the ObjVLisp Model*. Proc. of OOPSLA'89, SIGPLAN notices 24(10), pp. 156-167, 1989.

[4] S. Demphlous, *A Metaobject Protocol for Interoperability*, Proc. of the ISCA Int. Conf. on Parallel and Distributed Computing Systems, pp. 653-657, 1996.

[5] S. Demphlous, *Databases Evolution: An Approach by Metaobjects*, Proc. the third Int. Workshop on Databases and Information Systems, ACM SIGMOD Chapter, pp. 31-37, 1996.

[6] S. Demphlous, *Gestion de la persistance au sein de systèmes réflexifs à objets*, PhD thesis, University of Nice-Sophia Antipolis, France, 1998.

[7] J. Ferber, *Computational Reflection in Class based Object Oriented Languages*, Proc. of OOPSLA'89, SIGPLAN notices 24(10), pp. 317-326, 1989.

[8] I. Forman, *Putting Metaclasses to Work*, Addison-Wesley, 1998.

[9] A. Goldberg and D. Robson, *Smalltalk-80: the Language and its Implementation*, Addison-Wesley, 1983.

[10] N. Graube, *Metaclass Compatibility*, Proc. of OOPSLA'89, SIGPLAN notices 24(10), pp. 305-315, 1989.

[11] Ilog, *Ilog Talk/Power Classes Reference Manual v.1.3*, Gentilly, France, 1994.

[12] A. Keller, R. Jensen and S. Agarwal, *Persistence Software: Bridging Object-Oriented Programming and Relational Databases*, SIGMOD record, 22(2), pp. 215-230, 1993.

[13] G. Kiczales, J. des Rivières and D. Bobrow, *The Art of the Metaobject Protocol*, The MIT Press, 1991.

[14] W. Klas and M. Schref, *Metaclasses and their Application: Data Model Tailoring and Database Integration*, Lecture Notes in Computer Science n.943, Springer-Verlag, 1995.

[15] W. Klas, G. Fischer and K. Aberer, *Integrating Relational and Object-Oriented Databases using a Metaclass Concept*, Journal of Systems Integration, vol. 4, pp. 341-372, 1994.

[16] F. Lebastard, *DRIVER: une couche objet persistante pour le raisonnement sur les bases de données relationelles*, PhD thesis, INSA de Lyon / INRIA / CERMICS, 1993.

[17] F. Lebastard, S. Demphlous, V. Aguilera and O. Jautzy, *ObjectDriver: Reference Manual*, CERMICS, France, http://www.inria.fr/cermics/ dbteam/ObjectDriver, 1999.

[18] F. Lebastard, *Vues objets compatibles ODMG sur base de données relationnelles*, Actes des premières journées Ré-ingénierie des Systèmes d'Information, pp. 16-25, 1998.

[19] P. Maes, Concepts and Experiments in Computational Reflection, *Proc. of OOPSLA'87*, ACM SIGPLAN notices 22(12), pp. 147-155, 1987.

[20] C. Nicolle, D. Benslimane and K. Yetongnon, *Multi-Data Models Translation in Interoperable Information Systems*, Proc. of the 8th Intl Conf. on Advanced Information Systems Engineering (CAiSE'96), pp. 176-192, 1996.

[21] J. Padget, G. Nuyens and H. Bretthauer, *On Overview of EuLisp*, Lisp and Symbolic Computation, vol.6, n.1/2, pp. 9-99, 1993.

[22] A. Paepcke. *PCLOS: A Flexible Implementation of CLOS Persistence*, Proc. of ECOOP, Lecture Note in Computer Science n.322, pp. 374-389, Springer-Verlag, 1988;

[23] R. Peters, *Tigukat: a Uniform Behavioral Objectbase Management System*, PhD thesis, University of Alberta, Canada, 1994.

[24] Rational Software Corporation, *Unified Modeling Language, Notation Guide*, can be found at the URL: http://www.rational.com/, 1997.

[25] N. Revault, H. Sahraoui, G. Blain and J.-F. Perrot, *A Metamodeling Technique: the Metagen System*, Proc. of TOOLS Europe'95, pp. 127-139, 1995

Non-functional Policies

Bert Robben, Bart Vanhaute, Wouter Joosen, and Pierre Verbaeten

Distrinet
Computer Science Department
Katholieke Universiteit Leuven
Celestijnenlaan 200A, B-3001 Leuven BELGIUM
{ bert | bartvh | wouter | pv }@cs.kuleuven.ac.be

Abstract. It is well known that a meta-object protocol (MOP) is a powerful mechanism to control the behavior of an application and to implement non-functional requirements such as fault-tolerance and distributed execution. A key feature of these architectures is the strict separation between the application at the base-level and the non-functional concerns at the meta-level. This makes it possible to develop generic meta-programs that can be reused for many applications. However, an important difficulty with this approach is the expression of application specific policies with respect to non-functional behavior. In this paper, we show a new approach that solves this problem by clearly separating policy from both application and meta-level. In our approach, policies are expressed at a high-level of abstraction as separate strategies. This results in highly reusable meta-programs that take application specific characteristics into account. We have validated our approach in the Correlate prototype.

1 Introduction

Meta-level architectures have become an important research topic in object-oriented programming. Such architectures enable the development of highly flexible application programs that can manipulate the state of their own execution [6].

An important topic in this research domain is the study of meta-object protocols (MOPs hereafter). A MOP is a powerful mechanism that can be used to control the behavior of an application and to implement non-functional requirements such as fault-tolerance and distributed execution. This has already been extensively addressed in [1, 2, 8]. One particularly relevant problem is the complexity of the meta-programs that use these MOPs to reflect on the base-level behavior. This complexity results from the inherent complexity of reflective systems and from the non-trivial distributed protocols and algorithms that are used to meet the non-functional requirements. As a result, it is hard for the application programmer, who is typically not an expert in these domains, to specialize such meta-programs to the needs of the application.

Existing research on describing synchronisation constraints[5] has tried to solve this problem. In this work, the application programmer is provided with a high-level declarative language that can be used to express application specific synchronisation policies. Similar ideas have been used to specify concurrency semantics in the context of atomic data types [9]. However all these approaches propose domain specific policy languages and are as such not applicable in a general context. Aspect Oriented Programming (AOP) [7] addresses this problem and takes a more general approach. In AOP, multiple aspects can be described, each in their own special-purpose high-level aspect language. However, current state-of-the-art requires a dedicated aspect weaver for each aspect. This constrains the rapid development of new aspect languages. In addition, aspect languages are composed with the base-level component's code at compile-time. Therefore the possibility for run-time composition, a powerful feature of run-time MOPs, has been lost.

Here, a new approach is proposed which brings the ease-of-use of AOP to run-time reflection. Using this approach, meta-programmers use a specialized language to define a template. This template expresses how the meta-program can be configured. Application programmers instantiate these templates to define application specific policies. This way we can combine high-level declarative policies with reusable and flexible meta-programs. An important property of our approach is that it is not specific to a particular non-functional property. This means that it can be applied to any meta-program.

The rest of this paper is structured as follows. First, we describe how our work is related to other ongoing research. We then elaborate our approach in more detail. This is based on two examples: load balancing and secure execution. We briefly show how this work has been implemented in the Correlate prototype. We then discuss the composition of several non-functional requirements and finally conclude.

2 Problem Description

Run-time reflection is a powerful technique that can be used to control an application's behaviour. Existing research has shown how this technique is used successfully to implement non-functional requirements such as reliability, security and physical distribution [8]. In this approach, the code that realises the non-functional requirements is expressed as a meta-program. This meta-program consists of a collection of meta-level objects that use the MOP to control the application.

The major benefit of this approach is that all non-functional aspects are captured inside the meta-program. As such, an excellent separation of concerns is achieved where the base-level code is completely free of any non-functional concerns. This separation greatly reduces the overall complexity as both the base and the meta-level can be understood independently of each other. In addition, the reflective approach improves reusability and versatility. The meta-object protocol defines an abstract application-independent view on the base-level objects. Therefore, a meta-program can be reused for many different applications. Because the application code is separated from the meta-program, it is possible to use different meta-programs for a single application.

An important issue with this approach is the specification of the binding between base and meta-level program. One might think that it would be sufficient to simply choose a meta-program that realizes the required non-functional properties of the application. If an application needs for instance to be secure, we simply take the security meta-program and everything is fine. In practice however, things are much more complicated. Non-functional requirements are largely independent of an application but not completely. For example, to achieve optimal performance application-specific requirements have to be taken into account. This means for instance that some application objects are treated differently at the meta-level. In a dynamic environment, it might even mean that the treatment of a single application object depends on the current state. In such cases, a much more expressive specification of the binding is required. An alternative way of looking at this problem is to consider it as a parameterization of the meta-program with respect to the application. Current work on run-time reflection does not address this problem in a satisfactory way.

In OpenC++ Version1 [1], the application's source code is annotated with special comments. With these comments, an application programmer can indicate the binding between base and meta-level classes. In addition, methods of base-level classes can be annotated with a category name to enable their meta-level objects to recognize the role of the methods. Iguana [3] uses the same technique but also enables instances and expressions to be annotated. In our opinion, this approach is not satisfactory because the separation of concerns is violated. Indeed, the application's source code is tangled with references to the meta-program. Each time the binding between application and meta-program changes, the application's source code needs to be changed. In addition, the expressive power of these mechanisms is limited because the annotations only allow a static binding defined at compile-time.

A more modular solution is provided by Dalang [11]. In this system, a separate configuration file is used to specify the binding between the third party classes used by the application and the appropriate meta-object class. This file also specifies if all methods and constructors are to be reflected upon or only a subset of them. This yields a much better separation of concerns than the previous approaches. A change in the configuration files does not require a recompilation of the application classes. This leads to an approach where the programming task can be divided amongst three different roles. The application programmer is concerned with the application functionality. The meta-level programmer provides the meta-program that implements the non-functional behavior such as security and fault-tolerance. Finally, the system integrator configures the system to ensure that the overall system meets the organizational policy. It is the task of the latter person to ensure that application specific requirements are taken into account. However, support for system integration is very limited in Dalang. It is not possible to decide on configuration at run-time[1] or to provide detailed application specific information.

In the rest of this paper, we will present a new approach that provides high-level support for the integration of meta-program and application. We maintain the separation of concerns yet allow complex dependencies to be expressed. In our approach, meta-programmers create policy templates that define declarative languages. Application-specific policies can be specified in these languages at a high level of abstraction.

3 Examples

Throughout this paper, two examples of non-functional requirements are used to illustrate our approach. These examples are load balancing and security.

3.1 Load balancing

As a first example, consider the physical distribution of an application over a cluster of workstations. This requires the following mechanisms.

- *Location-transparent communication between objects.* Application objects interact with each other. This interaction must be possible independent of the location of the participating objects.
- *Load balancing.* The location of objects is an important factor in the global performance of an application. Because remote communication introduces a non-negligible overhead, objects that interact frequently should be allocated as close to each other as possible. However, to profit from the availability of multiple CPU's, CPU-intensive objects should be allocated on different hosts.

The first mechanism is independent of application specific characteristics[2] and can thus be applied in an application-independent way. The second one however needs application-specific information for optimal performance. Some applications for instance require a very specific object allocation where each object must be allocated on the correct host. Other applications are more dynamic and need reallocation at run-time to deal with ever-changing interaction patterns [4].

3.2 Secure execution

A second example is secure execution of an application. The core element here is to constrain the interaction between objects according to some policy. It also includes protection of communication from eavesdropping and tampering. Several mechanisms are used to reach these goals.

---

[1] This is in the assumption that the configuration files are created before the application starts.

[2] For this example, we don't take the occurrence of failures into account.

- *Principal authentication.* Each object in the application acts on behalf of a principal. This can be a user or some system service. When two objects start interacting, they need to authenticate each other before any security-related decision can be made.
- *Authorization.* Access to services can be restricted to a subset of privileged clients. In an object-oriented setting, these services correspond to methods of objects, and the clients are the objects invoking these methods. It is generally suitable to define roles for principals and define access according to these roles.
- *Encryption and hashing.* In a distributed application, a combination of encryption and hashing can be used to provide secure communication between communicating objects located on different nodes. The algorithms can be selected according to the cryptographic strength needed. Within a local trust domain, this could be weaker than inter-domain communication.
- *Auditing.* Some services may need to log all the incoming requests. In other cases, the requests that some client object makes may need to be logged.

Except maybe for the third, all of these mechanisms will normally be dependent on the application. Encryption and hashing could depend on the environment only. However, for performance reasons the strength of the encryption may depend on the data that is communicated, thus be specific for the application.

4 Application Policies

Meta-programs that implement non-functional requirements are often complex pieces of software that require specialized domain knowledge to construct and maintain. For optimal performance, these programs have to take application specific characteristics into account.

In our approach, application specific characteristics can be defined in policies. A policy specifies how the mechanisms that are provided by the meta-program should be applied for a specific application. Policies are strictly separated both from the application and from the meta-program. The idea is to use a separate policy object which is linked both to the application object and to the meta-level object. This strict separation enables the reuse of meta-programs for multiple applications.

The definition of policies is the task of the system integrator. They are declared at a high level of abstraction in specialized languages. These languages are defined by the meta-level programmer as general templates. From the point-of-view of the meta-level programmer, application policies are then specializations of these templates.

At run-time, policies are interpreted by the meta-program. This allows the meta-program to ensure that the required mechanisms are executed. Vice versa, it also means that the semantics of the templates is ultimately defined by the meta-program. Finally note that the interpretation is in terms of the general template which keeps meta-programs independent of specific applications.

This idea is explained in further detail in the following two sections. In section 5, the definition of policies is discussed in detail. Section 6 explains the interpretation.

5 Defining Policies

In this section we show how policies can be defined. First two examples are presented that illustrate the general idea. This is followed by a more abstract description of the proposed technique.

5.1 Load balancing

As a first example, consider a subsystem that performs load balancing. Such a subsystem requires application specific information for the allocation of new objects and for measuring the load. The following template expresses this.

```
distributor {

    constructorproperty creation = BALANCED | LOCAL | CUSTOMISED;

    constructorproperty Host allocate(Host[] h) { return h[0]; }

    objectproperty migration = NONE | BALANCED;

    objectproperty double getLoad() { return 1.0; }

}
```

The template defines four properties. The first, **creation**, is a constructor property. It indicates where a new object should be created. There are three possibilities.

- *BALANCED*: The static allocation of objects of this class should be under control of the load management system. This is the default option.
- *LOCAL*: The new object must be created on the local host, i.e. it should reside on the same host as its creator.
- *CUSTOMIZED*: The new object should be allocated on the host indicated by the application programmer.

In the case of customised allocation, the application programmer can implement the constructor property **allocate** to indicate the correct host. The implementation of this constructor property should be a side-effect free function that returns one of the hosts in the array that is passed as a parameter. The default behaviour of this operation is to return the first host in the array.

Dynamic load balancing is controlled through the **migration** property. Objects whose class has this property set to BALANCED, are dynamically migrated during their life-time to ensure a proper load balance over the different nodes of the distributed system. The object property **getLoad()** indicates the load the object generates. The implementation of this property can make use of the internal state of the (base-level) object. By default, the load generated by an object is 1.

System integrators can then instantiate these templates. As an example, consider the following allocation policy for class **WorkUnit**. This class performs an iterative calculation over a square area.

```
distributor WorkUnit {

  WorkUnit(int xPos, int yPos, Dimension size) {

    creation = CUSTOMISED;

    Host allocate(Host[] h) {

      return host[xPos % h.length];

    }

  }

  migration = BALANCED;

  double getLoad() { return mySize.x * mySize.y; }

}
```

This policy specifies that the allocation of new **WorkUnits** is customised and that objects of this class can be migrated for reasons of load management. A **WorkUnit** that is created with the indicated constructor shall be allocated on a host depending on the **xPos** constructor parameter. The load index of a **WorkUnit** instance is equal to the geometric surface of the object. This value can be easily computed based on **mySize**, which is an instance variable of the **WorkUnit** class.

5.2 Secure execution

A similar template can be constructed to specify a security policy.

```
securitypolicy {

  objectproperty principal = INHERITED | USER | NONE;

  objectproperty auditing = NONE | INCOMING | OUTGOING | BOTH;

  methodproperty security = NONE | WEAK | STRONG;

  methodproperty boolean allow(Principal mp, Principal sp,

      Object sender) { return true; }

}
```

This template defines two object properties. The **principal** property defines how a principal is attached to the object when it is created. There are three possibilities.

- *USER*: the object will be acting on behalf of a user.
- *INHERITED*: the new object will inherit the principal of the object that created it. This is useful if a several objects together form one logical client. The 'main' object in the cluster can delegate responsibilities to other objects it creates. This is the default.
- *NONE*: the object does not act on behalf of someone. In this case, an anonymous principle is attached to the object.

The **auditing** property specifies what interactions will be logged. Choices are: no logging, only invocations of other objects on this object (INCOMING), only invocations made by this object (OUTGOING) or both.

Two additional properties are specified on a per method basis. The first one, **security**, defines what security (secrecy, integrity, etc.) is applied to invocations of the method. This ranges from no security applied, over only weak security, to strong. The implementation of weak and strong is left to the security subsystem. Its selection of the algorithms (RSA, DES, ...) will depend on the environment of the involved objects.

Access control can be specified with the **allow()** method property. The parameters allow for a fine-grained specification of access control. The two principals, one for the sender and one for the receiver, make it possible to check role membership, compare identity, or query other attributes. The third parameter is a reference to the sending object. This can be used to extract application specific information in cases where a complex access control policy is needed.

This template can be instantiated as follows for a class in an electronic commerce application that manages electronic payment instruments.

```
securitypolicy UserPayment {

  String[] getPaymentMethods() {

    security = WEAK;

    boolean allow

      (Principal mp, Principal sp, Object sender) {

        return (sender instanceof User);

    }

  }

  UserPaymentInstrument create(String n) {

    security = STRONG;

    boolean allow

     (Principal mp, Principal sp, Object sender) {

        return mp.equals(sp);

    }

  }

}
```

Two important methods for this class have custom security requirements. The first method gives a list of available payment methods. As the names of these methods are not too critical, weak security is sufficient. For access control, the policy states that only users (objects of type **User**) can do the query. The other method is more critical, so it requires strong security measures. Only users acting on behalf of the same principal as the principal of the **UserPayment** object are able to ask to create a new payment instrument.

5.3 Definition

Our approach makes a difference between *templates* and *policies*. A template defines a declarative language that indicates the various possible customisations an application might require. A policy is an instantiation of such a template. Instantiating a template consists of making a selection between a number of possible customisations and completing certain missing information. The scope of the resulting policy is a single application class.

A template is expressed as a set of *properties*. In the simplest case, a property is an enumeration of a set of atomic values. In more complex cases, a property is expressed as a function of the internal state of the object and of the current state of the environment. In this context, the environment is defined as a set additional parameters that contain essential information for that specific property. The array of **Hosts** in the **Distributor** template is an example of such a parameter. It is the responsibility of the meta-program to provide these parameters. Orthogonal to this, a property can be specified for an entire application class or for a single method/constructor.

The template also defines the default value that is used in case no policy can be found for a certain class. For enumerations, the default value is always the first element. For properties that depend on the internal state of the object, a default implementation of the abstraction function has to be defined. Examples of this were given in the two previous subsections.

A policy is the instantiation of a template. It is always related to a single application class. A policy can instantiate any number of properties of its template. Properties that are not instantiated have the default value. Instantiating an enumeration consists of selecting a single value from the set. To instantiate a function, an alternative implementation must be given. This implementation can make use of the instance variables of the application class (as free variables).

A grammar for the syntax of templates and policies can be found in appendix A.

5.4 Conclusion

It is important to understand that the examples are not meant as the ultimate policy templates for distribution and security that fit every application. Developing a general template would also mean building a general subsystem for some non-functional requirement, foreseeing all possible demands applications can have. This is clearly a very difficult task. In practice, the template is usually constructed as a result of the dialog between system integrators, giving rough descriptions of the non-functional requirements, and meta-level programmers explaining the available options.

A second point is that the semantics of the various properties in a policy template is ultimately defined by the meta-level program that interprets the policy objects. This enables a declarative policy specification at a high level of abstraction. Only a high level of abstraction enables system integration without the need for highly detailed knowledge on algorithms and implementation strategies.

6 Interpreting Policies

In the previous section, we have shown how an application programmer can specify an application specific policy. We now show how such a specification is transformed into a class and then used by the meta-program at run-time.

Note that the transformation from policy and template to Java class is simple and can be handled automatically by a tool. This tool is independent of both applications and meta-programs.

6.1 Representing templates

Each template is transformed into an abstract class. This class serves as interface for the meta-program to query the policy an application wants. They don't contain any code related to the implementation of a certain policy.

The interface of a template class is fairly simple. Each property is represented as a public operation on this class. In case of an enumeration property, the operation returns a number that indicates which enumeration value the policy chooses. A state-dependent property has the return type that was defined in the template. All these operations have the appropriate parameters depending on the type of property. This is shown in table 6.1. As before, the environment is defined as the set of additional parameters that are delivered by the non-functional meta-program.

Table 1. Parameters of properties

	Enumeration	State-dependent value
Object property	/	Internal state of object
		Environment
Constructor property	Constructor	Constructor
		Constructor parameters
		Environment
Method property	Method	Internal state of object
		Method
		Method parameters
		Environment

Finally, a static operation is defined that can be used to get the policy object for a certain application class.

Figure 1 shows this class for the Distributor template. The **Distributor** class defines five integer constants, one for each enumeration value. Two get-operations are defined to retrieve respectively the creation and the migration property. The **getLoad** and the **allocate** property are implemented as operations on the **Distributor** class. The former property only depends on the internal state of the object. Therefore, the **getLoad()** operation has this object as

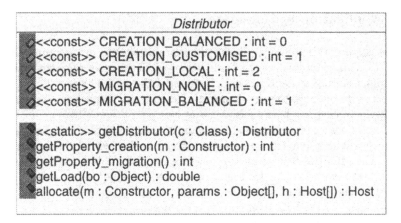

Fig. 1. Implementing the Distributor policy

only parameter. The latter is a constructor property and takes the constructor and the constructor parameters as parameters. In addition, as specified in the policy template, the operation has as final parameter an array of hosts.

6.2 Representing policies

Policies for application classes are transformed into specializations of the abstract template classes. Policy classes implement of course the property operations of the template class. Note that all **Policy** classes are singletons.

Figure 2 shows this for the **SecurityPolicy** template and two security policies of application classes (**User** and **UserPayment**).

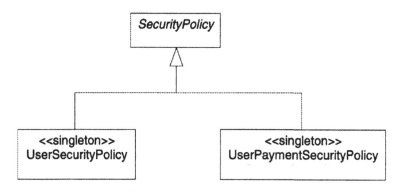

Fig. 2. Implementing templates and policies

Details on the implementation of properties can be found in appendix B.

7 Application in Correlate

We've applied this technique in the Correlate meta-level architecture. Correlate is a research project of the DistriNet research group of the department of Computer Science of the Katholieke Universiteit Leuven. The overall aim of the project is to support the development of distributed application software. A prototype in Java has been built and is available on the web[12].

Correlate is a concurrent object-oriented language extension based on Java. It supports a strictly implicit meta-object protocol for behavioral reflection at run-time. The MOP[13] focuses on the run-time events of object creation/deletion and object invocation. In this sense, it is related to OpenC++ version 1[1]. A Correlate meta-program reacts to these events and implements an execution environment for the base-level application objects.

Using this MOP, we have developed a customised execution environment that implements distributed execution. This meta-program implements a remote communication mechanism and a mechanism for object migration. The abstract interface defined by the MOP ensures a strict separation of concerns between application and execution environment. Therefore, this meta-program can be reused for several applications.

However, application specific requirements need to be taken into account. For example, a genetic search agent application[10] has been built that solves the traveling salesman problem (TSP). In this application, the optimal object allocation scheme is known to the application programmer before the execution of the program. A numerical solver for the heat equation, has a quite different policy. Dynamic refinement of objects at run-time causes major shifts in the work load generated by this application. Because these refinements cannot always be computed in advance, dynamic load balancing techniques have to be applied.

The distributor template has been successfully used to handle both these application-specific policies. As an example, we'll show how the creation property is implemented. The Correlate MOP lets a meta-program control the creation of new objects. In the distribution meta-program, this is implemented by the **handle**() operation which is invoked each time a new application object is created[13]. The following code fragment shows the simplified implementation.

```
void handle(ConstructionMessage msg) {

  Distributor d =

  Distributor.getDistributor(msg.getCorrelateClass());

  switch(d.getProperty_creation(msg.getConstructor())) {
```

```
case CREATION_BALANCED:

    location = loadManager.getNewLocation(...);

    break;

case CREATION_CUSTOMISED:

    location = d.allocate(msg.getConstructor(),

      msg.getParams(), Host.getHosts());

    break;

default:

    location = Host.getLocalHost();

  }

  ... // allocate new object at location

}
```

First, we search for the distributor object that implements the policy for the class of which a new instance must be created. Depending on the **creation** property, the location of the new object is then computed. In case of a balanced allocation, the local load manager is consulted to find a good location. In case of customized allocation, the location is computed based on the allocate object property. The third case, local allocation, is straightforward and needs no further explanation.

Other properties, such as dynamic load balancing and security for example, are more complex and require more sophisticated mechanisms at the meta-level. In the case of load balancing for instance, an information gathering component and a dealing component are necessary. The former component monitors the load distribution. This information is then used by the latter component that decides when to migrate which object(s) to which host. Nevertheless, the principle stays the same. The meta-program implements the mechanism and consults the policy objects whenever application-specific information is required.

At the moment, we only applied our approach to the Correlate prototype. Nevertheless, we believe that the technique as described is general and can therefore be applied in any sufficiently powerful meta-level architecture that supports run-time reflection.

8 Discussion

The major advantage of the approach as described in this paper, is that application specific policies can be expressed as a separate entity. The base application remains totally independent from any meta-program; no hooks or comment lines are present that link application code to meta-level objects. The meta-program contains no application specific code. The only links to the application it supports are through the abstract interface of the MOP and through a policy template, both independent of a specific application. Because of this separation, reuse of both parts is achieved more easily. In addition, changes in the meta-program will have no effect on the application, and vice versa. All modifications are concentrated in the set of policies for the application. However, the effort is reduced as a result of the high-level declarative style of the specifications. To help the system integrator manage the properties in all policies, a tool could even be constructed. For example, in the case of security specifications, the properties for access control would probably be derived from a more general policy statement.

In comparison to aspect-oriented programming, experimentation with the functionality of the meta-program and the expressions of the templates is less difficult. Instead of constantly having to rewrite the aspect weaver for every change in the aspect language, one only has to modify some property definitions in the template. The general parser will generate new policy objects so that the meta-program can query them in an object-oriented fashion. This flexibility of policy templates lets the meta-programmer focus on implementing the necessary algorithms instead of the adaptation of base application code.

Finally, consider the problem of composition. Suppose an application needs both security and distribution. A promising approach is to organize the meta-programs into a meta-tower. In this case, composition simply means describing an order of stacking the different meta-programs on each other. For instance, such a system is described in [2] for a combination of fault-tolerance, security and distributed execution. However, when two meta-programs need to control the same base application, there is a problem. As the meta-program only sees the level that lies directly beneath it, the higher meta-levels can make no decisions about the state of the base application. Although it is too early yet to make a definite statement, we claim our approach can overcome this latter problem for many practical cases. The reason for this is that a meta-program can define its policies based on the policies of the base-level that it controls.

For example, suppose the security meta-program is to be used together with the distribution meta-program. The distribution policy of a security meta-level object then depends on the distribution policy of the base-level object it controls. Consider for instance the allocation property. A particular security policy could be to only allow creation of **WorkUnit** instances on trusted hosts. The **allocation** property of the security policy will thus first query the property of its base object. If the host on which the base object wants to be created is trusted, that host is selected by the security policy. If not, a different but trusted host is selected. This means controlled access to the state of the base application is achieved, through mapping policies from one level onto the next. The complexity of the mapping will depend on how orthogonal the non-functional requirements and their meta-programs are.

9 Conclusion

This paper described a new approach that enables application-specific policies for non-functional requirements to be expressed at a high level of abstraction. These policies are represented as objects that are separated both from the base and the meta-level. Our approach has been applied in the Correlate meta-level architecture.

As part of our future work, we want to apply our approach in the domains of distributed security and real-time systems to validate its expressiveness. Also of particular interest is the applicability of our approach for the composition of complex non-orthogonal requirements. Another interesting track would be to apply this research to architectures that support compile-time reflection.

Acknowledgements

We gratefully thank all the anonymous reviewers for the many helpful comments that helped us to improve the presentation of this work.

References

1. Shigeru Chiba and Takashi Masuda. Designing an Extensible Distributed Language with a Meta-Level Architecture. In Proceedings ECOOP '93, pages 483-502, Kaiserslautern, July 1993. Springer-Verlag.
2. Jean-Charles Fabre and Tanguy Prennou. A Metaobject Architecture for Fault-Tolerant Distributed Systems: The FRIENDS Approach. In IEEE Transactions on Computers, 47(1), January 1998.
3. Brendan Gowing, Vinny Cahill. Meta-Object Protocols for C++: The Iguana Approach. In Proceedings of Reflection'96, San Francisco, 1996.
4. Wouter Joosen. Load Balancing in Distributed and Parallel Systems. PhD Thesis, Department Computer Science K.U.Leuven, 1996.
5. Ciaran McHale. Synchronisation in Concurrent, Object-oriented Languages: Expressive Power, Genericity and Inheritance. Phd Thesis, University of Dublin, Trinity College, 1994.
6. G. Kiczales, J. des Rivieres and D. Bobrow. The Art of the Meta-Object Protocol, MIT Press, 1991.
7. Christina Lopes. D: A Language Framework for Distributed Programming. PhD thesis, Graduate School of the College of Computer Science of Northeastern University, 1997.
8. Robert J. Stroud and Zhixue Wue. Using Metaobject Protocols to Satisfy Non-Functional Requirements. In Chris Zimmermann, editor, Advances in Object-Oriented Metalevel Architectures and Reflection, CRC Press, 1996.
9. R. J. Stroud and Z. Wu. Using Metaobject Protocols to Implement Atomic Data Types. In Proceedings of ECOOP'95, Lecture Notes in Computer Science 952, 168-189, 1995.

10. Romain Slootmaekers, Henk Van Wulpen, Wouter Joosen. Modeling Genetic Search Agents Using a Concurrent Object-Oriented Language. In Proceedings of HPCN Europe 1998, Lecture Notes in Computer Science 1401, Amsterdam 1998.
11. Ian Welch and Robert Stroud. Dalang - A Reflective Java Extension, OOPSLA'98 Workshop on Reflective Programming in C++ and Java, Vancouver, Canada, October 1998. To be published as part of the OOPSLA'98 Workshop Reader.
12. Correlate Home Page. http://www.cs.kuleuven.ac.be/x̄enoops/CORRELATE/.
13. Bert Robben, Wouter Joosen, Frank Matthijs, Bart Vanhaute, and Pierre Verbaeten. A Metaobject Protocol for Correlate. In ECOOP'98 Workshop on Reflective Object-Oriented Programming Systems, 1998.

Appendix A: Grammars

The grammar for policy templates is defined as follows. A template is written as a name followed by a sequence of properties surrounded by curly braces. A property is defined as a context modifier followed by either an enumeration or a state-function. In this context, a modifier is one of the keywords "constructorproperty", "objectproperty" or "methodproperty". An enumeration consists of a name and a sequence of identifiers separated by the | operator. A state-function is a simple Java method declaration. Simple in this context means that the method doesn't declare any thrown exceptions and doesn't have any method modifiers.

```
<template> = <name> "{" <property>+ "}"

<property> = <modifier>

   ( <enumeration> | <state-function> )

<modifier> = "constructorproperty" | "objectproperty" |

            "methodproperty"

<enumeration> = <identifier> "=" <value-list> ";"

<value-list> = <identifier> [ "|" <value-list> ]

<state-function> = <simple-method-declaration>
```

The grammar for a policy is similar to that for a template. The major difference is that constructor and method policies have to declare to which constructor or method they apply.

```
<policy> = <template-name> <application-class-name>

    "{" <policy-property>+ "}"

<policy-property> = <c-prop> | <m-prop> | <o-prop>

<c-prop> = <constructor-signature>

    "{" <simple-property>+ "}"

<m-prop> = <method-signature>

    "{" <simple-property>+ "}"

<o-prop> = <simple-property>

<simple-property> = <selection> | <completion>

<selection> = <identifier> "=" <identifier> ";"

<completion> = <simple-method-declaration>
```

The grammar for policies that is described here is independent of any template. For a policy to be valid, it must be an instantiation of a template for a certain application class. This means that the simple properties of the policy are defined in the policy template and that all methods and constructors that are mentioned refer to actual methods and constructors of the application class. Also, note that methods defined in policies access the instance variables of the application class. Completions for constructors and methods can use the constructor / method parameters.

Appendix B: Translating policies to classes

In section 6, we discussed the representation of policies and templates as classes. However, we only showed the external interface. This appendix explains a straightforward implementation.

While implementing policy classes, we face two interesting problems. On the one hand, we need to give an implementation for the three different kinds of properties. On the other hand, we must ensure that properties can access the environment (for instance the state of the base-level object).

The first problem is not very hard to solve in Java. A simple solution is to make use of the Java reflection feature that reifies an operation in a Method object. On the policy class, a single operation is defined for each method property. This operation takes a Method object as parameter. In its implementation, a simple if-then-else structure is used to select the appropriate code. The following code fragment shows this for the allow property. The code is for a policy that redefines the property for two operations. For a constructor property, a similar implementation strategy can be followed.

```
public boolean allow(Method m, ...) {

  if (m.equals(METHOD_1)) {

    ... // code for METHOD_1

  } else if (m.equals(METHOD_2)) {

    ... // code for METHOD_2

  }

  return super.allow(m, ...); // default property

}
```

The second problem concerns properties that are specified as state functions. The code of these functions can almost directly be used as implementation of the operation that implements the property. We must only ensure that references to instance variables and invocation parameter are correctly transformed. This is necessary because the operation that implements the property is defined on the policy class and not on the application class. To access instance variables, we define the policy class to be in the same package as the application class. All non-private instance variables are then reachable. To access private variables, the Correlate compiler generates special hidden get-functions on the application class. These functions have package visibility and can thus be used by the policy classes[3]. Consider for instance the **getLoad()** property for the **WorkUnit** class as discussed earlier. This property depends on the **mySize** instance variable of the **WorkUnit** class. The following code fragment shows the implementation.

```
public double getLoad(Object o) {

  return ((WorkUnit)o).mySize().x * ((WorkUnit)o).mySize().y;

}
```

We've developed a tool that automates this translation.

---

[3] Note that the Sun^{Tm} Java Compiler uses a similar solution when Java inner classes need to access instance variables of an outer class.

Invited Talk 2
On the reflective structure of Information Networks

Jean-Bernard Stefani
France Télécom - Centre National d'Etudes des Télécommunications (CNET)
28 Chemin du Vieux Chêne BP 98
38243 Meylan, FRANCE
E-mail : jeanbernard.stefani@cnet.francetelecom.fr

Introduction

The notion of information networking has been the subject of much work, in the past ten years, from the "classical" telecommunications community under the auspices of the TINA (Telecommunications Information Networking Architecture) Consortium. Although much of this work has turned up in the end to be predicated upon a relatively traditional view of networking, and has been overshadowed by the recent phenomenal growth of the Internet and the World Wide Web, the notion of an information network, as described e.g. in [1, 2], embodies a small but powerful set of architectural principles that have passed largely un-noticed. In this talk we will review these principles and spend some time reviewing the resulting network view, which characterizes an information network as an essentially reflective structure. In the process, we will end up discussing the significance of binding as a key constituency in a full-fledged reflective distributed system and pointing at relevant works in the area.

Information network architectural principles

The terms "information network" and "information networking" have been coined to emphasize the evolution of telecommunications networks towards communication systems providing a broad range of services, from standard, low-level transmission services — bit pipes — to high-level, value-added, information processing services — e.g. WWW-based services.

Briefly, an information network architecture can be generated by adopting three architectural principles :

- networks as open distributed systems ;
- reifying network resources as computational objects ;
- telecommunications services as binding services.

An information network can thus be seen as consisting in a superposition (in the technical sense of the term) of two different sub-systems: a transport network and a control system. The transport network corresponds to the set of network elements and communications resources that provide the transfer of information from one point of the network to another. The control system encompasses the set of information processing resources and capabilities that are used to manage and control the transport network, as well as to support services constructed on top of the transport network services.

The resulting structure is inherently reflective in that the effectiveness of the control system is predicated upon the ability to reify network elements as full-fledged programming objects. It is also inherently recursive in that several information networking structures may stack-up in a tower of transport/information networks.

Within such a structure, many different network views can be reconciled, from traditional signalling in POTS to active networks.

References

1. J.B. Stefani: "A reflexive architecture for intelligent networks" – 2nd TINA International Workshop, Chantilly, France, May 1991.
2. J.B. Stefani : "Open Distributed Processing: an architectural basis for information network" – Computer Communications vol. 18, no 11, November 1995.
3. D. Tennenhouse, J. Smith, W. Sincoskie, D. Wetherall, G. Minden : "A survey of active network research" – IEEE Communications Magazine, vol. 35, no 1, January 1997.

Reflective Media Space Management Using RASCAL

Wayne Robbins and Nicolas D. Georganas

Multimedia Communications Research Laboratory
Electrical and Computer Engineering
School of Information Technology and Engineering
University of Ottawa
161 Louis Pasteur
Ottawa, Ontario, Canada
K1N 6N5
{robbins, georganas}@mcrlab.uottawa.ca

Abstract. The advent of interactive shared media spaces has augmented the traditional role of multimedia by providing a natural and intuitive means for interpersonal communication. These shared media-rich environments serve as a natural basis for distributed collaboration through a seamless blend of presentational, conversational and interactive multimedia. This integration, however, presents challenges ranging from the need to support various media types to managing real-time object interaction. This work addresses how to facilitate media space design by employing reflection as a primary design, implementation and management technique within a pattern-based meta-level architecture. Reflection is used to isolate system-level issues such as behavioural coordination from low-level, media-specific computation as well as to facilitate dynamic adaptation of differing behavioural requirements. The architectural framework and underlying topology are illustrated along with the model's application to a distance education system. Finally, the prototype and its use of the ObjecTime CASE tool are overviewed.

1 Introduction

The traditional role of multimedia systems has been to disseminate information. From textual to graphical, auditory to visual, such systems were designed to augment the presentation of ideas by representing them in the most appropriate format(s). *Collaborative multimedia*, however, goes beyond the role of exposition to provide support for distributed work groups. By melding multimedia within computer-supported collaborative work (CSCW) environments, media offer a natural and intuitive means to facilitate group interaction and the collaborative exchange of ideas.

The classical model of collaborative computing offered by teleconferencing can be seen as multimedia. However, its potential falls short because it does not adequately allow users to mimic traditional shared work spaces. In real-world collaborative exchanges, people see and talk to each other, manipulate and point at shared props, sketch ideas on shared surfaces and view other media (such as film clips) in a mutually common environment. In short, participants and the objects they use form a *shared media space* in which users interact with each other through the experience

Collaborating group consisting of shared document editing and real-time audio/video conference

Collaborating group consisting of graphical editing and a synthetic audio/video movie playback

Fig. 1. Logical View of an Example Media Space

and manipulation of multiple media (Fig. 1). The expressiveness of a diverse media palette combined with a distributed work environment goes not only beyond the utility of teleconferencing, but also the conventional classifications of presentational, conversational and interactive multimedia.

In order to effectively utilize this expressive power, activities performed within the space must be understood by all those involved. That is, user actions must be integrated into a *semantically coherent workspace* that suits the needs and expectations of participants as they interact. An important part of maintaining semantic coherence is the very often subtle and implicit *coordination* of activities that is part of the collaborative process [1]. This coordination [2] is necessary to achieve an environment in which the actions performed upon objects and the interactions between them make sense; that is, meaning must be maintained through synchronizing participants and their actions.

These actions can be seen to constitute participant *behaviours* within the shared environment. Consequently, specific actions can be viewed as *behavioural components* within the collaborative scenario while well-defined groups of actions form the notion of *behavioural patterns*. While multimedia synchronization has traditionally referred to temporal relationships amongst media [3], collaborative systems must address participant behaviours (personal interaction, media processing, and so forth) in an integrated fashion to facilitate a naturally fluid, predictable and reasonable work environment. Behaviours must be coordinated to ensure that they maintain their own semantics (such as timeliness), while interacting activity patterns must also occur in the correct temporal order (precedence relationship) to ensure causal dependencies of collaborative actions are reflected and maintained throughout the shared space [2][4]. In short, the media space must provide a containment framework for the integration of diverse entities and behaviours used within a particular collaborative context. It must do so in a way that mirrors the dynamic way people work together as well as how their collaborative behaviours change over time.

This inherently open and dynamic nature of the media space, however, creates significant difficulty in the construction of such systems. In particular, how to best provide for the possible variety of entities and behaviours while still being able to enforce the rules and requirements governing them. This work proposes an infrastructural framework that facilitates both structural and behavioural flexibility based on a system that can potentially analyze and modify itself. Rather than retrofit concerns such as synchronization in an ad hoc "after the fact" manner, behaviour and structure are regarded as orthogonal building blocks from which systems can be built, modified or replaced throughout their lifetime.

To this end, this paper presents a work in progress that proposes a reflective meta-level approach to collaborative media space management. Emphasis is given to the design of an infrastructural framework for building a broad range of media-based collaborative environments, with specific support for addressing diverse behavioural requirements. How to provide for these various facets in a flexible and adaptive fashion illustrates the importance of addressing how "the pieces of the puzzle" are put together. Consequently, the architecture's design, its underlying software engineering and the role of its communication infrastructure are considered.

The remainder of this paper is organized as follows: section two overviews the definition and management of a media space while section three discusses the flexibility achieved through the use of patterns within a reflective, meta-level management architecture. Section four presents the proposed model, which is then illustrated in terms of a telelearning scenario. On-going work towards development of a prototype utilizing ObjecTime [5], a CASE tool for the design of real-time and distributed systems, is then discussed. Finally, the paper summarizes and concludes.

2 A Media Space and Its Management

The term *media space* originated from work at Xerox Parc [6][7] in the mid to late 80's. A broad discussion in [8] illustrated its potential group for supporting group interaction between co-workers at remote sites in both social and work settings. These initial media spaces were based on the use of an analog audio/video network in parallel with a digital network of workstations. In contrast, our work is based on the premise of an "all digital" media space and that users interact using an integrated, more closely unified "point of presence" within the space. Collaboration is facilitated via whatever *objects* (media, applications and so forth) are shared between users and how they are manipulated. Indeed, various media and interfaces (including user interface peripheral devices such as video capture/display) are integrated into the space as adjunct objects rather than separate parallel systems. Our approach attempts to provide an integrated solution so that different aspects of collaboration are sufficiently modular but not disjoint streams of activity.

Traditional collaborative space research has dealt with collaboration from process, psychological and technological perspectives: (1) specific application environments [9][10]; (2) human-computer interaction [1][11]; and (3) communication and/or application protocols [4][12]. The first perspective deals with a program's functionality, while the second addresses elements of the user interface. In each, coordination is often either ignored or statically embedded within the application. Additionally, collaborative potential is limited since an application's utility is "wrapped up" in its design and complexity. While protocol-based solutions are more versatile, their premise is that data exchange rules are the main issue, resulting in a "message sequence chart"-based approach. In all cases, there is little focus on extensibility, abstraction or adaptivity.

Of specific interest is the work by Dourish [13], in which reflection/meta-techniques are used to provide extensibility in CSCW toolkits. While borrowing some intent from Dourish's body of work, ours differs (in part) via its focus on multimedia systems and its emphasis on behavioural components. While not explored in this paper, a significant benefit of our approach is its potential to address mixed mode synchronization issues that are not well served by other approaches.

This work therefore addresses the need for a design framework and methodology which can be used to build a versatile and enabling infrastructure for user-level collaborative applications. The proposed work can be viewed as a potential a way to organize, relate and integrate different approaches (including user interface technologies, applications and protocols) as required. To facilitate this, the work observes a key underlying principle: management and domain functionality must be strictly separated to facilitate a flexible, modifiable and adaptive system. In particular, the coordination and synchronization of both the environment and individual entities within it should be managed separately from their domain functionality. To facilitate both the abstraction of these components as well as their integration in a mutually effective manner, reflection is employed to provide the "causally connected glue" between functional and behavioural components. In particular, the primary areas of concern include: (1) how to address behavioural characteristics within the space; and (2) how to facilitate a versatile and flexible infrastructure to accommodate new uses.

2.1 Characterizing Media Space Behaviours

The usual concern of multimedia synchronization has been to ensure timely media rendering. Collaborative multimedia, however, goes beyond simple presentation, and so too does its synchronization requirements. While traditional concerns are important, it is the coordination of the collaborative activities that ultimately defines media space utility. As discussed later, by representing behaviours as first-class building blocks, it is easier to address the variety of media, interaction styles and the typical characteristics of inter-personal communication. Shown in Fig. 2, these characteristics form a hierarchy which can parameterize and constrain the behavioural patterns used within the media space [14].

2.2 Extending the Media Space

A significant benefit of the media space approach is its integration of many different kinds of media and activities into a single environment. As such, it naturally suits the

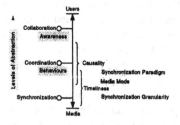

Fig. 2. Facets of Media Space Management

collaborative process by offering a "what you need is what you get" solution. However, even in a very feature-rich system, there will always be the need for another type of media, another application, the introduction of a new behaviour, a change in policy and so on. In other words, the utility of the space drives it to be a dynamic entity whose composition must be extensible and adaptive to different uses over time. Therefore, a media space framework must be able to facilitate changes both in terms structure and behaviour.

Structural extensibility means that the media space can be modified and extended through the introduction of new types of objects within the space. This is done by dynamically installing/replacing functional components, such as a new media type or application. For example, if users need to refer to a particular medium (e.g. use a particular codec) or perform a specific task (e.g. use a specific application) during a collaborative session, the media space integrates the required modules into its environment. This allows the media space framework to address real-world diversity and the "on-the-fly" nature of the collaborative process by "growing" the infrastructure as necessary. Such a *component-based* approach can also be applied to the user interface (UI) metaphors offered to media space users. By abstracting the manner in which users interact with the space, different types of physical interaction can be supported, ranging from common CSCW tools to virtual environments.

Behavioural adaptation primarily refers to modifying an object's coordination and synchronization within the media space. Examples range from changing the frame rate for video playback to modifying the rules which govern the interaction between users who are jointly editing a shared document. Behavioural adaptation can be seen to cover a broad range of activities including performance monitoring of object mechanisms to the specification and evolution of collaborative policies. By treating object behaviours separately from their functionality, descriptions of behaviours can be manipulated as first-class abstractions. The result is a *behavioural component* approach which mirrors the structural component model. Behavioural adaptation then becomes a task of dynamically installing/replacing/modifying the behavioural components which describe entity behaviour and interaction within the space.

3 Facilitating Management Through Design

As a real-time system, the viability of a media space can be significantly impacted by its ability to meet the specific needs of a usage scenario. For example, reliability is paramount in a tele-surgical application while much less important for video-on-demand. In each case, however, the details typical of real-time systems that must be addressed to "get the job done right" can cloud issues of proper system and software design. The very issues that are vital to system deployment are often over-complicated or inadequately addressed because they are all jumbled together; areas of concern are inextricably woven together rather than properly separated into disjoint areas of responsibility. In multimedia, system complexity is often exacerbated due to the desire for an immediate and sleek solution. Hence, it is extremely important to address the organization and management of a collaborative multimedia environment.

3.1 Responsibility-Driven Organization

Object orientation is a technique which attempts to address these concerns by considering a system as a collection of interacting objects, each of which represents and encapsulates the details of some (real-world) entity. Unfortunately, an object's complexity is often increased as a result of this composite view. A video-on-demand system, using a movie object with audio and video tracks, would address issues such as data retrieval, decoding, intra/inter-stream synchronization, user interface management and so forth. While most designs would not attempt a strictly monolithic solution, it is quite common to blend at least some of these aspects together in implementation-specific ways. The result is difficulty in isolating which aspects of the system deal with different parts of the problem, ultimately affecting how easy it is to debug, modify and maintain it. Levels of functionality are often woven together and blur the distinction between solution, policy and mechanism [15].

Within collaborative environments, this lack of separation affects the ability to scale and adapt such systems because the range of usage scenarios can be overwhelming. Combined with the integration of presentational techniques, live media and interactive exchanges, there is clearly a need to simplify when, where and how to address a system's overall design. Object orientation is a necessary but insufficient means of isolating system detail because such an object addresses issues relating to its own behaviour as well as its interaction with others. The result is a mesh of interacting objects, each communicating with the other in a very tangled manner. In general, objects are both busy doing their own work (i.e. domain computation) and telling others what to do (i.e. coordinating them), either explicitly or implicitly through their direct communication with each other. This leads to a system that is a highly interdependent and interconnected collection of objects which must directly deal with the coordination of other entities in its environment. Consequently, the entities within the space are highly configuration-dependent and their ability to be re-used within a general framework is reduced.

Therefore, there is a need to organize the system along lines of the responsibility in which a system's execution (i.e. domain computation) is separated from its coordination (i.e. the management of domain computation). The coordination meta level manages the base-level computation in which these two aspects of an entity are explicitly separated. Doing so facilitates cleaner system design and re-use at a behavioural level in addition to a structural (i.e. functional) level (as in the standard object-oriented paradigm). This takes the standard hierarchical approach to structure (e.g. classes, types, objects) and mirrors it in a behavioural context; that is, lower-level domain activities are managed by higher-level coordination activities.

In collaborative systems, this approach reflects the difference between the elements of a media space. Media are synchronized at multiple granularities (objects, frames, actions, groups of...) and in terms of their individual media-specific requirements. Collaborators who use these media must be coordinated according to their behaviours, which are oriented towards achieving a specific goal. Consequently, collaboration is achieved by coordinating users' behaviours via synchronizing the media they use. Since these tasks deals with different entities and at different levels of abstraction within the media space, each forms a meta level to the one below it.

This meta-level approach is the basis for applying *reflection* [16][17][18] as a technique to abstract and inter-relate different levels of functionality and behaviour within the media space. With the use of multiple meta levels, a *reflective tower* can be used to provide a dynamically extensible and adaptive model for both structure and behaviour. And as such, it can thought of as a *pattern* for structuring the organization of the system into causally connected levels of responsibility.

3.2 Employing a Pattern-Based Architecture

Increasingly prevalent within the domain of software engineering, *pattern-oriented software architectures* [19] are extending the notion of encapsulation and re-use from simple code modules (such as procedures and objects) to entire subsystems of interacting components (i.e. component-based systems). Each component is an independently developed and tested entity which also has well-defined interfaces to connect to and function as part of a larger system. Patterns offer a way to re-use a general solution methodology across a variety of specific problems, ranging from architectural patterns for software system organization, design patterns for detailing subsystem refinements and idioms which hilight implementation constructs. Well-known patterns include the client/server, proxy and broker models.

The structural view of an architecture is one in which an entity's functional role and interconnections are governed according to a specific well-known configuration. This view addresses the design of collaborative multimedia systems as patterns of collaborating entities, each of which support/enable a particular kind of collaborative activity or multimedia functionality. For example, a video-on-demand system would employ the client/server pattern using an video data server and playback client.

The behavioural view, however, constitutes a logical perspective of entities and their interaction as part of the collaborative process. The interaction between participants and the media they use is a highly purposeful dialogue in which participants' activities and the exchanges between them are part of a mutually understood "goal-oriented" behaviour. Participants can be seen to engage in specific collaborative *behavioural patterns* which guide their mutual understanding and

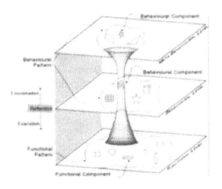

Fig. 3. Functional and Behavioural Patterns

activities, both as individuals as well as members of a collaborating group. Complex behaviours are a combination of simpler ones, with each behaviour being a pattern of entities which interact in a specific well-defined manner. The result is a composition of complex patterns from simpler ones, functioning much like *behavioural components* in the overall collaborative effort (Fig. 3).

The key benefit of this approach is the customization or *tailorability* offered to system designers, implementers and users. The different elements of the system can be integrated according to the requirements of the system at a range of granularities based on behavioural patterns (i.e. perform a required function, meet specific performance levels, work at a specific level of abstraction, etc.). The proposed architecture considers a media space as a collection of component entities which interact in a coordinated manner using an "intelligent" communications service. The space's coordination is separated from media-specific computations using patterns to specify policy and specific collaborative rules, in which behavioural components and patterns are first-class entities which are instantiated and manipulated in their own right. Rather than being an inherent part of the structural model, activity coordination involves behavioural (i.e. coordination/synchronization) meta-objects in which synchronization characteristics (Sect. 2.1) would be applied through the use of behavioural patterns.

An important aspect of this approach is its use of *active objects* to realize the environment's components. Each element, be it a user-level collaborative object or a part of the media space system itself, is considered an active object with its own run-time behaviour/thread of execution. Rather than use passive computational structures (i.e. traditional objects) to handle the system's various operational states, an entity's active nature allows it to perform computations and execute actions to fulfill its role. Changes in behaviour or function are achieved by using the appropriate active entity which "knows how" to perform a particular type of activity.

4 The RASCAL Collaborative Infrastructure

The proposed model [20][21][22][14] provides both a framework and a methodology from which to build collaborative media spaces. The *Reflectively Adaptive Synchronous Coordination Architectural framework* (more affectionately known as *RASCAL*) blends support for traditional multimedia synchronization with a more holistic approach to shared space coordination. The media space is taken as a collection of interacting objects which are managed using an "intelligent network coordination service" which separates the space's behavioural issues from its media-specific computation based on a reflective meta-architecture.

4.1 The RASCAL Media Space Topology

Based on the architectural premise of separating execution and coordination, data and control mechanisms form two distinct subsystems within the media space. As shown in Fig. 4, the architecture's topology can be represented as a collection of hosts (participants in the collaborative environment) joined by a *coordinated*

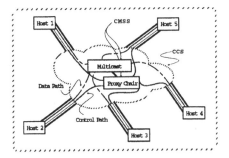

Fig. 4. RASCAL's Underlying Topology

communications subsystem (CCS). Most communications systems are simply viewed as a "passive" medium that link participants in a conference; however, the principle in RASCAL is to provide an "active" communications infrastructure which intelligently coordinates media space activities. The hosts are "points of presence" in the media space at which users connect to the collaborative environment. The basic element used to collaborate is the *object* which can represent a medium, application or other technological entity in the space, such as an autonomous intelligent agent. Users at different hosts manipulate and/or communicate through objects to interact with remote collaborators. Example objects include live audio/video objects (for conferencing), a shared editing application, a synthetic MPEG movie or a bitmap image. Objects are used in the context of a *collaborative session* which in which users participate and interact according to some behavioural pattern. Each of these objects has their own synchronization requirements and each collaborative session coordinates its constituent objects relative to the overall collaborative effort.

The CCS is divided into two complementary elements: a *coordination sphere* and an *execution sphere* (shown in Fig. 5). The execution sphere represents the flow of data, which is produced and consumed by objects within the collaborative environment; that is, execution constitutes the "media" within the media space. The data that forms this sphere are the media and interactions that compose the objects and the manipulations performed on them by participants. Coordination of these activities, on the other hand, is considered separately. The coordination of the activities addresses the notion of synchronization within the shared space. The coordination of execution (i.e. the synchronization of the media data) utilizes separate data and control paths within the CCS. The data from different participants is multicast to send and receive data between participants; the intention is to utilize an underlying network that would offer simultaneous data delivery as well as support for QoS guarantees [3]. Control information that describes the consumption of the generated data forms the execution sphere of the CCS. The control information is also multicast but under the auspices of the *collaborative multimedia support system*, or CMSS.

Coordination of the space, as performed by the CMSS, logically pairs a *dedicated coordinator* with the multicast switch. This coordinator, called the *Proxy Chair*, manages control messages that describe the data flowing through the multicast network. Data is not channeled through the Proxy Chair (abbreviated as *Proxy*), nor does the Proxy perform any other function other than coordinate the space through the synchronization of control messages. From the collaborator's perspective, the network is providing the necessary coordination and synchronization, while from the network's point of view, the coordinator is a specialized entity within it that offers a particular service, like those associated with *intelligent networks* [23]. Hence, the Proxy Chair is *not* a functionality to be assumed by a host participant; rather, it is to be a dedicated component of the CCS. Rather than waste resources, this separation offers the following benefits:

1. A complete and straight-forward separation of concerns in terms of communication. The separation of paths enables appropriate QoS levels for different objects' data as well as control messages. Multicasting is still used for transmitting coordination constructs but at the discrimination of the Proxy Chair.

2. A complete and straight-forward separation of concerns in terms of processing. End hosts are often taxed by the manipulation of media data (e.g. decoding and user interface); therefore, placing coordination in a subservient position to such variable and demanding duties is ill-considered. More than the use of a centralized architecture, it is this often-assumed multiplexing of functionality which leads to bottlenecks; in short, the temptation to minimize the number of components to perceive a more effective use of resources needs careful consideration.

3. The autonomy of coordination facilitates more straight-forward, scaleable and flexible designs for both end systems and the Proxy. End hosts typically function as input/output devices for participants within the shared space. For specific usage scenarios, the calibre of these machines could vary considerably. However, if considerable coordination logic is made part of the end host design, these machines necessarily become more complex and expensive. Furthermore, the potential orthogonality of host design is lessened because components are now context dependent as to their role within the media space; therefore, the adaptability and scalability of the architecture are now determined by application topology. As proposed, the architecture partitions system workload into two areas, each of which can be managed separately. The modification or addition of new coordination policies is more easily managed by using a central coordinator combined with host-independent, role-specific control software. The Proxy only functions as a "chairperson" for coordination purposes and is independent of any application-specific management or "chairperson" entity. While the Proxy forms a single, independent entity within the CCS, it can best be viewed as a *logical* entity. Should media space scale, performance or failure be an issue, a group of coordinators could be defined to function as a distributed Proxy Chair. In the case of failure, the Proxy could be dynamically replaced; or if the space scaled beyond the capacity of a single Proxy, multiple coordinators, each of which would manage a specific region of the media space, could be used to transparently migrate select sessions to another coordinator.

4.2 Applying the Meta-Level Approach

As part of the collaborative effort, the activities which ultimately achieve and affect the state of the collaboration can be seen to causally affect media space state (i.e. the users' environment). Therefore, in as much as participants and media interact in a coordinated manner, these entities can be modelled in a reflective relationship which maintains the semantics of the collaboration by using meta-information about their interactions. Hence the complexity of different entities (such as a particular medium or activity) is abstracted away and isolated from other parts of the system. The bi-directional nature of the reflective relationship allows the intention of more abstract layers to be reflected "down" to the lower implementation levels while their status is reflected "up" in order for the system to monitor and adapt itself.

The relationship between the coordination sphere (controlled by policy) and the execution sphere (enabled by mechanism) can be applied throughout the entire media space as shown in Fig. 5. The coordination meta level addresses issues of managing user behaviour (as well as media synchronization) according to collaborative policies (and associated goals). Meanwhile, the execution level deals with computations which realize the media and other "physical" components of the media space. The reflective relationship between the coordination and execution levels link the various entities within the space while still maintaining their encapsulation (both structurally and behaviourally) at different levels of abstraction.

Reflection can therefore be seen as an organizational pattern which bridges various levels of responsibility and function within the media space. While an important aspect of the architecture is to facilitate flexible and adaptive design through the explicit separation of concerns, there is a need to integrate them in a manner where changes in one area are "felt" in another; that is, there is a need to provide a *causal connection* between the various entities within the system. Fig. 6 illustrates (using pseudo-OMT notation [24]) different elements of a collaborative session within the space, ranging from users and mechanisms at the lowest base level to the abstract definition of collaborative rules (via patterns) at the highest meta level. The result is a reflective organization in which upper meta levels monitor and configure lower levels according to their status/performance. As with other reflective systems, each media space entity provides both a standard API by which specific domain functionality

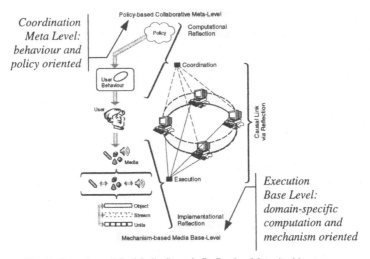

Fig. 5. Overview of the Media Space's Reflective Meta Architecture

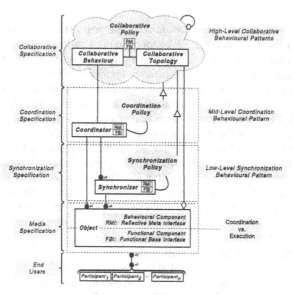

Fig. 6. Elements of a Collaborative Session

(such as media rendering) is accessed. In addition to this *functional base interface* (or FBI), a secondary interface is provided to manipulate and examine how the entity provides its base functionality. This *reflective meta interface* (or RMI) offers a structured way to detail how specific aspects of an entity's functionality are facilitated and managed through the use of appropriate meta objects. These interfaces are applied across the entire system, such that "physical" system entities (like the Proxy Chair) as well as the logical ones (like collaborative behaviours) are all subject to reflective manipulation.

This encapsulation of responsibility promotes flexibility and increased adaptability in terms of implementation, design and usage; for example, the ability to support different "awareness widgets" using adaptive user interface meta objects. It also allows for *self-adaptive behaviours* in which collaborative behaviour patterns can themselves be designed in a reflective manner (i.e. causally connected meta/base levels); that is, it facilitates a hierarchical behavioural specification in which more abstract collaborative levels can monitor and modify lower-level coordination and synchronization rules. Such a specification would utilize multiple meta levels to specify behavioural patterns in terms of other behavioural patterns. By reifying these behaviours, the system can examine and modify itself using behavioural components that can be dynamically added to/removed from a collaborative session. Since all media space components are "active", they can perform whatever computation is necessary to provide different kinds of collaborative services based on the semantics deemed appropriate by the users/designers of the collaborative session. Additionally, "physical" components could (conceivably) reconfigure themselves based on system performance to better meet the needs of the media space users (such as dynamic load balancing for a distributed Proxy Chair as mentioned in Sect. 4.1). The result is a *self-investigative collaborative environment* that can adapt itself to both system performance as well user-specific behavioural idiosyncrasies.

5 Telelearning: An Example Media Space

Given the proposed model, its application as the coordination infrastructure for a distributed telelearning system will now be illustrated. The telelearning system will consist of multiple students and a single lecturer interconnected by a communications network. The environment will constitute a media space in that real-time audio/visual capture and display will be used in combination with support for a shared whiteboard, the distributed playback of synthetic media such as video clips, and so forth.

In the proposed model, the primary coordination logic is contained in the CCS (i.e. network), while the standard "multiplexed" method has the coordination and synchronization logic placed in highly role-specific entities. The standard method results in a more complex and less orthogonal system where functionality is determined more by hardware and topological assumptions rather than software control mechanisms. The proposed model promotes an orthogonal system in which coordination is provided by a coordinated communications subsystem under the control of host-independent software. Therefore, the priority and management hierarchy of the media space is determined by control software at individual hosts which provide a management interface to the CCS. This provides more flexibility in development and extension of the system by encouraging high-level configuration of the media space using adaptable, policy-based software rather than application-dependent hardware. While end hosts require some secondary synchronization logic, coordination is primarily achieved through the intelligent communications system which is a more topological-independent location for policy-enabling mechanisms.

Consider a telelearning environment where rather than placing all the synchronization and coordination logic in a single, complex and expensive lecturer machine, the lecturer is a simple entity with an interface to the synchronization and coordination logic within the CCS/Proxy Chair. By increasing host equity (reducing differences in calibre between student and teacher machine requirements), the system's instructional policy can be enforced by role-based control software, rather than hardware layout. The ability to reduce the impact of resource requirements on student machines is also important given the burgeoning trend to low-cost network appliances such as set-top boxes or digital entertainment terminals (DETs). Consequently, by taking a network services approach, topology and functionality are more orthogonal and changes to either are easier. Specifically, the architecture offers more flexibility in the way that students can be involved within the media space. Since a participant's role is not determined by the complexity of synchronization mechanisms in their local host, the CMSS allows both students and lecturer to participate in or lead the "classroom" based on policy, not topology.

As an example, consider the collaborative scenario outlined in Fig. 1, which maps the media space to a virtual classroom. A pattern-based view of classroom entities and their relationships are shown in Fig. 7. Within this scenario, the highest meta level is a global "classroom policy" which guides all interactions in the classroom, such as regulations as to how individuals interact, what kinds of group activity are allowed (such as brain-storming or working at the blackboard) and so forth. These policies are represented as patterns which specify the role and interaction between entities within the media space. Therefore, if entity interaction at a given level of abstraction conforms to the (behavioural) pattern specified at its meta level, then the

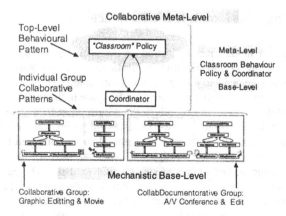

Fig. 7. High-Level Meta/Base Pattern View of Example Scenario

given entities are coordinated according to the intended collaborative behaviour. This argument can then be applied throughout the system at different levels of abstraction, including low-level media synchronization (Fig. 8).

The Proxy Chair functions as a *coordinator* who is the entity responsible for managing the coordination of the space (the classroom) according to its management policy (the classroom policy). It is important to note that the coordinator (i.e. Proxy Chair) does *not* represent the lecturer but an entity which enforces the guidelines of the space for all participants within it; therefore, the coordinator guides the lecturer as well as the students. Within the given scenario, there are two separate collaborating groups: (1) two participants with live audio/visual conferencing are jointly editing a (text) document; and (2) a graphic is being worked on while a movie is being played. In each case, other students can be observing these active collaborators and form passive participants in the collaborative effort.

While the classroom policy forms the meta level for the coordinator, the coordinator is itself a meta entity to the collaborating groups. The coordinator governs the coarse-grain behaviour of the individual groups using the classroom policy while individual groups are governed in a similar manner but at a finer

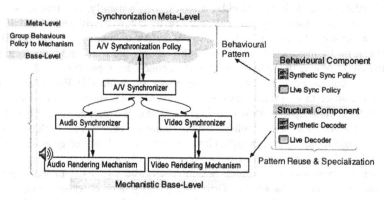

Fig. 8. Local Meta/Base View of an Audio/Video Collaborative Pattern

granularity and using the appropriate behavioural pattern. For example, while the maintenance of audio/video "lip-sync" is done on a per pair basis, it is coordinated with respect to sibling collaborators under the control of the coordinator using a "conversation" behavioural pattern. This non-monolithic approach enables different paradigms and granularities of synchronization to be specified as part of a specific group's local synchronization policy. Additionally, the appropriate considerations for specific mixed mode semantics (live and synthetic media combined) can also be dealt with in a similar manner. And finally, the mechanisms which actually perform the operations are at the lowest level and represent the media-specific execution sphere.

The tailorability offered by using such an approach means that different educational requirements can be met by integrating different components (i.e. specific demonstration applets or informational material, such as an on-line textbook). It also offers support for a wide range of classroom settings and learning styles, such as specifying interactions between students and the tools they can use. Such components could conceivably be intelligently modified or replaced under the control of the system itself (based on self-investigative meta-computations by higher-level entities). The ability to monitor and adapt based on the notion of reflection would effectively provide a media space which could dynamically "learn" how best to support its participants based on their usage characteristics. Possibilities include changes in synchronization granularity according to user satisfaction with the provided quality of service, switching to a less stringent synchronization paradigm based on frequency of access and the dynamic reconfiguration of how media objects are related (i.e. composition of the collaborative groupings in Fig. 7).

6 MSpace: The RASCAL Media Space Prototype

Currently, efforts are focusing on the creation of a prototype to illustrate the use of a reflective meta-architecture as applied to media space design and implementation. A major emphasis is being placed on providing for the flexible and adaptive coordination of the collaborative process involving both live and synthetic media.

Development is being done under Windows NT using MFC/C++ and ObjecTime Developer [5] in order to facilitate a *simulation-based prototype*. ObjecTime is a computer-assisted software engineering (CASE) tool designed for the design, implementation and simulation of object-oriented, distributed real-time systems. The given approach blends implementation of a user interface front-end and a distributed coordination/communications backbone; the former being implemented using OLE (Object Linking and Embedding) and ActiveX technologies under Windows while the latter is built with ObjecTime. Using a visual design paradigm, ObjecTime models are 'drawn' using the *Real-Time Object Oriented Modelling (ROOM)* technique. In addition to production-level code generation, the toolset supports internally built test harnesses as a means to validate its models. This offers the ability to independently simulate, test and analyze any of the prototype's ObjecTime-based components, including the reflection service and the behavioural pattern mechanism.

Figure 9 illustrates ObjecTime design metaphor as applied to the top-level structural definition of the media space. Each rectangle represents an entity in the

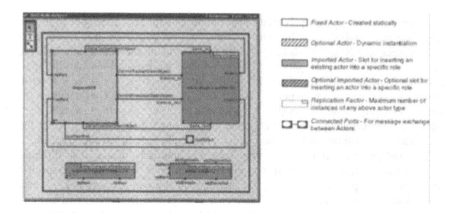

Fig. 9. Top-Level ObjecTime Structural Model of a RASCAL Media Space

system and is modelled by an *actor*. *Actor class*es define *active objects* (entities with their own run-time behaviour) that can be created statically or dynamically, in single or multiple instances and imported/exported to/from 'slots' as required. Each actor runs independently, can contain other actors using structural containment and communicates with others through the exchange of messages (using ports) defined via *protocol class*es. These messages (or events) then trigger changes in actor behaviour, which is specified using hierarchical finite state machines (FSMs). The definition of both actors and protocols is done in an object-oriented manner and uses inheritance in order to specialize their definitions. Therefore, a media space implementation that wishes to customize the types of entities within the space (for specific types of media or specific collaborative patterns) can take advantage of pre-existing designs and build upon them. This includes both structural and behavioural elements as well as protocols definitions, enabling the derivation of specialized meta-object protocols.

The ObjecTime model considers the media space as an instance of the actor class *RASCALMediaSpace* which acts as a container for all other actors in the system. This includes the CCS (*mspaceCCS* of class *RBE_CCS*) and a set of client "point of presence" workstations (*mspaceUserClientStations* of class *RBE_UserClient*). Each of these would also contain other active objects as part of their structural definition, such as the CCS which contains an instance of the multicast facility (*RBE_MulticastFacility*) and the Proxy Chair (*RBE_ProxyChair*). Other entities, such as *mspaceCollaborativeSessions* and *mspaceObjects*, would be built in a similar manner. These particular entities are kept as a "global pool" within the model such that they are potentially used by other entities within the space, including importation into collaborative sessions and behaviours.

While a complete examination of the RASCAL object framework (partially shown in Fig. 10) is beyond the scope of this paper, it can be seen that both structural (e.g. *RMSApplication*) and behavioural entities (e.g. *RMSCollaborativePattern*) are first-class objects than can be: (1) specialized through subclassing; (2) instantiated as active objects with their own thread of execution; and (3) have their own behavioural definition (via its FSM). For example, a video class could be defined based on the *RMSMediaObject* class and itself later subclassed to refer to a variety of synthetic or

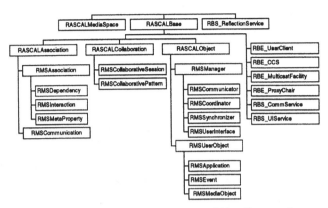

Fig. 10. Abbreviated RASCAL Active Object Framework

live video encoding standards. Similarly, different types of behaviours could be derived from a general audio/video synchronization pattern based on granularity, paradigm or media mode. As an active entity, a collaborative behavioural pattern is defined as a set of actor(s), each of which executes their own behaviour as specified by their individual finite state machines.

The flexibility of behaviours is brought about by the use of *behavioural slots* in which specific behaviour patterns and components can be inserted. Pools of collaborative behaviours can be predefined and brought into the ObjecTime environment and dynamically imported into slots which define policies and patterns for behaviours; Fig. 11 illustrates this technique as applied to the definition of the both collaborative session and collaborative pattern objects. This change would result from the system performing a reflective act in which the system would reify to the current object's meta level which would decide whether behavioural modifications were necessary and import an appropriate actor into the behavioural slot. Upon deification, (i.e. returning to the thread of execution belonging to the actor in the slot), the new behaviour would take effect. Consequently, by changing the actor whose execution is performing either a behavioural or functional role in the system, a natural causal link occurs relative to the system's execution when that slot resumes its base level computation (since it is now a different actor). Orthogonally applicable to policies, patterns and mechanisms at various levels in the architecture, Fig. 12 illustrates this notion with respect to changing the style of classroom discussion between the classic lecture style and group brainstorming.

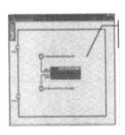

One or more top-level behavioural pattern slots

One or more object slots, their optional associations and a slot for this pattern's own meta-behaviour

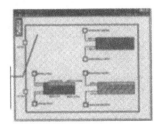

Fig. 11. ObjecTime View of a Collaborative Session (*left*) and Behavioural Pattern (*right*)

Fig. 12. Switching Classroom Behaviour Policies

As an alternative example, consider the physical entities within RASCAL's topology, such as the Proxy Chair. The software governing these entities (Fig. 10) is derived from *RASCALBase*, and from there they inherit support for reflection and the ability to perform reflective acts. They therefore have the means by which to monitor and potentially adapt themselves via reflection in order to meet the evolving needs of a media space. As a logical entity, the Proxy Chair could be designed in such a way that it could dynamically distribute its workload to sibling coordinators (moving from a strictly centralized to a distributed Proxy) based on issues such as type of media traffic, number of participants and so forth. Similarly, the multicast facility could adapt itself, with respect to QoS issues, to address particular types of traffic and/or congestion. The policies and mechanisms to address these kinds issues, however, could vary considerably and would best be provided using a meta-level approach.

This flexibility within the framework is mirrored in the prototype's user interface shown in Fig. 13. The prototype's main window represents the whole media space and functions as a container of different collaborative sessions (realized as child windows). Each session consists of objects that represent media and applications that the users utilize within the collaboration. To illustrate the notion of implementational reflection, the prototype utilizes OLE technology to facilitate inserting a wide variety of object types and functionality into the space. The sample screen shot illustrates the use of a graphic, textual document and live video camera input. Each of these objects is independently manipulated by its own application program. Events generated through the manipulation of these objects via the user interface, which is written in C++, are then passed to the ObjecTime backbone to be coordinated.

Therefore, the prototype clearly separates the system's coordination from its execution. Events generated through the manipulation of user interface elements

Fig. 13. Snapshot of Prototype's User Interface

represent media space activities which are coordinated according to the behavioural patterns governing a collaborative session. In both cases, the user interface and behavioural patterns form a meta-level which abstracts a specific aspect of a media space entity. Doing so simplifies their modification and promotes their re-use as structural and behavioural components. While shown through the use of different media and application objects via an OLE interface, the premise can be extended to support less conventional user interfaces, like those in virtual reality systems.

7 Summary and Conclusion

This paper has presented the notion of a collaborative media space and introduced RASCAL as a versatile and flexible foundation on which to build a broad range of media space systems. In particular, the framework was shown to provide for highly modular and adaptive systems, both in terms of structure and behaviour. As part of the framework's reflective meta-architecture, RASCAL explicitly separates the system's coordination from its execution. The architecture and its role as a management and support infrastructure for collaborative multimedia computing were presented along with the model's application to the field of distance education.

RASCAL provides a flexible and adaptive way to design, implement and extend a media space, both in terms of structure and behaviour. Both of these elements are regarded as orthogonal building blocks from which systems can be built, modified or replaced throughout their lifetime. Structural diversity is shown through the potential to address a variety of objects (media, applications and so forth) while behavioural aspects are shown in terms of how the model can supports various coordination strategies and synchronization mechanisms. The versatility of the proposed framework was shown amenable to a range of media space applications without the need to embed aspects of the system's coordination in its topology.

On-going work related to RASCAL includes development of the prototype along with continued evolution and exploration of its framework. The prototype is being developed under Windows NT using MFC/C++ and the ObjecTime Developer CASE tool. The dual approach blends an implementation of the user interface along with a model of the media space's communications system in order to concentrate on meta-architectural and behavioural issues rather than network-specific ones. Additionally, ObjecTime offers the potential to address performance analysis related to those components involved in using reflection as a behavioural management technique. A topic for future investigation may also be to assess the feasibility of integrating a collaborative knowledge base within a RASCAL media space so it can intelligently modify itself based on observing the behavioural patterns of its users.

As applied to the development of media space systems, RASCAL illustrates the importance of using design and implementation methods that inherently mirror the system being modelled. The highly dynamic and complex nature of multimedia systems needs to be addressed using techniques that can express this complexity in a simple and understandable manner. Consequently, RASCAL's use of reflection and its meta-architectural approach can be seen to offer an elegant way to deal with media space complexity in a straightforward, scalable, flexible and adaptive fashion.

References

[1] Gutwin, C., Greenberg, S.: Workspace Awareness in Real-Time Distributed Groupware. Technical Report 95-575-27, Dept of Computer Science, University of Calgary (1995)

[2] Malone, T. W., Crowston, K.: The Interdisciplinary Study of Coordination. ACM Computing Surveys 16.1 (1994) 87 – 119

[3] Steinmetz, R., Nahrstedt, K.: Multimedia: Computing, Communications and Application. Prentice-Hall, Upper Saddle River (1995)

[4] Yavatkar, R.: MCP: A Protocol for Coordination and Temporal Synchronization in Multimedia Collaborative Applications. Proc. ICDCS, IEEE Com. Soc. (1992) 606 – 613

[5] Selic, B., Gullekson, G., McGee, J., Engelberg, I.: ROOM: An Object-Oriented Methodology for Developing Real-Time Systems. Proc. CASE'92, IEEE Com. Soc. (1992)

[6] Stults, R.: Media Space. Technical Report, Xerox Corporation, Palo Alto (1986)

[7] Harrison, S., Minneman, S.: The Media Space: An Electronic Setting for Design. Technical Report SSL-89-63, Xerox Corporation, Palo Alto (1989)

[8] Bly, S. A., Harrison, S. R., Irwin, S.: Media Spaces: Bringing People Together in a Video, Audio and Computing Environment. Comm. of the ACM 36.1 (1993) 28 – 47

[9] Ahuja, S. R., Ensor, J. R., Horn, D. N.: The Rapport Multimedia Conferencing System. Proc. ACM COIS, ACM Press (1988) 1 – 8

[10] Eriksson, H.: MBone: The Multicast Backbone. Comm. of the ACM 37.8 (1994) 56 – 60

[11] Lauwers, J. C., Lantz, K. A.: Collaboration Awareness in Support of Collaboration Technology: Requirements for the Next Generation of Shared Window Systems. Proc. CHI'90, ACM Press (1990) 303 – 311

[12] Akyildiz, F., Yen, W.: Multimedia Group Synchronization Protocols for Integrated Services Networks. IEEE J. Selected Areas in Comm. 14.1 (1996) 162 – 173

[13] Dourish, P.: Open Implementation and Flexibility in CSCW Toolkits. Ph. D. Thesis, University College London (1996)

[14] Robbins, W., Georganas, N. D.: Reflective Pattern-Based Approach to Media Space Management. In: Kandlur, D., Jeffay, K., Roscoe, T. (eds.): Proc. MMCN'99, Vol. 3654. SPIE, Bellingham (1999) 29 – 40

[15] Crowley, T., Milazzo, P., Baker, E., Forsdick, H., Tomlinson, R.: MMConf: An Infrastructure for Building Shared Applications. Proc. CSCW'90, ACM Press (1990) 637 – 650

[16] Maes, P.: Computational Reflection. Ph. D. Thesis, Vrije Universiteit Brussel (1987)

[17] Ibrahim, M. H.: Reflection in Object-Oriented Programming. Intl. J. Artificial Intelligence Tools 1.1 (1992) 117 – 136

[18] Kiczales, G., Paepcke, A.: Open Implementations and Metaobject Protocols. Tutorial Notes, Xerox Corporation, Palo Alto (1996)

[19] Buschmann, F., Meunier, R., Rohnert, H., Sommerlad, P., Stal, M.: Pattern-Oriented Software Architecture: A System of Patterns. John Wiley & Sons Ltd., Chichester (1996)

[20] Robbins, W., Georganas, N. D.: Shared Media Space Coordination: Mixed Mode Synchrony in Collaborative Multimedia Environments. Proc. IEEE ICMCS'97, IEEE Com. Soc. (1997) 466 – 473

[21] Robbins, R. W.: Collaborative Media Space Coordination Using RASCAL. Ph. D. Candidacy Paper, School of Information Technology and Engineering (Electrical and Computer Engineering), University of Ottawa (1997)

[22] Robbins, W., Georganas, N. D.: Collaborative Media Space Architectures. Proc. CCBR'98, OCRI Publications (1998) 284 – 295

[23] ITU-T, Principles of Intelligent Network Architecture. Recomm. Q.1201, Geneva (1992)

[24] Rumbaugh, J., Blaha, M., Premerlani, W., Eddy, F., Lorensen, W.: Object-Oriented Modeling and Design. Prentice-Hall, Englewood Cliffs (1991)

The Design of a Resource-Aware Reflective Middleware Architecture

Gordon S. Blair[1], Fábio Costa[1], Geoff Coulson[1], Fabien Delpiano[2], Hector Duran[1],
Bruno Dumant[2], François Horn[2], Nikos Parlavantzas[1], Jean-Bernard Stefani[2]

[1]Computing Department, Lancaster University, Bailrigg, Lancaster LA1 4YR, UK.
{gordon, geoff, fmc, duranlim, parlavan}@comp.lancs.ac.uk

[2]CNET, France Télécom, 38-40 rue Général Leclerc, 92794 Issy les Moulineaux, CEDEX
9, Paris, France.
{fabien.delpiano, bruno.dumant, francois.horn, jeanbernard.stefani}@cnet.francetelecom.fr

Abstract. Middleware has emerged as an important architectural component in
supporting distributed applications. With the expanding role of middleware,
however, a number of problems are emerging. Most significantly, it is
becoming difficult for a single solution to meet the requirements of a range of
application domains. Hence, the paper argues that the next generation of
middleware platforms should be both configurable and re-configurable.
Furthermore, it is claimed that reflection offers a principled means of achieving
these goals. The paper then presents an architecture for reflective middleware
based on a multi-model approach. The main emphasis of the paper is on
resource management within this architecture (accessible through one of the
meta-models). Through a number of worked examples, we demonstrate that the
approach can support introspection, and fine- and coarse- grained adaptation of
the resource management framework. We also illustrate how we can achieve
multi-faceted adaptation, spanning multiple meta-models.

1. Introduction

Middleware has emerged as a key architectural component in supporting distributed
applications. The role of middleware is to present a unified programming model to
application writers and to mask out problems of heterogeneity and distribution. The
importance of the topic is reflected in the increasing visibility of industrial
standardisation activities such as OMG's CORBA and Microsoft's DCOM.

The expanding role of middleware is however leading to a number of problems.
Most importantly, middleware is now being applied to a wider range of application
domains, each imposing their own particular requirements on the underlying
middleware platform. Examples of this phenomenon include real-time multimedia
systems (requiring an element of quality of service management), and embedded
systems (requiring small footprint technologies). In our opinion, this implies that
future middleware platforms should be *configurable* in terms of the components used
in the construction of a given instance of a platform. With the advent of mobile

computing, changes may also occur in the underlying network environment. Given this, it is also becoming increasingly important that middleware platforms are *re-configurable*, i.e. underlying components can be changed at run-time. Finally, and of central importance to this paper, we also believe that future middleware platforms should provide sophisticated facilities for *resource management*, in terms of allocating (potentially) scarce resources, being aware of patterns of resource usage, and adapting to changes in resource patterns.

The authors believe the general solution to these problems is to introduce more openness and flexibility into middleware technologies. In particular, we advocate the use of reflection [Smith82, Kiczales91] as a means of achieving these goals. Reflection was first introduced in the field of programming languages and has recently been applied to a range of other areas including operating systems and windowing systems (see section 5). We believe that similar techniques can usefully be applied to middleware technology. This solution contrasts favourably with existing approaches to the construction of middleware platforms, which typically adopt a black box philosophy whereby design decisions are made by the platform developers in advance of installation and then hidden from the programmer at run-time.

Note that some flexibility has been introduced into middleware products. For example, CORBA now supports a mechanism of interception whereby wrappers can be placed round operation requests. However, this can be viewed as a rather ad hoc technique for achieving openness. The Portable Object Adaptor can also be criticised in this way. Some work has been carried out on developing more open ORBs. For example, the TAO platform from the University of Washington offers a more open and extensible structure, and also features the documentation of software patterns as used in the construction of TAO [Schmidt97]. TAO also offers access to key resource management functionality. Similarly, BBN's QuO platform employs techniques of open implementation to support quality of service management, in general, and adaptation, in particular [Vanegas98]. Finally, a number of researchers have recently experimented with reflective middleware architectures (see section 5). These platforms address many of the shortcomings of middleware platforms. However, none of these initiatives offer a complete and principled reflective architecture in terms of configurability, re-configurability and access to resource management.

Based on these observations, researchers at Lancaster University and CNET are developing a reflective middleware architecture as part of the Open ORB Project. This architecture supports introspection and adaptation of the underlying components of the middleware platform in terms of both structural and behavioural reflection [Watanabe88]. Crucially, the architecture also supports reification of the underlying resource management framework. This paper discusses the main features of this architecture with particular emphasis on the resource management aspect of our work.

The paper is structured as follows. Section 2 presents an overview of the reflective middleware architecture highlighting the multi-model approach that is central to our design. Section 3 then focuses on resource management, discussing the resource management framework in detail and considering the integration of this framework into the reflective architecture. Following this, section 4 presents three contrasting examples illustrating how our architecture can support introspection, fine- and coarse-grained adaptation, and resource-aware adaptation. Section 5 then discusses some related work and section 6 offers some concluding remarks.

2. Open ORB Architecture

2.1. Overall Approach

In common with most of the research on reflective languages and systems, we adopt an *object-oriented model of computation*. As pointed out by Kiczales et al [Kiczales91], there is an important synergy between reflection and object-oriented computing:

> "*Reflective techniques make it possible to open up a language's implementation without revealing unnecessary implementation details or compromising portability; and object-oriented techniques allow the resulting model of the language's implementation and behaviour to be locally and incrementally adjusted*".

The choice of object-orientation is important given the predominance of such models in open distributed processing [Blair97]. Crucially, we propose the use of the RM-ODP Computational Model, using CORBA IDL to describe computational interfaces. The main features of this object model are: i) objects interact with each other through *interfaces*, ii) objects can have *multiple interfaces*, iii) interfaces for *continuous media interaction* are supported, iv) interfaces are uniquely identified by *interface references*, and v) *explicit bindings* can be created between compatible interfaces (the result being the creation of a *binding object*). The object model also has a sophisticated model of quality of service including QoS annotation on interfaces. Further details of this object model can be found in [Blair97]. In contrast, with RM-ODP, however, we adopt a consistent object model throughout the design [Blair98].

As our second principle, we adopt a *procedural* (as opposed to a declarative) approach to reflection, i.e. the meta-level (selectively) exposes the actual program that implements the system. In our context, this approach has a number of advantages over the declarative approach. For example, the procedural approach is more primitive (in particular, it is possible to support declarative interfaces on top of procedural reflection but not vice versa[1]). Procedural reflection also opens the possibility of an infinite tower of reflection (i.e. the base level has a meta-level, the meta-level is implemented using objects and hence has a meta-meta-level, and so on). This is realised in our approach by allowing such an infinite structure to exist in theory but only to instantiate a given level on demand, i.e. when it is reified. This provides a finite representation of an infinite structure (a similar approach is taken in ABCL/R [Watanabe88]). Access to different meta-levels is important in our design although in practice most access will be restricted to the meta- and meta-meta-levels.

The third principle behind our design is to support *per object* (or *per interface*) meta-spaces. This is necessary in a heterogeneous environment where objects will have varying capacities for reflection. Such a solution also provides a fine level of control over the support provided by the middleware platform; a corollary of this is that problems of maintaining integrity are minimised due to the limited scope of

---

[1] Indeed, we have already experimented with constructing more declarative interfaces on top of our architecture in the context of the resources framework.

change. We do recognise however that there are situations where it is useful to be able to access the meta-spaces of sets of objects in one single action; to support this, we also allow the use of (meta-object) *groups* (see discussion in 2.2 below).

The final principle is to structure meta-space as a number of closely related but distinct *meta-space models*. This approach was first advocated by the designers of AL-1/D, a reflective programming language for distributed applications [Okamura92]. The benefit of this approach is to simplify the interface offered by meta-space by maintaining a separation of concerns between different system aspects. Further details of each of the various models can be found below.

2.2. The Design of Meta-space

2.2.1. Supporting Structural Reflection

In reflective systems, structural reflection is concerned with the content of a given object [Watanabe88]. In our architecture, this aspect of meta-space is represented by two distinct meta-models, namely the *encapsulation* and *composition* meta-models. We introduce each model in turn below.

The *encapsulation meta-model* provides access to the representation of a particular interface in terms of its set of methods and associated attributes, together with key properties of the interface including its inheritance structure. This is equivalent to the introspection facilities available, for example, in the Java language, although we go further by also supporting adaptation. Clearly, however, the level of access provided by the encapsulation model will be language dependent. For example, with compiled languages such as C access may be limited to introspection of the associated IDL interface. With more open (interpreted) languages, such as Java or Python, more complete access is possible such as being able to add or delete methods and attributes. This level of heterogeneity is supported by having a type hierarchy of encapsulation meta-interfaces ranging from minimal access to full reflective access to interfaces. Note however that it is important that this type hierarchy is open and extensible to accommodate unanticipated levels of access.

In reality, many objects will in fact be composite, using a number of other objects in their construction. In recognition of this fact, we also provide a *compositional meta-model* offering access to such constituent objects. Note that this meta-model is associated with each object and not each interface. More specifically, the same compositional meta-model will be reached from each interface defined on the object (reflecting the fact that it is the object that is composite). In the meta-model, the composition of an object is represented as an *object graph* [Hokimoto96], in which the constituent objects are connected together by *local bindings*[2]. The interface offered by the meta-model then supports operations to inspect and adapt the graph structure, i.e. to view the structure of the graph, to access individual objects in the graph, and to adapt the graph structure and content.

This meta-model is particularly useful when dealing with binding objects [Blair98]. In this context, the composition meta-model reifies the internal structure of the

---

[2]   This RM-ODP inspired concept of local binding is crucial in our design, providing a language-independent means of implementing the interaction point between interfaces.

binding in terms of the components used to realise the end-to-end communication path. For example the object graph could feature an MPEG compressor and decompressor and an RTP binding object. The structure can also be exposed recursively; for example, the composition meta-model of the RTP binding might expose the peer protocol entities for RTP and also the underlying UDP/IP protocol. It is argued in [Fitzpatrick98] that open bindings alone provide strong support for mobile computing.

2.2.2. Supporting Behavioural Reflection

Behavioural reflection is concerned with activity in the underlying system [Watanabe88]. This is represented by a single meta-model associated with each interface, the *environmental meta-model*. In terms of middleware, the underlying activity equates to functions such as message arrival, enqueueing, selection, unmarshalling and dispatching (plus the equivalent on the sending side) [Watanabe88, McAffer96].

Again, different levels of access are supported. For example, a simple meta-model may enable the insertion of pre- and post- methods. Such a mechanism can be used to introduce, for example, some additional levels of distribution transparency (such as concurrency control). In addition, additional functions can be inserted such as security functions. A more complex meta-model may allow the inspection or adaptation of each element of the processing of messages as described above. With such complexity, it is likely that such a meta-model would itself be a composite object with individual components accessed via the compositional meta-space of the environmental meta-space. As with the other meta-models, heterogeneity is accommodated within an open and extensible type hierarchy.

2.2.3. The Associated Component Library

To realise our open architecture, we provide an open and extensible library of components that can be assembled to build middleware platforms for a range of applications. By the term component, we mean a robust, packaged object that can be independently developed and delivered. Our components adhere to a component framework that offers a built in event notification service and also access to each of the meta-models.

The component library consists of both primitive and composite components, the distinction being that primitive components are not open to introspection or adaptation in terms of the compositional meta-model. Examples of primitive components include communication protocols such as UDP and TCP, and end system functions such as continuous media filters. Composite components then represent off-the-shelf configurations of components such as end-to-end stream bindings. Importantly, we also provide *group bindings* (or simply groups) as composite objects. The role of groups is to provide a uniform mechanism for invoking a set of interfaces whether they are at the base-level, meta-level, meta-meta-level, etc. Furthermore, through access to their underlying object graph of the group component, it is possible to tailor and adapt the semantics of group message distribution, e.g. by introducing a new ordering protocol.

2.3. Management of Consistency

In reflective architectures, care must be taken to ensure the consistency of the underlying virtual machine. This is particularly true in the reflective middleware architecture described above, as the internal structure of the underlying platform can be changed significantly by using the meta-object protocols associated with the meta-models. For example, using the encapsulation meta-model, it is possible to introduce new methods or attributes into a running object. Similarly, the compositional and environmental meta-models allow the programmer to change the construction of a composite object and the interpretation of method invocation respectively. Given this, steps must be taken to ensure that consistency constraints are maintained.

As can be seen from the architecture, the most common style of adaptation is to alter the structure of an object graph. Consequently, it is crucial that such run-time alterations can be made in a safe manner. Some support is provided by the strongly-typed object model in that local bindings will enforce type correctness across interacting objects. This is however not a complete solution to the problem. The following steps are also necessary[3]:

1. Any activity in the affected region of the graph must be suspended;
2. The state of such activity must be preserved;
3. Replacement components must maintain the desired level of quality of service.

In addition, it is also necessary to maintain global consistency across the graph, i.e. changes of one component may require changes to another component (as in the case when replacing a compression and decompression object).

Responsibility for enforcing consistency constraints may be left to the application in our architecture. However, it is much more likely that the application will devolve responsibility to QoS management components that monitor the underlying object graph and implement an appropriate adaptation policy. The design of such a QoS management infrastructure for our reflective architecture is discussed in [Blair99].

We return to this important issue in section 4 below.

3. Resource Meta-Model

3.1. The Resource Framework

3.1.1. The Overall Approach
The main aim of the resource framework is to provide a complete and consistent model of all resources in the system at varying levels of abstraction. For example, a consistent approach should be taken to the management of processing capacity, memory, and network resources. Similarly, the framework should encompass more abstract resources such as virtual memory, persistent virtual memory, connections, teams of threads, and more general collections of resources.

---

[3] This is similar to the problem of (nested) atomic transactions, but with the added requirement of maintaining the quality of service constraints [Mitchell98].

This is achieved by recursively applying the structure illustrated in figure 1.

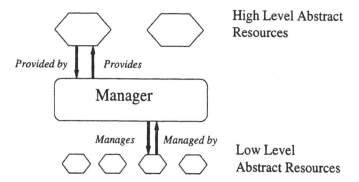

Fig. 1. The Overall Resource Framework

This diagram shows how higher level resources are constructed out of lower level resources by resource manager objects [ReTINA99]. Managers *provide* the higher level resources and *manage* the lower level resources. Similarly, higher level resources are *provided by* managers and lower level resources are *managed by* managers (we return to this in section 3.3). This structure maps naturally on to facilities offered by most modern operating systems. Note that there is an assumption that access to resource management is possible. At the very least, this will be possible in terms of user level resources such as user level threads. The level of access can also be enhanced through techniques such as split-level resource management [Blair97].

Both the high level and low level resources are of type AbstractResource as defined by the following interface:

```
interface AbstractResource {
  Manager provided_by();
  Manager managed_by();
  void release();
}
```

The provided_by() operation enables an application to locate the manager for a high level resource. Similarly, the managed_by() operation can be used to locate the manager for a given low level resource. Finally, release() should be called when the (abstract) resource is no longer needed.

Different styles of manager can be created. For example, some managers may multiplex high level resources on to the set of low level resources (e.g. schedulers), or they can map directly on to low level resources (e.g. memory allocation), with the set of available resources either being static or dynamic. Similarly, they can compose low level resources to create a more abstract high level resource (e.g. to create a Unix-like process), or they can provide direct access to a low level resource (cf binders).

In general, managers offer the following interface:

```
interface Manager {
  void register(Interface ref,...);
  void unregister(Interface ref);
```

```
AbstractResource[] manages(AbstractResource high);
AbstractResource[] provides();
}
```

The register() and unregister() operations allow a programmer to associate additional low level resources with the manager. The precise interpretation of this will vary between different styles of manager as seen when we consider factories and binders below. The manages() and provides() operations return the high level and low level abstract resources associated with this manager respectively. The high parameter to manages() enables the manager to return only the low level resources supporting that given high level resource.

Note that this approach treats resource as a relative term. An object *r* is a resource *for* another object *u* - a *user* -, that itself may be a resource for a third object *v*, or possibly for *r*. In other words, resource and user are roles, similar to server and client.

3.1.2. Factories and Binders

Overview
Suppose now that an object requires access to an abstract resource. There are two ways in which this can happen. Firstly, it can create a new instance of the required abstract resource. Secondly, it can locate and bind to an existing instance of an abstract resource. These two scenarios are supported in the framework by *factories* and *binders* respectively.

As will be seen, both factories and binders are specialisations of Manager in the architecture in that they both have the role of providing an AbstractResource for an object (the Manager() class described above should be viewed as an abstract class, which is realised by factories, binders, or indeed other styles of manager). In this way, they can be viewed as different *patterns* of object management.

We look at each in turn below.

Factories
As stated above, factories support the creation of new objects of type AbstractResource. In our architecture, they also have a second role, i.e. performing the run-time management of the resultant resource(s). Combining the two roles has a number of advantages, e.g. in integrating policies for static and dynamic resource management.

A factory must conform to the following interface:

```
interface Factory extends Manager {
  AbstractResource new(...);
}
```

The new() method returns a reference to an interface of an abstract resource. Its arguments may contain information needed by the factory to build and manage the new resource, like specifications of the type and quality of service of the expected resource, indications of lower level resources or factories to be used, etc. The register() operation defined in the super class effectively provides the factory with additional raw material to create the new high level abstract resource, e.g. in terms of providing a new virtual processor to support threads. The `unregister()` operation has the opposite effect of removing the low level abstract resource from the factory.

In a typical environment, an extensible range of factories will be provided corresponding to the various levels of abstract resources discussed in section 3.1.1.

Binders

As stated earlier (section 2.1), an object is only aware of other objects through knowledge of interface references. However, holding an interface reference does not mean that it is possible for the holder of the reference to interact with the corresponding object. The object may be inaccessible or unusable in its current form.

The role of a binder object is to make identified interfaces accessible to their user. More specifically, in the resources framework, they support the location of appropriate resources and also undertake the necessary steps to make the interface accessible. For example, if an interface is located on a remote machine, the binder will establish an appropriate communications path to the object or indeed migrate the remote object to the local site.

The interface for a binder object is shown below:

```
interface Binder extends Manager {
  AbstractResource bind(Interface ref,...);
}
```

To be managed by a binder, an interface must register itself using the inherited `register()` method. In this context, this is similar to registering an interface with a name server or trading service. This means that the binder is now entitled to let users access and interact with that interface. The binder may also take steps to make this resource accessible. The precise policies used for allocation may be implicit in the binder, encapsulated in the provided interface reference, or made explicit in parameters to the `register()` method. Additional parameters may also specify management policies (cf the policies provided in CORBA in the Portable Object Adapter specification). The corresponding `unregister()` method then removes this abstract resource from control of that binder.

The role of the `bind()` method is to allow the specified interface to be used. This method returns an interface reference that should then be used to interact with that object. This is likely to be an interface reference for the object itself. The architecture however also allows this to refer to an intermediary interface that will provide indirect access to the appropriate object (cf proxy mechanisms).

3.2. Application to Processing Resources

3.2.1. A Resource Framework for Processing

To illustrate the use of the resource management framework, we now discuss a particular instantiation of the framework to support the management of processing resources. As an example, we present a two-level structure whereby lightweight threads are constructed using virtual processors, which are themselves built on top of the underlying processor(s). The corresponding structure is illustrated in figure 2.

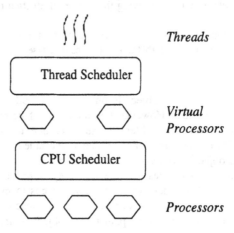

Fig. 2. An Example Scheduling Framework

From this diagram, it can be seen that *schedulers* fulfil the role of managers (more specifically factories). The CPU scheduler provides the abstraction of virtual processors out of the underlying physical processors. Similarly, the thread scheduler creates the abstraction of threads and maps them on to the underlying virtual processor(s). In both cases, the scheduling policy is encapsulated within each of the schedulers but may be changed dynamically (see below).

Processors, virtual processors and lightweight threads can all be viewed as a particular type of abstract resource that we refer to as a *machine*. In general terms, machines consume messages, act on these messages (possibly changing the state of the corresponding object), and then emit further messages. We also introduce a specialisation of a machine, called a *job*, which can be configured with scheduling parameters.

3.2.2. The Major Objects Revisited

Machines and Jobs
As mentioned above, machines are abstract resources that are responsible for carrying out some activity. They may be processors or sets of processors, or may represent more abstract execution environments such as virtual processors or indeed interpreters for high level languages. They may also be sequential or parallel.

Machines offer the following interface:

```
interface Machine {
  void run(Message);
}
```

The run() method provides a target machine with a new message (assuming the machine is in an appropriate state to accept the message). A Job is then an abstract machine that uses lower-level machines controlled by the scheduler to execute its messages. It offers the following interface:

```
interface Job extends Machine, AbstractResource {
SchedParams getSchedParams();
void setSchedParams(SchedParams params);
}
```

The two methods, getSchedParams() and setSchedParams() can be used to inspect the current scheduling parameters used by the underlying scheduler and to change these parameters dynamically.

Schedulers

The precise definition of a scheduler is that it is a machine factory that is able to create abstract machines (jobs) and then multiplex them on to lower-level machines. Its interface is as follows:

```
interface Scheduler extends Factory {
Job new(SchedParams params);
void notify(Event event);
void suspend(...);
void resume(...);
}
```

As can be seen, the interface supports a new() method that returns an object of type job. The params argument represents the initial *scheduling parameters* that will be used by the scheduler to control the multiplexing. These may be expressed in terms of priorities, deadlines, periods, etc. The scheduler implements a function to decide at any moment how jobs should be allocated to the various machines under its control[4] (according to these scheduling parameters). For instance, threads may be understood as jobs offered by a scheduler; the scheduler will then allocate the processor(s) (the lower-level machine(s)) to them according to their priority (the scheduling parameter). The scheduler may also use some dynamic information, like the timestamp on specific events, to control the multiplexing. Obviously, if there are fewer machines than jobs, the scheduler must maintain a job queue.

The decisions taken by a scheduler to multiplex jobs on machines may be triggered by different events such as interruptions or timer notifications. More generally, an event is an asynchronous occurrence in the system (message reception, message emission, object creation, etc).

The remaining methods defined on Scheduler provide a level of event management. The notify() method informs the scheduler of the occurrence of a specific event. The suspend() method then specifies that the execution of one or more jobs, as given by the arguments of the call, should be stopped and blocked. Finally, the resume() method is called to make blocked jobs eligible for re-

---

[4] Note that, in our framework, we enforce a restriction that a machine can be controlled by one and only one scheduler, this being the sole entity allowed to call the run() method. In contrast, a single scheduler may manage and use several machines.

execution. Parameters may include events that should trigger the suspend/resume mechanism. Locks may also be provided as specific instantiations of these operations.

3.3. Incorporation into Open ORB

The resource management framework is incorporated into the Open ORB architecture as an additional meta-model, referred to as the *resources meta-model*. The complete Open ORB architecture therefore consists of four meta-models as shown in figure 3.

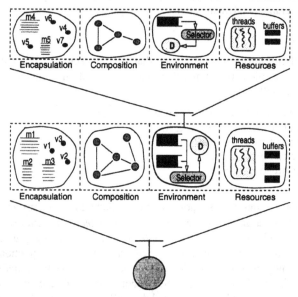

Fig. 3. The Open-ORB Reflective Architecture

It is important to stress that this meta-model is orthogonal to the others. For example, the environmental meta-model identifies the steps involved in processing an arriving message; the resources meta-model then identifies the resources required to perform this processing. More generally, the resources meta-model is concerned with the allocation and management of resources associated with any activity in the system. There is an arbitrary mapping from activity to resources. For example, all objects in a configuration could share a single pool of resources. Alternatively, each object could have its own private resources. All other combinations are also possible including objects partitioning their work across multiple resource pools and resources spanning multiple objects.

As an example, consider a configuration of objects providing an environmental model. One object could deal with the arrival and enqueuing of all messages from the network. This object could have a single high-priority thread and a dedicated pool of buffers associated with it. A further set of objects could deal with the selection, unmarshalling and dispatching of the message. In this case, the various objects could all share a pool of threads and a pool of buffers. Note that, once allocated to deal with a message, the thread (and associated buffer) will complete the entire activity, spanning multiple object boundaries. Synchronisation with other threads (and buffers) is only required when switching between abstract resources, e.g. when handing over from the arrival activity to the selection activity.

The resources meta-model supports the reification of the various objects in the resource framework. More specifically, the meta-model provides access to the (one or more) top-level abstract resources associated with a given interface. For example, a given interface might have a single abstract resource containing a global pool of threads and a dedicated buffer pool. It is then possible to traverse the management structure from the abstract resource(s). In particular, we can locate the manager for a given abstract resource by following a *provided by* link (see section 3.1.1). In turn, each manager maintains a list of resources that it *manages*, providing access to abstract resources one level down. This process can then be applied recursively to reach any particular object of the management structure. Similarly, from a resource, it is possible to follow a *managed by* link to locate the appropriate manager. It is then possible to trace the abstract resource that this manager *provides* (see figure 1).

Using such traversal mechanisms, it is possible to inspect and adapt the management structure associated with such abstract resources. We distinguish between fine-grained adaptation whereby the management structure remains intact and coarse-grained adaptation that makes changes to this structure. Examples of both styles of adaptation are given below.

4. Explanatory Examples

4.1. Introspection and Fine-grained Adaptation

This example demonstrates introspection and fine-grained adaptation for processing resources. We consider a single object, offering a single interface iref. This object is supported by a set of abstract resources that are bundled into a single top level abstract resource. In particular, this bundle contains a *team of threads* and some associated *virtual memory*. We assume a two-level management structure for threads as defined in section 3.2 above. We note that the threads are, in general, under-performing and decide to alter the priority of the underlying virtual processor (we assume that all threads in the team map on to one virtual processor).

This level of adaptation is achieved as follows:

```
top  = iref.Resources()[BUNDLE];
team = top.provided_by().manages(top)[THREADS];
vp   = team.provided_by().manages(top)[VP];
vp.setSchedParams (new_params);
```

The first line enters the resources meta-model, using a Resources() method as defined on all (reflective) objects. Note that this operation returns an array of all the top level abstract resources associated with the interface. We thus provide an index to select the appropriate resource (in this case the bundle, denoted by BUNDLE). From this, we can access the underlying team of threads and then the underlying virtual processor by using the provided_by() and manages() links. Note that we must also provide an index to select the appropriate low level resource from the array returned by the manages() operation. From there, it is straightforward to change the scheduling parameters on the appropriate virtual processor.

4.2. Coarse-grained Adaptation

In this example, we assume the same top-level abstract resource as before. This time, however, we want to change virtual memory to persistent virtual memory. This implies some fundamental changes to the management structure. In addition, this example raises important issues of consistency, i.e. the new persistent memory should mirror the original virtual memory and the change should be atomic.

We assume that virtual memory is provided by a single resource manager that maps to both the underlying physical memory and secondary storage resources. We also assume that we have access to a factory, denoted by pvm_factory, which can be used to create a new segment of persistent virtual memory.

The first few steps are similar to the example above:

```
top  = iref.Resources()[BUNDLE];
vm   = top.provided_by().manages(top)[VM];
team = top.provided_by().manages(top)[THREADS];
vp   = team.provided_by().manages();
```

In this case, however, we locate the virtual memory abstract resource *and* the underlying virtual processor. The latter is required as it is necessary to suspend all activity on the object while the changes are made, i.e. to make the change atomic. Note that this only works if we assume that no other threads will operate on the abstract resource. If this is not the case, then we must lock the resource instead.

We proceed as follows:

```
vp.suspend();
pvm  = pvm_factory.new(vm);
vm.release();
meta.provided_by().unregister(vm);
meta.provided_by().register(pvm);
vp.resume();
```

As can be seen, we use the state of the old virtual memory in the creation of the new persistent virtual memory (we assume that the factory supports this initialisation capability). The old virtual memory abstract resource can now be released. It then remains to alter the top level abstract resource (via its manager) to use the persistent virtual memory rather than the previous virtual memory.

4.3. Multi-faceted Adaptation

The final example illustrates how adaptation strategies can span multiple meta-models. In particular, we consider adaptation of a continuous media binding object, referring to the compositional and resources meta-models (the former provides access to the components used in the construction of the binding, and the latter provides information on underlying resource usage). The binding object is responsible for the delivery of audio in a mobile environment, where the available bandwidth may change significantly on roaming between different network types. The object has an initial structure as shown in figure 4.

As can be seen, the configuration contains a GSM encoder and decoder with a throughput requirement of approx. 13kbits/sec. The role of the monitoring object is to report if throughput drops below this threshold. Should this happen, the compression and decompression objects must be changed to a more aggressive scheme such as LPC-10 (which only requires 2.4kbits/sec). This is only feasible, however, if there is spare processing capacity as the computational overhead of LPC-10 is significantly greater than GSM. To support this, we assume the existence of a monitoring object in the resources meta-model that collects statistics on the available processing resources.

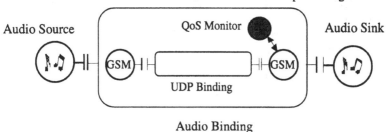

Audio Binding

Fig. 4. The Composite Binding Object

The solution is outlined below. (As this is a more complex example, we do not go to the level of providing code.)

Firstly, it is necessary to locate the relevant monitoring objects in the compositional and resource meta-spaces. On detecting a drop in available bandwidth, it is then necessary to check if there is spare processing capacity. If there is, then adaptation can proceed (if not, it may be possible to obtain additional processing capacity, e.g. by increasing the priority of the underlying virtual processor as described in section 4.1. above[5]).

To achieve adaptation, it is first necessary to suspend activity in the binding (as in section 4.2 above). With this being a distributed object, however, this will involve the suspension of activity in more than one abstract resource. We can then use graph manipulation operations to replace the encoder and decoder with the new LPC-10 components[6]. Following this, activity can be resumed. Note that suspension of activity may not be sufficient to ensure consistency, i.e. some GSM packets may remain in transit until after the change-over. For the sake of this example, we assume that decoders will discard invalid packets.

In general, this is an example of a *resource aware QoS management* strategy. As an extension of this strategy, we can implement adaptation policies that monitor and

---

[5]   Strictly speaking, such a step could violate QoS contracts in other parts of the system and so should involve QoS renegotiation [ReTINA99].

[6]   Again, this step could involve QoS re-negotiation.

adapt one or more meta-models. Further discussion of such multi-faceted adaptation and QoS management can be found in [Blair99].

5. Related Work

5.1. Reflective Architectures

As mentioned earlier, reflection was first introduced in the programming language community, with the goal of introducing more openness and flexibility into language designs [Kiczales91, Agha91, Watanabe88]. More recently, the work in this area has diversified with reflection now being applied to areas such as operating system design [Yokote92], atomicity [Stroud95] and atomic transactions [Barga96], windowing systems [Rao91], CSCW [Dourish95]. There is also growing interest in the use of reflection in distributed systems. Pioneering work in this area was carried out by McAffer [McAffer96]. With respect to middleware, researchers at Illinois have carried out initial experiments on reflection in Object Request Brokers (ORBs) [Singhai97]. The level of reflection however is coarse-grained and restricted to invocation, marshalling and dispatching. In addition, the work does not consider the reification of resource management. Researchers at APM have developed an experimental middleware platform called FlexiNet [Hayton97]. This platform allows the programmer to tailor the underlying communications infrastructure by inserting/ removing layers. Their solution is, however, language-specific, i.e. applications must be written in Java. Manola has carried out work in the design of a "RISC" object model for distributed computing [Manola93], i.e. a minimal object model which can be specialised through reflection. Researchers at the Ecole des Mines de Nante are also investigating the use of reflection in proxy mechanisms for ORBs [Ledoux97].

Our design has been influenced by a number of specific reflective languages. As stated above, the concept of multi-models was derived from AL/1-D. The underlying models of AL/1-D are however quite different; the language supports six models, namely operation, resource, statistics, migration, distributed environment and system [Okamura92]. Our ongoing research on the environment and encapsulation meta-models is also heavily influenced by the designs of ABCL/R [Watanabe88] and CodA [McAffer96]. Both these systems feature decompositions of meta-space in terms of the acceptance of messages, placing the message in a queue, their selection, and the subsequent dispatching. Finally, the design of ABCL/R2 includes the concept of groups [Matsuoka91]. However, groups in ABCL/R2 are more prescriptive in that they enforce a particular construction and interpretation on an object. The groups themselves are also primitive, and are not susceptible to reflective access.

5.2. Reflective Resource Management

In general, existing reflective architectures focus on structural reflection, behavioural reflection, or a combination of both. Most architectures do not address the reification of resource management. There are three notable exceptions, namely AL/1D, the ABCL/R* series of languages and Apertos. We consider each in turn below.

As mentioned above, Al/1D [Okamura92] offers a resource model as one of its six meta-models. This resource model focuses on resources on the local host and does not consider issues of distribution. AL1/D, like the other systems considered in this section, has an active object model. In terms of resources, this maps on to execution environments, called *contexts*, and memory abstractions, referred to as *segments*. These are managed by *schedulers* and *garbage collectors* respectively (with an object having precisely one of each). In terms of reflection, the resource model supports reification of contexts, segments, schedulers and garbage collectors. Consequently, this meta-model supports reification of only selected aspects of resource management; it does not attempt to provide as comprehensive a framework as we offer.

In ABCL/R2 [Matsuoka91], resource management is closely related to their concept of *groups* (see section 5.1). In their design, structural reflection is accessed through a meta-object, but behavioural reflection is controlled by a meta-group. This meta-group is implemented by a group kernel object offering a meta-object *generator* (for the creation of meta-objects), an evaluator (which acts as a sequential interpreter for the language), and a group manager (which bears the identity of the group and has reference to the meta-object generator and the evaluator). It is assumed that objects belonging to a group share a pool of common resources. Resource management policies are then contained within the various components of the group kernel object. For example, evaluators are responsible for scheduling of activity relating to the group. Such meta-behaviour can be changed dynamically. For example, as the evaluator is an object itself, the scheduling policy can be changed by inserting a call to a user-defined scheduler in the code of its meta-object. In contrast to ABCL/R2, our approach separates out the concepts of group and resource management, and also offers a more explicit resource management framework.

The successor, ABCL/R3 [Masuhara94] has a quite different resource model. In particular, the designers have added the concepts of node and node management to make the locality of computations more explicit at the meta-level (this is transparent to the base-level). A node is the meta-level representation of a processor element. Node management can then be used, for example, to control where objects are created, e.g. to introduce an element of load balancing. The language also makes node scheduling more explicit (again as a meta-level object on each node). This is an interesting development but again is less comprehensive than our proposed approach.

Finally, as a reflective operating system, one of the primary goals of Apertos is to provide open access to resource management [Yokote92]. In Apertos, every object has an associated meta-space offering an execution environment for that object (in terms of for example a particular scheduling policy, implementation of virtual memory, etc). This meta-space is accessed via a reflector object, which acts as a façade for the meta-space and offers a set of primitives for message passing, memory management, etc. Apertos adopts the computational model of active objects and pushes it to the limits. Every object managed by the system owns its computational resources, called a context), which includes, for example, memory chunks or disk blocks. This leads to prohibitive overheads in the system due to constant context switching. Our approach is more flexible with respect to active/ passive resource association, allowing high level active objects to co-exist with passive but efficient low level resources. In addition, in Apertos meta-space is structured as a set of interacting meta-objects, including resource objects and resource managers. These are not accessed directly; rather a form of coarse-grained adaptation is achieved by migrating an object from one meta-space to another (equivalent) meta-space (e.g. one that offers persistent virtual memory). The validity of migration is checked by calling a primitive defined on all reflectors called canSpeak(). The granularity of adaptation is therefore fixed by the class of the reflectors. In our framework, objects can gain direct access to the resources they use at the desired level of abstraction (e.g. an object may want to know at different times all the time-slices, threads or transactions executing its methods). Thus, we achieve dynamic reconfiguration at any level of expressiveness, the validity of adaptations being verified by type checking.

6. Concluding Remarks

This paper has discussed the design of next generation middleware platforms which we believe should be more configurable and re-configurable and should also provide access to the underlying resource management structure. We argue that this is best achieved through the use of reflection. More specifically, we advocate a reflective architecture where every object has its own meta-space. This meta-space is then structured as a series of orthogonal meta-models offering structural and behavioural reflection, and also reification of the resource management framework. Associated meta-object protocols support introspection and adaptation of the underlying middleware environment in a principled manner. This reflective architecture is supported by a component framework, offering a re-usable set of services for the configuration and re-configuration of meta-spaces. In general, re-configuration is achieved through reification and adaptation of object graph structures.

The main body of the paper concentrated on the resource model. The underlying resource management framework provides a uniform mechanism for accessing resources and their management at different levels of abstraction. We also presented a specialisation of this framework for activity management. We demonstrated, through a set of worked examples, that the approach can support introspection, fine- and coarse- grained adaptation, and also multi-faceted adaptation.

The work presented in this paper is supported by a number of prototype implementations. For example, the reflective middleware architecture has been implemented in the object-oriented, interpreted language Python [Watters96]. Currently, this particular implementation supports a full implementation of structural and behavioural reflection, together with an initial implementation of the resources meta-model. An earlier version of this platform (without the resources meta-model) is described in detail in [Costa98]. The resources framework is inspired by the underlying structure of Jonathan [Dumant97]. A more complete implementation of the resources framework is also being developed in Jonathan v2. A similar approach is also taken in GOPI [Coulson98].

Ongoing research is addressing two main distinct areas: i) further studies of consistency and adaptation, and ii) an examination of the support offered by the architecture for QoS-driven transaction mechanisms. This latter activity, in particular, should provide a demanding examination of the approach.

Acknowledgements

The research described in this paper is funded by CNET, France Telecom (Grant 96-1B-239). We would also like to thank a number of other people at CNET and Lancaster University who have contributed to the work described in this paper, including Anders Andersen, Lynne Blair, Mike Clarke, Tom Fitzpatrick, Lee Johnston and Katia Saikoski.

References

[Agha91] Agha, G., "The Structure and Semantics of Actor Languages", Lecture Notes in Computer Science, Vol. 489, pp 1-59, Springer-Verlag, 1991.

[Barga96] Barga, R., Pu,, C., "Reflection on a Legacy Transaction Processing Monitor", In Proceedings of Reflection 96, G. Kiczales (ed), pp 63-78, San Francisco; Also available from Dept. of Computer Science and Engineering, Oregon Graduate Institute of Science and Technology, P.O. Box 91000, Portland, OR 97291-1000, 1996.

[Blair97] Blair, G.S., Stefani, J.B., "Open Distributed Processing and Multimedia, Addison-Wesley, 1997.

[Blair98] Blair, G.S., Coulson, G., Robin, P., Papathomas, M., "An Architecture for Next Generation Middleware", Proc. IFIP International Conference on Distributed Systems Platforms and Open Distributed Processing (Middleware'98), pp 191-206, Springer, 1998.

[Blair99] Blair, G.S., Andersen, A., Blair, L., Coulson, G., "The Role of Reflection in Supporting Dynamic QoS Management Functions", Internal Report MPG-99-03, Computing Department, Lancaster University, Bailrigg, Lancaster, LA1 4YR, U.K., 199 January 1999.

[Costa98] Costa, F., Blair, G.S., Coulson, G., "Experiments with Reflective Middleware", Proceedings of the ECOOP'98 Workshop on Reflective Object-Oriented Programming and Systems, ECOOP'98 Workshop Reader, Springer-Verlag, 1998.

[Coulson98] Coulson, G., "A Distributed Object Platform Infrastructure for Multimedia Applications", Computer Communications, Vol. 21, No. 9, pp 802-818, July 1998.

[Dourish95] Dourish, P., "Developing a Reflective Model of Collaborative Systems", ACM Transactions on Computer Human Interaction, Vol. 2, No. 1, pp 40-63, March 1995.

[Dumant97] Dumant, B., Horn, F., Dang Tran, F., Stefani, J.B., "Jonathan: An Open Distributed Processing Environment in Java", Proc. IFIP International Conference on Distributed Systems Platforms and Open Distributed Processing (Middleware'98), Springer, September 1998.

[Hayton97] Hayten, R., "FlexiNet Open ORB Framework", APM Technical Report 2047.01.00, APM Ltd, Poseidon House, Castle Park, Cambridge, UK, October 1997.

[Hokimoto96] Hokimoto, A., Nakajima, T., "An Approach for Constructing Mobile Applications using Service Proxies", Proceedings of the 16th International Conference on Distributed Computing Systems (ICDCS'96), IEEE, May 1996.

[Fitzpatrick98] Fitzpatrick, T., Blair, G.S., Coulson, G., Davies N., Robin, P., "A Software Architecture for Adaptive Distributed Multimedia Systems", IEE Proceedings on Software, Vol. 145, No. 5, pp 163-171, October 1998.

[Kiczales91] Kiczales, G., des Rivières, J., and Bobrow, D.G., "The Art of the Metaobject Protocol", MIT Press, 1991.

[Ledoux97] Ledoux, T., "Implementing Proxy Objects in a Reflective ORB", Proc. ECOOP'97 Workshop on CORBA: Implementation, Use and Evaluation, Jyväskylä, Finland, June 1997.

[Manola93] Manola, F., "MetaObject Protocol Concepts for a "RISC" Object Model", Technical Report TR-0244-12-93-165, GTE Laboratories, 40 Sylvan Road, Waltham, MA 02254, USA, December 1993.

[Masuhara94] Masuhara, H., Matsuoka, S., Yonezawa, A., "An Object-Oriented Concurrent Reflective Language for Dynamic Resource Management in Highly Parallel Computing", IPSJ SIG Notes, Vol. 94-PRG-18 (SWoPP'94), pp. 57-64, July 1994.

[Matsuoka91] Matsuoka, S., Watanabe, T., and Yonezawa, A., "Hybrid Group Reflective Architecture for Object-Oriented Concurrent Reflective Programming", In Proceedings of the European Conference on Object-Oriented Programming (ECOOP'91), Geneva, Switzerland, LNCS 512, pp 231-250, Springer-Verlag, 1991.

[McAffer96] McAffer, J., "Meta-Level Architecture Support for Distributed Objects", In Proceedings of Reflection 96, G. Kiczales (ed), pp 39-62, San Francisco; Available from Dept of Information Science, Tokyo University, 1996.

[Mitchell98] Mitchell, S., Naguib, H., Coulouris, G., Kindberg, T., "Dynamically Reconfiguring Multimedia Components: A Model-based Approach", Proc. 8th ACM SIGOPS European Workshop, Lisbon, Sep. 1998.

[Okamura92] Okamura, H., Ishikawa, Y., Tokoro, M., "AL-1/d: A Distributed Programming System with Multi-Model Reflection Framework", Proceedings of the Workshop on New Models for Software Architecture, November 1992.

[Rao91] Rao, R., "Implementational Reflection in Silica", Proceedings of ECOOP'91, Lecture Notes in Computer Science, P. America (Ed), pp 251-267, Springer-Verlag, 1991.

[ReTINA99] ReTINA, "Extended DPE Resource Control Framework Specifications", ReTINA Deliverable AC048/D1.01xtn, ACTS Project AC048, January 1999.

[Schmidt97] Schmidt, D.C., Bector, R., Levine, D.L., Mungee, S., Parulkar, G., "Tao: A Middleware Framework for Real-time ORB Endsystems", IEEE Workshop on Middleware for Real-time Systems and Services, San Francisco, Ca, December 1997.

[Singhai97] Singhai, A., Sane, A., Campbell, R., "Reflective ORBs: Supporting Robust, Time-critical Distribution", Proc. ECOOP'97 Workshop on Reflective Real-Time Object-Oriented Programming and Systems, Jyväskylä, Finland, June 1997.

[Smith82] Smith, B.C., "Procedural Reflection in Programming Languages", PhD Thesis, MIT, Available as MIT Laboratory of Computer Science Technical Report 272, Cambridge, Mass., 1982.

[Stroud95] Stroud, R.J., Wu, Z., "Using Metaobject Protocols to Implement Atomic Data Objects", Proceedings of the European Conference on Object-Oriented Programming (ECOOP'95), pp 168-189, Aarhus, Denmark, August 1995.

[Vanegas98] Vanegas, R., Zinky, J., Loyall, J., Karr, D., Schantz, R., Bakken, D., "QuO's Runtime Support for Quality of Service in Distributed Objects", Proc. IFIP International Conference on Distributed Systems Platforms and Open Distributed Processing (Middleware'98), pp 207-222, Springer, 1998.

[Watanabe88] Watanabe, T., Yonezawa, A., "Reflection in an Object-Oriented Concurrent Language", In Proceedings of OOPSLA'88, Vol. 23 of ACM SIGPLAN Notices, pp 306-315, ACM Press, 1988; Also available as Chapter 3 of "Object-Oriented Concurrent Programming", A. Yonezawa, M. Tokoro (eds), pp 45-70, MIT Press, 1987.

[Watters96] Watters, A., van Rossum, G., Ahlstrom, J., "Internet Programming with Python", Henry Holt (MIS/M&T Books), September 1996.

[Yokote92] Yokote, Y., "The Apertos Reflective Operating System: The Concept and Its Implementation", In Proceedings of OOPSLA'92, ACM SIGPLAN Notices, Vol. 28, pp 414-434, ACM Press, 1992.

A Formal Analysis of Smithsonian Computational Reflection

Inge M.C. Lemmens and Peter J. Braspenning

University Maastricht, P.O. Box 616, 6200MD Maastricht, The Netherlands
lemmens@cs.unimaas.nl,
WWW home page: http://www.cs.unimaas.nl/~lemmens/

Etymologically, to be reflective means: "to apply to oneself"; i.e., reflectivity occurs when the subject and the object of some action are roughly the same. The notion of reflection has attracted the attention of researchers in the field of Computer Science. Consequently, several theories of computational reflection have been developed. In a sense, all these theories come down to applying the symbolic processing paradigm to the inner workings of computational engines. As fascinating as the topic may be, the interest in it within Computer Science is not so constant, albeit rather persistent. We think that this situation is likely caused by the inherent cognitive complexity of the topic. It is our belief that the use of standard modelling methods w.r.t. the issue of computational reflection can assist in decreasing this cognitive complexity. Therefore, as a first step, we applied the Booch method to the theory of B.C. Smith, as described in [2]. This theory relies on the application of the *reflection hypothesis* and the use of *meta-circular* processes.

Computational Processes

The notion of *computational process* is the fundamental subject matter. According to the interpretive reduction model, a process P consists of a structural field, S_P, and an ingredient process P'; i.e., the tupel $\langle S_P, P' \rangle$. The *structural field*, S_P, consists of data structures which specify a representation of the domain of process P. The *ingredient process* P' involves the dynamics of the process. This dynamics can be achieved by running a *program* on a *processor*. Thus, the ingredient process P' can be further decomposed into a program $S_{P'}$ and a processor P'' (the tupel $\langle S_{P'}, P'' \rangle$). The program of P', $S_{P'}$, is a particular kind of structural field, consisting of symbol structures that represent the intended virtual machine instructions whose processing by P'' engenders the process P' (see figure 1, in the middle).

Reflection Hypothesis Applied

Smith formulated a reflection hypothesis which in essence states that it is possible for a process to reason about itself, in the *same way* that a process can reason about some part of the external world ([2]).

The first part of the theoretical account relies on the development of a process Q which reasons about a process P'. This implies that the structural field of Q, i.e., S_Q should contain a representation of the objects and events in P' (see left side of figure 1).

In the *reflective process* we not only want to target something that reasons about itself, but we want something that is also affected by its ability to reason

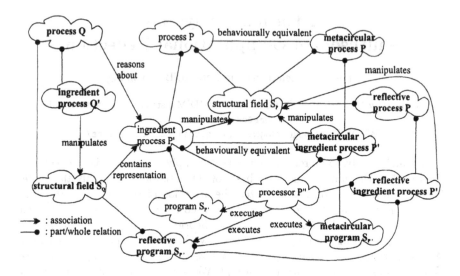

Fig. 1. The Booch method applied.

about itself. Therefore, in the end, we require the structural field S_Q to be *causally connected* to P'. This means that Q not only reasons about P', but that the results of the reasoning process have a direct impact on the process P'.

Note, that this process of "reasoning about" can be iterated: we could construct a third process, say R, which reasons about Q' in the same way that Q reasons about P'. With every iteration we are, in fact, shifting what is considered to be the *theory* w.r.t. which the reasoning process takes place. For that reason, the relationship of "reasoning about" is *not* transitive.

Meta-Circular Processes

The second part of the theoretical account is based on the use of meta-circular processes. In any computational formalism able to model its own syntax and structures, it is possible to construct what are commonly known as *meta-circular processes*: if *programs* are accessible as first class symbolic structural fields, it is possible to construct meta-circular processes. The term *circular* indicates that the meta-circular process does not constitute a definition of the process: they have to be executed by the underlying process in order to yield any sort of behaviour (since they are programs and thus static, not dynamic) and the behaviour they would thereby engender can only be known if one knows beforehand what the process does (since it refers to the process) (see figure 2).

If one would consider processes to be functions from structure onto behaviour, then one should be able to prove that $P''(MCP_{P'}) \cong P'$, where $\cong$ means *behaviourally* equivalent. Thus, if an entire computation is mediated by the explicit processing of the meta-circular process, then the result will be the same as if the entire computation had been carried out directly. A meta-circular process is *not* causally connected to the process to which it refers. The interpretive reduction model allows the construction of a tower of meta-circular processes.

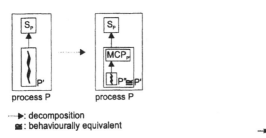

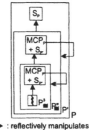

Fig. 2. A meta-circular process.

Fig. 3. A reflective process.

Reflective Processes

The tower of meta-circular processes is not yet reflective since the causal connection link is lacking. One can, however, combine the theory of meta-circular processes with the application of the reflection hypothesis. We have shown that in order for a process Q to reason about a process P', the structural field S_Q of Q should contain a representation of the relevant facts of P'. Suppose now that we incorporate within the meta-circular process $MCP_{P'}$ the structural field which contains a representation of the relevant facts of P' (a representation like in S_Q). Then this incorporation gives rise to a reflective process since the causal connection requirement is now fulfilled. This can be explained as follows: the underlying process, P'', manipulates the program, $MCP_{P'} + S_{P'}$, which may cause a change in $S_{P'}$. This change in $S_{P'}$ will, due to the circularity, change the process P'. Furthermore, $P''(MCP_{P'}) \cong P'$ and $P''(MCP_{P'} + S_{P'}) \cong P'$. This implies that a change of P' leads to a change of $P''(MCP_{P'} + S_{P'})$, and in particular in a change of $S_{P'}$.

Future Research

Research involved the comparison of different theories of computational reflection (see [1]). Future research will concentrate on the application of standard modelling techniques on the theories. It is our belief that some interesting differences will become apparent. This may lead to two possible research directions: the development of a unified theory, or the development of parallel theories of computational reflection.

References

1. Lemmens, I.M.C., Braspenning, P.J.: Computational Reflection: Different Theories Compared. Report CS99-02, University Maastricht (1999).
2. Smith, B.C.: Reflection and Semantics in Lisp. MIT Technical Report MIT/LCS/TRT-272, Massachusetts Institute of Technology (1982).

Reflection for Dynamic Adaptability: A Linguistic Approach Using LEAD++

Noriki Amano and Takuo Watanabe

Graduate School of Information Science,
Japan Advanced Institute of Science and Technology,
1-1 Asahidai, Tatsunokuchi, Ishikawa, 923-1292, Japan
Email: {n-amano, takuo}@jaist.ac.jp

Nowadays open-ended distributed systems and mobile computing systems have come into wide use. In such systems, we cannot obtain accurate information of dynamically changing runtime environments beforehand. The changes of runtime environments have given a strong influence on the execution of programs, which we cannot ignore. Thus, the software systems that can adapt themselves to dynamically changing runtime environments are required. We call such software systems *dynamically adaptable software systems*.

In this work, we propose a software model called *DAS* [1] and its description languages *LEAD++* for dynamically adaptable software systems. The DAS model has the mechanism to adapt software systems to dynamically changing runtime environments. We had designed & implemented the language *LEAD* [1] [2] based on the DAS model. We are currently working on object-oriented reflective language LEAD++. Its prototype is a pre-processor of Java. By using them, we can systematically describe dynamically adaptable software systems.

To realize dynamically adaptable software systems, it is an effective way to change the behaviors of each software system depending on the states of runtime environments. However, it is not practical to develop several versions of the same software system depending on each runtime environment and/or its states. Moreover, such behaviors of each software system depending on the states are related with any other parts of it. Thus, it is difficult to control such behaviors of each software system from its outside. From such reasons, each software system should have the ability that can adapt itself to dynamically changing runtime environments. We call such ability of software systems *dynamic adaptability*. The dynamically adaptable software systems (namely, software systems with dynamic adaptability) not only adapt themselves to dynamically changing runtime environments, but also change their own functionalities flexibly to make full use of the properties in the runtime environments.

However, there is a limitation on runtime environments and their states that software engineers can anticipate beforehand. Thus, there is also a limitation on the dynamic adaptability that the software engineers can give to software systems beforehand. From the reason, the mechanism of dynamic adaptability must be extensible. Namely, the mechanism must be able to change depending on various runtime environments and their states afterward.

---

[1] LEAD is based on the restricted DAS model and its prototype is an extension of Scheme.

We propose a software model with dynamic adaptability in extensible way called DAS. The following are main concepts of the DAS model.

- The basic components of adaptable behaviors in a software system are procedures, and the control of adaptable behaviors is based on procedure's invocation.
- The DAS model has a variant of generic procedures (functions) based on the states of runtime environments called *adaptable procedures*.
- The control mechanism of adaptable procedures (called *adaptation mechanism*) is realized by using reflection.
- A software system based on the DAS model forms a meta-level architecture.

These concepts are based on our following objectives.

- High compatibility for existing software systems.
- High flexibility of dynamic adaptability.
- High readability, maintainability and extensibility.

We have a great many requirements that we want to use many existing software systems effectively in open-ended distributed systems and mobile computing systems. Therefore, we require the methodology that we can introduce dynamic adaptability into software systems in existing languages. In the DAS model, adaptable behaviors in a software system are realized as *adaptable procedures*. An adaptable procedure consists of several *adaptable methods* that have runtime codes depending on the states of runtime environments. When an adaptable procedure is invoked, a well-suited adaptable method is selected depending on the states, and its runtime codes are executed. This approach can be applied to many existing languages that have the procedure invocation's mechanism in principle. Consequently, we have a great potentiality for effective utilization of existing software systems. Actually, we had applied the DAS model to two different languages Scheme and Java, and had designed & implemented the languages LEAD (based on Scheme) & LEAD++ (based on Java). Moreover, we had implemented a dynamically adaptable workflow system in LEAD++ by using an existing mobile code system in Java.

In our approach, to realize dynamic adaptability of software systems in flexible way, the adaptation mechanism must be able to change depending on the states of runtime environments. In the DAS model, the mechanism itself is realized using an adaptable procedure in reflective way. Therefore, it can adapt itself to the states (namely, it can change its own behaviors depending on the states). By changing the mechanism depending on the states, we can realize adaptable behaviors of software systems in flexible way such as the temporary restrictions & releases of their functionalities without modifying their original programs. Moreover, since the mechanism is realized by using an adaptable procedure, its customization is also realized by adding adaptable methods incrementally without modifying its structure.

A dynamically adaptable software system based on the DAS model forms a meta-level architecture. The descriptions of the mechanism that controls adaptable behaviors in the software system (meta-level) are completely separated from the descriptions of the primary subject domain in it (base-level). The descriptions of the control mechanism are hidden into the meta-level. This separation of concerns improves the readability, maintainability and extensibility of dynamically adaptable software systems.

Toward several related works, the following are features of the DAS model.

- It is a generic model that is independent of specific paradigms & description languages (such as object-oriented paradigm & languages, etc.).
- The adaptation mechanism can adapt itself to dynamically changing runtime environments.
- The adaptation mechanism (in other words, adaptation strategy) can be modified/extended by adding adaptable methods incrementally without modifying the structure.
- It provides asynchronous events mechanism (event object) depending on the abstractions of the virtual & local runtime environments.

Moreover, although existing reflective languages have potential for realizing dynamically adaptable software systems, their design is mainly aimed for language (or runtime) extension. On the contrary, the DAS model aims to realize dynamic adaptability of software systems using reflection. In the DAS model, reflection is used to realize the adaptation mechanism. Thus, the mechanism itself can also realize adaptable behaviors depending on the states of runtime environments. As the result, we can realize dynamic adaptability of software systems in flexible way.

However, there are also disadvantages of the DAS model. For example, when we develop dynamically adaptable software systems based on the DAS model in practice by using LEAD++, the following problems occur.

- When we describe adaptable procedures, we must consider the adaptation strategies for them.
- We must pay attention to the alteration of adaptation strategy sufficiently.
- It is difficult to apply the DAS model to software systems that require dynamic adaptability for the real time processing.

As the future works on this research, there are the following issues.

- Evaluation of dynamically adaptable software systems.
- Verification of dynamically adaptable software systems.
- Introducing concurrency & synchronization into the DAS model.

References

1. N. Amano and T. Watanabe. A Procedural Model of Dynamic Adaptability and its Description Language. In *Proceedings of the ICSE'98 International Workshop on Principles of Software Evolution*, pages 103–107, April 1998.
2. N. Amano and T. Watanabe. LEAD: Linguistic Approach to Dynamic Adaptability for Practical Applications. In *Proceedings of the System Implementation 2000*, pages 277–290. International Federation for Information Processing (IFIP), Chapman & Hall, February 1998.

Networking and Reflection: A Strong Combination

Frank Matthijs, Peter Kenens, Wouter Joosen, and Pierre Verbaeten

Distrinet - Computer Science Department
Katholieke Universiteit Leuven
Celestijnenlaan 200A, B-3001 Leuven BELGIUM
Frank.Matthijs@cs.kuleuven.ac.be

Abstract. Current meta-levels for distribution tend to ignore the networking aspect of distribution. The solution we propose is to build those meta-levels using a flexible protocol stack, which can be customised by specialised programmers. We present a framework with which such a protocol stack can be built, and briefly discuss some trade-offs and issues that have to be solved to make this approach feasible as a main-stream solution.

1 Introduction

Modern distributed systems run on a variety of hosts, from huge servers to credit card sized smart cards, with object invocations traveling over various communication technologies. Therefore, the need to control how those invocations are sent over the network becomes more and more apparent. Current meta-levels for distribution tend to ignore this aspect of distribution. The solution we propose is to construct a meta-level controlling the "execution" of base-level object invocations using a flexible protocol stack. Reflection can be used to dynamically reconfigure the protocol stack.

2 Protocol stacks at the meta-level

In the rest of this text, we assume we have available an object-oriented system with a meta-level architecture, where object invocations are reified and available at the meta-level. In our case, the meta-level for distribution will consist of protocol stack objects.

Such a meta-level can for example be built using our protocol stack framework [1]. The framework uses *components* as its basic building blocks. Each component is responsible for exactly one function in the stack, like fragmentation, encryption, flow control, etc. Components may be grouped in layers. Unlike in many other flexible protocol stack systems (e.g., microprotocols in [3]), the framework decouples header handling from protocol stack composition: any group of components (including layers but this is no requirement) can have its own header and a component does not necessarily have a header. Multiplexing is also decoupled from the other concepts, which avoids multiplexing problems [12] while still retaining layers as a unit of composition. Architecture wise, components are connected by *connectors*. Using different kinds of connectors, programmers can create their own protocol stack architecture, such as common layered stacks, or more horizontal configurations (like [10][11]). Network packets are explicitly passed between components as objects, according to the connectors between the components. Components can only communicate implicitly, through *meta-information* attached to packets. As a result, components can be added and removed dynamically, since there are no direct dependencies on other components.

One connector which deserves more attention is the *ReflectionPoint*. A ReflectionPoint observes the Packet objects flowing through and can decide to alter the destination component dynamically. As an illustration of what reflection points can do, consider an object oriented web server application. All object invocations flow through our meta-level for distribution. A reflection point in the metalevel could notice, by observing the object identifiers attached to the packets flowing through, that certain invocations tend to contain large amounts of data (probably invocations of graphics objects), and fine tune some parameters of the transport protocol or switch to a different transport protocol altogether (one which is optimized for bulk-data transfers) for these invocations. Somewhere else in the meta-level, a different reflection point could decide to apply encryption to certain invocations (for example only those which retrieve the contents of entry field objects in a secure page).

Note that this kind of dynamic behaviour on an invocation basis could also be achieved by setting up a separate, custom communication session for each object invocation. However, this approach prevents optimisations such as maintaining a communication channel pool which reuses open channels. Moreover, one would have to use a different endpoint identifier (e.g., port number) for each custom channel. This may lead to an exponential explosion of endpoint identifiers [10]. Our simple example would already require 4 different endpoint identifiers.

3 Discussion

ReflectionPoints introduce limited reflective capabilities in the protocol stack. They are very useful for normal stack reconfigurations. More sophisticated reconfigurations are probably handled better if the interactions between components are themselves reified and handled at the meta-meta-level. A potential disadvantage of this, however, is decreased performance. Using explicit reflection points as connectors between components allows specialised programmers to introduce them only where necessary (selective "inlining" of reflective parts).

Meta-levels for distribution like we propose here can also be constructed using other flexible protocol stack systems, such as Ensemble [6], Horus [5], x-kernel [3] / Morpheus [4], Scout [7], Plexus [2], DaCaPo [9], FCSS [8], Tau [10], HOPS [11], etc. Unlike our framework, these systems are in general not designed to form a meta-space. In our opinion, the most important requirement in this regard is the ability to convey control information between components, allowing application specific information to flow through the stack, and making specialised behaviour per invocation possible. This poses problems in many of these systems, certainly if we extend the requirement to the complete protocol stack, not just the upper layers (transport and above). Some systems, such as HOPS and the x-kernel can only be configured at bind time. Going meta-meta is also not trivial with many of these protocol stack systems.

Since applying flexible protocol stacks in a meta-level for distribution is not yet common practice (to say the least), many issues have to be studied in more detail. We believe that the protocol stack framework presented here, by decoupling concepts such as components, layers, multiplexing and encapsulation, and by its ability to attach any kind of meta-information to packets, is well suited as a basis for experimentation not only with protocol stack architecture and functionality, but also with dynamic reconfiguration, stability issues when reconfiguring the meta-level at run-time, usefulness of meta-meta levels, etc.

References

1. Frank Matthijs, Pierre Verbaeten. The Distrinet Protocol Stack framework. CW Report 276. 1999.
2. Marc Fiuczynski, Brian Bershad. "An Extensible Protocol Architecture for Application-Specific Networking." In Proceedings of the 1996 Winter USENIX Conference, 55-64. January 1996.
3. N. C. Hutchinson and L. L. Peterson. "The x-Kernel: An architecture for implementing network protocols." In IEEE Transactions on Software Engineering, 17(1), 64-76, Jan. 1991.
4. M. B. Abbott and L. L. Peterson. "A language-based approach to protocol implementation." In IEEE/ACM Transactions on Networking, 1(1), 4-19. Feb. 1993.
5. Robbert van Renesse, Kenneth P. Birman, Roy Friedman, Mark Hayden, and David A. Karr. "A Framework for Protocol Composition in Horus." In Proceedings of Principles of Distributed Computing. August 1995.
6. M. Hayden."The Ensemble System." PhD Dissertation, Dept. of Computer Science, Cornell University, USA. Hayton, 1997.
7. A. Montz, D. Mosberger, S. O'Malley, L. Peterson, T. Proebsting. "Scout: a communications-oriented operating system." In Proceedings of the Fifth Workshop on Hot Topics in Operating Systems, 1995.
8. M. Zitterbart, B. Stiller and A. Tantawy. "A Model for Flexible High-Performance Communication Subsystems." In IEEE Journal on Selected Areas in Communications 11(4), 507-518, 1993.
9. T. Plagemann, B. Plattner, M. Vogt and T. Walter. "Modules as Building Blocks for Protocol Configuration." In Proceedings of the IEEE International Conference on Network Protocols, San Francisco, 106-113, 1993.
10. R. Clayton, K. Calvert. "A Reactive Implementation of the Tau Protocol Composition Mechanism." In Proceedings of the First IEEE Conference on Open Architectures and Network Programming, San Francisco, California.
11. Z. Haas. "A protocol structure for high-speed communication over broadband ISDN." In IEEE Network 5(1), 64-70, January 1991.
12. D. L. Tennenhouse, "Layered Multiplexing Considered Harmful." In Protocols for High-Speed Networks, Rudin and Williamson (Ed.), North Holland, Amsterdam, 1989.

Towards Systematic Synthesis of Reflective Middleware

Petr Tůma, Valerie Issarny, Apostolos Zarras

INRIA/IRISA, Campus de Beaulieu, 35042 Rennes Cedex, France
{tuma, issarny, zarras}@irisa.fr
http://www.irisa.fr/solidor/work/aster.html

Abstract. In this paper, we present a method for systematic synthesis of middleware based on the meta-level requirements of the application that stands on top of it. Particular attention is paid to the ability to accommodate evolving requirements of a running application.

1 Introduction

Following the definition of programming languages supporting reflection [3], we say that a middleware supports *reflection* if the application that lies on top of it is provided with means for reasoning about the middleware properties and for customizing the properties as necessary. Many middleware infrastructures, such as FLEXINET and reflective ORBs, expose functionality in a way that can be used to customize the properties. This process is called *reification* [2] of the middleware functionality. Reification alone, however, does not equal reflection. What is missing are the means for reasoning about the properties of the middleware. The reasoning itself is left to the application designer, who is free to make unconstrained changes to the reified functionality and has to deduce the impact of the changes on the middleware properties himself. We remedy this drawback by designing a method for the systematic synthesis of middleware based on the application requirements, detailed in [4] and outlined in Section 2. Here, we concentrate more on how to use the systematic synthesis to accommodate changes in the requirements of a running application, as detailed in Section 3.

2 Systematic Middleware Synthesis

The systematic synthesis of middleware uses an architectural description of the application consisting of two views. The *structural view* describes interconnection of the individual components of the application; the *property view* describes meta-level properties of the middleware that implements the interconnections. The meta-level properties are described formally using temporal logic, a theorem prover is used to check the relationship between properties.

The available middleware services are stored in a middleware repository together with descriptions of the properties they provide. Based on the specification of requirements on the middleware properties, the appropriate middleware services are retrieved from the repository, assembled into a middleware and incorporated into the application [4].

3 Dynamic Reflection

Here, we extend the systematic synthesis of middleware with the ability to build middleware that can be dynamically exchanged so as to reflect changes in the requirements of a running application. The problem of exchanging the middleware is twofold. Immediately visible are the technical issues related to dynamic loading and unloading of the middleware code, where many solutions have been proposed. Less visible is the issue of what impact the dynamic change of the middleware code has on the properties provided by the middleware.

At the time a new middleware M' is to replace the old middleware M, there might be requests issued through M for which the application requirements are not satisfied yet. Examples of these requests include an unfinished remote procedure call when reliable delivery is required, or an open distributed transaction when some of the ACID transaction properties are required. The new middleware M' must guarantee that the requirements $R(req)$ valid at the time these *pending requests* were issued will be satisfied. During system execution, the information necessary to complete pending requests is a part of the middleware state. The new middleware should start from an initial state that contains this information and should be able to satisfy requirements related to the pending requests. Given a specific mapping $Map(\sigma)$ between the states of the old and the new middleware, we define a *safe state* σ_M in which it is possible to perform the exchange while satisfying the requirements:

$$SafeState(\sigma_M, M, M', Map) \equiv$$
$$[\sigma_M] \wedge \forall req \mid Pending_M(req) : [Map(\sigma_M)] \Rightarrow R(req)$$

A safe state is defined in relation to the ability to map the state from the old to the new middleware. When no state mapping is available, we refine the *SafeState* predicate into a stronger criterion, *IdleState*, defined only with respect to the old middleware properties. In an *idle state* [1], no requests are pending and hence no state needs to be mapped:

$$IdleState(\sigma_M, M) \equiv [\sigma_M] \wedge (\forall req : \neg Pending_M(req))$$

Based on a straightforward utilization of the safe state definition, the general strategy of the exchange is to reach the safe state of the middleware, block incoming requests to remain in the safe state during update, exchange the middleware implementation, and unblock incoming requests. To detect whether the middleware reached a safe state, an idle state detection code is incorporated into it at the time it is being synthesized. The definition of the idle state makes this code independent of the middleware implementation; it is retrieved from the repository based on the middleware properties only. During exchange, this code is used to determine when it is safe to perform it; alternatively, a safe state detection code specific to the particular update can be installed.

It is generally not guaranteed that the middleware will reach a safe state within finite time during normal execution. We therefore selectively block requests from the application, so as to prevent activities that do not participate in driving the middleware into a safe state from issuing requests that would keep the middleware away from the safe state. It can be shown that the decision whether to block a request depends only on the safe state used during the update. This decision is therefore taken by the safe state detectors associated with the update.

For the purpose of the exchange, the middleware is separated into a static and a dynamic part. The static part of the middleware contains the proxy through which the application accesses the middleware, and the code for blocking requests. The dynamic part contains the safe state detection code and the middleware itself, both retrieved from the repository based on the required properties. The exchange is directed by a coordinator component, responsible for exchange within the scope of the changed property. When requested to perform an exchange and given the new code of the dynamic middleware parts, the coordinator instructs the static middleware parts to block the requests as described above. After a safe state is reached, the coordinator directs the middleware to unload the existing dynamic parts and install the new code.

4 Conclusion

The approach presented in this paper tackles the problem of changing middleware properties in a running application. Its advantage is in synthesizing the middleware systematically based on the required properties, as opposed to only exposing the functionality through reification. The basic concepts of the approach were prototyped using several CORBA platforms and the STeP theorem prover. The current work focuses on improvements related to granularity and timing of the middleware exchange, and on using the approach to synthesize adaptive middleware.

Acknowledgement: this work has been partially supported the C3DS LTR Esprit project.

References

1. J. Kramer and J. Magee. The Evolving Philosophers Problem. *IEEE Transactions on Software Engineering*, 15(1):1293–1306, November 1990.
2. J. Malenfant, M. Jacques, and F.N. Demers. A Tutorial on Behavioral Reflection and its Implementation. In *Proceedings of REFLECTION '96*. ECOOP, 1996.
3. B. C. Smith. *Procedural Reflection in Programming Languages*. PhD thesis, MIT, 1982. Available as MIT Techical Report 272.
4. A. Zarras and V. Issarny. A Framework for Systematic Synthesis of Transactional Middleware. In *Proceedings of MIDDLEWARE '98*, pages 257–272. IFIP, Sept 1998.

An Automatic Aspect Weaver with a Reflective Programming Language

Renaud Pawlak, Laurence Duchien, and Gérard Florin
{pawlak, duchien, florin}@cnam.fr

Laboratoire CEDRIC-CNAM 292 rue St Martin, Fr 75141 Paris Cedex 03

Abstract. This short paper presents A-TOS (Aspect-TOS (TCL Object System)), an aspect-oriented framework that allows the programmer to define its own specialized aspects and to weave or remove them at runtime. Since A-TOS is based on a configurable and semantic-reliable object-wrapping technique, it is able to solve what we call the Aspect-Composition Issue (ACI), i.e., to detect and solve many semantic conflicts when weaving the different aspects together.

Keywords: Aspect-Oriented Programming, Weaver, Wrapping.

Introduction

Recent approaches like the Aspect-Oriented Programming approach [KLM+97] consist in finding an accurate and consistent mean to achieve separation of concerns within complex application programs.

However, since it does not exist any general and semantic reliable solution when aspects are composed together, existing weavers are *ad hoc* and fixed solutions to a given problem.

In this short paper, we present A-TOS (for Aspect-Tcl Object System), a general purpose Aspect-Oriented Framework that we have implemented with TOS [Paw99], a class-based reflective language. A-TOS uses wrappers [BFJR98] to ensure a sequential and ordered composition of the aspect codes by the weaver and allows the meta-programmer to easily add or remove any aspect in a controlled and semantic reliable way.

The first section presents the Aspect-Composition Issue and proposes an aspect-composition model based on wrapping. Section 2 briefly describes how the ACI is automatically solved in A-TOS (by ordering the wrappers).

1 A Wrapper-Based Composition Model

When programming with aspects, an application programmer can deal with different parts of the problem within different programs. However, none of the proposed solutions allows the programmer to easily add or remove aspects in a secure and automatic way — we say that a weaver is automatic when the programmer does not need to explicitly extend the weaver capabilities when a new aspect is added. For instance, D [LK97] fixes the number of aspects (two) that can be used to program an application. The main reason for this limitation comes from true difficulties to reliably control the resulting program semantics when a new aspect is added — we call this problem the *Aspect-Composition Issue* (ACI). For example, if the composition of a synchronization and an authentication aspects makes all the authentication processes to be synchronized, it can have tragic effects on the system performances.

Since it may be very difficult to solve the ACI in a general case, A-TOS proposes a wrapping-based system where the aspect composition is realized by some *WRAPS* links (see figure 1). In this system, wrappers are sequentially called in a given order so that the ACI is reduced to an ordering problem.

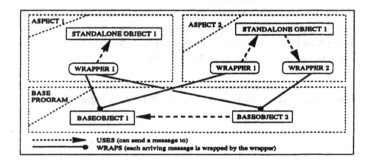

Fig. 1. An overview of an aspect system based on wrapping.

2 From Composition to Automatic Composition

Since our composition scheme consists in sequentially calling the wrappers, solving the object-level ACI (as defined in 1) consists in finding the good wrappers order to realize the required semantics. Many criteria may influence the way wrappers are composed with each other. However, those criteria can be reduced to four main wrapper properties:
- the wrapper does not always call the base object — it is a **conditional** wrapper,
- it always has to be called — it is a **mandatory** wrapper,
- it has to be called only if the base object is effectively called — it is an **exclusive** wrapper,
- it sends messages to other objects — it is a **modificator** wrapper.

Those properties can be composed[1] and finally give five different classes of wrappers: conditional wrappers (CW), mandatory w. (MW), exclusive w. (EW), mandatory conditional w. (MCW), and exclusive conditional w. (ECW).

---

[1] Mandatory and exclusive properties cannot be composed. Moreover, for simplification sake, we assume that the modificator property is not relevant for ordering the wrappers.

When knowing the wrapper classes, we can deduce ordering constraints when composing wrappers. For instance, a mandatory wrapper always has to be placed *before* a conditional wrapper to always respect the mandatory wrapper definition (i.e., it is always called).

Finally, to resolve the wrapper list order when adding a wrapper to a base object, A-TOS adds a new class-level property that represents the wrapper class and that must be filled by the wrapper programmer. When composing aspects, A-TOS respects the following ordering constraint that is a garantee for a correct resulted semantics ($C1 > C2$ means that class $C1$ wrappers must always be called before class $C2$ ones): MW > MCW > CM > ECW > EW.

Conclusion

In this paper, we propose A-TOS, a generic and automatic aspect-composition framework based on a simple wrapper classification. This classification determines automatic and semantic-reliable composition rules (by ordering the wrappers) and partially solves the Aspect-Composition Issue (ACI). This solution, by forcing the programmer to think about the objects semantics when programming an aspect, can be considered as a tradeoff between a fully automatic solution (where all the conflicts would be solved by the weaver) and with a handmade solution like D.

In the future, we will also address some difficult points. Especialy, since we assumed that all the modificators modifications are commutative (see section 2), we must now provide some support when it is not the case. Besides, this framework points out that, in an open environment, some aspect administration has to be done to prevent redundancies and semantics conflicts.

References

[BFJR98] J. Brant, B. Foote, R. E. Johnson, and D. Roberts. Wrappers to the rescue. In *Prodeedings of ECOOP'98*, 1998.

[KLM+97] G. Kiczales, J. Lamping, A. Mendhekar, C. Maeda, C.V. Lopes, J.M. Loingtier, and J. Irwin. Aspect-oriented programming. In *Proceedings of the European Conference on Object-Oriented Programming (ECOOP'97)*, 1997.

[LK97] C. V. Lopes and G. Kiczales. D: A language framework for distributed programming. Technical report, Xerox Palo Alto Research Center, 1997.

[Paw99] R. Pawlak. Tos: a class-based reflective language on tcl. Technical Report 9902, Laboratoire CEDRIC-CNAM, January 1999.

Using Compile-Time Reflection for Objects'State Capture[1]

Marc-Olivier Killijian, Juan-Carlos Ruiz-Garcia, Jean-Charles Fabre

LAAS-CNRS, 7 Avenue du Colonel Roche
31077 Toulouse cedex, France
{killijian, fabre, ruiz}@laas.fr

1 Motivations

Checkpointing is a major issue in the design and the implementation of dependable systems, especially for building fault tolerance strategies. Checkpointing a distributed application involves complex algorithms to ensure the consistency of the distributed recovery state of the application. All these algorithms make the assumption that the internal state of the application objects can be obtained easily. However, this is a strong assumption and, in practice, it is not so easy when complex active objects are considered. This is the problem we focus on in our current work. The available solutions to this problem either rely on :
- a specific hardware/operating-system/middleware that can provide runtime information about the mapping used between memory and application objects;
- a reflective runtime which provides access to class information, such as Java Serialization [1] based on the Java Reflection API;
- intervention at the language level, rewriting the original code to add checkpointing mechanisms (e.g. Porch [2] for C programs);
- the provision of state handling mechanisms by the user; since the implementation of these mechanisms must be error-free, this is a weak solution.

When neither the underlying system nor the language runtime is sufficiently reflective to provide type information about the object classes, the only solution is to obtain this information at the language level. Two approaches can be investigated here: (i) developing a specific compiler (as Porch does) or (ii) using a reflective compiler such as OpenC++ [3] or OpenJava [4]. Since diving into a compiler is very complex and can lead to the introduction of new software faults, we think that the latter is a better solution. Clearly, compile-time reflection opens up the compilation process without impacting the compiler itself. Off-the-shelf compilers can thus be used to produce the runtime entities.

---

[1] This work has been partially supported by the European Esprit Project n° 20072, DeVa, by a contract with FRANCE TELECOM (ref. ST.CNET/DTL/ASR/97049/DT) and by a grant from CNRS (National Center for Scientific Research in France) in the framework of international agreements between CNRS and JSPS (Japan Society for the Promotion of Science).

2 Approach Overview

To provide state handling facilities to target objects, we have to implement two new methods for each class: saveState and restoreState. The former is responsible for saving the state of an object and the latter for restoring this state; these methods are similar to the readObject and writeObject methods provided by the Java runtime.

These methods must save/restore the values of each attribute: basic and structured types of the language, arrays, and inherited fields. Furthermore, they must be able to traverse object hierarchies, i.e. save/restore the objects included in the object currently processed. To generate these methods we use OpenC++, an open-compiler for C++ which provides a nice API for both introspection and intercession of application classes. Thanks to the static type information it provides, we are able to analyse the structure of the classes and can thus generate the necessary methods for checkpointing.

However, since C++ is an hybrid between object-oriented and procedural languages, some of its features are very difficult to handle. Features which break the encapsulation principle must be avoided from a dependability viewpoint: friend classes or functions and the pointer model of C++. We decided to handle only a single level of indirection for pointers and to forbid the use of pointer arithmetic; pointers can thus be seen as simple object references as in Java.

Filtering programs and rejecting those that dont respect these restrictions is easy to implement using compile-time reflection. Enforcing other programming restrictions is also useful for validation aspects. Dependability can be significantly enhanced by restricting to a subset of a language [5] in many respects.

It is worth noting that this approach does not deal with multithreaded objects. Indeed, compile-time reflection is not sufficient to save the state of threads, thread introspection is needed [6].

3 Current Implementation Status

We have implemented this approach using OpenC++ 2.5.1 and GCC 2.8.1 on both Solaris and Linux operating systems. Firstly the application program is parsed by the metaclasses we designed, these metaclasses generate the necessary facilities (save/restore state methods and related state buffer classes). Secondly, the C++ compiler compiles the instrumented code.

We are currently working on the validation of this toolkit. We are using some application benchmarks in order to evaluate the correctness of the states obtained (the coverage of the class' structure analysis), and to evaluate the efficiency of the state capture/restoration compared to Java serialization and Porch checkpointing. The first efficiency results obtained on simple examples are promising.

We have also implemented an optimisation of this approach that saves only the modified attributes of an object. This technique uses runtime reflection in order to know which of the object's members have been modified since the last checkpoint.

The idea is to save/restore a delta-state instead of the full object state. Since an object's methods often modify only a small subset of its attributes, this approach is more efficient in practice. It is worth noting that this new technique can only be applied for checkpointing. Cloning an object requires its full state to be available.

4 Conclusion

The work briefly describe here is part of a reflective architecture for dependable CORBA applications [7] which implements fault-tolerance mechanisms as metaobjects on any off-the-shelf ORB. The metaobject protocol controls both object interaction and object state. It has been developed for C++ objects and is currently being ported for Java objects using OpenJava. The implementation relies on a combined use of tools and techniques, such as open compiler, IDL compiler and reflective runtime when available.

Acknowledgements. We would like to thank Shigeru Chiba and Michiaki Tatsubori for their contribution to this work and invaluable assistance in using OpenC++.

References

[1]   Sun Microsystems, "Java Object Serialization Specification".

[2]   V. Strumpen and B. Ramkumar , "Portable Checkpointing for Heterogeneous Architectures," in *Fault-Tolerant Parallel and Distributed Systems*, D. Avresky, R. and D. Keli, R., Eds.: Kluwer Academic Press, pp. 73-92, 1998.

[3]   S. Chiba, "A Metaobject Protocol for C++," presented at OOPSLA, Austin, Texas, USA, pp. 285-299, 1995.

[4]   M. Tatsubori, "An Extensible Mechanism for the Java Language", Master of Engineering Dissertation, Graduate School of Engineering, University of Tsukuba , University of Tsukuba, Ibaraki, Japan, Feb 2, 1999.

[5]   P. J. Plauger, "Embedded C++", appeared in C/C++ Users Journal, vol.15, issue 2, February 1997.

[6]   M. Kasbekar, C. Narayanan, and C. R. Dar, "Using Reflection for Checkpointing Concurrent Object Oriented Programs" Center for Computational Physics, University of Tsukuba, UTCCP 98-4, ISSN 1344-3135, October 1998.

[7]   M.-O. Killijian, J.-C. Fabre, J.-C. Ruiz-Garcia, and S. Chiba, "A Metaobject Protocol for Fault-Tolerant CORBA Applications," presented at IEEE Symposium on Reliable Distributed Systems, West Lafayette, Indiana, USA, pp. 127-134, 1998.

Invited Talk 3
Past, Present, and Future of Aperios

Yasuhiko Yokote
Sony Corporation
PSD Center, ESDL (3G5F)
6-7-35 Kitashinagawa, Shinagawa-ku,
Tokyo 141 JAPAN
E-mail : ykt@arch.sony.co.jp

Aperios is a software platform for Networked Consumer Devices such as STB, Digital TV, and Home Server. It has originally developed at Sony Computer Science Laboratory, and transferred to Sony Corporation as an operating system for an Interactive Videocommunication System in 1995. Since then, Aperios has been evolved to be used for software platform of consumer devices development and the first Aperios product has introduced in the Japan market on May 1999.

Firstly, some technical aspects of Aperios are presented in terms of reflection in an operating system. Then, our experience of Aperios introduction to the product development is discussed: How have we introduced a new idea, reflection, to engineers?; How has reflection contributed to the product?; What is the most difficulty in that process?; etc. Also, our policy of the Aperios release and some business related topics are presented. In conclusion, the next step (or direction) of Aperios is briefly described.

Yasuhiko Yokote got his PhD in Electrical Engineering from Keio University in 1988. From 1988 to 1996, he was a resarcher at the Sony Computer Science Laboratory in Tokyo. Then he joins Sony Corporation. His interests include object-oriented operating systems, programming languages, distributed computing, and embedded systems. He worked on the design and implementation of well known object-oriented systems including ConcurrentSmalltalk, the Muse Operating System, the Apertos Operating System, and Aperios. He is a member of ACM, IEEE Computer Society, and JSSST.

Reflecting Java into Scheme

Kenneth R. Anderson[1], Timothy J. Hickey[2]

[1]BBN Technologies, Cambridge, MA, USA KAnderson@bbn.com,
[2]Brandeis University, Waltham, MA, USA tim@cs.brandeis.edu

Abstract. We describe our experience with SILK, a Scheme dialect written in Java. SILK grazes symbiotically on Java's reflective layer, enriching itself with Java's classes and their behavior. This is done with three procedures. (constructor) and (method) provide access to a specific Java constructor or method respectively. (import) allows the entire behavior of a class to be imported easily. (import) converts Java methods into generic functions that take methods written in Java or Scheme. In return, SILK provides Java applications with an interactive development and debugging environment that can be used to develop graphical applications from the convenience of your web browser. Also, because SILK has introspective access into Java, it can also be used for compile time metaobject scripting. For example, it can generate a new class using an old one as a template.

1 Introduction

Java's reflective layer provides access to metaobjects that reflect primitive, class, array, field, constructor, and method objects. There are obvious limitations to its reflective capabilities. For example, one can only affect the behavior of the running program by invoking methods and accessing fields of objects. One cannot define or redefine a new class or method. Also, one cannot subclass any metaobjects.

Despite these restrictions, Java's reflective capabilities are used successfully by many Java facilities, such as serialization, remote method invocation (RMI), and Java Beans. However, programming in base Java, is different from programming in the reflective layer. While Java is a statically typed language, the reflective layer is more dynamic. This suggests that a dynamic language, such as Scheme, could be ideal for programming the reflective layer. Scheme could be used as a dynamic language at runtime, and as a dynamic metalanguage at compile time.

Here we describe SILK (Scheme in about 50 K), a compact Scheme dialect written in Java. Because Java is reflective, considerable power can be gained relatively easily. For example, only two functions, (constructor) and (method), need to be added to Scheme to provide complete access to the underlying Java.

Following Common Lisp, SILK provides generic functions. These generic functions accept several method types:
- Java static methods, instance methods, and constructors
- Methods written in Scheme that dispatch on Java classes

By arranging for Java to do most of the work, method dispatch is efficient. For most generic functions, the method dispatch overhead is only one Java method invocation beyond the normal overhead of invoking a reflected Java method through Scheme.

The foreign function interface between Scheme and Java is virtually transparent. The function (import <class name>) makes the methods and final static fields of the Java class named <class name> accessible to Scheme.

SILK started out simply as a Scheme implementation in Java. However, as its use of reflection has grown, it has become a powerful tool for controlling and developing Java applications. The following sections describe what programming in SILK is like, focusing on issues related to using reflection and the implementation of generic functions.

As this paper is concerned with Scheme, and Java reflection, we begin with a very brief introduction to the essential features of these topics. Anyone familiar with these topics can simply skip to the next section. Anyone with some knowledge of object-oriented programming and reflection should be able to follow this paper easily.

1.1 Java Reflection

Java is a statically typed object-oriented language, with a syntax similar to C. Java is a hybrid language with both primitive types, like int and double, and class based object types descending from the class Object. A Java program is built out of a set of classes. Java classes support single inheritance of implementation (extends) and multiple inheritance of interfaces (implements). An interface is a class that describes an object in terms of the protocol (set of methods) it most implement, but provides no implementation itself.

A class definition can contain other class definitions, static and instance fields, and static and instance methods.

A Java method has a signature, which is its name, and the types of each of its parameters. The signature is used at compile time to focus the choice of which method is to be invoked.

Java has two types of methods. An "instance method" has a distinguished first argument as well as possibly some parameters. When such a method is invoked, the dynamic type of this argument is used to select the appropriate method to invoke at runtime, while the declared types of the parameters are used to choose a signature at compile time.

A "static method" does not have a distinguished argument, but may have other parameters. It fills the role of a function in other languages. The choice of which static method to invoke is determined completely at compile time.

The java.lang and java.lang.reflect packages provide metaclasses that reflect the class and its components. To invoke a method, one must first ask the class that defined the method for the method's metaobject, using getMethod(), which takes the methods name, and an array of argument types as parameters. The method can be invoked by using its invoke() method which takes a parameter which is an object array of the arguments. Java provides a set of wrapper classes that let one convert a primitive type to an object. Thus for example, an int can be represented as an instance of class Integer. Here's an example of using the reflection layer to construct a hash table of size 10 and then invoke a put () method on it:

```
package elf;
import java.lang.reflect.*;
import java.util.Hashtable;

public class Reflect {
  public static void main(String[] args) {
    try {
      // Hashtable ht = new Hashtable(10);
      Class[] types1 = new Class[] { Integer.TYPE };
      Constructor c =
        Hashtable.class.getConstructor(types1);
      Object[] args1 = new Object[] {new Integer(10) };
      Hashtable ht = (Hashtable) c.newInstance(args1);

      // ht.put("Three", new Integer(3))
      Class[] types2 = new Class[] {Object.class,
                                    Object.class };
      Method m = Hashtable.class.getMethod("put",
                                           types2);
      Object[] args2 =
        new Object[] { "Three", new Integer(3) };
      m.invoke(ht, args2);

      System.out.println(ht);  // Prints: {Three=3}
    } catch (Exception e) { e.printStackTrace(); }}}
```

1.2 Scheme

Scheme is a dynamically typed language that uses simple Lisp syntax. A Scheme program is built out of a sequence of expressions. Each expression is evaluated in turn.

Scheme provides a set of primitive types. The following exhibit shows the Scheme type name and its Java implementation used in SILK:

Scheme	Java
boolean	Boolean
symbol	silk.Symbol
char	Character
vector	Object[]
pair	silk.Pair
procedure	silk.Procedure
number	Number
exact	Integer
inexact	Double
string	char[]
port	
inputport	silk.InputPort
outputport	java.io.PrintWriter

A Scheme procedure takes arguments of any type. Type predicates can be used to identify the type of an object at runtime.

While Scheme would not be considered "object oriented", the Scheme community has developed SLIB [1], a standard library that provides more complex data structures built from these types, including several object oriented extensions.

The power of Scheme comes from such features as:

1. A compact and clear definition, requiring only 50 pages, including its denotational semantic, example, references, and index.
2. A procedure can construct and return a new procedure, as you would expect from a functional language.
3. The syntax is so simple that new minilanguages can extend the language easily using functions or Scheme's macro facility, (define-syntax).

Both Java and Scheme provide garbage collection.

2 SILK's Access to Java

SILK offers two distinct interface to Java which are discussed in the following sections.

2.1 Primitive Access to Java is Easy

Originally, SILK provided two primitive procedures for accessing Java behavior:
```
(constructor CLASSNAME ARGTYPE1 ...)
(method METHODNAME CLASSNAME ARGTYPE1 ...)
```
The (constructor) procedure is given a specification of a Java constructor, in terms of a class name and a list of argument type names, and returns a procedure implementing that constructor. The (method) is given a specification of a Java method, in terms of a method name, class name, and a list of argument type names, and returns a procedure implementing that method.

So, for example, we can use the `java.math.BigInteger` package to see if the number, 12345678987654321, is probably prime (with a probability of error of less than 1 part in 2^{-10} when the result is #t):

```
> (define isProbablePrime
    (method "isProbablePrime" "java.math.BigInteger"
            "int"))
isProbablePrime
> (define BigInteger
    (constructor "java.math.BigInteger"
                 "java.lang.String"))
BigInteger
> (isProbablePrime (BigInteger "12345678987654321") 10)
#f
```

It is useful to have additional access to Java's reflection layer. Here we define the procedure (`class`) that returns a class object given its full name string:

```
> (define class (method "forName" "java.lang.Class"
                        "java.lang.String"))
class
> (define HT (class "java.util.Hashtable"))
HT
> HT
class java.util.Hashtable
```

Here we define a procedure, (`get-static-value`) that given a class and a string naming a static field, returns the value of the corresponding static field. We then ask for the value of the `TYPE` field of the class `Void`. In Java, that would be simply `Void.TYPE`.

```
>(define get-field
    (method "getField" "java.lang.Class"
            "java.lang.String"))
get-field
>(define get-field-value
    (method "get" "java.lang.reflect.Field"
                  "java.lang.Object"))
get-field-value
>(define (get-static-value class field-name)
   (get-field-value (get-field class field-name) '()))
get-static-value
>(get-static-value (class "java.lang.Void") "TYPE")
void
>
```

2.2 But, Procedures Aren't Generic Enough

This approach was used extensively for a year. However, two problems became apparent:

1. Procedures are not generic. Procedures must be carefully named apart to avoid name conflicts. There are many potential conflicts, such as:
   - classes `java.util.Hashtable` and `java.lang.reflect.Field` both provide a `put` method.
   - class `java.lang.Object` provides a `toString` method, while `java.lang.reflect.Modifier` provides a static `toString` method.
   - methods can be overloaded, so for example, class `java.lang.StringBuffer` provides 10 methods named `append`.

2. For each Java method or constructor one needs, it must be named and defined separately. Even if only a few methods of a class are used, this can be a fair amount of work.

2.3 (import) Lifts Java Classes into SILK Wholesale

To overcome this problem, an (import) function was added used to import the static and instance methods of a class. The goal was to make this similar to the import statement in Java. Here we import Hashtable:

```
> import "java.util.Hashtable")
importing java.util.Hashtable in 161 ms.
#t
>
```

The result of the (import) is that:
- The global variable `Hashtable.class` is given the value of the class `Hashtable`.
- Each public instance method applicable to `Hashtable` is made a generic function. This includes inherited methods, such as `clone()`, and `toString()` that are inherited from `java.lang.Object`. Generic functions, whose name conflicts with an existing Scheme procedure, have "#" add to the name as a suffix. Such conflicts include `load#`, `substring#`, `length#`, `apply#`, `list#`, `append#`, and `print#`.
- Generic functions are also made for each static method, but they must be named apart from instance methods. They are given a name that looks like `Class.method`. See the example uses of such methods below.
- A generic constructor function named after the class, `Hashtable`, is defined. Thus one does not need to say "new", just use the name of the class, `Hashtable`. This approach is similar to Haskell or ML. It makes con-

structing nested objects a bit more compact. It also fits well with Scheme's syntax.

- Each global constant is represented in Java as a `public static final` field is assigned to a global variable of the form `Class.field`.

We can immediately start using Hashtables:

```
>(define ht (Hashtable 20))
ht
>ht
{}
>(put ht 'clone 1)
()
>ht
{clone=1}
>(put ht 'zone 2)
()
>ht
{clone=1, zone=2}
>(get ht 'clone)
1
>
```

The procedure (import) creates generic functions. For example, (get) is a generic function with three methods:

```
> get
{silk.Generic get[3]}
> (for-each print (methods get))
{InstanceMethod Object Map.get(Object)}
{InstanceMethod Object silk.GlobalEnv.get(Symbol)}
{InstanceMethod Object Field.get(Object)}
#t
>
```

Here's an example of using a static method:
```
> (import "java.lang.Float")
importing java.lang.Float in 81 ms.
#t
> (Float.parseFloat "17.42")
17.42
```

2.4 Here's an Example of Using (import)

To show what programming with (import) and generic functions is like, here's a simple applet:

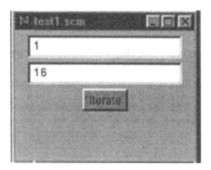

To use it, type a number into the second textfield. The top textfield contains the current estimate of its square root. Each time the "iterate" button is pressed, an iteration of Newton's method is performed to better approximate the square root.

Here's the code. The EasyWin class is borrowed from JLIB.

```
(import "java.lang.Double")
(import "java.awt.Color")
(import "java.awt.Button")
(import "java.awt.TextField")
(import "jlib.EasyWin")

(define (test1)
  ;; Construct a test window.
  (let ((win (EasyWin "test1.scm" this-interpreter))
        (g (TextField "1" 20))
        (x (TextField "16" 20))
        (go (Button "Iterate")))
    (define (action e)               ; Define call back.
      (setText g
               (toString
                (f
                 (Double.valueOf (getText g))
                 (Double.valueOf (getText x))
                 ))))
    (define (f g x)                  ; Newton's method.
      (/ (+ g (/ x g)) 2.0))
    (resize win 200 200)             ; Size the window.
    (add win g)                      ; Add the components.
    (add win x)
    (add win go)
    (addActionCallback win action)
    (setBackground win (Color 200 200 255))
    (show win)))

(test1)                              ; Try it out.
```

3 The Generic Function Protocol

Compared to Common Lisp, or even Tiny CLOS, the SILK generic function protocol is simple. Because the protocol is defined in terms of non generic Java methods, metacircularity is not an issue [3]. Here are the essential abstract classes and methods:

```
public abstract class Procedure extends SchemeUtils {
  // Apply the Procedure to a list of arguments.
  public abstract Object apply(Pair args, Engine eng);
}


public abstract class Generic extends Procedure {
  // Add a method to the generic.
  public abstract void addMethod(GenericMethod m);
}

public abstract class GenericMethod extends Procedure {
  // Two GenericMethod's match if they have equal
  // lists of parameterTypes.
  public abstract boolean match(GenericMethod x);

  // Is the method applicable to the list of arguments?
  public abstract boolean isApplicable(Pair args);

  // Returns the method that is more applicable.
  public abostract GenericMethod moreApplicableMethod
                              (GenericMethod m2);
}
```

A `Procedure` is an object that can be applied to a list of arguments. It is the basis for function calling in SILK. Class `SchemeUtil` simply provides many convenient utilities (a common Java idiom). `Engine` is used to execute code fragments that allows tail call optimization and need not be considered further here.

A `Generic` is a `Procedure` defined in terms of a set of `GenericMethod`'s The `addMethod()` method is used to add a `GenericMethod` to the set. No two `GenericMethod`'s in the set are allowed to `match()`.

There are currently four classes of `GenericMethod`. `ConstructorMethod`, `StaticMethod`, and `InstanceMethod` are wrapper classes for each of the corresponding Java metaobjects. A `SchemeMethod` is used to define methods whose behavior is written in Scheme.

Since (`import`) assigns constructors, static methods and instance methods to different generic functions, the methods in a generic function tend to be of only one type. However, a generic function can have any subclass of `GenericMethod`. This allows `Scheme` methods to be added to any `Generic`, for example.

3.1 Choosing the Applicable Method

To choose the applicable method, we follow Java semantics closely. This may seem surprising since Java chooses a method based on the dynamic type of its first argument, and the declared type of its other arguments. SILK simply makes this choice at runtime based on the types of arguments passed to the `Generic`.

For example, here are the methods for the `(list#)` Generic looks like after importing `java.io.file` and `javax.swing.JFrame`:

```
> list#
{silk.Generic list#[7]}
> (for-each print (methods list#))
{InstanceMethod String[] File.list(FilenameFilter)}
{InstanceMethod String[] File.list()}
{InstanceMethod void Component.list(PrintStream, int)}
{InstanceMethod void Component.list(PrintWriter, int)}
{InstanceMethod void Component.list()}
{InstanceMethod void Component.list(PrintWriter)}
{InstanceMethod void Component.list(PrintStream)}
```

To list the contents of a directory, the second method would be chosen:

```
> (define f (File "d:/java/jlib3/src/silk/"))
f
> (for-each* print (list# f))
Closure.java
Code.java
ConstructorMethod.java
...
>
```

The only complication with this approach is Scheme datatypes must be mapped to an appropriate Java type during method invocation. Currently, there are two issues.

1. SILK's numeric types include only `Integer` and `Double`. So, methods such as `java.util.Hashtable(int, float)` can't be invoked directly. One must first convert the required `float`, using `(Float 0.75)` for example. While SILK does not use `Float` or `Long` objects, once such objects are constructed it treats them as normal numbers.

2. Scheme symbols and strings (represented as Java `char[]`) are mapped to class `String` during method invocation. This can lead to an ambiguity, such as in the `append()` method of `java.lang.StringBuffer`:

```
>(import "java.lang.StringBuffer")
importing java.lang.StringBuffer in 70 ms.
#t
>append#
{silk.Generic append#[10]}
>(for-each print (methods append#))
{InstanceMethod StringBuffer.append(char[], int, int)}
```

```
{InstanceMethod StringBuffer.append(char[])}    ; ***
{InstanceMethod StringBuffer.append(boolean)}
{InstanceMethod StringBuffer.append(String)}    ; ***
{InstanceMethod StringBuffer.append(Object)}
{InstanceMethod StringBuffer.append(char)}
{InstanceMethod StringBuffer.append(long)}
{InstanceMethod StringBuffer.append(int)}
{InstanceMethod StringBuffer.append(float)}
{InstanceMethod StringBuffer.append(double)}
```

Since this `Generic` has methods on both `String` and `char[]`, SILK can't decide which to use. In such a case, the user must invoke a particular method using `(method)`.

3.2 Use Only The Most General Method

To minimize the method lookup overhead, for Java instance methods we let Java's single argument dispatch do most of the work. To do that, we only store the most general Java methods in a generic function. For example, for the generic function `(toString)` we only need the `Object.toString()` method:

```
>(methods toString)
({InstanceMethod String Object.toString()})
>
```

We call such a method, a "most general method".

The feasibility of this approach was studied using the 494 classes reachable from the class `javax.swing.Jframe`. Here are some statistics:

```
Count What
 494   classes
 458   public classes
  52   Exception classes
 176   static most general methods
2759   instance most general methods.
2935   total most general methods.
```

There were 134 generic functions that contain only static methods. 93% of them have two or fewer methods:

```
Count          # Methods, Cumulative % and examples
    110          1 82.1%
     15          2 93.3%
      6          3
      1          4 createPackedRaster
      1          5 getKeyStroke
      1          9 valueOf
```

The 2,759 most general instance methods fall into 1525 generic functions. 91% of these have three or fewer methods:

```
Count          # Methods, Cumulative % and examples
   1058        1  69.4%
    255        2  86.1%
     75        3  91.0%
     39        4
     24        5
     23        6
     17        7
     10        8
      6        9
      1       10
      5       11
      1       12
      1       13
      2       16
      1       17 get
      1       18 contains
      3       20 clone insert print
      1       22 println
      1       24 remove
      1       36 add
```

So, most generic functions have one or two methods so our approach favors such situations.

Methods are only added to a generic function when a class is imported. So, the above statistics reflect what you get if you imported all 494 classes. The number of actual methods is likely to be substantially lower than this. For example, when using only javax.swing.JFrame, (add) only has six methods, not 36.

3.3 A Few Discriminator States Are Adequate

Since the number of methods per generic function tends to be small, we focus on optimizing the method lookup for such cases. We use a discriminator function with a small number of states. The state of the discriminator is recomputed whenever a method is added to the generic function. The states are chosen based on the static statistical analysis above. In contrast, Common Lisp chooses discriminator states dynamically so performance is adapted to each run of an application [4]. Here is a description of the states:

1. NOMETHODS - No methods, an error occurs if invoked. The discriminator is in this state when the generic function is first constructed, before any methods have been added to it.
2. ONEMETHOD - One method simply invoke the method.
3. TWOMETHODINSTANCEFIXED - Two instance methods with the same number of arguments. Check the first argument of the first method. If it is appliable, apply it, otherwise apply the second method. This works because the types of the first arguments are disjoint because of the most general method requirement.

4. TWOMETHODNOTFIXED - Two methods of any type with different numbers of arguments. Choose the method based on the number of arguments.
5. GENERAL - Most general lookup. Compute the most applicable method based on all of the arguments of all methods.

For the most likely case of a generic function only having one or two methods, discrimination is little more than a switch jump and a subclass test or two. For cases where an error would occur, we simply invoke the wrong method and let Java signal the error.

Most of the cost of invoking a generic function is in crossing the Scheme/Java frontier to actually apply the method. Currently this involves converting a list of arguments from the Scheme side to an array of arguments on the Java side. String and symbol arguments are also converted to appropriate Java types. The return value must also be converted. For example, a boolean result must be inverted to either #t or #f.

3.4 Scheme Methods

Besides using Java methods in generic functions, it is useful to define methods directly in Scheme, using the (define-method) macro:

```
(define-method name ((arg class) ...)
  (form) ..)
```

Where class names a Java class.

For example, here we define the generic function (iterate collection action) that maps the function action over the elements of collection:

```
(import "java.util.Iterator")
(import "java.util.Collection")
(import "java.util.Map")
(import "java.util.Vector")
(import "java.util.Hashtable")

(define-method iterate ((items java.util.Iterator)
                        action)
  (if (hasNext items)
      (begin (action (next items))
             (iterate items action)))))

(define-method iterate ((items java.util.Collection)
                        action)
  (iterate (iterator items) action))

(define-method iterate ((items java.util.Map) action)
  (iterate (entrySet items) action))
```

```
(define-method iterate ((items silk.Pair) action)
  (action (car items))
  (let ((items (cdr items)))
    (if (pair? items) (iterate items action)))))

(define-method iterate ((items java.lang.Object[])
                action)
  (let loop ((i 0)
             (L (vector-length items)))
    (if (< i L) (begin (action (vector-ref items i))
             (loop (+ i 1) L)))))
```

The collection argument can be an array, a Scheme list (of type silk.Pair), or any of the Java 1.2 collection types. This type of integration is not easy in Java because new instance methods cannot be added to existing classes. Here's an example use:

```
>(define h (Hashtable 50))
h
>(put h 'fred 3)
()
>(put h 'mary 4)
()
>(iterate h print)
fred=3
mary=4
()
>
```

Scheme methods are treated like Java static methods. Currently, there is no provision for (call-next-method). One must invoke such a method directly using (method).

Java classes can be defined directly in Scheme using a (define-class) macro, using the compiling technique described below. Such classes only have constructor and field accessor methods. Scheme methods can be added to the class using (define-method).

4 Creating New Code From Old

It should be clear that SILK fulfills one of Scheme's important roles as an embedded scripting and prototyping language [5]. Perhaps a greater strength is that Scheme can be used as a compile time scripting language to generate new code, perhaps in another language, such as C or Java. Two examples of this are described in references [6] and [7] where Scheme is used to set up a complex numerical problem such as a complex computer visualization. Partial evaluation is then used to generate an efficient algorithm to compute the solution of the problem, in C.

Java development environments, such as Sun's Java Bean box, compile small glue classes automatically. This generated code usually follows a standard template and requires some introspection of an existing class. We can do the same thing in SILK. Essentially, Scheme becomes a macro language for Java.

For example, the normal Java runtime environment does not provide a way to trace individual methods. Here we sketch how to add such tracing capability. The basic idea is to generate a subclass of an existing class which allows its methods to be traced. If SILK has enough access to the Java application, an instance of this traceable class can be substituted into the application without changing any Java code. As part of this process, we would have a method, m2, say the method `Hashtable.put()`, and generate a traced method from it using `(gen-trace-method m2)`:

```
>m2
public synchronized Object Hashtable.put(Object,
                                          Object)
>(emit (gen-trace-method m2))
public synchronized java.lang.Object
    put(java.lang.Object a1, java.lang.Object a0) {
  if(trace) Trace.enter(this + ".put(" + a1 + ", " +
                        a0 + "}");
  java.lang.Object result = super.put(a1, a0);
  if(trace) Trace.exit(result);
  return result;
  }
#t
```

Here's some Scheme code that does this:

```
(define-method method-return-type
  (m java.lang.reflect.Method)
  (getName (getReturnType m)))

(define-method gen-trace-method
  (m java.lang.reflect.Method)
  `(,(gen-method-signature m)
    { ,(gen-trace-method-body m) }))

(define-method gen-method-signature
  (m java.lang.reflect.Method)
  `(,(Modifier.toString (getModifiers m))
    ,(method-return-type m)
    ,(getName m) "("
    ,(map-args
      (lambda (arg) `(,(arg-type arg) ,(arg-name arg)))
```

```
       ","
       (arg-types m))
    ")"))

(define-method gen-trace-method-body
  (m java.lang.reflect.Method)
  `(if "(" trace ")"
       Trace.enter "(" this +
       ,(quotify "." (getName m) "(")
       ,(map-args (lambda (arg) `(+ ,(arg-name arg)))
                  "+ \", \""
                  (arg-types m))
       + ,(quotify "}") ")" ";"
       ,(method-return-type m) result = super.
       ,(getName m) "("
       ,(map-args arg-name "," (arg-types m))
       ")" ";"
       if "(" trace ")" "Trace.exit(result)" ";"
       return result ";"))
```

This code generation system is extremely basic. (emit) takes a list structure, produced by (gen-trace-method) here, and formats it into readable Java code. Scheme's backquote macro characters, ` (, ,@) are used to construct the necessary list structures. (map-args) is like (map) but adds a separator between each argument, to generate a comma separated argument list, for example.

SILK can automatically compile Java files using:

```
(import "java.lang.String")
(import "java.lang.reflect.Array")
(import "sun.tools.javac.Main")
(import "java.lang.System")
(define (compile-file file)
  ;; Compile the *.java file, file,
  ;; using the current CLASSPATH.
  (let ((as (Array.newInstance String.class 3))
        (main (Main (get-field System.class 'out)
                    'silkc)))
    (vector-set! as 0 "-classpath")
    (vector-set! as 1 (System.getProperty
                        "java.class.path"))
    (vector-set! as 2 file)
    (compile main as)))
```

In this simple example, Java's Method metaclass was used directly to generate the traced code. A more realistic example would provide a compile time metaobject protocol that would be used to do code generation more formally. While this example is simple, it should be clear that SILK can be used as a useful compile time software development environment without a substantial amount of work.

5 Related Work

5.1 Other Scheme Implementations

There are three other Scheme implementations in Java we are aware of, which we briefly describe: The following exhibit shows statistics from these implementations.

Scheme implementation statistics

Implementation	java files	lines	Scheme files	lines	Generics
Silk 1.0	12	1905	0	0	No
Silk 2.0	20	2778	0	0	No
Generic Silk 2.0	28	3508	5	510	Yes
Skij [8]	27	2523	44	2844	Yes
Jaja [9]	66	5760	?	?	No
Kawa [10]	273	16629	14	708	No

Skij: Skij is a Scheme advertised as a scripting extension for Java. It is similar in capabilities to SILK and has extensive Java support including (peek) and (poke) for reading and writing slots, (invoke) and (invoke-static) for invoking methods, and *(new)* for constructing new instances of a Java class.

(new) (invoke) and (invoke-static) invoke the appropriate Java method using runtime looked up based on all of its arguments. This approach is similar to SILK's. However, SILK's generic functions also allow Scheme methods to be added.

Jaja: Jaja is a Scheme based on the Christian Queinnec's wonderful book "Lisp in Small Pieces"[11]. It includes a Scheme to Java compiler written in Scheme, because it requires only 1/3 the code of a Java version. Compared to Silk, Jaja is written in a more object oriented style. Like Silk, Jaja uses a super class (`Jaja` in `Jaja`, and `SchemeUtils` in `Silk`) to provide globals and utilitiy functions. Unlike Silk, in Jaja, each Scheme type has one or more Java classes defined for it. Also, in Jaja, the empty list `'()` is represented as an instance of the class `EmptyList`, while in Silk it is represented by null. All Jaja objects are serializable.

Kawa: Kawa is an ambitious Scheme implementation. It includes a Scheme to Java byte code compiler. Each function becomes a Java class compiled and loaded at runtime.

5.2 Generic Function Dispatch

In any language that uses generic functions, efficient method lookup is extremely important. Method lookup is basically a two-dimensional table lookup in a very sparse table. There has been extensive research recently on table compression methods [12] [13] [14][15].

While these techniques are quite interesting, they seemed too complex to implement for our tiny Scheme environment. Instead, we follow the approach taken in Common Lisp, and associate each generic function with a list of its methods. The trick then becomes, given a generic function and a set of arguments, choose the appropriate method.

In Common Lisp, [4] a generic function does method lookup using one of several strategies. The strategy used is based on the number of different methods the generic function has actually invoked. Backing up these strategies is a per generic function caching scheme. The advantage of such a dynamic approach is that it tailors itself to the running application.

In SILK, a generic function uses a static strategy based on the number and types of methods that have been added to the generic function, as described above. This approach seems to work well, but we have not had a chance to analyze this in any detail. However, other evidence suggests that a static approach such as ours is not unreasonable.

For example, STK[14] is a Scheme dialect that uses an object system based on Tiny CLOS [3]. Method lookup is done by searching for the appropriate method each time, without any caching. Our belief is that this approach works reasonably because most methods only have a few methods.

We have verified this with one typical Common Lisp application (Allegro CL 5.0 + CLIM). There were 1,568 generic functions and 952 classes. The following is a cumulative histogram of the number of methods per generic function.

```
#methods  Cumulative %
   1          59.3
   2          79.6
   3          89.1
   4          91.7
   5          94.4
  10          97.6
  20          99.1
 100         100.0
```

From this we see that 59% of the generic functions have one method. These are likely to be assessor methods. 89% of the methods have three or fewer methods. However, one generic function, (print-object) has 100 methods.

Thus we expect our static approach to be reasonable. However, adding a Scheme method to a generic function can often force a full lookup to be done. Thus as more Scheme methods are used over Java methods, exploring other approaches will become important. Queinnec [9] describes a method lookup approach that uses discrimination net. This approach looks promising for SILK.

6 Conclusion

There are many Scheme implementations, This is partly because it relatively easy to implement a reasonably efficient implementation, and techniques to build a high performance implementation are well understood. It is also partly because, while Scheme is a useful language in its own right, it has found and important role as a scripting language embedded in an application. Guile and STK are two examples of embeddable Schemes implemented in C [16].

Beckman argues that scripting languages are inevitable [5]. In the 80's Jon Bently popularized the idea of Little Languages [17]. Such a language can be used to describe in a compact way, one aspect of your project, graphical layout for example. Beckman argues that this decoupling of aspects is essential, because the only other option is to keep changing all the source code. He also argues that little languages often grow to become more complete languages, adding control structure, classes, etc. TCL and Visual Basic are unfortunate examples of this trend. Beckman further argues that Scheme is an excellent choice for a little language, because it is also a complete language in which other extension languages can be easily embedded.

We have tried to show that SILK makes effective use of Java's reflective capabilities:

1. The implementation of its data types were carefully chosen to match those of Java closely. This minimizes the impedance mismatch between Scheme and Java. Currently the main remaining mismatch is that strings in Scheme are represented as char[] because strings are mutable in Scheme. Making Scheme strings immutable, as they are in Java would allow us to use the String class. This change would only require dropping the procedure (string-set!) from SILK.

2. Using (import) SILK has almost transparent access to Java. A Scheme implemented in another languages requires substantial foreign function interface to be written. While it is possible to automatically generate this interface from C headers files, for example, it is a fair amount of work.

3. Once SILK is available, it can be used for scripting in the base language, providing the benefits that Beckman suggests. For example, a SILK extension is used to layout Java Swing components. A graphical designer lays out the components and a Java programmer wires in the underlying behavior.

4. Because SILK has direct access to the reflection of any Java class, SILK can be used as a metalevel scripting language to generate new Java classes at compile or runtime. While other Java systems have similar capabilities, we've tried to show that the amount of work required in SILK is small.

5. Reflection could be used more aggressively in the implementation of the underlying Scheme interpreter itself. For example, the Scheme primitives could be implemented as Java classes and imported into a kernel language. The Scheme interpreter and Scheme-to-Java compiler, which are written in Java, could also be accessed via reflection, and even modified at runtime using a custom classloader.

Acknowledgments

The authors wish to thank Peter Norvig for developing the first version of SILK and for keeping it simple enough that we could easily use and extend it. We thank Geoffrey S. Knauth, Richard Shapiro, Tom Mitchell, Bruce Roberts, and Jeff Tustin for reviewing drafts of this paper. We thank Rusty Bobrow who thought SILK was simple enough that he suggested it to his daughter for programming a High School science project. And we'd like to thank Rusty's brother, Danny Bobrow for long ago teaching us that "Meta is Beta!" That two generations of one family use reflection, reflects well on reflection.

References

1. http://www-swiss.ai.mit.edu/~jaffer/SLIB.html
2. Aubrey Jaffer, r4rstest.scm, ftp://ftp-swiss.ai.mit.edu/pub/scm/r4rstest.scm.
3. Gregor Kiczales, Tiny CLOS, file://parcftp.xerox.com/pub/mops/tiny/
4. Gregor Kiczales and Luis Rodriguez, Efficient method dispatch in PCL, proceedings 1990 ACM Conference on LISP and Functional Programming, Nice, France, June 1990, 99-105.
5. Brian Beckman, A scheme for little languages in interactive graphics, Software Practice and Experience, 21, 2, p. 187-208, Feb, 1991.
6. A. Berlin and D. Weise, Compiling scientific code using partial evaluation. Technical Report CSL-TR 90-422, Artificial Intelligence Laboratory, Massachusetts Institute of Technology, 1990.

7. Clifford Beshers Steven Feiner, Generating efficient virtual worlds for visualization using partial evaluation and dynamic compilation, ACM SIGPLAN Symposium on Partial Evaluation and Semantics-Based Program Manipulation (PEPM'97), p. 107-115.

8. Mike Travers, Skij, IBM alphaWorks archive, http://www.alphaworks.ibm.com/formula/Skij

9. Christian Queinnec, JaJa: Scheme in Java, http://www-spi.lip6.fr/~queinnec/WWW/Jaja.html

10. Per Bothner, Kawa the Java-based Scheme System, http://www.cygnus.com/~bothner/kawa.html

11. http://www-spi.lip6.fr/~queinnec/Papers/dispatch.ps.gz

12. Shih-Kun Huang and Deng-Jyi Chen, Efficient algorithms for method dispatch in object-oriented programming systems, Journal of Object-Oriented Programming, 5(5):43-54, September 1992.

13. E.Amiel, O. Gruber, and E. Simon, Optimmizing multi-method dispatch using compressed dispatch tables. In OOPSLA '94, October 1994.

14. Jan Vitek and R. Nigel Horspool, Taming message passing: Efficien method lookup for dynamically typed languages. ECOOP '94 - 8th European Conference on Object-Oriented Programming, Bologna (Italy), 1994.

15. Weimin Chen and Volker Turau, Multiple-dispatching base on automata, Theory and Practice of Object Systems, 1(1):41-60, 1995.

16. http://kaolin.unice.fr/STk/

17. J.L. Bentley, More Programming Pearls, Addison-Wesley, Reading, MA, 1988.

jContractor: A Reflective Java Library to Support Design by Contract

Murat Karaorman[1,2], Urs Hölzle[2], John Bruno[2]

[1]Texas Instruments Inc.,
315 Bollay Drive, Santa Barbara, California 93117
muratk@ti.com

[2]Department of Computer Science,
University of California, Santa Barbara, CA 93106
{murat,urs,bruno}@cs.ucsb.edu

Abstract. *jContractor* is a purely library based approach to support Design By Contract specifications such as preconditions, postconditions, class invariants, and recovery and exception handling in Java. *jContractor* uses an intuitive naming convention, and standard Java syntax to instrument Java classes and enforce Design By Contract constructs. The designer of a class specifies a contract by providing contract methods following *jContractor* naming conventions. *jContractor* uses Java Reflection to synthesize an instrumented version of a Java class by incorporating code that enforces the present *jContractor* contract specifications. Programmers enable the run-time enforcement of contracts by either engaging the *jContractor* class loader or by explicitly instantiating objects using the *jContractor* object factory. Programmers can use exactly the same syntax for invoking methods and passing object references regardless of whether contracts are present or not. Since *jContractor* is purely library-based, it requires no special tools such as modified compilers, modified JVMs, or pre-processors.

1 Introduction

One of the shortcomings of mainstream object-oriented languages such as C++ and Java is that class or interface definitions provide only a signature-based application interface, much like the APIs specified for libraries in procedural languages. Method signatures provide limited information about the method: the types of formal parameters, the type of returned value, and the types of exceptions that may be thrown. While type information is useful, signatures by themselves do not capture the essential semantic information about what the method does and promises to deliver, or what conditions must be met in order to use the method successfully. To acquire this information, the programmer must either analyze the source code (if available) or rely on some externally communicated specification or documentation, none of which is automatically checked at compile or runtime.

A programmer needs semantic information to correctly design or use a class. Meyer introduced *Design By Contract* as a way to specify the essential semantic information and constraints that govern the design and correct use of a class [6]. This information includes assertions about the state of the object that hold before and after each method call; these assertions are called *class invariants*, and apply to the public interface of the class. The information also includes the set of constraints that must be satisfied by a client in order to invoke a particular method. These constraints are specific to each method, and are called *preconditions* of the method. Each precondition specifies conditions on the state of the object and the argument values that must hold prior to invoking the method. Finally, the programmer needs assertions regarding the state of the object after the execution of a method and the relationship of this state to the state of the object just prior to the method invocation. These assertions are called the *postconditions* of a method. The assertions governing the implementation and the use of a class are collectively called a *contract*. Contracts are specification constructs which are not necessarily part of the implementation code of a class, however, a runtime monitor could check whether contracts are being honored.

In this paper we introduce *jContractor*, a purely library-based system and a set of naming conventions to support *Design By Contract* in Java. The *jContractor* system does not require any special tools such as modified compilers, runtime systems, modified JVMs, or pre-processors, and works with any pure Java implementation. Therefore, a programmer can practice *Design By Contract* by using the *jContractor* library and by following a simple and intuitive set of conventions.

Each class and interface in a Java program corresponds to a translation unit with a machine and platform independent representation as specified by the Java Virtual Machine (JVM) `class` file format [10]. Each class file contains JVM instructions (bytecodes) and a rich set of meta-level information. *jContractor* utilizes the meta-level information encoded in the standard Java class files to instrument the bytecodes on-the-fly during class loading. During the instrumentation process *jContractor* parses each Java class file and discovers the *jContractor* contract information by analyzing the class meta-data.

The *jContractor* design addresses three key issues which arise when adding contracts to Java: how to express preconditions, postconditions and class invariants and incorporate them into a standard Java class definition; how to reference entry values of attributes, to check method results inside postconditions using standard Java syntax; and how to check and enforce contracts at runtime.

An overview of *jContractor*'s approach to solving these problems is given below:

1. Programmers add contract code to a class in the form of methods following *jContractor*'s naming conventions: *contract patterns.* The *jContractor* class loader recognizes these patterns and rewrites the code to reflect the presence of contracts.

2. Contract patterns can be inserted either directly into the class or they can be written separately as a *contract class* where the contract class' name is derived from the target class using *jContractor* naming conventions. The separate contract class approach can also be used to specify contracts for interfaces.

3. The *jContractor* library instruments the classes that contain *contract patterns* on the fly during class loading or object instantiation. Programmers enable the run-time enforcement of contracts either by engaging the *jContractor* class loader or by explicitly instantiating objects from the *jContractor* object factory. Programmers can use exactly the same syntax for invoking methods and passing object references regardless of whether contracts are present or not.

4. *jContractor* uses an intuitive naming convention for adding *preconditions, postconditions, class invariants, recovery* and *exception handling* in the form of `protected` methods. Contract code is hence distinguished from the functional code. The name and signature of each contract method determines the actual method with which the contract is associated.

5. Postconditions and exception handlers can access the *old* value of any attribute by using a special object reference, `OLD`. For example `OLD.count` returns the value of the attribute `count` just prior to the execution of the method. *jContractor* emulates this behavior by transparently rewriting class methods during class loading so that the entry values of `OLD` references are saved and then made available to the postcondition and exception handling code.

6. *jContractor* provides a class called `RESULT` with a `static boolean` method, `Compare`. Inside a method's postcondition it is possible to check the *result* associated with the method's execution by calling `RESULT.Compare(<expression>)`. The call returns true or false by comparing the value of the `<expression>` with the current result.

This paper presents an extension to Java to support Design By Contract by introducing *jContractor* as a pure library-based approach which utilizes the meta-level information found in Java class files and takes advantage of dynamic class loading in order to perform "reflective", on-the-fly bytecode modification.

2 *jContractor* Library and Contract Patterns

jContractor is a purely library-based approach to support Design By Contract constructs using standard Java. Table 1 contains a summary of key Design By Contract constructs and the corresponding *jContractor* patterns. One of the key contributions of *jContractor* is that it supports all Design By Contract principles using a *pure-Java, library-based* approach. Therefore, any Java developer can immediately start using Design By Contract without making any changes to the test, development, and deployment environment after obtaining a copy of *jContractor* classes.

Table 1. Summary of *jContractor* Design By Contract Constructs

Construct	jContractor Pattern	Description

Precondition
 	
(Client's obligation)
	`protected boolean`
	`methodName_PreCondition(`
	`<arg-list>)`
		Evaluated just before `methodName` with matching signature is executed. If the precondition fails the method throws a `PreConditionException` without executing the method.

Postcondition
(Implementor's promise)
	`protected boolean`
	`methodName_PostCondition(`
	`<arg-list>)`
		Evaluated just before `methodName` returns (i.e. *normal termination*). If the postcondition fails, a `PostConditionException` gets thrown.

Exception Handler
 	
(Implementor's attempt)
	`protected Object`
	`methodName_OnException(`
	`Exception e)`
	`throws Exception`
		Called when `methodName's` execution ends in *abnormal termination*, throwing an Exception. The exception handler provides an opportunity to do recovery by restoring invariants, resetting state, etc.,

Class invariant
 	
(Implementor's promise)
	`protected boolean`
	`className_ClassInvariant(`
	`)`
		Evaluated once before each invocation of a public method, *m*, <u>and</u> once before *m* is about to return -- *normal termination*. If class invariant fails, a `ClassInvariantException` is thrown instead of returning the result.

old	`OLD.attr` `OLD.foo( )`	Expression evaluates to *value* of `attr` on method entry. `OLD` methods can only be used inside postcondition and exception handler methods; `attr` can be any non-private class attribute.
Result	`RESULT.compare(expr)`	Evaluates true/false depending on if current result matches the expr. RESULT class is part of *jContractor* distribution.

```
class Dictionary ... {
    protected Dictionary OLD;

    Object put(Object x, String key)
    {
        putBody();
    }
    protected boolean put_PreCondition(Object x,
                                       String key)
    {
        return ( (count <= capacity)
            &&   !(key.length()==0)   );
    }
    protected boolean put_PostCondition(Object x,
                                        String key)
    {
        return (    (has (x))
                &&  (item (key) == x)
                &&  (count == OLD.count + 1) )
    }
    protected Object put_OnException(Exception e)
                throws Exception
    {
        count =  OLD.count;
        throw e;           //rethrow exception.
    }
    protected boolean Dictionary_ClassInvariant()
    {
        return (count >= 0);
    }
...}
```

Figure 1-a. Dictionary Class Implementing Contract for *put* Method

A programmer writes a contract by taking a class or method name, say *put*, then appending a suffix depending on the type of constraint, say *_PreCondition*, to write the *put_PreCondition*. Then the programmer writes the method body describing the precondition. The method can access both the arguments of the *put* method with the identical signature, and the attributes of the class. When jContractor instrumentation is engaged at runtime, the precondition gets checked each time the *put* method is called, and the call throws an exception if the precondition fails.

The code fragment in Figure 1-a shows a *jContractor* based implementation of the put method for the *Dictionary* class. An alternative approach is to provide a separate *contract class*, *Dictionary_CONTRACT*, as shown in Figure 1-b, which

```
class Dictionary_CONTRACT extends Dictionary ...
{
    protected boolean put_PostCondition(Object    x,
                                        String key)
    {
        return (    (has (x))
                && (item (key) == x)
                && (count == OLD. count + 1) )
    }

    protected boolean Dictionary_ClassInvariant() {
            return (count >= 0);
    }
}
```

Figure 1-b. Separate Contract Class for Dictionary

contains the contract code using the same naming conventions. The contract class can (optionally) extend the target class for which the contracts are being written, which is the case in our example. For every class or interface X that the *jContractor ClassLoader* loads, it also looks for a separate contract class, X_CONTRACT, and uses contract specifications from both X and X_CONTRACT (if present) when performing its instrumentation. The details of the class loading and instrumentation will be presented in subsequent sections.

Table 2 shows the informal contract specifications for inserting an element into the *dictionary*, a table of bounded capacity where each element is identified by a certain character string used as key.

Table 2. Contract Specification for Inserting Element to Dictionary

	Obligations	*Benefits*
Client	(Must ensure precondition) Make sure table is *not full* & key is a *non-empty* string	(May benefit from postcondition) Get updated table where the given element now appears, associated with the given key.
Supplier	(Must ensure postcondition) Record given element in table, associated with given key.	(May assume precondition) No need to do anything if table given is *full*, or key is *empty* string.

2.1 Enabling Contracts During Method Invocation

In order to enforce contract specifications at run-time, the contractor object must be instantiated from an instrumented class. This can be accomplished in two possible ways: (1) by using the *jContractor class loader* which instruments all classes containing contracts during class loading; (2) by using a factory style instantiation using the *jContractor* library.

The simplest and the preferred method is to use the *jContractor class loader*, since this requires no changes to a client's code. The following code segment shows how a client declares, instantiates, and then uses a Dictionary object, *dict*. The client's code remains unchanged whether *jContractor* runtime instrumentation is used or not:

```
Dictionary  dict;          // Dictionary (Figure-1) defines contracts.

dict = new Dictionary();  // instantiates dict from instrumented or
                           // non- instrumented class depending on
                           // jContractor classloader being engaged.
dict.put(obj1,"name1");   // If jContractor is enabled, put-contracts
                           // are enforced, i.e. contract violations
                           // result in an exception being thrown.
```

The second approach uses the *jContractor* object factory, by invoking its *New* method. The factory instantiation can be used when the client's application must use a custom (or third party) class loader and cannot use *jContractor class loader*. This approach also gives more explicit control to the client over *when* and *which* objects to instrument. Following code segment shows the client's code using the *jContractor* factory to instantiate an instrumented Dictionary object, *dict*:

```
dict = (Dictionary) jContractor.New("Dictionary");
                     // instruments Dictionary

dict.put(obj1,"name1"); // put-contracts are enforced
```

Syntactically, any class containing *jContractor* design-pattern constructs is still a pure Java class. From a client's perspective, both instrumented and non-instrumented instantiations are still Dictionary objects and they can be used interchangeably, since they both provide the same interface and functionality. The only semantic difference in their behavior is that the execution of instrumented methods results in evaluating the contract assertions, (e.g., *put_PreCondition*) and throwing a Java runtime exception if the assertion fails.

Java allows method overloading. *jContractor* supports this feature by associating each method variant with the pre- and postcondition functions with the matching argument signatures.

For any method, say `foo`, of class X, if there is no `boolean` method by the name, `foo_PreCondition` with the same argument signature, in either X, $X\_CONTRACT$ or one of their descendants then the default precondition for the `foo` method is "true". The same "default" rule applies to the postconditions and class invariants.

2.2 Naming Conventions for Preconditions, Postconditions and Class Invariants

The following naming conventions constitute the *jContractor* patterns for pre- and postconditions and class invariants:

Precondition: protected boolean methodName + _PreCondition + (<arg-list>)
Postcondition: protected boolean methodName + _PostCondition + (< arg-list >)
ClassInvariant: protected boolean className   + _ClassInvariant ( )

Each construct's method body evaluates a `boolean` result and may contain references to the object's internal state with the same scope and access rules as the original method. Pre- and postcondition methods can also use the original method's formal arguments in expressions. Additionally, postcondition expressions can refer to the old values of object's attributes by declaring a pseudo object, `OLD`, with the same class type and using the `OLD` object to access the values.

2.3 Exception Handling

The postcondition for a method describes the contractual obligations of the contractor object only when the method terminates successfully. When a method terminates abnormally due to some exception, it is not required for the contractor to ensure that the postcondition holds. It is very desirable, however, for the contracting (supplier) objects to be able to specify what conditions must still hold true in these situations, and to get a chance to restore the state to reflect this.

jContractor supports the specification of general or specialized exception handling code for methods. The instrumented method contains wrapper code to catch exceptions thrown inside the original method body. If the contracts include an exception-handler method for the type of exception caught by the wrapper, the exception handler code gets executed.

If exception handlers are defined for a particular method, each exception handler must either re-throw the handled exception or compute and return a valid result. If the exception is re-thrown no further evaluation of the postconditions or class-invariants is carried out. If the handler is able to recover by generating a new result, the postcondition and class-invariant checks are performed before the result is returned, as if the method had terminated successfully.

The exception handler method's name is obtained by appending the suffix, *"_OnException"*, to the method's name. The method takes a single argument whose type belongs to either one of the exceptions that may be thrown by the original method, or to a more general exception class. The body of the exception handler can include arbitrary Java statements and refer to the object's internal state using the same scope and access rules as the original method itself. The *jContractor* approach is more flexible than the Eiffel's *"rescue"* mechanism because separate handlers can be written for different types of exceptions and more information can be made available to the handler code using the exception object which is passed to the handler method.

2.4 Supporting Old Values and Recovery

jContractor uses a clean and safe instrumentation "trick" to mimic the Eiffel keyword, *old*, and support Design By Contract style postcondition expressions in which one can refer to the *"old"* state of the object just prior to the method's invocation. The trick involves using the "syntax notation/convention", `OLD.x` to mean the value that x had when method body was entered. Same notation is also used for method references as well, e.g., `OLD.foo()` is used to refer to the result of calling the member `foo()` when entering the method. We will later explain how the *jContractor* instrumentation process rewrites expressions involving `OLD` to achieve the desired effect. First we illustrate its usage from the example in Figure 1. The class Dictionary first declares *OLD*.

```
private Dictionary OLD;
```

Then, in the postcondition of the put method taking `<Object x, String key>` arguments, the following subexpression is used

```
(count == OLD.count + 1)
```

to specify that the execution of the corresponding put method increases the value of the object's `count` by 1. Here `OLD.count` refers to the value of `count` at the point just before the `put`-method began to execute.

jContractor implements this behavior using the following instrumentation logic. When loading the Dictionary class, *jContractor* scans the postconditions and exception handlers for `OLD` usage. So, when it sees the `OLD.count` in `put_PostCondition` it inserts code to the beginning of the put method to allocate a unique temporary and to save count to this temporary. Then it rewrites the expression in the postcondition replacing the `OLD.value` subexpression with an access to the temporary. In summary, the value of the expression `OLD.expr` (where `expr` is an arbitrary sequence of field dereferences or method calls) is simply the value of `expr` on entry to the method.

It is also possible for an exception handler or postcondition method to revert the state of `attr` to its old value by using the `OLD` construct. This may be used as a basic recovery mechanism to restore the state of the object when an invariant or postcondition is found to be violated within an exception-handler. For example,

```
attr = OLD.attr;
```

or

```
attr = OLD.attr.Clone();
```

The first example restores the object reference for `attr` to be restored, and the second example restores the object state for `attr` (by cloning the object when entering the method, and then attaching the object reference to the cloned copy.)

2.5 Separate Contract Classes

jContractor allows contract specifications for a particular class to be externally provided as a separate class, adhering to certain naming conventions. For example, consider a class, *X*, which may or may not contain *jContractor* contract specifications. *jContractor* will associate the class name, *X_CONTRACT*, with the class *X*, as a potential place to find contract specifications for *X*. *X_CONTRACT* must extend class *X* and use the same naming conventions and notations developed earlier in this paper to specify pre- and postconditions, exception handlers or class invariants for the methods in class *X*.

If the implementation class *X* also specifies a precondition for the same method, that precondition is *logical-AND*'ed with the one in *X_CONTRACT* during instrumentation. Similarly, postconditions, and class invariants are also combined using *logical-AND*. Exception handlers in the contract class override the ones inherited from *X*.

The ability to write separate contract classes is useful when specifying contracts for legacy or third party classes, and when modifying existing source code is not possible or viable. It can be used as a technique for debugging and testing system or third-party libraries.

2.6 Contract Specifications for Interfaces

Separate contract classes also allow contracts to be added to interfaces. For example, consider the `interface IX` and the class *C* which implements this interface. The class *IX_CONTRACT* contains the pre- and postconditions for the methods in *IX*. Methods defined in the contract class are used to instrument the class "implementing" the interface.

```
interface IX {

        int foo(<args>);
}

class IX_CONTRACT  {

    protected boolean foo_PreCondition(<args>) { … }
    protected boolean foo_PostCondition(<args>){ … }
}
```

Contracts for interface classes can only include pre- and postconditions, and can only express constraints using expressions involving the method's arguments or interface method calls, without any references to a particular object state. If the implementation class also specifies a precondition for the same method, the conditions are *logical-AND*'ed during instrumentation. Similarly, postconditions are also combined using *logical-AND*.

3 Design and Implementation of *jContractor*

The *jContractor* package uses *Java Reflection* to detect Design By Contract patterns during object instantiation or class loading. Classes containing contract patterns are instrumented on the fly using the *jContractor* library. We begin by explaining how instrumentation of a class is done using the two different mechanisms explained in section 2.1. The rest of this section explains the details of the instrumentation algorithm.

The primary instrumentation technique uses the *jContractor class loader* to transparently instrument classes during class loading. The scenario depicted in Figure 2 illustrates how the *jContractor Class Loader* obtains instrumented class bytecodes from the *jContractor instrumentor* while loading class Foo. The *jContractor class loader* is engaged when launching the Java application. The instrumentor is passed the name of the class by the class loader and in return it searches the compiled class, Foo, for *jContractor* contract patterns. If the class contains contract methods, the instrumentor makes a copy of the class bytecodes, modifying the public methods with wrapper code to check contract violations, and returns the modified bytecodes to the class loader. Otherwise, it returns the original class without any modification. The object instantiated from the instrumented class is shown as the Foo<Instrumented> object in the diagram, to highlight the fact that it is instrumented, but syntactically it is a Foo object.

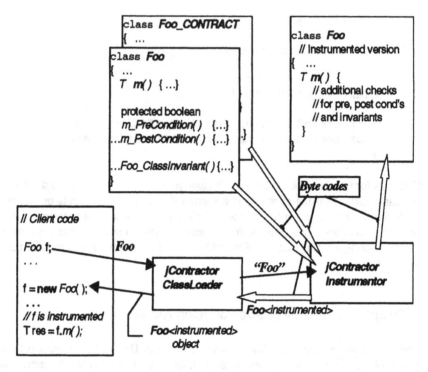

Figure 2. *jContractor* Class Loader based Instrumentation

If the command line argument for *jContractor* is not present when starting up the application, the user's own (or the default) class loader is used, which effectively turns off the *jContractor* instrumentation. Since contract methods are separate from the public methods, the program's behavior remains exactly the same except for the runtime checking of contract violations. This is the preferred technique since the client's code is essentially unchanged and all that the supplier has to do is to add the *jContractor* contract methods to the class.

The alternative technique is a factory style object instantiation using the *jContractor* library's New method. New takes a class name as argument and returns an instrumented object conforming to the type of requested class. Using this approach the client explicitly instructs *jContractor* to instrument a class and return an instrumented instance. The factory approach does not require engaging the *jContractor* class loader and is safe to use with any pure-Java class loader. The example in Figure 3 illustrates the factory style instrumentation and instantiation using the class Foo. The client invokes *jContractor*.New() with the name of the class, "Foo". The New method uses the *jContractor* Instrumentor to create a subclass of Foo, with the name, Foo_Contractor which now contains the instrumented version of Foo. New instantiates and returns a Foo_Contractor object to the client. When the client

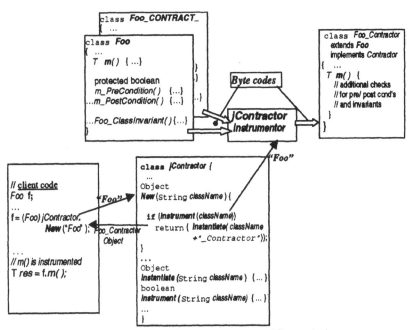

Figure 3 *jContractor* **Factory Style Instrumentation and Instantiation**

invokes methods of the returned object as a `Foo` object, it calls the instrumented methods in `Foo_Contractor` due to the polymorphic assignment and dynamic binding.

The remainder of this section contains details of the instrumentation algorithm for individual *jContractor* constructs.

3.1 Method Instrumentation

jContractor instruments contractor objects using a simple code rewriting technique. Figure 4 illustrates the high level view of how code segments get copied from original class methods into the target instrumented version. *jContractor's* key instrumentation policy is to inline the contract code for each method within the target method's body, to avoid any extra function call. Two basic transformations are applied to the original method's body. First, `return` statements are replaced by an assignment statement – storing the result in a method-scoped temporary – followed by a labeled `break`, to exit out of the method body. Second, references to "old" values, using the `OLD` object reference are replaced by a single variable – this is explained in more detail in a subsection. After these transformations, the entire method block is placed inside a wrapper code as shown in the instrumented code in Figure 4.

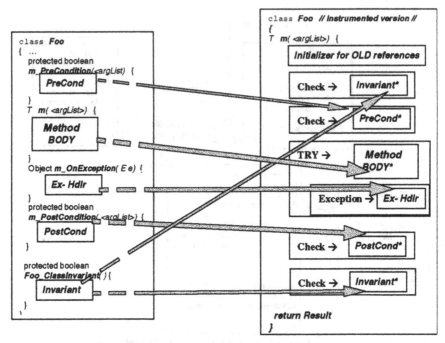

Figure 4. *jContractor* Instrumentation Overview

A *check wrapper* checks the boolean result computed by the wrapped block and throws an exception if the result is *false*. A *TRY wrapper* executes the wrapped code inside a try-catch block, and associates each exception handler that the contract specifies with a catch phrase inside an exception wrapper. *Exception wrappers* are simple code blocks that are inserted inside the catch clause of a try-catch block with the matching *Exception* type. Typically, exception handlers re-throw the exception, which causes the instrumented method to terminate with the thrown exception. It is possible, however, for the exception handler to recover from the exception condition and generate a result. Figure 5 shows a concrete example of the instrumented code that is generated.

3.2 Instrumentation of OLD References

jContractor takes the following actions for each unique *OLD-expression* inside a method's postcondition or exception handler code. Say the method's name is *m ( )* and the expression is *OLD.attr*, and *attr* has type T, then *jContractor* incorporates the following code while rewriting *m ( )* :

```
T  $OLD_$attr = this.attr;
```

```
class Dictionary_Contractor   extends Dictionary ...{
 ...
   Object put(Object x, String key)
   {
       Object    $put_$Result;
       boolean   $put_PreCondition,
                 $put_PostCondition,
                 $ClassInvariant;

       int       $OLD_$count = this.count;

       $put_PreCondition = (   (count <= capacity)
                           && (! key.length()==0) );

       if (!$put_PreCondition) {
           throw new PreConditionException();
       }
       $ClassInvariant = (count >= 0);
       if (!$ClassInvariant) {
           throw new ClassInvariantException();
       }
       try {
           $put_$Result = putBody();
       }
       catch (Exception e) {        // put_OnException
           count = $OLD_$count; //restore(count)
           throw e;
       }
       $put_PostCondition =((has(x)) &&
                           (item (key) == x) &&
                           (count == $OLD_$count + 1));
       if (!$put_PostCondition) {
           throw new PostConditionException();
       }
       $ClassInvariant = (count >= 0);
       if (!$ClassInvariant) {
           throw new ClassInvariantException();
       }
       return $put_$Result;
   }
 }
```

Figure 5. Factory Instrumented Dictionary Subclass.

The effect of this code is to allocate a temporary, $OLD_$attr, and record the value of the expression, attr, when the method code is entered. The code rewriting logic then replaces all occurrences of OLD.attr inside the contract code with the temporary variable $OLD_$attr whose value has been initialized once at the beginning of the method's execution.

3.3 Instrumentation of RESULT References

jContractor allows the following syntax expression inside a method's postcondition method to refer to the result of the current computation that led to its evaluation:

> RESULT.Compare(expression)

RESULT is provided as part of the jContractor library package, to facilitate this syntax expression. It exports a single static boolean method, Compare(), taking a single argument with one variant for each built-in Java primitive type and one variant for the Object type. These methods never get invoked in reality, and the sole purpose of having them (like the OLD declarations discussed earlier) is to allow the Java compiler to legally accept the syntax, and then rely on the instrumentation logic to supply the right execution semantics.

During instrumentation, for each method declaration, T m(), a temporary variable $m_$Result is internally declared with the same type, T, and used to store the result of the current computation. Then the postcondition expression shown above is rewritten as:

> ($m_$Result == (T)(expression))

3.4 Use of Reflection

Each class and interface in a Java program corresponds to a translation unit with a machine and platform independent representation as specified by the Java Virtual Machine class file format. Each class file contains JVM instructions (bytecodes) and a rich set of meta-level information. During the instrumentation process jContractor parses and analyzes the meta-information encoded in the class byte-codes in order to discover the jContractor contract patterns. When the class contains or inherits contracts, jContractor instrumentor modifies the class bytecodes on the fly and then passes it to the class loader. The class name and its inheritance hierarchy; the method names, signatures and code for each class method; the attribute names found and referenced in class methods constitute the necessary and available meta information found in the standard Java class files. The presence of this meta information in standard Java class byte codes and the capability to do dynamic class loading are essential to our way building a pure-library based jContractor implementation.

Core Java classes include the `java.lang.reflect` package which provides reflection capabilities that could be used for parsing the class information, but using this package would require prior loading of the class files into the JVM. Since jContractor needs to do its instrumentation *before* loading the class files, it cannot use core reflection classes directly and instead uses its own class file parser.

4 Discussion

4.1 Interaction Of Contracts With Inheritance And Polymorphism

Contracts are essentially specifications checked at run-time. They are not part of the functional implementation code, and a "correct" program's execution should not depend on the presence or enabling of the contract methods. Additionally, the exceptions that may be thrown due to runtime contract violations are not checked exceptions, therefore, they are not required to be part of a method's signature and do not require clients' code to handle these specification as exceptions. In the rest of this section we discuss the contravariance and covariance issues arising from the way contracts are inherited.

The inheritance of preconditions from a parent class follows *contravariance*: as a subclass provides a more specialized implementation, it should weaken, not strengthen, the preconditions of its methods. Any method that is redefined in the subclass should be able to at least handle the cases that were being handled by the parent, and in addition handle some other cases due to its specialization. Otherwise, polymorphic substitution would no longer be possible. A client of X is bound by the contractual obligations of meeting the precondition specifications of X. If during runtime an object of a more specialized instance, say of class Y (a subclass of X) is passed, the client's code should not be expected to satisfy any stricter preconditions than it already satisfies for X, irrespective of the runtime type of the object.

jContractor supports contravariance by evaluating the a *logical-OR* of the precondition expression specified in the subclass with the preconditions inherited from its parents. For example, consider the following client code snippet:

```
// assume that class Y extends class X
X x;
Y y = new Y();       // Y object instantiated
x = y;               // x is polymorphically attached
                     // to a Y object
int i = 5; ...
x.foo(i);            // only PreCondition(X,[foo,int i]) should be met
```

When executing $x.foo()$, due to dynamic binding in Java, the *foo()* method that is found in class Y gets called, since the dynamic type of the instance is Y. If *jContractor* is enabled this results in the evaluation of the following precondition expression:

$$PreCondition(X,[foo,int\ i]) \lor PreCondition(Y,[foo,int\ i])$$

This ensures that no matter how strict *PreCondition(Y,foo)* might be, as long as the *PreCondition(X,foo)* holds true, $x.foo()$ will not raise a precondition exception.

While we are satisfied with this behavior from a theoretical standpoint, in practice a programmer could violate contravariance. For example, consider the following precondition specifications for the *foo()* method defined both in X and Y, still using the example code snippet above:

PreCondition(X, [foo,int a]):	$a > 0$	*(I)*
PreCondition(Y, [foo,int a]):	$a > 10$	*(II)*

From a specification point of view *(II)* is stricter than *(I)*, since for values of a: $0 < a <= 10$, *(II)* will fail, while *(I)* will succeed, and for all other values of a, *(I)* and *(II)* will return identical results. Following these specifications, the call of previous example:

```
x.foo(i);    // where i is 5
```

does not raise an exception since it meets *PreCondition(X,foo,int a)*. However, there is a problem from an implementation view, that Y's method $foo(int\ a)$ effectively gets called even though its own precondition specification, *(II)*, is violated. The problem here is one of a design error in the contract specification. Theoretically, this error can be diagnosed from the specification code using formal verification and by validating whether following *logical-implication* holds for each redefined method $m()$:

$$PreCondition(ParentClass,m) \Rightarrow PreCondition(SubClass,m)$$

For the previous example, it is easy to prove that *(I)* does not logically-imply *(II)*. It is beyond the scope of *jContractor* to do formal verification for logical inference of specification anomalies. *jContractor* does, however, diagnose and report these types of design anomalies, where any one of the *logical-OR*'ed precondition expressions evaluates to *false*. In the above example, *jContractor* would throw an exception to report that the precondition has been illegally strengthened in the subclass, thus forcing the programmer to correct the precondition.

A similar specification anomaly could also occur when a subclass strengthens the parent class's invariants, since *jContractor* checks the class invariants when preconditions are evaluated. The subclass' invariant's runtime violation is caught by *jContractor* instrumented code as an exception, with the correct diagnostic explanation.

The inheritance of postconditions is similar: as a subclass provides a more specialized implementation, it should strengthen, not weaken, the postconditions of its interface methods. Any method that is redefined in the subclass should be able to guarantee at least as much as its parent's implementation, and then perhaps some more, due to its specialization. *jContractor* evaluates the *logical-AND* of the postcondition expression found in the subclass with the ones inherited from its parents. Similar anomalies as discussed above for preconditions can also appear in postcondition specifications due to programming errors. *jContractor* will detect these anomalies should they manifest during runtime execution of their respective methods.

4.2 Factory Style Instrumentation Issues

When factory style instrumentation is used, *jContractor* constructs a contractor subclass as a direct descendant of the original base class. Therefore, it is possible to pass objects instantiated using the instrumented subclass to any client expecting an instance of the base class. Other than enforcing the contract specifics, an instrumented subclass, say `Foo_Contractor`, has the same interface as the base class, `Foo`, and type-wise conforms to `Foo`. This design allows the contractor subclasses to be used with any polymorphic substitution involving the base class. Consider the following class hierarchy:

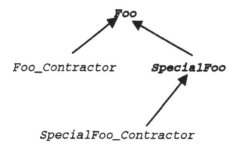

jContractor allows for the polymorphic substitution of either `SpecialFoo` objects or the instrumented `SpecialFoo_Contractor` objects with `Foo` objects.

5 Related Work

The idea of associating boolean expressions (assertions) with code as a means to argue the code's correctness can be traced back to Hoare [2] and others who worked in the field of program correctness. The idea of extending an object-oriented language using only libraries and naming conventions appeared in [3]. The notion of compiling assertions into runtime checks first appeared in the *Eiffel* language [7].

Eiffel is an elegant language with built-in language and runtime support for Design By Contract. *Eiffel* integrates preconditions (*require-clause*), postconditions (*ensure-clause*), class invariants, *old* and *rescue/retry* constructs into the definition of methods and classes. *jContractor* is able to provide all of the contract support found in *Eiffel*, with the following differences: *jContractor* supports exception-handling with finer exception resolution – as opposed to a single *rescue* clause; *jContractor* does not support the *retry* construct of *Eiffel*. We believe that if such recovery from an exception condition is possible, it is better to incorporate this handler into the implementation of the method itself, which forestalls throwing the exception at all. *jContractor'* support for *old* supports cloning semantics where references are involved, while Eiffel does not.

Duncan & Hölzle introduced Handshake[1], which allows a programmer to write external contract specifications for Java classes and interfaces without changing the classes themselves. Handshake is implemented as a dynamically linked library and works by intercepting the JVM's file accesses and instrumenting the classes on the fly using a mechanism called binary component adaptation (BCA). BCA is developed for on the fly modification of pre-compiled Java components (class bytecodes) using externally provided specification code containing directives to alter the pre-compiled semantics [5]. The flexibility of the approach allows Handshake to add contracts to classes declared `final`; to system classes; and to interfaces as well as classes. Some of the shortcomings of the approach are that contract specifications are written externally using a special syntax; and that Handshake Library is a non-Java system that has to be ported to and supported on different platforms.

Kramer's *iContract* is a tool designed for specifying and enforcing contracts in Java [4]. Using *iContract*, pre-, postconditions and class invariants can be annotated in the Java source code as "comments" with tags such as: @pre, @post. The *iContract* tool acts as a pre-processor, which translates these assertions and generates modified versions of the Java source code. *iContract* uses its own specification language for expressing the boolean conditions.

Mannion and Philips have proposed an extension to the Java language to support Design By Contract [8], employing *Eiffel*-like keyword and expressions, which become part of a method's signature. Mannion's request that Design By Contract be directly supported in the language standard is reportedly the most popular "non-bug" request in the Java Developer Connection Home Page (bug number 4071460).

Porat and Fertig propose an extension to C++ class declarations to permit specification of pre- and postconditions and invariants using an assertion-like semantics to support *Design By Contract* [9].

6 Conclusion

We have introduced *jContractor*, a purely library-based solution to write Design By Contract specifications and to enforce them at runtime using Java. The *jContractor* library and naming conventions can be used to specify the following Design By Contract constructs: pre- and postconditions, class invariants, exception handlers, and *old* references. Programmers can write contracts using standard Java syntax and an intuitive naming convention. Contracts are specified in the form of protected methods in a class definition where the method names and signatures constitute the *jContractor* naming conventions. *jContractor* checks for these patterns in class definitions and rewrites those classes on the fly by instrumenting their methods to check contract violations at runtime.

The greatest advantage of *jContractor* over existing approaches is the ease of deployment. Since *jContractor* is purely library-based, it does not require any special tools such as modified compilers, runtime systems, pre-processors or JVMs, and works with any pure Java implementation.

The *jContractor* library instruments the classes that contain *contract patterns* during class loading or object instantiation. Programmers enable the run-time enforcement of contracts by using a command line switch at start-up, which installs the *jContractor* instrumenting class loader. *jContractor* object factory provides an alternative mechanism that does not require engaging the *jContractor* ClassLoader to instantiate instrumented objects. Clients can instantiate objects directly from the *jContractor* factory, which can use any standard class loader and does not require a command line switch. Either way, clients can use exactly the same syntax for invoking methods or passing object references regardless of whether contracts are present or not. Contract violations result in the method throwing proper runtime exceptions when instrumented object instances are used.

We also describe a novel instrumentation technique that allows accessing the *old* values of variables when writing postconditions and exception handling methods. For example, `OLD.count` returns the value of the attribute `count` at method entry. The instrumentation arranges for the attribute values or expressions accessed through the `OLD` reference to be recorded at method entry and replaces the `OLD` expressions with automatically allocated unique identifiers to access the recorded value.

References

1. Andrew Duncan and Urs Hölzle. *Adding Contracts to Java with Handshake.* Technical Report TRC98-32, University of California, Santa Barbara, 1998.

2. C.A.R. Hoare. An Axiomatic Basis for Computer Programming. *Communications of the ACM*, 12(10), October 1969.

3. Murat Karaorman and John Bruno. Introducing Concurrency to a Sequential Language. *Communications of the ACM.* Vol.36, No.9, September 1993, pp.103-116.

4. Reto Kramer. *iContract – The Java Design by Contract Tool.* Proc. of TOOLS '98, Santa Barbara, CA August 1998. Copyright IEEE 1998.

5. Ralph Keller and Urs Hölzle. *Binary Component Adaptation.* Proc. of ECOOP '98, Lecture Notes in Computer Science, Springer Verlag, July 1998.

6. Bertrand Meyer. *Applying Design by Contract.* In Computer IEEE), vol. 25, no. 10, October 1992, pages 40-51.

7. Bertrand Meyer: *Eiffel: The Language,* Prentice Hall, 1992.

8. Mike Mannion and Roy Phillips. *Prevention is Better than a Cure.* Java Report, Sept.1998.

9. S.Porat and P.Fertig. *Class Assertions in C++.* Journal of Object Oriented Programming, 8(2):30-37, May 1995.

10. Tim Lindholm and Frank Yellin. *The Java Virtual Machine Specification.* Addison-Wesley, 1996.

OpenCorba: A Reflective Open Broker

Thomas Ledoux

École des Mines de Nantes
4 rue Alfred Kastler
F-44307 Nantes cedex 3, France
Thomas.Ledoux@emn.fr

Abstract. Today, CORBA architecture brings the major industrial solution for achieving the interoperability between distributed software components in heterogeneous environments. While the CORBA project attempts to federate distributed mechanisms within a unique architecture, its internal model is not very flexible and seems not to be suitable for future evolutions. In this paper, we present OpenCorba, a *reflective open broker*, enabling users to adapt dynamically the representation and the execution policies of the software bus.

We first expose the reflective foundations underlying the implementation of OpenCorba: i) metaclasses which provide a better separation of concerns in order to improve the class reuse; ii) a protocol which enables the dynamic changing of metaclass in order to allow run-time adaptation of systems.

Based on this reflective environment, OpenCorba enables the adaptability of the internal characteristics of the broker in order to change its run-time behavior (e.g. remote invocation, IDL type checking, IR error handling). OpenCorba gives a clear example of the benefits of reflective middleware.

1   Introduction

In the last couple of years, the success of the Internet emphasizes the need to quickly find solutions for interoperability between distributed heterogeneous environments. Reusability and composability of software components are one of the main concerns for the computer industry dealing with different languages, systems and locations.

By supporting specifications for portable and interoperable object components, the OMG (Object Management Group) consortium proposes a solution to deal with the construction of object-oriented distributed applications [OMG 95]. Indeed, OMG's standardization efforts led to the definition of a whole modular architecture approved by the computer industry. The specifications describe independent modules of a large system, from technical aspects to business objects, reviewing essential distributed services such as security, transactions, event notification, etc. known as the CORBA Services [OMG 97]. The CORBA (Common Object Request Broker Architecture) software bus is the main module of this architecture and has the responsibility of achieving a transparent communication between remote objects [OMG 98]. The *modularity* of this architecture is a major advantage of the OMG solution.

However, the complexity of the broker specifications negatively impacts in the intended flexibility of the CORBA model. For example, the invocation mechanism is a "black box" described by fixed specifications. The introduction of a small evolution leads to a new version of the specifications, making obsolete the last one. Dealing with the invocation, the introduction of the interceptors mechanism in CORBA 2.2 and the request for proposal Messaging Service for CORBA 3.0, attempt to improve the existing specifications (and resulting applications). Thus, we can be sceptical about the stability of such improvement. In the current style of distributed systems, we must support the *dynamic* modification of the broker mechanisms to deal with changing contexts of execution (e.g. load balancing, fault tolerance). This dynamic capability of the bus makes possible the evolution of execution policies (e.g. object migration).

We propose an overall solution that allows the object bus to be *adaptive*, making the broker "plug and play". The classification of concurrent and distributed programming proposed by Briot et al. [BRI 98] constitutes an interesting framework for tackling the adaptive issue. The authors distinguish three approaches:

- *library* approach applies object-oriented concepts in order to structure the concurrent and distributed systems through class libraries;

- *integrative* approach consists in unifying concurrent and distributed systems concepts with object-oriented ones;

- *reflective* approach integrates protocol libraries dealing with concurrency and distribution within an object-based programming system.

Using this classification, we can notice that the OMG model both corresponds to an integrative and a library approach, with the minimal object model and the CORBA services perspective respectively. In this taxonomy, the reflective approach is presented as a solution for combining the advantages of the two previous approaches. So, reflection is the best choice for handling the adaptability of the object bus. Reflection [SMI 82] [MAE 87] [KIC 91] allows the extension of the initial OMG model with libraries of meta-protocols customizing mechanisms of distributed programming. Then, it is possible to introduce – in a transparent way – new semantics on the initial model such as concurrency, replication, security, etc. including ones currently unthought of.

In this paper, we present an overview of OpenCorba [LED 98]: a CORBA broker based on a reflective approach. Its architecture enables the reification of the internal characteristics of the software bus in order to modify and adapt them at *run-time*. Then, OpenCorba allows introspection and dynamic modification of the representation and the execution policies of the CORBA bus. Its implementation is based on the reflective language NeoClasstalk [RIV 97]. This language results from an implementation of a MOP (Meta Object Protocol) [KIC 91] in Smalltalk [GOL 89]. Its main contribution consists of an extension of dynamic aspects in Smalltalk: an efficient solution for handling message sending and a way of achieving dynamic behavior of a class.

This paper is presented as follows. In section 2, we explain the reflective foundations underlying the making of OpenCorba and show the advantages of reflection for building open systems. In section 3, after an introduction of OpenCorba itself, we present three possible reflective aspects of the bus. In section 4, we present related work, and in section 5, we discuss about our works in progress. Finally, we draw our conclusions on the contribution of *dynamic adaptability* to middleware.

2 Reflective Foundations for Building Open Systems

In this section, we show the benefits of the paradigm of metaclasses for building reusable and adaptable architectures.

2.1 Metaclasses and Separation of Concerns

Reflection allows us to separate what an object does (the base level) from how it does it (its meta level) [McA 95]. A reflective language encourages a clean separation between the basic functionalities of the application from its representations and controls. In class-based languages integrating reflective features [COI 87] [DAN 94], the class of a class – a *metaclass* – defines some properties concerning object creation, encapsulation, inheritance rules, message handling, etc. We call *class properties* the properties that denote behavior for classes themselves, independently from the behavior for their instances. In [LED 96], we present a taxonomy of reusable metaclasses which represent class properties such as ensuring that a class has one sole instance (like the pattern Singleton [GAM 95]), a class cannot be subclassed (like Java final [GOS 96]), a class provides pre/post conditions for its methods (like the Eiffel assertions [MEY 92]), etc.

The previous taxonomy was implemented in the MOP NeoClasstalk, which is a based on a new kernel of metaclasses inside the Smalltalk world [RIV 96]. An additional metaclass named StandardClass, is defined and strapped into the initial Smalltalk meta-level architecture. StandardClass provides a starting point to the NeoClasstalk system. Then, new metaclasses can be derived from StandardClass, which describes common behavior for classes, by subclassing it.

Fig. 1 shows a class Account, instance of the metaclass BreakPoint that owns the responsibility to set breakpoints in the methods of the class Account[1]. Message sending is handled by the method #execute:receiver:arguments: of the MOP NeoClasstalk: the metaclass BreakPoint intercepts messages received by the instances of Account.

---

[1] It could be interesting to control class interactions with the rest of the system during the debugging phase.

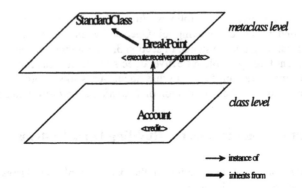

Fig. 1. Class properties and (meta)classes

The method #execute:receiver:arguments: described above, opens a debugger with the execution context of the trapped method (e.g. #credit:), then performs the originally intended method via traditional inheritance mechanisms.

metaclass code
```
BreakPoint>>execute: cm receiver: rec arguments: args
   "Set a breakpoint on my instance methods"
   self halt: 'BreakPoint for ', cm selector.
   ^super execute: cm receiver: rec arguments: args
```

class code
```
Account>>credit: aFloat
   "Make a credit on the current balance"
   self balance: self balance + aFloat
```

In this way, we avoid the mixing between the business code (bank account) and the code describing a specific property on it (breakpoints). By increasing the separation of concerns, class properties encourage readability, reusability and quality of code. Then, reusable metaclasses propose a better organisation of class libraries for designing open architectures.

2.2 Dynamic Change of Metaclass

The dynamic change of class introduced by NeoClasstalk is a protocol that makes it possible for the objects to change their class at run-time [RIV 97][2]. The purpose of

---

[2] This protocol compensates for the restrictions imposed by the method #changeClassToThatOf: found in Smalltalk.

this protocol is to take into account the evolution of the behavior of the objects during their life in order to improve their class implementations. The association of first class objects with this protocol allows the dynamic change of metaclass at run-time. Therefore, it is possible to dynamically add and remove class properties without having to regenerate code.

By taking again the previous example, we can temporarily associate the BreakPoint property with a class during its development. The class Account changes its original metaclass towards metaclass BreakPoint[3] for debugging the messages, then returns towards its former state reversing its change of class (cf. **Fig. 2**).

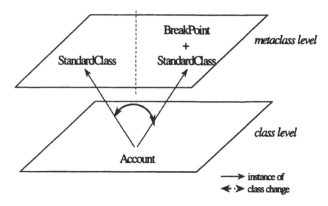

Fig. 2. Dynamic adaptability of class properties

The protocol for dynamically changing the class of a class (the metaclass) allows us to replace a class property by another, during execution. In our work dealing with adaptive brokers, this protocol is extremely helpful because it provides a "plug and play" environment for enabling the *run-time* modification of the distributed mechanisms.

3 OpenCorba

Our first implementation of an open architecture dealt with the CORBA platform [OMG 98] and gave place to the implementation of a software bus named OpenCorba. The goal of this section is to expose the major reflective aspects of OpenCorba. Others features of OpenCorba like the IDL compiler or the different layers of the broker are described in details in [LED 98].

---

[3] Or a composition of metaclasses dealing with BreakPoint and other class properties (cf. 5.1).

3.1 Introduction

OpenCorba is an application implementing the API CORBA in NeoClasstalk. It reifies various properties of the broker – by the means of explicit metaclasses – in order to support the separation of the internal characteristics of the ORB. The use of the dynamic change of metaclass allows to modify the ORB mechanisms represented by metaclasses. Then, OpenCorba is a reflective ORB, which allows to *adapt* the behavior of the broker at *run-time*.

In the following paragraphs, we present three aspects of the bus that have been reified:

1. the mechanism of remote invocation via a proxy;

2. the IDL type checking on the server class;

3. the management of exceptions during the creation of the interface repository[4].

First, we introduce the two basic concepts for creating classes in OpenCorba. This creation deals directly with the reflective aspects.

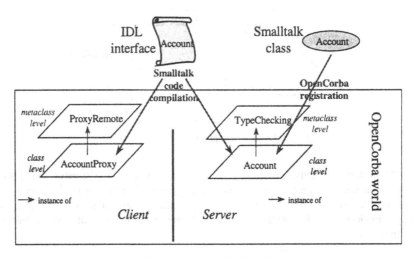

Fig. 3. Creation of OpenCorba classes

IDL Mapping in OpenCorba.

Following the Smalltalk mapping described in the CORBA specifications [OMG 98], the OpenCorba IDL compiler generates a proxy class on the client side and a template class on the server side. The proxy class is associated with the metaclass

---

[4] Let us recall that the interface repository (IR) is similar to a run-time database containing all the IDL specifications reified as objects.

ProxyRemote implementing the remote invocation mechanisms; the template class, with the metaclass TypeChecking which implements the IDL type checking on the server. The left hand of **Fig. 3** shows the results from IDL mapping of the Account interface in OpenCorba: the proxy class AccountProxy is instance of ProxyRemote and the template class Account is instance of TypeChecking.

Feature Smalltalk2OpenCorba.

OpenCorba allows the Smalltalk developers to transform any Smalltalk standard class into a Smalltalk server class in the ORB. This feature was introduced to reuse existing Smalltalk code, and to free the programmer from the writing of the bulk of IDL specification. Technically, a semi-automatic process is applied to the Smalltalk class in order to generate the interface repository and the IDL file. Then, to become a server class in OpenCorba, the class must be an instance of TypeChecking (cf. **Fig. 3**, right hand). By analogy with similar techniques, we called this special feature Smalltalk2OpenCorba.

3.2   The OpenCorba Proxy

In distributed architectures, the proxy object is a local representation in the client side of the server object. Its purpose is to ensure the creation of the requests and their routing towards the server, then to turn over the result to the client. In order to remain transparent, a proxy class adapts the style of local call to the mechanism of remote invocation [SHA 86].

Separation of Concerns.

The remote invocation mechanism is completely independent of the semantics of the IDL interface (e.g. Account). That is, remote invocation refers to the control of the application and not to the application functionality; it deals with meta-level programming. The OpenCorba IDL compiler automatically generates the proxy class on the basic level of the application and associates the proxy class with the metaclass ProxyRemote in charge of calling the real object. The remote invocation remains thus transparent for the client. We can manipulate the proxy class with the traditional Smalltalk tools (browser, inspector).

Base level features. Methods of the proxy class are purely descriptive and represent interfaces like IDL operations [LED 97]. In the Smalltalk browser, the methods do not contain any code, only one comment denoting that OpenCorba generated them. **Table 1** presents some examples of mapping for OpenCorba. The type of the returned values is put in comments to announce IDL information to the programmer.

Table 1. Examples of IDL mapping

IDL attribute/operation	Methods of a proxy class OpenCorba
readonly attribute float balance;	balance "Generated by OpenCORBA *** DO NOT EDIT **** ^^aFloat *
void credit(in float amount);	credit: aFloat "Generated by OpenCORBA *** DO NOT EDIT **** ^^nil*

Meta level features. By definition, the sending of a message to a proxy object involves a remote message send to the server object it represents. The idea is to intercept the message at its reception time by the proxy object and to launch a remote invocation. Thus, the control of the message sending is suitable for our purpose. The metaclass ProxyRemote redefines the method #execute:receiver:arguments: of the MOP NeoClasstalk to intercept the messages received by a proxy. This redefinition carries out the remote invocation by using the DII CORBA API according to [OMG 98].

Dynamic Adaptability.

To allow the dynamic adaptability of the invocation mechanisms in OpenCorba, it is possible to develop others metaclasses. We distinguished them in two categories:

- The first one deals with the possible variations on the proxy mechanisms. We think of policies modelling Java RMI [SUN 98], a future version of the CORBA DII or a local invocation. This last mechanism was implemented in OpenCorba in order to model proxies with cache.

- The second category considers extensions of the proxy concept for introducing new mechanisms like object migration [JUL 88] [OKA 94] or active replication [BIR 91] [GUE 97].
    - Object migration consists in transferring a server object towards the client side in order to optimize the performances of the distributed system. This mechanism reduces the bottlenecks of the network and minimizes the remote communications.
    - Replication is another mechanism of administration of the objects distribution. It consists of a duplication of the server in several replicas, which are the exact representation of the original server object. The mechanism of active replication supposes that the message is sent by the client to the replicas – via the proxy – thanks to an atomic protocol of diffusion (broadcast).

Thus, the dynamic adaptability of metaclasses allows to implement some variations on the remote invocation mechanism, without upsetting existing architecture.

3.3   IDL Type Checking on the Server Classes

The CORBA standard [OMG 98] specifies that the server side uses the interface repository to check the conformity of the signature of a request by checking the argument and return objects. On the other hand, it does not specify how it must be carried out.

Separation of Concerns.

We are convinced that it falls within the competence of the server class to check if one of its methods can be applied or not. Indeed, if this kind of checking could be carries out more upstream by the ORB (during the unmarshalling of request by the server for example), that would introduce a more inflexible management: a little change in the mechanism of control involves a rewriting of the lower layers of the broker. On the contrary, we propose an externalisation of the control of these layers towards the server class, which will test if the application of a method is possible or not.

Moreover, the type checking is independent of the functionalities defined by the server class: it can be separated from the base code and constituted as a class property that will be implemented by a metaclass. Thus, the code of the server class does not carry out any test on the type of the data in arguments. The developer can then write, modify or recover its code without worrying about the control of the type handled by the metaclass `TypeChecking`.

Technically, this metaclass controls the message sending on the server class – via the method `#execute:receiver:arguments:` – to interrogate the interface repository before and after application of its methods. This query enables us to check the type of the arguments and the type of the result of the method.

In conclusion, OpenCorba externalises the type checking, at the same time from the lower layers of the ORB, and from the server class.

Dynamic Adaptability.

Thanks to our approach, we can bring new mechanisms for type checking, without modifying the existing implementation. For example, we can develop a new metaclass managing a system of cache for the types of the parameters. During the first query of the interface repository, OpenCorba locally backs up the type of each argument of the method[5]. Then, with the next invocations of the method, the metaclass questions memorized information in order to carry out the type checking.

Another example: we can also remove the control of the type for reasons of performance or when the type of the parameters is known before hand. A dynamic

---

[5] For example, in a Smalltalk shared dictionary or in the byte code of the compiled method.

change of metaclass allows then to associate the server class with the default metaclass of the OpenCorba system (i.e. StandardClass).

3.4 Interface Repository and Error Handling

There are two ways used to populate the interface repository: the IDL mapping and the feature Smalltalk2OpenCorba. In the first case, the generation of each proxy class is handled in the creation of the objects in the repository. In the second case, this creation is allowed by a table of Smalltalk equivalence towards IDL (*retro-mapping*). Technically, these two mechanisms do not have the same degree of intercession:

- In the case of Smalltalk2OpenCorba, the Smalltalk compiler already carried out the syntactic analysis and the semantic checking of the class. Also, the installation of a Smalltalk class in the ORB does not cause errors during the creation of the objects in the repository;

- On the other hand, in the IDL case, it is an authentic compilation where the semantic actions check the integrity of IDL specifications before the creation of objects in the repository (e.g. the same attribute duplicated).

Thus, in order to distinguish the Smalltalk case from the IDL case where creation can lead to error handling, we must encapsulate the CORBA creational APIs of the interface repository. Let us recall that these creational APIs are implemented by the *container* classes of the interface repository specified by CORBA standard [OMG 98].

Separation of Concerns.

By analyzing the tests of integrity necessary for the IDL compilation, it appears that they are generic and independent from the creational APIs of the *containers*. Thus, they can be externalized from the *container* classes to constitute a class property which will be implemented by a metaclass. The code of the *container* classes does not carry out any tests. It is then helpful to differentiate the IDL case from the Smalltalk case, in order to associate a given metaclass or not to the *container* classes.

The metaclass IRChecking plays this role. It specializes the method #execute:receiver:arguments: of the MOP NeoClasstalk in order to intercept the messages received by the instances of the *container* class. For the creational APIs, the integrity tests are carried out and an exception is raised if an error occurs.

Dynamic Adaptability.

Our design leads to a greater flexibility to carry out or transform the integrity tests without having to modify the creational APIs. Thus, it allows the distinction between the Smalltalk case and the IDL case at run-time. In the Smalltalk case, creation is carried out normally (default metaclass StandardClass); in the IDL case, there is a dynamic adaptability of the behavior to carry out creation only if the integrity tests do not raise an error (metaclass IRChecking). OpenCorba connects the appropriate metaclasses at run-time according to needs of the system.

3.5   Implementation and Performance Issues

Reflective aspects of OpenCorba are essentially based in the ability of handling message sends. Therefore, the extra cost of the reflective broker is highly dependent on the performance of the message sending.

The implementation of this control in NeoClasstalk is based on a technique called *method wrappers* [BRA 98]. The main idea of this feature is the following: rather than changing the method lookup process directly at run-time, we modify the compiled method objects that the lookup process returns. In NeoClasstalk, the method wrappers deal both with compile-time and run-time reflection. We briefly describe the two steps involved:

* *At compile-time*

    The original method defined in a class is wrapped so that it sends to the class itself the message #execute:receiver:arguments: defined in its class (the metaclass). The arguments are i) the original compiled method which is stored in the method wrapper, ii) the object originally receiving the message, iii) the arguments of the message.

* *At run-time*

    Method lookup is unmodified: the activation of the method wrapper does the call to the metaclass and starts the meta-level processing.

By analysing these two steps, we conclude that the cost is actually significant. First, the meta-level indirection occurring at run-time involves additional method invocations. Since the meta-level indirection is applied to each message send, the performance of the whole system decreases. However, we can notice that since OpenCorba deals with distributed environment, the network traffic moderates the impact of this overhead.

Secondly, at compile-time, there is a real difficulty in applying the method wrappers concept: which are the methods that we need to wrap? It depends on the problem at hand. For example, in OpenCorba, all the methods of a server class and all the inherited ones must be wrapped. Thus, the technique of method wrappers imposes some decisions at design time, which imply a cost that should not be overlooked.

In summary, the flexibility provided by reflection impacts on the system efficiency. Many works attempt to find a way for efficient reflective systems such as the optimization of virtual machine for meta-programming, the reification categories which provide the opportunity to specifically reify a given class [GOW 96], the partial evaluation for MOP [MAS 98], etc.

4 Related Work

4.1 Reflective Adaptive Middleware

Like the OpenCorba broker, other research projects are under development in the field of adaptive middleware. The ADAPT project of the University of Lancaster has investigated the middleware implementation for mobile multimedia applications which are capable of dynamically adapting to QoS fluctuations [BLA 97]. Its successor, the OpenORB project, studies the role of reflection in the design of middleware platforms [BLA 98]. The implementation of the current reflective architecture is based on a per-object meta-space (structured as three distinct meta-space models) and on the concept of open bindings, differing from the per-class reflective environment and the MOP of OpenCorba. These two design approaches result in two different ways of investigating reflective middleware.

The FlexiNet platform [HAY 98], a Java middleware, proposes to reify the layers of the communication stack into different meta-objects (in order to customize them). Each meta-object represents a specific aspect such as call policy, serialization, network session, etc. OpenCorba currently reifies characteristics dealing the upper layers of the invocation mechanism, and could reify the lower layers (e.g. marshalling, transport).

Researchers at the University of Illinois developed dynamicTAO, a CORBA-compliant reflective ORB that supports run-time reconfiguration [ROM 99]. Specific strategies are implemented and packed as dynamically loadable libraries, so they can be linked to the ORB process at run-time. Rather than implementing a new ORB from scratch as done in OpenCorba, they chose to use TAO [SCH 99], causing a dependency to this ORB.

Finally, since its experiment in the development of MOP [GOW 96], the distributed system team of the Trinity College of Dublin has recently started the Coyote project whose goal is to provide the adaptation of distributed system (e.g. administration of telecommunication network, CORBA bus).

4.2 Reflection in Distributed Systems

The use of reflection in the concurrent and distributed systems is certainly not recent [WAT 88], but seems to take a new rise in the last years. Indeed, many research projects in the field of reflection or in the distributed domain use the reification of the distributed mechanisms to modify them and specialize them. Let us quote the mechanisms of migration [OKA 94], marshalling [McA 95], replication [GOL 97], security [FAB 97], etc. The CORBA architecture is a federate platform of the various mechanisms of distribution. Also, it seems interesting to study these projects to implement their mechanisms within OpenCorba.

4.3 Programming with Aspects

The mixing in the system's basic functionality of several technical aspects (e.g. distribution, synchronization, memory management) dealing with the application domain, constitutes one of the major obstacles to the reusability of the software components. A possible solution is then to consider the isolation of these specific aspects for their individual reuse. The "tangled" code is separated and aspects can evolve independently thus formulating the paradigm of separation of concerns [HUR 95].

There are some models and techniques allowing the separation of concerns: composition filters [BER 94], adaptive programming [LIE 96], aspect-oriented programming (AOP) [KIC 97]. However, the latter implement particular constructs to achieve the programming with aspects. We preferred a reflective approach that does not impose a new model, but extends the existing languages to open them. Moreover, contrary to these models, our solution allows the dynamic adaptability of aspects.

5 Work in Progress

5.1 Metaclass Composition

Distributed architectures are complex and require many mechanisms for their implementation. The question of how to compose these mechanisms is essential. For example, the functionality of "logging within a class the remote invocations" uses the mechanism of "logging" combined with the mechanism of "remote invocation". As we have seen previously, each of these mechanisms corresponds with a class property and is implemented by a metaclass. Thus, the combination of several mechanisms raises the problem of the composition of the metaclasses: this composition causes conflicts a priori when there is a behavior overlap.

To tackle this problem, our recent work consists in the definition of a "metaclass compatibility model" in order to offer a reliable framework for the composition of the metaclasses [BS 98]. We attempt to define a classification of the various distribution mechanisms to prevent possible overlappings of behavior.

5.2 Towards Specifications of a Reflective Middleware

By studying concurrent and distributed architectures, we can notice that they deal with well-known mechanisms and policies, which are independent from the system's basic functionality (i.e. business objects) and could be implemented at the meta-level. Then, we can suggest a first classification of middleware features related to reflective components:

- Distribution
  proxy mechanism, replication, migration, persistence, etc.

- Communication
  synchronous, asynchrounous, no reply, future, multicast, etc.

- Object concurrency
  inter-objects, intra-object (readers/writer model, monitor), etc.

- Reliability
  exceptions, transactions, etc.

- Security
  authentification, authorisation, licence, etc.

- Thread management
  single-threaded, thread-per-message, thread-pool, etc.

- Data transport
  sockets, pipes, shared memory, etc.

The richness of future middlewares will depend on their capabilities to dynamically adapt and (fine) tune such features. Then, we are strongly convinced that the first step to build such a middleware is to find a good reflective model and environment.

In OpenCorba, we experimented with a per-class reflective environment on the top of Smalltalk. We are currently investigating other models like meta-object or message reification models in order to compare them with our metaclass approach. We noticed that the design of reflective distributed mechanisms could be common to any reflective language dealing with similar features. For example, the handling of the message sending is an important feature because several mechanisms have to deal with it (in their implementation). Then, most of the reflective languages support the *same design* of the meta-level in order to implement a given distributed mechanism (e.g. primary replication [CHI 93] [McA 95] [GOL 97]).

To reason about a language independent environment, we sketched out an abstract MOP allowing the control and customization of the message sending and state accessing. Thus, we plan to describe the specifications of distributed mechanisms in the context of meta-programming, i.e. reflective distributed components.

6 Conclusion

In this paper, we developed the idea in which reflection is a tremendous vector for the building of open architectures. Languages considering classes as full entities allow separation of concerns through metaclasses, improving reusability and quality of code. Then, associated to the dynamic change of class, metaclasses offer an exclusive reflective scheme for the building of reusable and adaptable, open architectures.

In the context of distributed architectures, these reflective foundations offer a dynamic environment allowing the reuse and the adaptability of mechanisms related to the distribution. Our first experimentation enabled us to "open" some internal characteristics of the CORBA software bus, such as the invocation mechanism. The result – OpenCorba – is an open broker capable of dynamically adapting the policies of representation and execution within the CORBA middleware.

Acknowledgements

The research described in this paper was funded by IBM Global Services (France) during the author's PhD (1994-1997). The author wishes to thanks Noury Bouraqadi-Saâdani, Pierre Cointe, Fred Rivard for many discussions about OpenCorba, Xavier Alvarez for his reviewing of the final version of the paper.

References

[BER 94]   BERGMANS L. — *Composing Concurrent Objects.* PhD thesis, University of Twente, Enschede, Netherlands, June 1994.

[BIR 91]   BIRMAN K., SCHIPER A., STEPHENSON P. — Lightweight Causal and Atomic Group Multicast. In *ACM Transactions on Computer Systems*, vol.9, n°3, p.272-314, 1991.

[BLA 97]   BLAIR G.S., COULSON G., DAVIES N., ROBIN P., FITZPATRICK T. — Adaptive Middleware for Mobile Multimedia Applications. In *Proceedings of the 8th International Workshop on NOSSDAV'97*, St-Louis, Missouri, May 1997.

[BLA 98]   BLAIR G.S., COULSON G., ROBIN P., PAPATHOMAS M. — An Architecture for Next Generation Middleware. In *Proceedings of Middleware'98*, Springer-Verlag, p.191-206, N. Davies, K. Raymond, J. Seitz Eds, September 1998.

[BRA 98]   BRANT J., FOOTE B., JOHNSON R., ROBERTS D. — Wrappers to the Rescue. In *Proceedings of ECOOP'98*, Springer-Verlag, Brussels, Belgium, July 1998.

[BRI 98]   BRIOT J.P., GUERRAOUI R., LÖHR K.P. — Concurrency and Distribution in Object-oriented Programming. In *ACM Computer Surveys*, vol.30, n°3, p.291-329, September 1998.

[BS 98]   BOURAQADI-SAÂDANI N., LEDOUX T., RIVARD F. — Safe Metaclass Programming. In *Proceedings of OOPSLA'98*, ACM Sigplan Notices, Vancouver, Canada, October 1998.

[CHI 93]   CHIBA S., MASUDA T. — Designing an Extensible Distributed Language with a Meta-Level Architecture. In *Proceedings of ECOOP'93*, p.482-501, LNCS 707, Springer-Verlag, Kaiserslautern, Germany, 1993.

[COI 87]   COINTE P. — Metaclasses are First Class : the ObjVlisp Model. In *Proceedings of OOPSLA'87*, ACM Sigplan Notices, p.156-167, Orlando, Florida, October 1987.

[DAN 94]   DANFORTH S., FORMAN I.R. — Reflections on Metaclass Programming in SOM. In *Proceedings of OOPSLA '94*, ACM Sigplan Notices, Portland, Oregon, October 1994.

[FAB 97]   FABRE J.C, PÉRENNOU T. — A metaobject architecture for fault tolerant distributed systems: the FRIENDS approach. In *IEEE Transactions on Computers*. Special Issue on Dependability of Computing Systems, vol.47, n°1, p.78-95, January 1998

[GAM 95]   GAMMA E., HELM R., JOHNSON R., VLISSIDES John — *Design Patterns*, Addison-Wesley Reading, Massachusetts, 1995.

[GOL 89]   GOLDBERG A., ROBSON D. — *Smalltalk-80 : The Language*, Addison-Wesley, Reading, Massachusetts, 1989.

[GOL 97]   GOLM M. — *Design and Implementation of a Meta Architecture for Java*. Master's Thesis, University of Erlangen, Germany, January 1997.

[GOS 96]   GOSLING J., JOY B., STEELE G. — *The Java Language Specification*. The Java Series, Addison-Wesley, Reading, Massachusetts, 1996.

[GOW 96]   GOWING B., CAHILL V. — Meta-Object Protocols for C++ : The Iguana Approach. In *Proceedings of Reflection'96*, Ed. Kiczales, San Francisco, California, April 1996.

[GUE 97]   GUERRAOUI R., SCHIPER A. — Software Based Replication for Fault Tolerance. In *IEEE Computer*, vol.30 (4), April 1997.

[HAY 98]   HAYTON R., HERBERT A., DONALDSON D. — FlexiNet - A flexible component oriented middleware system. In *Proceedings of ACM SIGOPS European Workshop*, Sintra, Portugal, September 1998.

[HUR 95]   HÜRSH W.L., LOPES C.V. — *Separation of Concerns*. Technical Report NU-CCS-95-03, College of Computer Science, Northeastern University, Boston, MA, February 1995.

[JUL 88]   JUL E., LEVY H., HUTCHINSON N., BLACK A. — Fine-grained mobility in the Emerald system. In *ACM Transactions on Computer Systems*, vol.6(1), p.109-133, February 1988.

[KIC 91]   KICZALES G., DES RIVIERES J., BOBROW D.G.— *The Art of the Metaobject Protocol*. The MIT Press, 1991.

[KIC 97]   KICZALES G., LAMPING J., MENDHEKAR A., MAEDA C., LOPES C., LOINGTIER J.M, IRWIN J. — Aspect-Oriented Programming. In *Proceedings of ECOOP'97*, LNCS 1241, Springer-Verlag, p.220-242, Jyväskyla, Finland, June 1997.

[LED 96]   LEDOUX T., COINTE P. — Explicit Metaclasses as a Tool for Improving the Design of Class Libraries. In *Proceedings of ISOTAS'96*, LNCS 1049, p.38-55, Springer-Verlag, Kanazawa, Japan, March 1996.

[LED 97]   LEDOUX T. — Implementing Proxy Objects in a Reflective ORB. In *Workshop CORBA : Implementation, Use and Evaluation*, ECOOP'97, Jyväskylä, Finland, June 1997.

[LED 98]   LEDOUX T. — *Réflexion dans les systèmes répartis : application à CORBA et Smalltalk.* PhD thesis, Université de Nantes, École des Mines de Nantes, March 1998. *(in french)*

[LIE 96]   LIEBERHERR K.J. — *Adaptive Object-Oriented Software : The Demeter Method with Propagation Patterns.* PWS Publishing Company, Boston, 1996.

[MAE 87]   MAES P. — Concepts and Experiments in Computational Reflection. In *Proceedings of OOPSLA'87*, ACM Sigplan Notices, p.147-155, Orlando, Florida, October 1987.

[MAS 98]   MASUHARA H., YONEZAWA A. — Design and Partial Evaluation of Meta-objects for a Concurrent Reflective Language. In *Proceedings of ECOOP'98*, LNCS 1445, p.418-439, Springer-Verlag, Brussels, Belgium, July 1998.

[McA 95]   McAFFER J. — Meta-level architecture support for distributed objects. In *Proceedings of IWOOOS'95*, p.232-241, Lund, Sweden, 1995.

[MEY 92]   MEYER B. — *Eiffel: The Language.* Prentice Hall, second printing, 1992.

[OKA 94]   OKAMURA H., ISHIKAWA Y. — Object Location Control Using Meta-level Programming. In *Proceedings of ECOOP'94*, p.299-319, LNCS 821, Springer-Verlag, July 1994.

[OMG 95]   OBJECT MANAGEMENT GROUP — *Object Management Architecture Guide*, Revision 3.0. OMG TC Document ab/97-05-05, June 1995.

[OMG 97]   OBJECT MANAGEMENT GROUP — *CORBAservices: Common Object Services Specification.* OMG TC Document formal/98-07-05, November 1997.

[OMG 98]   OBJECT MANAGEMENT GROUP — *The Common Object Request Broker : Architecture and Specification*, Revision 2.2. OMG TC Document formal/98-07-01, February 1998.

[RIV 96]   RIVARD F. — A New Smalltalk Kernel Allowing Both Explicit and Implicit Metaclass Programming. In *Workshop "Extending the Smalltalk Language"*, OOPSLA'96, San Jose, California, October 1996.

[RIV 97]   RIVARD F. — *Évolution du comportement des objets dans les langages à classes réflexifs.* PhD thesis, Université de Nantes, École des Mines de Nantes, June 1997. *(in french)*

[ROM 99]   ROMAN M., KON F., CAMPBELL R.H. — Design and Implementation of Runtime Reflection in Communication Middleware: the dynamicTAO Case. In *Workshop on Middleware*, ICDCS'99, Austin, Texas, May 1999.

[SCH 99]   SCHMIDT D., CLEELAND C. — Applying Patterns to Develop Extensible ORB Middleware. In *IEEE Communications Magazine*, 1999. (to appear)

[SHA 86]   SHAPIRO M. — Structure and Encapsulation in Distributed Systems : The Proxy Principle. In *Proceedings of the 6th International Conference on Distributed Computer Systems*, p.198-204, Cambridge, MA, May 1986.

214

[SMI 82]   SMITH B.C. — *Reflection and Semantics in a Procedural Programming Language.* PhD thesis, MIT, January 1982.

[SUN 98]   SUN MICROSYSTEMS — *Java Remote Method Invocation (RMI).* At http://java.sun.com/products/jdk/rmi/index.html

[WAT 88]   WATANABE T., YONEZAWA A. — Reflection in an Object-Oriented Concurrent Language. In *Proceedings of OOPSLA'88*, ACM Sigplan Notices, p.306-315, San Diego, California, September 1988.

OMPC++ – A Portable High Performance Implementation of DSM Using OpenC++ Reflection

Yukihiko Sohda, Hirotaka Ogawa, and Satoshi Matsuoka

Department of Mathematical and Computing Sciences
Tokyo Institute of Technology
2-12-1 Oo-okayama, Meguro-ku, Tokyo 152-8552
TEL: (03)5734-3876   FAX: (03)5734-3876
email: {sohda,ogawa,matsu}@is.titech.ac.jp

Abstract. Platform portability is one of the utmost demanded properties of a system today, due to the diversity of runtime execution environment of wide-area networks, and parallel programs are no exceptions. However, parallel execution environments are VERY diverse, could change dynamically, while performance must be portable as well. As a result, techniques for achieving platform portability are sometimes not appropriate, or could restrict the programming model, e.g., to simple message passing. Instead, we propose the use of *reflection* for achieving platform portability of parallel programs. As a prototype experiment, a software DSM system called OMPC++ was created which utilizes the compile-time metaprogramming features of OpenC++ 2.5 to generate a message-passing MPC++ code from a SPMD-style, shared-memory C++ program. The translation creates memory management objects on each node to manage the consistency protocols for objects arrays residing on different nodes. Read- and write- barriers are automatically inserted on references to shared objects. The resulting system turned out to be quite easy to construct compared to traditional DSM construction methodologies. We evaluated this system on a PC cluster linked by the Myrinet gigabit network, and resulted in reasonable performance compared to a high-performance SMP.

1 Introduction

Due to rapid commoditization of advanced hardware, parallel machines, which had been specialized and of limited use, are being commoditized in the form of workstation and PC clusters. On the other hand, commodity software technologies such as standard libraries, object-orientation, and components are not sufficient for guaranteeing that the same code will work across all parallel platforms not only with the same set of features but also similar performance characteristics, similar fault guarantees, etc. Such *performance portability* is fundamentally difficult because platforms differ in processors, number of nodes, communication hardware, operating systems, libraries, etc., despite commoditization.

Traditionally, portability amongst diverse parallel computers have been either achieved by standard libraries such as MPI, or parallel programming languages and compilers such as HPF and OpenMP[Ope97]. However, such efforts will could require programming under a fixed programming model. Moreover, portable implementation of such systems themselves are quite difficult and require substantial effort and cost. Instead, *Reflection* and *open compilers* could be alternative methodologies and techniques for *performance portable* high-performance programs.

Based on such a belief, we are currently embarked on the OpenJIT[MOS+98] project. OpenJIT is a (reflective) Just-In-Time open compiler written almost entirely in Java, and plugs into the standard JDK 1.1.x and 1.2 JVM. At the same time, OpenJIT is designed to be a compiler framework similar to Stanford SUIF[Suif], in that it facilitates user-customizable high-level and low-level program analysis and transformation frameworks. With OpenJIT, parallel programs of various parallel programming models in Java compiled into Java bytecode, will be downloaded and executed on diverse platforms over the network, from single-node computers to large-scale parallel clusters and MPPs, along with customization classes for respective platforms and programming models using compiler metaclasses[1].

The question is, will such a scheme be feasible, especially with strong requirements for performance of high-performance parallel programs? Moreover, how much metaprogramming effort would such an approach take? So, as a precursor work using OpenC++, we have employed reflection to implement DSM (distributed shared memory) in a portable way, to support Java's chief model of parallel programming i.e., the multithreaded execution over shared memory. More specifically, we have designed a set of compiler metaclasses and the supportive template classes and runtimes for OpenC++2.5[Chi95, Chi97] that implements necessary program transformations with its compile-time MOP for efficient and portable implementation of software-based DSM for programs written in (shared-memory) SPMD style, called *OMPC++*. A multithreaded C++ program is transformed into message-passing program in MPC++[Ish96] level0 MTTL (multithread template library), and executed on our RWC(Real-World Computing Partnership)-spec PC-cluster, whose nodes are standard PCs but interconnected with the Myrinet[Myr] gigabit network, and running the RWC's SCore parallel operating system based on Linux.

The resulting OMPC++ is quite small, requiring approximately 700 lines of metaclass, template class, and runtime programming. Also, OMPC++ proved to be competitive with traditional software-based DSM implementations as well as hardware-based SMP machines. Early benchmark results using numerical core programs written in shared-memory SPMD-style programs (a fast parallel CG-kernel, and parallel FFT from SPLASH2) shown that, our reflective DSM implementation scales well, and achieves performance competitive with that of high-performance SMPs (SparcServer 4000, which has dedicated and expensive

---

[1] OpenJIT is in active development, and is currently readying the first release as of Feb. 1, 1999.

hardware for maintaining hardware memory consistency). Not only this result serves as a solid groundwork for OpenJIT, but OMPC++ itself serves as a high-performance and portable DSM in its own right.

2 Implementation of a Portable, High-Performance Software DSM

DSM (Distributed Shared Memory) has had multitudes of studies since its original proposal by Kai Li[LH89], with proposals for various software as well as hardware assisted coherency protocols, techniques for software-based implementation, etc. However, there have not been so much work with platform (performance) portability in mind. In order for a program to be portable, one must not extensively alter the underlying assumptions on the hardware, OS, the programming language, which are largely commoditized. Moreover, as a realistic parallel system, one must achieve high performance and its portability across different platforms.

Below, we give an outline of our OMPC++ system with the above requirements in mind, as well as the building blocks we have employed.

2.1 Overview of the OMPC++ system

OMPC++ takes a parallel multithreaded shared-memory C++ program, transforms the program using compile-time metaprogramming, and emits an executable depending on various environments, those with fast underlying message passing in particular(Fig. 2). OMPC++ itself does not extend the C++ syntax in any way.

More concretely, OMPC++ defines several template classes (distributed shared array classes), and OpenC+ metaclasses for performing the necessary program transformations for implementing software DSM (such as read/write barriers to shared regions, and initialization/finalization). The OpenC++ compiler generates a customized program transformer, which then transforms the program into message-passing MPC++ program, which is further compiled into C++ and then onto a binary, and finally linked with DSM template libraries as well as MPC++ runtime libraries, resulting in an executable on the RWC cluster.

Our system exhibits competitive and sometimes superior performance to software DSM systems implemented as class libraries. This is because OMPC++ can analyze and pinpoint at compile time, exactly where we should insert runtime meta-operations (such as read/write barriers) that would result in performance overhead. Thus, we only incur the overhead when it is necessary. On the other hand, for traditional class-based DSM systems, either the programmer must insert such meta-operations manually, or it would incur unnecessary runtime overhead resulting in loss of performance.

2.2 Underlying 'Building-Blocks'

We next describe the underlying 'building-blocks', namely OpenC++, MPC++, SCore, and the PC Cluster hardware(Fig. 1). We note that, aside from OpenC++, the components could be interchanged with those with similar but different functionalities and/or interfaces, and only the metaclasses have to be re-written. For example, one could easily port OMPC++ to other cluster environments, such as Beowulf[Beo].

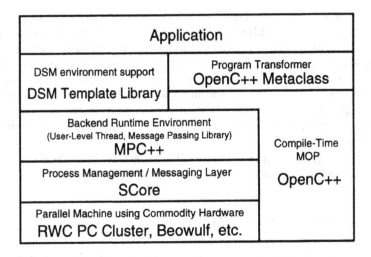

Fig. 1. Building-blocks hierarchy

OpenC++ OpenC++ provides a compile-time MOP capability for C++. By defining appropriate compiler metaclasses, the OpenC++ compiler effectively generates a preprocessor that performs the intended program transformations. The preprocessor then can be applied to the base program for appropriate meta-operations. Compile-time MOP could eliminate much of the overhead of reflection, and coupled with appropriate runtime, could simulate the effects of traditional run-time MOPs. (OMPC++ currently employs OpenC++ 2.5.4.)

MPC++ MPC++ 2.0 Level 0 MTTL is a parallel object-based programming language which supports high-level message-passing using templates and inheritance. MTTL is solely implemented using language features of C++, and no custom language extensions are done. For OMPC++, we employ most of the features of MTTL, such as local/remote thread creation, global pointers, and reduction operations[2].

---

[2] MPC++ Level 1[Ie96] supports compile-time MOP features similar to OpenC++. The reason for not utilizing them was not a deep technical issue, but rather for

RWC PC Cluster and SCore The default OMPC++ library emits code for RWC PC cluster, although with a small amount of metaclass reprogramming it could be ported to other cluster platforms. The cluster we employed is a subset of the RWC cluster II, with 8–10 Pentium Pro (200MHz) PC nodes interconnected with Myrinet gigabit LAN. The nodes in the cluster communicate with each other using PM, a fast message-passing library, and the whole cluster acts as one parallel machine using the SCore operating system based on Linux. SCore is portable in that it only extends Linux using daemons and device drivers.

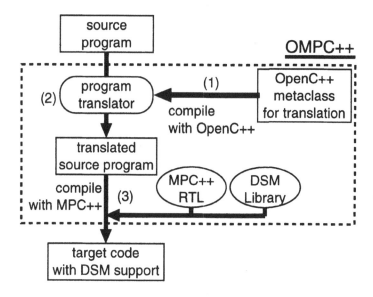

Fig. 2. Program Transformation and Compilation

3 Implementation of Software DSM in OMPC++

We outline the process of compilation and execution in OMPC++(Fig. 2).

- OpenC++ generates a preprocessor from the OMPC++ metaclasses (1).
- The source program is transformed using the preprocessor (2). The transformed program is a message-passing MPC++ program.
- MPC++ adds compiler variables such as the SCore library, and hands it off to the backend C++, which generates the executable (3).

---

practicality at the time of OMPC++ development such as stability and compilation speed. In theory we could replicate our work using MPC++ Level 1.

A real compilation session is depicted in Fig. 3. The numbers correspond to those in Fig. 2.

```
% ompc++ -m -- SharableClass.mc              |(1)

% ompc++ -v -- -o cg cg.cc problem.o         |
[Preprocess...  /usr/score/bin/mpc++         |
  -D__opencxx -E -o cg.occ -x c++ cg.cc]     |
compiling  cg.cc                             |(2)
[Translate... cg.occ into: cg.ii]            |
Load SharableClass-init.so.. Load            |
  SharableClass.so.. Initialize.. Done.      |

[Compile...  /usr/score/bin/mpc++            |
                 -o cg cg.ii problem.o]      |
compiling  cg.ii                             |(3)
[done.]                                      |
[GC happened 10 times.]                      |
```

Fig. 3. A Compilation Session for OMPC++

3.1 Program Transformation

There are 3 steps in the program transformation for implementing the DSM functionality:

1. Initialization and finalization of memory management objects created on each node.
2. Initialization of shared memory regions (creation of management tables, allocation of local memory).
3. Insertion of locks and read/write barriers to shared variables in the program.

The examples of program transformations are depicted in Fig. 4 and Fig. 5[3]. The program transformation possible with OpenC++ is restricted to transformation of base programs, and in particular those of class·methods; so, for OMPC++, we assume the user program to conform to the following structure:

```
sdsm_main() { .. };   // main computing code
sdsm_init() { .. };   // application-specific initialization
sdsm_done() { .. };   // application-specific finalization
```

---

[3] Note that, there are restrictions of the template features in the metaclasses for the current version of OpenC++, forcing us to do some template expansions manually.

sdsm_init() is called following the system-level DSM initialization. sdsm_main() function is the body of parallel code, and is called independently in parallel on each PE after initialization of the shared memory region. sdsm_done() is called after sdsm_main() terminates, followed by system-level DSM finalization, after which the whole program terminates. sdsm_init() and sdsm_done() is sequentially executed on a single PE (normally PE 0), while sdsm_main() is executed on all the PEs.

The following functions are added as a result of program transformation:

```
mpc_main() { .. };        // the main MPC++ function
Initialize() { .. };      // initialization of shared region
Finalize() { .. };        // finalization: freeing of shared region
```

Because the resulting code of program transformation is MPC++ code, the program starts from mpc_main(). This in turn calls Initialize(), which then calls the application-specific sdsm_init(). After the computation completes, sdsm_done() is called, and finally Finalize() is executed on all the processors, and the program terminates.

```
Shared<double> a(100);                    // ..(1)
Shared<double> b;
sdsm_main() {
  b = (double*)malloc(sizeof(double) * 10); // ..(2)
  b[0] = a[0];  ...
};
sdsm_init() { a[0] = 10.0; ... };
sdsm_done() { ... };
```

Fig. 4. OMPC++ Program before Transformation

Initialization and Finalization The initialization process initializes the memory management object and the DSM objects. These are quite straightforward, and only involve initialization of locks (the MPC++ Sync object). Finalization involves freeing of all the memory regions and the associated management objects, and are also straightforward.

Initialization of Shared Regions There are two types of initialization of shared regions, depending on when the memory is allocated by the user. Type 1 is when the size of the shared region (on variable definition) is fixed, and initialization is done in Initialize(). Transformation from Fig. 4-(1) to Fig. 5-(1) is an example. Type 2 is when the user does not specify the size on variable definition, but instead dynamically allocates a memory region within sdsm_init, sdsm_main(); in this case, allocation is done on the spot as we see in Fig. 4-(2) to Fig. 5-(2).

```
Shared<double> a(100);
Shared<double> b;
sdsm_main() { b.allocate(10);              // ..(2)
             { double _sym52501_8 = a[0]; // ..(5)
               b.WriteStart(0);            // ..(3)
               b(0) = _sym52501_8;
               b.WriteEnd(0); } ... };     // ..(3)
sdsm_init() { { a.WriteStart(0);           // ..(4)
               a(0) = 10.0;
               a.WriteEnd(0); } ... };     // ..(4)
sdsm_done() { ... };
Initialize() { a.allocate(100); };         // ..(1)
Finalize() { a.free();
             b.free(); };
mpc_main() {
  invoke Initialize() on all PEs.
  sdsm_init();
  invoke sdsm_main() on all PEs.
  sdsm_done();
  invoke Finalize() on all PEs.
};
```

Fig. 5. After Transformation

Access to Shared (Memory) Regions For accessing shared regions, lock/unlock are inserted on writes. Fig. 5-(3),(4)). When a shared variable occurs on the RHS expression, writes are first performed to a temporary variable to avoid duplicate lockings (Fig. 5-(5)) on further RHS evaluation. Read access does not require any locks.

3.2 Program Transformation Metaclasses

In OpenC++, metaclasses are defined as subclasses of class Class, and by overriding the methods, one could change the behavior of programs. OMPC++ overrides the following three OpenC++ methods:

TranslateInitializer Called when the shared class object is created. We can then obtain the name, type, size, and other information of the distributed shared array object, and are used for initialization of the shared regions.

TranslateAssign Called when there is an assignment to the shared class object. We can then transform the initialization and the writes of the distributed shared array objects. We analyze the expression which is passed as a parameter by the OpenC++, and if there is an malloc (or other registered allocation functions), then we perform similar task as the TranslateInitializer to obtain the necessary information, and if it is within sdsm_main(), the initialization code for shared regions directly replaces the allocation. When a shared variable occurs on the RHS expression, TranslateAssign generates a new statement which assigns it to a temporary variable. For assignments to shared variables, their operators [] are transformed to operators (), and the WriteStart() and WriteEnd() methods are inserted to sandwitch the assignment.

FinalizeInstance Called upon the end of transformation. Here, we insert the initialization and finalization functions discussed earlier. More concretely, we generate Initialize(), Finalize() based on the information obtained with TranslateInitializer and TranslateAssign, and also generate mpc_main(), obtaining the whole program.

We illustrate a sample metaprogram of TranslateAssign in Fig. 6. Here, we sandwitch the assignment with lock method calls. Metaprograms are quite compact, with only 250 lines of code (does not include runtime as well as template code, etc.).

```
Ptree* SharedClass::
  TranslateAssign(Environment* env,
    Ptree* obj, Ptree* op, Ptree* exp){
      Ptree* exp0 = ReadExpressionAnalysis(env, exp);
      Ptree* obj0 = WriteExpressionAnalysis(env,obj);
      return Ptree::List(obj0, op, exp0);  };
Ptree* SharedClass::
  WriteExpressionAnalysis(Environment* env, Ptree* exp){
    Ptree *obj = exp->First();
    Ptree *index = exp->Nth(2);
    if (!index->IsLeaf())
      index = ReadExpressionAnalysis(env, index);
    InsertBeforeStatement(env,
      Ptree::qMake("'obj'.WriteStart('index');\n"));
    AppendAfterStatement(env,
      Ptree::qMake("\n'obj'.WriteEnd('index');\n"));
    return Ptree::qMake("'obj'('index')");  };
```

Fig. 6. Metaprogram Example

3.3 Distributed Shared Memory

OMPC++ does not implement DSM transformation with OpenC++ compile-time MOP alone; rather, it also utilizes C++ templates and operator overloading. Also, in OMPC++, read/write barriers are performed in software, instead of (traditional) hardware page-based strategies such as TreadMarks[ACD+96]. Although such checks are potential sources of overhead, they provide the benefit of maintaining the coherency blocks small, avoiding false sharing. Recent work in Shasta[SGT96] has demonstrated that, with low-latency networks, software-based checks do not incur major overhead, even compared to some hardware

Table 1. Entry of the management table

addr	pointer into the real (local) memory (4)
copyowner	pointer to a list of PEs holding a copy (4)
owner	the block owner (2)
copyowers	# of PEs with copies (2)
havedata	A flag indicating whether data is present (1)
lock	Lock (1)
dummy	Padding (2)

() indicates the number of bytes for the field

based DSMs. Moreover, for portability, software-based checks are substantially better than paged-based checks, as the latter would incur adapting to differing APIs and semantics of trapping page faults and upcalling into the user code for a variety of operating systems.

We note that, with languages such as Java which does not have templates, more program transformation responsibility will be delegated to metaprogramming. It would be interesting to compare the real tradeoffs of the use of templates versus metaprograms from the perspective of performance, code size, ease-of-programmability, etc.

Distributed Shared Array Class Distributed Shared Array Class is a template class written in MPC++. The class implements a shared array as the name implies, and objects are allocated on all the PEs. For the current version, the memory consistency protocol is write-invalidate with sequential consistency, and weaker coherence protocols and algorithms such as LRC[Kel94] are not employed. The array elements are organized in terms of consistency block size, which is the unit of memory transfer among the nodes. The size of the block can be specified with BlockSize, and can be of arbitrary 2^n size. The management tables of the block resides entirely within the class. Each entry in the table is as shown in Table 1, and is aligned to 16 bytes to minimize the cost of address calculations. When the memory allocation method allocate(size) is called, (size/BlockSize) entry management table is created, and each PE allocates (size/#PE) memory for storage (excluding the copies).

Read Access Processing Because we employ the array access operator [], we overload the [] operator in the distributed shared array class. The overloaded behavior is as follows:

1. If the havedata flag is true, then return that address.
2. If the havedata flag is not true, then allocate the necessary copy block, and request for copying of the block contents to the block owner by passing the MPC++ global pointer to the owner.
3. The requested owner of the block remotely writes the contents of the block onto the copy block pointed to by the global pointer.
4. After the write is finished, the local address of the copy block is returned.

Write Access Processing The write access overloads the () operator, but recall that the OMPC++ metaclasses have inserted the lock methods WriteStart() and WriteEnd(). The overloaded behavior is as follows, for write invalidation. Other protocols could be easily accommodated.

1. WriteStart() sets the `lock` flag of the corresponding management table entry. If it is already locked, then wait.
2. If the PE is the block owner, and there are copies elsewhere, then issue invalidation messages to the PEs with copies.
3. If the PE does not have the block data, then request for a copy in the same manner as the read.
4. If the PE is not the block owner, then transfer the ownership. The previous owner notifies to the other PEs that the ownership change has occurred.
5. The operator () checks the `havedata` flag, and returns its address.
6. WriteEnd() resets the `lock` flag.

Optimizations Minimizing software overhead is essential for the success of software DSM algorithms. Upon analysis, one finds that the overhead turns out to not be caused by invalidation, but primarily due to the reads/writes which require address translation and barrier checks. In OMPC++, we optimize this in the following way. For accessing the management table entries, we have made the entry size to be 2^n so that shifts could be used instead of multiplications and divisions. The overloaded [] and () operators as well as WriteStart() and WriteEnd() are inlined. Moreover, the block address computed in the last access is cached; as a result, if one accesses the same block repeatedly (which is the assumed action of "good" DSM programs in any case), read/write access speed are substantially improved.

One could further define sophisticated metaclasses to perform more through analysis and program transformation to physically eliminate coherency messages, as is seen in [LJ98]. As to whether such analysis are easily encodable in terms of compiler metaclasses of OpenC++ is an interesting issue, and we are looking into the matter.

4 Performance Evaluation

The current version of OMPC++ is approximately 700 lines of code, which consists of 250 lines of metaclass code, and 450 lines of template runtime code. This shows that, by the use of reflection, we were able to implement a portable DSM system with substantially less effort compared to traditional systems.

In order to investigate whether OMPC++ is sufficiently fast for real parallel programs, we are currently undertaking extensive performance, analysis, pitting OMPC++ with other software-based DSM algorithms, as well as large-scale SMP systems such as the 64-node Enterprise 10000. Here we report on some of our preliminary results on the PC cluster, including the basic, low-level benchmarks, as well as some parallel numerical application kernels, namely the CG kernel, and the SPLASH2[WOT+95] FFT kernel and LU.

4.1 Evaluation Environment

Evaluation environment is a small subset of the PC Cluster II developed at RWCP (Real-World Computing Partnership) in Tsukuba, Japan. The subset embodies 8–10 200MHz Pentium Pro PC nodes with 64MB memory (of which 8 is used for benchmarking), and interconnected by the Myrinet Gigabit network (LinkSpeed 160MB/s). The OS for this system is the Linux 2.0.36-based version of SCore, and uses MPC++ Version 2.0 Level 0 MTTL as mentioned. The underlying compiler is pgcc 1.1.1, and the optimization flags are "-O6 -mpentiumpro -fomit-frame-pointer -funroll-loops -fstrength-reduce -ffast-math -fexpensive-optimizations". For comparative environment, we use the Sparc Enterprise Server 4000, with 10 250MHz UltraSparc II/1Mb, and 1Gb of memory. The Sun CC 4.2 optimization options are "-fast -xcg92 -xO5".

4.2 Basic Performance

As a underlying performance basis, we measured the read/write access times. For access patterns to shared arrays, we measured continues access, strided access, and write access with invalidation.

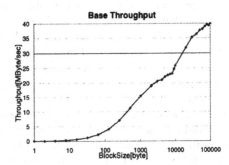

Fig. 7. Throughput of basic remote memory operations

Continuous Read/Write Accesses We measured the total read/write access times of size 1024×1024 double shared array. All the blocks are setup so that they reside on other PEs; in other words, none of the blocks are initially owned or cached. For reads, this obviously means that accesses must first start by fetching the copies. For writes, since none of the blocks are cached on any of the PEs, write access does not involve invalidation, and thus most of the incurred overhead is remote writes.

We show the averaged times of a single access for different block sizes in Fig. 8. For both reads and writes, average access time decreases with increased block size. This is naturally due to amortization of message handling and lock processing overhead. When block size increases further, we see a falloff due such amortization has mostly making the overhead negligible, and the speed is primarily determined by the network bandwidth. For `BlockSize` 64kbytes, it is 0.34μsec/1dword, which corresponds to 23.5Mbytes/sec. By comparison, raw MPC++ RemoteMemoryRead is approximately 40Mbytes/sec (Fig. 7). The difference here is the cost of address translation and barrier on the read operation.

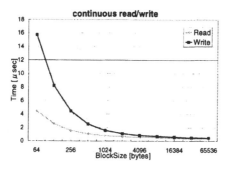

Fig. 8. Cost of Continuous Reads and Writes Accesses

Strided Read/Write Accesses Strided Access is a worse-case scenario where the arrays are serially accessed at a stride, and the stride is equal to `BlockSize`. As a result, no cached access can occur, but rather the entire block must be transferred per each memory access. The size and the initialization of memory is identical to the continuous access. However, the number of elements accessed would differ according to the stride. The results are shown in Fig. 9. As we can see, the access times increase along with the increase in `BlockSize`. This is due to increased memory transfer per each access. Also, the difference between read and write diminishes; this is because the transfer times become dominant, despite using a very fast network, as opposed to software overhead such as address translation and locking.

Accesses with Invalidation Because we currently employ the standard write-invalidate algorithm, the read cost will remain constant, while the write cost could increase as the number of shared copies of the block increases, as invalidate message has to be broadcast to all the PEs holding the copy. In order to measure the overhead, we varied the number of PEs with copies to 0,1,2,6, and the `BlockSize` to 1kbytes and 16kbytes, whose result is shown in Table 2. Here, we observe that for such small number of sharings, the differences are negligible. This is because message passing of MPC++ on SCore is physically

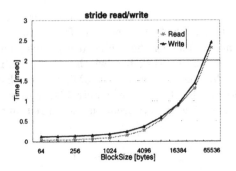

Fig. 9. Cost of Strided Read and Write Accesses

asynchronous, and as a result, multiple invalidations are being effectively issued in parallel. Also, access times is independent of block size, as invalidation does not transfer any memory, so its cost is independent of the BlockSize.

One might argue that for a larger number of sharing, parallelism in the network interface would saturate, resulting in increased cost. While this is true, research has shown that average number of sharing for invalidation-based protocol is typically below 3. This is fundamental to the nature of the write-invalidate algorithm, as shared blocks are thrown away per each write.

Table 2. Cost of Write Accesses with Invalidation (BlockSize=1kbytes,16kbytes)

	Time(μsec)	
Sharings (#PEs)	BlockSize 1kbytes	BlockSize 16kbytes
0	4.80	5.26
1	31.27	33.05
2	46.06	48.27
6	76.68	78.24

4.3   CG (Conjugate Gradient Solver Kernel)

As a typical parallel numerical application, we employ the CG (Conjugate Gradient) Solver Kernel, without preconditioning. As a comparative basis, we execute the equivalent sequential program on one of the nodes of the PC cluster, and also on the Sun Ultra60(UltraSPARC II 300MHz, 256Mbytes, Sun CC 4.2). Here are the parameters for the measurements:

- Problem sizes: 16129 (197 iterations), 261121 (806 iterations)
- BlockSizes: 256, 1k, 4k, 16kbytes
- Number of PEs: 1, 2, 4, 8

The results are shown in Fig. 10 and Fig. 11.

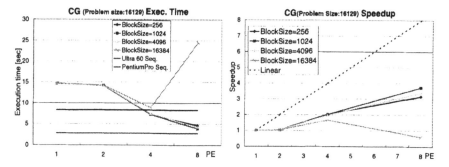

Fig. 10. CG Kernel Result, Problem Size=16129

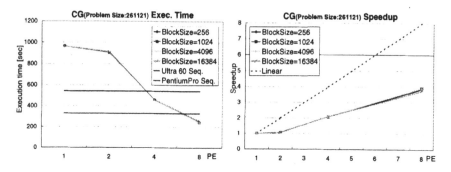

Fig. 11. CG Kernel Result, Problem Size=261121

According to the results of Fig. 10, we obtain only about 5% speedup from 1PE to 2PEs, whereas we observe approximately linear speedups from 2PEs to 8PEs. This is primarily due to the software overhead of DSM, in particular write-invalidation does not occur for 1PE, whereas they do occur for 2PEs and above. Even with 8PEs, we do not match the speed of sequential UltraSparc II 300MHz, which has much faster floating performance than a Pentium Pro 200MHz. We do attain about factor of 2 speedup over a sequential execution on a cluster PC node. For BlockSize of 16KB, we see that performance degrades significantly. This is due to the overhead of excessive data transfer.

With larger problem size as in Fig. 11, the overall characteristics remain the same. We still see speedups of range 3.8 to 4.0 with 8 processors. Here, BlockSize is almost irrelevant for overall performance; this is because, as the amount of data required for computation is substantially larger than BlockSize, and thus we do not have wasteful internote data transfers. On the other hand, compared to overall computation, the software overhead of message handling is negligibly small.

We also executed the same program on the Sun Enterprise 4000 (UltraSPARC II 250MHz, 10PEs). There the speedup was approximately 6 with 8 processors. The overhead is primarily due to barrier operations.

4.4 SPLASH2 FFT and LU

Finally, we tested the SPLASH2 [WOT+95] FFT and LU kernel (Fig. 12) with 1kbytes BlockSize. In FFT, the problem size is 64Kpoints. In LU, the matrix size is 512.

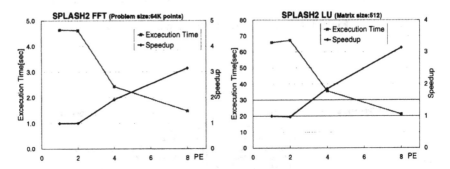

Fig. 12. SPLASH2 FFT and LU

As was with the CG kernel, speedup curves are similar. The required change to the original SPLASH2 was approximately 70 lines out of the 1008 in FFT, 80 lines out of the 1030 in LU, mostly the required top-level program structure (with sdsm_main, etc.) and memory allocations.

Shasta employs various low-level optimization strategies, that have not been implemented on OMPC++, such as bunching multiple read-/write-accesses. As an experiment, to qualify the effect of bunching technique, we manually applied it to the daxpy function in the LU kernel on OMPC++, attaining about factor of 2 speedup in terms of the total execution time(Fig. 13).

5   Related Work

There are several work on implementing DSM features using program trans-formations [SGT96]. All of them have had to develop their own preprocessor,

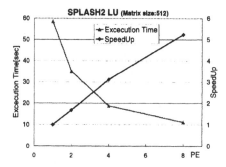

Fig. 13. SPLASH2 LU with bunched read-/write-accesses

and is thus expensive, and furthermore not portable nor adaptable to complex programming languages such as C++. By utilizing the reflective features of OpenC++, we have demonstrated that, developing a program transformer for an efficient DSM system was an easy effort with a small number of metaclass customizations, much easier to maintain and tune the code. In fact, substantial tuning and experimentation was possible by small changes to the metacode.

Shasta [SGT96] is a DSM system that performs program transformation at program load time, and is thus more language independent than other program transformation systems. Shasta is specifically tailored to work on DEC Alpha PEs interconnected by the MemoryChannel low-latency gigabit network. Shasta is extremely efficient, in that it optimizes the read/write barrier overhead for common cases down to two instructions. This is currently possible because Shasta performs program transformation at the binary level. On the other hand, Shasta is much harder to port to other platforms, as it is hardware and processor-binary dependent. There are numerous low-level optimization techniques that Shasta uses, that have not been implemented on OMPC++. We are planning to exploit such techniques with more metaprogramming, with the aid of better optimizing compilers such as Kai C++.

Midway[BZS93] and CRL[JKW95] are object-based DSM systems. Midway employs entry consistency as the coherency protocol, and read/write barriers are inserted by a special compiler. Thus, one must craft such a compiler, and as such portability and extensibility suffers. For example, it is difficult to add a new coherency protocol or porting to different hardware platform without detailed knowledge of the compiler. On the other hand, in CRL, the barriers must be inserted by the user. This is quite error-prone, and such bugs would be very hard to detect, as they will be dynamic, transient memory bugs. By using reflection, OMPC++ was created by only small set of customization in the underlying workings of the C++, and is easily understandable, thus being easily maintainable, customizable, and portable.

As a common shared memory programming API, OpenMP[Ope97] has been proposed as a standard. In OpenMP, the user adds appropriate annotations to the source code to indicate potential SPMD parallelism and distribution to sequential code, and the compiler emits the appropriate parallel code. OpenMP suffers from the same problem as Midway, as customized preprocessor/compiler must be built. It would be interesting to investigate whether OpenMP (or at least, its subset) could be implemented using reflective features to indicate DSM optimizations.

In perspective, with respect to the maintainability, customizability, and portability of DSM systems,

- Traditional page-based DSM systems must have OS-dependent code to trap memory reference via a page fault. Also, overhead is known to be significant.
- Link-time DSM systems such as Shasta is efficient, but is platform and processor-binary dependent.
- Class-based systems requires the user to insert appropriate read/write barriers, and is thus error prone and/or only a certain set of classes can be shared.
- Macros or ad-hoc preprocessor are hard to build and maintain, let alone customize or be portable, and complete support of complex programming languages such as C++ is difficult.

6 Conclusion and Future Work

We have described OMPC++, a portable and efficient DSM system implemented using compile-time reflection. OMPC++ consists of a small set of OpenC++ 2.5 metaclasses and template classes and is thus easy to customize and port to different platforms. OMPC++ is a first step to realization of reflective framework for portable and efficient support of various parallel programming models across a wide variety of machines. Such characteristics are necessary as increasingly in the days of network-wide computing, where a piece of code could be executed anywhere in a diverse network.

OMPC++ was shown to be efficient for a set of basic as well as parallel numerical kernel benchmarks on the RWC PC cluster platform.

As a future work, we are pursuing the following issues:

More comprehensive benchmarking The number of benchmarked programs, processors, and comparative platforms, are still small. We are currently conducting a set of comprehensive benchmarks by adding more SPLASH2 benchmarks (Water, Barnes), on larger platforms (64-processor RWCP cluster and 64-processor Sparc Enterprise Server 10000), pitting against other DSM platforms (developed at RWCP). We are also attempting alternative algorithms, both for coherency and barriers. We will report the findings in another paper after more analysis is done.

More efficient implementation Although OMPC++ went under some tuning process, the read/write barriers and locks are still expensive. Although in our preliminary benchmarks we are finding that OMPC++ is competitive with other DSM implementations, we need to further enhance efficiency. For example, Shasta only requires two instructions for barriers, much smaller than ours, and employs various low-level optimization strategies such as bunching multiple read-/write-accesses. Also, raw MPC++ Remote-MemoryRead throughput is 40MByte/sec, whereas OMPC++ throughput is 23.5MByte/sec. This is due to address translation and table accesses. We are considering altering the runtime data structures to further eliminate the overhead.

Porting to other platforms OMPC++ currently is implemented on top of MPC++ and RWC cluster. In order to port to different platforms, one must alter the dependency on MPC++, if it is not available. In principle this is simple to do, as one must only provide (1) threads, (2) remote memory read/write, and (3) global barriers. This can be easily implemented using MPI or other message passing platforms such as Illinois Fast Messages. Alternatively one could make MPC++ to be more portable, which is our current project in collaboration with RWC. In all cases, we must analyze and exhibit the portability and efficiency of OMPC++ to validate that implementing DSM systems with reflection is the right idea.

Other coherency protocols On related terms, we should support other coherency protocols, such as write-update, as well as weak coherency models such as LRC and ALRC. The latter will fundamentally require changes to the source code, and it would be interesting to investigate how much of this simplified using open compilers.

Portable DSM on Java using OpenJIT Finally, we are planning to implement a Java version of DSM using OpenJIT, our reflective Java Just-In-Time compiler. As of Feb. 1, 1999, We have almost completed the implementation of OpenJIT, and will start our implementation as soon as OpenJIT is complete.

Acknowledgment

We would like to thank Shigeru Chiba for his support in the use of OpenC++, and the members of RWCP for their support in the usage of MPC++ plus the RWC cluster. Also, we would like to thank the Dept. of Information Science, the Univ. of Tokyo for allowing experiments on their Sparc Enterprise Server 10000. We finally thank the members of the Tsukuba TEA group for fruitful discussions on performance analysis of SPMD and DSM systems.

References

[ACD+96] C. Amza, A.L. Cox, S. Dwarkadas, P. Keleher, H. Lu, R. Rajamony, W. Yu, and W. Zwaenepoel. TreadMarks: Shared Memory Computing on Networks of Warkstations. *IEEE Computer*, 29(2):18–28, Feb. 1996.

[Beo] Beowulf Project. Beowulf Homepage. http://beowulf.gsfc.nasa.gov/.

[BZS93] Brain N. Bershad, Matthew J. Zekauskas, and Wayne A. Sawdown. The Midway Distributed Shared Memory System. In *Proceedings of the IEEE CompCon Conference*, 1993.

[Chi95]   Shigeru Chiba. A Metaobject Protocol for C++. In *Proceedings of OOP-SLA '95*, pages 285–299, 1995.

[Chi97]   Shigeru Chiba. *OpenC++ 2.5 Reference Mannual*, 1997.

[Ie96]   Yutaka Ishikawa and et.al. Design and Implementation of Metalevel Architecture in C++ – MPC++ Approach –. In *Proceedings of Reflection'96*, Apr. 1996.

[Ish96]   Yutaka Ishikawa. Multiple Threads Template Library – MPC++ Version2.0 Level 0 Document –. TR 96012, RWCP, 1996.

[JKW95]   Kirk L. Johnson, M. Frans Kaashoek, and Deborah A. Wallach. CRL: High-Performance All-Software Distributed Shared Memory. In *Proceedings of the Fifteenth Symosium on Operating Systems Principles*, Dec. 1995.

[Kel94]   Pete Keleher. *Lazy Release Consistency for Distributed Shared Memory*. PhD thesis, Dept. of Computer Science, Rice University, Dec. 1994.

[LH89]   K. Li and P. Hudak. Memory Coherence in Shared Virtual Memory Systems. *ACM Transactions on Computer Systems*, 7(4):321–359, Nov 1989.

[LJ98]   Jae Bum Lee and Chu Shik Jhon. Reducing Coherence Overhead of Barrier Synchronization in Software DSMs. In *SC'98*, Nov. 1998.

[MOS+98]   Satoshi Matsuoka, Hirotaka Ogawa, Kouya Shimura, Yasunori Kimura, and Koichiro Hotta. OpenJIT — A Reflective Java JIT Compiler. In *Proceedings of OOPSLA'98 Workshop on Reflective Programming in C++ and Java*, pages 16–20, Oct. 1998.

[Myr]   Myricom, Inc. Myricom Homepage. http://www.myri.com/.

[Ope97]   OpenMP Architecture Review Board. *OpenMP: A Proposed Industry Standard API for Shared Memory Programming.*, Oct. 1997.

[SGT96]   Daniel J. Scales, Kourosh Gharachorloo, and Chandramohan A. Thekkath. Shasta: A Low Overhead, Software-Only Approach for Supporting Fine-Grain Shared Memory. In *Proceedings of ASPLOS VII*, Oct. 1996.

[Suif]   Stanford Univ. SUIF Homepage. http://www-suif.stanford.edu/.

[WOT+95]   Steven Cameron Woo, Moriyoshi Ohara, Evan Torrie, Jaswinder Pal Singh, and Anoop Gupta. The SPLASH-2 Programs: Characterization and Methodological Considerations. In *Proceedings of the 22nd Annual International Symposium on Computer Architecture*, pages 24–36, Jun. 1995.

Metaprogramming Domain Specific Metaprograms

Tristan Cazenave

Laboratoire d'Intelligence Artificielle,
Département Informatique, Université Paris 8,
2 rue de la Liberté,
93526 Saint Denis, France.
cazenave@ai.univ-paris8.fr

Abstract. When a metaprogram automatically creates rules, some created rules are useless because they can never apply. Some metarules, that we call impossibility metarules, are used to remove useless rules. Some of these metarules are general and apply to any generated program. Some are domain specific metarules. In this paper, we show how dynamic metaprogramming can be used to create domain specific impossibility metarules. Applying metaprogramming to impossibility metaprogramming avoids writing specific metaprogram for each domain metaprogramming is applied to. Our meta-metaprograms have been used to write metaprograms that write search rules for different games and planning domains. They write programs that write selective and efficient search programs.

1 Introduction

Knowledge about the moves to try enables to select a small number of moves from a possibly large set of possible moves. It is very important in complex games and planning domains where search trees have a large branching factor. Knowing the moves to try drastically cuts the search trees. Metaprogramming can be used to automatically create the knowledge about interesting and forced moves, only given the rules about the direct effects of the moves [4],[5]. Impossibility metaprograms enable to remove useless rules from the set of unfolded rules. These metaprograms can themselves be written by metametaprograms. From a more general point of view, metaknowledge itself can be very useful for a wide range of applications [23], and one of its fascinating characteristic is that it can be applied to itself to improve itself. We try to experimentally evaluate the benefits one can get from this special property.

The second section describes metaprogramming and especially metaprogramming in games. The third section uncovers how metametaprograms can be used to write impossibility metaprograms. The fourth section gives experimental results.

2 Metaprogramming in games and planning domains

Our metaprograms write programs that enable to safely cut search trees, therefore enabling large speedups of search programs. In our applications to games, metarules are used to create theorems that tell the interesting moves to try to achieve a tactical goal (at OR nodes). They are also used to create rules that find the complete set of forced moves that prevent the opponent to achieve a tactical goal (at AND nodes). Metaprogramming in logic has already attracted some interest [11],[2],[9]. More specifically, specialization of logic program by fold/unfold transformations can be traced back to [26], it has been well defined and related to Partial Evaluation in [15], and successfully applied to different domains [9]. The parallel between Partial Evaluation and Explanation-Based Learning [21],[18],[6],[13],[24] is now well-known [28],[7]. As Pitrat [23] points it, the ability for programs to reason on the rules of a game so as to extract useful knowledge to play is a problem essential for the future of AI. It is a step toward the realization of efficient general problem solvers.

In our system, two kinds of metarules are particularly important : impossibility metarules and monovaluation metarules. Other metarules such as metarules removing useless conditions or ordering metarules are used to speed-up the generated programs.

Impossibility metarules find which rules can never be applied because of some properties of the game, or because of more general impossibilities. An example of a metarule about a general impossibility is the following one :

```
impossible(ListAtoms):-
        member(N=\=N1,ListAtoms),var(N),var(N1),N==N1.
```

This metarule tells that if a rule created by the system contains the condition 'N=\=N1' and the metavariables N and N1 contain the same variable, then the condition can never be fulfilled. So the rule can never apply because it contains a statement impossible to verify. These metarule is particularly simple, but this is the kind of general knowledge a metasystem must have to be able to reason about rules and to create rules given the definition of a game.

Some of the impossibility metarules are more domain specific. For example the following rule is specific to the game of Go :

```
impossible(ListAtoms):-
        member(color_string(B,C),ListAtoms),C==empty.
```

It tells that the color of a string can never be the color 'empty'.

The other important metarules in our metaprogramming system are the monovaluation metarules. They apply when two variables in the same rules always share the same value. Monovaluation metarules unify such variables. They enable to simplify the rules and to detect more impossible rules. An example of a monovaluation metarule is :

```
monovaluation(ListAtoms):-
        member(color_string(B,C),ListAtoms),
        member(color_string(B1,C1),ListAtoms),
        B==B1,C\==C1,C=C1.
```

It tells that a string can only have one color. So if the system finds two conditions 'color_string' in a rule such that the variables contained in the metavariables 'B' and 'B1' are equals, and if the corresponding color variables contained in the metavariables 'C' and 'C1' are not the same, it unifies C and C1 because they always contain the same value.

Impossible and monovaluation metarules are vital rules of our metaprogramming system. They enable to reduce significantly the number of rules created by the system, eliminating many useless rules. For example, we tested the unfolding of six rules with and without these metarules. Without the metarules, the system created 166 391 568 rules by regressing the 6 rules on only one move. Using basic mono-valuation and impossible metarules shows that only 106 rules where valid and different from each other.

The experiments described here use the goal of taking enemy stones to create rules for the game of Go. The game of Go is known to be the most difficult game to program [27],[1],[25]. Experiments in solving problems for the hardest game benefit to other games, and to other planning domains, especially if these experiments use general and widely applicable methods as it is the case for our metaprogramming methods.

3 Programs that write programs that write programs

Works on writing programs that write programs that write programs often refer to the third Futamura projection. Their goal is to speed up programs that write programs using self-application of Partial Evaluation. Self-applicable partial evaluators such as Goëdel [11] usually use a ground representation to enable self-application (a ground representation consists in representing variables in the programs by numbers, a parallel can be made with the numbering technique used by the mathematician Kurt Gödel to prove his famous theorem [10]). Our choice is rather to use general non-ground metaprograms that find domain specific metaknowledge to write the programs that write programs. On the contrary of fold/unfold/generalization and other program transformation techniques [20], our system only uses unfolding, and simple metaprograms can be written to decide when to stop unfolding: typically when generated rules have more condition than a pre-defined threshold.

Domain specific metarules in games and planning domains can be divided in different categories. We will focus on the 'board topology metarules' category in this section. Other categories that are often used are 'move metarules' or 'object metarules' for example.

The essential property of a game board is that it never changes whatever the moves are. The set of facts describing the board is always the same. Moreover it is a complete set: no facts can be added or removed.

In this paper, we will use a fixed grid to give examples of metaprogram generation. Grids are used in planning domains, for example for a robot to plan a path through a building, and in games such as Go or Go-Moku.

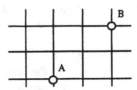

Fig. 1. A robot at point A has to choose a path on the grid to go to point B

The grid task consists in finding a path of length four between point A and point B in the figure 1. This task is easier to understand than the game of Go which is our principal application. A Go board is also a grid, and all the mechanisms described in this paper also apply to the rules generated by our metaprogram for the game of Go.

3.1 Metaprogramming impossibility metarules

The figure 2 gives all the points that are at distance three of point A. After each new instanciation of a variable containing a point, the rule verifies that the instanciated point is different from any previously instanciated one.

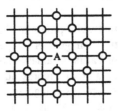

Fig. 2. All the points at a distance three of point A are marked.

The rule that find all these points is generated as follows:

```
distance(X,W,3):-
            connected(X,Y),connected(Y,Z),connected(Z,W).
```

This rule is generated unfolding the goal 'distance(X,W,3)' defined below:

```
distance(X,X,0).
distance(X,W,N1):-
            N is N1-1,distance(X,Z,N),connected(Z,W).
```

On a grid, all the points that are at a distance two of X are not at a distance three. Moreover, when unfolding definitions in more complex domains, it often happens that two variables are unified, there is only one variable left after unfolding. Unfolding can lead to generate rules similar to this one:

```
distance(X,X,3):-
        connected(X,Y),connected(Y,Z),connected(Z,X).
```

This rule has been correctly generated by a correct metaprogram on a correct domain theory, but it is a rule that will never be applied, because no point on a grid is at a distance three of itself.

We can detect that this rule cannot be fired because we have access to the complete set of facts representing the topology of the board in this domain. In the generated rules, we only select the conditions that are related to the topology of the board (the connected predicates and the test that are done on the variables representing intersections of the grid). Then we fire this set of conditions on the complete set of facts. If the set of conditions never matches, we are confident that the system has generated an impossible set of conditions. In order to find the minimal set of impossible conditions, the system tries to remove the conditions one by one until each removed condition leads to a possible set of conditions. We now have a minimal set of conditions representing a subset of the initial rule that is impossible to match. In our simple example of the distance three goal, it is composed of the three conditions of the rule.

Once this subset is created, it is used to generate a new impossibility metarule. Impossibility metarules match generated rules to find subsets of impossible conditions. If an impossibility metarule succeeds, the generated rule is removed. The impossibility metarule generated in our example is:

```
impossible(ListAtoms):-
        member(connected(X,Y),ListAtoms),
        var(X),var(Y),X\==Y,
        member(connected(A,Z),ListAtoms),
        A==Y,var(A),var(Z),A\==Z,
        member(connected(B,C),ListAtoms),
        B==Z,var(B),var(C),B\==C,C==X.
```

The generation of impossibility metarules is useful in almost all the planning domains we have studied. Here is another example of its usefulness for the game of Abalone.

Fig. 3. An abalone board at the beginning of the game

The figure 3 represents an Abalone board, on this board, each position has six neighbors instead of four for the grid board. Each neighbor is associated to one of the six directions represented by numbers ranging from 1 to 6.

Fig. 4. The directions a stone can be moved to are marked, ranging from one to six.

In the rules of the game and therefore in the rules generated by our metaprogram, the connected predicates contain a slot for the direction. Here is an example of an impossible set of conditions in the game of Abalone :

```
connected(X,Y,Direction),connected(Y,X,Direction),
```

The corresponding impossibility metarule for the game of Abalone is:

```
impossible(ListAtoms):-
          member(connected(X,Y,D),ListAtoms),
          member(connected(A,B,C),ListAtoms),
          A==Y,B==X,C==D.
```

It is also generated using our metametaprogram that generate impossibility metarules.

3.2 Metaprogramming simplifying metarules

The system sometimes generates some rules that contain useless conditions. We give below a rule that finds a path of length four to go from one point of a grid to another one without going twice through the same point. After each new instanciation of a variable in the conditions, the rule verifies that the instanciated point is different from any previously instanciated one.

After each condition in the rule, we give the number of times the condition has been verified when matching the rule once on a set of facts.

```
distance(X,D,4):-
        connected(X,Y),                     4
        X=\=Y,                              4
        connected(Y,Z),                     16
        Z=\=X,                              12
        Z=\=Y,                              12
        connected(Z,W),                     48
        W=\=X,                              48
        W=\=Y,                              36
        W=\=Z,                              36
        connected(W,D).                     144
```

However, in some cases, it is useless to verify that some points are different due to the topology of the grid. For example, two connected points are always different. We can use a metarule that tells to remove the condition 'X=\=Y' if the condition 'connected(X,Y)' is also present in the rule:

```
useless(X=\=Y,ListAtoms):-
        member(connected(X,Y),ListAtoms),
        member(A=\=B,ListAtoms),A==X,B==Y.
```

Another metarule, given below, removes the condition 'X=\=Y' when there is a path of length three between the two points contained in X and Y, this is a consequence of the figure 2 that shows all the points that are at a three step path from point A: A is not at a three step path of itself.

```
useless(X=\=Z,ListAtoms):-
        member(connected(X,Y),ListAtoms),
        var(X),var(Y),X\==Y,
        member(connected(Y,Z),ListAtoms),
        var(Y),var(Z),Y\==Z,
        member(connected(Z,A),ListAtoms),
        var(Z),var(A),Z\==Y,A==X.
```

The initial rule makes 361 instanciations and tests. After firing the metarule of deletion on the initial rule, we obtain the rule below that only makes 261 instanciations or tests with the same results.

```
distance(X,D,4):-
        connected(X,Y),                     4
        connected(Y,Z),                     16
        Z=\=X,                              12
        connected(Z,W),                     48
```

```
W=\=Y,                                    36
connected(W,D).                           144
```

The simplifying metarules described here can also be generated using a complete set of facts representing the board topology.

For example, if our system analyzes a rule containing the conditions:

```
connected(X,Y),X=\=Y,
```

in this order. It observes that the condition `'X=\=Y'` is always fulfilled. So it tries to remove all the conditions of the rule one by one, provided the condition `'X=\=Y'` is always fulfilled when matching the set of remaining conditions. At the end of this process, the final set of conditions only contains the two above conditions, and the condition `'X=\=Y'` is always fulfilled for all the complete set of facts in the working memory. As the set of fact representing the topology of the board is complete, it can generate a new simplifying metarule that will apply to all the generated rules of this domain. This simplifying metarule is the one given above.

This method works in all planning domains where a complete set of facts can be isolated, such as the topology of the board, for games where the topology cannot be changed by the moves.

3.3 Metaprogramming ordering metarules

Related Work
P. Laird [14] uses statistics on some runs of a program to reorder and to unfold clauses of this program. T. Ishida [12] also dynamically uses some simple heuristics to find a good ordering of conditions for a production system. Our approach is somewhat different, it takes examples of working memories to create metarules that will be used to reorder the clauses. What we do, is automatically creating a metaprogram that is used to reorder the clauses, and not dynamically reordering conditions of the rules. One advantage is that we can create this metaprogram independently. Moreover, once the metaprogram is created, running it to reorder learned rules is faster than dynamically optimizing the learned rules. This feature is important for systems that use a large number of generated rules. The creation of the metaprogram is also fast.

We rely on the assumption that domain-dependent information can enhance problem solving [16]. This assumption is given experimental evidence on constraint satisfaction problems by S. Minton [17]. On the contrary of Minton, we do not specialize heuristics on specific problems instances, we rather create metaprograms according to specific distributions of working memories.

Reordering conditions
Reordering conditions is very important for the performance of generated rules. The two following rules are simple examples that show the importance of a good order

of conditions. The two rules give the same results but do not have the same efficacy when X is known and Y unknown:

```
sisterinlaw(X,Y):-brother(X,X1),married(X1,Y),woman(Y).
sisterinlaw(X,Y):-woman(Y),brother(X,X1),married(X1,Y).
```

Reordering based only on the number of free variables in a condition does not work for the example above. In the constraint literature, constraints are reordered according to two heuristics concerning the variables to bind [17] : the range of values of the variables and the number of other variables it is linked to. These heuristics dynamically choose the order of constraints. But to do so, they have to keep the number of possible bindings for each variable, and to lose time when dynamically choosing the variable. It is justified in the domain of constraints solving because the range of value of a variable, affects a lot efficiency, and can change a lot from one problem to another. It is not justified in some other domains where the range of value a variable can take is more stable. We have chosen to order conditions, and thus variables, statically by reordering once for all and not dynamically at each match because it saves more time in the domains in which we have tested our approach.

Reordering optimally the conditions in a given rule is an NP-complete problem. To reorder conditions in our generated rules, we use a simple and efficient algorithm. It is based on the estimated number of following nodes the firing of a condition will create in the semi-unification tree. Here are two metarules used to reorder conditions of generated rules in the game of Go:

```
branching(ListAtoms,ListBindVariables,
          connected(X,Y),3.76):-
          member(connected(X,Y),ListAtoms),
          member_term(X,ListBindVariables),
          non_member_term(Y,ListBindVariables).

branching(ListAtoms,ListBindVariables,
          elementstring(X,Y),94.8):-
          member(elementstring(X,Y),ListAtoms),
          non_member_term(X,ListBindVariables),
          non_member_term(Y,ListBindVariables).
```

A metarule evaluates the branching factor of a condition based on the estimated mean number of facts matching the condition in the working memory. Metarules are fired each time the system has to give a branching estimation for all the conditions left to be ordered. When reordering a rule containing N conditions, the metarule will be fired N times: the first time to choose the condition to put at first in the rule, and at time number T to choose the condition to put in the Tth place. In the first reordering metarule above, the variable X is already present in some of the conditions preceding the condition to be chosen. The variable Y is not present in the preceding conditions. The condition 'connected(X,Y)' is therefore estimated to have a branching factor of 3.76 (this is the mean number of neighbor intersections of an intersection on a 19*19 grid, this number can vary from 2 to 4), this is the mean number of bindings of Y.

The branching factors of all the conditions to reorder are compared and the condition with the lowest branching factor is chosen. The algorithm is very efficient, it orders rules better than humans do and it runs fast even for rules containing more than 200 conditions.

Generating ordering metarules
For each predicate in the domain theory that has an arity less or equal than three. Each variable of the predicate free or not, leading to $2^3=8$ possibilities for the three variables. So, for each predicate, we create between 1 and 8 metarules.

For predicates of arity greater than three, we only create the metarules that corresponds to the bindings of all but one of the variables of the predicate.

All the metarules are tested on some working memories. This enables to conclude on the priority to give to the metarule. The priority is the mean number of bindings the condition will create. The lower the priority, the sooner the condition is to be matched. When all the variables of a condition are instanciated, it is a test and it has a priority between zero and one, whereas predicates containing free variables have, most of the time, a priority greater than one.

4 Results

This section gives the results and the analysis of some experiments in generating metaprograms. We used a Pentium 133 with SWI-Prolog for testing.

4.1 Metaprogramming impossibility metarules

In the figure 5, the horizontal axis represents the number of rules unfolded by our metaprogram on one move. This experiment was realized using the game of Go domain theory associated to the subgoal of taking stones of the opponent. There are six unfolded rules, it means that six rules concluding on a won subgoal of taking stones where randomly chosen out of the total number of such rules created by our system. Each of these six rules has been unfolded using the rules of the game of Go, without the cuts of impossibility and monovaluation metarules. All of the six rules to unfold, match Go boards where the friend color can take the opponent string in less than two moves, whatever the opponent plays. The goal of the unfolding was to find all the rules that find a move that lead to match one of the six rules concluding on a won state. The vertical axis of the figure 5 represents the cumulated number of rules that have been created for each of the six rules. We did not match the impossible and monovaluation metarules on the resulting rules because it would have been to time consuming.

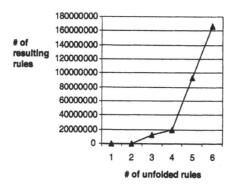

Fig. 5. Number of rules generated when unfolding six simple rules without impossibility and monovaluation metarules.

Instead of unfolding all the rules one move ahead and then destroying useless rules, we matched the monovaluation and impossibility metarules after each unfolding step (an unfolding step is the replacement of a predicate by one of its definitions). Each unfolding step is considered as a node in the unfolding tree.

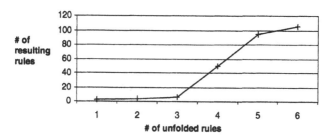

Fig. 6. Number of rules generated when unfolding six simple rules with impossibility and monovaluation metarules

This resulted in a very significant improvement of the specialization program, it was much faster and completely unfolding the six rules only gave 106 resulting rules concluding on winning moves to take stones 3 moves in advance. The results are shown in the figure 6, and can be compared with the results of the figure 5. It is important to see that among all the resulting rules of the figure 5, only the 106 resulting rules of the figure 6 are valid and different from each other.

This experiment also stresses the importance of the impossibility metarules. Without them, unfolding a goal on a domain theory is not practically feasible. Therefore impossibility metarules are necessary for such programs, and automatically generating them is a step further in the automatisation of planning programs development.

4.2 Metaprogramming ordering metarules

When no metarule concludes on the priority of the conditions left to be ordered, simple reordering heuristics are used. For example, the condition containing the less variables is chosen.

Following are two equivalent rules. The first one is ordered without metarules, and the second one is ordered using the learned metarules :

```
threattoconnect(C,B,B1,I):-
        colorintersection(I1,empty),          55
        connected(I,I1),                      208
        connected(I1,I2),                     796
        I=\=I2,                               588
        liberty(I2,B1),                       306
        colorblock(B1,C),                     140
        liberty(I,B),                          84
        colorblock(B,C),                       36
        color(C).                              36
                                             ____
                                             2249
```

```
threattoconnect(C,B,B1,I):-                    1
        color(C),                              2
        colorblock(B,C),                      14
        liberty(I,B),                         68
        connected(I,I1),                     240
        colorintersection(I1,empty),          96
        connected(I1,I2),                    350
        I=\=I2,                              254
        liberty(I2,B1),                       84
        colorblock(B1,C).                     36
                                            ____
                                            1145
```

Each condition is followed by the number of time it has been accessed during the matching of the rule. In this example, when choosing the first condition, a classic order gives 'colorintersection(I,empty)' in the first rule. In the second rule, the two following metarules where matched among others to assign priorities to conditions :

```
branching(ListAtoms,ListBindVariables,
          colorintersection(I,C),240.8):-
          member(colorintersection(I,C),ListAtoms),
          C==empty,
          non_member_term(I,ListBindVariables).
```

```
branching(ListAtoms,ListBindVariables,color(C),2):-
          member(color(C),ListAtoms),
          non_member_term(C,ListBindVariables).
```

Therefore, the condition 'color(C)' has been chosen because it has the lowest branching factor.

The two rules given in the example are simple rules. Speedups are more important with rules containing more conditions.

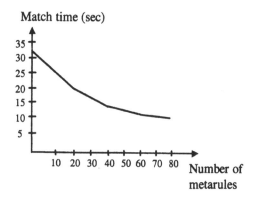

Fig. 7. The match time of generated rules decreases when more ordering metarules are generated and used.

The figure 7 gives the evolution of the matching time of a set of generated rules with the number of metarules generated. The evolution is computed on a test set of 50 problems. Problems in the test set are different from the problems used to generate the metarules.

5 Conclusion

Metaprogramming games and planning domains is considered as an interesting challenge for AI [19],[23]. Moreover it has advantages over traditional approaches: metaprograms automatically create the rules that otherwise take a lot of time to create, and the results of the search trees developed using the generated programs are more reliable than the results of the search trees developed using traditional heuristic and hand-coded rules.

The Go program that uses the rules resulting of the metaprogramming has good results in international competitions (6 out of 40 in 1997 FOST cup [8], 6 out of 17 in 1998 world computer Go championship). The metaprogramming methods presented here can be applied in many games and in other domains than games. They have been applied to other games like Abalone and Go-Moku, and to planning problems [3]. Using metaprogramming this way is particularly suited to automatically create complex, efficient and reliable programs in domains that are complex enough to require a lot of knowledge to cut search trees.

However metaprogramming large programs can be itself time consuming. We have proposed and evaluated methods to apply metaprogramming to itself so as to

make it more efficient. These methods gave successful results. Moreover they tend
to give even better results when generated programs become more complex.

6 References

1. Allis, L. V.: Searching for Solutions in Games an Artificial Intelligence. Ph.D. diss., Vrije
   Universitat Amsterdam, Maastricht 1994.
2. Barklund J. : Metaprogramming in Logic. UPMAIL Technical Report N° 80, Uppsala,
   Sweden, 1994.
3. Cazenave, T.: Système d'Apprentissage par Auto-Observation. Application au Jeu de Go.
   Ph.D. diss., Université Paris 6, 1996.
4. Cazenave T.: Metaprogramming Forced Moves. Proceedings ECAI98, Brigthon, 1998.
5. Cazenave T.: Controlled Partial Deduction of Declarative Logic Programs. ACM Computing Surveys, Special issue on Partial Evaluation, 1998.
6. Dejong, G. and Mooney, R.: Explanation Based Learning : an alternative view. Machine
   Learning 1 (2), 1986.
7. Etzioni, O.: A structural theory of explanation-based learning. Artificial Intelligence 60
   (1), pp. 93-139, 1993.
8. Fotland D. and Yoshikawa A.: The 3rd fost-cup world-open computer-go championship.
   ICCA Journal 20 (4):276-278, 1997.
9. Gallagher J.: Specialization of Logic Programs. Proceedings of the ACM SIGPLAN
   Symposium on PEPM'93, Ed. David Schmidt, ACM Press, Copenhagen, Danemark,
   1993.
10. Gödel K.: 'Über formal unentscheidbare Sätze der Principia Mathematica und verwandter
    Systeme I', Monatsh. Math. Phys. 38, 173-98, 1931.
11. Hill P. M. and Lloyd J. W.: The Gödel Programming Language. MIT Press, Cambridge,
    Mass., 1994.
12. Ishida T.: Optimizing Rules in Production System Programs, AAAI 1988, pp 699-704,
    1988.
13. Laird, J.; Rosenbloom, P. and Newell A. Chunking in SOAR : An Anatomy of a General
    Learning Mechanism. Machine Learning 1 (1), 1986.
14. Laird P.: Dynamic Optimization. ICML-92, pp. 263-272, 1992.
15. Lloyd J. W. and Shepherdson J. C.: Partial Evaluation in Logic Programming. J. Logic
    Programming, 11 :217-242., 1991.
16. Minton S.: Is There Any Need for Domain-Dependent Control Information : A Reply.
    AAAI-96, 1990.
17. S. Minton. Automatically Configuring Constraints Satisfaction Programs : A Case Study.
    Constraints, Volume 1, Number 1, 1996.
18. Mitchell, T. M.; Keller, R. M. and Kedar-Kabelli S. T.: Explanation-based Generaliza-
    tion : A unifying view. Machine Learning 1 (1), 1986.
19. Pell B.: A Strategic Metagame Player for General Chess-Like Games. Proceedings of
    AAAI'94, pp. 1378-1385, 1994. ISBN 0-262-61102-3.
20. Pettorossi, A. and Proietti, M.: A Comparative Revisitation of Some Program Transfor-
    mation Techniques. Partial Evaluation, International Seminar, Dagstuhl Castle, Germany
    LNCS 1110, pp. 355-385, Springer 1996.

21. Pitrat J.: Realization of a Program Learning to Find Combinations at Chess. Computer Oriented Learning Processes, J. C. Simon editor. NATO Advanced Study Institutes Series. Series E: Applied Science - N° 14. Noordhoff, Leyden, 1976.

22. Pitrat, J.: Métaconnaissance - Futur de l'Intelligence Artificielle. Hermès, Paris, 1990.

23. Pitrat, J.: Games: The Next Challenge. ICCA journal, vol. 21, No. 3, September 1998, pp.147-156, 1998.

24. Ram, A. and Leake, D.: Goal-Driven Learning. Cambridge, MA, MIT Press/Bradford Books, 1995.

25. Selman, B.; Brooks, R. A.; Dean, T.; Horvitz, E.; Mitchell, T. M.; Nilsson, N. J.: Challenge Problems for Artificial Intelligence. In Proceedings AAAI-96, 1340-1345, 1996.

26. Tamaki H. and Sato T.: Unfold/Fold Transformations of Logic Programs. Proc. 2nd Intl. Logic Programming Conf., Uppsala Univ., 1984.

27. Van den Herik, H. J.; Allis, L. V.; Herschberg, I. S.: Which Games Will Survive ? Heuristic Programming in Artificial Intelligence 2, the Second Computer Olympiad (eds. D. N. L. Levy and D. F. Beal), pp. 232-243. Ellis Horwood. ISBN 0-13-382615-5. 1991.

28. Van Harmelen F. and Bundy A.: Explanation based generalisation = partial evaluation. Artificial Intelligence 36:401-412, 1988.

Aspect-Oriented Logic Meta Programming

Kris De Volder and Theo D'Hondt
{kdvolder|tjdhondt}@vub.ac.be

Programming Technology Lab, Vrije Universiteit Brussel

Abstract. We propose to use a logic meta-system as a general framework for aspect-oriented programming. We illustrate our approach with the implementation of a simplified version of the COOL aspect language for expressing synchronization of Java programs. Using this case as an example we illustrate the principle of *aspect-oriented logic meta programming* and how it is useful for implementing weavers on the one hand and on the other hand also allows users of AOP to fine-tune, extend and adapt an aspect language to their specific needs.

1 Introduction

The notion of aspect-oriented programming (AOP) [MLTK97,KLM⁺97] is motivated by the observation that there are concerns of programs which defy the abstraction capabilities of traditional programming languages. At present the main idea behind software engineering is hierarchical (de)composition. Not surprisingly, current programming languages are designed from this perspective and provide mechanism of abstraction such as procedures, classes and objects, that constitute units of encapsulation specifically aimed at top-down refinement or bottom-up composition.

These abstraction mechanism however do not align well with what AOP terminology calls *cross-cutting design concerns*, such as synchronization, distribution, persistence, debugging, error handling etc. which have a wider, more systemic impact. Precisely because of their wider impact on the system, the code dealing with cross-cutting concerns can not be neatly packaged into a single unit of encapsulation. This results in their implementation being scattered throughout the source code and this severely harms the readability and maintainability of the program. Aspect-oriented programming addresses this problem by designing *aspect languages* which offer new language abstractions that allow cross-cutting aspects to be expressed separately from the base functionality. A so called *aspect weaver* generates the actual code by intertwining basic functionality code with aspect code.

Early instances of aspect languages where limited in scope and dealt only with very specific aspects in very specific contexts. The D [LK97] system for example proposes specific aspect languages to handle the aspects of synchronization and replication of method arguments in distributed Java programs. Similarly [ILGK97] describes an aspect-oriented approach in the specific context of sparse matrix algorithms. More recently, with AspectJ [LK98], AOP has taken a turn towards a more general aspect language applicable in a broader context.

What all aspect languages have in common is that they are declarative in nature, offering a set of declarations to direct code generation. Earlier incarnations of AOP support only specific declarations suited to one particular context, e.g. synchronization in Java. Typically these stand at a high level of abstraction, avoiding specific implementation details of the weaver. Consequently they are formulated in terms of concepts linked to their context, e.g. mutual exclusion in the context of synchronization. AspectJ on the other hand provides more generally applicable but at the same time also more low-level declarations which are more intimately linked with the weaving algorithm, directly affecting code generation. Typical AspectJ declarations provide code to be executed upon entry and exit of methods, variables to be inserted into classes, etc. The universal declarative nature of aspect languages begs for a single uniform declarative formalism to be used as a general uniform aspect language. This paper proposes to use a logic programming language for this purpose. Thus, aspect declarations are not expressed by means of a specially designed aspect language but are simply logic assertions expressed in a general logic language. These logic facts function as hooks into a library of logic rules implementing the weaver.

The objective of this paper is to clearly demonstrate the advantage gained by unifying the aspect declaration language and the weaver implementation language and using a logic language for both purposes. There are two points of view from which the advantages will be discussed: the side of the AOP implementor and the side of the AOP user. The *implementor* is responsible for identifying what kind of aspects he wants to tackle. He subsequently devises a set of aspect declarations that allows expressing the aspects conveniently. Then he implements a *weaver* that takes base functionality and aspects into account and produces code that integrates them. The *user* on the other hand, is a programmer who declares base functionality and aspects by means of the special purpose languages provided by the AOP implementor.

We have called our approach *aspect-oriented logic meta programming* (AOLMP), because it depends highly on using the logic meta language to reason *about aspects*. On the one hand the logic language can be used merely as a simple general purpose declaration language, using only facts, but more importantly, it can also be used to express *queries about aspect declarations* or to declare rules which *transform aspect declarations*.

To illustrate the advantages of AOLMP from both the user's and the implementor's point of view, we will look at one aspect: the aspect of synchronization. The concern for synchronization, to ensure integrity of data accessible simultaneously by several threads, is more or less orthogonal to the program's functionality. Nevertheless, synchronization code is spread all over the program thus making it completely unintelligible. Lopes [LK97] proposed a solution for the synchronization problem using the aspect-oriented approach. She defined the aspect language COOL for expressing the synchronization aspect separately from the base functionality. We will present an implementation for COOL-like aspect declarations, using the logic meta programming approach. Note that it is not the goal of this paper to propose a better solution to the particular problem of synchronization. Instead, the emphasis of the paper is on the technique of logic meta programming and how it relates to AOP. For reasons of clarity we therefore only provide support for a simplified subset of Lopes' declarations in our example implementation. Nevertheless, the extra flexibility of our logic meta programming approach will allow us to recover some of the omitted features and even go beyond. This results in clearer synchronization declarations because the reasoning underlying them can be made explicit through a logic program.

We used the TyRuBa system to conduct the experiments upon which this paper is based. TyRuBa was designed as an experimental system to explore the use of logic meta programming for code generation in our recent Ph.D. dissertation [DV98].

The structure of the paper is as follows. We start by briefly introducing logic meta programming and the TyRuBa system in section 2. Section 3 explains the synchronization problem and how it can be tackled using an AOP approach. This section is mostly based on Lopes' work on the COOL aspect language [LK97]. We show how it is possible to express the synchronization aspect by means of logic facts that represent COOL-like aspect declarations. Section 4 illustrates the usefulness of AOLMP from the viewpoint of an AOP user. Section 5 discusses the relevance of AOLMP for weaver implementation. Section 6 discusses related work. Section 7 summarizes the conclusions.

2 TyRuBa and Logic Meta Programming

2.1 The TyRuBa core language

The TyRuBa system is built around a core language which is basically a simplified Prolog variant with a few special features to facilitate Java-code manipulation. We assume some familiarity with Prolog and will only briefly discuss the most important differences with it. For more information about standard Prolog we refer to [DEDC96,SS94]. For more information about the TyRuBa language we refer to [DV98]. The examples throughout the paper are simple enough and sufficiently explained to be understandable to a reader not familiar with Prolog.

Quoted code blocks The most important special feature of TyRuBa is its quoting mechanism which allows pieces of Java code to be used as terms in logic programs. Quoted pieces of code may in turn contain references to logic variables or other compound terms. Pieces of quoted code containing logic variables can be used as a kind of code templates and are very useful in implementing code generators.

In the version of TyRuBa presented and used in this text the quoting mechanism is rudimentary. Basically a quoted Java term is nothing more than a kind of string starting after a "{" and ending just before the next balanced "}". Unlike a string it is not composed of characters but of Java tokens, logic variables, constant terms and compound terms. The Java tokens are treated as special name constants whose name is equal to the printed representation of the token. The following example of a quoted Java term illustrates most kinds of quoted elements:

```
{ void foo() { Array<?El> contents  = new Array<?El>[5];
                ?El         anElement = contents.elementAt(1); }
}
```

In the above example we see a compound term "Array<?El>". We find several name constants "contents", "new", "anElement", ... There are two integer literals 5 and 1. The remainder of the tokens such as "=", "." and "(" are Java tokens treated as name constants with "strange names". Note that a quoted code block may contain "{" and "}" tokens, as long as these are properly balanced. Let it be clear that a nested "{" or "}" is treated just as any other token and does *not* introduce a nested quoted code block.

The meaning of a quoted Java term in the context of a TyRuBa program is derived directly from its internal representation. A quoted Java term corresponds to a compound term of arity 1 with a special qualifier. Its single subterm is a TyRuBa list of quoted elements. The example given above is internally represented by the following compound term:

```
'{}'([void, foo, '(', ')', '{', Array<?El>, contents, '=', ... ])
```

Note that in this example the term Array<?El> is used in place of an identifier. Compound terms which occur inside blocks of quoted code are printed as mangled identifier names. This is very convenient for code generation purposes. It can be used to parameterize names for types, variables or methods. The term Array<?El> for example can be thought of as the name of a template class for representing arrays of type ?El. Also variable's and method's names can be parameterized this way. In the weaver implementation presented in section 5 we make explicit use of this feature to declare a synchronization variable per method by parameterizing the variable name with the method name.

Lexical Conventions Because terms and variables may occur inside of quoted code, TyRuBa's lexical conventions differ somewhat from Prolog's to avoid confusion. Variables are identified by a leading "?" instead of starting with a capital. This avoids confusion between Java identifiers and Prolog variables. Some examples of TyRuBa variables are: ?x, ?Abc12, etc. Consequently, any identifier, including identifiers starting with a capital, is considered to be a constant. Some examples constants are: x, 1, Abc123, etc. To avoid confusion with function or procedure calls in Java, TyRuBa compound terms are written with "<" and ">" instead of "(" and ")" as in Prolog.

2.2 Logic Meta Programming

The idea of logic meta-programming is very simple. A base program is represented indirectly by means of a set of logic propositions. The relationship between the base program and its logic representation is concretized under the form of a code generator: a program that queries the logic data repository and outputs source code in the base language.

Logic meta-programming is thus achieved because a logic program can be thought of as representing the set of logic propositions that can be proven from its facts and rules. These facts in turn can be thought of as indirectly representing a base-language program. The full power of the logic paradigm may thus be used to describe base-language programs indirectly. This offers great potential as we will try to illustrate in the rest of this paper.

The mapping scheme between logic representation and base program may vary and determines the kind of information that is reified and accessible to meta programs. In this paper we assume a mapping that represents classes by means of facts which state that the class has certain methods, instance variables or constructors.

The presence of a variable declaration in a class is represented by a fact of the form:

```
var(?Class,?VarType,?VarName,{...declaration code...}).
```

A method declaration is asserted by a fact of the following form:

```
method(?Class,?ReturnType,?MethodName,?ArgTypeList,
    {...declaration head...},
    {...method body...}).
```

Below is an example Java class declaration and its corresponding representation as a set of TyRuBa propositions.

```
class Stack {
  int pos = 0 ;
  Stack() {
    contents = new Object[SIZE];}
  public Object peek ( ) {
    return contents[pos];  }
  public Object pop ( ) {
    return contents[--pos];  }
  ... }
```

```
class(Stack).
var(Stack,int,pos,{int pos = 0;}).
constructor(Stack,[],{public Stack()},
  {contents = new Object[SIZE]; }).
method(Stack,Object,peek,[],
  {public Object peek()},{return...}).
method(Stack,Object,pop,[],
  {public Object pop()},{return...}).
...
```

3 The Synchronization Problem and AOP

In this section we introduce the example used throughout the rest of this paper: a simple aspect language and weaver for solving the problems involved in writing synchronization code for multi-threaded Java applications. Subsection 3.1 sketches the problem and subsection 3.2 describes the aspect declarations supported by our simple weaver.

3.1 The Synchronization Problem

The problem in writing multi-threaded Java applications is that synchronization code ensuring data integrity tends to dominate the source code completely. As a result it becomes entangled and unmanageable. As an illustration of the problem, consider the implementation of a Stack abstract data type which is given in figure 1. The figure just lists the "bare bones" version without synchronization code. This code is simple, straightforward and easy to read.

```
class Stack  {
   static final int MAX = 10 ;
   int pos = 0 ;
   Object[] contents = new Object [ MAX ] ;

   public void print ()  {
      System.out.print("[");
      for (int i=0 ; i<pos ; i++ ) {
         System.out.print(contents[i]+" ") ; }
      System.out.print("]"); }
   public Object peek ()  {
      return contents[pos];  }
   public Object pop ()  {
      return contents[--pos];  }
   public void push (Object e)  {
      contents [pos++]=e ;  }
   public boolean empty ()  {
      return pos == 0 ;  }
   public boolean full ()  {
      return pos == MAX ;  }
}
```

Fig. 1. The "bare bones" version of the class Stack

The readability of the class Stack with synchronization code added is much worse. It is even too complicated to fit comfortably onto a single page. Therefore we will only take a look at one of the methods in it. The other methods are messed up in a similar way. Figure 2 lists the declaration of the peek method, complete with synchronization code.

To implement synchronization at the granularity of methods, a number of counter instance variables will be added to the Stack class. One such counter will be declared for each method. A counter instance variable will therefore have a name such as BUSY_pop, BUSY_peek etc. Code must be added to the start and end of each method to increment and decrement these counters. Also added to the start of the method is a "guard condition" which verifies whether the method may start executing. If the guard is not satisfied the method must wait for the guard to become true. The peek method for example waits until there are no

```
public Object peek ( ) {
    while ( true ) {
      synchronized ( this ) {
        if ( ( BUSY_pop == 0  ) && ( BUSY_push == 0 )  ) {
          ++ BUSY_peek ; break ; } }
      try { wait ( ) ; }
      catch ( InterruptedException COOLe ) { } }
    try {
     return contents [ pos ] ;  }
    finally {
      synchronized ( this ) {
        -- BUSY_peek ;
        notifyAll ( ) ; } } }
```

Fig. 2. The peek method with synchronization code

more threads currently executing a push or a pop method. It is obvious from figure 2 that the synchronization code completely dominates the source code: almost all of the code in the figure is synchronization code. Aspect oriented programming solves this problem by providing a special purpose language, called an *aspect language*, with which the synchronization aspect can be described separately from the base functionality. A code generator, called an *aspect weaver* takes a base program without aspects and an aspect program and generates output code integrating both.

3.2 Synchronization-aspect Declarations

Our TyRuBa weaver for generating synchronization code supports a simplified version of the COOL aspect language proposed by Lopes [LK97]. The COOL aspect language is used to specify the synchronization aspect of a Java base program. Our approach differs from the traditional AOP approach. Instead of defining a special purpose aspect language we assume that the AOP programmer provides aspect declarations under the form of TyRuBa logic facts. The weaver is consequently implemented as a library of logic rules for generating code from the facts describing the aspects and the base functionality. We defer treatment of the weaver's implementation to section 5. In this section we introduce the various aspect declarations that are recognized and supported by it.

Mutual exclusion between methods is expressed by a logic fact as illustrated by the following example.

```
mutuallyExclusive(Stack,push,pop).
```

The same kind of declaration is also used to declare that a method should never be run concurrently with itself. For example, to declare that the method push is not allowed to be run concurrently with itself, one asserts a fact:

```
mutuallyExclusive(Stack,push,push).
```

Declaration of mutually exclusive methods triggers the weaver to insert the appropriate guard expressions at the beginning of methods. Additional guards, other than those derived from the above synchronization declarations, may be added to a method by declaring a fact:

```
requires(?c,?m,?condition).
```

This means that the method ?m in class ?c may not be started unless the ?condition expression evaluates to true. The following example declarations ensure that no elements are ever popped from an empty stack nor pushed onto a stack which is full.

```
requires(Stack,push,{!full()}).
requires(Stack,pop,{!empty()}).
```

Finally, declarations of facts **onEntry** and **onExit** can be used to specify synchronization related actions that have to be performed upon entry and exit of a method.

```
onEntry(?class,?method,?statements).
onExit(?class,?method,?statements).
```

4 Aspect-Oriented Meta Programming

The fundamental advantage of using logic facts to declare aspects instead of a special-purpose aspect language is that aspect declarations can be accessed and declared by logic rules. This enables what we call *aspect-oriented logic meta programming*, i.e. writing logic programs which reason about aspect declarations. This technique is useful because it allows the user to extend or adapt the aspect language. This section presents two examples of the usefulness of AOLMP from the user's point of view.

4.1 Example: Self-exclusive and Mutually-exclusive Lists

The first example is a simple extension of the aspect language which adds some syntactic sugar on top of the pairwise declaration of mutually exclusive methods. This syntactic sugar allows expressing mutual exclusion by means of lists of mutually-exclusive and self-exclusive methods, in the same style as the declarations in Lopes' system. For example, mutual exclusion of three methods can be declared using the syntactic sugar as follows:

```
mutuallyExclusiveList(Stack,[push,pop,peek]).
```

This single declaration implies that any method in the given list is mutually exclusive with any other method in the list. A similar syntactic sugar is supported to assert that methods should not run concurrently with themselves:

```
selfExclusiveList(Stack,[push,pop,print]).
```

When the list of `mutuallyExclusive` methods is long the pairwise notation becomes cumbersome and less readable because of a combinatorial explosion of pairwise combinations. We would therefore like to be able to use the list notation as syntactic sugar. It is fairly easy to add support for this. All we need to do is include two simple rules into our aspect (meta) program. The first rule expresses that two methods ?m1 and ?m2 should be declared (pairwise) mutually exclusive if they both occur together as elements in the same mutually-exclusive list ?l.

```
mutuallyExclusive(?c,?m1,?m2)  :- mutuallyExclusiveList(?c,?l),
    element(?m1,?l),
    element(?m2,?l),
    NOT(equal(?m1,?m2)).
```

Note that the above rule checks that the method ?m1 and ?m2 are not one and the same method. To actually infer that a method is mutually exclusive with itself, it must occur in a self exclusive list. This is taken care of by the following rule:

```
mutuallyExclusive(?c,?m,?m)  :- selfExclusiveList(?c,?l),
    element(?m,?l).
```

The aspect program that describes the synchronization aspect of the Stack class, using the list-like notation is given in figure 3.

```
selfExclusiveList(Stack,[push,pop,print]).

mutuallyExclusiveList(Stack,[push,pop,peek]).
mutuallyExclusiveList(Stack,[push,pop,empty]).
mutuallyExclusiveList(Stack,[push,pop,full]).
mutuallyExclusiveList(Stack,[push,pop,print]).

requires(Stack,push,{!full()}).
requires(Stack,pop,{!empty()}).
```

Fig. 3. The Stack synchronization-aspect program

4.2 Example: Modifies and Inspects Declarations

This second example is a somewhat more sophisticated variation of the aspect language. The goal is to allow declaring synchronization of methods in an entirely different way. Rather than declaring which methods are mutually or self exclusive one may declare how methods modify or inspect state. This is often more convenient. For example in the Stack, when reasoning about what methods should be declared mutually exclusive with one another, one depends entirely on the knowledge of which methods inspect or modify what state. It would therefore be preferable to declare this information directly and explicitly. Therefore, instead of using exclusiveness declarations, we would like to write the following:

```
modifies(Stack,push,this).
modifies(Stack,pop,this).
inspects(Stack,peek,this).
inspects(Stack,empty,this).
inspects(Stack,full,this).
modifies(Stack,print,SystemOut).
inspects(Stack,print,this).
```

This style of declarations is much more convenient than exclusiveness declarations because they relate more closely to the semantics of the methods rather than to the way that synchronization is implemented. These declaration are also clearer because they explicitly reveal which is otherwise left implicit: the reason why synchronization code must be added.

This example really highlights the advantages of declaring aspects by means of a general purpose logic language. Using logic rules which reason about and declare aspects, we can easily provide support for these alternative synchronization aspect declarations, thereby explicitizing the reasoning underlying the aspect declarations. It is also important to note that we can do this aspect-language extension without having to reimplement the weaver! We can regard the modifies and inspects aspect declarations again as syntactic sugar on top of pairwise mutual exclusive declarations. This is possible because the modifies and inspects declarations provide sufficient information to derive mutuallyExclusive properties. Using AOLMP we can express elegantly and concisely how both kinds of declarations relate to one another by means of two simple logic rules. The first rule expresses that any two methods are mutually exclusive if one method inspects a state modified by the other one.

```
mutuallyExclusive(?class,?inspector,?modifier) :-
    inspects(?class,?inspector,?thing),
    modifies(?class,?modifier,?thing).
```

The second rule takes care of mutual exclusion between methods which modify the same state. This rule states that modification is implicitly a kind of inspection.

```
inspects(?class,?method,?thing) :- modifies(?class,?method,?thing).
```

The examples given so far illustrate how AOLMP is useful from the AOP user's point of view. They show how expressing aspects by means of logic assertions in combination with the availability of a full-fledged logic language fosters an enormous potential for the aspect-oriented programmer. It allows him to build on top of the existing aspect declarations in order to extend or modify the aspect language. It is important to note in these examples that in order to extend the aspect language, the aspect programmer did not have to descend to the level of the weaver's implementation. The core of the weaver's implementation has never been touched and consequently knowledge about its internal workings is not required. Extensions are simply defined as sophisticated syntactic sugar on top of already existing aspect declarations.

It might be argued that inspects/modifies declarations are less general and not able to express the synchronization aspect in some situations where exclusiveness style declarations could. This however only further highlights the power of our AOLMP approach: on the fly extensions of the aspect language can be implemented fairly easily and can be as general or as specific as a particular situation requires.

5 AOLMP and Weaver implementation

In this section we will have a look at the usefulness of AOLMP from the viewpoint of the AOP implementor. We will present the implementation of a weaver for the synchronization declarations proposed in section 3.2. For easy reference we have summarized these declarations in figure 4.

Declaration	Meaning
mutuallyExclusive(?c,?m1,?m2)	The method ?m1 in class ?c should not be run concurrently with the method ?m2.
requires(?c,?m,?e)	The method ?m in class ?c should not be started unless expression ?e evaluates to true.
onEntry(?c,?m,?s)	Execute the statement ?s upon entry of method ?m.
onExit(?c,?m,?s)	Execute the statement ?s upon exit of method ?m.

Fig. 4. Basic synchronization-aspect declarations

5.1 Layers of Code-to-code Transformations

The architecture of the COOL weaver implementation in TyRuBa is depicted in figure 5. This is a layered architecture of code-to-code transformations. Every layer consists of logic facts describing Java source code. The Java input program with only the base functionality is parsed and turned into a set of logic facts which are inserted into the TyRuBa fact and rule base in the JCore[1] layer. A set of logic rules describes how to copy the code on the basic layer onto the COOL layer. Another set of rules describes how code is added (woven) into the COOL layer to support the aspect declarations. Finally there is one more set of rules which describes how the thus produced facts on the COOL layer should be "unparsed" into a form printable as Java source code.

---

[1] Named after JCore, the simplified Java language which is used in Lopes' system to express basic functionality.

Many of these rules, such as for example the copying rules and the unparsing rules just implement the general architecture and are not directly dependent on the aspect language. We will only discuss the set of rules which handles weaving of COOL aspect declarations into the COOL layer. For a more complete description we refer to [DV98].

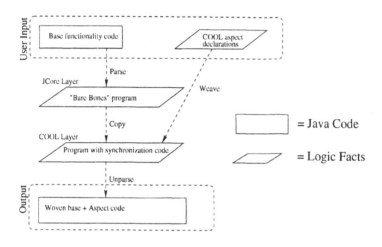

Fig. 5. The COOL code generator

Because the TyRuBa language is an experimental and simple logic language, without a module system, we could not rely on modules to divide the facts and rules into layers. We therefore partition the logic facts by adopting the convention that the first argument of every fact indicates the layer it belongs to. The JCore parser for example will insert the following fact into the rule base to indicate that the Stack has a peek method. The first argument is a symbol JCore indicating that this fact belongs to the JCore layer.

```
method(JCore,Stack,Object,peek,[],
  {public Object peek()},   //signature
  {return contents[pos]; }  //body
).
```

5.2 Synchronization-aspect Code

We will now have a look at the most important rules in the COOL weaver implementation: the rules that describe how the code on the COOL layer is generated, based on the code on the JCore layer and the synchronization aspect declarations.

Before continuing we note that part of the aspect language can be defined in terms of the more low-level features of the aspect language itself. The synchronization code for maintaining the counters could be added by means of **onEntry** and onExit declarations. Likewise, the guard conditions that prevent methods from being started based on the value of these counters can be added by means of requires declarations. This is a very important observation because it implies that the task of implementing the weaver is greatly simplified using AOLMP. We only need to provide support for generating code for the low-level features and can then implement the higher level declarations in terms of the more low-level declarations, in a similar way as in the previous examples. We therefore start by implementing support for the more low-level aspect declarations onExit, onEntry, and requires. Afterwards we will implement the mutuallyExclusive declaration easily in terms of the more low-level declarations.

Low-level Aspect Declarations The core of the COOL code generator is very simple. Basically it merely adds some wrapper code around the body of a JCore method declaration. Below is the rule which adds wrapper code around a method in the COOL layer. This wrapper code should look familiar since it has roughly the same layout as the example synchronization code we presented for the peek method in figure 2.

```
method(COOL,?class,?Return,?name,?Args,?head,{
    while (true) {
      synchronized ( this ) {
        if (?condition) {
           ?atStart
           break; } }
      try { wait ( ) ; }
      catch ( InterruptedException COOLe ) { } }
    try {?body}
    finally {
      synchronized(this) {
       ?atEnd
       notifyAll();} }}
) :- method(JCore,?class,?Return,?name,?Args,?head,?body),
     COOL_allRequired(?class,?name,?condition),
     COOL_atStartStatements(?class,?name,?atStart),
     COOL_atEndStatements(?class,?name,?atEnd).
```

A number of auxiliary predicates computes the ?condition expression and the ?atStart and ?atEnd statement lists to be inserted into the template wrapper code.

The auxiliary predicate COOL_allRequired collects all of the conditions declared by requires aspect declarations for a certain method. All of these are combined into a conjunction, i.e. a list of Java expressions combined together by means of the Java "&&" logical "and" operator.

```
COOL_allRequired(?class,?name,?exp) :-
  FINDALL(NODUP(?cond,requires(?class,?name,?cond)),
         ?cond,?conditions),
  JavaConjunction(?conditions,?exp).
```

The meta predicate FINDALL is a standard Prolog feature which can be used to collect results from a given query into a list. Here it is used to collect all of the guard conditions declared in **requires** declaration into the list ?conditions.

The meta predicate NODUP is a feature of TyRuBa to filter out duplicate solutions based on a comparison key. It was added to facilitate code generation. The use of NODUP here avoids duplicate conditions from being included more than once.

Two other auxiliary rules collect the statements to be inserted at the start and end of a method.

```
COOL_atStartStatements(?class,?name,?statements) :-
    FINDALL(onEntry(?class,?name,?stat),
            ?stat,?statements).


COOL_atEndStatements(?class,?name,?statements) :-
    FINDALL(onExit(?class,?name,?stat),
            ?stat,?statements).
```

Higher-level Aspect Declarations The rules presented in the previous section implement the core of the COOL code generator which supports the more low-level aspect declarations that insert synchronization statements and conditions at the right places into the synchronization wrapper code of a method. We can now relatively easily provide support for pairwise mutuallyExclusive declarations in terms of these.

First we observe that the mutuallyExclusive relationship is a symmetric relationship: whenever mutuallyExclusive(?c,?m1,?m2) holds this also implies mutuallyExclusive(?c,?m2,?m1). Rather than requiring the user to declare the symmetric pairs we let the weaver implementation take care of it and declare the symmetric closure of the mutuallyExclusive relationship declared by the user as follows[2].

```
mutuallyExclusiveSym(?c,?m1,?m2) :-
    mutuallyExclusive(?c,?m1,?m2);mutuallyExclusive(?c,?m2,?m1).
```

The following declaration adds the guard condition that makes sure that a method ?name is not started when another method with which it is mutuallyExclusive is already running[3].

```
requires(?class,?name,{BUSY<?other> == 0}) :-
    mutuallyExclusiveSym(?class,?name,?other).
```

---

[2] The ";" denotes a logical "or"

[3] The implementation of our simplified code generator also prohibits recursive calls from the same thread. This is usually not the intention. In Lopes' work this is patched by using a more complicated Lock object instead of a simple int counter. The Lock object also records which thread is locking the object and allows calls from the same thread explicitly. We could also support this more complicated locking strategy. All we need to change are the guard conditions and the declarations of the counter instance variables.

The guard expression consults a counter variable BUSY<?x> which registers how many times a method ?x has been entered. We still have to declare these variables and the onEntry and onExit code to increment and decrement the counters appropriately. The following rule adds a counter variable for every method which needs to be counted, i.e. every method that must conform to a mutuallyExclusive constraint. Note that the use of NODUP serves to avoid declaring the variable multiple times.

```
var(COOL,?class,int,BUSY<?name>,{
  private int BUSY<?name> = 0;
}) :- NODUP([?class,?name],
          mutuallyExclusiveSym(?class,?name,?other)).
```

Finally we present the rules that add administrative code for incrementing and decrementing the counter variables. Administrative code is added to every method for which a counter variable has been defined.

```
onEntry(?class,?name,{
        ++BUSY<?name>;
}) :- var(COOL,?class,int,BUSY<?name>,?declaration).
onExit(?class,?name,{
        --BUSY<?name>;
}) :- var(COOL,?class,int,BUSY<?name>,?declaration).
```

This concludes the implementation of our simplified version of the COOL aspect language and code generator. Due to lack of space we will not present the actually generated code. To get an idea of the the generated code, reexamine the peek method in figure 2. This is actually an excerpt taken from the generated code with only minor cosmetic changes to the indentation and renaming of messy "mangled TyRuBa-term identifiers" such as BUSY_Lpeek_R.

6 Related Work

6.1 Logic Meta Programming

To our knowledge, the connection between aspect-oriented programming and logic meta programming has never before been discussed or examined in the literature. The idea of logic meta programming itself, i.e. using a logic language as an expressive and powerful means to reason about programs is not new. A recent survey of the field can be found in [HG98,Bar95]. Logic programming languages are known to be good for implementing various kinds of meta programs, such as compilers, interpreters, type checkers, type inferencers etc. It's powerful unification and backtracking mechanism make it especially suitable for implementing these kinds of programs. Also, many features have been added to logic languages to facilitate meta programming. Prolog [DEDC96,CM81,SS94] for example has features to support meta programming. It offers definite clause grammars for example, a feature that facilitates the implementation of parsers. The programming language Gödel [HL94] is a declarative higher-order logic language designed for meta programming. Lambda Prolog [FGH+90] is an extension of Prolog with unification of lambda terms. Lambda terms are an extension specifically intended to facilitate the manipulation of formulas and programs [MN87]. It is especially useful in manipulating functional programs.

A logic programming approach has also been proposed for expressing sophisticated pattern matching and verification of programs [Wuy98,Cre97,BGV90,CMR92,Min96]. The power of the logic paradigm is exploited in two major ways in these approaches: as a verification/enforcing tool (e.g. Law Governed Architectures [Min96]), or as an information gathering tool [Cre97,BGV90,CMR92], or both at the same time (e.g. SOUL [Wuy98]). Both kinds of uses of logic are complementary to AOP. All deal with code tangling. AOP tries to avoid code tangling, by allowing aspects to be expressed separately. Using logic language as an information gathering tool on the other hand, its powerful pattern matching capabilities are exploited in recovering lost information from already tangled code. As a verification tool, a logic language is used in yet another way to deal with error prone tangled code by enforcing global correctness or consistency constraints.

6.2 AspectJ

The recent developments around AspectJ [KL98] concur with our ideas in many ways. Just like our approach, AspectJ moves away from the approach of only offering a fixed set of special purpose aspect languages. Instead, it tries to capture them as particular instantiations of a more general notion of an aspect. The major difference with our approach is that AspectJ is not offering a meta-programming language in order to achieve generality. Instead, a much more restricted extension mechanism, resembling a form of subclassing on aspects, is offered. Incidentally AspectJ also incorporates a simple form of pattern matching using wild cards as an alternative for the pattern matching power we get almost for free through unification and backtracking. Our approach is more general and more expressive than AspectJ because our extension language is a general full-fledged (logic) programming language. Of course, telling which approach is best is not as clear cut as that and other criteria besides generality and expressiveness are also important. The AspectJ team explicitly does not want to offer the full power of a real meta-programming language to the AOP user and strives to obtain a simpler and more manageable extension language.

The question remains open however whether the simplicity and manageability is worth sacrificing the expressiveness. We feel given the experimental stage of development of AOP that a more liberal more expressive formalism, such as ours, might be more suitable, at least as means of exploration and experimentation. Also, extensions and adaptation of the logic meta language towards better AOP support, such as special syntactic sugar and a scoping and module mechanism to make it more closely resemble an AspectJ like syntax might eliminate the drawbacks of a more complicated notation for simple uses altogether.

Last but not least, the `modifies/inspects` example, is at least one compellingly simple application of AOLMP for extending an aspect language. This alone earns some merit for AOLMP as a suitable alternative for AspectJ's approach.

6.3 Reflection

Reflection is also a mechanism that can be used to deal with cross cutting. In our opinion there is however a large difference between true reflection and simpler forms of meta programming. Meta programs are programs which reason about *other* programs or aspects thereof. Reflection however, means programs which reason about *themselves*. Following the treatment of [Smi82] a reflective system has a "causally connected self representation". This means that a program has access to some kind of data structure which represents (reifies) its computational system or aspects thereof. This can be inspected or it can be acted upon. "Causally connected" means that acting upon the self representation directly affects the computational system (this is sometimes called absorption). For a more detailed explanation of this terminology and theory we refer to [Smi82,Ste94].

The self-referential nature of reflective systems makes them very complex both theoretically and with respect to implementation. Issues such as reflective overlap, meta-stability, infinite towers etc. need to be considered [Smi82,Smi84,Mae87,WF88,KdRB91,Ste94,DVS95]. The complications with reflection mainly have one common cause: its self-referential nature creates confusion between what is "meta" and what is "base". Sometimes what is "meta" can be "base" at the same time and vice versa. This confusion inevitably has its impact on the usability of reflective systems and programs because they tend to be very hard to understand. A "simple" meta system is much easier to understand and use because it has a clean separation of meta level and base level.

Our approach clearly falls into the category of "simple" meta programming. There is a very clear separation between the base program and the meta program. This can be seen easily because the base language and the meta language are actually different programming languages. The base language is Java and the meta language is a logic programming language.

This places our approach of AOLMP somewhere in between AOP and full reflection. Aspect-oriented programming is not really programming, in the sense that an aspect language is typically a restricted declarative formalism that allows asserting things about base programs, without offering the power of a programming language. Therefore aspect programs are "meta" since they are *about* programs. However, they are not real programs themselves. Our approach replaces the multitude of restricted declarative formalisms, that special purpose aspect languages typically are, by one general purpose (also declarative!) logic programming language. We however purposefully do not provide a fully reflective system because we want to keep a clear separation between meta level and base level. Mixing the two in moving towards full-fledged reflection would add confusion and complications without significantly improving the generality or expressive power of the system.

6.4 Synchronization

We have based the simple example weaver used throughout this paper on Lopes' work on D [LK97,Lop97]. The weaver presented in this text only serves as an example to illustrate the principle of AOLMP and its advantages. We did not intend to give a better solution to the particular problem of synchronization. Our example therefore is greatly simplified omitting many important features such as synchronization between multiple classes, distinction between synchronization per-class or per-instance, a more complicated and realistic locking strategy etc. However, all of these could be implemented with not too much difficulty in the logic framework we presented.

A great deal of the work involved in defining an aspect language for solving a particular problem, for example synchronization, is in deciding how exactly to describe a particular aspect. For the example of synchronization we were relieved of this task because we borrowed Lopes' design. Our approach does not offer a magical solution here: the AOP implementor still has a large responsibility in analyzing the problem and designing an aspect language for it. In this respect, the only difference is that one is designing an interface to a library of rules rather than inventing specialized syntax. Our example does illustrate how AOLMP simplifies weaver implementation once the interface to it has been designed. It also facilitates user defined variations of the aspect language. This alone may indirectly help in designing aspect languages by making it easier to experiment with alternatives.

6.5 The Transformational Approach to AOP

Work in progress by Fradet and Südholt [FS98] proposes a transformational approach to AOP. They focus on an interesting class of aspects which can be described by source to source program transformations. It is difficult to make very punctual comparisons with our approach because their work is still very much in progress. Nevertheless, we want to compare the approaches on some conceptual points because of the obvious similarities.

To a large extent our approach has a lot in common with their approach especially when considered from the AOP implementors point of view, which they seem to have focussed on. Our approach to weaver implementation in the given example is indeed a form of source to source transformation. From this point of view we simply use the logic language as a general purpose programming language which happens to be convenient as a transformation language because of its powerful pattern matching capabilities.

The transformational approach of Fradet and Südholt is based on a special purpose transformation language, specially designed for expressing transformations on abstract syntax trees. New kinds of aspect declarations consist of extensions to the abstract syntax and consequently also the concrete syntax of the language. They point out that only pattern matching on syntactic properties is not always sufficient to describe or guide the transformation and they propose to use static program analysis to remedy this.

Summarizing the above we discern three essential components in the system they envision:

1. A special purpose transformation language: To specify the aspect language. It can also serve as a generic weaver implementation language.
2. A static program analyzer construction toolkit: To deduce different kinds of static information needed in different kinds of aspects.
3. A parser generator toolkit: For creating new syntax for declaring aspects.

From the implementor's viewpoint, the added potential of our approach is found in its uniformity: the logic formalism provides a convenient substitute for all three components. A logic language can serve not only as a transformation language, but also as a general meta-programming language, well suited for implementing other kinds of meta programs, such as for example static program analyzers.

It might be useful to occasionally define special purpose syntax for some aspects. Therefore including a parser generator toolkit is not useless and could also be a useful addition to our approach. There is however no real need for it since the logic language itself can serve as a general-purpose aspect declaration language.

In many ways our work and their work is complementary in nature. Their approach is more ambitious with respect to formal underpinnings for transformational aspects, whereas ours is more directly inspired from a concrete implementation viewpoint. They also focus mostly on the aspect implementors viewpoint and consider an aspect language itself immutable once it has been defined. In contrast, this paper stresses the importance of user level programmability of aspects, for the purpose of extending the aspect language.

While it is not an central issue in this paper that the example weaver is transformational, this is still an interesting observation. It is to be expected that theoretical results from the transformational approach will be directly applicable in constructing a generic-weaver library of logic rules.

7 Conclusion

We have illustrated how an aspect language can be embedded in the logic paradigm by representing aspect declarations as logic facts. We illustrated this for a simplified version of the COOL aspect language proposed by Lopes.

That aspects are expressed by means of a full-fledged logic language represents an important advantage over using more limited special-purpose aspect languages: the logic language can serve uniformly as a formalism to declare aspects as logic facts and as a meta language for aspect-oriented logic meta programming using rules.

Aspect-oriented meta programming is useful for both users and implementors of AOP. AOP users can extend the aspect language on the fly, defining new kinds of aspect declarations. Some interesting examples where shown which do not require the user to descend to the level of the weaver implementation. This was possible because the new declarations could be defined in terms of already existing ones. Thus, the new declarations could be defined as a kind of sophisticated syntactic sugar and implemented by means of logic rules transforming new declarations into already existing ones. This kind of programming is very interesting because it allows making the reasoning underlying the aspect declarations explicit. This was illustrated clearly by the example, where AOLMP made it possible to explicitly capture the reasoning about how modification and inspection of state is the underlying motivation for the synchronization code in a Stack class. The same technique is also useful at the level of the weaver implementation because often some of the aspect declarations can be defined in terms of other more low-level aspect declarations.

7.1   About the generality of the conclusions

Despite the restricted and simplified nature of the example given in this paper, we can draw some conclusions about AOLMP which are valid in a broader context because:

1. The logic language is a full-fledged (Turing complete) programming language. Consequently, it is theoretically possible to implement any conceivable weaver in it. Some weavers will be harder to implement than others, but the same is true for weaver implementation in any other language.
2. There are other known aspects which have join points very similar to the synchronization aspect such as debugging and tracing. These at least would be equally easy to implement.
3. From the user's points of view, any aspect language implemented as a library of logic rules benefits from AOLMP for building on top of the aspect language, since this is independent of the internal complexity of the library implementation itself. In an extreme case, the library may also be a logic "front end" to a weaver implemented in another programming language altogether. This would yield the advantages of user-level AOLMP without requiring a logic implementation for the weaver itself.

It is important to realize that there is no magic. Designing a good aspect language is tricky business regardless of what medium is being used to implement it. This is also true when implementing them as libraries of logic rules. For example, one of the features omitted from our simplified example weaver is inter-class synchronization. Theoretically implementing it in the logic language is not a problem. However, it is not possible to implement it by only building on top of the simplistic library exemplified in this paper. It would require the rewriting of at least a small portion of the library of rules since an inter-class synchronization policy would require a more general form of synchronization declaration which names the class together with the method:

```
mutuallyExclusive(Stack<push>,Stack<pop>).
```

The more general use of this type of declaration with methods in two distinct classes cannot be defined in terms of the building blocks provided by the simplified library. Note that it would be easy to go the other way around and provide the intra-class syntax on top of the more general inter-class syntax:

```
mutuallyExclusive(?cls<?m1>,?cls<?m2>) :- mutuallyExclusive(?cls,?m1,?m2).
```

This merely shows that aspect languages should be designed with care, just like every other programming language, library or software system.

8 Acknowledgments

I offer my gratitude to Kim Mens, Tom Tourwé, Tom Mens, Wolfgang De Meuter and Rob Nebbe for their proofreading and valuable comments on this paper and for the many inspiring discussions.

I also thank the organizers of the third AOP workshop: Cristina Lopes, Gregor Kiczales, Bedir Tekinerdogan and Wolfgang de Meuter, for their comments on an earlier version of this paper.

I thank Pascal Fradet and Mario Südholt for their comments on section 6.5 and for an interesting discussion about the subject over email.

References

[Bar95]   J. Barklund. Metaprogramming in logic. *Encyclopedia of Computer Science and Technology*, 33:205–227, 1995. Also available as UPMAIL Technical Report No. 80.

[BGV90]   R. Ballance, S. Graham, and M. VanDeVanter. The Pan Language-Based Editing System for Integrated Development Systems. In *Proc. 4th ACM SIGSOFT Symp. on Software Development Environments*, volume 15:6 of *ACM SIGSOFT Software Engineering Notes*, pages 77–93, 1990.

[CM81]   W.F. Clocksin and C.S. Mellish. *Programming in Prolog*. Springer-Verlag, 1981.

[CMR92]   M. Consens, A. Mendelzon, and A. Ryman. Visualizing and Querying Software Structures. In *Proceedings of the 14th International Conference on Software Engineering*, pages 138–156, May 1992.

[Cre97]   R.F. Crew. Astlog: A language for examining abstract syntax trees. In *Proceedings of the USENIX Conference on Domain-Specific Languages*, Santa Barbara, California, October 1997.

[DEDC96] P. Deransart, A. Ed-Dbali, and L. Cervoni. *Prolog: The Standard*. Springer-Verlag, New York, 1996.

[DV98]   Kris De Volder. *Type-Oriented Logic Meta Programming*. PhD thesis, Vrije Universiteit Brussel, Programming Technology Laboratory, June 1998.

[DVS95]   Kris De Volder and Patrick Steyaert. Construction of the Reflective Tower Based on Open Implementations. Technical Report vub-prog-tr-95-01, Programming Technology Lab, Vrije Universiteit Brussel, 1995.

[FGH+90] Amy Felty, Elsa Gunter, John Hannan, Dale Miller, Gopalan Nadathur, and Andre Scedrov. λ Prolog: An extended logic programming language. In M. Stickel, editor, *Proceedings of the Tenth International Conference on Automated Deduction (Kaiserslautern, West Germany)*, volume 449 of *lncs*, pages 754–755, Berlin, 1990. sv.

[FS98] Pascal Fradet and Mario Südholt. Aop: towards a generic framework using program transformation and analysis. In Serge Demeyer and Jan Bosch, editors, *ECOOP 98 Workshop Reader*, volume 1543 of *Lecture Notes in Computer Science*, pages 394–397. Springer Verlag, 1998.

[HG98] P. M. Hill and J. Gallagher. Meta-programming in logic programming. *Handbook of Logic in Artificial Intelligence and Logic Programming*, 5:421–498, January 1998.

[HL94] P. Hill and J. Lloyd. *The Gödel Programming Language*. MIT Press, Cambridge, MA, 1994.

[ILGK97] J. Irwin, J.-M. Loingtier, J. R. Gilbert, and G. Kiczales. Aspect-oriented programming of sparse matrix code. *Lecture Notes in Computer Science*, 1343:249–??, 1997.

[KdRB91] Gregor Kiczales, Jim des Rivières, and Daniel G. Bobrow. *The Art of the Metaobject Protocol*. MIT Press, 1991.

[KL98] Gregor Kiczales and Cristina Videira Lopes. Tutorial 64: Aspect-oriented programming using aspectj. *OOPSLA'98 Tutorial Notes*, 1998.

[KLM+97] Gregor Kiczales, John Lamping, Anurag Mendhekar, Chris Maeda, Cristina Lopes, Jean-Marc Loingtier, and John Irwin. Aspect-oriented programming. In Mehmet Aksit and Satoshi Matsuoka, editors, *ECOOP'97—Object-Oriented Programming, 11th European Conference*, volume 1241 of *Lecture Notes in Computer Science*, pages 220–242, Jyväskylä, Finland, 9–13 June 1997. Springer.

[LK97] Cristina Videira Lopes and Gregor Kiczales. D: A language framework for distributed programming. Technical Report SPL97-007 P9710047, Xerox Palo Alto Research Center, http://www.parc.xerox/aop, 1997.

[LK98] Cristina Videira Lopes and Gregor Kiczales. Recent developments in aspectj. In Serge Demeyer and Jan Bosch, editors, *ECOOP 98 Workshop Reader*, volume 1543 of *Lecture Notes in Computer Science*, pages 398–401. Springer Verlag, 1998.

[Lop97] Cristina Videira Lopes. *D: A Language Framework for Distributed Programming*. PhD thesis, College of Computer Science, Northeastern University, November 1997.

[Mae87] Patti Maes. *Computational Reflection*. Phd thesis, Vrije Universiteit Brussel, Artificial Intelligence Lab., Brussels, Belgium, January 1987.

[Min96] Naftaly H. Minsky. Law-governed regularities in object systems, part 1: An abstract model. *Theory and Practice of Object Sytems*, 2(4):283–301, 1996.

[MLTK97] K. Mens, C. Lopes, B. Tekinerdogan, and G. Kiczales. Aspect-oriented programming. In Jan Bosch and Stuart Mitchell, editors, *ECOOP 97 Workshop Reader*, Lecture Notes in Computer Science, pages 483–496. Springer Verlag, 1997.

[MN87] Dale Miller and Gopalan Nadathur. A logic programming approach to manipulating formulas and programs. In Seif Haridi, editor, *IEEE Symposium on Logic Programming*, pages 379–388, San Francisco, September 1987.

[Smi82] Brian C. Smith. *Reflection and Semantics in a Procedural Language*. PhD thesis, MIT, January 1982. Also available as MIT/LCS/TR-272.

[Smi84]   Brian C. Smith. Reflection and semantics in LISP. Report ISL-3, ACM/ Xerox PARC, Intell. Systems Lab., Palo Alto, CA, June 1984.

[SS94]   Leon Sterling and Ehud Shapiro. *The Art of Prolog*. The MIT Press, Cambridge, Mass., second edition, 1994.

[Ste94]   Patrick Steyaert. *Open Design of Object-Oriented Languages, A Foundation for Specialisable Reflective Language Frameworks*. PhD thesis, Vrije Universiteit Brussel, 1994.

[WF88]   Mitchell Wand and Daniel P. Friedman. The mystery of the tower revealed: A non-reflective description of the reflective tower. In P. Maes and D. Nardi, editors, *Meta-Level Architectures and Reflection*, pages 111–134. Elsevier Sci. Publishers B.V. (North Holland), 1988.

[Wuy98]   Roel Wuyts. Declarative reasoning about the structure of object-oriented systems. In *Proceedings of TOOLS USA '98*, 1998.

Author Index

Lecture Notes in Computer Science

For information about Vols. 1–1562
please contact your bookseller or Springer-Verlag

Vol. 1606: J. Mira, J.V. Sánchez-Andrés (Eds.), Foundations and Tools for Neural Modeling. Proceedings, Vol. I, 1999. XXIII, 865 pages. 1999.

Vol. 1607: J. Mira, J.V. Sánchez-Andrés (Eds.), Engineering Applications of Bio-Inspired Artificial Neural Networks. Proceedings, Vol. II, 1999. XXIII, 907 pages. 1999.

Vol. 1608: S. Doaitse Swierstra, P.R. Henriques, J.N. Oliveira (Eds.), Advanced Functional Programming. Proceedings, 1998. XII, 289 pages. 1999.

Vol. 1609: Z. W. Raś, A. Skowron (Eds.), Foundations of Intelligent Systems. Proceedings, 1999. XII, 676 pages. 1999. (Subseries LNAI).

Vol. 1610: G. Cornuéjols, R.E. Burkard, G.J. Woeginger (Eds.), Integer Programming and Combinatorial Optimization. Proceedings, 1999. IX, 453 pages. 1999.

Vol. 1611: I. Imam, Y. Kodratoff, A. El-Dessouki, M. Ali (Eds.), Multiple Approaches to Intelligent Systems. Proceedings, 1999. XIX, 899 pages. 1999. (Subseries LNAI).

Vol. 1612: R. Bergmann, S. Breen, M. Göker, M. Manago, S. Wess, Developing Industrial Case-Based Reasoning Applications. XX, 188 pages. 1999. (Subseries LNAI).

Vol. 1613: A. Kuba, M. Šámal, A. Todd-Pokropek (Eds.), Information Processing in Medical Imaging. Proceedings, 1999. XVII, 508 pages. 1999.

Vol. 1614: D.P. Huijsmans, A.W.M. Smeulders (Eds.), Visual Information and Information Systems. Proceedings, 1999. XVII, 827 pages. 1999.

Vol. 1615: C. Polychronopoulos, K. Joe, A. Fukuda, S. Tomita (Eds.), High Performance Computing. Proceedings, 1999. XIV, 408 pages. 1999.

Vol. 1616: P. Cointe (Ed.), Meta-Level Architectures and Reflection. Proceedings, 1999. XI, 273 pages. 1999.

Vol. 1617: N.V. Murray (Ed.), Automated Reasoning with Analytic Tableaux and Related Methods. Proceedings, 1999. X, 325 pages. 1999. (Subseries LNAI).

Vol. 1618: J. Bézivin, P.-A. Muller (Eds.), The Unified Modeling Language. Proceedings, 1998. IX, 443 pages. 1999.

Vol. 1619: M.T. Goodrich, C.C. McGeoch (Eds.), Algorithm Engineering and Experimentation. Proceedings, 1999. VIII, 349 pages. 1999.

Vol. 1620: W. Horn, Y. Shahar, G. Lindberg, S. Andreassen, J. Wyatt (Eds.), Artificial Intelligence in Medicine. Proceedings, 1999. XIII, 454 pages. 1999. (Subseries LNAI).

Vol. 1621: D. Fensel, R. Studer (Eds.), Knowledge Acquisition Modeling and Management. Proceedings, 1999. XI, 404 pages. 1999. (Subseries LNAI).

Vol. 1622: M. González Harbour, J.A. de la Puente (Eds.), Reliable Software Technologies – Ada-Europe'99. Proceedings, 1999. XIII, 451 pages. 1999.

Vol. 1625: B. Reusch (Ed.), Computational Intelligence. Proceedings, 1999. XIV, 710 pages. 1999.

Vol. 1626: M. Jarke, A. Oberweis (Eds.), Advanced Information Systems Engineering. Proceedings, 1999. XIV, 478 pages. 1999.

Vol. 1627: T. Asano, H. Imai, D.T. Lee, S.-i. Nakano, T. Tokuyama (Eds.), Computing and Combinatorics. Proceedings, 1999. XIV, 494 pages. 1999.

Col. 1628: R. Guerraoui (Ed.), ECOOP'99 - Object-Oriented Programming. Proceedings, 1999. XIII, 529 pages. 1999.

Vol. 1629: H. Leopold, N. García (Eds.), Multimedia Applications, Services and Techniques - ECMAST'99. Proceedings, 1999. XV, 574 pages. 1999.

Vol. 1631: P. Narendran, M. Rusinowitch (Eds.), Rewriting Techniques and Applications. Proceedings, 1999. XI, 397 pages. 1999.

Vol. 1632: H. Ganzinger (Ed.), Automated Deduction – Cade-16. Proceedings, 1999. XIV, 429 pages. 1999. (Subseries LNAI).

Vol. 1633: N. Halbwachs, D. Peled (Eds.), Computer Aided Verification. Proceedings, 1999. XII, 506 pages. 1999.

Vol. 1634: S. Džeroski, P. Flach (Eds.), Inductive Logic Programming. Proceedings, 1999. VIII, 303 pages. 1999. (Subseries LNAI).

Vol. 1636: L. Knudsen (Ed.), Fast Software Encryption. Proceedings, 1999. VIII, 317 pages. 1999.

Vol. 1638: A. Hunter, S. Parsons (Eds.), Symbolic and Quantitative Approaches to Reasoning and Uncertainty. Proceedings, 1999. IX, 397 pages. 1999. (Subseries LNAI).

Vol. 1639: S. Donatelli, J. Kleijn (Eds.), Application and Theory of Petri Nets 1999. Proceedings, 1999. VIII, 425 pages. 1999.

Vol. 1640: W. Tepfenhart, W. Cyre (Eds.), Conceptual Structures: Standards and Practices. Proceedings, 1999. XII, 515 pages. 1999. (Subseries LNAI).

Vol. 1643: J. Nešetřil (Ed.), Algorithms – ESA '99. Proceedings, 1999. XII, 552 pages. 1999.

Vol. 1644: J. Wiedermann, P. van Emde Boas, M. Nielsen (Eds.), Automata, Languages, and Programming. Proceedings, 1999. XIV, 720 pages. 1999.

Vol. 1645: M. Crochemore, M. Paterson (Eds.), Combinatorial Pattern Matching. Proceedings, 1999. VIII, 295 pages. 1999.

Vol. 1647: F.J. Garijo, M. Boman (Eds.), Multi-Agent System Engineering. Proceedings, 1999. X, 233 pages. 1999. (Subseries LNAI).

Vol. 1649: R.Y. Pinter, S. Tsur (Eds.), Next Generation Information Technologies and Systems. Proceedings, 1999. IX, 327 pages. 1999.

Vol. 1650: K.-D. Althoff, R. Bergmann, L.K. Branting (Eds.), Case-Based Reasoning Research and Development. Proceedings, 1999. XII, 598 pages. 1999. (Subseries LNAI).

Vol. 1651: R.H. Güting, D. Papadias, F. Lochovsky (Eds.), Advances in Spatial Databases. Proceedings, 1999. XI, 371 pages. 1999.

Vol. 1653: S. Covaci (Ed.), Active Networks. Proceedings, 1999. XIII, 346 pages. 1999.

Vol. 1654: E.R. Hancock, M. Pelillo (Eds.), Energy Minimization Methods in Computer Vision and Pattern Recognition. Proceedings, 1999. IX, 331 pages. 1999.

Vol. 1663: F. Dehne, A. Gupta. J.-R. Sack, R. Tamassia (Eds.), Algorithms and Data Structures. Proceedings, 1999. X, 367 pages. 1999.

Lecture Notes in Computer Science 1589

Edited by G. Goos, J. Hartmanis and J. van Leeuwen

Springer
Berlin
Heidelberg
New York
Barcelona
Hong Kong
London
Milan
Paris
Singapore
Tokyo

José Luiz Fiadeiro (Ed.)

Recent Trends in Algebraic Development Techniques

13th International Workshop, WADT'98
Lisbon, Portugal, April 2-4, 1998
Selected Papers

 Springer

Series Editors

Gerhard Goos, Karlsruhe University, Germany
Juris Hartmanis, Cornell University, NY, USA
Jan van Leeuwen, Utrecht University, The Netherlands

Volume Editor

José Luiz Fiadeiro
University of Lisbon, Department of Informatics
Campo Grande, 1700 Lisbon, Portugal
E-mail: llf@di.fc.ul.pt

Cataloging-in-Publication data applied for

Die Deutsche Bibliothek - CIP-Einheitsaufnahme

Recent trends in algebraic development techniques : 13th international workshop
;.selected papers / WADT '98, Lisbon, Portugal, April 2 - 4, 1998. José Luiz
Fiadeiro (ed.). - Berlin ; Heidelberg ; New York ; Barcelona ; Hong Kong ;
London ; Milan ; Paris ; Singapore ; Tokyo : Springer, 1999
(Lecture notes in computer science ; Vol. 1589)
ISBN 3-540-66246-4

CR Subject Classification (1998): D.1.1-2, D.2.4, D.2.m, D.3.1, F.3.1-2

ISSN 0302-9743
ISBN 3-540-66246-4 Springer-Verlag Berlin Heidelberg New York

© Springer-Verlag Berlin Heidelberg 1999
Printed in Germany

Typesetting: Camera-ready by author
SPIN: 10704101   06/3142 – 5 4 3 2 1 0   Printed on acid-free paper

Foreword

The European conference situation in the general area of software science has long been considered unsatisfactory. A fairly large number of small and medium-sized conferences and workshops take place on an irregular basis, competing for high-quality contributions and for enough attendees to make them financially viable. Discussions aiming at a consolidation have been underway since at least 1992, with concrete planning beginning in summer 1994 and culminating in a public meeting at TAPSOFT'95 in Aarhus.

On the basis of a broad consensus, it was decided to establish a single annual federated spring conference in the slot that was then occupied by TAPSOFT and CAAP/ESOP/CC, comprising a number of existing and new conferences and covering a spectrum from theory to practice. ETAPS'98, the first instance of the European Joint Conferences on Theory and Practice of Software, is taking place this year in Lisbon. It comprises five conferences (FoSSaCS, FASE, ESOP, CC, TACAS), four workshops (ACoS, VISUAL, WADT, CMCS), seven invited lectures, and nine tutorials.

The events that comprise ETAPS address various aspects of the system development process, including specification, design, implementation, analysis and improvement. The languages, methodologies and tools which support these activities are all well within its scope. Different blends of theory and practice are represented, with an inclination towards theory with a practical motivation on one hand and soundly-based practice on the other. Many of the issues involved in software design apply to systems in general, including hardware systems, and the emphasis on software is not intended to be exclusive.

ETAPS is a natural development from its predecessors. It is a loose confederation in which each event retains its own identity, with a separate programme committee and independent proceedings. Its format is open-ended, allowing it to grow and evolve as time goes by. Contributed talks and system demonstrations are in synchronized parallel sessions, with invited lectures in plenary sessions. Two of the invited lectures are reserved for "unifying" talks on topics of interest to the whole range of ETAPS attendees. The aim of cramming all this activity into a single one-week meeting is to create a strong magnet for academic and industrial researchers working on topics within its scope, giving them the opportunity to learn about research in related areas, and thereby to foster new and existing links between work in areas that have hitherto been addressed in separate meetings.

ETAPS'98 has been superbly organized by José Luis Fiadeiro and his team at the Department of Informatics of the University of Lisbon. The ETAPS steering committee has put considerable energy into planning for ETAPS'98 and its successors. Its current membership is:

André Arnold (Bordeaux), Egidio Astesiano (Genova), Jan Bergstra (Amsterdam), Ed Brinksma (Enschede), Rance Cleaveland (Raleigh), Pierpaolo Degano (Pisa), Hartmut Ehrig (Berlin), José Fiadeiro (Lisbon), Jean-Pierre Finance (Nancy), Marie-Claude Gaudel (Paris), Tibor Gyimothy (Szeged), Chris Hankin (London), Stefan Jähnichen (Berlin), Uwe Kastens (Paderborn), Paul Klint (Amsterdam), Kai Koskimies (Tampere), Tom Maibaum (London), Hanne Riis Nielson (Aarhus), Fernando Orejas (Barcelona), Don Sannella (Edinburgh, chair), Bernhard Steffen (Dortmund), Doaitse Swierstra (Utrecht), Wolfgang Thomas (Kiel)

Other people were influential in the early stages of planning, including Peter Mosses (Aarhus) and Reinhard Wilhelm (Saarbrücken). ETAPS'98 has received generous sponsorship from:

Portugal Telecom
TAP Air Portugal
the Luso-American Development Foundation
the British Council
the EU programme "Training and Mobility of Researchers"
the University of Lisbon
the European Association for Theoretical Computer Science
the European Association for Programming Languages and Systems
the Gulbenkian Foundation

I would like to express my sincere gratitude to all of these people and organizations, and to José in particular, as well as to Springer-Verlag for agreeing to publish the ETAPS proceedings.

Edinburgh, January 1998   Donald Sannella
                                            ETAPS Steering Committee chairman

Preface

This volume contains papers selected from WADT'98 the 13th Workshop on Algebraic Development Techniques. Like its predecessors, WADT'98 focused on the algebraic approach to the specification and development of systems, an area that was born around the algebraic specification of abstract data types and encompasses today the formal design of integrated hardware and software systems, new specification frameworks, and a wide range of applications.

WADT'98 was organized as part of the first European Joint Conferences on Theory and Practice of Software (ETAPS). It took place at the Gulbenkian Foundation in Lisbon, Portugal, April 2-4, 1998.

The program of WADT'98 consisted of 43 presentations. The main topics addressed during the workshop were: algebraic and other approaches to system specification; algebraic combination of logics; algebraic structures and logics for concurrency; other algebraic structures and their logics; specification languages and their associated methods and tools; term rewriting and theorem proving.

A committee consisting of Bernd Krieg-Brückner, José Luiz Fiadeiro, Peter Mosses, Fernando Orejas, Francesco Parisi Presicce, Don Sannella, and Andrzej Tarlecki, with the help of Marie-Claude Gaudel and Hélène Kirchner, selected a number of papers based on the abstracts and the presentations at the workshop, and invited their authors to submit a written version of their talks for possible inclusion in this volume. All the submissions underwent a careful refereeing process. The selection committee then made the final decisions. This volume contains the final versions of the contributions that were accepted.

We are very grateful to all the referees that helped the selection committee in reviewing the submissions: Marek Bednarczyk, Michel Bidoit, Tomasz Borzyszkowski, Roberto Bruni, Luca Cardelli, Maura Cerioli, Christine Choppy, Pierpaolo Degano, Alessandro Fantechi, Nicoletta De Francesco, Martin Hofmann, Hans-Jörg Kreowski, Neil Ghani, Jo Hannay, Stefan Kahrs, Manuel Koch, Alfio Martini, Wieslaw Pawlowski, Adolfo Piperno, Gianna Reggio, Horst Reichel, Pino Rosolini, H. Schlingloff, Aleksy Schubert, Patrick Viry, Martin Wirsing, and Uwe Wolter.

Being part of ETAPS'98, the workshop shared the generous sponsorship acknowledged in the foreword and the dedication of the organization committee. As organizing chair of ETAPS'98, I would like to take the opportunity to express my deepest thanks to Antnia Lopes, whose help made it all feel so easy, as well as M.Costa, S.Jourdan, E.Moita, I.Nunes, L.Pires, J.Ramos, P.Resende, O.Torres, and M.Wermelinger.

January 1999   José Luiz Fiadeiro

Table of Contents

An Algebraic Framework for Separate Type-Checking*

Davide Ancona

Dipartimento di Informatica e Scienze dell'Informazione
Via Dodecaneso, 35
16146 Genova (Italy)
davide@disi.unige.it

Abstract. We address the problem of defining an algebraic framework for modularization supporting separate type-checking. In order to do that we introduce the notions of abstract type system and logic of constraints and we present a canonical construction of a model part, on top of a logic of constraints. This canonical construction works under standard assumptions on the underlying type system.
We show that the framework is suitable for defining the static and dynamic semantics of module languages, by giving a concrete example of construction on top of the type system of a simple typed module language. As a result, the subtyping relation between module interfaces is captured in a natural way by the notion of signature morphism.

Introduction

Modularization has been considered since the early 70s an essential principle for managing the complex task of software development [29]. Nowadays there exist many modular programming languages offering rather advanced features for modularization. Nevertheless, many recent papers [21,22,6,12,19,20,24,9,10] have shown that many of the modular mechanisms provided by them turn out to be inadequate in the light of the new software technology.

Object-oriented and distributed programming have promoted a stronger demand for more flexible modularization mechanisms able to face the problem of software reuse, maintenance and extensibility. As a consequence, *true separate compilation* and *linking* are becoming more and more important issues which must be taken into account in order to successfully deal with complex system libraries. In particular, *separate type-checking* turns out to be an essential phase of separate compilation, both from the point of view of software *reliability*, since it allows compilers to statically detect many subtle errors due to incompatibility between modules, and of *efficiency*, since compilers may take advantage of the information about the external components modules depend on.

---

* This work has been partially supported by Murst 40% - Modelli della computazione e dei linguaggi di programmazione and CNR - Formalismi per la specifica e la descrizione di sistemi ad oggetti.

J.L. Fiadeiro (Ed.): WADT'98, LNCS 1589, pp. 1–15, 1999.

Another important consideration that has emerged in the last years is related to the notion of *modular module system* [23]: following the approach of SML [27], many authors [8,6,23,11] have recognized the usefulness both from the practical and the theoretical point of view of considering a module language as a language on its own which is independent of the underlying core language.

The algebraic framework for modularization developed in [4,3,2] partially fulfills the characteristics exposed above. It is based on the well-established theory of *institutions* [15] which allows an abstract approach to modularization [31,13]. Indeed, the framework is parametric in the algebraic framework used for modeling the underlying core language. The framework allows to deal with mixins [8] and generic modules (e.g., SML functors) in a uniform way and to define three primitive operations from which many higher-level operators commonly used in module languages can be derived [4,2]. Since their semantics abstracts from a particular underlying language, they actually correspond to linking operations.

What the framework does not directly support, because of its generality, is the notion of type system, which is essential for dealing with type-checking.

The aim of this paper is to define an algebraic framework supporting static and dynamic semantics of parametric modules in an arbitrary type system. In order to do that we introduce the notions of *abstract type system* and *logic of constraints*. Then, on top of a fixed logic of constraints, a model part (in the sense of institutions) can be canonically built; standard requirements over the logic ensure the model part to satisfy the amalgamation property and, therefore, to be suitable for defining static and dynamic semantics of module languages.

The intuitive idea behind this construction is to consider a separately compiled module as a program fragment containing all the type information needed to successfully perform the inter-module type-checking (what is called *inter-check* in [9]) in order to link the module in a type-safe way. This information can be abstractly modeled by a set of type constraints whose form depends on the underlying type system. In this way it is possible to deal uniformly with several linguistic mechanisms adopted in module languages. For instance, if a generic module G is parametric in a type t s.t. t$\leq$real (bounded types mechanism), then t$\leq$real belongs to the set of constraints associated with G. This happens also for the types defined in G; if G exports the implementation of a type u=int*int (manifest types mechanism) then u=int*int is another constraint for G. Depending on the core language we consider, we have to specify which are the possible forms of constraints and how these constraints are translated when we rename the type symbols contained in them (e.g., t and u in the example of G). The logic of constraints has to be completed by adding an *entailment* relation between set of constraints (essential for dealing with inter-check), obtaining in this way an *abstract type system*, and, finally, by considering a *satisfaction* relation which introduces the notion of model.

In Sect.1 we present two motivating examples showing the usefulness of type constraints in the context of separate type-checking. The definitions of abstract type system and logic of constraints together with the canonical construction of the model part are given in Sect.2. In the same section we give some standard conditions needed for the construction to work and for the amalgamation lemma to hold. In Sect.3 we show how on top of the model part defined in Sect.2 we can conveniently define static and dynamic semantics of module languages. A simple instantiation of the model is presented in Sect.4, formalizing the concepts introduced in the examples of Sect.1. Sect.5 briefly discusses some related work and draws some conclusions.

1   Two Motivating Examples

In this section we show the usefulness of the notion of *type constraint* for separate type-checking by means of two motivating examples, written in SML.

The first example deals with *manifest types* and *type information propagation*, whereas the second deals with *bounded polymorphism*.

In both cases we show how these mechanisms allows one to gain flexibility in the context of module languages with separate type-checking and how they can be formalized in a uniform way by means of the general notion of *type constraint*.

Manifest Types The notion of *manifest type* has been introduced by Leroy [21] in the context of separate type-checking for SML; a completely equivalent approach can be found also in [16]. Roughly speaking, manifest types correspond to the ability of interfaces to contain type definitions, so that additional information can be recovered by the compiler when performing separate type-checking. Consider, for instance, the following definitions:

```
signature TwiceSig = sig type t; val f:t->t end;
functor TwiceFun(structure S:TwiceSig):TwiceSig =
 struct type t=S.t; fun f(x)=S.f(S.f(x)) end;
structure Succ:TwiceSig = struct type t=int; fun f(x)=x+1 end;
structure TwiceSucc:TwiceSig = TwiceFun(structure S=Succ);
```

Since we are interested in separate type-checking, the compiler can inspect the signatures (i.e., the interfaces) of Succ and TwiceFun, but not their code; for this reason, it can infer that TwiceSucc matches the signature (i.e., has the interface) TwiceSig, but it cannot infer (as we would like in this case) that TwiceSucc matches the signature sig val f:int->int end.

As a consequence, the module TwiceSucc is of little use. The solution to this problem consists in adding the information t=int and t=S.t in the signature of Succ and in the interface of TwiceFun, respectively:

```
functor TwiceFun(structure S:TwiceSig):sig type t=S.t;val f:t->t end =...
structure Succ:sig type t=int; val f:t->t end = ...
```

The information t=int is necessary for the compiler to know how t is implemented in Succ, whereas t=S.t expresses type information propagation.

Bounded Polymorphism Consider the following definitions:

```
signature RealSig = sig val plus:real*real->real end;
signature ComplexSig = sig type cpx; val plus:cpx*cpx->cpx end;
functor Complex(structure S:RealSig):ComplexSig =
  struct type cpx=real*real;
         fun plus((x1,y1),(x2,y2))=(S.plus(x1,x2),S.plus(y1,y2)) end;
```

The functor `Complex` allows one to build complex number on top of a given implementation for real numbers. This definition has the drawback that `Complex` cannot be applied to structures (i.e., modules) implementing other kinds of numbers (e.g., natural, integer and rational numbers). We can solve this problem by changing the signature of the parameter of `Complex` in this way:

```
signature PlusSig = sig type t; val plus:t*t->t end;
functor Complex2(structure S:PlusSig):ComplexSig =
  struct type cpx=S.t*S.t; ... end;
```

However, this is not a completely satisfactory solution, since now our functor can be applied to too many structures (namely, also to non-numeric ones). A better solution consists in adding to `PlusSig` the subtyping constraint $t \leq real$. Obviously, one can take advantage of these kinds of constraints only for module languages whose core language supports subtyping, typically, the object oriented ones. For instance, the language Eiffel [26] supports this approach by allowing the definition of generic classes to depend on a bounded object type; even more advanced is the F-bounded polymorphism of generics in the language Pizza [28].

What should be clear from these examples is that modular programming in the context of separate type-checking becomes more flexible when we have the possibility of enriching interfaces with some information about types in the form of type constraints. What is more interesting, this is a general approach that, in principle, can be applied to any typed core language, independently of its particular type system. Indeed, a particular type system being fixed, one can easily define the set of equality and subtyping constraints over it. Furthermore, equality and subtyping are two possible kinds of constraints, but many others can arise in practice. Consider, for instance, constraints over the structure of types, in order to ensure recursive types to be well defined (see [1]); another example is given by Pizza generics which can contain constraints of the form C implements I(C), where C is a class and I a generic interface.

2   Abstract Type Systems and Logic of Constraints

This section is devoted to the notion of *abstract type system* and *logic of constraints*. Abstract type systems are characterized by the notions of *constraint*, *translation* of a constraint along a function and *constraint entailment*. On top of this notion we can build a category of signatures, where subtyping between signatures is modeled by inclusion morphisms.

A logic of constraints is an abstract type system equipped with a satisfaction relation for constraints which is used for defining the model functor; this is essential for ensuring that the typing rules of the module language (constraint entailment) are sound w.r.t. its semantics (constraint satisfaction).

A set of minimal requirements on the abstract type system and on the logic of constraints must hold in order to be able to define a model part on top of them; we prove that such requirements corresponds to very natural properties of type systems by providing a set of stronger requirements which we expect to be satisfied in a type system (e.g., soundness of the entailment relation w.r.t. the satisfaction relation). Furthermore, such requirements allow logics of constraints to determine model parts where the signature category is finitely cocomplete and the model functor preserves such colimits, an essential property for dealing with modularization [13].

Abstract Type System The notion of abstract type system is strictly based on the concept of type constraint which is crucial when dealing with modules and separate type-checking. Indeed, this turns to be a very general notion which does not need to introduce the concept of type, which is "encapsulated" in that of constraint: this allows to define a general framework which can be instantiated with many different type systems and kinds of constraints.

Definition 1. *An abstract type system $\mathcal{T}$ is a pair $<Con, \vdash>$ where:*

- *Con: **Set** $\rightarrow$ **Set** is a functor over the category **Set** of small sets, mapping sets of type symbols into sets of constraints. For any set T in **Set**, we call $Con(T)$ the set of all constraints over T; similarly, each subset C of $Con(T)$ is called a set of constraints over T and each element belonging to it is called a constraint over T. For each morphism $f: T_1 \rightarrow T_2$ in **Set**, $Con(f): Con(T_1) \rightarrow Con(T_2)$ is a function associating with each constraint $c \in Con(T_1)$ its translation via f, denoted by fc (rather than $Con(f)(c)$). For each set C of constraints over T_1, we denote by fC the set of constraints over T_2 defined by $\{fc \mid c \in C\}$;*
- *$\vdash$ is a family of entailment relations $\vdash_T \subseteq \mathcal{P}(Con(T)) \times Con(T)$ indexed over sets of type symbols. If $C \vdash_T c$ then we say that the set of constraints C entails the constraint c.*
- *the following two properties are satisfied:*
    1. *for any set of constraints C, $C \vdash C$;*
    2. *for any set of constraints C_1, C_2, C_3 over T_1, T_2, T_3, respectively, and any function $f_1: T_1 \rightarrow T_2$ and $f_2: T_2 \rightarrow T_3$, if $C_3 \vdash f_2C_2$ and $C_2 \vdash f_1C_1$ then $C_3 \vdash (f_2 \circ f_1)C_1$.*

We also write $C_1 \vdash_T C_2$ if C_2 is a set of constraints over T s.t. for all $c \in C_2$, $C_1 \vdash_T c$. In the following we will omit the subscripts from the entailment relation.

A similar notion of constraint was introduced in [13] in the context of specification modules. However, here the intention is to focus on the notion of type. Therefore we avoid the more general notion of constraint over a signature and assume that constraints specify only properties about types. The entailment relation is at the basis of the notion of type system. If $C_1 \vdash C_2$ holds, then we expect C_2 to be a logical consequence of C_1, hence, when considering models, we expect that every solution for C_1 is also a solution for C_2.

We now prove that an abstract type system determines a category of signatures.

Proposition 2. *Let $\mathcal{T} = <Con, \vdash>$ be an abstract type system. Then $\mathcal{T}$ determines a category of signatures $\mathbf{Sig}_{\mathcal{T}}$ where objects are all the triples $<T, O, C>$, with C over T and O a T-family of sets of symbols, morphisms from $<T_1, O_1, C_1>$ to $<T_2, O_2, C_2>$ are all the pairs $<f^t, f^o>$ with $f^t: T_1 \to T_2$ s.t. $C_2 \vdash f^t C_1$ and f^o a T_1-family of functions $\{f_t^o: (O_1)_t \to (O_2)_{f^t(t)}\}_{t \in T_1}$ and identities and composition are defined in the obvious way.*

If $\Sigma = <T, O, C>$ is a signature, then we say that Σ *is over T*.

Logic of Constraints We turn now to define a model functor over a category of signatures defined on top of an abstract type system in order to obtain a model part.

A satisfaction relation for sets of constraints is at the basis of the notion of model.

Definition 3. *A logic of constraints $\mathcal{L}$ is a triple $<Con, \vdash, \models>$, where:*

- *$<Con, \vdash>$ is an abstract type system (denoted by $\mathcal{T}(\mathcal{L})$);*
- *$\models$ is a family of satisfaction relations $\models_T \subseteq [T \to \mathbf{Set}] \times Con(T)$ indexed over sets of type symbols, where $[T \to \mathbf{Set}]$ denotes the class of all T-families of sets (i.e., all functors from the discrete category T into $\mathbf{Set}$), called carriers over T. If $A \models_T c$, then we say that the carrier A over T satisfies the constraint c;*
- *the following property is satisfied:*

   3. for any C_1, C_2 over T_1, T_2, respectively, and for any $f: T_1 \to T_2$ and A over T_2, if $A \models C_2$ and $C_2 \vdash fC_1$ then $A_{|f} \models C_1$.

We could consider a more general notion of carrier by replacing $[T \to \mathbf{Set}]$ with $[T \to \mathbf{Cat}]$; this choice should be better for dealing with advanced semantics of types (e.g., CPO and PER models). However, here we prefer to restrict ourselves to sets in order to make the presentation simpler.

We write $A \models_T C$ if C is a set of constraints over T s.t. for all $c \in C$, $A \models_T c$. We also write $C_1 \models_T C_2$ if C_1 and C_2 are sets of constraints over T s.t. for any carrier A over T, $A \models C_1 \Rightarrow A \models C_2$. In the following we will always omit the subscript from the satisfaction relation. Furthermore, if A is over T_1 and $f: T_2 \to T_1$, we will adopt the more standard notation $A_{|f}$ for denoting $A \circ f = \{A_{f(t)}\}_{t \in T_2}$; we also use $A_{|T_2}$ when f is the inclusion of T_2 into T_1.

There exists a clear connection between the notion of abstract type system and logic of constraints and those of *entailment system* [25], *π-institution* [14] and *logical system* [18]. The main difference is that here we focus on the notion of type and type system of a programming language. Hence, defining a logic of constraints means to fix a particular type system and its associate semantics. Once these "ingredients" are fixed, it is possible to define a model part on top of them.

Proposition 4. *Let $\mathcal{L} = \;<Con, \vdash, \models>$ be a logic of constraints. Then $\mathcal{L}$ determines a model part $<\mathbf{Sig}_{\mathcal{L}}, Mod_{\mathcal{L}}>$, where $\mathbf{Sig}_{\mathcal{L}}$ is the signature category $\mathbf{Sig}_{T(\mathcal{L})}$ determined by $T(\mathcal{L})$ and $Mod_{\mathcal{L}}: \mathbf{Sig}_{\mathcal{L}}^{op} \to \mathbf{Class}$ is defined in the following way:*

- *$Mod_{\mathcal{L}}(<T, O, C>)$ is the class of pairs $<A, \mathcal{I}>$, with A carrier over T s.t. $A \models C$ and $\mathcal{I}$ a T-family of functions $\{\mathcal{I}_t: O_t \to A_t\}_{t \in T}$ called interpretation;*
- *if $\;<f^t, f^o>: <T_1, O_1, C_1> \to <T_2, O_2, C_2>$ then $Mod_{\mathcal{L}}(<f^t, f^o>)$ is the function defined by $Mod_{\mathcal{L}}(<f^t, f^o>)(<A, \mathcal{I}>) = <A_{|f^t}, \{\mathcal{I}_{f^t(t)} \circ f_t^o\}_{t \in T_1}>$, for any model $<A, \mathcal{I}>$ over $<T_2, O_2, C_2>$.*

By an abuse of notation, in the following we will often denote a model $<A, \mathcal{I}>$ simply by A and use the standard notation $A_{|<f^t, f^o>}$ for denoting $Mod_{\mathcal{L}}(<f^t, f^o>)(<A, \mathcal{I}>)$. Furthermore, we will also write g^A instead of $\mathcal{I}_t(g)$.

Conditions 1, 2, and 3 ensure that the model part construction is correct. However, even though minimal, conditions 2 and 3 are not standard. Therefore we prefer to replace them with a set of more restrictive but standard conditions ensuring the correctness of our construction.

Proposition 5. *Let $\mathcal{L} = \;<ConSetSet, \vdash, \models>$ be a triple satisfying the following properties:*

- *(reflexivity of entailment) for any set of constraints C, $C \vdash C$;*
- *(transitivity of entailment) for any set of constraints C_1, C_2 and C_3 over T, if $C_1 \vdash C_2$ and $C_2 \vdash C_3$ then $C_1 \vdash C_3$;*
- *(preservation of entailment under translation) for any set of constraints C_1 and C_2 over T_1 and any function $f: T_1 \to T_2$, if $C_1 \vdash C_2$ then $fC_1 \vdash fC_2$;*
- *(soundness) for any set of constraints C_1 and C_2 over T, if $C_1 \vdash C_2$ then $C_1 \models C_2$;*
- *(satisfaction condition) for any set of constraints C over T_1, any function $f: T_1 \to T_2$ and any carrier A over T_2, $A \models fC$ iff $A_{|f} \models C$.*

Then $\mathcal{L}$ determines a logic of constraints.

Note that here, by contrast with the notion of entailment system, π-institution and logical system, we do not require monotonicity of the entailment relation, therefore the framework is suitable also for supporting non-monotonic reasoning. Note also that for the proof of Prop.5 we need only one side of the satisfaction condition (actually, it suffices to assume that reduct preserves satisfaction); the other side is needed for proving that $Mod_{\mathcal{L}}$ preserves finite colimits (Prop.10).

Proposition 6. *Let $\mathcal{L} = \;<Con, \vdash, \models>$ be a logic of constraints satisfying the five properties of Prop.5. Then the signature category $\mathbf{Sig}_{\mathcal{L}}$ determined by $\mathcal{L}$ is finitely cocomplete.*

We have shown that we can combine signatures together in $\mathbf{Sig}_{\mathcal{L}}$; we turn now to consider models and wonder whether it is possible to combine models, too, by means of the *amalgamated sum*. Fortunately, the answer is affirmative, since it can be proved that for any logic of constraints $\mathcal{L}$, $Mod_{\mathcal{L}}$ preserves finite colimits and, therefore, the amalgamation lemma holds [13]. In order to prove this fact, we first need to show that the model functor $UMod$, obtained from $Mod_{\mathcal{L}}$ by simply forgetting type constraints, preserves finite colimits. In the following we denote by $\mathbf{SSet}$ the category of many-sorted sets (see [32] for a formal definition); furthermore, we recall that $\mathbf{SSet}$ is (finitely) cocomplete.

Definition 7. *Let* $UMod: \mathbf{SSet} \to \mathbf{Class}$ *be the functor defined by:*

- *$UMod(<T, O>)$ is the class of pairs $<A, \mathcal{I}>$, with A a carrier over T and $\mathcal{I}$ a T-family of functions $\{\mathcal{I}_t: O_t \to A_t\}_{t \in T}$;*
- *if $<f^t, f^o>: <T_1, O_1> \to <T_2, O_2>$ then $UMod(<f^t, f^o>)$ is the function defined by $UMod(<f^t, f^o>)(<A, \mathcal{I}>) = <A_{|f^t}, \{\mathcal{I}_{f^t(t)} \circ f_t^o\}_{t \in T_1}>$, for any model $<A, \mathcal{I}>$ over $<T_2, O_2>$.*

Note that, if $\mathcal{L}$ is a logic of constraints, then, trivially, for any morphism $f: \Sigma_1 \to \Sigma_2$ in $\mathbf{Sig}_{\mathcal{L}}$, the equality $i_1 \circ Mod_{\mathcal{L}}(f) = (UMod \circ U_{\mathcal{L}})(f) \circ i_2$, holds, where $i_k: Mod_{\mathcal{L}}(\Sigma_k) \hookrightarrow (UMod \circ U_{\mathcal{L}})(\Sigma_k)$, $k = 1, 2$, denotes the obvious inclusions.

Let $<\mathbf{AlgSig}, Alg>$ be the model part of many-sorted algebras (see [32]); it is well-known that Alg preserves finite colimits [7]; furthermore there exists an embedding functor E from $\mathbf{SSet}$ into $\mathbf{AlgSig}$ s.t. E preserves finite colimits and $Alg \circ E$ is naturally isomorphic to $UMod$, hence $UMod$ preserves finite colimits, too. That is formalized by the following propositions.

Proposition 8. *Let* $E: \mathbf{SSet} \to \mathbf{AlgSig}$ *be the functor defined by:*

$$E(<T, O>) = <T, O'>, \ O'_{<\bar{t}, t>} = \begin{cases} O_t & \text{if } \bar{t} = \Lambda \\ \emptyset & \text{otherwise} \end{cases} \text{ for each } <\bar{t}, t> \in T^* \times T$$

$$E(<f^t, f^o>) = <f^t, f'^o>, \ f'^o_{<\bar{t}, t>} = \begin{cases} f_t^o & \text{if } \bar{t} = \Lambda \\ id_{\emptyset} & \text{otherwise} \end{cases} \text{ for each } <\bar{t}, t> \in T^* \times T$$

Then E has a right-adjoint and $UMod$ is naturally isomorphic to $Alg \circ E$.

Corollary 9. *The functor $UMod$ preserves finite colimits.*

Proposition 10. *Let $\mathcal{L} = <Con, \vdash, \models>$ be a logic of constraints satisfying the five properties of Prop.5. Then the functor $Mod_{\mathcal{L}}$ determined by $\mathcal{L}$ preserves finite colimits.*

3   Modeling Generic Modules in an Arbitrary Type System

In this section we show how it is possible to model constant (i.e., non parametric) and generic (i.e., parametric) modules defined on top of a typed core language.

In order to be able to do this, we only need the type system of the underlying core language to give rise to a logic of constraints satisfying the five properties of Prop.5. Indeed, the models are directly defined on top of the model part determined by the logic of constraints, and the semantics of generic module application is based on the amalgamation sum.

For reasons of space we consider a very simple module language supporting constant and generic modules and application as the only possible operation over modules. However, we see no restrictions in defining a richer language, with more sophisticated operators and features, as investigated in [4,2].

Static Semantics The entities denoted by the module typed language we are going to define are constant and generic modules, whereas types are their interfaces. Types for constant modules are the objects $<T, O, C>$ of the signature category $\mathbf{Sig}_{\mathcal{L}}$: T represents the exported type components, whereas O represents all the other exported components (associated with their corresponding types); C represents the set of constraints over the exported type components that are assumed to be statically satisfied by the module.

The type for a generic module is of the form $\Sigma^{in} \to \Sigma^{out}$, with Σ^{in} and Σ^{out} the type of the parameter and of the body of the generic, respectively.

Definition 11. *All generic module types are of the form $\Sigma^{in} \to \Sigma^{out}$, with Σ^{in} and Σ^{out} signatures in $\mathbf{Sig}_{\mathcal{L}}$ over T^{in} and T^{out}, respectively, and $T^{in} \subseteq T^{out}$.*

The condition $T^{in} \subseteq T^{out}$ is essential for dealing with type information propagation. However, such a condition corresponds to automatically export all the type components of the parameter; by slightly complicating Def.11 we could also manage with situations where one wants to hide some types of the parameter, but here we prefer to avoid such a complication in favor of a clearer presentation.

As already stated, the module language supports subtyping: intuitively, a generic module G can be applied to a module whose interface is larger and have more restrictive requirements than the parameter interface. This is formalized by the notion of *inclusion morphism*.

Definition 12. *An inclusion morphism $<i^t, i^o>:<T_1, O_1, C_1> \hookrightarrow <T_2, O_2, C_2>$ in $\mathbf{Sig}_{\mathcal{L}}$ is a morphism s.t. $i^t:T_1 \hookrightarrow T_2$ is the inclusion function from T_1 into T_2 and i^o is the family of inclusions $\{i_t:(O_1)_t \hookrightarrow (O_2)_t\}_{t \in T_1}$.*

If $<i^t, i^o>:\Sigma_1 \hookrightarrow \Sigma_2$ is an inclusion morphism, then we will often use the notation $A_{|\Sigma_1}$ instead of $A_{|<i^t,i^o>}$.

Definition 13. *The type Σ_1 is a subtype of Σ_2 iff there exists an inclusion morphism (necessarily unique) from Σ_2 into Σ_1.*

By definition of $\mathbf{Sig}_{\mathcal{L}}$ (see Prop.2) and by Def.12 and Def.13 we can easily derive the rule for subtyping (Fig.1).

The typing rule for application is given in Fig.1. Note that no subsumption rule has been given, since in rule $(A\tau)$ we need to know the most specific type of M, in order to properly deal with type information propagation. More precisely, the types of M and their associated constraints are propagated to the outside by putting together the interface of the body (Σ^{out}) with the type information of M ($<T, \emptyset, C>$) by means of the pushout operator $+_{T^{in}}$ (note that, by contrast, the other components of M are not propagated):$\Sigma^{out} +_{T^{in}} <T, \emptyset, C>$ denotes the pushout for the pair of (inclusion) morphisms $<T^{in}, \emptyset, \emptyset> \hookrightarrow \Sigma^{out}$ and $<T^{in}, \emptyset, \emptyset> \hookrightarrow <T, \emptyset, C>$.

$$\text{(S)} \quad \frac{}{\Sigma_1 \leq \Sigma_2} \quad <i^t, i^o>:\Sigma_2 \hookrightarrow \Sigma_1$$

$$\text{(A}\tau\text{)} \quad \frac{G: \Sigma^{in} \to \Sigma^{out} \quad M:\Sigma}{G(M):\Sigma^{out} +_{T^{in}} <T, \emptyset, C>} \quad \begin{array}{l} \Sigma \leq \Sigma^{in} \\ \Sigma^{in} = <T^{in}, O^{in}, C^{in}> \\ \Sigma = <T, O, C> \end{array}$$

Fig. 1. Typing rule for application

Dynamic Semantics We turn now to consider the entities denoted by the module language. Constant modules of type Σ are simply modeled by models in $Mod_{\mathcal{L}}(\Sigma)$; recall that such models provide interpretations for the types in T which are consistent with the set of constraint C and for the other components in O (see Prop.4).

Intuitively, one expects generic modules of type $\Sigma^{in} \to \Sigma^{out}$ to be modeled by functions from $Mod_{\mathcal{L}}(\Sigma^{in})$ into $Mod_{\mathcal{L}}(\Sigma^{out})$. But this is a too coarse domain since type propagation implies that for any constant module M and generic module G which are type-compatible, M and $G(M)$ must coincide over the type components in T^{in}.

Definition 14. *For any module type $\Sigma^{in} \to \Sigma^{out}$, its class of models is defined by all functions $F: Mod_{\mathcal{L}}(\Sigma^{in}) \to Mod_{\mathcal{L}}(\Sigma^{out})$ s.t. $\forall A \in Mod_{\mathcal{L}}(\Sigma^{in})$ $A = (F(A))_{|T^{in}}$.*

The semantic clause for application is given in Fig.2. It is assumed that G and M satisfy the typing rule $(A\tau)$ of Fig.1. The semantics of M must be explicitly coerced to the supertype of the parameter by means of the reduct operator $(A_{|\Sigma^{in}})$, then F can be safely applied. Finally, the result must be "augmented" by the types introduced by the actual parameter by means of the amalgamated sum operator $\oplus_{T^{in}}$ (the model counter-part of the $+_{T^{in}}$ operator over signatures); note that the types in T^{in} must be shared.

We finish this section by showing that the semantics of application is well-defined.

Proposition 15. *For any well-typed expression $G(M)$, $[\![G(M)]\!]$ is well-defined.*

$$(A\sigma) \qquad \frac{[\![G]\!] = F \quad [\![M]\!] = A}{[\![G(M)]\!] = F(A_{|\Sigma^{in}}) \oplus_{T^{in}} A_{|<T,\emptyset,C>}}$$

Fig. 2. Semantic clause for application

4   Fixing a Logic of Constraints

In this section we instantiate the framework presented in Sect.2 and 3 over a particular logic of constraints (henceforth denoted by $\mathcal{L}_0$) in order to define a model for the module language presented in Sect.1. We give a concrete definition of abstract type system and of logic of constraints and prove that these definitions verify the requested properties of Prop.5.

Finally, we show how the two examples presented in Sect.1 are mapped into the model.

Constraints A constraint over $\{t_1, \ldots, t_n\}$ is either of the form $\tau_1 = \tau_2$ or $\tau_1 \leq \tau_2$, where τ_1 and τ_2 range over the type expressions inductively defined over basic types (unit, bool, int, real), the type variables $t_1, \ldots, t_n$ and the constructors $*$ and $\rightarrow$. For reasons of space and for sake of simplicity we have not not considered polymorphic types, which, obviously should be taken into account when dealing with SML-like core languages.

Translation is straightforward: $f(\tau_1 = \tau_2) \equiv f^\#(\tau_1) = f^\#(\tau_2)$, $f(\tau_1 \leq \tau_2) \equiv f^\#(\tau_1) \leq f^\#(\tau_2)$, where $\equiv$ denotes syntactic equivalence and $f^\#$ is the homomorphic extension of f to type expressions.

The entailment relation is defined in Fig.3.

$$\frac{}{C \vdash \tau \leq \tau} \qquad \frac{C \vdash \tau_1 \leq \tau_2 \quad C \vdash \tau_2 \leq \tau_1}{C \vdash \tau_1 = \tau_2} \qquad \frac{C \vdash \tau_1 \leq \tau_2 \quad C \vdash \tau_2 \leq \tau_3}{C \vdash \tau_1 \leq \tau_3}$$

$$\frac{C \vdash \tau_1 = \tau_2}{C \vdash \tau_2 = \tau_1} \qquad \frac{C \vdash \tau_1 = \tau_2}{C \vdash \tau_1 \leq \tau_2} \qquad \frac{}{C \vdash \text{int} \leq \text{real}}$$

$$\frac{C \vdash \tau_1 \leq \tau_1' \quad C \vdash \tau_2 \leq \tau_2'}{C \vdash \tau_1 * \tau_2 \leq \tau_1' * \tau_2'} \qquad \frac{C \vdash \tau_1' \leq \tau_1 \quad C \vdash \tau_2 \leq \tau_2'}{C \vdash \tau_1 \rightarrow \tau_2 \leq \tau_1' \rightarrow \tau_2'} \qquad \frac{}{\{c\} \cup C \vdash c}$$

Fig. 3. Constraint entailment

Satisfaction The relation is defined by $A \models \tau_1 \leq \tau_2 \iff [\![\tau_1]\!](A) \subseteq [\![\tau_2]\!](A)$ and $A \models \tau_1 = \tau_2 \iff [\![\tau_1]\!](A) = [\![\tau_2]\!](A)$, where $[\![\tau]\!](A)$ denotes the semantics of τ w.r.t. the carrier A and is defined in Fig.4. The notation $A \rightharpoonup B$ denotes the set of all partial functions from A to B and $A \times B$ the Cartesian product of A and B. Again, for reasons of space, we have preferred a simple semantics avoiding to introduce CPO models, which, however, are essential ingredients when dealing with recursive type expressions.

$$\llbracket \text{unit} \rrbracket (A) = \{*\} \qquad \llbracket \text{bool} \rrbracket (A) = \{f,t\} \qquad \llbracket \text{int} \rrbracket (A) = \mathbb{Z} \qquad \llbracket t \rrbracket (A) = A_t$$
$$\llbracket \tau_1 * \tau_2 \rrbracket (A) = \llbracket \tau_1 \rrbracket (A) \times \llbracket \tau_2 \rrbracket (A) \qquad \llbracket \tau_1 \rightarrow \tau_2 \rrbracket (A) = \llbracket \tau_1 \rrbracket (A) \rightharpoonup \llbracket \tau_2 \rrbracket (A)$$

Fig. 4. Semantics of types

Proposition 16. *The logic $\mathcal{L}_0$ satisfies the five properties of Prop.5.*

Mapping modules into models We conclude this section by showing how the modules presented in Sect.1 are mapped into models of the form defined in Sect.3, instantiated over $\mathcal{L}_0$. We stress again that in this case $\mathcal{L}_0$ turns out to be adequate, since the examples given in Sect.1 do not deal with polymorphism and recursive types; however, for more sophisticated examples, more advanced logics are needed.

Manifest types The interface of Succ corresponds to the signature $\Sigma_S = <\{t,t'\}, \{f:t'\}, \{t = \text{int}, t' = t \rightarrow t\}>$, where $\{f:t'\}$ denotes the family O s.t. $O_t = \emptyset$, $O_{t'} = \{f\}$ (we keep using this notation in the examples that follow below). The signature $\Sigma_{TF}^{in} \rightarrow \Sigma_{TF}^{out}$ of TwiceFun is defined by
$$\Sigma_{TF}^{in} = <\{t,t'\}, \{f:t'\}, \{t' = t \rightarrow t\}>,$$
$$\Sigma_{TF}^{out} = <\{t,t',t'',t'''\}, \{f:t'''\}, \{t'' = t, t''' = t'' \rightarrow t''\}>, \text{ where } t, t'' \text{ corre-}$$
spond to S.t and t in the first example of Sect.1, respectively.

Since $\{t = \text{int}, t' = t \rightarrow t\} \vdash \{t' = t \rightarrow t\}$, we have, by (S) of Fig.1, $\Sigma_S \leq \Sigma_{TF}^{in}$, therefore, applying $(A\tau)$ of Fig.1 we can derive that TwiceFun(Succ) has the signature
$<\{t,t',t'',t'''\}, \{f:t'''\}, \{t'' = t, t''' = t'' \rightarrow t'', t = \text{int}, t' = t \rightarrow t\}>$, which is a subtype of $<\{t'',t'''\}, \{f:t'''\}, \{t'' = \text{int}, t''' = t'' \rightarrow t''\}>$, since, clearly, $\{t'' = t, t''' = t'' \rightarrow t'', t = \text{int}, t' = t \rightarrow t\} \vdash \{t'' = \text{int}, t''' = t'' \rightarrow t''\}$.

The module Succ denotes the model A_S defined by $(A_S)_t = \mathbb{Z}$, $(A_S)_{t'} = \mathbb{Z} \rightharpoonup \mathbb{Z}$ and $f^{A_S} = \lambda x.x + 1$, whereas the generic module TwiceFun denotes the function F, mapping each model A^{in} (over Σ_{TF}^{in}) to the model A^{out} (over Σ_{TF}^{out}) defined by $A_t^{out} = A_{t''}^{out} = A_t^{in}$, $A_{t'}^{out} = A_{t'''}^{out} = A_{t'}^{in}$, $f^{A^{out}} = f^{A^{in}} \circ f^{A^{in}}$. By clause $(A\sigma)$ of Fig.2, TwiceFun(Succ) denotes the model B defined by $B_t = B_{t''} = \mathbb{Z}$, $B_{t'} = B_{t'''} = \mathbb{Z} \rightharpoonup \mathbb{Z}$, $f^B = \lambda x.x + 2$.

Bounded Polymorphism. The signature $\Sigma_C^{in} \rightarrow \Sigma_C^{out}$ of Complex2 is defined by
$$\Sigma_C^{in} = <\{t,t'\}, \{plus:t'\}, \{t' = t * t \rightarrow t, t \leq \text{real}\}>,$$
$$\Sigma_C^{out} = <\{t,t',t'',t'''\}, \{plus:t'''\}, \{t'' = t * t, t''' = t'' * t'' \rightarrow t''\}>, \text{ where } t, t''$$
correspond to S.t and cpx in the second example of Sect.1, respectively. Let $\Sigma_I = <\{t,t'\}, \{plus:t'\}, \{t' = t * t \rightarrow t, t = \text{int}\}>$ be the signature of a module I implementing integer numbers. Then $\Sigma_I \leq \Sigma_C^{in}$, since
$$\{t' = t * t \rightarrow t, t = \text{int}\} \vdash \{t' = t * t \rightarrow t, t \leq \text{real}\}.$$
Note that subtyping could not be inferred if the constraint $t = \text{int}$ were not present in the signature Σ_I. Finally, Complex2(I) has the signature
$<\{t,t',t'',t'''\}, \{plus:t'''\}, \{t'' = t * t, t''' = t'' * t'' \rightarrow t'', t' = t * t \rightarrow t, t = \text{int}\}>$.

Analogously to the previous example, we can easily derive the models denoted by Complex2, I and Complex2(I).

5 Conclusion and Related Work

We have defined an algebraic framework directly supporting the notion of *type* and *separate type-checking*. More precisely, we have shown how it is possible to construct a model part on top of a given type system by introducing the notions of abstract type system and logic of constraints.

We have proved that, under standard requirements over the logic, such a model part satisfies the usual properties needed for defining the semantics of module systems. Indeed, following the technique developed in [4,2], we have defined over this model part the static and dynamic semantics of a typed module language with generic modules; as a consequence, the definition of such a language is independent of the underlying core language and its type system. A simple module language has been considered, but one could define richer languages, with more sophisticated operators and features, as investigated in [4,2].

Finally, we have presented an instantiation of the framework able to model a module language over a simple typed functional language supporting manifest types, type information propagation and bounded polymorphic generics.

The notion of logic of constraints has been inspired by [13] where it was introduced in the context of specification modules; however, even though the approach is similar in the spirit (and, for this reason, we have used the same terminology), here the technical details are different, since we are interested in type constraints over programs, rather than generic constraints over specifications.

As already stated, the notions of abstract type system and logic of constraints have a strict connection with those of entailment system [25], π-institution [14] and logical system [18]. Our approach, however, is different from the others since it privileges the aspects connected with the notion of type system and separate type-checking. For instance, we do not need to assume monotonicity of the entailment relation, as it happens in the other mentioned approaches.

The PhD thesis of Aspinall ([5], Chap.6 and 7) and the related paper [30] is without any doubt the most related work to this paper: the instantiation of ASL+ over the institution $\mathcal{FPC}$ allows Aspinall to define a powerful type-checking system for modules. However, such a system deals with type equalities, but not with more general type constraints like subtyping; furthermore, the choice of the specific $\mathcal{FPC}$ institution prevents from defining module systems over arbitrary core languages.

Finally, many other interesting theoretical papers can be found about modularization and separate type-checking [17,16,21,22,20,33]. However, this paper differs from them since it proposes a general framework bound to neither any particular language nor type system and able to embody some of the techniques proposed in them. For instance, the several subtyping relations on polymorphic constrained types defined in [33] in the context of constrained type inference, have also interesting applications to separate type-checking of modules, as recognized by the authors themselves.

Acknowledgments

Special thanks to Elena Zucca for her suggestions and corrections to early drafts to this paper; many thanks also to Maura Cerioli, whose technical suggestions helped me in the development of some proofs. Finally, I am also in debt with Xavier Leroy and Didier Rémy, for their interesting discussions about preliminary versions of this paper.

References

1. R. Amadio and L. Cardelli. Subtyping recursive types. *ACM Transactions on Programming Languages and Systems*, 15(4):575–631, September 1993. Extended abstract in POPL 1991.
2. D. Ancona. *Modular Formal Frameworks for Module Systems*. PhD thesis, Dipartimento di Informatica, Università di Pisa, March 1998.
3. D. Ancona and E. Zucca. An algebra of mixin modules. In F. Parisi-Presicce, editor, *Proc. 12th International Workshop, WADT '97, Tarquinia, Italy, June 1997. Selected Papers*, volume 1376 of *Lecture Notes in Computer Science*, Berlin, 1998. Springer Verlag. To appear.
4. D. Ancona and E. Zucca. A theory of mixin modules: basic and derived operators. *Mathematical Structures in Computer Science*, 1998. To appear.
5. D. Aspinall. *Type Systems for Modular Programs and Specifications*. PhD thesis, Department of Computer Science, University of Edinburgh, August 1997.
6. G. Banavar and G. Lindstrom. An application framework for module composition tools. In *Proc. of European Conference on Object-Oriented Programming*, number 1098 in Lecture Notes in Computer Science, pages 91–113. Springer Verlag, July 1996.
7. S. Bloom and E. Wagner. Many-sorted theories and their algebras, with examples from computer science. In *US-French Joint Symp. on the Applications of Algebra to language definition and Compilation, Fontainebleau*, 1982.
8. G. Bracha and G. Lindstrom. Modularity meets inheritance. In *Proc. International Conference on Computer Languages*, pages 282–290, San Francisco, April 1992. IEEE Computer Society.
9. L. Cardelli. Program fragments, linking, and modularization. In *Proc. 24th ACM Symp. on Principles of Programming Languages*, pages 266–277. ACM Press, January 1997.
10. J. Courant. An applicative module calculus. In M. Bidoit and M. Dauchet, editors, *Proc. TAPSOFT '97: Theory and Practice of Software Development*, number 1217 in Lecture Notes in Computer Science, pages 622–636. Springer Verlag, April 1997.
11. J. Courant. *MC: un calcul de modules pour les systèmes de types purs*. PhD thesis, École normale supérieure de Lyon, 1998.
12. D. Duggan and C. Sourelis. Mixin modules. In *Intl. Conf. on Functional Programming*, Philadelphia, May 1996. ACM Press.
13. H. Ehrig and B. Mahr. *Fundamentals of Algebraic Specification 2. Module Specifications and and Constraints*, volume 21 of *EATCS Monograph in Computer Science*. Springer Verlag, 1990.
14. J. Fiadeiro and A. Sernadas. Structuring theories on consequence. In *Selected Papers from the 5th Workshop on Specification of Abstract Data Types*, number 332 in Lecture Notes in Computer Science, pages 44–72. Springer Verlag, 1988.

15. J. A. Goguen and R. Burstall. Institutions: abstract model theory for specification and programming. *Journ. ACM*, 39(1):95–146, 1992.
16. R. Harper and M. Lillibridge. A type theoretic approach to higher-order modules with sharing. In *Proc. 21st ACM Symp. on Principles of Programming Languages*, pages 127–137. ACM Press, 1994.
17. R. Harper, M. Lillibridge, and E. Moggi. Higher-order modules and the phase distinction. In *Proc. 17th ACM Symp. on Principles of Programming Languages*, pages 341–354, S. Francisco, CA, January 1990. ACM Press.
18. R. Harper, D. Sannella, and A. Tarlecki. Structure theory presentations and logic representations. *Annals of Pure and Applied Logic*, 67:113–160, 1994.
19. M. P. Jones. A system of constructor classes: Overloading and implicit higher-order polymorphism. *Journal of Functional Programming*, 5(1), January 1995.
20. M. P. Jones. Using parameterized signatures to express modular structure. In *Proc. 23rd ACM Symp. on Principles of Programming Languages*, pages 68–78, St. Petersburg Beach, Florida, Jan 1996. ACM Press.
21. X. Leroy. Manifest types, modules and separate compilation. In *Proc. 21st ACM Symp. on Principles of Programming Languages*, pages 109–122. ACM Press, 1994.
22. X. Leroy. Applicative functors and fully transparent higher-order modules. In *Proc. 22nd ACM Symp. on Principles of Programming Languages*. ACM Press, 1995.
23. X. Leroy. A modular module system. Technical Report 2866, INRIA, April 1996.
24. M. Van Limberghen and T. Mens. Encapsulation and composition as orthogonal operators on mixins: a solution to multiple inheritance problems. *Object Oriented Systems*, 3:1–30, 1996.
25. J. Meseguer. General logic. In *Logic Colloquium '87*, pages 275–329. North Holland, 1989.
26. B. Meyer. *Eiffel: The language*. Prentice Hall, 1992.
27. R. Milner, M. Tofte, and R. Harper. *The Definition of Standard ML*. The MIT Press, Cambridge, Massachussetts, 1990.
28. M. Odersky and P. Wadler. Pizza into Java: Translating theory into practice. In *Proc. 24th ACM Symposium on Principles of Programming Languages*, January 1997.
29. D.L. Parnas. On the criteria to be used in decomposing systems into modules. *Communications of the ACM*, 5(12):1053–1058, December 1972.
30. D. Sannella, S. Sokołowoski, and A. Tarlecki. Toward formal development of programs from algebraic specifications: Parameterisation revisited. *Acta Informatica*, 29:689–736, 1992.
31. D. Sannella and A. Tarlecki. Specification in an arbitrary institution. *Information and Computation*, 76:165–210, 1988.
32. A. Tarlecki, R.M. Burstall, and J.A. Goguen. Some fundamental algebraic tools for the semantics of computation - Part III: Indexed categories. *TCS*, 91:239–264, 1991.
33. V. Trifonov and S. Smith. Subtyping constrained types. In *Proc. of the Third International Static Analysis Symposium*, volume 1145 of *Lecture Notes in Computer Science*, pages 349–365. Springer Verlag, 1996.

Moving Specification Structures Between Logical Systems *

Tomasz Borzyszkowski

Institute of Mathematics, University of Gdańsk
T.Borzyszkowski@guests.ipipan.gda.pl

Abstract. The conditions under which a formal system for reasoning about structural specifications, built over one logical system could be reused for reasoning about structured specifications built over another logical system are formulated and studied. Following Goguen and Burstall, the notion of a logical system is formalized as an institution and extended to a $\mathcal{D}$-institution. A new function between classes of specifications, inspired by a similar function from [HST 94], is defined as a natural extension of *institution representations* to structured specifications.

1 Introduction

In the process of software specification and development, we often have to use various logical systems to capture various aspects of software systems and various programming paradigms. The problem which arises during such processes (see also [Tar 95]) can be formulated as follows:

> Can we reuse various tools, libraries and proof strategies available for different logical systems in the context of other logical systems?

Attempts to find a positive answer to this question could be found in various works on logical systems and specifications built over them (see e.g. [CM 97,HST 94,Mossa 96,Tar 95]).

In this paper we extend *institution representation* to *specification representation* and formulate conditions under which a complete and sound proof system for reasoning about logical consequences (and also about refinement) of structured specifications can be reused for a sound, but not necessarily complete, proof system for reasoning about logical consequences (and also about refinement) of structured specifications. The conditions under which a proof system for structured specifications is sound and complete can be found in [Wir 91,Cen 94,Borz 97].

The main theorems of this paper were inspired by similar theorems presented in [HST 94] on the theory level and also in [Tar 95] for *flat specifications* and extend them to structured specifications. Relationships presented in section 5 were also studied in [AC 94].

---

* This research was partially supported by KBN grant 8 T11C 018 11 and ESPRIT CRIT2 program.

In last sections, we demonstrate "how and while" the results presented in this paper are stronger then those presented in [HST 94] and also compare them with similar results presented in other papers.

2 Institutions

While developing a specification system independently of the underlying logical system, it is necessary to formalize an abstract mathematical concept of what a logical system is. Our choice of an abstract formalization depends on what we mean by a logical system. Following [GB 92] in the model–theoretic tradition of logic:

> "One of the most essential elements of a logical system is its relationship of *satisfaction* between its *syntax* (i.e. its sentences) and its *semantics* (i.e. models)..."

Based on this principle, the notion of a logical system is formalized as a mathematical object called *institution* in [GB 92].

An institution consists of a collection of signatures, together with a set of Σ-sentences and a collection of Σ-models for each signature Σ, and a satisfaction relation between Σ-models and Σ-sentences. The only requirement is that when we change signatures (by signature morphisms), the induced translations of sentences and models preserve the satisfaction relation.

Definition 1 (Institution [GB 92]). *An institution I consists of:*

- *a category $\mathbf{Sign}_I$ of signatures;*
- *a functor $\mathbf{Sen}_I : \mathbf{Sign}_I \to \mathbf{Set}$, giving a set $\mathbf{Sen}_I(\Sigma)$ of Σ-sentences for each signature $\Sigma \in |\mathbf{Sign}_I|$;*
- *a functor $\mathbf{Mod}_I : \mathbf{Sign}_I^{op} \to \mathbf{Cat}$, giving a category $\mathbf{Mod}_I(\Sigma)$ of Σ-models for each signature $\Sigma \in |\mathbf{Sign}_I|$;*
- *for each $\Sigma \in |\mathbf{Sign}_I|$, a satisfaction relation $\models_\Sigma^I \subseteq |\mathbf{Mod}_I(\Sigma)| \times \mathbf{Sen}_I(\Sigma)$ such that for any signature morphism $\sigma : \Sigma \to \Sigma'$, Σ-sentence $\varphi \in \mathbf{Sen}_I(\Sigma)$ and Σ'-model $M' \in |\mathbf{Mod}_I(\Sigma')|$:*

$$M' \models_{\Sigma'}^I \mathbf{Sen}_I(\sigma)(\varphi) \quad iff \quad \mathbf{Mod}_I(\sigma)(M') \models_\Sigma^I \varphi \quad (Satisfaction\ condition)$$

□

In the rest of the paper, the following abbreviations are used:

- for every set of sentences $\Phi \subseteq \mathbf{Sen}_I(\Sigma)$ and $M \in \mathbf{Mod}_I(\Sigma)$, we define $M \models_\Sigma^I \Phi$ as an abbreviation for *for all $\varphi \in \Phi$ $M \models_\Sigma^I \varphi$* and similarly for every class of models $\mathcal{M} \subseteq \mathbf{Mod}_I(\Sigma)$ and sentence $\varphi \in \mathbf{Sen}_I(\Sigma)$ we define $\mathcal{M} \models_\Sigma^I \varphi$ as an abbreviation for *for all $M \in \mathcal{M}$ $M \models_\Sigma^I \varphi$*;
- the following abbreviations will be used: $\sigma\,\varphi$ for $\mathbf{Sen}_I(\sigma)(\varphi)$, $M|_\sigma$ for $\mathbf{Mod}_I(\sigma)(M)$ and $\models$ or $\models_\Sigma$ for $\models_\Sigma^I$ when it is clear what they mean.

Examples of various logical systems viewed as institutions can be found in [GB 92]. In this paper we recall a few examples of institutions. The first two were presented also in [Tar 95]:

Example 1. The institution **EQ** of equational logic: Signatures are the usual many-sorted algebraic signatures; sentences are (universally quantified) equations with translations along a signature morphism essentially by replacing the operation names as indicated by the signature morphism; models are many-sorted algebras with reducts along a signature morphism defined in the usual way; and satisfaction relations are given as the usual satisfaction of an equation in an algebra.   □

Example 2. The institution **FOEQ** of first-order logic with equality: Signatures are first-order many-sorted signatures (with sort names, operation names and predicate names); sentences are the usual closed formulae of first-order logic built over atomic formulae given either as equalities or atomic predicate formulae; models are the usual first-order structures; satisfaction of a formula in a structure is defined in the standard way.   □

Example 3. The institution **PEQ** of partial equational logic: Signatures are (as in **EQ**) many-sorted algebraic signatures; sentences are (universally quantified) equations and definedness formulae with translations along a signature morphism defined similarly as in institution **EQ**; models are partial many-sorted algebras with reducts along a signature morphism defined in the usual way; and satisfaction relations are defined as the satisfaction of an equation[1] and a definedness formula in a partial many-sorted algebra.   □

Definition 2 (D-institution). *An institution I (as in Definition 1) with a fixed class of signature morphisms $\mathcal{D}_I \subseteq \mathbf{Sign}_I$ will be called $\mathcal{D}$-institution.*
                                                                                       □

3   Institution representations

The notion of an institution representation introduced below is a special case of a *map of institutions* (see [Mes 89]). A similarly motivated notion was introduced in [Tar 95].

Definition 3 (Institution representation). *Let*
$I = \langle \mathbf{Sign}, \mathbf{Sen}, \mathbf{Mod}, \langle \models_\Sigma \rangle_{\Sigma \in |\mathbf{Sign}|} \rangle$ *and*
$I' = \langle \mathbf{Sign}', \mathbf{Sen}', \mathbf{Mod}', \langle \models'_\Sigma \rangle_{\Sigma \in |\mathbf{Sign}'|} \rangle$ *be arbitrary institutions. An institution representation $\rho : I \to I'$ consists of:*

---

[1] The satisfaction of an equation is strong, i.e. the equation $t_1 = t_2$ holds if t_1 and t_2 are either both undefined or both defined and equal.

- a functor $\rho^{\mathbf{Sign}} : \mathbf{Sign} \to \mathbf{Sign}'$; and
- a natural transformation: $\rho^{\mathbf{Sen}} : \mathbf{Sen} \to \rho^{\mathbf{Sign}}; \mathbf{Sen}'$, that is, a family of functions $\rho_{\Sigma}^{\mathbf{Sen}} : \mathbf{Sen}(\Sigma) \to \mathbf{Sen}'(\rho^{\mathbf{Sign}}(\Sigma))$, natural in $\Sigma \in |\mathbf{Sign}|$:

$$
\begin{array}{ccc}
\Sigma_2 & \mathbf{Sen}(\Sigma_2) \xrightarrow{\rho_{\Sigma_2}^{\mathbf{Sen}}} \mathbf{Sen}'(\rho^{\mathbf{Sign}}(\Sigma_2)) \\[2ex]
\sigma \uparrow & \mathbf{Sen}(\sigma) \uparrow \qquad\qquad\qquad \uparrow \mathbf{Sen}'(\rho^{\mathbf{Sign}}(\sigma)) \\[2ex]
\Sigma_1 & \mathbf{Sen}(\Sigma_1) \xrightarrow{\rho_{\Sigma_1}^{\mathbf{Sen}}} \mathbf{Sen}'(\rho^{\mathbf{Sign}}(\Sigma_1))
\end{array}
$$

- a natural transformation $\rho^{\mathbf{Mod}} : (\rho^{\mathbf{Sign}})^{op}; \mathbf{Mod}' \to \mathbf{Mod}$, that is, a family of functors $\rho_{\Sigma}^{\mathbf{Mod}} : \mathbf{Mod}'(\rho^{\mathbf{Sign}}(\Sigma)) \to \mathbf{Mod}(\Sigma)$, natural in $\Sigma \in |\mathbf{Sign}|$:

$$
\begin{array}{ccc}
\Sigma_2 & \mathbf{Mod}(\Sigma_2) \xleftarrow{\rho_{\Sigma_2}^{\mathbf{Mod}}} \mathbf{Mod}'(\rho^{\mathbf{Sign}}(\Sigma_2)) \\[2ex]
\sigma \uparrow & \mathbf{Mod}(\sigma) \downarrow \qquad\qquad\qquad \downarrow \mathbf{Mod}'(\rho^{\mathbf{Sign}}(\sigma)) \\[2ex]
\Sigma_1 & \mathbf{Mod}(\Sigma_1) \xleftarrow{\rho_{\Sigma_1}^{\mathbf{Mod}}} \mathbf{Mod}'(\rho^{\mathbf{Sign}}(\Sigma_1))
\end{array}
$$

such that for any signature $\Sigma \in |\mathbf{Sign}|$ the translations $\rho_{\Sigma}^{\mathbf{Sen}} : \mathbf{Sen}(\Sigma) \to \mathbf{Sen}'(\rho^{\mathbf{Sign}}(\Sigma))$ of sentences and $\rho_{\Sigma}^{\mathbf{Mod}} : \mathbf{Mod}'(\rho^{\mathbf{Sign}}(\Sigma)) \to \mathbf{Mod}(\Sigma)$ of models preserve the satisfaction relation, that is, for any $\varphi \in \mathbf{Sen}(\Sigma)$ and $M' \in |\mathbf{Mod}'(\rho^{\mathbf{Sign}}(\Sigma))|$:

$$M' \models'_{\rho^{\mathbf{Sign}}(\Sigma)} \rho_{\Sigma}^{\mathbf{Sen}}(\varphi) \quad \text{iff} \quad \rho_{\Sigma}^{\mathbf{Mod}}(M') \models_{\Sigma} \varphi \qquad \text{(Representation condition)}$$

□

An institution representation $\rho : I \to I'$ shows how the institution I is encoded in the institution I'. It means that all parts of I are represented, but only some parts of I' are used for representing various parts of I. The above definition can be easily extended to $\mathcal{D}$-institutions. A $\mathcal{D}$-institution representation $\rho : I \to I'$ is a usual institution representation $\rho : I \to I'$ which additionally satisfies:

$$\rho^{\mathbf{Sign}}(\mathcal{D}_I) \subseteq \mathcal{D}_{I'}.$$

The following example was also presented in [Tar 95]:

Example 4. The institution representation $\rho_{\mathbf{EQ}\to\mathbf{FOEQ}} : \mathbf{EQ} \to \mathbf{FOEQ}$ is given by the embedding of the category of algebraic signatures into the category of first-order signatures which equips algebraic signatures with the empty set of predicate names. The translation of sentences is an inclusion of (universally quantified) equations as first-order logic sentences, and the translation of models is the identity. □

It is also possible to represent a richer logic in a poorer one.

Example 5. The institution representation $\rho_{\mathbf{PEQ} \rightarrow \mathbf{EQ}} : \mathbf{PEQ} \rightarrow \mathbf{EQ}$ is given by the identity on the category of algebraic signatures. Translation of an equality from $\mathbf{PEQ}$ is the corresponding equality in $\mathbf{EQ}$. Translation of the definedness formulae $D(t)$ is the equality $t = t$. Translation of models is the embedding of the category of total many-sorted algebras into the category of partial many-sorted algebras. □

The institution representation presented in the above example does not fit to our expectations (see the explanations after Definition 3). To improve this situation we put some extra condition on the model part of institution representations.

Definition 4 (ρ-expansion). *An institution representation $\rho : I \rightarrow I'$, has the ρ-expansion property, if for any signature $\Sigma \in |\mathbf{Sign}|$, any Σ-model M has a ρ-expansion to a $\rho^{\mathbf{Sign}}(\Sigma)$-model, that is, there exists a $\rho^{\mathbf{Sign}}(\Sigma)$-model M' such that $\rho_{\Sigma}^{\mathbf{Mod}}(M') = M$.* □

Example 6. The institution representation $\rho_{\mathbf{EQ} \rightarrow \mathbf{FOEQ}} : \mathbf{EQ} \rightarrow \mathbf{FOEQ}$ has the ρ-expansion property, whereas the institution representation $\rho_{\mathbf{PEQ} \rightarrow \mathbf{EQ}} : \mathbf{PEQ} \rightarrow \mathbf{EQ}$ does not. □

Definition 5 (Weak-$\mathcal{D}$-amalgamation). *Let $\rho : I \rightarrow I'$ be an institution representation and $\mathcal{D}$ be a class of signature morphisms in I. We say that the institution representation ρ has the weak-$\mathcal{D}$-amalgamation property iff for every signatures $\Sigma_1, \Sigma_2 \in |\mathbf{Sign}|$, $(d : \Sigma_2 \rightarrow \Sigma_1) \in \mathcal{D}$, $M_1 \in \mathbf{Mod}(\Sigma_1)$ and $M_2 \in \mathbf{Mod}'(\rho^{\mathbf{Sign}}(\Sigma_2))$, if $\rho_{\Sigma_2}^{\mathbf{Mod}}(M_2) = M_1|_d$ there exists $M \in \mathbf{Mod}'(\rho^{\mathbf{Sign}}(\Sigma_1))$ such that $\rho_{\Sigma_1}^{\mathbf{Mod}}(M) = M_1$ and $M|_{\rho^{\mathbf{Sign}}(d)} = M_2$.* □

Example 7. The institution representation $\rho_{\mathbf{EQ} \rightarrow \mathbf{FOEQ}} : \mathbf{EQ} \rightarrow \mathbf{FOEQ}$ presented in Example 4 has the weak-$\mathcal{D}$-amalgamation property for the class $\mathcal{D}$ being the class of all inclusions in the category of algebraic signatures. □

Example 8. The institution representation $\rho_{\mathbf{PEQ} \rightarrow \mathbf{EQ}} : \mathbf{PEQ} \rightarrow \mathbf{EQ}$ defined in Example 5, for $\mathcal{D}$ being class of all inclusions in the category of algebraic signatures, does not have the weak-$\mathcal{D}$-amalgamation property (see Appendix B for details). □

4 Specifications

In the rest of the paper we will work with specifications similar to specifications defined in [ST 88].

As in [ST 88], we assume that software systems described by specifications are adequately represented by models of institutions. This means that a specification must describe a signature and a class of models over this signature. We call this class *the class of models of the specification.* For any specification SP, we denote its signature by $\mathbf{Sig}[SP]$ and the collection of its models by $\mathbf{Mod}[SP]$. We also have $\mathbf{Sig}[SP] \in |\mathbf{Sign}_I|$ and $\mathbf{Mod}[SP] \subseteq |\mathbf{Mod}(\mathbf{Sig}[SP])|$. If $\mathbf{Sig}[SP] = \Sigma$, we will call SP a Σ-specification.

Definition 6 (Specifications). *Specifications over a $\mathcal{D}$-institution I and their semantics are defined inductively as follows:*

1. *Any pair $\langle \Sigma, \Phi \rangle$, where $\Sigma \in |\mathbf{Sign}|$ and $\Phi \subseteq \mathbf{Sen}(\Sigma)$, is a specification, called also* flat specification, *with the following semantics:*
   $\mathbf{Sig}[\langle \Sigma, \Phi \rangle] = \Sigma$;
   $\mathbf{Mod}[\langle \Sigma, \Phi \rangle] = \{M \in |\mathbf{Mod}(\Sigma)| \mid M \models_\Sigma \Phi\}$.
2. *For any signature Σ and Σ-specifications SP_1 and SP_2, $SP_1 \cup SP_2$ is a specification with the following semantics:*
   $\mathbf{Sig}[SP_1 \cup SP_2] = \Sigma$;
   $\mathbf{Mod}[SP_1 \cup SP_2] = \mathbf{Mod}[SP_1] \cap \mathbf{Mod}[SP_2]$.
3. *For any morphism $(\sigma : \Sigma \to \Sigma') \in \mathbf{Sign}$ and Σ-specification SP,* **translate** SP **by** σ *is a specification with the following semantics:*
   $\mathbf{Sig}[\textbf{translate } SP \textbf{ by } \sigma] = \Sigma'$;
   $\mathbf{Mod}[\textbf{translate } SP \textbf{ by } \sigma] = \{M' \in |\mathbf{Mod}_I(\Sigma')| \mid M'|_\sigma \in \mathbf{Mod}[SP]\}$.
4. *For any morphism $(d : \Sigma \to \Sigma') \in \mathcal{D}_I$ and Σ'-specification SP',* **derive from** SP' **by** d *is a specification with the following semantics:*
   $\mathbf{Sig}[\textbf{derive from } SP' \textbf{ by } d] = \Sigma$;
   $\mathbf{Mod}[\textbf{derive from } SP' \textbf{ by } d] = \{M'|_d \mid M' \in \mathbf{Mod}[SP']\}$.

$\square$

A definition of structured specifications similar to that presented above can be found in [Borz 97].

Definition 7 (Semantic consequence). *A Σ-sentence φ is a semantic consequence of a Σ-specification SP (written $SP \models_\Sigma \varphi$) if $\mathbf{Mod}[SP] \models_\Sigma^I \varphi$.* $\square$

Definition 8 (Semantic refinement). *A Σ-specification SP_2 is a semantic refinement of a Σ-specification SP_1 (written $SP_1 \leadsto_\Sigma SP_2$) if $\mathbf{Mod}[SP_1] \supseteq \mathbf{Mod}[SP_2]$.* $\square$

Definition 9 (Specification representation). *For any $\mathcal{D}$-institution representation $\rho : I \to I'$, the specification representation $\hat{\rho}$ is a family of functions $\{\hat{\rho}_\Sigma\}_{\Sigma \in |\mathbf{Sign}|}$ between classes of specifications defined as follows:*

1. *If SP is a Σ-specification of the form $\langle \Sigma, \Phi \rangle$, then*
   $\hat{\rho}_\Sigma(SP) = \langle \rho^{\mathbf{Sign}}(\Sigma), \rho^{\mathbf{Sen}}_\Sigma(\Phi) \rangle$;
2. *If SP is a Σ-specification of the form $SP_1 \cup SP_2$, then*
   $\hat{\rho}_\Sigma(SP) = \hat{\rho}_\Sigma(SP_1) \cup \hat{\rho}_\Sigma(SP_2)$;
3. *If SP is a Σ-specification of the form* **translate** SP_1 **by** $(\sigma : \Sigma_1 \to \Sigma)$, *then*
   $\hat{\rho}_\Sigma(SP) = \textbf{translate } \hat{\rho}_{\Sigma_1}(SP_1) \textbf{ by } \rho^{\mathbf{Sign}}(\sigma : \Sigma_1 \to \Sigma)$;
4. *If SP is a Σ-specification of the form* **derive from** SP_1 **by** $(d : \Sigma \to \Sigma_1)$, *then $\hat{\rho}_\Sigma(SP) = \textbf{derive from } \hat{\rho}_{\Sigma_1}(SP_1) \textbf{ by } \rho^{\mathbf{Sign}}(d : \Sigma \to \Sigma_1)$.*

For a Σ-specification SP we will write $\hat{\rho}(SP)$ as an abbreviation for $\hat{\rho}_\Sigma(SP)$.

$\square$

Remark 1. For any $\mathcal{D}$-institution representation $\rho : I \to I'$ and Σ-specification SP over $\mathcal{D}$-institution I, $\hat{\rho}(SP)$ is a $\rho^{\mathbf{Sign}}(\Sigma)$-specification over $\mathcal{D}$-institution I'.

5   Mod[SP] vs. Mod[$\hat{\rho}(SP)$]

In this section we study mutual relationships between models of a given specification SP and the specification $\hat{\rho}(SP)$.

Lemma 1. *For any $\mathcal{D}$-institutions I and I', $\mathcal{D}$-institution representation ρ : $I \to I'$, signature $\Sigma \in |\mathbf{Sign}|$, Σ-specification SP over the $\mathcal{D}$-institution I and $\rho^{\mathbf{Sign}}(\Sigma)$ model $M' \in \mathbf{Mod}[\hat{\rho}(SP)]$, we have $\rho_{\Sigma}^{\mathbf{Mod}}(M') \in \mathbf{Mod}[SP]$.*

Proof. By induction on the structure of the specification SP. Let us assume that $M' \in \mathbf{Mod}[\hat{\rho}(SP)]$.

1. If $SP = \langle \Sigma, \Phi \rangle$:
   By assumption and Definition 9 we have: $M' \in \mathbf{Mod}[\langle \rho^{\mathbf{Sign}}(\Sigma), \rho_{\Sigma}^{\mathbf{Sen}}(\Phi) \rangle]$. This is equivalent to $M' \models'_{\rho^{\mathbf{Sign}}(\Sigma)} \rho_{\Sigma}^{\mathbf{Sen}}(\Phi)$ and by the representation condition to $\rho_{\Sigma}^{\mathbf{Mod}}(M') \models_{\Sigma} \Phi$. Finally, we obtain $\rho_{\Sigma}^{\mathbf{Mod}}(M') \in \mathbf{Mod}[\langle \Sigma, \Phi \rangle]$.
2. If $SP = SP_1 \cup SP_2$:
   By assumption: $M' \in \mathbf{Mod}[\hat{\rho}(SP_1)] \cap \mathbf{Mod}[\hat{\rho}(SP_2)]$. Now, by the induction hypothesis, we obtain $\rho_{\Sigma}^{\mathbf{Mod}}(M') \in \mathbf{Mod}[SP_1] \cap \mathbf{Mod}[SP_2] = \mathbf{Mod}[SP]$.
3. If $SP = \mathbf{translate}\ SP_1\ \mathbf{by}\ (\sigma : \Sigma_1 \to \Sigma)$:
   By assumption: $M' \in \mathbf{Mod}[\mathbf{translate}\ \hat{\rho}(SP_1)\ \mathbf{by}\ \rho^{\mathbf{Sign}}(\sigma)]$. By definition, $M'|_{\rho^{\mathbf{Sign}}(\sigma)} \in \mathbf{Mod}[\hat{\rho}(SP_1)]$. Now, by the induction hypothesis

$$\rho_{\Sigma_1}^{\mathbf{Mod}}(M'|_{\rho^{\mathbf{Sign}}(\sigma)}) \in \mathbf{Mod}[SP_1]$$

and because the following diagram commutes

$$(1)$$

$$
\begin{array}{ccc}
\mathbf{Mod}(\Sigma) & \xleftarrow{\ \rho_{\Sigma}^{\mathbf{Mod}}\ } & \mathbf{Mod}'(\rho^{\mathbf{Sign}}(\Sigma)) \\
{\scriptstyle -|_{\sigma}}\downarrow & & \downarrow{\scriptstyle -|_{\rho^{\mathbf{Sign}}(\sigma)}} \\
\mathbf{Mod}(\Sigma_1) & \xleftarrow{\ \rho_{\Sigma_1}^{\mathbf{Mod}}\ } & \mathbf{Mod}'(\rho^{\mathbf{Sign}}(\Sigma_1))
\end{array}
$$

we have $\rho_{\Sigma_1}^{\mathbf{Mod}}(M'|_{\rho^{\mathbf{Sign}}(\sigma)}) = (\rho_{\Sigma}^{\mathbf{Mod}}(M'))|_{\sigma}$, hence $\rho_{\Sigma}^{\mathbf{Mod}}(M')|_{\sigma} \in \mathbf{Mod}[SP_1]$ and finally $\rho_{\Sigma}^{\mathbf{Mod}}(M') \in \mathbf{Mod}[SP]$.
4. If $SP = \mathbf{derive\ from}\ SP_1\ \mathbf{by}\ d : \Sigma \to \Sigma_1$:
   By assumption: $M' \in \mathbf{Mod}[\mathbf{derive\ from}\ \hat{\rho}(SP_1)\ \mathbf{by}\ \rho^{\mathbf{Sign}}(d)]$. Now, there exists $M'' \in \mathbf{Mod}[\hat{\rho}(SP_1)]$ such that $M''|_{\rho^{\mathbf{Sign}}(d)} = M'$. By the induction hypothesis, $\rho_{\Sigma_1}^{\mathbf{Mod}}(M'') \in \mathbf{Mod}[SP_1]$. Then, since $\rho_{\Sigma_1}^{\mathbf{Mod}}(M'')|_d \in \mathbf{Mod}[SP]$ and because the following diagram commutes:

$$(2)$$

$$
\begin{array}{ccc}
\mathbf{Mod}(\Sigma_1) & \xleftarrow{\ \rho_{\Sigma_1}^{\mathbf{Mod}}\ } & \mathbf{Mod}'(\rho^{\mathbf{Sign}}(\Sigma_1)) \\
{\scriptstyle -|_{d}}\downarrow & & \downarrow{\scriptstyle -|_{\rho^{\mathbf{Sign}}(d)}} \\
\mathbf{Mod}(\Sigma) & \xleftarrow{\ \rho_{\Sigma}^{\mathbf{Mod}}\ } & \mathbf{Mod}'(\rho^{\mathbf{Sign}}(\Sigma))
\end{array}
$$

we have $\rho_{\Sigma_1}^{\mathbf{Mod}}(M'')|_d = \rho_{\Sigma}^{\mathbf{Mod}}(M''|_{\rho^{\mathbf{Sign}}(d)}) = \rho_{\Sigma}^{\mathbf{Mod}}(M') \in \mathbf{Mod}[SP]$.

□

As a consequence we obtain:

Corollary 1. *For any $\mathcal{D}$-institutions I and I', $\mathcal{D}$-institution representation ρ : $I \to I'$, signature $\Sigma \in |\mathbf{Sign}|$ and Σ-specification SP over $\mathcal{D}$-institution I, we have:*
$$\rho_{\Sigma}^{\mathbf{Mod}}(\mathbf{Mod}[\hat{\rho}(SP)]) \subseteq \mathbf{Mod}[SP].$$

□

Now, we present conditions ensuring the inclusion in the opposite direction. Let us first consider a more basic property:

Lemma 2. *For any $\mathcal{D}$-institutions I and I', $\mathcal{D}$-institution representation ρ : $I \to I'$, if ρ satisfies the weak-$\mathcal{D}_I$-amalgamation then for every signature $\Sigma \in |\mathbf{Sign}|$, Σ-specification SP over the $\mathcal{D}$-institution I and $\rho^{\mathbf{Sign}}(\Sigma)$-model M'*

$$\rho_{\Sigma}^{\mathbf{Mod}}(M') \in \mathbf{Mod}[SP] \qquad implies \qquad M' \in \mathbf{Mod}[\hat{\rho}(SP)].$$

Proof. By induction on the structure of SP.

1. If $SP = \langle \Sigma, \Phi \rangle$:
   By assumption: $\rho_{\Sigma}^{\mathbf{Mod}}(M') \in \mathbf{Mod}[\langle \Sigma, \Phi \rangle]$. It is equivalent to $\rho_{\Sigma}^{\mathbf{Mod}}(M') \models_{\Sigma} \Phi$. By the representation condition, we obtain $M' \models'_{\rho^{\mathbf{Sign}}(\Sigma)} \rho_{\Sigma}^{\mathbf{Sen}}(\Phi)$, which is equivalent to $M' \in \mathbf{Mod}[\hat{\rho}(\langle \Sigma, \Phi \rangle)]$.

2. If $SP = SP_1 \cup SP_2$:
   By assumption: $\rho_{\Sigma}^{\mathbf{Mod}}(M') \in \mathbf{Mod}[SP_1] \cap \mathbf{Mod}[SP_2]$. Next, by the induction hypothesis, we obtain $M' \in \mathbf{Mod}[\hat{\rho}(SP_1)] \cap \mathbf{Mod}[\hat{\rho}(SP_2)] = \mathbf{Mod}[\hat{\rho}(SP_1 \cup SP_2)]$.

3. If $SP = \mathbf{translate}\ SP_1\ \mathbf{by}\ (\sigma : \Sigma_1 \to \Sigma)$:
   By assumption: $\rho_{\Sigma}^{\mathbf{Mod}}(M') \in \mathbf{Mod}[\mathbf{translate}\ SP_1\ \mathbf{by}\ \sigma]$. Next, by Definition 6, $\rho_{\Sigma}^{\mathbf{Mod}}(M')|_{\sigma} \in \mathbf{Mod}[SP_1]$, which by the commutativity of the diagram (1) (see the proof of Lemma 1) is equivalent to $\rho_{\Sigma_1}^{\mathbf{Mod}}(M'|_{\rho^{\mathbf{Sign}}(\sigma)}) \in \mathbf{Mod}[SP_1]$. Now, by the induction hypothesis we obtain:
   $M' \in \mathbf{Mod}[\mathbf{translate}\ \hat{\rho}(SP_1)\ \mathbf{by}\ \rho^{\mathbf{Sign}}(\sigma)] = \mathbf{Mod}[\hat{\rho}(\mathbf{translate}\ SP_1\ \mathbf{by}\ \sigma)]$.

4. If $SP = \mathbf{derive\ from}\ SP_1\ \mathbf{by}\ (d : \Sigma \to \Sigma_1)$:
   By assumption: $\rho_{\Sigma}^{\mathbf{Mod}}(M') \in \mathbf{Mod}[\mathbf{derive\ from}\ SP_1\ \mathbf{by}\ d]$. There exists $M_1 \in \mathbf{Mod}[SP_1]$ such that $M_1|_d = \rho_{\Sigma}^{\mathbf{Mod}}(M')$. Now, because ρ has the weak-$\mathcal{D}_I$-amalgamation property, there exists $M_1' \in |\mathbf{Mod}(\rho^{\mathbf{Sign}}(\Sigma_1))|$ such that $\rho_{\Sigma_1}^{\mathbf{Mod}}(M_1') = M_1$ and $M_1'|_{\rho^{\mathbf{Sign}}(d)} = M'$ (see diagram (2) from the proof of Lemma 1). By the induction hypothesis, we obtain $M_1' \in \mathbf{Mod}[\hat{\rho}(SP_1)]$, and finally $M_1'|_{\rho^{\mathbf{Sign}}(d)} \in \mathbf{Mod}[\hat{\rho}(SP)]$.

□

Now, we are ready to prove the expected inclusion.

Lemma 3. *For any $\mathcal{D}$-institutions I and I', $\mathcal{D}$-institution representation ρ : $I \to I'$, if ρ has the weak-$\mathcal{D}_I$-amalgamation property, then for every signature $\Sigma \in |\mathbf{Sign}|$, Σ-specification SP over the $\mathcal{D}$-institution I, if each model $M \in \mathbf{Mod}[SP]$ has a ρ-expansion to a $\rho^{\mathbf{Sign}}(\Sigma)$-model, then*

$$\mathbf{Mod}[SP] \subseteq \rho_\Sigma^{\mathbf{Mod}}(\mathbf{Mod}[\hat{\rho}(SP)]).$$

Proof. Let $M \in \mathbf{Mod}[SP]$. By the ρ-expansion, there exists a $\rho^{\mathbf{Sign}}(\Sigma)$-model M' such that $\rho_\Sigma^{\mathbf{Mod}}(M') = M$. By Lemma 2, we have $M' \in \mathbf{Mod}[\hat{\rho}(SP)]$. Finally, since $\rho_\Sigma^{\mathbf{Mod}}(M') = M$, we have $M \in \rho_\Sigma^{\mathbf{Mod}}(\mathbf{Mod}[\hat{\rho}(SP)])$. $\qquad\qquad\square$

The following example shows that the ρ-expansion property is needed as an assumption in Lemma 3.

Example 9. In this example we will write ρ for the institution representation $\rho_{\mathbf{PEQ} \to \mathbf{EQ}}$ defined in Example 5. Let $SP = \langle \Sigma, true \rangle$ be a Σ-specification over the $\mathcal{D}$-institution $\mathbf{PEQ}$, where $\Sigma \in |\mathbf{Sign}_{\mathbf{PEQ}}|$ and $true$ is sentence satisfied by each Σ-model $M \in \mathbf{Mod}_{\mathbf{PEQ}}(\Sigma)$. It means that $\mathbf{Mod}[SP] = \mathbf{Mod}_{\mathbf{PEQ}}(\Sigma)$. Similarly, the sentence $\rho_\Sigma^{\mathbf{Sen}}(true)$ is satisfied by each $\rho^{\mathbf{Sign}}(\Sigma)$-model $M' \in \mathbf{Mod}_{\mathbf{EQ}}(\rho^{\mathbf{Sign}}(\Sigma))$ and so $\mathbf{Mod}[\hat{\rho}(SP)] = \mathbf{Mod}_{\mathbf{EQ}}(\rho^{\mathbf{Sign}}(\Sigma))$. Now, by definition of ρ, we have that $\mathbf{Mod}[SP]$ is not included in $\rho_\Sigma^{\mathbf{Mod}}(\mathbf{Mod}[\hat{\rho}(SP)])$. $\qquad\square$

Corollary 2. *For any $\mathcal{D}$-institutions I and I', $\mathcal{D}$-institution representation ρ : $I \to I'$, if ρ has the weak-$\mathcal{D}_I$-amalgamation property, then for every signature $\Sigma \in |\mathbf{Sign}|$, Σ-specification SP over the $\mathcal{D}$-institution I, if each model $M \in \mathbf{Mod}[SP]$ has a ρ-expansion to a $\rho^{\mathbf{Sign}}(\Sigma)$-model, then*

$$\mathbf{Mod}[SP] = \rho_\Sigma^{\mathbf{Mod}}(\mathbf{Mod}[\hat{\rho}(SP)]).$$

$\qquad\qquad\qquad\qquad\qquad\qquad\qquad\qquad\qquad\qquad\qquad\qquad\qquad\qquad\square$

6   Reusing proof systems

The following result was presented in [Tar 95] for the case of flat specifications (cf. Definition 6).

Theorem 1. *For any $\mathcal{D}$-institutions I and I', $\mathcal{D}$-institution representation ρ : $I \to I'$, if ρ has the weak-$\mathcal{D}_I$-amalgamation property, then for every signature $\Sigma \in |\mathbf{Sign}|$, Σ-specification SP over $\mathcal{D}$-institution I and Σ-sentence φ, if each Σ-model M has ρ-expansion to a $\rho^{\mathbf{Sign}}(\Sigma)$-model, then:*

$$SP \models_\Sigma \varphi \quad \textit{iff} \quad \hat{\rho}(SP) \models'_{\rho^{\mathbf{Sign}}(\Sigma)} \rho_\Sigma^{\mathbf{Sen}}(\varphi).$$

Proof. $\Rightarrow$: Let $M' \in \mathbf{Mod}[\hat{\rho}(SP)]$. Then $\rho_\Sigma^{\mathbf{Mod}}(M') \in \rho_\Sigma^{\mathbf{Mod}}(\mathbf{Mod}[\hat{\rho}(SP)])$. By Lemma 1, we obtain $\rho_\Sigma^{\mathbf{Mod}}(M') \in \mathbf{Mod}[SP]$, which implies $\rho_\Sigma^{\mathbf{Mod}}(M') \models_\Sigma \varphi$. By the representation condition, this is equivalent to $M' \models'_{\rho^{\mathbf{Sign}}(\Sigma)} \rho_\Sigma^{\mathbf{Sen}}(\varphi)$.

$\Leftarrow$: Let $M \in \mathbf{Mod}[SP]$. Then by Lemma 3 $M \in \rho_\Sigma^{\mathbf{Mod}}(\mathbf{Mod}[\hat\rho(SP)])$. This means that there exists $M' \in \mathbf{Mod}[\hat\rho(SP)]$ such that $\rho_\Sigma^{\mathbf{Mod}}(M') = M$ and $M' \models'_{\rho^{\mathbf{Sign}}(\Sigma)} \rho_\Sigma^{\mathbf{Sen}}(\varphi)$. By the representation condition, we obtain $\rho_\Sigma^{\mathbf{Mod}}(M') \models_\Sigma \varphi$, that is $M \models_\Sigma \varphi$. $\qquad\square$

Let us see what the advantages of Theorem 1 are. First of all it ensures soundness of the following scheme of rules[2]:

$$(\rho\text{-join}) \quad \frac{\hat\rho(SP) \vdash'_{\rho^{\mathbf{Sign}}(\Sigma)} \rho_\Sigma^{\mathbf{Sen}}(\varphi)}{SP \vdash_\Sigma \varphi}$$

where ρ and SP satisfy the assumptions of Theorem 1. Now, let us assume that we have:

1. A sound and complete set of rules for proving logical consequences of specifications over $\mathcal{D}$-institution I';
2. A $\mathcal{D}$-institution representation: $\rho : I \to I'$ satisfying assumptions of Theorem 1.

We can construct a sound and complete set of rules for the logical system for reasoning about specifications over $\mathcal{D}$-institution I from rules from point 1 and the (ρ-join) rule schema for ρ from point 2 (see Example 10 below for usage in a particular case).

The next theorem allows us to repeat the above argumentation also for the refinement relation (see [Cen 94] for the completeness result for the refinement relation in the context of **FOEQ**).

Theorem 2. *For any $\mathcal{D}$-institutions I and I', $\mathcal{D}$-institution representation $\rho : I \to I'$, if ρ has the weak-$\mathcal{D}_I$-amalgamation property, then for every signature $\Sigma \in |\mathbf{Sign}|$ and Σ-specifications SP_1 and SP_2 over $\mathcal{D}$-institution I, if any Σ-model has ρ-expansion to a $\rho^{\mathbf{Sign}}(\Sigma)$-model, then:*

$$SP_1 \leadsto_\Sigma SP_2 \quad \textit{iff} \quad \hat\rho(SP_1) \leadsto_{\rho^{\mathbf{Sign}}(\Sigma)} \hat\rho(SP_2).$$

Proof. $\Rightarrow$: Assumption: $\mathbf{Mod}[SP_2] \subseteq \mathbf{Mod}[SP_1]$.
Let $M \in \mathbf{Mod}[\hat\rho(SP_2)]$. Then by Lemma 1, we have $\rho_\Sigma^{\mathbf{Mod}}(M) \in \mathbf{Mod}[SP_2]$ and next, by the assumption $\rho_\Sigma^{\mathbf{Mod}}(M) \in \mathbf{Mod}[SP_1]$. Now, by Lemma 2, we obtain $M \in \mathbf{Mod}[\hat\rho(SP_1)]$.
$\Leftarrow$: Assumption: $\mathbf{Mod}[\hat\rho(SP_2)] \subseteq \mathbf{Mod}[\hat\rho(SP_1)]$.
Let $M \in \mathbf{Mod}[SP_2]$. Then by Lemma 3, we have $M \in \rho_\Sigma^{\mathbf{Mod}}(\mathbf{Mod}[\hat\rho(SP_2)])$. There exists $M' \in \mathbf{Mod}[\hat\rho(SP_2)]$ such that $\rho_\Sigma^{\mathbf{Mod}}(M') = M$ and by the assumption $M' \in \mathbf{Mod}[\hat\rho(SP_1)]$. Now, by Corollary 1:

$$M = \rho_\Sigma^{\mathbf{Mod}}(M') \in \rho_\Sigma^{\mathbf{Mod}}(\mathbf{Mod}[\hat\rho(SP_1)]) \subseteq \mathbf{Mod}[SP_1].$$

$\qquad\square$

---

[2] The entailment relations $\vdash$ and $\vdash'$ are defined in Appendix A.

7   Examples

Example 10. This (positive) example is inspired by a (negative) example for logic representations presented in [HST 94] and also mentioned in [ST 97].

Let us consider a specification SP over $\mathcal{D}$-institution **EQ**, where $\mathcal{D}_{\mathbf{EQ}}$ is the class of signature inclusions, and also:

$$SP_0 = \langle \Sigma_0, \emptyset \rangle, \qquad SP_1 = \textbf{derive from } SP_0 \textbf{ by } \imath,$$
$$SP_2 = \langle \Sigma_1, \forall_{x:s}.b = c \rangle, \; SP = SP_1 \cup SP_2,$$

where:

- $\Sigma_0 = \textbf{sig sorts } s, s' \textbf{opns } a : s; \; b, c : s' \textbf{ end};$
- $\Sigma_1 = \textbf{sig sorts } s, s' \textbf{opns } b, c : s' \textbf{ end};$
- $\imath : \Sigma_1 \hookrightarrow \Sigma_0.$

As shown in [ST 97]:

$$SP \models_{\Sigma_1} b = c, \tag{3}$$

whereas the judgment:

$$SP \vdash_{\Sigma_1} b = c \tag{4}$$

cannot be proved in **EQ** logic by using rules similar to presented in Appendix A, because the sentence $b = c$ cannot be derived from the sentence $\forall_{x:s}.b = c$ (the nonemptiness of the carrier of sort s, ensured by the hidden constant a, cannot be expressed using equations, cf. [GM 85]).

Let us try to prove judgment (4) by using rules from Appendix A and the ($\rho_{\mathbf{EQ} \rightarrow \mathbf{FOEQ}}$-join) rule schema, where $\rho_{\mathbf{EQ} \rightarrow \mathbf{FOEQ}}$ is the institution representation defined in Example 4. Let us notice, that the institution representation $\rho_{\mathbf{EQ} \rightarrow \mathbf{FOEQ}}$ and the specification SP satisfy assumptions of Theorem 1. Therefore we can prove (4) (details in Appendix C). □

Example 11. Let $\rho_{\mathbf{EQ} \rightarrow \mathbf{FOEQ}}$ be the institution representation defined in Example 4, $\Sigma \in |\mathbf{Sign}_{\mathbf{EQ}}|$, SP be any Σ-specification over the $\mathcal{D}$-institution **EQ** and φ be a Σ-sentence, then by Theorem 1 and completeness of the logical system for structured specifications over the $\mathcal{D}$-institution **FOEQ** (see [Cen 94]) we have:

$$SP \models_{\Sigma} \varphi \quad \text{implies} \quad SP \vdash_{\Sigma} \varphi.$$

□

8   Conclusions

Results similar to Theorems 1 and 2 for the case of flat specifications are presented in [CM 97, Tar 95]. As presented there, the ρ-expansion property is a sufficient condition for Theorems 1 and 2 to hold for flat specifications. In this paper, we present that in order to extend these results to structural specifications, we need an additional condition: weak-$\mathcal{D}$-amalgamation. This gives a solution for some of the problems presented in [AC 94].

Similar results to these presented in our paper, but on the theory level, can also be found in [HST 94]. The main difference between our paper and [HST 94] is the way of lifting the logic representation to the level of structured theory presentations, in the case of [HST 94], and to the level of structured specifications, in our case. The natural lifting similar to that presented in Definition 9 fails in [HST 94], as demonstrated there by a counterexample similar to Example 10. Another difference is in the "proof power". The proof rules given in [HST 94] are more restricted then our proof strategy presented in Section 6. For instance Example 10 is example of a successful use of our strategy, whereas when using the strategy proposed in [HST 94], we are not able to complete the proof of a judgment similar to presented in Example 10 (in fact, this is necessary, since this judgment is not sound under the theory level semantics considered there).

An interesting task could be to work out examples of universal logics (cf. [Tar 95]), in which we will represent simpler logics in order to reuse for them strategies known/worked out for stronger universal logics. Theorem 1 together with results of [Borz 97] gives us the interpolation property as the required property of a reasonable universal logic. It will be also fine if some of known logical frameworks turn out to satisfy this property. Proper candidates seem to be for instance LF and HOL.

Acknowledgments

I would like to thank Andrzej Tarlecki for encouragement, support and helpful comments, Till Mossakowski and Grigore Rosu for pointing me at interesting examples, Wiesław Pawłowski for useful discussions, and also people from the Institute of Computer Science of the Polish Academy of Sciences for stimulating atmosphere.

References

AC 94.   E. Astesiano, M. Cerioli. Multiparadigm Specification Languages: a First Attempt at Foundations. In C.A. Middelburg D.J. Andrews, J.F. Groote, editor, *Semantics of Specification Languages (SoSL'93), Workshops in Computing*, pages 168–185. Springer Verlag, 1994.

BHK 90.   J. A. Bergstra, J. Heering, P. Klint. Module algebra. *Journal of the ACM*, 37(2):335-372, April 1990.

Borz 97. T. Borzyszkowski. Completeness of the logical system for structured specifications. *Recent Trends in Algebraic Development Techniques, Selected Papers, 12th International Workshop WADT'97*, Tarquinia, Italy, June 1997, ed. Francesco Parisi-Presicce, Springer LNCS 1376, pages 107-121, 1997.

Bur 82.   P. Burmeister. Partial algebras — survey of a unifying approach towards a two-valued model theory for partial algebras. *Algebra Universalis*, 15:306-358, 1982.

Bur 86.   P. Burmeister. A model theoretic approach to partial algebras. *Akademie Verlag*, Berlin, 1986.

Cen 94.   M. V. Cengarle. Formal Specifications with High-Order Parameteriza-
           tion. *Ph.D. thesis*, Institut für Informatik, Ludwig-Maximilians-Universität
           Müenchen, 1994.

CM 97.   M. Cerioli, J. Meseguer. May I Borrow Your Logic? (Transporting Logi-
           cal Structures along Maps) *Theoretical Computer Science*, 173(2):311–347,
           1997.

DGS 93.   R. Diaconescu, J. Goguen, P. Stefaneas. Logical Support for Modularization.
           In: G. Huet, G. Plotkin, editors *Logical Environments, Proceedings of a
           Workshop held in Edinburgh, Scotland, May 1991*, Cambridge University
           Press, pp. 83–130, 1993.

GB 92.   J. A. Goguen, R. M. Burstall. Institutions: abstract model theory for specifi-
           cations and programming. *Journal of the Assoc. for Computing Machinery*,
           39:95-146, 1992.

GM 85.   J. A. Goguen, J.Meseguer. Completeness of many–sorted equational logic.
           Houston Journal of Mathematics, volume 11(3), pages 307–334, 1985.

HST 94.   R. Harper, D. Sannella, A. Tarlecki. Structured theory presentations and
           logic representations. *Annals of Pure and Applied Logic*, volume 67, pages
           113–160, North-Holland 1994.

Mes 89.   J. Meseguer, General logic. *Logic Colloquium'87*, eds. H. D. Ebbinghaus et
           al., pages 279–329, North-Holland 1989.

Mossa 96. T. Mossakowski. Representations, Hierarchies, and Graphs of Institutions.
           Ph.D. thesis, Fachbereich Mathemetik und Informatik der Universität Bre-
           men, 1996.

Mosse 97. P. D. Mosses. CoFI: The Common Framework Initiative for Algebraic Spec-
           ification and Development. *Theory and Practice of Software Development*,
           volume 1214 of LNCS, pages 115–137, Springer-Verlag, 1997.

SST 92.   D. Sannella, S. Sokołowski, A. Tarlecki. Towards formal development of
           programs from algebraic specification: parameterization revised. *Acta In-
           formatica*, volume 29, pages 689–736, 1992.

ST 88.   D. Sannella, A. Tarlecki. Specifications in an Arbitrary Institution. *Infor-
           mation and Computation*, volume 76, pages 165–210, 1988.

ST 97.   D. Sannella, A. Tarlecki. Essential concepts of algebraic specification and
           program development. *Formal Aspects of Computing*, vol. 9, pages 229–269,
           1997.

Tar 86.   A. Tarlecki. Bits and pieces of the theory of institutions. *Proc. Workshop
           on Category Theory and Computer Programming*, Guildford. Springer LNCS
           240, pages 334–363, 1986.

Tar 95.   A. Tarlecki. Moving between logical systems. *Recent Trends in Data Type
           Specifications. Selected Papers. 11th Workshop on Specification of Abstract
           Data Types ADT'95*, Olso, September 1995, eds. M. Haveraaen, O. J. Dahl,
           O. Owe, Springer LNCS 1130, pages 478–502, 1996.

Wir 91.   M. Wirsing. Structured Specifications: Syntax, Semantics and Proof Calcu-
           lus. In F. L. Bauer, W. Brauer, and H. Schwichtenberg, editors, *Logic and
           Algebra of Specification*, volume 94 of *NATO ASI Series F: Computer and
           Systems Sciences*, pages 411–442. Springer Verlag, 1991.

A Inference rules for structured specifications

The entailment relation $\vdash_\Sigma \subseteq \mathbf{Spec}_\Sigma \times \mathbf{Sen}(\Sigma)$ between specification over $\mathcal{D}$-institution I, where $\mathcal{D}_I \subset \mathbf{Sign}$ and Σ-sentence φ is defined by the following set of rules:

$$(\text{CR}) \quad \frac{\{SP \vdash_\Sigma \varphi_j\}_{j\in J} \quad \{\varphi_j\}_{j\in J} \vdash^I_\Sigma \varphi}{SP \vdash_\Sigma \varphi} \qquad (\text{basic}) \quad \frac{\varphi \in \Phi}{\langle \Sigma, \Phi \rangle \vdash_\Sigma \varphi}$$

$$(\text{sum1}) \quad \frac{SP_1 \vdash_\Sigma \varphi}{SP_1 \cup SP_2 \vdash_\Sigma \varphi} \qquad (\text{sum2}) \quad \frac{SP_2 \vdash_\Sigma \varphi}{SP_1 \cup SP_2 \vdash_\Sigma \varphi}$$

$$(\text{trans}) \quad \frac{SP \vdash_\Sigma \varphi}{\mathbf{translate}\ SP\ \mathbf{by}\ \sigma \vdash_{\Sigma'} \sigma\varphi} \qquad (\text{derive}) \quad \frac{SP' \vdash_{\Sigma'} d\varphi}{\mathbf{derive\ from}\ SP'\ \mathbf{by}\ d \vdash_\Sigma \varphi}$$

where $d \in \mathcal{D}_I$. A similar set of rules was presented in [ST 88] and also in [Borz 97].

B Example 8: continued

In this appendix, we will write ρ as an abbreviation for the institution representation $\rho_{\mathbf{PEQ}\to\mathbf{EQ}}$ defined in Example 5.

Let:

- $\Sigma = \mathbf{sig\ sorts}\ s\ \mathbf{opns}\ op : s \to s\ \mathbf{end}$ and
- $\Sigma' = \mathbf{sig\ sorts}\ s\ \mathbf{opns}\ op : s \to s; pop : s \to s\ \mathbf{end}$

be signatures in **PEQ** and $\imath : \Sigma \hookrightarrow \Sigma'$ an inclusion, then in the model part of representation ρ, we have the following diagram:

$$
\begin{array}{ccc}
\mathbf{Mod}_{\mathbf{PEQ}}(\Sigma') & \xleftarrow{\ \rho^{\mathbf{Mod}}_{\Sigma'}\ } & \mathbf{Mod}_{\mathbf{EQ}}(\rho^{\mathbf{Sign}}(\Sigma')) \\
{\scriptstyle \mathbf{Mod}_{\mathbf{PEQ}}(\imath)}\big\downarrow & & \big\downarrow{\scriptstyle \mathbf{Mod}_{\mathbf{EQ}}(\rho^{\mathbf{Sign}}(\imath))} \\
\mathbf{Mod}_{\mathbf{PEQ}}(\Sigma) & \xleftarrow[\ \rho^{\mathbf{Mod}}_{\Sigma}\ ]{} & \mathbf{Mod}_{\mathbf{EQ}}(\rho^{\mathbf{Sign}}(\Sigma))
\end{array}
$$

Let us take $M \in \mathbf{Mod}_{\mathbf{PEQ}}(\Sigma)$ such that it interpretes operation $op : s \to s$ as a total operation, and $M' \in \mathbf{Mod}_{\mathbf{PEQ}}(\Sigma')$ interpreting operation $op : s \to s$ in the same way as M and operation $pop : s \to s$ as a partial operation. The forgetful functor $\mathbf{Mod}_{\mathbf{PEQ}}(\imath)$ just forgets interpretation of $pop : s \to s$. From the definition of ρ (cf. Example 5), we know that $\rho^{\mathbf{Sign}}(\Sigma)$ and $\rho^{\mathbf{Sign}}(\Sigma')$ are just Σ and Σ', but considered as signatures in **EQ**. Now, if $\bar{M} \in \mathbf{Mod}_{\mathbf{EQ}}(\rho^{\mathbf{Sign}}(\Sigma))$ interpretes $op : s \to s$ in the same way as M, then

$$\rho^{\mathbf{Mod}}_{\Sigma}(\bar{M}) = M = \mathbf{Mod}_{\mathbf{PEQ}}(\imath)(M').$$

On the other hand, from the definition of ρ we know that

$$\text{for any } \quad \bar{M}' \in \mathbf{Mod}_{\mathbf{EQ}}(\rho^{\mathbf{Sign}}(\Sigma')) \quad \rho_{\Sigma'}^{\mathbf{Mod}}(\bar{M}') \quad \text{is total}$$

hence there is no $\bar{M}' \in \mathbf{Mod}_{\mathbf{EQ}}(\rho^{\mathbf{Sign}}(\Sigma'))$ such that $\rho_{\Sigma'}^{\mathbf{Sign}}(\bar{M}') = M'$. It means that ρ does not have the weak-$\mathcal{D}_{\mathbf{PEQ}}$-amalgamation property for $\mathcal{D}_{\mathbf{PEQ}}$ being the class of all inclusions in the category of algebraic signatures.

C   Example 10: a direct proof

In this appendix we present the direct proof of the following judgment:

$$SP \vdash_{\Sigma_1} b = c$$

from Example 10.

Proof. In the following proof, we will use the inference rules from Appendix A and the (ρ-join) rule schema. We will also write ρ as an abbreviation for $\rho_{\mathbf{EQ} \to \mathbf{FOEQ}}$.

The following tree makes the proof:

$$
\text{(CR)} \frac{
\dfrac{(1)}{\hat{\rho}(SP) \vdash'_{\rho^{\mathbf{Sign}}(\Sigma_1)} \forall_{x:s}.\rho_{\Sigma_1}^{\mathbf{Sen}}(b = c)} \quad \dfrac{(2)}{\hat{\rho}(SP) \vdash'_{\rho^{\mathbf{Sign}}(\Sigma_1)} \exists_{x:s}.true} \quad (3)
}{
\text{(ρ-join)} \dfrac{\hat{\rho}(SP) \vdash'_{\rho^{\mathbf{Sign}}(\Sigma_1)} \rho_{\Sigma_1}^{\mathbf{Sen}}(b = c)}{SP \vdash_{\Sigma_1} b = c}
}
$$

where (1) is:

$$
\text{(sum2)} \frac{
\text{(basic)} \dfrac{\forall_{x:s}.\rho_{\Sigma_1}^{\mathbf{Sen}}(b = c) \in \{\rho_{\Sigma_1}^{\mathbf{Sen}}(\forall_{x:s}.b = c)\}}{\hat{\rho}(\langle \Sigma_1, \forall_{x:s}.b = c\rangle) \vdash'_{\rho^{\mathbf{Sign}}(\Sigma_1)} \forall_{x:s}.\rho_{\Sigma_1}^{\mathbf{Sen}}(b = c)}
}{
\hat{\rho}(SP_1) \cup \hat{\rho}(SP_2) \vdash'_{\rho^{\mathbf{Sign}}(\Sigma_1)} \forall_{x:s}.\rho_{\Sigma_1}^{\mathbf{Sen}}(b = c)
}
$$

(2) is:

$$
\text{(sum1)} \frac{
\text{(derive)} \dfrac{
\text{(CR)} \dfrac{\vdots \quad \emptyset \vdash_{\rho^{\mathbf{Sign}}(\Sigma_0)}^{\mathbf{FOEQ}} \exists_{x:s}.true}{\hat{\rho}(\langle\langle\{\{s,s'\},\{a:s,b,c:s'\}\},\emptyset\rangle) \vdash'_{\rho^{\mathbf{Sign}}(\Sigma_0)} \exists_{x:s}.true}
}{
\text{derive from } \hat{\rho}(SP_0) \text{ by } \rho^{\mathbf{Sign}}(\iota) \vdash'_{\rho^{\mathbf{Sign}}(\Sigma_1)} \exists_{x:s}.true
}
}{
\hat{\rho}(SP_1) \cup \hat{\rho}(SP_2) \vdash'_{\rho^{\mathbf{Sign}}(\Sigma_1)} \exists_{x:s}.true
}
$$

and finally, (3) is:

$$\{\forall_{x:s}.\rho_{\Sigma_1}^{\mathbf{Sen}}(b = c), \exists_{x:s}.true\} \vdash_{\rho^{\mathbf{Sign}}(\Sigma_1)}^{\mathbf{FOEQ}} \rho_{\Sigma_1}^{\mathbf{Sen}}(b = c)$$

$\square$

Normal Forms for Partitions and Relations*

Roberto Bruni[1], Fabio Gadducci[2], and Ugo Montanari[1]

[1] Univ. of Pisa, Dipartimento di Informatica,
Corso Italia 40, I-56125 Pisa, Italia.
{bruni,ugo}@di.unipi.it
[2] TU Berlin, Fach. 13 Informatik,
Franklinstr. 28/29, D-10587 Berlin, Germany.
gfabio@cs.tu-berlin.de

Abstract. Recently there has been a growing interest towards algebraic structures that are able to express formalisms different from the standard, tree-like presentation of terms. Many of these approaches reveal a specific interest towards their application in the "distributed and concurrent systems" field, but an exhaustive comparison between them is difficult because their presentations can be quite dissimilar. This work is a first step towards a unified view, which is able to recast all those formalisms into a more general one, where they can be easily compared. We introduce a general schema for describing a characteristic normal form for many algebraic formalisms, and show that those normal forms can be thought of as arrows of suitable concrete monoidal categories.

1 Introduction

Since models of computation based on the notion of free and bound *names* are widespread, the notion of *name sharing* is essential for several applications ranging from logic programming, λ-calculus, functional programming and process algebra with restriction (or name hiding mechanisms) to mobile processes (where local names may be communicated to the external world, thus becoming global names). We can think of names as links to communication channels, or to objects, or to locations, or to remote shared resources, or also to some *cause* in the event history of the system. In general, names can be freely α-converted, because the only important information they offer is *sharing*.

An informal "wire and box notation" gives an intuitive understanding of the name sharing mechanism, and of the role played by *auxiliary* term-structure: Wires represents variables and the operators of the signature are denoted by boxes labeled with the corresponding operation symbols. For instance, the term $f(x_1, g(x_2), h(x_1, a))$ over the signature $\Sigma = \{a : 0 \longrightarrow 1, g : 1 \longrightarrow 1, h : 2 \longrightarrow 1, f : 3 \longrightarrow 1\}$ and variables x_1, x_2 admits the graphical representation

---

* Research partly supported by the EC TMR Network *GETGRATS* through the Technical University of Berlin and the University of Pisa; and by Esprit Working Groups *CONFER2* and *COORDINA*, through the University of Pisa.

J.L. Fiadeiro (Ed.): WADT'98, LNCS 1589, pp. 31–47, 1999.
© Springer-Verlag Berlin Heidelberg 1999

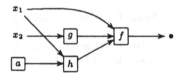

Notice that wire duplications (e.g., of x_1) and wires swapping (e.g., of x_2 and a copy of x_1) are auxiliary, in the sense that they belong to any wire and box model, independently from the underlying signature. The properties of the auxiliary structure are far from trivial and could lead to somehow misleading system representations, when their interpretation is not well formalized. For example, let us consider the wire and box diagrams c_1 and c_2 in the picture below:

In a *value-oriented* interpretation, both c_1 and c_2 yield the same term $h(a, a)$. Instead, in a *reference-oriented* interpretation, c_1 and c_2 define different situations: in the former the two arguments of the h operator are uncorrelated, while in the latter they point to the same *shared* location.

Term graphs [32] are a reference-oriented generalization of the ordinary (value-oriented) notion of term, where the sharing of sub-terms can be specified also for closed (i.e., without variables) terms.[1] The distinction is made precise by the axiomatization of *algebraic theories*: Terms and term graphs differ for two axioms, representing, in a categorical setting, the *naturality* of transformations for copying and discharging arguments [8]. Many other mathematical structures have been proposed, for expressing formalisms different from the ordinary tree-like presentation of terms. They range from the *flownomial calculus* of Stefanescu [6,34], to the *bicategories of processes* of Walters [18,19], to the *pre-monoidal categories* of Power and Robinson [28], to the *action structures* of Milner [24], to the *interaction categories* of Abramsky [1], to the *sharing graphs* of Hasegawa [16] and to the *gs-monoidal categories* of Corradini and Gadducci [7,8], just to mention a few (see also [9,11,15,29]). All these structures can be seen as enrichments of symmetric monoidal categories, which give the basis for the description of a distributed environment in terms of a wire and box diagram.

We propose a schema for describing normal forms for this kind of structures, generalizing the one in [12] (and that bears some similarity to the *equational term graph* of [2]), thus obtaining a universal framework where each structure finds its unique standard representation. We describe distributed spaces as sets of *assignments* over sets of variables, distinguishing between four different kinds

---

[1] Terms may share variables, but shared sub-terms of a closed term can be freely copied, always yielding an equivalent term.

of assignment, each representing a basic functionality of the space, namely *input* and *output interfaces, basic modules,* and *connections.* Changing the constraints on the admissible connections is the key to move between formalisms. We call Σ-spaces the distributed spaces over a signature Σ, and show that the classes of Σ-spaces we are interested in always form a symmetric monoidal category. We then establish a sort of triangular correspondence between various formalisms proposed in the literature (usually in a set-theoretical way), different classes of Σ-spaces and suitable enriched symmetric monoidal categories.

The structure of the paper is as follows: In Section 2 we give a categorical account of the various formalisms presented in the literature that we want to embed in our concrete normal-form representation. All of them are suitably enriched symmetric monoidal categories. In section 3 we formally define Σ-spaces, and equip them with two operations of parallel and sequential composition, yielding a monoidal category structure. In Section 4 we show how it is possible to have a normal form representation for net processes, relations, labeled partial orders, partitions, and contextual nets using suitable classes of Σ-spaces. We want to remark that all the classes under consideration are characterized by simple restrictions on the admissible links of Σ-spaces. In Section 5 we draw some conclusion and sketch a promising future research aimed at the *integration* of the mathematical structures considered in this paper via an implementation of their uniform normal form representations offered by Σ-spaces.

2   A Categorical View for Different Formalisms

We recall here a few categorical definitions, which allow to recast the usual notion of term over a signature in a more general setting. Moreover, the progressive enrichment of a basic theory with different auxiliary mathematical constructors generates a great variety of different model classes, where the usual notions of relation, partial order, partition, and many other can be represented.

Definition 1 (Signatures). *A many-sorted hyper-signature Σ over a set S_Σ of sorts is a family $\{\Sigma_{\omega,\omega'}\}_{\omega,\omega' \in S_\Sigma^*}$ of sets of operators. If S_Σ is a singleton, we denote the hyper-signature Σ by the family $\{\Sigma_{n,m}\}_{n,m \in \mathbf{N}}$.*

We usually omit the prefix "hyper". When it is clear from the context that a set S is the underlying set of sorts of a signature Σ, we drop the subscript $\_\Sigma$.

Definition 2 (Graphs). *A graph G is a 4-tuple $(O_G, A_G, \partial_0, \partial_1)$, where O_G is the set of objects, A_G is the set of arrows, and $\partial_0, \partial_1 : A_G \longrightarrow O_G$ are functions, called respectively source and target. We use the standard notation $f : a \longrightarrow b$ to denote an arrow f with source a and target b. A graph G is with pairing if O_G is a monoid.*

A many-sorted signature Σ over S is a graph with pairing G_Σ, where its objects are strings on S ($O_{G_\Sigma} = S^*$, string concatenation $\_\cdot\_$ yields the monoidal operator, and the empty string ϵ is the neutral element), and its edges are the operators of the signature (i.e., $f : \omega \longrightarrow \omega' \in A_{G_\Sigma}$ iff $f \in \Sigma_{\omega,\omega'}$).

A chain of structural enrichments enhances the expressiveness of different classes of models, e.g., the usual algebraic notion of terms over a signature. However, we are interested in weaker theories, where name sharing finds a natural embedding. The first enrichment is common to all the formalisms we will consider, and introduces the sequential and parallel compositions between arrows together with all the arrows necessary for arbitrary permutations of objects (corresponding to the swappings of wires in the wire and box presentation). Then, the models of the resulting *symmetric theory* of Σ are just suitable symmetric monoidal categories [21] (i.e., also equipped with the Σ-structure).

Definition 3 (Symmetric Monoidal Categories). *A monoidal category is a triple $\langle C, \_\otimes\_, e \rangle$, where C is the underlying category, $\_\otimes\_ : C \times C \longrightarrow C$ is a functor satisfying the associative law $(t_1 \otimes t_2) \otimes t_3 = t_1 \otimes (t_2 \otimes t_3)$, and e is an object of C satisfying the identity law $t \otimes e = t = e \otimes t$, for all arrows $t, t_1, t_2, t_3 \in C$. A symmetric monoidal category is a 4-tuple $\langle C, \_\otimes\_, e, \gamma \rangle$, where $\langle C, \_\otimes\_, e \rangle$ is a monoidal category, and $\gamma : \_1 \otimes \_2 \Rightarrow \_2 \otimes \_1 : C \times C \longrightarrow C$ is a natural transformation satisfying the coherence axioms*

$$
\begin{array}{ccc}
 & a\otimes\gamma_{b,c} & \\
a\otimes b\otimes c & \longrightarrow & a\otimes c\otimes b \\
 & & \downarrow \gamma_{a,c}\otimes b \\
\gamma_{a\otimes b,c} \searrow & & \\
 & c\otimes a\otimes b &
\end{array}
\qquad
\begin{array}{ccc}
 & \gamma_{a,b} & \\
a\otimes b & \longrightarrow & b\otimes a \\
 & & \downarrow \gamma_{b,a} \\
a\otimes b \searrow & & \\
 & a\otimes b &
\end{array}
$$

*A functor $F : C \longrightarrow C'$ between two (symmetric) monoidal categories is called monoidal if $F(t_1 \otimes t_2) = F(t_1) \otimes' F(t_2)$, and $F(e) = e'$; it is symmetric if $F(\gamma_{a,b}) = \gamma'_{F(a),F(b)}$. We denote by **SMCat** the category of symmetric functors.*

Among the uses of symmetric monoidal categories as a semantics framework, we recall the characterization of *concatenable processes* for Petri nets in [10], and the description of a *basic network algebra* for data-flows in [3,34].

2.1   Enriching the Monoidal Structure

The constructive definition of algebraic theories [20] as enriched monoidal categories dates back to the mid-Seventies [17,27], even if it has received a new stream of attention in these days. In our opinion, it separates very nicely the auxiliary structure from the Σ-structure (better than the ordinary description involving the meta-operation of substitution). Moreover, the naturality axioms for *duplicator* and *discharger* express a controlled form of data-sharing and data-garbaging. If these axioms are missing, then the corresponding theory, called *gs-monoidal*, is the natural framework for the representation of *term-graphs* rather than terms, as shown in [8].

Definition 4 (Share and GS-Monoidal Categories). *A share category is a 5-tuple $\langle C, \_\otimes\_, e, \gamma, \nabla \rangle$, where $\langle C, \_\otimes\_, e, \gamma \rangle$ is a symmetric monoidal category and $\nabla : 1 \Rightarrow \_1 \otimes \_1 : C \longrightarrow C$ is a transformation such that $\nabla_e = e$, and satisfying the coherence axioms (the first two diagrams express a sort of "output"* *associativity and commutativity for the duplicator, and the third diagram tells how the duplicator of a composed object $a \otimes b$ can be obtained by composing the duplicators of the subcomponents)*

$$
\begin{array}{ccc}
a & \xrightarrow{\nabla_a} & a \otimes a \\
{\scriptstyle \nabla_a}\downarrow & & \downarrow{\scriptstyle a \otimes \nabla_a} \\
a \otimes a & \xrightarrow{\nabla_a \otimes a} & a \otimes a \otimes a
\end{array}
\qquad
\begin{array}{ccc}
a & \xrightarrow{\nabla_a} & a \otimes a \\
 & {\scriptstyle \nabla_a}\searrow & \downarrow{\scriptstyle \gamma_{a,a}} \\
 & & a \otimes a
\end{array}
\qquad
\begin{array}{ccc}
a \otimes b & \xrightarrow{\nabla_a \otimes \nabla_b} & a \otimes a \otimes b \otimes b \\
 & {\scriptstyle \nabla_{a \otimes b}}\searrow & \downarrow{\scriptstyle a \otimes \gamma_{a,b} \otimes b} \\
 & & a \otimes b \otimes a \otimes b
\end{array}
$$

A share functor $F : C \longrightarrow C'$ between two share categories is a symmetric functor such that $F(\nabla_a) = \nabla'_{F(a)}$. We denote by **ShCat** the category of share functors.

A gs-monoidal category is a 6-tuple $\langle C, \_\otimes\_, e, \gamma, \nabla, ! \rangle$, where $\langle C, \_\otimes\_, e, \gamma, \nabla \rangle$ is a share category, and $! : 1 \Rightarrow e : C \longrightarrow C$ is a natural transformation such that $!_e = e$ and satisfying the coherence axioms (the first diagram says that creating two links to a and then discharging one of them just yields the identity on a, the second diagram expresses the monoidality of the discharger)

$$
\begin{array}{ccc}
a & \xrightarrow{\nabla_a} & a \otimes a \\
 & {\scriptstyle a}\searrow & \downarrow{\scriptstyle a \otimes !_a} \\
 & & a = a \otimes e
\end{array}
\qquad
\begin{array}{ccc}
a \otimes b & \xrightarrow{!_a \otimes !_b} & e \otimes e \\
 & {\scriptstyle !_{a \otimes b}}\searrow & \downarrow{\scriptstyle e} \\
 & & e \otimes e = e
\end{array}
$$

A gs-monoidal functor $F : C \longrightarrow C'$ is a share functor such that $F(!_a) = !'_{F(a)}$. We denote by **GSCat** the category of gs-monoidal functors.

Interesting applications often require the presence of the categorical opposite of duplicators, which may be used to express a sort of *data-matching*. Analogously, co-dischargers are introduced to represent the explicit *creation* of data. Several combinations are then possible, where only some of the operators are considered, and their mixed compositions are differently axiomatized, ranging from the *match-share* categories of [14] to the *dgs-monoidal* categories of [13,18]. Here we just sketch a survey of the categorical framework, and briefly comment their role in the literature and the main differences between similar models. We start with what we call a *r-monoidal category*: One of the various extensions, albeit with a different name, proposed in [5,33,34].

Definition 5 (R-Monoidal Categories). *A* r-monoidal category *is an 8-tuple* $\langle C, \_\otimes\_, e, \gamma, \nabla, !, \Delta, \dagger \rangle$ *such that* $\langle C, \_\otimes\_, e, \gamma, \nabla, ! \rangle$ *and* $\langle C^{op}, \_\otimes^{op}_{}\_, e, \gamma^{op}, \Delta^{op}, \dagger^{op} \rangle$ *are both gs-monoidal categories, and satisfying the additional coherence axioms (expressing the interplay between the gs and co-gs structures)*

$$
\begin{array}{ccc}
a \otimes a & \xrightarrow{\Delta_a} a \xrightarrow{\nabla_a} & a \otimes a \\
{\scriptstyle \nabla_a \otimes \nabla_a}\downarrow & & \uparrow{\scriptstyle \Delta_a \otimes \Delta_a} \\
a \otimes a \otimes a \otimes a & \xrightarrow{a \otimes \gamma_{a,a} \otimes a} & a \otimes a \otimes a \otimes a
\end{array}
\qquad
\begin{array}{ccc}
a & \xrightarrow{\nabla_a} & a \otimes a \\
 & {\scriptstyle a}\searrow & \downarrow{\scriptstyle \Delta_a} \\
 & & a
\end{array}
$$

$$
\begin{array}{ccc}
e & \xrightarrow{\dagger_a} & a \\
 & {\scriptstyle e}\searrow & \downarrow{\scriptstyle !_a} \\
 & & e
\end{array}
\qquad
\begin{array}{ccc}
e & \xrightarrow{\dagger_a} & a \\
 & {\scriptstyle \dagger_a \otimes \dagger_a}\searrow & \downarrow{\scriptstyle \nabla_a} \\
 & & a \otimes a
\end{array}
\qquad
\begin{array}{ccc}
a \otimes a & \xrightarrow{\Delta_a} & a \\
 & {\scriptstyle !_a \otimes !_a}\searrow & \downarrow{\scriptstyle !_a} \\
 & & e
\end{array}
$$

A r-monoidal functor $F : C \longrightarrow C'$ is a gs-monoidal functor such that also F^{op} is so. We denote by **RMCat** the category of r-monoidal functors.

The axioms we considered naturally embed the properties of relations, and the (partial) algebraic structure of r-monoidal categories yields a useful mathematical tool for their representation [5]. A stronger version of the axiom involving the composite $\Delta; \nabla$ is the basis for a different family of structures. In a certain sense, the stronger axiom establishes that duplicators and co-duplicators embed a sort of transitive and symmetric closure of the relation, i.e., it does not matter how two objects are connected, but just the fact that they are connected.

Definition 6 (Match-Share Categories). A match-share category is a 6-tuple $\langle C, \_ \otimes \_, e, \gamma, \nabla, \Delta \rangle$ such that $\langle C, \_ \otimes \_, e, \gamma, \nabla \rangle$ and $\langle C^{op}, \_ \otimes^{op}_-, e, \gamma^{op}, \Delta^{op} \rangle$ are both share categories, and satisfying the additional coherence axioms

$$
\begin{array}{ccc}
a \otimes a & \xrightarrow{\ \Delta_a\ } & a \\
{\scriptstyle \nabla_a \otimes a} \downarrow & & \downarrow {\scriptstyle \nabla_a} \\
a \otimes a \otimes a & \xrightarrow[a \otimes \Delta_a]{} & a \otimes a
\end{array}
\qquad\qquad
\begin{array}{ccc}
a & \xrightarrow{\ \nabla_a\ } & a \otimes a \\
& {\scriptstyle a} \searrow & \downarrow {\scriptstyle \Delta_a} \\
& & a
\end{array}
$$

A match-share functor $F : C \longrightarrow C'$ is a share functor such that also F^{op} is so. We denote by **MShCat** the category of match-share functors.

Match-share categories have been introduced in [14], and used to embed the algebraic properties of *processes* for *contextual nets* [25]. They are the basis for a class of categories where suitable models of partition-based structures can live.

Definition 7 (Part-Monoidal Categories). A part-monoidal category is an 8-tuple $\langle C, \_ \otimes \_, e, \gamma, \nabla, !, \Delta, \dagger \rangle$ such that both $\langle C, \_ \otimes \_, e, \gamma, \nabla, ! \rangle$ and $\langle C^{op}, \_ \otimes^{op}_-, e, \gamma^{op}, \Delta^{op}, \dagger^{op} \rangle$ are gs-monoidal categories, $\langle C, \_ \otimes \_, e, \gamma, \nabla, \Delta \rangle$ is a match-share category, and satisfying the additional coherence axiom

$$
\begin{array}{ccc}
e & \xrightarrow{\ \dagger_a\ } & a \\
& {\scriptstyle e} \searrow & \downarrow {\scriptstyle !_a} \\
& & e
\end{array}
$$

A part-monoidal functor $F : C \longrightarrow C'$ is a gs-monoidal functor such that also F^{op} is so. We denote by **PartMCat** the category of part-monoidal functors.

Differently from the previous structures, part-monoidal categories, as far as we know, has never been explicitly analyzed in the literature. The leading idea is that a generic arrow from $a_1 \otimes \cdots \otimes a_n$ to $b_1 \otimes \cdots \otimes b_m$ (where the a_i's and the b_i's are "basic" objects) represents some kind of partition of $\{a_1, ..., a_n, b_1, ..., b_m\}$. For example, the axiom $\Delta_a; !_a =\ !_a \otimes !_a$ of r-monoidal categories does not hold for partitions, because in the partition $\Delta_a; !_a$ both a sources belong to the same class, whereas in partition $!_a \otimes !_a$ they belong to disjoint classes.

3 The General Model: Σ-Spaces

We introduce now a concrete representation for the several formalisms discussed in the previous sections. It can be thought of as a normal form presentation of the less formal wire and box diagrams illustrated in the introduction. Basically, we split the operative components from the logical connectivity of a diagram. The typical operative components of a distributed system are the *input* and *output interfaces*, and the *basic functional modules* (n-to-m transforming black-boxes which give the building blocks of the wire and box notation). The way these components can interact constitutes the logical part of the system. Suitable *link-channels* can faithfully express this connectivity-related aspect. As a matter of notation, we write $z : s$ to say that the variable z has sort s.

Definition 8 (Σ-Spaces). *Let Σ be a signature. A Σ-assignment over a bipartite set $\mathcal{Z} = \mathcal{X} \uplus \mathcal{Y}$ ($\mathcal{X}$ is called the set of* names, *and $\mathcal{Y}$ the set of* results*) of typed variables is any of the following sentences, where the x's, the y's and the z's range over $\mathcal{X}$, $\mathcal{Y}$ and $\mathcal{Z}$ respectively.*

Generator: $x_1...x_n \overset{f}{\longmapsto} y_1...y_m$, *where $x_i : s_i$ for $i = 1...n$, $y_j : s'_j$ for $j = 1...m$, and $f \in \Sigma_{\omega,\omega'}$ with $\omega = s_1...s_n$, and $\omega' = s'_1...s'_m$,*
Link: $z_1 \longmapsto z_2$, *where $z_1 : s$ and $z_2 : s$,*
Input: $\square \longmapsto y_1...y_n$, *where $n \geq 0$,*
Output: $x_1...x_n \longmapsto \square$, *where $n \geq 0$.*
We say that a variable z is used *(respectively* assigned*) if it appears in the left-hand (respectively right-hand) side of a sentence.*
   A distributed space *over Σ is a set G of Σ-assignments such that*

1. *G contains exactly one input sentence $\square \longmapsto \alpha_{in}(G)$, denoted by $in(G)$,*
2. *G contains exactly one output sentence $\alpha_{out}(G) \longmapsto \square$, denoted by $out(G)$,*
3. *all the variables in $in(G)$, $out(G)$ and $gen(G) = \{ x_1...x_n \overset{f}{\longmapsto} y_1...y_m \in G \}$ are different,*
4. *all the variables in $link(G) = \{ z_1 \longmapsto z_2 \in G \}$ occur also in either $gen(G)$, $in(G)$ or $out(G)$.*

Given a distributed space G, its flow relation *F_G is the pre-order induced over variables by (the reflexive and transitive closure of) the set of sentences; its* link-flow relation *LF_G is the pre-order induced over variables by the set of links.*
   We call Σ-spaces the equivalence classes of distributed spaces over Σ up to α-conversion. Abusing the notation, we denote a generic Σ-space by the same symbols of the distributed spaces in the equivalence class it represents.

Σ-spaces yield a monoidal category. Indeed, let G be any Σ-space, and let $st : V^* \longrightarrow S^*$ be the function mapping a list of typed variables into the corresponding list of types, e.g. $st(z_1...z_n) = s_1...s_n$ if $z_i : s_i$ for $i = 1...n$. The objects are the elements of S^* (the free monoid over the set of sorts S), while each G is viewed as an arrow $G : st(\alpha_{in}(G)) \longrightarrow st(\alpha_{out}(G))$.

The parallel composition of two Σ-space G_1 and G_2 is always defined, yielding as a result the Σ-space $G_1 \otimes G_2$ that can be constructed as follows: Choose two distributed spaces in the classes of G_1 and G_2 such that their underlying sets of variables are disjoint (we can assume without loss of generality that G_1 and G_2 are already variable-disjoint), then take the following distributed space

$$\alpha_{in}(G_1 \otimes G_2) = \alpha_{in}(G_1) \cdot \alpha_{in}(G_2),$$
$$\alpha_{out}(G_1 \otimes G_2) = \alpha_{out}(G_1) \cdot \alpha_{out}(G_2),$$
$$gen(G_1 \otimes G_2) = gen(G_1) \cup gen(G_2),$$
$$link(G_1 \otimes G_2) = link(G_1) \cup link(G_2),$$

where $\_ \cdot \_$ denotes ordinary string concatenation.

Proposition 1. *Let G_1, G_2 be two Σ-spaces. Then $G_1 \otimes G_2$ is a Σ-space.*

The empty Σ-space $G_\epsilon = \{\, \Box \longmapsto \epsilon, \ \epsilon \longmapsto \Box \,\}$, where ϵ denotes the empty list of variables, is the unit element for parallel composition.

Proposition 2. *Let G be a Σ-space. Then $G \otimes G_\epsilon = G = G_\epsilon \otimes G$.*

The sequential composition of G_1 and G_2 is defined if and only if $st(\alpha_{out}(G_1)) = st(\alpha_{in}(G_2))$. As before, we assume G_1 and G_2 to be variable-disjoint and take the distributed space $G_1; G_2$ defined by

$$\alpha_{in}(G_1; G_2) = \alpha_{in}(G_1),$$
$$\alpha_{out}(G_1; G_2) = \alpha_{out}(G_2),$$
$$gen(G_1; G_2) = gen(G_1) \cup gen(G_2),$$
$$link(G_1; G_2) = [link(G_1)/\alpha_{out}(G_1)][link(G_2)/\alpha_{in}(G_2)],$$

where the composition of links is defined as

$$[L_1/X][L_2/Y] = I_1 \cup I_2 \cup F_{fw} \cup F_{bw} \cup D_1 \cup D_2$$

(but in all the cases we consider, except for *partitions* in Section 4.5 and Section 4.6, the three sets F_{bw}, D_1, and D_2 are empty), and if we denote by $X[i]$ the i-th variable of the list X, the formal definition of each subset of links is

$$I_1 = \{\, z_1 \longmapsto z_1' \in L_1 \},$$

$$I_2 = \{\, z_2 \longmapsto z_2' \in L_2 \},$$

$$F_{fw} = \{\, z_1 \longmapsto z_2 \mid z_1 \longmapsto X[i] \in L_1, \ Y[i] \longmapsto z_2 \in L_2 \},$$

$$F_{bw} = \{\, z_2 \longmapsto z_1 \mid z_2 \longmapsto Y[i] \in L_2, \ X[i] \longmapsto z_1 \in L_1 \},$$

$$D_1 = \{\, z_1 \longmapsto z_1' \mid z_1 \longmapsto X[i], \ X[j] \longmapsto z_1' \in L_1, \ Y[i] \longmapsto Y[j] \in L_2 \}$$

$$D_2 = \{\, z_2 \longmapsto z_2' \mid z_2 \longmapsto Y[i], \ Y[j] \longmapsto z_2' \in L_2, \ X[i] \longmapsto X[j] \in L_1 \}.$$

with $z_1, z_1' \notin X$ and $z_2, z_2' \notin Y$.

Intuitively, variables in $\alpha_{out}(G_1)$ and $\alpha_{in}(G_2)$ are removed from the composition $G_1; G_2$, but their ingoing and outgoing links are propagated to the remaining variables, with respect to the matching $\alpha_{out}(G_1)[i] \leftrightarrow \alpha_{in}(G_2)[i]$, for $i = 1...n$, of the variables in the "merged" interfaces of G_1 and G_2. Therefore, $link(G_1; G_2)$ contains: (1) the *internal* links I_1 of G_1, and I_2 of G_2, i.e. those links not involving removed variables, (2) the *forward* and *backward fusion* links F_{fw} and F_{bw}, and (3) the *forward* and *backward derived* links D_1 and D_2, propagating links involving only removed variables. However, as said before, most of the classes of Σ-spaces that we consider are acyclic, and define an intuitive *information flow* from left ($in(G)$) to right ($out(G)$): in this case, $F_{bw} \cup D_1 \cup D_2 = \emptyset$.

Proposition 3. *Let G_1, G_2 be two Σ-spaces, such that $st(\alpha_{out}(G_1)) = st(\alpha_{in}(G_2))$. Then $G_1; G_2$ is a Σ-space.*

For each $\omega \in S^*$, the Σ-space G_ω such that $st(\alpha_{in}(G)) = st(\alpha_{out}(G))$, $gen(G) = \emptyset$ and $link(G) = \{ \alpha_{in}(G)[i] \mapsto \alpha_{out}(G)[i] \mid i = 1...|\omega|\}$, behaves as the identity with respect to the sequential composition.

Proposition 4. *Let G be a Σ-space. Then $G; G_{st(\alpha_{out}(G))} = G_{st(\alpha_{in}(G))}; G = G$.*

Also the other properties of monoidal categories (e.g., $G_\omega \otimes G_{\omega'} = G_{\omega \cdot \omega'}$, and $(G_1; G_1') \otimes (G_2; G_2') = (G_1 \otimes G_2); (G_1' \otimes G_2')$, giving the functoriality of the tensor product $\_ \otimes \_$) are trivially satisfied by the definitions.

4   A Unified View for Nets, Relations and Partitions

In this section we show that all the models presented in Section 2 can be characterized as suitable Σ-spaces, simply imposing different requirements over the set of links. Moreover, such properties are preserved by the parallel and sequential composition as defined in Section 3, so that those spaces can be considered as concrete representations of their categorical counterparts.

4.1   Symmetric Monoidal

We begin by providing the class of Σ-spaces which characterize symmetric monoidal categories: its elements must satisfy a tight requirement over links.

Definition 9 (Symmetric Σ-space). *A Σ-space G is called* symmetric *if and only if each variable is used and assigned exactly once in G, and the flow relation induced by the assignment in G is acyclic.*

Or, in other words, the flow relation is actually a *partial order*.

Proposition 5. *If G is a symmetric Σ-space, then*

- *the only kind of link sentences allowed consists of sentences of the form $y \mapsto x$ where y is a result and x is a name,*

- *no result can be discharged in G,*
- *no name can be created in G,*
- *parallel and sequential composition of symmetric Σ-spaces yield symmetric Σ-spaces.*

Note that the restrictions always imply that $F_{bw} = D_1 = D_2 = \emptyset$, whenever two symmetric spaces are sequentially composed. To show that each symmetric Σ-space G defines a concrete symmetric monoidal category, we have to show what the symmetries are. For each pair of string $\omega, \omega' \in S^*$, with $|\omega| = n$, and $|\omega|' = m$, we define the symmetric Σ-space $G_{\omega,\omega'}$ as follows: Let Y and X be two lists of (pairwise disjoint) names such that $|Y| = |X| = n + m$, $Y[i] : (\omega \cdot \omega')[i]$, and $X[i] : (\omega' \cdot \omega)[i]$ for $i = 1...n + m$, then

$$G_{\omega,\omega'} = \{\, \square \longmapsto Y,\ X \longmapsto \square \,\} \cup \{\, Y[i] \longmapsto X[i+m] \mid i = 1...n \,\} \cup$$

$$\cup \{\, Y[i] \longmapsto X[i-n] \mid i = n+1...n+m \,\}.$$

Theorem 1. *Symmetric Σ-spaces are the arrows of a concrete symmetric monoidal category, which is (isomorphic to) the one freely generated by Σ.*

Proof sketch. From the last property of Proposition 5, we have just to show that the family of Σ-spaces $\{G_{\omega,\omega'}\}_{\omega,\omega' \in S^*}$ is a natural isomorphism from $_{-1} \otimes _{-2}$ to $_{-2} \otimes _{-1}$, and verifies the coherence axioms of Def. 3. This can be easily done by exploiting the definition of $G_{\omega,\omega'}$ and applying the definition of parallel and sequential composition. The initiality result relies on previous characterization results for symmetric monoidal categories as suitable *Petri processes* [31,30], to which our spaces are equivalent. $\square$

4.2 GS-Monoidal

As illustrated in Section 2, gs-monoidal categories are symmetric monoidal categories enriched with suitable transformations for copying and discharging information, which lack the naturality axiom. In our setting, this enrichment reflects into a relaxation of the previous constraints over symmetric Σ-spaces.

Definition 10 (GS-Monoidal Σ-space). *A Σ-space G is called gs-monoidal if and only if each variable is assigned exactly once in G, and the flow relation induced by the assignment in G is acyclic.*

Proposition 6. *If G is a gs-monoidal Σ-space, then*

- *the only kind of link sentences allowed consists of sentences of the form $y \longmapsto x$ where y is a result and x is a name,*
- *no name can be created in G,*
- *parallel and sequential composition of gs-monoidal Σ-spaces yield gs-monoidal Σ-spaces.*

The characterization of duplicators and dischargers is intuitive. For each string $\omega \in S^*$, with $|\omega| = n$, we define the gs-monoidal Σ-spaces G_ω^2, and G_ω^0 as follows: Let Y and X be list of names such that $|Y| = n$, $|X| = 2n$, $Y[i] : \omega[i]$, $X[i] : \omega[i]$, and $X[i + n] : \omega[i]$, for $i = 1...n$. Then

$$G_\omega^0 = \{ \Box \longmapsto Y, \; \epsilon \longmapsto \Box \},$$
$$G_\omega^2 = \{ \Box \longmapsto Y, \; X \longmapsto \Box \} \cup \{ Y[i] \longmapsto X[i] \mid i = 1...n \} \cup$$
$$\cup \{ Y[i] \longmapsto X[i + n] \mid i = 1...n \},$$

where we recall that ϵ denotes the empty list of variables.

Theorem 2. *GS-Monoidal Σ-spaces are the arrows of a concrete gs-monoidal category, which is (isomorphic to) the one freely generated by Σ.*

Proof sketch. From the last property of Proposition 6, we have just to show that the families of Σ-spaces $\{G_\omega^2\}_{\omega \in S^*}$, and $\{G_\omega^0\}_{\omega \in S^*}$ are transformation from $_{-1}$ to $_{-1} \otimes _{-1}$, and to G_ϵ, respectively, verifying the coherence axioms of Def. 4. This can be easily done exploiting the definition of G_ω^2, and G_ω^0. As an important remark, it is trivial to verify that the naturality axioms are not satisfied by $\{G_\omega^2\}_{\omega \in S^*}$, and $\{G_\omega^0\}_{\omega \in S^*}$. To show the initiality of our model we rely on the results of [8], since gs-monoidal Σ-spaces offer a concrete mathematical structure corresponding to a normalized representation for *gs-graphs*. □

The main result of [8] states that the free gs-monoidal category over a (ordinary) signature is isomorphic to the class of (ranked) *term graphs* labeled over it. Such a property is exploited in [7] to give an inductive, algebraic account of term graph *rewriting*. It is in this setting that we recover the intuitive interpretation of copying and discharging as suitable operations over graphical structures.

Also the *open graphs* of [26] form a free gs-monoidal category: The one generated by the one-sorted signature Σ such that $\Sigma_{h,k} = \emptyset$ if $k \neq 0$, and $\Sigma_{h,0} = L_h$ for $h \in \mathbb{N}$, where $L = \{L_h\}_{h \in \mathbb{N}}$ is the set of labels for the edges of the graph. Therefore, they find a normalized presentation in terms of Σ-spaces.

4.3   Relations

Due to the presence of both co-duplicators and co-dischargers in the relational model, we have no restriction on the number of ingoing and outgoing links in the corresponding version of Σ-spaces. The weaker constraint considered here just involves the global structure of the link sentences.

Definition 11. *A Σ-space G is called relational if and only if its link sentences have the form $y \longmapsto x$ where y is a result and x is a name, and the flow relation induced by the assignments in a relational Σ-space G is acyclic.*

For example, in a relational Σ-space, each variable can be assigned and used as many times as necessary.

Proposition 7. *The parallel and sequential composition of relational Σ-spaces yield relational Σ-spaces.*

For each string $\omega \in S^*$, with $|\omega| = n$, we define the relational Σ-spaces $\overline{G}_\omega^2$, and $\overline{G}_\omega^0$ as follows: Let Y and X be list of names such that $|Y| = 2n$, $|X| = n$, $Y[i] : \omega[i]$, $Y[i+n] : \omega[i]$, and $X[i] : \omega[i]$, for $i = 1...n$. Then

$$\overline{G}_\omega^0 = \{\, \square \longmapsto \epsilon, \ X \longmapsto \square \,\},$$

$$\overline{G}_\omega^2 = \{\, \square \longmapsto Y, \ X \longmapsto \square \,\} \cup \{\, Y[i] \longmapsto X[i] \mid i = 1...n \,\} \cup$$

$$\cup \{\, Y[i+n] \longmapsto X[i] \mid i = 1...n \,\},$$

Families $\{\overline{G}_\omega^2\}_{\omega \in S^*}$, and $\{\overline{G}_\omega^0\}_{\omega \in S^*}$ are the co-duplicators and the co-dischargers.

Theorem 3. *Relational Σ-spaces are the arrows of a concrete r-monoidal category, which is (isomorphic to) the one freely generated by Σ.*

Therefore, relational Σ-spaces define an initial relational model for Σ.

Theorem 4. *Given any two strings $\omega, \omega' \in S^*$, the class of relational Σ-spaces G from ω to ω' such that $gen(G) = \emptyset$ is isomorphic to the class of possible type-preserving relations between the components of ω and those of ω'.*

The proof relies on Theorem 3 and on the results of [5,34].

4.4   Partial Orders

If Σ is a one-sorted signature that contains only unary operators, then we may use relational Σ-spaces for the representation of labeled partial orders.

Definition 12. *A relational Σ-space G is called po_Σ-space if $S_\Sigma = \{s\}$, and $\Sigma = \Sigma_{s,s}$.*

Let $(P, \sqsubseteq, \ell, A)$, where $\ell : P \longrightarrow A$, be a generic partial order labeled over the set A, and let us consider the Σ-spaces over the signature $\Sigma_A = \{a : 1 \longrightarrow 1 \mid a \in A\}$. In a similar fashion to the proposal of [14], the basic ingredients are the Σ_A-spaces in the family $\{G_a\}_{a \in A}$, where

$$G_a = \{\, \square \longmapsto y_1, \ x \overset{a}{\longmapsto} y, \ x_1 \longmapsto \square, \ y_1 \longmapsto x, \ y \longmapsto x_1, \ y_1 \longmapsto x_1 \,\}.$$

Intuitively, each Σ-space G_a represents the label a in parallel with an identity. The presence of the links $y_1 \longmapsto x$ and $y_1 \longmapsto x_1$, acting as a duplicator of the input position, together with the presence of the links $y \longmapsto x_1$ and $y_1 \longmapsto x_1$, acting as a match in the output position, creates a sort of implicit transitive closure of identities whenever the sequential composition is applied. As a result, the ordering relation of the partial order, say between e and e', is represented by propagating a copy of the identity of e in parallel with e'. The Σ_A-space associated to P is obtained by composing the G_a's following the intuitive correspondence with the labeled elements of P.

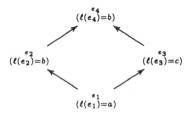

Fig. 1. A partial order $P = \{e_i\}_{i=1\ldots4}$ with labels over the set $A = \{a, b, c\}$.

Example 1. The Σ_A-space $G^0; G_a; G^2; (G_b \otimes G_c); \overline{G}^2; G_b; \overline{G}^0$ corresponds to the partial order in Fig. 1. The explicit construction for a sub-term is given in Fig. 2.

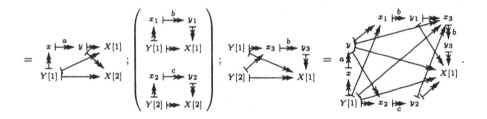

Fig. 2. Step-by-step illustration of $G_a; G^2; (G_b \otimes G_c); \overline{G}^2; G_b$. For simplicity we adopt a self-explanatory vector notation for the input and output variables.

Proposition 8. *Let G be a po_{Σ_A}-space. Then the class of arrows in the hom-set $G[\epsilon, \epsilon]$ are in one-to-one correspondence with the partial orders labeled on A.*

We believe that our characterization of partial orders as "closed elements" of an axiomatically defined algebra of relations is new.

4.5 Partitions

The most complex class of Σ-spaces we consider gives a framework for partitions.

Definition 13. *A Σ-space G is called* partition space *if and only if the link-flow relation is an equivalence relation.*

Proposition 9. *The parallel and sequential composition of partition spaces yield partition spaces as a result.*

Due to the peculiar nature of partition space, symmetries, (co)duplicators, and (co)dischargers still exist, but the constraints of partition spaces force some of them to have a richer structure than the one previously considered. In fact, they can be obtained freely adding link sentences, in order to obtain the minimal equivalence relation.

For each pair of string $\omega, \omega' \in S^*$, with $|\omega| = n$, and $|\omega|' = m$, the partition space $G_{\omega, \omega'}$ (which plays the role of the symmetry) is explicitly described as follows: Let Y and X be list of (pairwise disjoint) names such that $|Y| = |X| = n + m$, $Y[i] : (\omega \cdot \omega')[i]$, and $X[i] : (\omega' \cdot \omega)[i]$ for $i = 1...n + m$. Then

$$G_{\omega, \omega'} = \{ \square \longmapsto Y,\ X \longmapsto \square \} \cup \{ Y[i] \longmapsto X[i - n] \mid i = n + 1...n + m \} \cup$$

$$\cup \{ Y[i] \longmapsto X[i + m] \mid i = 1...n \} \cup \{ X[i + m] \longmapsto Y[i] \mid i = 1...n \} \cup$$

$$\cup \{ X[i - n] \longmapsto Y[i] \mid i = n + 1...n + m \}$$

where we skipped all the reflexive links, for the sake of readability. For each string $\omega \in S^*$, with $|\omega| = n$, the partition spaces G_ω^2, and G_ω^0 are as follows: Let Y and X be list of names such that $|Y| = n$, $|X| = 2n$, $Y[i] : \omega[i]$, $X[i] : \omega[i]$, and $X[i + n] : \omega[i]$, for $i = 1...n$. Then

$$G_\omega^0 = \{ \square \longmapsto Y,\ \epsilon \longmapsto \square \},$$

$$G_\omega^2 = \{ \square \longmapsto Y,\ X \longmapsto \square \} \cup \{ Y[i] \longmapsto X[i] \mid i = 1...n \} \cup$$

$$\cup \{ Y[i] \longmapsto X[i + n] \mid i = 1...n \} \cup \{ X[i] \longmapsto X[i + n] \mid i = 1...n \} \cup$$

$$\cup \{ X[i] \longmapsto Y[i] \mid i = 1...n \} \cup \{ X[i + n] \longmapsto Y[i] \mid i = 1...n \} \cup$$

$$\cup \{ X[i + n] \longmapsto X[i] \mid i = 1...n \}.$$

And similarly for their co-version.

Theorem 5. *Partition spaces are the arrows of a concrete part-monoidal category which is isomorphic to the one freely generated from Σ.*

Next correspondence theorem justifies the name part-monoidal.

Theorem 6. *Let G be a relational Σ-space with no generators. Then for each sort s and each $n, m \in \mathbb{N}$ the class of arrows in the hom-set $G[s^n, s^m]$ are in one-to-one correspondence with the partitions over $\{1...n + m\}$.*

We believe that our algebraic characterization of partitions is new.

4.6   Contextual Nets

As a last case we consider a subclass of partition Σ-spaces, which embeds processes of contextual nets.

Definition 14. *A partition Σ-space G is called* contextual *if and only if each variable is used and assigned at least once in G.*

Proposition 10. *If G is a contextual Σ-space, then*

- *no result can be discharged in G,*
- *no name can be created in G,*
- *parallel and sequential composition of contextual Σ-spaces yield contextual Σ-spaces.*

Theorem 7. *Contextual Σ-spaces are the arrows of a concrete match-share category, which is (isomorphic to) the one freely generated from Σ.*

Contextual nets extend ordinary Petri nets with *read arcs*, following the paradigm of read-write access to shared resources, where readers are allowed to progress in parallel. The axioms of match-share categories faithfully embed the compositional properties of contextual net processes [14]. In fact, the basic process associated to a transition t (with pre-set ${}^{\bullet}t$, context $\hat{t}$ and post-set $t^{\bullet}$) corresponds to the arrow $c(t) = ({}^{\bullet}t \otimes \nabla_{\hat{t}}); (t \otimes \hat{t}); (t^{\bullet} \otimes \Delta_{\hat{t}})$, where $t : {}^{\bullet}t \otimes \hat{t} \longrightarrow t^{\bullet} \otimes \hat{t}$. Intuitively this means that first a copy of the resources in the context $\hat{t}$ is created, then the firing of t consumes both its pre-set and a copy of the context, producing its post-set and a *fresh* copy of the context, which is then matched (and thus identified) with the initial copy left. For example, consider two transitions t_1 and t_2 such that $\hat{t_1} = a = \hat{t_2}$, then the following diagram commutes, and represents the concurrent access of t_1 and t_2 to the shared context a.

It follows that creating a copy of the context, firing t_1, matching the contexts, creating another copy of the context, firing t_2 and matching the contexts (upper path in the diagram) is equivalent to creating two copies of the context, concurrently firing t_1 and t_2 and matching the three copies of the context left, namely the one produced by t_1, the one produced by t_2 and the initial one (central path), and this is also equivalent to creating a copy of the context, firing t_2, matching the contexts, creating another copy of the context, firing t_1 and matching the contexts (lower path in the diagram).

5   Conclusion

We have investigated many of the numerous algebraic structures related to the "concurrent and distributed systems" representation, which have been proposed in the recent literature. Since all of them admit a presentation in terms of enriched symmetric monoidal categories, we have looked for a unifying concrete framework based on the same concepts. This has led us to a precise characterization of four fundamental aspects of an abstract distributed system: the *input* and *output interfaces*, the *basic functionalities* provided by the system (i.e., the constructors) and the *links* for the connection of subsystems.

As a main result, many of the algebraic approaches found in the literature are precisely characterized in our framework by considering different restrictions on the link sentences. We plan to show how these representation results allow for a uniform translation of these theories into a suitable specification formalism already available for partial algebras [22], as proved for a class of these structures in [23,4], the main point being the availability of tools supporting executability.

References

1. S. Abramsky, S. Gay, and R. Nagarajan. Interaction categories and the foundations of typed concurrent programming. In *Deductive Program Design*, Nato ASI Series, pages 403–442. Springer Verlag, 1994.
2. Z.M. Ariola and J.W. Klop. Equational term graph rewriting. *Fundamenta Informaticae*, 26:207–240, 1996.
3. J.A. Bergstra and G. Stefanescu. Network algebra for synchronous and asynchronous dataflow. Technical Report Logic Group Preprint Series n.122, Department of Philosophy, University of Utrecht, 1994.
4. R. Bruni, J. Meseguer, and U. Montanari. Process and term tile logic. Technical Report SRI-CSL-98-06, SRI International, 1998.
5. V.A. Cazanescu and G. Stefanescu. Classes of finite relations as initial abstract data types I. *Discrete Mathematics*, 90:233–265, 1991.
6. V.E. Cazanescu and G. Stefanescu. Towards a new algebraic foundation of flowchart scheme theory. *Fundamenta Informaticae*, 13:171–210, 1990.
7. A. Corradini and F. Gadducci. A 2-categorical presentation of term graph rewriting. In *Category Theory and Computer Science*, volume 1290 of *LNCS*. Springer Verlag, 1997.
8. A. Corradini and F. Gadducci. An algebraic presentation of term graphs, via gs-monoidal categories. *Applied Categorical Structures*, 1998. To appear.
9. A. Corradini and F. Gadducci. Functorial semantics for multi-algebras. Presented at WADT'98, 1998.
10. P. Degano, J. Meseguer, and U. Montanari. Axiomatizing the algebra of net computations and processes. *Acta Informatica*, 33:641–647, 1996.
11. G. Ferrari and U. Montanari. A tile-based coordination view of the asynchronous π-calculus. In *Mathematical Foundations of Computer Science*, volume 1295 of *LNCS*, pages 52–70. Springer Verlag, 1997.
12. G. Ferrari and U. Montanari. Tiles for concurrent and located calculi. In C. Palamidessi and J. Parrow, editors, *Expressiveness in Concurrency*, volume 7 of *Electronic Notes in Computer Science*. Elsevier Sciences, 1997.

13. F. Gadducci and R. Heckel. An inductive view of graph transformation. In F. Parisi-Presicce, editor, *Recent Trends in Algebraic Development Techniques*, volume 1376 of *LNCS*, pages 219–233. Springer Verlag, 1998.

14. F. Gadducci and U. Montanari. Axioms for contextual net processes. In *Automata, Languages and Programming*, volume 1443 of *LNCS*, pages 296–308. Springer Verlag, 1998.

15. F. Gadducci and U. Montanari. The tile model. In G. Plotkin, C. Stirling, and M. Tofte, editors, *Proof, Language and Interaction: Essays in Honour of Robin Milner*. MIT Press, 1999. to appear.

16. M. Hasegawa. Recursion from cyclic sharing: Traced monoidal categories and models of cyclic lambda-calculus. In *Typed Lambda Calculi and Applications*, volume 1210 of *LNCS*, pages 196–213. Springer Verlag, 1997.

17. H.-J. Hoenke. On partial recursive definitions and programs. In M. Karpinski, editor, *Fundamentals of Computations Theory*, volume 56 of *LNCS*, pages 260–274. Springer Verlag, 1977.

18. P. Katis, N. Sabadini, and R.F.C. Walters. Bicategories of processes. *Journal of Pure and Applied Algebra*, 115:141–178, 1997.

19. P. Katis, N. Sabadini, and R.F.C. Walters. SPAN(Graph): A categorical algebra of transition systems. In M. Johnson, editor, *Algebraic Methodology and Software Technology*, volume 1349 of *LNCS*, pages 307–321. Springer Verlag, 1997.

20. F.W. Lawvere. Functorial semantics of algebraic theories. *Proc. National Academy of Science*, 50:869–872, 1963.

21. S. Mac Lane. *Categories for the working mathematician*. Springer Verlag, 1971.

22. J. Meseguer. Membership algebra as a logical framework for equational specification. In F. Parisi-Presicce, editor, *Recent Trends in Algebraic Development Techniques*, volume 1376 of *LNCS*. Springer Verlag, 1998.

23. J. Meseguer and U. Montanari. Mapping tile logic into rewriting logic. In F. Parisi-Presicce, editor, *Recent Trends in Algebraic Development Techniques*, volume 1376 of *LNCS*. Springer Verlag, 1998.

24. R. Milner. Calculi for interaction. *Acta Informatica*, 33:707–737, 1996.

25. U. Montanari and F. Rossi. Contextual nets. *Acta Informatica*, 32:545–596, 1995.

26. U. Montanari and F. Rossi. Graph rewriting, constraint solving and tiles for coordinating distributed systems. *Applied Categorical Structures*, 1998. To appear.

27. M. Pfender. Universal algebra in s-monoidal categories. Technical Report 95–22, University of Munich - Department of Mathematics, 1974.

28. J. Power and E. Robinson. Premonoidal categories and notions of computation. *Mathematical Structures in Computer Science*, 7:453–468, 1998.

29. E. Robinson and G. Rosolini. Categories of partial maps. *Information and Computation*, 79:95–130, 1988.

30. V. Sassone. *On the Semantics of Petri Nets: Processes, Unfolding and Infinite Computations*. PhD thesis, University of Pisa - Department of Computer Science, 1994.

31. V. Sassone. An axiomatization of the algebra of Petri net concatenable processes. *Theoret. Comput. Sci.*, 170:277–296, 1996.

32. M.R. Sleep, M.J. Plasmeijer, and M.C. van Eekelen, editors. *Term Graph Rewriting: Theory and Practice*. Wiley, London, 1993.

33. G. Stefanescu. On flowchart theories: Part II. The nondeterministic case. *Theoret. Comput. Sci.*, 52:307–340, 1987.

34. G. Stefanescu. Algebra of flownomials. Technical Report SFB-Bericht 342/16/94 A, Technical University of München, Institut für Informatik, 1994.

Parameterisation of Logics*

Carlos Caleiro, Cristina Sernadas, and Amílcar Sernadas

Departamento de Matemática, Instituto Superior Técnico
Av. Rovisco Pais, 1096 Lisboa Codex, Portugal
{ccal,css,acs}@math.ist.utl.pt

Abstract. Combined logics have recently deserved much attention. In this paper we develop a detailed study of a form of combination that generalises the temporalisation construction proposed in [16]. It consists of replacing an atomic part (formal parameter) of one (parameterised) logic by another (actual parameter) logic. We provide a categorial characterisation of parameterisation and illustrate it with an example. Under reasonable assumptions, we show that the result logic is a conservative extension of both the parameterised and parameter logics and also that soundness, completeness and decidability are transferred.

1 Introduction

We need to work with evermore complex systems. The challenge is to identify abstractions that may lead to a modular and integrated management of this complexity. One such approach is the combination of logics. In practice, it is geared by the need for integrating heterogeneous platforms and tools. Theoretically, the study of logics for combined structures has been a topic of recurrent interest [5]. In [18], we presented a categorial study of fibring [12]. Here, we apply similar techniques to characterise another form of combination: parameterisation.

Parameterisation deals with refined structures [5], a kind of one-way fibring, and has temporalisation [16] as a particular case. The underlying idea is very simple: suppose that we want to describe a state based system (e.g., a database) and we know of two logics, one suited for describing its states (e.g., first-order logic [*fol*]) and the other its dynamics (e.g., propositional modal logic [*pml*]). Parameterisation builds up a new logic (e.g., modalised first-order logic [*mfol*]) that encompasses both, and whose properties capitalise on properties of the given logics in the lines of [16]. Formulae are obtained by replacing propositional symbols in *pml* formulae by *fol* formulae. Indeed, "monolithic" [16] *fol* formulae are enough: those whose principal constructor is not a propositional connective

---

* We are grateful to our colleagues in the ACL and FLIRTS initiatives for many discussions on the role of categories in the combination of logics. This work was partially supported by the PRAXIS XXI Program and FCT, by PRAXIS XXI Projects 2/2.1/MAT/262/94 SitCalc, PCEX/P/MAT/46/96 ACL and 2/2.1/TIT/1658/95 LogComp, the ProbLog initiative of CMA, and ESPRIT IV Working Groups 22704 ASPIRE and 23531 FIREworks.

J.L. Fiadeiro (Ed.): WADT'98, LNCS 1589, pp. 48–62, 1999.

(shared by *pml*). So, we can freely apply modalities but we cannot apply quantifiers to modal formulae. This asymmetry embodies the essential distinction between parameterisation and fibring. Models are Kripke frames, but the usual valuation for atoms is replaced by a "zoom in" [8] map associating a model of *fol* with a fixed assignment to each state. Proof-theoretically, we must be able to instantiate *pml* axioms and rules with *fol* monoliths but forbid *fol* reasoning to be applied to formulae with modalities. Note that issues like the Barcan formulae are meaningless here. First-order modal logic is, instead, a fibred logic [20].

Clearly, parameterisation requires a notion of logic where constructors and their evaluation are first class concepts, and inference rules allow for schematic substitutions. A flattening mechanism to obtain the required monoliths, models with selected item and restricted reasoning out of the parameter logic is also mandatory. Note that, despite the importance of the principle of invariance captured by the usual translation axiom [4], we are interested in a non-relativised notion of logic. We believe that by fixing the language we can better solve the problem at hand, and later on lift the results to the indexed case in a way similar to [21,14]. The use we make of categorial techniques is well justified by their extensively recognised utility in the study of logics and their combination [4,6,13,1,22,7,3,15,19,23]. As textbooks on category theory we suggest [9,17], and [11] as far as (co)cartesian liftings are concerned. The "pushout approach" to parameterised algebraic specifications [24] was also inspiring.

In section 2 we present the desired notion of logic universe and corresponding flattening mechanism, and state some technical results. In section 3, we define parameterisation and give it a categorial characterisation. We use *mfol* for illustration. In section 4, we prove that parameterisation extends both the parameter and parameterised logics, identify sufficient conditions for these extensions to be conservative, and establish transference results for soundness, completeness and decidability. We conclude with an outline of limitations and future work.

2   Logic universes

The above mentioned desired properties of logic universes are similar to those required for fibring. Thus, we adopt a slightly simplified version of the logic system presentations used in [18]. To cope with the asymmetric nature of parameterisation we further endow them with a flattening mechanism. Logic system presentations have both a proof and a model-theoretic component, each inducing a consequence (closure) operator.

Definition 1. *A consequence system C is a pair $\langle F, \_^\dagger \rangle$ where F is a set and $\_^\dagger : 2^F \to 2^F$ is such that:*

- $\Phi \subseteq \Phi^\dagger$;
- $\Phi^\dagger \subseteq (\Phi \cup \Psi)^\dagger$;
- $(\Phi^\dagger)^\dagger \subseteq \Phi^\dagger$.

Definition 2. *A morphism $h : C^1 \to C^2$ of consequence systems is a map $h : F^1 \to F^2$ such that $h(\Phi^{\dagger^1}) \subseteq h(\Phi)^{\dagger^2}$.*

Proposition 3. *Consequence systems and their morphisms constitute the category Csy.*

2.1 Signatures

Signatures are just ranked alphabets of *constructors*. Morphisms preserve rank.

Definition 4. *A signature Σ is an indexed family of sets $\{\Sigma_k\}_{k \in \mathbb{N}}$. A morphism $h : \Sigma^1 \to \Sigma^2$ of signatures is an indexed family of maps $\{h_k : \Sigma_k^1 \to \Sigma_k^2\}_{k \in \mathbb{N}}$.*

Proposition 5. *Signatures and their morphisms constitute the category Sig. Moreover, Sig is small cocomplete.*

As in *Set*, coproducts correspond to disjoint unions, coequalisers to quotients.

We use the natural extension to signatures of some usual operations on sets and functions: inclusion, complement, (disjoint) union, (back-)image. We promote sets X to signatures $@(X)$ by $@(X)_0 = X$ and $@(X)_{k+1} = \emptyset$, and functions $f : X \to Y$ to morphisms $@(f) : @(X) \to @(Y)$ by $@(f)_0 = f$ and $@(f)_{k+1} = \emptyset$.

From now on we consider fixed a set Ξ of *schema variables*.

Definition 6. *The set $F(\Sigma, \Xi)$ of schema formulae over signature Σ is defined inductively by Σ on Ξ. The elements of $F(\Sigma) = F(\Sigma, \emptyset)$ are just called formulae.*

Definition 7. *The* translation *$h : F(\Sigma^1, \Xi) \to F(\Sigma^2, \Xi)$ induced by a Sig morphism $h : \Sigma^1 \to \Sigma^2$ is defined inductively by letting $h(\xi) = \xi$ for each $\xi \in \Xi$.*

Since $h(F(\Sigma^1)) \subseteq F(\Sigma^2)$, it is trivial to set up the following functor.

Proposition 8. *The maps*

- $\mathcal{F}(\Sigma) = F(\Sigma)$;
- $\mathcal{F}(h : \Sigma^1 \to \Sigma^2) = h$,

constitute the (syntax) functor $\mathcal{F} : Sig \to Set$.

2.2 Hilbert calculi

The proof-theoretic component is captured by the notion of Hilbert calculus.

Definition 9. *A Hilbert calculus H is a pair $\langle \Sigma, R \rangle$ where Σ is a signature and $R \subseteq \wp_{\mathrm{fin}}(F(\Sigma, \Xi)) \times F(\Sigma, \Xi)$.*

We say that $r = \langle Prem(r), Conc(r) \rangle \in R$ is a (finitary) *schema rule*, $Prem(r)$ its *premises* and $Conc(r)$ its *conclusion*. If $Prem(r) = \emptyset$, r is a schema *axiom*.

Morphisms of Hilbert calculi preserve rules under translation.

Definition 10. *A morphism $h : H^1 \to H^2$ of Hilbert calculi is a Sig morphism $h : \Sigma^1 \to \Sigma^2$ such that $h(R^1) \subseteq R^2$.*

Proposition 11. *Hilbert calculi and their morphisms constitute the category Hil. Moreover, Hil is small cocomplete.*

Trivially, colimits in *Hil* are concrete on the forgetful functor $S_{Hil} : Hil \to Sig$.

We use *substitutions* $\varrho : \Xi \to F(\Sigma, \Xi)$, and call them *ground* if $\varrho(\Xi) \subseteq F(\Sigma)$. The *instance* $\gamma\varrho$ of a schema formula γ by ϱ is obtained by replacing in γ each occurrence of a schema variable ξ by $\varrho(\xi)$.

Definition 12. *The* derivation $\vdash \subseteq 2^{F(\Sigma, \Xi)} \times F(\Sigma, \Xi)$ *induced by* H *is such that* $\Gamma \vdash \delta$ *iff there exists a sequence* $\delta_1 \ldots \delta_n$ *of schema formulae with* $\delta_n = \delta$ *and, for each* i, *either* $\delta_i \in \Gamma$, *or there exist a substitution* ϱ *and a rule* $r \in R$ *such that* $\delta_i = Conc(r)\varrho$ *and every element of* $Prem(r)\varrho$ *occurs in* $\delta_1 \ldots \delta_{i-1}$.

If $\emptyset \vdash \delta$ we call δ a *theorem schema* (*theorem* if $\delta \in F(\Sigma)$) and just write $\vdash \delta$.

Proposition 13. *Given a Hil morphism* $h : H^1 \to H^2$ *and a substitution* ϱ *on* Σ^1, *if* $\Gamma \vdash^1 \delta$ *then* $h(\Gamma)(h \circ \varrho) \vdash^2 h(\delta)(h \circ \varrho)$.

Thus, we can define the following functor.

Proposition 14. *The maps*

- $C_{Hil}(H) = \langle F(\Sigma), \_^\vdash \rangle$ *where* $\Phi^\vdash = \{\varphi \in F(\Sigma) : \Phi \vdash \varphi\}$;
- $C_{Hil}(h : H^1 \to H^2) = h$,

constitute the (*syntactic consequence*) *functor* $C_{Hil} : Hil \to Csy$.

2.3   Interpretation systems

Finally, interpretation systems capture the model-theoretic component.

Definition 15. *An* interpretation system I *is a triple* $\langle \Sigma, M, A \rangle$ *where* Σ *is a signature,* M *a class and* $A : M \to Str(\Sigma)$ *a map, where* $Str(\Sigma)$ *is the class of all* Σ-*structures* $\langle U, \nu \rangle$ *with:*

- $U \neq \emptyset$;
- ν *an indexed family of maps* $\{\nu_k : \Sigma_k \to [(2^U)^k \to 2^U]\}_{k \in \mathbb{N}}$,

such that, denoting each $A(m)$ *by* $\langle U_m, \nu_m \rangle$, *for every* $m_1 \in M$ *and bijection* $f : U_{m_1} \cong U$ *there exists* $m_2 \in M$ *with* $U_{m_2} = U$ *and*

- $\nu_{m_2 k}(c)(b_1, \ldots, b_k) \circ f = \nu_{m_1 k}(c)(b_1 \circ f, \ldots, b_k \circ f)$.

We say that M is the class of *models*, and U_m and ν_m, respectively, the *pointspace* and *evaluator* of each model m. Note that the closure condition, being harmless for entailment [18], is necessary to the universality of our constructions.

Morphisms associate to each target model a set of source models inducing a partition of its pointspace and agreeing on the evaluators.

Definition 16. *A* morphism $h : I^1 \to I^2$ *of interpretation systems is a pair* $h = \langle \overline{h}, \underline{h} \rangle$ *where* $\overline{h} : \Sigma^1 \to \Sigma^2$ *is a Sig morphism and* $\underline{h} = \{\underline{h}_{mu}\}_{m \in M^2, u \in U_m}$ *with each* $\underline{h}_{mu} \in M^1$, *such that, being* $i^h_{mu} : U_{\underline{h}_{mu}} \hookrightarrow U_m$ *the inclusion:*

- $U_{\underline{h}_{mu}} = \{v \in U_m : \underline{h}_{mv} = \underline{h}_{mu}\}$;
- $\nu_{mk}(\overline{h}_k(c))(b_1, \ldots, b_k)(u) = \nu_{\underline{h}_{mu} k}(c)(b_1 \circ i^h_{mu}, \ldots, b_k \circ i^h_{mu})(u)$.

Proposition 17. *Interpretation systems and their morphisms constitute the category Int. Moreover, Int has all finite coproducts.*

For a detailed account on coproducts in *Int* we refer the reader to [18].

We denote by $S_{Int} : Int \rightarrow Sig$ the obvious forgetful functor. We use *assignments* $\alpha : \Xi \rightarrow 2^{U_m}$ over each $m \in M$. The *interpretation* $[\![.]\!]_{\alpha}^m : F(\Sigma, \Xi) \rightarrow 2^{U_m}$ is defined inductively by ν_m on α. *Satisfaction*, $\Vdash_{\alpha} \subseteq M \times F(\Sigma, \Xi)$, is defined by: $m \Vdash_{\alpha} \gamma$ iff $[\![\gamma]\!]_{\alpha}^m = U_m$. For formulae, α is useless and thus omitted.

Definition 18. *The entailment* $\vDash \subseteq 2^{F(\Sigma, \Xi)} \times F(\Sigma, \Xi)$ *induced by I is such that $\Gamma \vDash \delta$ iff for each assignment α, $m \Vdash_{\alpha} \delta$ whenever $m \Vdash_{\alpha} \gamma$ for every $\gamma \in \Gamma$.*

In case Γ is empty, we call δ a *valid* schema formula and simply write $\vDash \delta$.

Proposition 19. *Given a Int morphism $h : I^1 \rightarrow I^2$, if $\Gamma \vDash^1 \delta$ then $\overline{h}(\Gamma) \vDash^2 \overline{h}(\delta)$.*

Thus, we can define the following functor.

Proposition 20. *The maps*

- $C_{Int}(I) = \langle F(\Sigma), \_^{\vDash} \rangle$ *where* $\Phi^{\vDash} = \{\varphi \in F(\Sigma) : \Phi \vDash \varphi\}$;
- $C_{Int}(h : I^1 \rightarrow I^2) = h$,

constitute the (semantic consequence) functor $C_{Int} : Int \rightarrow Csy$.

2.4   Logic system presentations

The envisaged notion of logic universe can now be defined.

Definition 21. *A logic system presentation L is a tuple $\langle \Sigma, R, M, A \rangle$ where $\langle \Sigma, R \rangle$ is a Hilbert calculus and $\langle \Sigma, M, A \rangle$ an interpretation system.*

Note that soundness of the deductive component with respect to the semantics is not required. Obviously, we are "much more" interested in sound logic system presentations. However, for the moment, it is not essential to our constructions.

Definition 22. *A morphism $h : L^1 \rightarrow L^2$ of logic system presentations is a Int morphism $h : \langle \Sigma^1, M^1, A^1 \rangle \rightarrow \langle \Sigma^2, M^2, A^2 \rangle$ such that $\overline{h} : \langle \Sigma^1, R^1 \rangle \rightarrow \langle \Sigma^2, R^2 \rangle$ is a Hil morphism.*

Proposition 23. *Logic system presentations and their morphisms constitute the category Lsp. Moreover, Lsp has all finite coproducts.*

Such coproducts were used in [18] to characterise free fibring.

We consider the obvious forgetful functors S_{Lsp}, $\mathcal{H}_{Lsp}$ and $\mathcal{I}_{Lsp}$ from *Lsp* to *Sig*, *Hil* and *Int* respectively.

Proposition 24. *For each logic system presentation L^1 and Sig morphism $\overline{h} : \Sigma^1 \rightarrow \Sigma^2$ with each $\overline{h}_k$ surjective, the Lsp morphism $h : L^1 \rightarrow L^2$ where:*

- $R^2 = \overline{h}(R^1)$;
- M^2 is the class of $m \in M^1$ such that $\nu_{mk}(c) = \nu_{mk}(c')$ if $\overline{h}_k(c) = \overline{h}_k(c')$;
- $A^2(m) = \langle U_m, \nu^2 \rangle$ where $\nu_k^2(\overline{h}_k(c)) = \nu_{mk}(c)$;
- $\underline{h}_{mu} = m$,

is cocartesian by $\mathcal{S}_{Lsp}$ for $\overline{h}$ on L^1.

Constrained fibring was characterised in [18] using such cocartesian liftings.

As usual, a logic system presentation L is said to be (weakly) *sound* if $\vdash \varphi$ implies $\vDash \varphi$, and (weakly) *complete* if $\vDash \varphi$ implies $\vdash \varphi$. We also say that a rule $r \in R$ is *sound* if $Prem(r) \vDash Conc(r)$. It is easy to show that L is sound whenever all its rules are. The following result is a trivial corollary of proposition 19.

Proposition 25. *Given a Lsp morphism $h : L^1 \to L^2$, if $r \in R^1$ is sound in L^1 then $\overline{h}(r) \in R^2$ is sound in L^2.*

2.5 Flattening

As explained before, parameterisation requires a reshaping, flattening, of the parameter logic, taking into account a family of distinguished (shared) constructors. The following categories and functors are needed in the sequel.

Definition 26. *The categories $Sig^\bullet$, $Hil^\bullet$, $Int^\bullet$ and $Lsp^\bullet$ of, respectively, signatures, Hilbert calculi, interpretation systems and logic system presentations with distinguished subsignature are the following comma categories:*

- $Sig^\bullet$ is $(\mathcal{ID}_{Sig} \downarrow \mathcal{ID}_{Sig})$;
- $Hil^\bullet$ is $(\mathcal{ID}_{Sig} \downarrow \mathcal{S}_{Hil})$;
- $Int^\bullet$ is $(\mathcal{ID}_{Sig} \downarrow \mathcal{S}_{Int})$;
- $Lsp^\bullet$ is $(\mathcal{ID}_{Sig} \downarrow \mathcal{S}_{Lsp})$.

Clearly, $Sig^\bullet$ is the arrow category of Sig. Given $\langle S, h : S \to \Sigma, \Sigma \rangle$ in $Sig^\bullet$ we say that Σ is the *underlying signature* and $h(S)$ its *distinguished subsignature*. We consider the forgetful functor $\mathcal{U}_{Sig} : Sig^\bullet \to Sig$ which extracts the underlying signatures from $Sig^\bullet$. The same applies to $Hil^\bullet$, $Int^\bullet$ and $Lsp^\bullet$ with corresponding forgetful functors $\mathcal{U}_{Hil}$, $\mathcal{U}_{Int}$ and $\mathcal{U}_{Lsp}$. We also consider the obvious forgetful functors $\mathcal{S}_{Hil}^\bullet : Hil^\bullet \to Sig^\bullet$, $\mathcal{S}_{Int}^\bullet : Int^\bullet \to Sig^\bullet$, $\mathcal{S}_{Lsp}^\bullet : Lsp^\bullet \to Sig^\bullet$, $\mathcal{H}_{Lsp}^\bullet : Lsp^\bullet \to Hil^\bullet$ and $\mathcal{I}_{Lsp}^\bullet : Lsp^\bullet \to Int^\bullet$. These functors enjoy several nice properties. However, since they are not essential to this paper, we omit them.

At the signature level, only shared constructors are kept by flattening. However, monoliths are promoted to constructors. Given $\langle S, h, \Sigma \rangle$ in $Sig^\bullet$, the corresponding set of *monoliths* is $(F(\Sigma) \upharpoonright h) = \{c(\varphi_1, \ldots, \varphi_k) \in F(\Sigma) : c \notin h(S)_k\}$.

Proposition 27. *The maps*

- $\mathcal{F}_{Sig}(\langle S, h, \Sigma \rangle) = \Sigma^\flat(h)$;
- $\mathcal{F}_{Sig}(\langle h^S, h^\Sigma \rangle : \langle S^1, h^1, \Sigma^1 \rangle \to \langle S^2, h^2, \Sigma^2 \rangle) = h^\flat(\langle h^S, h^\Sigma \rangle)$,

where:

- $\Sigma^b(h) = h(S) \uplus @(F(\Sigma) \upharpoonright h)$;
- $h^b(\langle h^S, h^\Sigma \rangle) = h^\Sigma \uplus @(h^\Sigma)$,

constitute the (flattening) functor $\mathcal{F}_{Sig} : Sig^\bullet \to Sig$.

Although quite different, Σ and $\Sigma^b(h)$ induce the same set of formulae.

Proposition 28. $\mathcal{F} \circ \mathcal{F}_{Sig} = \mathcal{F} \circ \mathcal{U}_{Sig}$.

With respect to Hilbert calculi, rules over distinguished constructors are kept. The remaining rules are "closed" by ground substitutions thus preventing further instantiations (after the combination). The set $(R \upharpoonright h)$ of *rules on distinguished constructors* determined by $h : S \to \Sigma$ on a set R of rules over Σ is $h(h^{-1}(R))$.

Proposition 29. *The maps*

- $\mathcal{F}_{Hil}(\langle S, h, \langle \Sigma, R \rangle \rangle) = \langle \Sigma^b(h), R^b(h) \rangle$;
- $\mathcal{F}_{Hil}(\langle h^S, h^\Sigma \rangle : \langle S^1, h^1, H^1 \rangle \to \langle S^2, h^2, H^2 \rangle) = h^b(\langle h^S, h^\Sigma \rangle)$,

where:

- $R^b(h) = (R \upharpoonright h) \cup \{r\sigma : r \in (R \setminus (R \upharpoonright h)),\ \sigma \text{ is a ground substitution over } \Sigma\}$,

constitute the (flattening) functor $\mathcal{F}_{Hil} : Hil^\bullet \to Hil$.

We denote $\mathcal{F}_{Hil}(\langle S, h, H \rangle)$ by $H^b(h)$. As before, H and $H^b(h)$ induce the same syntactic consequence.

Proposition 30. $\mathcal{C}_{Hil} \circ \mathcal{F}_{Hil} = \mathcal{C}_{Hil} \circ \mathcal{U}_{Hil}$.

With respect to interpretation system, flat models are models with a singular selected point from its pointspace. However, the evaluation of a distinguished constructor on a flat model can only be appropriately defined if, for each original model, the evaluation of the constructor on one point does not depend on any other point. This is made precise using the functor $S^\bullet_{Int} : Int^\bullet \to Sig^\bullet$.

Proposition 31. $S^\bullet_{Int}$ *is a split fibration with a unique cleavage. In particular, for each* $\langle S^2, h^2, I^2 \rangle$ *in* $Int^\bullet$ *and* $Sig^\bullet$ *morphism* $\langle h^S, h^\Sigma \rangle : \langle S^1, h^1, \Sigma^1 \rangle \to \langle S^2, h^2, \Sigma^2 \rangle$, *the* $Int^\bullet$ *morphism* $\langle h^S, \langle h^\Sigma, \underline{h} \rangle \rangle : \langle S^1, h^1, I^1 \rangle \to \langle S^2, h^2, I^2 \rangle$ *where:*

- $M^1 = M^2$;
- $A^1(m) = A^2(m) \circ h^\Sigma$;
- $\underline{h}_{mu} = m$,

is cartesian by $S^\bullet_{Int}$ *for* $\langle h^S, h^\Sigma \rangle$ *on* $\langle S^2, h^2, I^2 \rangle$.

Definition 32. $\langle \Sigma, M, A \rangle$ *in* Int *is pointwise definable iff* $\nu_{mk}(c)(b_1, \ldots, b_k)(u) = \nu_{mk}(c)(d_1, \ldots, d_k)(u)$ *whenever each* $b_i(u) = d_i(u)$.

Definition 33. $\langle S, h, I \rangle$ *in* $Int^\bullet$ *is pointwise definable iff* $\mathcal{U}_{Int}$ *applied to the domain of the cartesian morphism by* $S^\bullet_{Int}$ *for* $\langle id_S, h \rangle : \langle S, id_S, S \rangle \to \langle S, h, \Sigma \rangle$ *on* $\langle S, h, I \rangle$ *yields a pointwise definable interpretation system.*

We denote by Int° the full subcategory of $Int^\bullet$ whose objects are all the pointwise definable interpretation systems with distinguished subsignature.

Proposition 34. *The maps*

- $\mathcal{F}_{Int}(\langle S, h, \langle \Sigma, M, A \rangle \rangle) = \langle \Sigma^\flat(h), M^\flat(h), A^\flat(h) \rangle$;
- $\mathcal{F}_{Int}(\langle h^S, \langle h^\Sigma, \underline{h} \rangle) : \langle S^1, h^1, I^1 \rangle \to \langle S^2, h^2, I^2 \rangle) = \langle h^\flat(\langle h^S, h^\Sigma \rangle), \underline{h}^\flat \rangle$,

where:

- $M^\flat(h) = \{\langle m, u \rangle : m \in M, \ u \in U_m\}$;
- $A^\flat(h)(\langle m, u \rangle) = \langle \{u\}, \nu \rangle$ *such that, being* $i^u : \{u\} \hookrightarrow U_m$ *the obvious inclusion,* $\nu_k(h_k(s))(b_1 \circ i^u, \ldots, b_k \circ i^u)(u) = \nu_{mk}(h_k(s))(b_1, \ldots, b_k)(u)$ *and* $\nu_0(\varphi)(u) = [\![\varphi]\!]^m(u)$;
- $\underline{h}^\flat_{\langle m, u \rangle u} = \langle \underline{h}_{mu}, u \rangle$,

constitute the (flattening) functor $\mathcal{F}_{Int} : Int^\circ \to Int$.

We denote $\mathcal{F}_{Int}(\langle S, h, I \rangle)$ by $I^\flat(h)$.

Unfortunately, the entailments in I and $I^\flat(h)$ are not the same. Indeed, $\vDash^\flat(h)$ is smaller than $\vDash$. Still, they coincide with respect to validity.

Proposition 35. *The map*

- $\eta(\langle S, h, I \rangle) = id_{F(\Sigma)} : \langle F(\Sigma), \_^{\vDash^\flat(h)} \rangle \to \langle F(\Sigma), \_^{\vDash} \rangle$,

constitutes the natural transformation $\eta : \mathcal{C}_{Int} \circ \mathcal{F}_{Int} \to \mathcal{C}_{Int} \circ \mathcal{U}_{Int} \circ J$, *where* $J : Int^\circ \hookrightarrow Int^\bullet$ *is the corresponding inclusion functor. Moreover,* $\emptyset^{\vDash^\flat(h)} = \emptyset^\vDash$.

We can now flatten logic system presentations. Obviously, we consider Lsp° to be the full subcategory of $Lsp^\bullet$ whose objects are mapped by $\mathcal{I}^\bullet_{Lsp}$ into Int°.

Proposition 36. *The maps*

- $\mathcal{F}_{Lsp}(\langle S, h, \langle \Sigma, R, M, A \rangle \rangle) = \langle \Sigma^\flat(h), R^\flat(h), M^\flat(h), A^\flat(h) \rangle$;
- $\mathcal{F}_{Lsp}(\langle h^S, \langle h^\Sigma, \underline{h} \rangle) : \langle S^1, h^1, L^1 \rangle \to \langle S^2, h^2, L^2 \rangle) = \langle h^\flat(\langle h^S, h^\Sigma \rangle), \underline{h}^\flat \rangle$,

constitute the (flattening) functor $\mathcal{F}_{Lsp} : Lsp^\circ \to Int$.

We denote $\mathcal{F}_{Lsp}(\langle S, h, L \rangle)$ by $L^\flat(h)$.

3   Parameterisation

At last, we can define parameterisation.

Definition 37. *A* parameterised logic system presentation $L(S, P)$ *is a triple* $\langle S, P, L \rangle$ *where* $L = \langle \Sigma, R, M, A \rangle$ *is a logic system presentation,* $S \subseteq \Sigma$ *and* $P \subseteq \Sigma_0$ *with* $P \cap S_0 = \emptyset$.

Expectedly, L is said to be the *body* and P the *formal parameter* of $L(S, P)$, while S designates the *shared constructors*.

From now on we fix a parameterised logic system presentation $L(S, P)$.

Definition 38. *An* actual parameter *for $L(S, P)$ is a logic system presentation $L_P = \langle \Sigma_P, R_P, M_P, A_P \rangle$ plus a pair $\langle h_S, h_P \rangle$ where $h_S : S \to \Sigma_P$ is a Sig morphism such that $\langle S, h_S, L_P \rangle$ is in $Lsp°$, and $h_P : P \to (F(\Sigma_P) \upharpoonright h_S)$ is surjective.*

We say that h_S is the *shared constructors matching* and h_P the *parameter passing map.* Surjectivity of h_P guarantees that the whole of L_P is used, and not just a sublogic possibly with quite specific properties.

Once again, we fix an actual parameter L_P and $h = \langle h_S, h_P \rangle$ for $L(S, P)$.

Given $\gamma \in F(\Sigma, \Xi)$, let γ^h be obtained from γ by replacing the occurrences of S and P symbols by their images under h_S and h_P, respectively.

Definition 39. *The* result logic system presentation *for $L(S, P)$ on L_P and h is*

$$L^h(L_P) = \langle \Sigma^h(\Sigma_P), R^h(R_P), M^h(M_P), A^h(A_P) \rangle$$

where:

- $\Sigma^h(\Sigma_P) = (\Sigma \setminus (S \uplus @(P))) \uplus \Sigma_P^\flat(h_S)$;
- $R^h(R_P) = R^h \cup R_P^\flat(h_S)$;
- $M^h(M_P)$ *is the class of pairs $\langle m, \theta : U_m \to M_P^\flat(h_S) \rangle$ with $m \in M$ such that $\nu_{mk}(s)(b_1, \ldots, b_k)(u) = \nu_{\theta(u)k}(h_{Sk}(s))(b_1(u), \ldots, b_k(u))$ and $[\![p]\!]^m(u) = [\![h_P(p)]\!]^{\theta(u)}$, noting that $U_{\theta(u)}$ is a singleton;*
- $A^h(A_P)(\langle m, \theta \rangle) = (U_m, \nu)$ *where $\nu_k(c) = \nu_{mk}(c)$, $\nu_k(h_{Sk}(s)) = \nu_{mk}(s)$ and $\nu_0(\varphi)(u) = [\![\varphi]\!]^{\theta(u)}$.*

Let $i_S : S \hookrightarrow \Sigma$ and $i_P : P \hookrightarrow \Sigma_0$ be the obvious inclusions. Noting that $\Sigma \uplus \Sigma_P^\flat(h_S)$ is a coproduct in *Sig* with corresponding injections j_Σ and $j_{\Sigma_P^\flat(h_S)}$, we call $q : \Sigma \uplus \Sigma_P^\flat(h_S) \to \Sigma^h(\Sigma_P)$ to the coequaliser of $j_\Sigma \circ (i_S \uplus @(i_P))$ and $j_{\Sigma_P^\flat(h_S)} \circ (h_S \uplus @(h_P))$. Note that this amounts to a pushout in *Sig* of the morphisms $i_S \uplus @(i_P) : S \uplus @(P) \to \Sigma$ and $h_S \uplus @(h_P) : S \uplus @(P) \to \Sigma_P^\flat(h_S)$. Clearly, $\gamma^h = (q \circ j_\Sigma)(\gamma)$. Moreover, it is trivial that $F(\Sigma^h(\Sigma_P), \Xi) = F(\Sigma, \Xi)^h$.

Proposition 40. *$L^h(L_P)$ is the codomain of the cocartesian lifting by S_{Lsp} for q on the coproduct in Lsp of L and $L_P^\flat(h_S)$.*

In the lines of [18], parameterisation is a particular case of constrained fibring.

We now present, in detail, the parameterisation of propositional modal logic with first-order logic outlined in the introduction.

Example 41. Propositional modal logic. The propositional modal logic system presentation pmL over the set Π of propositional symbols is such that:

- $pm\Sigma_0 = \Pi$, $pm\Sigma_1 = \{\neg, \square\}$, $pm\Sigma_2 = \{\Rightarrow\}$;
- pmR includes the usual axioms of propositional logic:
    $(\xi_1 \Rightarrow (\xi_2 \Rightarrow \xi_1))$;
    $((\xi_1 \Rightarrow (\xi_2 \Rightarrow \xi_3)) \Rightarrow ((\xi_1 \Rightarrow \xi_2) \Rightarrow (\xi_1 \Rightarrow \xi_3)))$;
    $(((\neg \xi_1) \Rightarrow (\neg \xi_2)) \Rightarrow (\xi_2 \Rightarrow \xi_1))$,

modus ponens (**MP**): $\langle\{\xi_1,(\xi_1\Rightarrow\xi_2)\},\xi_2\rangle$,
the axiom of normality (**K**): $((\Box(\xi_1\Rightarrow\xi_2))\Rightarrow((\Box\xi_1)\Rightarrow(\Box\xi_2)))$,
and necessitation (**Nec** $\Box$): $\langle\xi,\{(\Box\xi)\}\rangle$;

- pmM is the class of Kripke structures $K=\langle W,S,V\rangle$ with $W\neq\emptyset$, $S\subseteq W^2$ and $V:\Pi\to 2^W$;
- $pmA(K)=\langle W,\nu\rangle$ with:
  - $\nu_0(\pi)=V(\pi)$;
  - $\nu_1(\neg)(b)=\lambda w\,.\,1-b(w)$, $\nu_1(\Box)(b)=\lambda w\,.\,\Pi_{\langle w,w'\rangle\in S}\,b(w')$;
  - $\nu_2(\Rightarrow)(b_1,b_2)=\lambda w\,.\,b_1(w)\leq b_2(w)$.

Example 42. First-order logic. The first-order logic system presentation foL over the indexed families of sets $\{F_k\}_{k\in I\!N}$ and $\{P_k\}_{k\in I\!N}$ of function and predicate symbols, respectively, and the set of variables X is such that:

- $fo\Sigma_0=Atom$, $fo\Sigma_1=\{\neg\}\cup\{\forall x_x\in X\}$, $fo\Sigma_2=\{\Rightarrow\}$ with:
  - T_X defined inductively by $\{F_k\}_{k\in I\!N}$ on X;
  - $Atom=\{p(t_1,\ldots,t_k):p\in P_k,\ t_1,\ldots,t_k\in T_X\}$;
- foR includes the axioms of propositional logic, (**MP**), the first-order axioms:
  $((\forall x\,\varphi)\Rightarrow\varphi_t^x)$ for $t\in T_X$ free for $x\in X$ in $\varphi\in F(fo\Sigma)$;
  $((\forall x\,(\varphi\Rightarrow\xi))\Rightarrow(\varphi\Rightarrow(\forall x\,\xi)))$ for $x\in X$ not free in $\varphi\in F(fo\Sigma)$,
  and first-order necessitation (**Nec** $\forall$): $\langle\{\xi\},(\forall x\,\xi)\rangle$ for $x\in X$;
- foM is the isomorphism closure of the class of interpretations $I=\langle D,\_^I\rangle$ with $U\neq\emptyset$, $f^I:D^k\to D$ for $f\in F_k$ and $p^I:D^k\to 2$ for $p\in P_k$;
- $foA(I)=\langle U^X,\nu\rangle$ where:
  - $\nu_0(p(t_1,\ldots,t_k))(\rho)=p^I([\![t_1]\!]^{\langle I,\rho\rangle},\ldots,[\![t_k]\!]^{\langle I,\rho\rangle})$ with $[\![.]\!]^{\langle I,\rho\rangle}:T_X\to D$ inductively defined by $\_^I$ on each $\rho:X\to D$;
  - $\nu_1(\neg)(b)=\lambda\rho\,.\,1-b(\rho)$, $\nu_1(\forall x)(b)=\lambda\rho\,.\,\Pi_{\rho'\equiv_x\rho}\,b(\rho')$;
  - $\nu_2(\Rightarrow)(b_1,b_2)=\lambda\rho\,.\,b_1(\rho)\leq b_2(\rho)$.

Note that the two first-order axioms are not represented using schema variables. Indeed, arbitrary substitution is not allowed due to the freeness conditions. This difficulty can be overcome, as done in [20], by further adding explicit substitution requirements to schema variables in rules.

Example 43. Modalised first-order logic. The result $mfoL$ of parameterising pmL with first-order logic foL by sharing $\neg$ and $\Rightarrow$, according to any adequately surjective parameter passing map from Π to the corresponding set of monoliths $Mon=Atom\cup\{(\forall x\,\varphi):(\forall x\,\varphi)\in F(fo\Sigma)\}$ is such that:

- $mfo\Sigma_0=Mon$, $mfo\Sigma_1=\{\neg,\Box\}$, $mfo\Sigma_2=\{\Rightarrow\}$;
- $mfoR$ includes the axioms of propositional logic, (**MP**), (**K**), (**Nec** $\Box$), the flattened first-order axioms:
  $((\forall x\,\varphi)\Rightarrow\varphi_t^x)$ for $t\in T_X$ free for $x\in X$ in $\varphi\in F(fo\Sigma)$;
  $((\forall x\,(\varphi\Rightarrow\psi))\Rightarrow(\varphi\Rightarrow(\forall x\,\psi)))$ for $\varphi,\psi\in F(fo\Sigma)$ and $x\in X$ not free in φ,
  and a flattened version of (**Nec** $\forall$): $\langle\{\varphi\},(\forall x\,\varphi)\rangle$ for $x\in X$ and $\varphi\in F(fo\Sigma)$;
- $mfoM$ is the class of tuples $\langle W,S,\theta:W\to foM^\flat\rangle$ where $\langle W,S\rangle$ is a Kripke frame and $foM^\flat$ is the class of all pairs $\langle\langle D,\_^I\rangle,\rho:X\to D\rangle$, being $I=\langle D,\_^I\rangle$ a first-order interpretation;

- $mfoA(\langle W, S, \theta \rangle) = \langle W, \nu \rangle$ with:
  - $\nu_0(\varphi) = \lambda w . [\![\varphi]\!]^{\theta(w)}$;
  - $\nu_1(\neg)$, $\nu_1(\Box)$ and $\nu_2(\Rightarrow)$ as in example 41.

The results in the next section will show that $mfoL$ is a conservative extension of both pmL and foL, and also that $mfoL$ is sound and complete. It is not decidable, as expected, since foL is not decidable.

4 Transference theorems

We start by showing that $L^h(L_P)$ extends both L (under renaming) and L_P theorems. We then establish transference of soundness by requiring soundness of both R_P and R. Just soundness is not enough because of schema rules. We then state sufficient conditions for $L^h(L_P)$ to be a conservative extension of L and L_P: shared symbols must have the same meaning in both logics and P symbols must be free within L. Finally, we prove preservation of completeness and decidability. We further assume that shared symbols can express the interdependences between any finite number of formulae, and that L has implication, modus ponens and the ability to express the "accessibility" implied by each formula.

4.1 Extension and soundness

Proposition 44. $L^h(L_P)$ *theorems extend both* L *(under renaming by* h*) and* L_P *theorems:*

- *if* $\vdash_L \varphi$ *then* $\vdash_{L^h(L_P)} \varphi^h$;
- *if* $\vdash_{L_P} \varphi$ *then* $\vdash_{L^h(L_P)} \varphi$.

Proof. Both are corollaries of 13. The latter also requires 30.   □

Proposition 45. *If both* L *and* L_P *have sound rules then* $L^h(L_P)$ *is sound.*

Proof. The rules R^h *are sound, according to 25. Soundness of* $L^h(L_P)$ *then follows from the fact that* $L_P^b(h_S)$ *is sound, as a consequence of 30 and 35.*   □

It is quite fair to require soundness of rules. Proving that rules are sound is the obvious way to prove soundness of a deductive system.

4.2 Conservativeness

To prove that $L^h(L_P)$ theorems somehow conservatively extend both L and L_P theorems we need to consider two further assumptions.

Assumption A: Coincident evaluation of S.
There exists a singleton S-structure $\langle \{1\}, \nu \rangle$ such that:

- $\nu_{mk}(s)(b_1, \ldots, b_k)(u) = \nu_k(s)(b_1(u), \ldots, b_k(u))$, *for* $m \in M$, $u \in U_m$;
- $\nu_{mpk}(h_{Sk}(s))(d_1, \ldots, d_k)(u) = \nu_k(s)(d_1(u), \ldots, d_k(u))$, *for* $m_P \in M_P$, $u \in U_{m_P}$.

This condition requires the coincident interpretation of shared symbols. It holds, for instance, whenever S only contains propositional connectives.

Assumption B: Free evaluation of P.
For every $m_1 \in M$ and function $\pi : P \to 2^{U_{m_1}}$, there exists $m_2 \in M$ such that:

- $U_{m_2} = U_{m_1}$;
- ν_{m_2} *coincides with* ν_{m_1} *except that* $\nu_{m_2 0}(p) = \pi(p)$.

This condition is also not too restrictive. It holds whenever L is propositional based and P a set of (independent) propositional symbols.

Proposition 46. *Under assumptions A and B, whenever $L^h(L_P)$ is sound:*

- *if $\vdash_{L^h(L_P)} \varphi$ then $\vdash_{L_P} \varphi$, provided that L_P is complete;*
- *if $\vdash_{L^h(L_P)} \varphi^h$ then $\vdash_L \varphi$, provided that $\varphi \in F(\Sigma \setminus @(P))$ and L is complete.*

Proof. A and B together ensure that every $L^b_P(h_S)$ model can be found locally at some $L^h(L_P)$ model, proving the former, and also that every L model (except possibly its P evaluation) is represented in $L^h(L_P)$, which proves the latter. $\square$

4.3   Completeness and decidability

We now need three further assumptions.

Assumption C: Implication.
L has implication and "modus ponens":

- $\Rightarrow \in \Sigma_2$ *with* $\nu_{m2}(\Rightarrow)(b_1, b_2)(u) = b_1(u) \leq b_2(u)$;
- $\langle \{\xi_1, (\xi_1 \Rightarrow \xi_2)\}, \xi_2 \rangle \in R$.

This just restricts our attention to logics L with a classical implication.

Assumption D: Shared expressibility.
For every $p_1, \ldots, p_n \in P$ there exist $\varphi_1, \ldots, \varphi_k \in F(S \uplus @(P))$ such that:

- $\vDash_{L_P} (h_S \uplus @(h_P))(\varphi_1), \ldots, (h_S \uplus @(h_P))(\varphi_k)$;
- *for each $m \in M$ and $u \in \bigcap_{1 \leq i \leq k} [\![\varphi_i]\!]^m$ there exist $m_P \in M_P$ and $u_P \in U_{m_P}$ where $u_P \in [\![h_P(p_i)]\!]^{m_P}$ iff $u \in [\![p_i]\!]^m$.*

This condition is more restrictive. It requires that a finite set of L_P h-valid φ_j over only S and P can distinguish local L-evaluations of the symbols p_i that have a corresponding L_P model. This is true, for instance, whenever classical negation and implication are both expressible using constructors in S.

The last assumption relies on the possibility of associating to each formula $\varphi \in F(\Sigma)$, $m \in M$ and $u \in U_m$ a set $\varphi(m, u) \subseteq U_m$ whose points contain all the necessary information to evaluate whether or not $u \in [\![\varphi]\!]^m$. This can be done if we are able to associate a similar "reachability" set to each constructor in Σ, that is, for each $c \in \Sigma_k$ we must identify a set $c(m, u) \subseteq U_m$ such that $\nu_{mk}(c)(b_1, \ldots, b_k)(u) = \nu_{mk}(c)(d_1, \ldots, d_k)(u)$ whenever each $b_i \cap c(m, u) = d_i \cap c(m, u)$. If that is possible, we define $\varphi(m, u)$ inductively by:

- $c(\varphi_1, \ldots, \varphi_k)(m, u) = c(m, u) \cup (\bigcup_{1 \leq i \leq k, v \in c(m, u)} \varphi_i(m, v))$.

Assumption E: *L* **reachability.**

For every φ there exist $\gamma^1, \ldots, \gamma^l$ with at most one schema variable ξ such that:

- $\xi \vdash_L \gamma^1, \ldots, \gamma^l$;
- $\bigcap_{1 \leq j \leq l} [\![\gamma^j]\!]_\alpha^m = \{u \in U_m : \varphi(m, u) \subseteq \alpha(\xi)\}$.

The simplest form of this assumption corresponds to the case when an "every-where" modality is expressible in L. But it also holds for any modal like logic by analysing the nested modalities inside φ.

Proposition 47. *Under assumptions A-E, if both L and L_P are complete then $L^h(L_P)$ is complete.*

Proof. Assume that $\vDash_{L^h(L_P)} \varphi^h$ and let $p_1, \ldots, p_n$ be the P symbols occurring in φ. By using assumption D, we obtain $\varphi_1, \ldots, \varphi_k$. By using assumption E on φ we obtain $\gamma^1, \ldots, \gamma^l$ on ξ. Their combined conditions together with assumptions A and B and a simple missing symbols lemma, that we omit, imply that $\vDash_L (\gamma^1 \varrho^1 \Rightarrow (\ldots \Rightarrow (\gamma^l \varrho^1 \Rightarrow (\ldots \Rightarrow (\gamma^1 \varrho^k \Rightarrow (\ldots \Rightarrow (\gamma^l \varrho^k \Rightarrow \varphi) \ldots)) \ldots)) \ldots))$, where each $\varrho_i(\xi) = \varphi_i$. Therefore, using the hypothesis of completeness for L we have that $\vdash_L (\gamma^1 \varrho^1 \Rightarrow (\ldots \Rightarrow (\gamma^l \varrho^1 \Rightarrow (\ldots \Rightarrow (\gamma^1 \varrho^k \Rightarrow (\ldots \Rightarrow (\gamma^l \varrho^k \Rightarrow \varphi) \ldots)) \ldots)) \ldots))$. Since assumption E guarantees that $\xi \vdash_L \gamma^1, \ldots, \gamma^l$, by using modus ponens and 13, we also have that $\{\varphi_1, \ldots, \varphi_k\} \vdash_L \varphi$. Additionally, assumption D also guarantees $\vDash_{L_P} (h_S \cup @(h_P))(\varphi_1), \ldots, (h_S \cup @(h_P))(\varphi_k)$ thus, by completeness of L_P, $\vdash_{L_P} (h_S \cup @(h_P))(\varphi_1), \ldots, (h_S \cup @(h_P))(\varphi_k)$. Therefore, again by proposition 13, $\{\varphi_1^h, \ldots, \varphi_k^h\} \vdash_{L^h(L_P)} \varphi^h$ and $\vdash_{L^h(L_P)} \varphi_1^h, \ldots, \varphi_k^h$. Easily then, $\vdash_{L^h(L_P)} \varphi^h$. □

Proposition 48. *Under assumptions A-E, if L is decidable and both L and L_P are complete then $L^h(L_P)$ is decidable provided that there exist algorithms to build the formulae required by assumptions D and E.*

Proof. The proof amounts to using L decidability to determine whether or not $\vDash_L (\gamma^1 \varrho^1 \Rightarrow (\ldots \Rightarrow (\gamma^l \varrho^1 \Rightarrow (\ldots \Rightarrow (\gamma^1 \varrho^k \Rightarrow (\ldots \Rightarrow (\gamma^l \varrho^k \Rightarrow \varphi) \ldots)) \ldots)) \ldots))$ The rest of the proof follows the same lines of 47 above. □

Note that L_P is not assumed to be decidable. In any case, an algorithm to build the formulae required by assumption D seems to rely heavily on it.

5   Concluding remarks

It is our firm belief that the study of combination mechanisms in a categorial setting is essential to their full understanding. Herein, we have presented a categorial characterisation of parameterisation of logics, a mechanism that generalises the temporalisation construction proposed in [16]. Methodologically, our rationale was to use coproducts of logics and cocartesian liftings for signature coequalisers as combination tools, thus avoiding the (possibly complex) construction of the vertex of the required pushout.

Furthermore, we have identified sufficient conditions for parameterisation to conservatively extend both the parameter and parameterised logics and established transfer results for soundness, completeness and decidability. Our proofs follow ideas similar to those in [16]. We stress that the expressibility of the "everywhere" modality used in [16] is a very special case of our, much more general, assumption E. All the other assumptions are trivial if we assume that both logics are extensions of classical propositional logic and that the propositional connectives are shared, as in [16]. However, they deliver results even if that is not the case. For instance, completeness of the modalisation of conditional equational logic by just collapsing the conditional and implication follows from 47. The only proviso is that we cannot represent conditional equational logic as a logic system presentation with the conditional as an explicit constructor. To do that, we need a slightly more general notion of signature: e.g., a multi-sorted signature with a distinguished sort for formulae. For the sake of simplicity, we refrained from doing so in this paper but such an approach was followed in [20], further encompassing an adequate treatment of schema rules with requirements.

Our interpretation systems have similarities with the various notions of room for parchments [21,19,23,2] appearing in the literature. A detailed comparison of the concepts is needed, but some tentative ideas are outlined in [20]. The relationship of parameterisation with other combination mechanisms should also deserve attention. Some of our ideas are clearly related to the work on representation of logics reported in [25] and therefore, this connection should be explored. More specific links can be found with respect to fibring and synchronisation [14,26]. On one hand, it seems that fibring can be seen as a limit of adequate parameterisation constructions. On the other hand, it also seems to be possible to give an account of parameterisation using a generalized form of synchronisation. Thus, by making the parallel with [10], we hope to be able to obtain some consequent transfer results for fibring by capitalising on those for parameterisation, and similarly for parameterisation over synchronisation.

References

1. J. Meseguer. General logics. In H.-D. Ebbinghaus et al, editor, *Proceedings of the Logic Colloquium, 1987*, pages 275–329. North-Holland, 1989.
2. W. Pawłowski. Context parchments. In *Recent trends in abstract data types. Proceedings of the 12th Workshop on Algebraic Development Techniques, Tarquinia 1997*, volume 1376 of *Lecture Notes in Computer Science*. Springer-Verlag, 1998.
3. A. Tarlecki. Moving between logical systems. In M. Haveraaen, O. Owe, and O.-J. Dahl, editors, *Recent Trends in Data Type Specification*, volume 1130 of *Lecture Notes in Computer Science*, pages 478–502. Springer-Verlag, 1996.
4. J. Barwise. Axioms for abstract model theory. *Annals of Mathematical Logic*, 7:221–265, 1974.
5. P. Blackburn and M. de Rijke. Why combine logics? *Studia Logica*, 59(1):5–27, 1997.
6. J. Goguen and R. Burstall. Introducing institutions. In E. Clarke and D. Kozen, editors, *Proceedings of the Logics of Programming Workshop*, volume 164 of *Lecture Notes in Computer Science*, pages 221–256. Springer-Verlag, 1984.
7. M. Cerioli and J. Meseguer. May I borrow your logic? In A. Borzyszkowski and S. Sokolowski, editors, *Mathematical Foundations of Computer Science 1993*, volume 711 of *Lecture Notes in Computer Science*, pages 342–351. Springer-Verlag, 1993.

8. P. Blackburn and M. de Rijke. Zooming in, zooming out. *Journal of Logic, Language and Information*, 6:5–31, 1997.
9. S. MacLane. *Categories for the Working Mathematician*. Springer-Verlag, 1971.
10. M. Finger and D. Gabbay. Combining temporal logic systems. *Notre Dame Journal of Formal Logic*, 37(2):204–232, 1996.
11. M. Barr and C. Wells. *Category Theory for Computing Science*. Prentice Hall, 1990.
12. D. Gabbay. Fibred semantics and the weaving of logics: part 1. *Journal of Symbolic Logic*, 61(4):1057–1120, 1996.
13. J. Fiadeiro and A. Sernadas. Structuring theories on consequence. In D. Sannella and A. Tarlecki, editors, *Recent Trends in Data Type Specification*, volume 332 of *Lecture Notes in Computer Science*, pages 44–72. Springer-Verlag, 1988.
14. A. Sernadas, C. Sernadas, and C. Caleiro. Synchronization of logics. *Studia Logica*, 59(2):217–247, 1997.
15. A. Jánossy, Á. Kurucz, and Á. E. Eiben. Combining algebraizable logics. *Notre Dame Journal of Formal Logic*, 37(2):366–380, 1996.
16. M. Finger and D. Gabbay. Adding a temporal dimension to a logic system. *Journal of Logic, Language and Information*, 1:203–233, 1992.
17. J. Adámek, H. Herrlich, and G. Strecker. *Abstract and concrete categories*. John Wiley, 1990.
18. A. Sernadas, C. Sernadas, and C. Caleiro. Fibring of logics as a categorial construction. *Journal of Logic and Computation*, 8(10):1–31, 1998.
19. T. Mossakowski, A. Tarlecki, and W. Pawłowski. Combining and representing logical systems. In *Category Theory and Computer Science 97*, volume 1290 of *Lecture Notes in Computer Science*, pages 177–196. Springer-Verlag, 1997.
20. A. Sernadas, C. Sernadas, C. Caleiro, and T. Mossakowski. Categorial fibring of logics with terms and binding operators. In *Frontiers of Combining Systems - FroCoS'98*. Kluwer Academic Publishers, 1998. To appear in Applied Logic Series.
21. J. Goguen and R. Burstall. A study in the foundations of programming methodology: Specifications, institutions, charters and parchments. In D. Pitt, S. Abramsky, A. Poigné, and D. Rydeheard, editors, *Proceedings of the Conference on Category Theory and Computer Programming*, volume 240 of *Lecture Notes in Computer Science*, pages 313–333. Springer Verlag, 1986.
22. J. Goguen and R. Burstall. Institutions: Abstract model theory for specification and programming. *Journal of the ACM*, 39(1):95–146, 1992.
23. T. Mossakowski, A. Tarlecki, and W. Pawłowski. Combining and representing logical systems using model-theoretic parchments. In *Recent trends in abstract data types. Proceedings of the 12th Workshop on Algebraic Development Techniques, Tarquinia 1997*, volume 1376 of *Lecture Notes in Computer Science*. Springer-Verlag, 1998.
24. H.-D. Ehrich. On the theory of specification, implementation and parameterisation of abstract data types. *Journal of the ACM*, 29:206–227, 1982.
25. Robert Harper, Donald Sannella, and Andrzej Tarlecki. Structured theory presentations and logic representations. *Annals of Pure and Applied Logic*, 67(1–3):113–160, 1994.
26. A. Sernadas, C. Sernadas, and C. Caleiro. Synchronization of logics with mixed rules: Completeness preservation. In M. Johnson, editor, *AMAST'97 - 6th International Conference on Algebraic Methodology and Software Technology*, volume 1349 of *Lecture Notes in Computer Science*, pages 465–478. Springer-Verlag, 1997.

Semantic Constructions for Hidden Algebra

Corina Cîrstea*

Oxford University Computing Laboratory
Wolfson Building, Parks Road, Oxford OX1 3QD, UK
Corina.Cirstea@comlab.ox.ac.uk

Abstract. Hidden algebra is a behavioural algebraic specification formalism for objects. It captures their constructional aspect, concerned with the initialisation and evolution of their states, as well as their observational aspect, concerned with the observable b ehaviour of such states. When attention is restricted to the observational aspect, final/cofree constructions provide suitable denotations for the specification techniques involved. However, when the constructional aspect is integrated with the observatio nal one, the presence of nondeterminism in specifications prevents the existence of final/cofree algebras. It is shown here that *final/cofree families of algebras* exist in this case, with each algebra in such a family resolving the nondetermi nism in a particular way. Existence of final/cofree families yields a canonical way of constructing algebras of structured specifications from algebras of the component specifications. Finally, a layered approach to specifying complex objects in hidden al gebra is presented, with the semantics still involving final/cofree families.

1 Introduction

The use of algebra in the semantics of computation goes back to the 1970s and the use of initial algebras as denotational semantics for data types [9]. The constructional nature of data types makes algebra particularly suitable for their specification – the emphasis is on *generating* the elements of data types by means of *constructor operations*, with minimal structures such as initial or free algebras providing suitable denotations for data type specifications. Recently, the theory of *coalgebras* (the formal duals of algebras) has been used for the specification of state-based systems in general [5], and of objects in particular [4]; here, the emphasis is on *observing* system states by means of *destructor operations*, and maximal structures such as final or cofree coalgebras, incorporating possible behaviours, are used as denotations.

Objects are characterised by a state together with an interface which provides (limited) access to this state. Specifically, the object interface can be used to initialise its state in a particular way, to perform certain changes on its current state, or to observe certain properties of this state. One can identify a constructional aspect of objects, concerned with the initialisation and evolution of their

---

* Research supported by an ORS Award and an Oxford Bursary.

J.L. Fiadeiro (Ed.): WADT'98, LNCS 1589, pp. 63–78, 1999.

states, and an observational aspect of objects, concerned with the observations that can be made about such states.

Hidden algebra [1] combines concepts from algebra and coalgebra in order to capture the two aspects of objects and the relationship between them. One can argue that hidden algebra lies at the intersection of algebra and coalgebra, as its syntax is (a restricted version of) the syntax of many-sorted algebra, while its semantics is behavioural (coalgebraic). Consequently, the behaviours specifiable in hidden algebra are, in a sense, both algebraic and coalgebraic.

The coalgebraic nature of hidden algebra, already observed in [1], has been further investigated in [8], where the relevance of final/cofree constructions to coalgebraic hidden specifications and their reuse along specification maps has been emphasised. *Final hidden algebras* have been shown to provide a characterisation of the abstract behaviours associated to such specifications, while *cofree hidden algebras* have been used as formal denotations for their reuse.

When arbitrary hidden specifications are considered, the nondeterminism arising from underspecifying the behaviour of the constructor operations prevents the existence of final/cofree hidden algebras. It has been suggested in [8] that in this case, *final/cofree families* of hidden algebras should be taken as denotations, since such constructions can be used to characterise the ways of resolving the nondeterminism involved. Final/cofree families generalise final/cofree objects in a category, while still retaining their universal properties. The present paper gives a detailed account of the existence of such families in hidden algebra, illustrating their suitability as semantic constructions for hidden specifications. Existence of final/cofree families also yields a canonical way of constructing algebras of structured specifications from algebras of the component specifications.

Due to restrictions on its syntax, triggered by the coalgebraic nature of the approach, hidden algebra only provides limited support for the specification of *complex objects* (objects having other objects as components). In particular, neither can previously specified objects be used to specify the construction of new objects, nor can such objects be passed as arguments to the destructor operations of other objects. This paper also integrates complex objects in the hidden algebra formalism.

The paper is structured as follows. After recalling some category-theoretic concepts that will be used later in the paper, Section 2 introduces the hidden algebra formalism and briefly summarises the results in [8] regarding the existence of final/cofree constructions in *coalgebraic hidden algebra* (a restricted version of hidden algebra used to specify coalgebraic behaviours). Section 3 focuses on the existence of final/cofree families of hidden algebras and on their suitability as denotations for hidden specifications and their reuse. Section 4 uses a generalisation of the category-theoretic notion of limit to define a canonical way of combining algebras of component specifications into algebras of structured specifications. Section 5 presents a layered approach to the specification of complex objects in hidden algebra, with final/cofree families still providing appropriate denotations for the specification techniques involved. Finally, Section 6 summarises the results presented and briefly outlines future work.

2   Preliminaries

The first part of this section introduces some categorical concepts that will be used later in the paper, while the second part gives an outline of the hidden algebraic approach to object specification and of some existing results regarding the existence of final/cofree constructions in coalgebraic hidden algebra.

2.1   Some Category-Theoretic Notions

A *final object* in a category C is an object F of C such that any other object of C has a unique arrow into F. The notion of *final family of objects* generalises the notion of final object by requiring the existence of a unique arrow from any other object of C into an object in the final family.

Definition 1. *Given a category* C, *a family* $(F_j)_{j \in J}$ *of* C-*objects is a* **final family of** C-**objects** *if and only if, for any* C-*object* C, *there exist unique* $j \in J$ *and* C-*arrow* $f : C \to F_j$ *in* C.

Remark 1. A final family of C-objects determines a partition of C into subcategories with final objects (given by objects in the family). For $j \in J$, C_j is given by the full subcategory of C whose objects have an arrow into F_j.

[3] presents a generalisation of the category-theoretic notion of limit, called a *multi-limit*, which enjoys a universal property similar to that of a limit.

Definition 2. *Given a diagram* d : D → C *in a category* C, *a* **multi-limit for** d *consists of a family* $(L^i, (l_D^i : L^i \to \mathsf{d}(D))_{D \in |\mathsf{D}|})_{i \in I}$ *of cones for* d, *having the property that given any other cone* $(C, (c_D)_{D \in |\mathsf{D}|})$ *for* d, *there exist unique* $i \in I$ *and* C-*arrow* $c : C \to L^i$ *such that* $l_D^i \circ c = c_D$ *for each* D-*object* D.

Then, final families of objects appear as multi-limits of empty diagrams.

A *couniversal arrow* from a functor U : D → C to a C-object C is a C-arrow of form $\epsilon_C : \mathsf{U}\bar{C} \to C$ for some D-object $\bar{C}$, having the property that given any D-object D and C-arrow $f : \mathsf{U}D \to C$, there exists a unique factorisation of f through ϵ_C of form $f = \mathsf{U}\bar{f}; \epsilon_C$ with $\bar{f} : D \to \bar{C}$. ($\bar{C}$ is called a *cofree* D-*object over* C w. r.t. U.) The notion of *couniversal family of arrows* [3] generalises that of couniversal arrow as follows.

Definition 3. *Given a functor* U : D → C *and a* C-*object* C, *a family of* C-*arrows* $(\epsilon_{C,j} : \mathsf{U}\bar{C}_j \to C)_{j \in J}$ *with* $\bar{C}_j$ *a* D-*object for each* $j \in J$ *is a* **couniversal family of arrows fr om** U *to* C *if and only if, for any* D-*object* D *and* C-*arrow* $f : \mathsf{U}D \to C$, *there exist unique* $j \in J$ *and* D-*arrow* $\bar{f} : D \to \bar{C}_j$ *such that* $\mathsf{U}\bar{f}; \epsilon_{C,j} = f$. *The family* $(\bar{C}_j)_{j \in J}$ *is called a* **cofree family of** D-**objects over** C **w.r.t.** U. *If, for any* C-*object* C, *there exists a couniversal family of arrows from* U *to* C, *then* U *is said to have a* **right multi-adjoint**.

Remark 2. The concepts of multi-limit and couniversal family of arrows can be subsumed under the ordinary concepts of limit and couniversal arrow by considering *categories of families.* Given a category C, one can define a category Fam(C) wh ose objects are indexed families $(C_i)_{i \in I}$ of C-objects, and whose arrows from $(C_i)_{i \in I}$ to $(D_j)_{j \in J}$ are given by a reindexing function $h : I \to J$ together with an I-indexed family $(f_i : C_i \to D_{h(i)})_{i \in I}$ of C-arrows. C has a canonical embedding into Fam(C) which regards C-objects/arrows as families of C-objects/arrows indexed by a one-element set. Then, multi-limits of C-diagrams correspond to limits in Fam(C) of the translations of these diagrams along the embedding of C into Fam(C), while couniversal families of arrows from U : D → C to C-objects corresponds to couniversal arrows from Fam(U) : Fam(D) → Fam(C) to the translations of these objects along the embedding of C into Fam(C) (where Fam(U) takes $(D_i)_{i \in I}$ to $(U(D_i))_{i \in I}$, and $\langle h, (f_i)_{i \in I} \rangle : (D_i)_{i \in I} \to (D'_j)_{j \in J}$ to $\langle h, (U(f_i))_{i \in I} \rangle$).

2.2   Hidden Algebra

This section recalls the underlying definitions of the hidden algebra formalism, as well as some earlier results regarding the existence of semantic constructions based on finality in coalgebraic hidden algebra.

The fundamental distinction between data values and object states is reflected in the syntax of hidden algebra in the use of visible sorts/operation symbols for the data, and of hidden sorts/operation symbols for the objects. A *data universe*, given by an algebra D (the **data algebra**) of a many-sorted signature (V, Ψ) (the **data signature**) is fixed beforehand, with the additional constraint that each element of D is named by some constant in Ψ. For convenience, we assume $D_v \subseteq \Psi_{[],v}$ for each $v \in V$.

The operations available for creating and accessing the states of objects are specified using *hidden signatures*, while translations from one signature to another are captured by *hidden signature maps*.

Definition 4. *A (hidden) signature over* (V, Ψ) *is a pair* (H, Σ) *with* H *a set of* **hidden sorts***, and* Σ *a* $V \cup H$*-sorted signature satisfying: (i)* $\Sigma_{w,v} = \Psi_{w,v}$ *for* $w \in V^*$ *and* $v \in V$*, and (ii) for* $\sigma \in \Sigma_{w,s}$*, at most one sort appearing in* w *(by convention, the first one) is hidden.* $\Sigma \setminus \Psi$*-operation symbols having exactly one hidden-sorted argument are called* **destructor symbols***, while those having only visible-sorted arguments are called* **constructor symbols***. A (hidden) signature map* $\phi : (H, \Sigma) \to (H', \Sigma')$ *is a many-sorted signature morphism* $\phi : (V \cup H, \Sigma) \to (V \cup H', \Sigma')$ *such that* $\phi\!\restriction_{(V,\Psi)} = 1_{(V,\Psi)}$ *and* $\phi(H) \subseteq H'$.

An *algebra* of a hidden signature agrees with the data algebra on the interpretation of the visible sorts/operation symbols and, in addition, provides interpretations for the hidden sorts/operation symbols.

Definition 5. *A (hidden)* Σ*-algebra is a many-sorted* $(V \cup H, \Sigma)$*-algebra* A *such that* $A\!\restriction_\Psi = D$*. A (hidden)* Σ*-homomorphism between* Σ*-algebras* A *and* B *is a many-sorted* Σ*-homomorphism* $f : A \to B$ *such that* $f_v = 1_{D_v}$ *for* $v \in V$.

Σ-algebras and Σ-homomorphisms form a category, denoted $\mathsf{Alg}(\Sigma)$. Hidden signature maps $\phi : \Sigma \to \Sigma'$ then induce reduct functors $\mathsf{U}_\phi : \mathsf{Alg}(\Sigma') \to \mathsf{Alg}(\Sigma)$. For a Σ'-algebra A' (Σ'-homomorphism f'), we write $A'{\upharpoonright}_\Sigma$ (respectively $f'{\upharpoonright}_\Sigma$) for $\mathsf{U}_\phi(A')$ (respectively $\mathsf{U}_\phi(f')$) whenever ϕ is clear from the context.

Definition 6. *Given a hidden signature map $\phi : (H, \Sigma) \to (H', \Sigma')$ and a Σ-algebra A, a Σ'-algebra A' is a* **coextension** *of A along ϕ if and only if there exists a Σ-homomorphism $f : \mathsf{U}_\phi(A') \to A$.*

Hidden algebra takes a behavioural approach to specifying objects – their states are only specified *up to observability*. State observations are formalised by *contexts*, while indistinguishability of states by observations is captured by *behavioural equivalence*.

Definition 7. *Given a hidden signature (H, Σ), a Σ-**context** for sort $s \in V \cup H$ is an element of $T_\Sigma(\{z\})_v$, with z an s-sorted variable and $v \in V$. Given a Σ-algebra A,* **behavioural equivalence** *on A (denoted $\sim_A$) is given by: $a \sim_{A,s} a'$ if and only if $c_A(a) = c_A(a')$ for all contexts c for s, $s \in V \cup H$ and $a, a' \in A_s$.*

One uses (many-sorted) equations to specify correctness properties of object behaviour. However, one only requires the two sides of an equation to be indistinguishable by observations, rather than to coincide.

Definition 8. *A* **(hidden) specification** *is a triple (H, Σ, E) with (H, Σ) a hidden signature and E a set of (many-sorted) Σ-equations. A Σ-algebra A* **behaviourally satisfies** *a Σ-equation e of form $(\forall X)\ l = r$ if $l_1 = r_1, \ldots, l_n = r_n$ (written $A \models_\Sigma e$) if and only if, for any assignment $\theta : X \to A$ of values in A to the variables in X, $\bar\theta(l) \sim_A \bar\theta(r)$ whenever $\bar\theta(l_i) \sim_A \bar\theta(r_i)$ for $i = 1, \ldots, n$. Given a set E of Σ-equations and a Σ-equation e, one writes $E \models_\Sigma e$ if $A \models_\Sigma E$ implies $A \models_\Sigma e$ for any Σ-algebra A.*

The following properties of behavioural satisfaction will be used later.

Proposition 1. *Let A, B be Σ-algebras and $f : A \to B$ be a Σ-homomorphism.*

1. *$B \models_\Sigma e$ implies $A \models_\Sigma e$ for each Σ-equation e.*
2. *$A \models_\Sigma e$ implies $B \models_\Sigma e$ for each Σ-equation e in visible-sorted variables.*

We let $\mathsf{Alg}(\Sigma, E)$ denote the full subcategory of $\mathsf{Alg}(\Sigma)$ having Σ-algebras that behaviourally satisfy E as objects.

Proposition 2. *The category $\mathsf{Alg}(\Sigma, E)$ has pullbacks.*

Proof (sketch). Pullbacks in $\mathsf{Alg}(\Sigma, E)$ are constructed as pullbacks in the category of many-sorted Σ-algebras and Σ-homomorphisms.

We restrict our attention to specifications whose equations have visible-sorted conditions, if any. Given an equation e of form $(\forall V)\ l = r$ if $l_1 = r_1, \ldots, l_n = r_n$ such that $l_1, r_1, \ldots, l_n, r_n$ are visible-sorted, the *visible consequences* of e are of form: $(\forall V)\ c[l] = c[r]$ if $l_1 = r_1, \ldots, l_n = r_n$ ($c[e]$ for short), with $c \in T_\Sigma(\{z\})$ appropriate for l, r. Then, $A \models_\Sigma e$ if and on ly if $A \models_\Sigma c[e]$ for any $c \in T_\Sigma(\{z\})$.

Hidden algebra provides support for the reuse of specifications through the notion of *hidden specification map*.

Definition 9. *A hidden signature map* $\phi : \Sigma \to \Sigma'$ *defines a* (hidden) **speci-fication map** $\phi : (\Sigma, E) \to (\Sigma', E')$ *if and only if* $E' \models_{\Sigma'} \phi(c[e])$ *for each* $e \in E$ *and each* Σ*-context* c *for* e.

Given a specification map $\phi : (\Sigma, E) \to (\Sigma', E')$, the reduct functor $U_\phi :$ $\mathsf{Alg}(\Sigma') \to \mathsf{Alg}(\Sigma)$ induced by the signature map $\phi : \Sigma \to \Sigma'$ takes hidden (Σ', E')-algebras to hidden (Σ, E)-algebras.

The following result allows a finite number of specifications related via specification maps to be combined in a canonical way.

Theorem 1. *The category* Spec *of hidden specifications and specification maps is finitely cocomplete.*

The rest of this section briefly recalls some existing results regarding the existence of semantic constructions based on finality in coalgebraic hidden algebra.

Definition 10. *A hidden signature* (H, Σ) *is a* **destructor signature** *if and only if* $\Sigma \backslash \Psi$ *consists of destructor symbols only. A hidden specification* (H, Σ, E) *is a* **destructor specification** *if and only if* (H, Σ) *is a destruct or signature, and each equation in* E *contains exactly one hidden-sorted variable.*

Any destructor specification admits a final algebra. This appears as a consequence of the existence of a one-to-one correspondence between hidden algebras of destructor signatures and coalgebras of endofunctors induced by such signatures on one hand, and of the equations in destructor specifications defining predicates on the carriers of algebras of the underlying signatures on the other. The elements of the final algebra of a destructor specification describe all possible behaviours under the specified d estructors that satisfy the constraints imposed by the equations.

The main result in [8] shows the existence of cofree constructions w.r.t. reduct functors induced by destructor specification maps. Given destructor specifications (Δ, E), (Δ', E') and a hidden specification map $\phi : (\Delta, E) \to (\Delta', E')$, the reduct functor $U_\phi : \mathsf{Alg}(\Sigma', E') \to \mathsf{Alg}(\Sigma, E)$ is shown to have a right adjoint C_ϕ. The counit of the adjunction yields, for each (Δ, E)-algebra A, a couniversal arrow $\epsilon_A : U_\phi(C_\phi(A)) \to A$ from U_ϕ to A. That is, $C_\phi(A)$ coextends A along ϕ and furthermore, the universal property of ϵ_A makes $C_\phi(A)$ final (most general) among the (Δ', E')-coextensions of A along ϕ. $C_\phi(A)$ is called a **cofree coextension of** A **along** ϕ.

3   Semantics with Final/Cofree Families

Due to the possibility of underspecifying constructor operations, existence of final/cofree hidden algebras does not generalise to arbitrary hidden specifications/specification maps. However, as already suggested in [8], final/cofree families of hidden algebras can be used to characterise all possible ways of resolving the nondeterminism arising from underspecification. Here we prove the existence of such constructions in hidden algebra and emphasise their suitability as denotations for hi dden specifications/specification maps.

Theorem 2. *Let* (Σ, E) *denote a hidden specification. If each equation in* E *contains at most one hidden-sorted variable, then there exists a final family of hidden* (Σ, E)*-algebras.*

Proof. We define a relation $\sim$ on hidden (Σ, E)-algebras and use it to partition $\mathsf{Alg}(\Sigma, E)$ into subcategories. Next, we show that each of these subcategories has a final object. It then follows that $\mathsf{Alg}(\Sigma, E)$ has a final family of objects.

Given (Σ, E)-algebras A and B, we let $A \sim B$ if and only if there exist a (Σ, E)-algebra C and Σ-homomorphisms $f : C \to A$ and $g : C \to B$. Since $\mathsf{Alg}(\Sigma, E)$ has pullbacks (see Proposition 2), it follows that $A \sim B$ holds if and only if A and B are *connected* in $\mathsf{Alg}(\Sigma, E)$, i.e. there exists a *zigzag morphism* from A to B in $\mathsf{Alg}(\Sigma, E)$ (see [2], page 58). Hence, $\sim$ determines a partition $\mathcal{C}$ of $\mathsf{Alg}(\Sigma, E)$ into subcategories.

We now show that each category C in $\mathcal{C}$ has a final object. We let Δ denote the destructor subsignature of Σ and let F_Δ denote a final Δ-algebra. We define a many-sorted subset F_{C} of F_Δ as follows: $F_{\mathsf{C},v} = D_v$ for $v \in V$, and $F_{\mathsf{C},h} = \{f \in F_{\Delta,h} \mid f = f_A(a) \text{ for some } A \in |\mathsf{C}| \text{ and } a \in A_h\}$ for $h \in H$ (where, for a Σ-algebra A, $f_A : A{\upharpoonright}_\Delta \to F_\Delta$ denotes the unique Δ-homomorphism of its Δ-reduct into F_Δ). Then, F_{C} defines a Δ-subalgebra of F_Δ: given $f \in F_{\mathsf{C},h}$ with $f = f_A(a)$ for some $A \in |\mathsf{C}|$ and $a \in A_h$, and given $\delta \in \Delta_{hw,h'}$ with $h, h' \in H$ and $w \in V^*$, we have: $\delta_{F_\Delta}(f, \bar{d}) = f_A(\delta_A(a, \bar{d}))$, and hence $\delta_{F_\Delta}(f, \bar{d}) \in F_{\mathsf{C},h'}$ for each $\bar{d} \in D_w$. Moreover, F_{C} can be given the structure of a Σ-algebra by arbitrarily choosing $A \in |\mathsf{C}|$ and then letting $\gamma_{F_{\mathsf{C}}}(\bar{d}) = f_A(\gamma_A(\bar{d}))$ for each $\gamma \in \Sigma_{w,h}$ with $w \in V^*$ and $h \in H$, and each $\bar{d} \in D_w$. The definition of $\sim$ together with uniqueness of a Δ-homomorphism into a final Δ-algebra ensure that the definition of $\gamma_{F_{\mathsf{C}}}$ does not depend on the choice of A. Then, $F_{\mathsf{C}} \models_\Sigma E$ follows from each $e \in E$ containing at most one hidden-sorted variable: in this case, any assignment of values in F_{C} to the variables in e is obtained by post-composing a similar assignment into some $A \in |\mathsf{C}|$ with f_A; behavioural satisfaction of e in (a state f of) F_{C} then follows from its behavioural satisfaction in (a state a of) A, with $A \in |\mathsf{C}|$.

Hence, $F_{\mathsf{C}} \in |\mathsf{C}|$; furthermore, F_{C} is final in C: given A in $|\mathsf{C}|$, $A{\upharpoonright}_\Delta$ has a unique Δ-homomorphism f_A into F_Δ which, by the definition of F_{C}, defines a Σ-homomorphism $f_A : A \to F_{\mathsf{C}}$. Uniqueness of such a Σ-homomorphism follows from uniqueness of a Δ-homomorphism into F_Δ.

It then follows that $(F_{\mathsf{C}})_{\mathsf{C} \in \mathcal{C}}$ is a final family of hidden (Σ, E)-algebras: given any (Σ, E)-algebra A, say $A \in |\mathsf{C}|$ for some $\mathsf{C} \in \mathcal{C}$, there exists a unique Σ-homomorphism $f_A : A \to F_{\mathsf{C}}$; also, for $\mathsf{C}' \neq \mathsf{C}$, there exists no Σ-homomorphism of A into $F_{\mathsf{C}'}$, as C and C' are disjoint.

The existence of a final family of (Σ, E)-algebras results in the existence of a final object in the category $\mathsf{Fam}(\mathsf{Alg}(\Sigma, E))$ (see Remark 2), given by $(F_{\mathsf{C}})_{\mathsf{C} \in \mathcal{C}}$.

The next result states an important property of final families.

Theorem 3. *Let* (Σ, E) *denote a hidden specification,* $(F_i)_{i \in I}$ *denote a final family of hidden* (Σ, E)*-algebras, and* e *denote an arbitrary* Σ*-equation. Then,* e *is behaviourally satisfied by all* (Σ, E)*-algebras if and only if* e *is behaviourally satisfied by each* F_i*, with* $i \in I$.

Proof. The **only if** direction follows by each F_i being a (Σ, E)-algebra. For the **if** direction, given an arbitrary (Σ, E)-algebra A, existence of a Σ-homomorphism from A to one of the F_is together with Proposition 1 and $F_i \models_\Sigma e$ yield $A \models_\Sigma e$.

The above result justifies the use of final families as denotations for hidden specifications satisfying the hypothesis of Theorem 2.

The proof of Theorem 2 also gives some information about how the algebras in the final family look like: for a hidden specification (Σ, E), the Δ-reduct of each algebra in the final family is a Δ-subalgebra of the final Δ-algebra (with Δ denoting the destructor subsignature of Σ). However, in most cases, the final family has a more concrete representation than the one above. Such cases correspond to *split specifications*.

Definition 11. *Given a hidden signature Σ with destructor subsignature Δ, a hidden specification (Σ, E) is called* **split** *if and only if $E = E_\Delta \cup E_\Sigma$, with E_Δ consisting of Δ-equations in one hidden-sorted var iable and E_Σ consisting of Σ-equations in no hidden-sorted variables.*

The intuition behind the above definition is that E_Δ constrains the behaviour of hidden states (by means of equations that use Δ-symbols only), while E_Σ constrains the interpretation of the constructor symbols in the state space defined by E_Δ, without imposing further constraints to this state space.

Proposition 3. *Let (Σ, E) denote a split hidden specification (with $E = E_\Delta \cup E_\Sigma$), let F_{Δ, E_Δ} denote a final (Δ, E_Δ)-algebra and let $\mathcal{F} = \{F \in \mathsf{Alg}(\Sigma) \mid F\restriction_\Delta = F_{\Delta, E_\Delta}, F \models_\Sigma E_\Sigma\}$. Then, $\mathcal{F}$ defines a final family of hidden (Σ, E)-algebras.*

Proof. We must show that an arbitrary (Σ, E)-algebra A has exactly one Σ-homomorphism into an $F \in \mathcal{F}$. Any such homomorphism must extend the unique Δ-homomorphism $f_A : A\restriction_\Delta \to F_{\Delta, E_\Delta}$ resulting from $A\restriction_\Delta \models_\Delta E_\Delta$ on one hand, and must preserve the $\Sigma \setminus \Delta$-structure on the other. Hence, the only $F \in \mathcal{F}$ that A can have a Σ-homomorphism into has its $\Sigma \setminus \Delta$-structure induced by the $\Sigma \setminus \Delta$-structure of A: given $\gamma \in (\Sigma \setminus \Delta)_{w,h}$ with $w \in V^*$ and $h \in H$, $\gamma_F(\bar{d}) = f_A(\gamma_A(\bar{d}))$ for each $\bar{d} \in D_w$. Since all the equations in E_Σ are quantified over data only and since $A \models_\Sigma E_\Sigma$, it follows by Proposition 1 that $F \models_\Sigma E_\Sigma$. This concludes the proof.

Therefore, the carriers of all algebras in the final family of a split hidden specification coincide with the carrier of the final algebra of its destructor subspecification.

Finally, it is worth noting that given a hidden specification (Σ, E), the final family of (Σ, E)-algebras may be empty – this happens precisely when the specification (Σ, E) is *inconsistent*, i.e. there are no (Σ, E)-algebras.

In coalgebraic hidden algebra, cofree algebras provided suitable denotations for hidden specification maps. When specifications comprising both algebraic and coalgebraic structure are considered, the semantics involves *cofree families*.

Theorem 4. *Let $\phi : (H, \Sigma, E) \to (H', \Sigma', E')$ denote a hidden specification map. If each equation in E' contains at most one hidden-sorted variable, then the reduct functor $U_\phi : \mathsf{Alg}(H', \Sigma', E') \to \mathsf{Alg}(H, \Sigma, E)$ has a righ t multi-adjoint.*

Proof. We let Δ and Δ' denote the destructor subsignatures of Σ and Σ' respectively, and $\phi_\Delta : \Delta \to \Delta'$ denote the restriction of the signature map $\phi : \Sigma \to \Sigma'$ to destructor subsignatures. We fix a (Σ, E)-algebra A and construct a cofree family of (Σ', E')-algebras over A. We let $\bar{A}$ denote the cofree coextension of $A{\restriction}_\Delta$ along ϕ_Δ, with $\epsilon_A : \bar{A}{\restriction}_\Delta \to A{\restriction}_\Delta$ as the associated couniversal arrow.

The proof now follows the same line as the proof of Theorem 2. We consider a category $\mathsf{Alg}(\Sigma', E', A)$ whose objects correspond to (Σ', E')-coextensions of A along ϕ, and use a relation $\sim$ on its objects to partitio n it into subcategories with final objects. These final objects then yield a final family for $\mathsf{Alg}(\Sigma', E', A)$, which at the same time defines a cofree family of (Σ', E')-algebras over A.

$\mathsf{Alg}(\Sigma', E', A)$ is the category whose objects are pairs $\langle A', f \rangle$ with A' a (Σ', E')-algebra and $f : A'{\restriction}_\Sigma \to A$ a Σ-homomorphism, and whose arrows from $\langle A'_1, f_1 \rangle$ to $\langle A'_2, f_2 \rangle$ are Σ'-homomorphisms $g : A'_1 \to A'_2$ such that $\bar{f}_1 = \bar{f}_2 \circ g{\restriction}_{\Delta'}$ (where $\bar{f}_1 : A'_1{\restriction}_{\Delta'} \to \bar{A}$ and $\bar{f}_2 : A'_2{\restriction}_{\Delta'} \to \bar{A}$ denote the unique Δ'-homomorphisms satisfying $\epsilon_A \circ \bar{f}_1{\restriction}_\Delta = f_1{\restriction}_\Delta$, respectively $\epsilon_A \circ \bar{f}_2{\restriction}_\Delta = f_2{\restriction}_\Delta$). Given $\langle A'_1, f_1 \rangle$ and $\langle A'_2, f_2 \rangle$ in $\mathsf{Alg}(\Sigma', E', A)$, $\langle A'_1, f_1 \rangle \sim \langle A'_2, f_2 \rangle$ if and only if there exist $\langle A', f \rangle$ together with $g_1 : \langle A', f \rangle \to \langle A'_1, f_1 \rangle$, $g_2 : \langle A', f \rangle \to \langle A'_2, f_2 \rangle$ in $\mathsf{Alg}(\Sigma', E', A)$. One can easily show that $\mathsf{Alg}(\Sigma', E', A)$ has pullbacks, and therefore $\langle A'_1, f_1 \rangle \sim \langle A'_2, f_2 \rangle$ holds if and only if $\langle A'_1, f_1 \rangle$ and $\langle A'_2, f_2 \rangle$ are connected in $\mathsf{Alg}(\Sigma', E', A)$. Hence, $\sim$ determines a partition $\mathcal{C}$ of $\mathsf{Alg}(\Sigma', E', A)$ into subcategories. Furthermore, each subcategory C in $\mathcal{C}$ has a final object $\langle \bar{A}_\mathsf{C}, \epsilon_{A,\mathsf{C}} \rangle$. Its carriers are given by: $\bar{A}_{\mathsf{C},h} = \{ a \in \bar{A}_h \mid a = \bar{f}(a')$ for some $\langle A', f \rangle \in |\mathsf{C}|$ and $a' \in A'_h \}$ for $h \in H$, with $\bar{f} : A'{\restriction}_{\Delta'} \to \bar{A}$ denoting the unique Δ'-homomorphism satisfying $\epsilon_A \circ \bar{f}{\restriction}_\Delta = f{\restriction}_\Delta$. The Δ'-structure of $\bar{A}_\mathsf{C}$ coincides with the Δ'-structure of $\bar{A}$, while its $\Sigma' \setminus \Delta'$-structure is induced by the $\Sigma' \setminus \Delta'$-structure of (any of) the (Σ', E')-algebras in C. Also, $\bar{A}_\mathsf{C}$ behaviourally satisfies E', since each algebra in C does and since each equation in E' contains at most one hidden-sorted variable. Finally, the Δ-homomorphism $\epsilon_A : \bar{A}{\restriction}_\Delta \to A$ defines a Σ-homomorphism $\epsilon_{A,\mathsf{C}} : \bar{A}_\mathsf{C}{\restriction}_\Sigma \to A$. (The way $\Sigma' \setminus \Delta'$-operation symbols are interpreted in $\bar{A}_\mathsf{C}$ is used to prove this.) Hence, $\langle \bar{A}_\mathsf{C}, \epsilon_{A,\mathsf{C}} \rangle \in |\mathsf{C}|$.

It then follows easily that $\langle \bar{A}_\mathsf{C}, \epsilon_{A,\mathsf{C}} \rangle_{\mathsf{C} \in \mathcal{C}}$ defines a final $\mathsf{Alg}(\Sigma', E', A)$-family, while $(\epsilon_{A,\mathsf{C}} : \bar{A}_\mathsf{C}{\restriction}_\Sigma \to A)_{\mathsf{C} \in \mathcal{C}}$ defines a couniversal family of arrows from U_ϕ to A.

Right multi-adjoints to the reduct functors induced by specification maps satisfying the hypothesis of Theorem 4 provide suitable denotations for specification steps given by such specification maps. Given an algebra A of the source specification, the right multi-adjoint yields a family of algebras of the target specification which coextend A; furthermore, each algebra in this family is *most general*, in that no algebra of the target specification which coextends A strictly extends it.

We conclude this section by noting that initial/free families of hidden algebras also exist (no restriction on the specifications involved is needed in this case). Although initial families do not satisfy properties similar to the ones stated in

Theorem 3, they are relevant for characterising behaviours which are reachable through ground Σ-terms. A consequence of the existence of both initial and final families of hidden specifications is the existence of a partition of the category of hidden algebras of such specifications into subcategories, with each subcategory corresponding to a particular behaviour for the constructor operations, and having an initial as well as a final representative.

4   Semantics with Multi-limits

Algebraic approaches to the specification of data types use colimit constructions to define canonical ways of combining specifications, and free extensions of algebras to define the semantics of combined specifications purely at the model level [10], [11]. In hidden algebra, colimits are used in a similar way at the specification level. However, at the model level the interest is in *coextending* (restricting) collections of behaviours, rather than in *extending* collections of values, and consequently dual constructions should be considered. Multi-limits are an obvious candidate for such constructions, as they define final solutions to categorically formulated constraints. Here we prove the existence of multi-limits in a general category of hidden algebras. This then yields a canonical construction for algebras of combined specifications from algebras of the component specifications.

It is shown in [3] that the standard results regarding the existence of limits (see e.g. [2]) generalise to multi-limits. In particular, existence of finite multi-limits in a category is a consequence of the existence of a final f amily of objects and of multi-pullbacks. We have already seen that final families of (Σ, E)-algebras exist, provided that the equations in E contain at most one hidden-sorted variable. Also, multi-pullbacks exist in $\mathsf{Alg}(\Sigma, E)$, since st andard pullbacks exist (see Proposition 2). Hence, we immediately obtain the following result.

Theorem 5. *Let (Σ, E) denote a hidden specification such that each equation in E contains at most one hidden-sorted variable. Then, the category $\mathsf{Alg}(\Sigma, E)$ has finite multi-limits. Furthermore, if (Σ, E) is a destructor specification, then f inite multi-limits coincide with finite limits.*

Theorem 5 will be used to prove a similar result for a general category Alg, whose objects are hidden algebras and whose arrows correspond to coextension relations between their source and target. One can also consider a subcategory CoAlg of Alg whose objects are hidden algebras of destructor specifications. CoAlg will be shown to have finite limits, while Alg will be shown to have finite multi-limits.

Theorem 6. *Let Alg denote the category having:*

- *objects: pairs $\langle P, A \rangle$, with P a hidden specification whose equations contain at most one hidden-sorted variable, and A a P-algebra*
- *arrows from $\langle P', A' \rangle$ to $\langle P, A \rangle$: pairs $\langle \phi, f \rangle$, with $\phi : P \to P'$ a hidden specification map, and $f : A'\!\upharpoonright_P \to A$ a P-homomorphism.*

Also, let CoAlg *denote the full subcategory of* Alg *whose objects are such that their first component is a destructor specification. Then,* CoAlg *has finite limits, while* Alg *has finite multi-limits.*

Proof (sketch). Existence of finite limits in CoAlg follows from a general result in [6] regarding the existence of limits in the structure category of a fibration. This result states that if both the base category of a fibration and each of its fibres have a certain kind of limits, and if the reindexing functors between the fibres preserve that kind of limits, then the structure category also has those limits; furthermore, the limit of a diagram in the structure category is computed by first computing the limit of the underlying diagram in the base category, then lifting the initial diagram to the fibre over this limit, and finally computing the limit of the resulting diagram in this fibre. All the hypotheses of the result in [6] are satisfied by the fibration CoSp : CoAlg $\to$ Spec^{op} mapping $\langle P, A \rangle$ to P and $\langle \phi, f \rangle : \langle P', A' \rangle \to \langle P, A \rangle$ to $\phi : P \to P'$. First, the fact that CoSp is a fibration is an immediate consequence of the existence of cofree constructions along destructor specification maps – cartesian liftings are given by the couniversal arrows. Then, the first two hypotheses are guaranteed by Theorem 1 and respectively Proposition 2 together with the existence of final algebras of destructor specifications, while preservation of finite limits by the reindexing functors (the right adjoints to the reduct functors induced by the underlying specification maps) follows from the limit-preservation property of right adjoints.

The functor Sp : Alg $\to$ Spec^{op} defined similarly to CoSp is not a fibration, since cofree constructions do not exist for arbitrary specification maps. However, one can use a similar strategy to construct multi-limits of diagrams in Alg: given such a diagram $\mathcal{D}$, its multi-limit is obtained by first constructing the limit P of Sp $\circ \mathcal{D}$ in Spec^{op}, then cofreely coextending each algebra in $\mathcal{D}$ to a family of P-algebras, and finally computing some multi-limits in Alg(P). The couniversal property of the multi-limit then follows from the couniversal properties of limits in Spec^{op}, cofree families, and respectively multi-limits in Alg(P).

Limits in CoAlg / multi-limits in Alg provide canonical ways of constructing algebras of structured specifications from algebras of the component specifications.

We conclude this section by illustrating the pullback construction in Coalg. Given destructor specification maps $\phi_i : P_0 \to P_i$ with $i = 1, 2$, P_i-algebras A_i with $i = 0, 1, 2$ and P_0-homomorphisms $f_i : A_i \upharpoonright_{P_0} \to A_0$ with $i = 1, 2$ (defining a V-shaped diagram d in Coalg), a pullback for d is obtained by:

1. constructing the pushout $(P, (\phi_i' : P_i \to P)_{i=1,2})$ of ϕ_1, ϕ_2 in Spec
2. cofreely coextending A_0 along $\phi_1' \circ \phi_1 = \phi_2' \circ \phi_2$ to A_0' and A_i along ϕ_i' to A_i', $i = 1, 2$ (with $\epsilon_i : A_i' \upharpoonright_{P_i} \to A_i$ as couniversal arrows, $i = 0, 1, 2$)
3. taking the pullback of f_1', f_2' in Alg(P), with $f_i' : A_i' \to A_0'$ denoting the unique P_i'-homomorphism satisfying $f_i \circ \epsilon_i \upharpoonright_{P_0} = \epsilon_0 \circ f_i' \upharpoonright_{P_0}$, $i = 1, 2$.

Then, $\langle \phi_1', f_1' \rangle$, $\langle \phi_2', f_2' \rangle$ define a pullback for $\langle \phi_1, f_1 \rangle$, $\langle \phi_2, f_2 \rangle$.

5   Complex Objects in Hidden Algebra

The coalgebraic nature of hidden algebra comes as a consequence of all the operations specified by hidden signatures taking at most one argument of hidden sort. This means that only data values can be passed as arguments to either constructors or destruct ors, becoming particularly restrictive for specifying objects that have other objects as components. This section outlines a way to overcome this problem, with final/cofree families still providing appropriate denotations for the specification techniques involved.

There are at least two alternatives for solving the problem described above. One of them is to simply drop the restriction regarding the presence of at most one argument of hidden sort in operations. Such an approach is taken in [7], where be havioural equivalence is defined only in terms of operations taking one argument of hidden sort, while its preservation by the remaining operations becomes a requirement on algebras. (The satisfaction of this requirement by algebras can either appear as a consequence of the satisfaction of the equations in the specification, or be imposed as a restriction on algebras.)

The other alternative is to retain (a version of) the restriction regarding the arity of operations, by making it *relative* to the already defined object types. Syntactically, this amounts to generalising the importation of the data signature into a hidden signature to the importation of a number of hidden signatures into another hidden signature, with similar restrictions on the kinds of importations allowed. Semantically, this involves fixing implementations for existing specifications befor e importing them into more structured specifications, in the same way in which a data algebra was fixed before importing the data signature into a hidden signature. However, complex objects should only have limited access to their component objects (whose implementation details should be abstracted away). That is, the operations of complex objects should use, for hidden arguments other than the object itself, abstractions (w.r.t behavioural equivalence) of the corresponding hidden carriers, rather than th e carriers themselves.

Then, object specification becomes layered, with the first layer consisting of a specification for the data, the next layer consisting of specifications for simple objects, and the upper layers consisting of specifications of increasingly complex objects, that use the specifications situated at previous layers. This approach has the advantage of preserving the coalgebraic nature of the approach, including the existence of semantic constructions based on finality.

We let $\mathsf{Sign}^{\hookrightarrow}$ denote the category of many-sorted signatures and inclusion signature morphisms. The operations provided by a layered object system are specified using *system signatures*.

Definition 12. *A system signature is a finite partial order diagram* $\Sigma : \mathsf{I} \to \mathsf{Sign}^{\hookrightarrow}$, *with* $\Sigma(i) = (S_i, \Sigma_i)$, *such that if* $\Sigma(i)$ *includes* $\Sigma(j_1), \ldots, \Sigma(j_n)$, *then: (i)* Σ_i *adds no operation symbols to* $\bigcup \Sigma_{j_k}$ *whose argument/result sorts are all in* $\bigcup S_{j_k}$, *and (ii) the operation symbols of* Σ_i *have at most one argument sort not from* $\bigcup S_{j_k}$. $\Sigma_i \setminus \bigcup \Sigma_{j_k}$*-operation symbols having an argument of a sort not from* $\bigcup S_{j_k}$ *are called* Σ_i**-destructor symbols**, *while the remaining operation symbols are called* Σ_i**-constructor symbols**.

Ordinary hidden signatures (H, Σ) over (V, Ψ) then correspond to system signatures $(V, \Psi) \hookrightarrow (V \cup H, \Sigma)$.

An *algebra of a system signature* provides interpretations for the sorts and operation symbols at each layer, by abstracting away the implementation details of sorts from lower layers. *Behavioural equivalence* on such an algebra is defined as indistinguishability by contexts that use operation symbols from the current layer. The only difference w.r.t. the standard notion of behavioural equivalence is that variables of imported sorts are now allowed in contexts, since reachability of data values by constants of the data signature does not generalise to arbitrary layers.

Definition 13. *Given a system signature Σ, a Σ-algebra is an I-indexed family $(A_i)_{i \in I}$, with A_i a Σ_i-algebra for each $i \in I$, such that:*

1. *If Σ_i does not include any other signature, then behavioural equivalence on A_i coincides with equality: $\sim_{A_{i,s}} = =_{A_{i,s}}$ for $s \in S_i$.*
2. *If Σ_i includes $\Sigma_{j_1}, \ldots, \Sigma_{j_n}$, and $s \in S_{j_k}$ with $k \in \{1, \ldots, n\}$, then $A_{i,s} = A_{j_k,s}/\sim_{A_{j_k,s}}$. Behavioural equivalence on A_i is defined as follows:*
   (a) *for $s \in \bigcup S_{j_k}$, $\sim_{A_{i,s}} = =_{A_{i,s}}$.*
   (b) *for $s \in S_i \setminus \bigcup S_{j_k}$ and $a, a' \in A_s$, $a \sim_{A_{i,s}} a'$ if and only if $c_{A_i}(\overline{x}, a) = c_{A_i}(\overline{x}, a')$ for each Σ_i-context $c \in T_{\Sigma_i}(X)(\{z\})_{s_l}$, with z an s -sorted variable, X a $\bigcup S_{j_k}$-sorted set of variables, and $s_l \in S_{j_l}$ for some $l \in \{1, \ldots, n\}$, and each assignment of values $\overline{x}$ in A_i to the variables in X.*

Behavioural equivalence on A is given by $(\sim_{A_i})_{i \in I}$. Given Σ-algebras $A = (A_i)_{i \in I}$ and $B = (B_i)_{i \in I}$, a Σ-**homomorphism** *from* A *to* B is an I-indexed mappi ng $f = (f_i)_{i \in I}$ with $f_i : A_i \to B_i$ a Σ_i-homomorphism for each $i \in I$, such that $f_i = 1_{A_i}$ for each $i \in I$ which is not maximal.

That is, for $i \in I$, $\sim_{A_i}$ coincides with equality for sorts imported by $\Sigma(i)$, and with indistinguishability by contexts with variables and result of imported sorts, for sorts that are specific to $\Sigma(i)$. Also, Σ-homomorphisms only relate Σ-algebras that coincide on all layers which are not maximal.

It is worth noting that, by considering abstractions of the lower-layer behaviours at the upper-layers, there is no need for additional constraints to ensure that behavioural equivalence is a congruence relation – the upper layers simply can not distinguish between behaviourally equivalent states at lower layers.

We now let $\mathsf{Spec}^{\hookrightarrow}$ denote the category of many-sorted specifications and inclusion specification morphisms, and $U : \mathsf{Spec}^{\hookrightarrow} \to \mathsf{Sign}^{\hookrightarrow}$ denote the functor taking specifications to their underlying signatures.

Definition 14. *A system specification is a finite diagram $\mathsf{P} : I \to \mathsf{Spec}^{\hookrightarrow}$, such that $U \circ \mathsf{P}$ is a system signature. For $i \in I$, we let $\mathsf{P}(i) = (\Sigma_i, E_i)$.*

A Σ-algebra A behaviourally satisfies a system specification P if and only if $A_i \models_{\Sigma_i} e_i$ for each $e_i \in E_i$ and each $i \in I$.

Ordinary hidden specifications (H, Σ, E) correspond to system specifications $(V, \Psi, E_D) \hookrightarrow (V \cup H, \Sigma, E_D \cup E)$, with $E_D = \{e \mid D \models_\Psi e\}$.

All the techniques for proving behavioural satisfaction (see [1]) apply to system specifications, the only difference being in the use, in contexts, of variables of imported sorts. Furthermore, behavioural satisfaction of an equation at a given layer implies its (standard) satisfaction at the upper layers.

Horizontal specification steps involve extending the module structure, while protecting the existing modules. They correspond to inclusions of diagrams in $\mathsf{Spec}^{\hookrightarrow}$ of the following kind:

and are formally captured by the notion of *system specification morphism*.

Definition 15. *A **system specification morphism** from* $\mathsf{P} : \mathsf{I} \to \mathsf{Spec}^{\hookrightarrow}$ *to* $\mathsf{P}' : \mathsf{I}' \to \mathsf{Spec}^{\hookrightarrow}$ *is an inclusion of partial orders (i.e. an inclusion* $\iota : \mathsf{I} \hookrightarrow \mathsf{I}'$ *such that* $\mathsf{P}'(\iota(i)) = \mathsf{P}(i)$ *for each* $i \in \mathsf{I}$*), with* I *and* I' *additionally satisfying* $\mathsf{I}'(\_,\iota(i)) \simeq \mathsf{I}(\_,i)$ *(with* $\mathsf{I}(\_,i)$ *consisting of all* I*-arrows with codomain* i*).*

Final families of hidden algebras yield suitable denotations for system specification morphisms: given a system specification morphism $\iota : \mathsf{P} \to \mathsf{P}'$ and a P-algebra A, a final family of P'-algebras over A can be obtained b y combining the final families of $\mathsf{P}'(i')$-algebras over A, with $i' \not\in \iota(\mathsf{I})$.

Vertical specification steps involve specialising some of the existing modules, and are formally captured by the notion of *system specification map*.

Definition 16. *Given system specifications* $\mathsf{P} : \mathsf{I} \to \mathsf{Spec}^{\hookrightarrow}$ *and* $\mathsf{P}' : \mathsf{I} \to \mathsf{Spec}^{\hookrightarrow}$ *with* $\mathsf{P}(i) = \mathsf{P}'(i)$ *for each* $i \in \mathsf{I}$ *which is not maximal in* I*, a **system specification map** from* P *to* P' *is given by a family of many-sorted signature morphisms* $\phi_i : \Sigma_i \to \Sigma_i'$*, with* i *maximal in* I*, such that* $E_i' \models_{\Sigma_i'} \phi_i(c[e_i])$ *for each* $e_i \in E_i$*, each context* c *for* e_i*, and each* i *maximal in* I*.*

That is, only modules which are maximal w.r.t. the partial order structure can be specialised. The following depicts a system specification map:

System specification maps $\phi : \mathsf{P} \to \mathsf{P}'$ induce reduct functors $U_\phi : \mathsf{Alg}(\mathsf{P}') \to \mathsf{Alg}(\mathsf{P})$, mapping $(A_i')_{i \in \mathsf{I}}$ to $(A_i' \restriction_{\Sigma_i})_{i \in \mathsf{I}}$. Cofree f amilies of algebras w.r.t. the maximal components of ϕ yield suitable denotations for system specification maps: they induce right multi-adjoints to the reduct functors U_ϕ.

One can alternate horizontal and vertical steps to specify arbitrarily complex objects: while horizontal steps correspond to importing existing specifications along protecting inclusion morphisms, vertical steps protect the lower layers of system specific ations and specialise the upper-most layers.

We conclude this section by commenting on the relationship between the approach taken here and the one of [7]. In a sense, our approach is less general, as it does not support algebraic operations of arbitrary form (each operation can only ta ke one argument of a non-imported sort). However, the approach here is more suitable for the specification of complex objects. It is often the case that the destructors associated to such objects take other objects as arguments; in this case, the notion o f behavioural equivalence should depend on such destructors. While this is captured here (by layering the specification), in [7] it is prevented by the requirement that any operation which takes more than one hidden argument preserves behavio ural equivalence, rather than influences it.

6   Conclusions and Future Work

Hidden specifications comprising both algebraic and coalgebraic structure and maps between such specifications have been considered, and final/cofree families of hidden algebras have been shown to provide appropriate denotations for them. A canonical way of combining algebras of component specifications into algebras of structured specifications has also been derived. Finally, an extension of hidden algebra that supports the specification of arbitrarily complex objects, with the semantics still given by f inal/cofree families, has been presented.

The use of an algebraic syntax together with a coalgebraic semantics restricts the form of constructors/destructors one can specify in hidden algebra. Other ways of combining algebra and coalgebra for objects should also be investigated, possibly by makin g the separation between their algebraic and coalgebraic aspects more explicit, in order to allow the specification of more general behaviours.

Acknowledgement I would like to thank my supervisor, Dr Grant Malcolm, for his continuous advice and encouragement.

References

1. J. Goguen and G. Malcolm. A hidden agenda. Technical Report CS97-538, UCSD, 1997.
2. F. Borceux. *Handbook of Categorical Algebra*, volume I. Cambridge University Press, 1994.
3. Y. Diers. Familles universelles de morphismes. *Annales de la Société Scientifique de Bruxelles*, 93(3), 1979.
4. B. Jacobs. Objects and classes, coalgebraically. In B. Freitag, C. B. Jones, C. Lengauer, and H.-J. Schek, editors, *Object Orientation with Parallelism and Persistence*. Kluwer Academic Publishers, 1996.
5. J. Rutten. Universal coalgebra: a theory of systems. Technical Report CS-R9652, CWI, 1996.

6. C. Hermida. On fibred adjunctions and completeness for fibred categories. In H. Ehrig and F. Orejas, editors, *Recent Trends in Data Type Specification*, volume 785 of *LNCS*. Springer, 1993.

7. R. Diaconescu. Behavioural coherence in object-oriented algebraic specification. Technical Report IS-RR-98-0017F, Japan Adv. Instit. for Sci. and Tech., 1998.

8. C. Cîrstea. Coalgebra semantics for hidden algebra: parameterised objects and inheritance. In F. Parisi-Presicce, editor, *Recent Trends in Algebraic Development Techniques*, volume 1376 of *LNCS*. Springer, 1998.

9. J. Goguen, J. Thatcher, and E. Wagner. An initial algebra approach to the specification, correctness, and implementation of abstract data types. In R. Yeh, editor, *Current Trends in Programming Methodology*, volume 4. Prentice-Hall, 1978.

10. H. Ehrig and B. Mahr. Fundamentals of algebraic specification 1: Equations and initial semantics. In W. Brauer, G. Rozenberg, and A. Salomaa, editors, *EATCS Monographs on TCS, Volume 6*. Springer, 1985.

11. H. Ehrig, M. Baldamus, and F. Orejas. New concepts for amalgamation and extension in the framework of specification logics. In M. Bidoit and C. Choppy, editors, *Recent Trends in Data Type Specification*, volume 655 of *LNCS*. Springer, 1993.

Functorial Semantics for Multi-algebras*

Andrea Corradini[1] and Fabio Gadducci[2]

[1] University of Pisa, Dipartimento di Informatica,
andrea@di.unipi.it
[2] Technical University of Berlin, Fach. 13 · Informatik,
gfabio@cs.tu-berlin.de

Abstract. Multi-algebras allow to model nondeterminism in an algebraic framework by interpreting operators as functions from individual arguments to sets of possible results. We propose a functorial presentation of various categories of multi-algebras and partial algebras, analogous to the classical presentation of algebras over a signature Σ as cartesian functors from the algebraic theory of Σ, $\mathbf{Th}(\Sigma)$, to **Set**. The functors we introduce are based on variations of the notion of theory, having a structure weaker than cartesian, and their target is **Rel**, the category of sets and relations. We argue that this functorial presentation provides an original abstract syntax for partial and multi-algebras.

1 Introduction

Nondeterminism is a fundamental concept in Computer Science. It arises not only from the study of intrinsically nondeterministic computational models, like Turing machines and various kinds of automata, but also in the study of the behaviour of deterministic systems when one desires to abstract out from some irrelevant implementation or physical details. As an example, concurrent systems are often presented as nondeterministic, essentially because one intends to abstract out from timing considerations.

Among the great variety of formal models that have been proposed in the literature to deal with nondeterminism, we consider in this paper *multi-algebras*, which is certainly the most common among the approaches to nondeterminism in the algebraic specification or Universal Algebra framework (see [18] for an overview of the various algebraic approaches). The basic idea is that an operator of a multi-algebra is interpreted as a function from individual arguments to sets of possible results, as opposed to the usual interpretation in algebras as a function from individuals to individuals. Equivalently, one can say that a nondeterministic operator is interpreted as a deterministic, but set-valued, function.

In the works on algebraic semantics one recognizes two main streams of development: The classical, set-theoretical one, based on Universal Algebra, and

---

* Research partly supported by the EC TMR Network GETGRATS (General Theory of Graph Transformation Systems) through the Technical University of Berlin and the University of Pisa.

J.L. Fiadeiro (Ed.): WADT'98, LNCS 1589, pp. 79–91, 1999.

the categorical one based on *algebraic theories* and on a functorial view of algebras. In the latter, an algebra over a given signature Σ is regarded as a functor from a cartesian category "freely generated" by Σ to the category of sets, and Σ-homomorphisms are viewed as natural transformations, yielding a category that is equivalent to the standard category of Σ-algebras and Σ-homomorphisms. It is argued, for example in [16], that algebraic theories are a much richer framework than Universal Algebra. Indeed, they provide a context where both the syntax and the semantics of a variety of programming languages can be handled in a uniform way, including those involving variables of higher type (function, functional, etc.). Also, by replacing the category of sets with another universe, they give a precise meaning to the notion of algebra with a carrier equipped with an additional structure (e.g., continuous algebras, where the carrier is a CPO).

In this paper we have a rather straightforward aim: To show that, like algebras, also multi-algebras (and *partial* algebras, which are just a special case) have a functorial presentation. More precisely, we show that the category of multi-algebras and their homomorphisms is equivalent to a suitable category of functors and natural transformations from the category **GS-Th**(Σ), the *gs-monoidal theory* over Σ, to the category **Rel** of sets and relations. Actually, many definitions of homomorphisms are possible for multi-algebras: We consider some variations of the most natural case, showing that also for them a functorial presentation is possible, by resorting to looser kinds of natural transformations. Similar results are presented for partial algebras as well, by slightly changing the structure of the theory and by considering functors to **Par**, the category of sets and partial functions.

From a methodological point of view, one relevant aspect of the functorial representation of multi-algebras that we present is that, in a sense, it provides an *abstract syntax* for multi-algebras, exactly in the sense in which the algebraic theory provides an abstract syntax for algebras. Also, it defines a formal framework where at least part of the categorical structure of the category of Σ-algebras could be lifted functorially to the categories of partial and multi-algebras. We hope to provide in our presentation enough material to sustain those claims.

After a short summary on multi-algebras in Section 2, in Section 3 we discuss why a functorial semantics of multi-algebras could not be based on the standard notion of algebraic theories. Simple counterexamples will show indeed that neither multi-algebras nor partial algebras enjoy the categorical product structure which characterizes those theories. This motivates the presentation in Section 4 of weaker notions of theories for a signature, that will be used in Section 5 and Section 6 to present our characterization results.

2 A short recap on multi-algebras

By interpreting the operators of a signature as relations, instead of as functions, one easily models in an algebraic framework some sort of nondeterministic behaviour [18]. For *multi-algebras*, the relation associated with an operator is regarded as a function mapping each input value to a *set* of (possible) output values.

Quite obviously, this is just an alternative definition of relation, equivalent to the standard one as subset of the cartesian product.

Definition 1 (relations). *Let A and B be two sets. A relation $R : A \to B$ is a function $R : A \to \mathcal{P}(B)$, where $\mathcal{P}$ is the power-set operator. A relation is* total *if $|R(a)| \geq 1$ for all $a \in A$; it is* functional *if $|R(a)| \leq 1$ for all $a \in A$. Given two relations $P : A \to B$, $R : B \to C$, their* composition *$P; R : A \to C$ denotes the relation obtained by composing P with the function $\mathcal{P}(R) : \mathcal{P}(B) \to \mathcal{P}(C)$, the point-wise extension of R.*

In other words, a total relation is a function $R : A \to \mathcal{P}^+(B)$; while a functional relation is a partial function $R : A \rightharpoonup B$. A functional and total relation is then just a function $R : A \to B$. In the following, we denote with **Rel** and **Par** the categories having sets as objects, and relations or functional relations, respectively, as arrows; clearly, there are obvious inclusion functors **Set** $\hookrightarrow$ **Par** and **Par** $\hookrightarrow$ **Rel**.

We assume the reader to be familiar with the usual definition of signature, (term) algebra, and so on: For the sake of clarity, we will restrict our analysis to the one-sorted case. Our starting points are [18] and [17], and in particular the taxonomy for the notion of multi-algebra proposed in the latter.

Definition 2 (multi-algebras). *Let Σ be a signature. A* multi-algebra *A over Σ is a pair $\langle |A|, \rho_A \rangle$, where $|A|$ is a set, called the* carrier, *and $\rho_A = \{f_A \mid f \in \Sigma\}$ is a family of relations, such that, for every $f \in \Sigma_n$, $f_A : |A|^n \to |A|$. A* partial algebra *$\langle |A|, \rho_A \rangle$ over Σ is a multi-algebra such that f_A is a functional relation for all $f \in \Sigma$.*

Unlike the case of algebras, for multi-algebras many different definitions of homomorphisms are possible: We postpone their presentation to Section 6.

3   Why algebraic theories do not work for multi-algebras

We briefly recall the definition of *algebraic theory* over a signature —a category whose arrows represent (tuples of) terms, introduced in Lawvere's thesis [13]— and its use in providing a functorial view of algebras. As Kock and Reyes summarize, *the right way of conceiving the totality of operations for an equational theory was found by Lawvere, who realized that* substitution *should be viewed as the composition of arrows on a certain kind of category* [11].

Definition 3 (algebraic theories). *An* algebraic theory *$\mathbf{C}$ is a category whose objects are (underlined) natural numbers, such that for each $\underline{n}$ it is equipped with an n-tuple of* distinguished morphisms *(or* projections*) $\{\pi_i^n : \underline{n} \to \underline{1} \mid i = 1 \ldots n\}$, making $\underline{n}$ the n-fold categorical product of $\underline{1}$, that is, $\underline{n} = \underline{1}^n$.*

Given a signature Σ, the algebraic theory over Σ, *$\mathbf{Th}(\Sigma)$, is defined as follows. For each pair of objects $\underline{n}$ and $\underline{m}$, the hom-set $\mathbf{Th}(\Sigma)[\underline{n}, \underline{m}]$ is the set of m-tuples of terms over Σ with variables in $\{x_1, \ldots, x_n\}$; arrow composition is term substitution; and for each $n \in \mathbf{N}$, $i \in \{1, \ldots, n\}$, the distinguished morphism π_i^n is $\langle x_i \rangle : \underline{n} \to \underline{1}$.*

Theorem 1 (algebras as functors). *Let Σ be a signature. The category* $[\mathbf{Th}(\Sigma) \to \mathbf{Set}]^c$ *of cartesian functors[1] from the algebraic theory over Σ to the category of sets, having natural transformations as arrows,[2] is equivalent to* $\mathbf{Alg}_\Sigma$, *the category of Σ-algebras and Σ-homomorphisms.* ☐

It is worth recalling how the correspondence between algebras and functors works. A Σ-algebra $A = \langle |A|, \{f_A \mid f \in \Sigma\}\rangle$ determines a cartesian functor $M_A : \mathbf{Th}(\Sigma) \to \mathbf{Set}$ as follows. On objects, let $M_A(\underline{1}) = |A|$; this determines $M_A(\underline{n})$ for each $n \in Nat$, as $M_A(\underline{n}) = M_A(\underline{1})^n = |A|^n$. On arrows, for each $f \in \Sigma_n$ let $M_A(\langle f(x_1, \ldots, x_n)\rangle : \underline{n} \to \underline{1}) = f_A : |A|^n \to |A|$; then M_A is determined uniquely on all arrows of $\mathbf{Th}(\Sigma)$ by closing under composition and tupling, and observing that the distinguished morphisms have to be mapped to projections. Vice-versa, and similarly, given a cartesian functor $M : \mathbf{Th}(\Sigma) \to \mathbf{Set}$, a Σ-algebra A_M is easily defined as $A_M = \langle M(\underline{1}), \{M(\langle f(x_1, \ldots, x_n)\rangle) \mid f \in \Sigma\}\rangle$.

Evidently, in this functorial presentation of algebras every arrow of the algebraic theory is mapped to an arrow of $\mathbf{Set}$, i.e., to a function. In particular, arrows of the form $\langle f(x_1, \ldots, x_n)\rangle$, which faithfully represent operators of Σ, are interpreted as n-ary functions on the carrier $M(\underline{1})$. This fact suggests that if we want to interpret the operators as relations, we should use $\mathbf{Rel}$, instead of $\mathbf{Set}$, as the target category of our functorial representation, because relations are arrows of $\mathbf{Rel}$. As a first, naïve attempt, we may consider cartesian functors from $\mathbf{Th}(\Sigma)$ to $\mathbf{Rel}$, trying to understand if they correspond to multi-algebras. But we have the following:

Fact 2 (products in Rel). *Let A and B be two sets. Their categorical product in $\mathbf{Rel}$ is their disjoint union $A \uplus B$, with projection $\pi_A : A \uplus B \to A$ defined as $\pi_A(x) = \{x\}$ if $x \in A$ and $\pi_A(x) = \emptyset$ if $x \in B$, and symmetrically for π_B. For, if $f : C \to A$ and $g : C \to B$ are two relations, the only relation $\langle f, g \rangle : C \to A \uplus B$ such that $\langle f, g\rangle; \pi_A = f$ and $\langle f, g\rangle; \pi_B = g$ is clearly $\langle f, g\rangle(c) = f(c) \uplus g(c)$ for all $c \in C$.* ☐

As a consequence, if Σ contains, say, a binary operator f, a cartesian functor $M : \mathbf{Th}(\Sigma) \to \mathbf{Rel}$ would interpret it as a relation $M(\langle f(x_1, x_2)\rangle) : M(\underline{1}) \uplus M(\underline{1}) \to M(\underline{1})$. This is in contrast with the intuition that binary operators, even if nondeterministic, should have as domain the cartesian product of the carrier with itself; more explicitly, this is inconsistent with the notion of multi-algebras as introduced in Definition 2.

Therefore we find convenient to insist interpreting the product of the algebraic theory as the cartesian product in $\mathbf{Rel}$, and the distinguished morphisms as projections, regarded as total and functional relations. This way, we are able to

---

[1] We denote as *cartesian* those functors F that preserve the n-fold product of $\underline{1}$ *on the nose*, that is, such that $F(\underline{n}) = F(\underline{1})^n$, and each distinguished morphism π_i^n is mapped to the corresponding i-th projection of $F(\underline{n})$.

[2] Given functors $F, G : \mathbf{A} \to \mathbf{B}$, a *transformation* $\tau : F \Rightarrow G : \mathbf{A} \to \mathbf{B}$ is a family of arrows of $\mathbf{B}$ indexed by objects of $\mathbf{A}$, $\tau = \{\tau_a : F(a) \to G(a) \mid a \in |\mathbf{A}|\}$. Transformation τ is *natural* if for every arrow $f : a \to a'$ in $\mathbf{A}$, $\tau_a; G(f) = F(f); \tau_{a'}$.

recover the fact that "any algebra is also a multi-algebra", simply post-composing each functor between $\mathbf{Th}(\Sigma)$ and $\mathbf{Set}$ with the inclusion functor (preserving the cartesian product) from $\mathbf{Set}$ to $\mathbf{Rel}$. The resulting functors from $\mathbf{Th}(\Sigma)$ to $\mathbf{Rel}$ are not anymore cartesian (because the cartesian product is not the categorical product in $\mathbf{Rel}$). But we obtain the following, perhaps a bit surprising, result.

Theorem 3 (models of $\mathbf{Th}(\Sigma)$ in Rel are algebras). *Let $M : \mathbf{Th}(\Sigma) \to \mathbf{Rel}$ be a functor such that $M(\underline{n})$ is the n-fold cartesian product of $M(\underline{1})$, and such that for each $n \in \mathbf{N}$, $i \in \{1, \ldots, n\}$, $M(\langle x_i \rangle) : M(\underline{n}) \to M(\underline{1}) : \langle a_1, \ldots, a_n \rangle \mapsto \{a_i\}$. Then for each arrow g of $\mathbf{Th}(\Sigma)$, $M(g)$ is a total function.* □

Consequently, such functors determine *algebras*, and not multi-algebras, over Σ. Let us explain why this happens. Firstly, notice that $\underline{0}$ is the terminal object of an algebraic theory (for example, in $\mathbf{Th}(\Sigma)$ there is only one arrow from $\underline{n}$ to $\underline{0}$, namely the empty tuple). As in any category with terminal object, if $!_{\underline{n}} : \underline{n} \to \underline{0}$ denotes the unique arrow, it holds that $f; !_{\underline{n}} = !_{\underline{m}}$ for every $f : \underline{m} \to \underline{n}$, or, in other words, the transformation $!_{\_} : Id \Rightarrow \underline{0}$ is natural, where Id is the identity functor on $\mathbf{Th}(\Sigma)$ and $\underline{0}$ is the constant functor mapping all objects to $\underline{0}$ and all arrows to its identity.

Secondly, for each object $\underline{n}$ of $\mathbf{Th}(\Sigma)$, let $\nabla_{\underline{n}} : \underline{n} \to \underline{n} \times \underline{n} = \underline{n+n}$ be the arrow $\langle id_{\underline{n}}, id_{\underline{n}} \rangle$. Again, it is easy to check that for every arrow $f : \underline{m} \to \underline{n}$ it holds $\nabla_{\underline{m}}; (f \times f) = f; \nabla_{\underline{n}}$, i.e., that transformation $\nabla_{\_} : Id \Rightarrow \times \circ D$ is natural, where $D : \mathbf{Th}(\Sigma) \to \mathbf{Th}(\Sigma)^2$ is the diagonal functor.

Since these equalities hold in $\mathbf{Th}(\Sigma)$, they must also hold in $\mathbf{Rel}$ for every arrow in the image of a functor M as above. But we have the following easy fact.

Proposition 1 (on naturality). *For every set A, let $!_A : A \to \{*\}$ be the only total relation, and let $\nabla_A : A \to A \times A : a \mapsto \{\langle a, a \rangle\}$. Now let $f : A \to B$ be a relation. Then f is total if and only if $f; !_B = !_A$. It is functional if and only if $\nabla_A; (f \times f) = f; \nabla_B$.* □

It follows that every relation in the image of $\mathbf{Th}(\Sigma)$ must be a total function, as stated in Theorem 3. These considerations suggest that in order to characterize multi-algebras, one should get rid of the cartesian category structure of the algebraic theory over Σ in some way. One possibility would be to consider, for example, suitable *monoidal* (instead of cartesian) functors from the algebraic theory to $\mathbf{Rel}$ (such an approach is suggested for example in [15]). In our opinion, even if this technique could work for characterizing multi-algebras functorially, it would not be completely satisfactory in a functorial semantic framework.

In fact, we think that in functorial semantics, the "theory" on which the collection of functors corresponding to a category of models is based should be understood as an "abstract syntax" for that class of models. Such an abstract syntax must contain only the really necessary structure that one wants to interpret in all the models. Therefore, the functors must preserve ALL such structure.

Consistently with this intuition, in the next section we introduce a different notion of theory over a signature having a structure weaker than the cartesian one, and we require that this structure is preserved completely by the functors we define, that are shown to correspond to multi-algebras.

4   GS-monoidal theories

From the discussion in the last section, it follows that the cartesian product in **Rel** fails to be also the categorical product, since the naturality of the associated transformations $!_-$ and ∇_- does not hold. The interesting fact is that among the rich structural properties of cartesian categories, these naturality laws are the only ones which are missing in **Rel**. Therefore we introduce here *gs-monoidal theories*, which essentially enjoy all properties of algebraic ones, but for those naturality laws, and we will consider *gs-monoidal functors* to **Rel**, i.e., functors preserving all the structure of the theories.

Definition 4 (gs-monoidal categories). *A strict gs-monoidal category* **C** *is a six-tuple* $\langle \mathbf{C}_0, \otimes, e, \rho, \nabla, ! \rangle$, *where* $\langle \mathbf{C}_0, \otimes, e, \rho \rangle$ *is a symmetric strict monoidal category (see [14]) and* $! : Id \Rightarrow e : \mathbf{C}_0 \to \mathbf{C}_0$, $\nabla : Id \Rightarrow \otimes \circ D : \mathbf{C}_0 \to \mathbf{C}_0$ *are two transformations (D is the diagonal functor), such that* $!_e = \nabla_e = id_e$ *and they satisfy the* coherence *axioms*

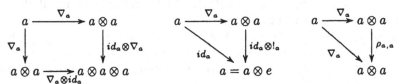

and the monoidality axioms

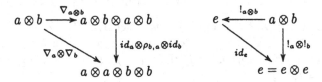

A gs-monoidal functor $\langle F, \phi, \phi_e \rangle : \mathbf{C} \to \mathbf{C}'$ *is a symmetric monoidal functor (that is, a functor F equipped with two natural isomorphisms* $\phi_e : F(e) \to e'$ *and* $\phi : F(a \otimes b) \to F(a) \otimes' F(b)$*) such that* $F(!_a); \phi_e =!'_{F(a)}$ *and* $F(\nabla_a); \phi = \nabla'_{F(a)}$; *it is strict if* ϕ *and* ϕ_e *are identities. The category of small strict gs-monoidal categories and their strict functors is denoted by* **GSM-Cat**.

Strict gs-monoidal categories have been introduced in [2] for reasons apparently quite unrelated to the topic of the present paper, namely to provide an algebraic characterization of *term graphs* as arrows of a suitable theory, in the same way *terms* over a signature are represented by arrows of its algebraic theory. The prefix *gs-* stays indeed for *graph substitution*, and is justified by the main characterization result of [2] (analogous correspondence results for other graph-like structures, like cyclic term graphs and directed graphs, can be found in [3,5]). The non-strict version is presented in [4], and it is based on non-strict monoidal categories, where associativity and unit only hold up to natural isomorphism. Unless otherwise specified, in this paper with gs-monoidal we always intend the strict case.

The categories just introduced fill the gap between monoidal and carte-sian categories: It can be considered categorical folklore [9,12] that equipping a monoidal category with suitable *natural* transformations, one obtains a carte-sian category: See for example [2] for a recollection. Using our terminology, a cartesian category is just a gs-monoidal category where transformations ∇ and ! are natural. Instead, by requiring just ∇ to be natural (and not !), we ob-tain structures which are very similar to the *dht-categories* of the pioneering [7,8]. More recently, analogous constructions are the *p-categories* of [15], or the *copy-categories* of [6]: We call them *g-monoidal categories*, where "g" stays for *garbage*, for reasons that will be explained later on.

Definition 5 (from gs-monoidal to cartesian categories). *A g-monoidal category is a gs-monoidal category where transformation ∇ is natural. The full sub-category of* **GSM-Cat** *containing all g-monoidal categories is denoted* **GM-Cat**. *Similarly,* **C-Cat** *is the full sub-category of* **GSM-Cat** *containing all cartesian categories, i.e., those where both ∇ and ! are natural.*

The inclusion functors **C-Cat** $\hookrightarrow$ **GM-Cat** $\hookrightarrow$ **GSM-Cat** have obvious left adjoints: They turn, for example, a gs-monoidal category into a cartesian one by imposing the missing naturality laws. It is worth revisiting the relationship between the categories **Set**, **Par** and **Rel** in view of the notions just introduced.

Fact 4 (on functors relating Set, Par and Rel). *Let $\times$ denote the cartesian product bifunctor on* **Rel**, *defined as $A \times B = \{\langle a, b \rangle \mid a \in A, b \in B\}$ on objects, and such that if $R_i : A_i \to B_i$ for $i = 1, 2$, then $R_1 \times R_2 : A_1 \times A_2 \to B_1 \times B_2$ is defined as $(R_1 \times R_2)\langle a_1, a_2 \rangle = R_1(a_1) \times R_2(a_2) \in \mathcal{P}(B_1 \times B_2)$ for all $a_1 \in A_1, a_2 \in A_2$. It is easy to check that $\times$ restricts to a bifunctor (denoted in the same way) on the sub-categories* **Set** *and* **Par** *of* **Rel**, *because the product of two (partial) functions is again a (partial) function. Then the following holds:*

- $\langle$**Set**, $\times\rangle$ *is a (non-strict) cartesian category.*[3]
- $\langle$**Par**, $\times\rangle$ *is a (non-strict) g-monoidal category.*
- $\langle$**Rel**, $\times\rangle$ *is a (non-strict) gs-monoidal category.*

As a consequence, the inclusion functors **Set** $\hookrightarrow$ **Par** *and* **Par** $\hookrightarrow$ **Rel** *are actually gs-monoidal functors, but obviously not cartesian ones.* $\square$

Let us explain how a free gs-monoidal category is generated from a (one-sorted) signature Σ, obtaining its gs-monoidal theory. Every gs-monoidal cate-gory **C** has an underlying graph having a monoid of nodes (the objects of **C**) and all the arrows of **C** as arcs. This defines a forgetful functor from **GSM-Cat** to **GenSig**, a category of *generalized signatures* that we are going to define. This functor has an obvious left adjoint (denoted *GSM*) that preserves the monoidal structure of the nodes, and generates in a free way all the missing structure on arrows. We define the gs-monoidal theory over a signature Σ as the action of *GSM* over a graph G_Σ that faithfully represents Σ.

---

[3] Since all the structures we consider here are gs-monoidal categories, they should be presented as six-tuples according to Definition 4: We only indicate the relevant bifunctor because the rest of the structure can be recovered easily.

Definition 6 (generalized signatures). *A generalized signature Σ is a four-tuple $\langle M, T, s, t \rangle$, where M is a monoid, T a set of operators, and $s, t : T \to U(M)$ are (the source and target) functions, where $U(M)$ is the underlying set of M. A morphism of generalized signatures $f : \Sigma \to \Sigma'$ is a pair $\langle f_M : M \to M', f_T : T \to T' \rangle$, where f_M is a monoid homomorphism and f_T a function preserving sources and targets. Generalized signatures and their morphisms form a category, denoted* **GenSig**.

Note that a one-sorted signature is a generalized signature where M is the free monoid generated by a singleton (whose elements we denote by natural numbers), and $f : n \to 1$ if the *arity* of f is n.

Proposition 2 (free theories). *Let $V_s :$ **GSM-Cat** $\to$ **GM-Cat** be the functor mapping a gs-monoidal category to the underlying g-monoidal one, and let $V_g :$ **GM-Cat** $\to$ **GenSig** be the functor mapping a g-monoidal category to the underlying generalized signature (forgetting all the structure but the monoidal structure on objects). Both functors admit a left (free) adjoint, denoted $G :$ **GenSig** $\to$ **GM-Cat** and $S :$ **GM-Cat** $\to$ **GSM-Cat**, respectively.*

The g-monoidal theory **G-Th**(Σ) *of a given (one-sorted) signature Σ is defined as $G(\Sigma)$; its gs-monoidal theory* **GS-Th**(Σ) *as $S(G(\Sigma))$.*   □

5   On the structure of theories

For a given signature, all the theories introduced so far are related by the obvious functors induced by the various adjunctions.

Fact 5 (relating theories). *Consider again the chain of adjunctions* **C-Cat** $\leftrightarrows$ **GM-Cat** $\leftrightarrows$ **GSM-Cat** *mentioned in Definition 5. By uniqueness of free constructions (up to isomorphism) one can easily show that there are full functors* **GS-Th**$(\Sigma) \to$ **G-Th**$(\Sigma) \to$ **Th**(Σ), *which are components of the units of the mentioned adjunctions. Such functors impose the missing naturality law on the argument category.*   □

Here we also used the fact that the algebraic theory over Σ can be characterized via a free construction exactly like the other theories, considering the forgetful functor from **C-Cat** to **GenSig**: The presentation of Definition 3 was preferred for its simplicity.

Interestingly, also the gs-monoidal theory over a signature can be presented in the style of Definition 3, by exploiting the main result of [2]. In fact, it is shown there that the hom-set **GS-Th**$(\Sigma)[\underline{n}, \underline{m}]$ is isomorphic to the set of "term graphs over Σ with n variables and m roots". Informally, such term graphs are defined as isomorphism classes of directed acyclic graphs with nodes partially labeled on Σ, having two sequences of distinguished nodes, the variables (which are unlabeled) and the roots. We could have used this result to define a gs-monoidal theory by providing directly the hom-sets, as in Definition 3, but we would have been forced to introduce term graphs formally, tackling a few difficult issues regarding the syntactical presentation, which we preferred to avoid: An alternative presentation for various graph-like structures can be found in [1].

Concerning the g-monoidal theory, instead, the situation is simpler. It follows by easy considerations that each arrow of $\mathbf{G\text{-}Th}(\Sigma)[\underline{n}, \underline{m}]$ corresponds to a pair of the form $\langle t, s \rangle$, where t is an m-tuple and s is a set of terms over n-variables. Intuitively, the terms in s are "garbage" that would have been thrown away if "!" were natural (whence the "g-" prefix).

Definition 7 (g-monoidal theories). *A g-monoidal theory $\mathbf{C}$ is a category whose objects are (underlined) natural numbers, such that $\underline{m} \otimes \underline{n} = \underline{m+n}$, and for each n it is equipped with two distinguished morphisms, the duplicator $\nabla_n : \underline{n} \to \underline{n+n}$ and the discharger $!_n : \underline{n} \to \underline{0}$, making $\mathbf{C}$ a g-monoidal category.*

Given a signature Σ, the g-monoidal theory over Σ, $\mathbf{G\text{-}Th}(\Sigma)$, is defined as follows. For each pair of objects $\underline{n}$ and $\underline{m}$, the hom-set $\mathbf{G\text{-}Th}(\Sigma)[\underline{n}, \underline{m}]$ is the set of pairs (t, s), where t is a m-tuple of terms over Σ and s is a set of terms, all of them with variables in $\{x_1, \ldots, x_n\}$, and satisfying the conditions

- *$t_i \in s$ for all $i = 1, \ldots, m$;*
- *s is closed with respect to sub-terms;*
- *$\bigcup_j \{var(s_j)\} = \{x_1, \ldots, x_n\}$.*[4]

Arrow composition is term substitution, plus the union of the two sets of terms: That is, given $(t, s) : \underline{n} \to \underline{m}$ and $(t', s') : \underline{m} \to \underline{p}$, if we denote with σ the substitution $\{x_1/t_1, \ldots, x_m/t_m\}$, then $(t, s); (t', s') = (t'\sigma, s'\sigma \cup s)$; and for each $n \in \mathbf{N}$, $i \in \{1, \ldots, n\}$, the distinguished morphisms are $\nabla_n = (\langle x_1, \ldots, x_n, x_1, \ldots, x_n \rangle, \{x_1 \ldots x_n\})$ and $!_n = (\lambda, \{x_1, \ldots, x_n\})$, for λ the empty tuple.

We defer to the last section an informal discussion about the meaning of such an explicit description for the g-monoidal theory of a signature, that we consider a suitable syntactical presentation for *partial* terms. For the time being, please note that with those representation of the arrows of the various theories in mind, one can easily explain the effect of functors $\mathbf{GS\text{-}Th}(\Sigma) \to \mathbf{G\text{-}Th}(\Sigma) \to \mathbf{Th}(\Sigma)$ on arrows: their composition maps a term graph with m roots to the m-tuple of terms obtained by "unraveling" it; and the second functor maps a pair $\langle t, s \rangle$ to the tuple t, thus discarding the garbage.

6 Partial algebras and multi-algebras, functorially

In the previous sections we have introduced all the technical machinery needed to extend to partial and multi-algebras the functorial representation of algebras briefly described in Theorem 1. As mentioned in Section 2, unlike the case of algebras, for partial and multi-algebras many different definitions of homomorphisms are possible. They depend on how two orthogonal issues are handled.

---

[4] This is not the only possible choice for the normal form of arrows, neither the most compact. Nevertheless, it assures a smooth definition for arrow composition.

The first issue is if a homomorphism should be a function or a relation over the underlying carriers. The second is whether the set of possible values associated to an element by an operator of the source multi-algebra should be strictly preserved by the homomorphism, or should be allowed to shrink or to increase. We stick here to the case where homomorphisms are relations (the point-to-set homomorphisms of [18], as opposed to point-to-point ones).[5]

Definition 8 (homomorphism). *Let A and B be multi-algebras over Σ. A tight (weak, or closed) homomorphism $\phi : A \to B$ is a relation $\phi : |A| \to |B|$ such that $\phi^n; f_B = f_A; \phi$ ($\phi^n; f_B \subseteq f_A; \phi$, or $\phi^n; f_B \supseteq f_A; \phi$, respectively) for all $f \in \Sigma_n$.*

We will denote by $\mathbf{MAlg}_\Sigma$ ($\mathbf{MAlg}_\Sigma^\subseteq$, or $\mathbf{MAlg}_\Sigma^\supseteq$) the category of multi-algebras over Σ and tight (weak, or closed, respectively) homomorphisms, and similarly by $\mathbf{PAlg}_\Sigma$ ($\mathbf{PAlg}_\Sigma^\subseteq$, or $\mathbf{PAlg}_\Sigma^\supseteq$) the category of partial algebras and tight (weak, or closed, respectively) functional homomorphisms.

Theorem 6 (functorial representation, tight homomorphism). *Let Σ be a signature. Then there exists an equivalence of categories between the category $\mathbf{MAlg}_\Sigma$ of multi-algebras and tight homomorphisms and the category of gs-monoidal functors $[\mathbf{GS\text{-}Th}(\Sigma) \to \langle \mathbf{Rel}, \times \rangle]^{gs}$ and natural transformations.[6]*

Similarly, there exists an equivalence between the category $\mathbf{PAlg}_\Sigma$ of partial algebras and tight homomorphisms and the category of gs-monoidal functors $[\mathbf{G\text{-}Th}(\Sigma) \to \langle \mathbf{Par}, \times \rangle]^{gs}$ and natural transformations.

Proof. The correspondence between functors and multi-algebras is analogous to that between functors and algebras described after Theorem 1. In particular, when showing that every multi-algebra can be represented as a functor one needs the fact that the theory is just gs-monoidal, because so is the cartesian product in **Rel**. The fact that tight, point-to-set homomorphisms correspond to natural transformations is trivial because the arrows of **Rel** are relations. Similar arguments hold for the second part of the statement.   □

The observations that every algebra is a partial algebra and that every partial algebra is a multi-algebra can now be recast easily in the functorial framework.

Proposition 3 (algebras are multi-algebras). *There are faithful functors $[\mathbf{Th}(\Sigma) \to \mathbf{Set}]^c \to [\mathbf{G\text{-}Th}(\Sigma) \to \langle \mathbf{Par}, \times \rangle]^{gs} \to [\mathbf{GS\text{-}Th}(\Sigma) \to \langle \mathbf{Rel}, \times \rangle]^{gs}$.*

---

[5] This choice is the most natural, as far as our functorial representation is concerned. The other case could be recovered *via* a suitable restriction on the kind of natural transformations considered, that is, by choosing suitable sub-categories of the functor categories introduced in Theorem 6.

[6] As for algebraic theories, we consider here only those non-strict, gs-monoidal functors that preserve the n-fold cartesian product *on the nose*, i.e., such that $F(\underline{n}) = F(\underline{1})^n$. Note also that we indicate explicitly that the relevant gs-monoidal structure of category **Rel** is the one based on the cartesian product, because there are two different gs-monoidal structures in **Rel**, the other induced by the categorical product structure (see Fact 2). The same observation holds for the g-monoidal structure of **Par**.

Proof. Note that each cartesian functor representing an algebra can be pre-composed with the gs-monoidal functor $\mathbf{G\text{-}Th}(\Sigma) \to \mathbf{Th}(\Sigma)$ and post-composed with $\mathbf{Set} \hookrightarrow \langle \mathbf{Par}, \times \rangle$ obtaining a gs-monoidal functor representing a partial algebra, and similarly for multi-algebras. Faithfulness of such functors follows from the fact that the functors relating the theories are full, and those relating the model categories are faithful.   □

Let us consider now the categories of partial algebras and multi-algebras with weak or closed homomorphisms. Since in the functorial presentation homomorphisms correspond to natural transformations, we only need some variation of this categorical notion which matches the looser commutativity requirement for weak or closed homomorphisms. The notion of *lax* and *op-lax* natural transformation for order-enriched categories is exactly what we need.[7]

Fact 7 (Rel and Par are order enriched). *An order enriched category is a category* $\mathbf{C}$ *where each "hom-set" is a preorder, and such that if* $f \sqsubseteq f' \in \mathbf{C}[a, b]$ *and* $g \sqsubseteq g' \in \mathbf{C}[b, c]$, *then* $f; g \sqsubseteq f'; g'$.
Category $\mathbf{Rel}$ *has a natural order enriched structure, where for relations* $f, g :$ $A \to B$, $f \sqsubseteq g$ *iff for all* $a \in A$ *it holds* $f(a) \subseteq g(a)$. *This ordering restricts to partial functions in the expected way (* $f \sqsubseteq g : A \rightharpoonup B$ *iff for all* $a \in A$ $f(a) \downarrow$ *implies* $f(a) = g(a)$*) making* $\mathbf{Par}$ *order enriched as well.*   □

Definition 9 (lax and op-lax natural transformations for order enriched categories). *Let* $F, G : \mathbf{A} \to \mathbf{B}$ *be two functors where* $\mathbf{B}$ *is an order enriched category (with order* $\sqsubseteq$*). A transformation* $\tau : F \Rightarrow G$ *is lax natural if for every arrow* $f : a \to a'$ *in* $\mathbf{A}$, $\tau_a; G(f) \sqsupseteq F(f); \tau_{a'}$. *It is op-lax natural if for every arrow* $f : a \to a'$ *in* $\mathbf{A}$, $\tau_a; G(f) \sqsubseteq F(f); \tau_{a'}$.

With this notion we immediately obtain the following.

Theorem 8 (functorial representation, weak and closed homomorphism). *There is an equivalence between the category* $\mathbf{MAlg}_\Sigma^{\supseteq}$ *and the category* $[\mathbf{GS\text{-}Th}(\Sigma) \to \langle \mathbf{Rel}, \times \rangle]_{lax}^{gs}$ *of gs-monoidal functors and lax natural transformations. Similarly, there are equivalences* $\mathbf{MAlg}_\Sigma^{\subseteq} \cong [\mathbf{GS\text{-}Th}(\Sigma) \to \langle \mathbf{Rel}, \times \rangle]_{op-lax}^{gs}$, $\mathbf{PAlg}_\Sigma^{\supseteq} \cong [\mathbf{G\text{-}Th}(\Sigma) \to \langle \mathbf{Par}, \times \rangle]_{lax}^{gs}$, *and* $\mathbf{PAlg}_\Sigma^{\subseteq} \cong [\mathbf{G\text{-}Th}(\Sigma) \to \langle \mathbf{Par}, \times \rangle]_{op-lax}^{gs}$.   □

7 Conclusions

The main contribution of this paper is the proposal of a functorial presentation for various categories of partial algebras and multi-algebras, analogous to the presentation of algebras using algebraic theories, by means of suitable free categories called g-monoidal and gs-monoidal theories, respectively.

---

[7] Lax and op-lax natural 2-transformations for 2-functors between 2-categories are presented in [10]. We tailor the definition according to our limited needs.

Our starting point was the observation that the cartesian structure of the algebraic theory over a signature was not suitable as source of functors to **Rel** intended to represent multi-algebras, because the categorical product structure on **Rel** is not compatible with that of **Set**. Therefore we introduced two different theories over a signature with a somewhat weaker structure, namely the gs-monoidal and g-monoidal theory, respectively, showing that structure-preserving functors from the first to **Rel** model multi-algebras, and from the second theory to **Par** model partial algebras. Different notions of homomorphisms for such structures are closely related to different notions of natural transformations in the corresponding functor categories.

A relevant aspect of our functorial presentation of multi-algebras and partial algebras, is that it provides an abstract syntax for such structures. More to the point, think for a minute of the classical functorial presentation of algebras. One can recognize that the algebraic theory over Σ provides an abstract syntax for algebras. In fact, given a cartesian functor to **Set** (which determines an algebra), such functor maps all the arrows of the theory to corresponding functions. Since the arrows of the theory are generated freely from the operators of the signature, one can consider them as "derived operators", whose interpretation for a specific algebra is given by the image, which is indeed a function. Actually, there is also a corresponding "concrete syntax", because we know that arrows of the algebraic theory are in one-to-one correspondence with tuples of terms over Σ, meaning that the concrete syntax of derived operators are terms, as expected.

A similar fact holds also for partial algebras. In fact, developing an intuition in [15], it is clear that, for a term $t : \underline{n} \to \underline{1}$, the arrow $\nabla_{\underline{n}}; (id_{\underline{n}} \otimes t; !_{\underline{1}})$ (or equivalently, in our representation, $(\langle x_1, \ldots, x_n \rangle, \bar{t})$ for $\bar{t}$ the set of sub-terms of t) abstractly denotes for each partial algebra F the identity over the domain of $F(t)$ (that is, a partial function over the n-fold cartesian product $F(\underline{1})^n$ of the carrier of the algebra). Let us denote by $dom_F(t)$ the domain of the partial term $F(t)$. As shown in Definition 7, each arrow of $\mathbf{G\text{-}Th}(\Sigma)[\underline{n}, \underline{m}]$ can be described as a pair of the form (t, s), where t is an m-tuple $\langle t_1, \ldots, t_m \rangle$ and s is a set $\{s_1, \ldots, s_k\}$ of k terms over n-variables: It abstractly represents the restriction of the m-tuple of partial functions $\langle F(t_1), \ldots, F(t_m) \rangle$ to $dom_F(s_1) \cap \ldots \cap dom_F(s_k)$.

By analogy, we claim that such a property holds also for each gs-monoidal theory, whose arrows are abstract syntax for the "derived relations" generated by the operators of the signature, which are mapped by functors to their interpretation as relations in a multi-algebra. The elements of the abstract syntax are in this case expressed as term graphs: The involved technical definitions impose to delay the precise correspondence to the full paper.

References

1. R. Bruni, F. Gadducci, and U. Montanari. Normal forms for partitions and relations. In J. L. Fiadeiro, editor, *Recent Trends in Algebraic Development Techniques*, LNCS. Springer Verlag, 1999. This volume.
2. A. Corradini and F. Gadducci. An algebraic presentation of term graphs, via gs-monoidal categories. *Applied Categorical Structures*, 1998. To appear.

3. A. Corradini and F. Gadducci. Rewriting on cyclic structures. Technical Report TR-98-05, Dipartimento di Informatica, Pisa, 1998. Extended abstract in *Fixed Points in Computer Science*, satellite workshop of MFCS'98.
4. F. Gadducci. *On the Algebraic Approach to Concurrent Term Rewriting*. PhD thesis, University of Pisa - Department of Computer Science, 1996.
5. F. Gadducci and R. Heckel. An inductive view of graph transformation. In F. Parisi-Presicce, editor, *Recent Trends in Algebraic Development Techniques*, volume 1376 of *LNCS*, pages 219–233. Springer Verlag, 1998.
6. U. Hensel and D. Spooner. A view on implementing processes: Categories of circuits. In M. Haveraaen, O. Owe, and O. Dahl, editors, *Recent Trends in Data Types Specification*, volume 1130 of *LNCS*, pages 237–255. Springer Verlag, 1995.
7. H.-J. Hoenke. On partial algebras. In *Universal Algebra*, volume 29 of *Colloquia Mathematica Societatis János Bolyai*, pages 373–412. 1977.
8. H.-J. Hoenke. On partial recursive definitions and programs. In M. Karpinski, editor, *Fundamentals of Computation Theory*, volume 56 of *LNCS*, pages 260–274. Springer Verlag, 1977.
9. B. Jacobs. Semantics of weakening and contraction. *Annals of Pure and Applied Logic*, 69:73–106, 1994.
10. G.M. Kelly and R.H. Street. Review of the elements of 2-categories. In G.M. Kelly, editor, *Sydney Category Seminar*, volume 420 of *Lecture Notes in Mathematics*, pages 75–103. Springer Verlag, 1974.
11. A. Kock and G.E. Reyes. Doctrines in categorical logic. In J. Barwise, editor, *Handbook of Mathematical Logic*, pages 283–313. North Holland, 1977.
12. Y. Lafont. Equational reasoning with 2–dimensional diagrams. In H. Comon and J-P. Jouannaud, editors, *Term Rewriting*, volume 909 of *LNCS*, pages 170–195. Springer Verlag, 1995.
13. F.W. Lawvere. Functorial semantics of algebraic theories. *Proc. National Academy of Science*, 50:869–872, 1963.
14. S. Mac Lane. *Categories for the working mathematician*. Springer Verlag, 1971.
15. E. Robinson and G. Rosolini. Categories of partial maps. *Information and Computation*, 79:95–130, 1988.
16. E.G. Wagner, S.L. Bloom, and J.W. Thatcher. Why algebraic theories? In M. Nivat and J.C. Reynolds, editors, *Algebraic methods in semantics*, pages 607–634. Cambridge University Press, 1985.
17. M. Walicki and M. Bialasik. Categories of relational structures. In F. Parisi-Presicce, editor, *Recent Trends in Algebraic Development Techniques*, volume 1376 of *LNCS*, pages 418–433. Springer Verlag, 1998.
18. M. Walicki and S. Meldal. Algebraic approaches to nondeterminism: An overview. *ACM Computing Surveys*, 29:30–81, 1997.

An Algebra of Graph Derivations Using Finite (co–) Limit Double Theories

Andrea Corradini[1], Martin Große–Rhode[2], and Reiko Heckel[3] *

[1] Dip. Informatica, Università di Pisa,
andrea@di.unipi.it
[2] TU Berlin, FB Informatik,
mgr@cs.tu-berlin.de
[3] Universität–GH Paderborn, FB Mathematik–Informatik,
reiko@uni-paderborn.de

Abstract. Graph transformation systems have been introduced for the formal specification of software systems. States are thereby modeled as graphs, and computations as graph derivations according to the rules of the specification. Operations on graph derivations provide means to reason about the distribution and composition of computations. In this paper we discuss the development of an algebra of graph derivations as a descriptive model of graph transformation systems. For that purpose we use a categorical three level approach for the construction of models of computations based on structured transition systems. Categorically the algebra of graph derivations can then be characterized as a free double category with finite horizontal colimits.

One of the main objectives of this paper is to show how we used algebraic techniques for the development of this formal model, in particular to obtain a clear and well structured theory. Thus it may be seen as a case study in theory design and its support by algebraic development techniques.

1 Introduction

Our main concern with this paper is to document a case study on the use of algebraic specifications or, more generally, algebraic development techniques. However, the application in this case is not the development of a software system or its specification, but rather the development of a theory that shall then be used for system specification and design. We are convinced that in order for a theory to be applicable it must itself have a clear and manageable structure, which can be obtained by a good theory design. This is particularly important for complex theories that aim at a wide range of aspects of formal system specification. Carrying over the *separation of concerns* principle from software engineering it

---

* This work has been carried out during a stay of the second and third author at the University of Pisa, supported by the EEC TMR network GETGRATS (General Theory of Graph Transformation Systems) ERB-FMRX-CT960061.

means that the different aspects or levels of the theory must be well separated and encapsulated in order to allow for a focusing on the particular aspect concerned.

Algebraic development techniques provide powerful tools for the formal specification, structuring, model construction, and formal verification for a wide range of systems. To discuss the applicability of algebraic techniques to theory design let us briefly sketch the formal model we are developing, the algebra of graph derivations, and its intended meaning.

Graph grammars are a further development of usual string or tree grammars for formal languages, that allow to handle more complex structures — graphs instead of words — as intuitive representations of system, program, or data states for example. Using this approach for the specification of the dynamic behaviour of systems, i.e., their computations, the emphasis shifts from the consideration of the language generated by a grammar to its *derivations*, that model the computations. Thus, under this perspective, *graph transformation systems* are considered rather than graph grammars. A semantical model of graph transformation systems can then be given by an algebra whose elements are graph derivations and whose operations describe how graph derivations can be composed sequentially (in time) and in parallel (in space). The main feature of the theory we are developing is the precise definition of this algebra of derivations.

A general method for the development of models of computations from given formal models of programs that supports the above mentioned algebraic structure has been introduced in [Cor90,CM92]. Models of computations are there given by categories with algebraic structure on objects and morphisms. The categorical composition operation models the sequential composition of computations, whereas the algebraic structure is used to express the distribution of states and computations. In order to apply this method to a particular domain, such as graph transformation systems, only the algebraic structure of the states and the atomic state transitions have to be given. The model of computations is fully determined by these data. Thus the purpose is to find the right algebraic structure of graphs to obtain the appropriate notion of computations.

Altogether both the domain we address and the method we use are well suited for an algebraic specification approach: the domain is an *algebra* of graph derivations, the method makes use of *algebraic* and categorical (*essentially algebraic*) structures.

In the following sections we introduce the method, the domain, and the application of the method to the domain and discuss some problems and their consequences for the development and structure of our theory. Then we sketch the algebra of graph derivations in this framework, and discuss the benefits of this model. The full formal definitions and results are presented in [Hec98].

2 The Method: Structured Transition Systems

In [Cor90,CM92] a method for the construction of models of computations from given formal models of programs has been introduced.

The first level is given by the **programs**, i.e., the syntactic entities that represent the behaviour of the system. A program is given by a transition system whose set of states comes equipped with an algebraic structure. The state operations are composition operations that indicate how larger states can be put together from smaller ones. To reduce the complexity the whole algebra of states is considered already on the level of programs, although it is in general infinite. The transitions however are an unstructured set on this level, that describe the atomic steps the systems can perform. This set can be assumed to be finite.

Consider as examples of programs in this sense P/T–nets $N = (P, T, pre, post)$, given by sets P and T of places and transitions respectively, and functions $pre, post : T \to P^\oplus$ that assign to each transition multisets of places, the pre and post conditions ([MM90]). The states are then given by multisets of places, i.e., markings of the net, with addition and empty set as algebraic operations. Note that this algebra of states is the free commutative monoid over the set P of places. Distribution of states is directly modeled via the markings; correspondingly addition of multisets is the composition operation for (distributed) states. The transition system associated to a P/T–net has the set $P^\oplus$ of multisets of places as set of states. Its transitions are given by $t : pre(t) \to post(t)$ for each $t \in T$. In this case, as in many other examples, the algebra of states is a free algebra over a given set. For the general methodology this assumption however is not necessary.

In the second level, given by **structured transition systems**, distributed computation steps, corresponding to the distribution of the states, are introduced. First the transition system given on the first level is extended by idle steps for all states. Then the state operations are extended to the transitions. Formally this construction is obtained by replacing the set of transitions by the free algebra generated by this set, including the idle transitions. For the P/T–net example this means to construct the free commutative monoid over transitions and places, with set $(T \cup P)^\oplus$ of multisets of transitions and places as carrier. The functions pre and $post$ are then extended accordingly, i.e., the pre and post conditions of a multiset are given by the sums of the pre and post conditions of its elements. The composed transitions correspond to the parallel composition of the atomic transitions.

Finally the third level, introducing the **models of computations**, is given by the categories freely generated by the structured transition systems. These categories inherit the algebraic structure both on objects (states) and arrows (computations), and have implicit compatibility laws for sequential and parallel composition given by the categorical axioms. The model of computations of a P/T–net for example is given by the set of multisets of places (=markings) as states as before, and sequential compositions of parallel transitions as computations. These are subject to the categorical axioms, such as associativity and neutrality of the empty set, and the interchange law for sequential and parallel composition. This means e.g. $(t_1 + t_2); (t_3 + t_4) = (t_1; t_3) + (t_2; t_4)$, provided both sides are well defined (where ; and + denote sequential and parallel composition respectively). More precisely, the algebraic structure of the model of computations of a net is a *strict symmetric, strict monoidal category*, and as such it is perfectly consistent with the corresponding models as defined in [MM90].

The STS–method just described has been applied successfully to various computational formalisms just by changing the basic algebraic structure of states. As we just outlined, in the case of P/T Petri nets the relevant structure is that of commutative monoids; other applications include Phrase Structure Grammars, for which the algebraic structure is that of monoids, Term Rewriting Systems, where states are represented as arrows of a small cartesian category, Term Graph Rewriting, where *gs-monoidal* categories are used [CG97], and pure Logic Programming, where the models turn out to be *indexed monoidal* categories [CA93]. Concerning our application the STS–method has three main advantages:

1. Both steps, the construction of the structured transition system from the program and the construction of the model of computations from the structured transition system, are *free constructions*. Since free constructions preserve colimits the construction of the model of computations is also compositional w.r.t. all composition operations for programs that can be modeled by colimits. (Recall that colimits are the general categorical construction to 'put things together' [Gog91], thus the restriction is acceptable.)
2. Applying the STS–method to a suitable algebraic presentation of graphs we obtain an algebra of graph derivations with sequential and parallel composition operations for free, given by the model of computations delivered by the method.
3. The categorical axioms induce an equivalence (actually a congruence) on computations, that coincides with important given notions of *behavioural equivalence*, i.e., an equivalence up to the rearrangement of independent steps, in the concrete applications of the method. This yields a clear semantical interface for notions of behavioural equivalence that appear more complicated in the special instances.

3   The Domain: DPO–Graph Rewriting

In this section we briefly review the main definitions and facts of graph rewriting in the double pushout (DPO) approach ([Ehr79,Roz97]). A *graph* $G = (N, E, src, tar)$ is given by a set N of nodes, a set E of edges, and functions $src, tar : E \to N$ that assign source and target nodes to each edge. Thus graphs are unlabeled directed graphs that may have multiple edges and loops. A *graph morphism* $f = (f_N, f_E) : G \to G'$ is given by functions $f_N : N \to N'$ and $f_E : E \to E'$ such that $src' \circ f_E = f_N \circ src$ and $tar' \circ f_E = f_N \circ tar$. With identities and composition being defined component-wise this defines the category **Graph**. The approach can be easily extended to labeled or typed graphs, or arbitrary *graph structures*. These are total algebras to a signature that contains only unary operation symbols. Such a signature is called *hierarchical* if it does not yield loops of operation symbols.

A *graph rewriting rule* $p = (L \xleftarrow{l} K \xrightarrow{r} R)$ is given by a left graph L, that is matched to the actual state graph when the rule is applied, a right graph R

by which the occurrence of L is replaced, and a span $L \leftarrow K \rightarrow R$, given by a gluing graph K and injective graph morphisms to L and R. The span expresses which items of L are related to which items of R, thus defining how R will be connected to the host graph G to which the rule is applied. Intuitively, items related by the span are preserved in a rewriting, and items in $L - K$ are deleted. A *rule morphism* $mp = (mp_L, mp_K, mp_R) : p \rightarrow p'$ is given by graph morphisms $mp_L : L \rightarrow L'$, $mp_K : K \rightarrow K'$, and $mp_R : R \rightarrow R'$, that commute with l and l', and r and r' respectively, i.e., $mp_L \circ l = l' \circ mp_K$ and $mp_R \circ r = r' \circ mp_K$. With component-wise identities and composition this defines the category **Rule**. The *amalgamation* of two rules w.r.t. a common subrule is their pushout in **Rule**.

A *graph transformation system* $\mathbf{G} = (P, \pi)$ is given by a set P of names, that is considered as its signature, and a mapping $\pi : P \rightarrow |\mathbf{Rule}|$ that assigns to each name a rule, thus specifying the atomic steps. A *morphism of graph transformation systems*, $f : \mathbf{G} \rightarrow \mathbf{G}'$ is a mapping $f : P \rightarrow P'$ between the sets of rule names that is compatible with π and π', i.e., $\pi' \circ f = \pi$. With composition and identity inherited from **Set** this defines the category **GTS**.

Since **Graph** is (isomorphic to) a functor category to **Set**, **Rule** is the restriction of such a functor category to monomorphisms in the images of the functors, and **GTS** is a comma category to **Set** all three categories are cocomplete.

Given a graph transformation system $\mathbf{G} = (P, \pi)$ a *direct derivation* $p/m : G \Rightarrow H$ from a graph G via a rule p and a matching morphism $m : L \rightarrow G$ is a pair (p, S), where $p \in P$, S is a double pushout diagram

$$
\begin{array}{ccccc}
L & \xleftarrow{\;l\;} & K & \xrightarrow{\;r\;} & R \\
{\scriptstyle m}\downarrow & (po) & \downarrow {\scriptstyle d} & (po) & \downarrow {\scriptstyle n} \\
G & \xleftarrow{\;g\;} & D & \xrightarrow{\;h\;} & H
\end{array}
$$

in **Graph**, and $\pi(p) = (L \xleftarrow{l} K \xrightarrow{r} R)$. G is called the *input*, and H the *output* of $p/m : G \Rightarrow H$. Note that, due to the pushout construction, D and H are only determined up to isomorphism by G, p and m. A *derivation* $p_1/m_1; \dots ; p_n/m_n : G \Rightarrow H$ from a graph G via rules $p_1, \dots, p_n$ and matching morphisms $m_1, \dots, m_n$ is a sequence of direct derivations w.r.t. $\mathbf{G}$, such that the output of the i'th direct derivation is the input of the $(i + 1)$'st direct derivation. The span relating the input G and the output H of two consecutive direct derivations $p/m : G \Rightarrow G'$ and $p'/m' : G' \Rightarrow H$ is defined via the pullback of the embeddings of the context graphs D and D' of the single steps into the intermediate graph G'.

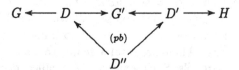

Behavioural equivalence of graph derivations in the DPO–approach is given by the so called *shift equivalence*. Consider again two consecutive direct graph derivations $p/m : G \Rightarrow G'$ and $p'/m' : G' \Rightarrow H$.

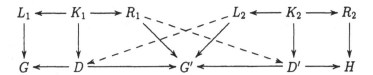

If there is a morphism $L_2 \to D$ such that $L_2 \to D \to G' = L_2 \to G'$, then this states that the part of G' to which p' is applied is already present in G, i.e., p' can be applied to G. Vice versa, if $R_1 \to G'$ factorizes through D', then all of the right hand side R_1 of the first rule application is still present in the final output graph H. In this case the direct derivations $p/m : G \Rightarrow G'$ and $p'/m' : G' \Rightarrow H$ are called *sequentially independent*. The *parallelism theorem* of DPO–graph rewriting states that under these conditions the order of the derivations can be reversed, i.e., there are a graph G'' and matchings $n' : L_2 \to G$ and $n : L_1 \to G''$ such that $p'/n' : G \Rightarrow G''$ and $p/n : G'' \Rightarrow H$ are derivations. Moreover, the same effect can be obtained by applying immediately the parallel rule $p + p'$ to G, i.e., there is a parallel direct derivation $p + p'/k : G \Rightarrow H$. The essential idea of the proof is, that two sequentially independent rule applications only overlap in the context that both derivations leave unchanged. That means, the input G can be decomposed as a pushout of two local graphs overlapping in a common part, such that each rule applies to one local graph and both are identity transformations on the common part. Finally two *derivations are shift equivalent*, if one can be obtained from the other by repeatedly exchanging the order of sequentially independent consecutive direct derivations. Normal forms can be obtained by applying each rule in a derivation as early as possible.

The three levels of the STS–method roughly correspond to the elements of DPO–graph rewriting as follows. (1) Programs are graph transformation systems, (2) structured transition systems are parallel direct derivations (i.e. double pushouts), and (3) models of computations are shift equivalence classes of derivations. We will make this correspondences more precise in section 5.

4   The Application of the STS–Method to DPO–Graph Rewriting

To apply the STS–method now the algebraic structure of graphs has to be made explicit, i.e., the composition (and construction) operations for graphs — as representatives of distributed states — have to be defined.

Many papers in the literature propose some (essentially) algebraic presentation of suitable classes of graphs (see for example [BC87,EV97,GH98]). Clearly, the choice of the right algebraic presentation of graphs is fundamental for our goals, because the STS–method will lift via a free construction this structure to the transitions and then to the computations of a system. We do not discuss here what would be the result of applying the method to the various presentations of graphs proposed in the literature, because this goes beyond the scope of the paper. Instead, we will introduce directly the algebraic structure of graphs that we shall use, and that will be shown to induce correct structure on transitions

and computations. For that purpose the following observation is crucial. Graphs
are total algebras to the algebraic specification $GRAPH$ with two sorts E and N
and two operations $src, tar : E \to N$. More generally (hierarchic) graph structures are total algebras to a (hierarchic) graph signature GS. The specification
generates a *finite limit theory* $FL(GS)$, which is a category with finite limits that
is universal among the categories with finite limits containing the specification
GS. Its objects are basically sets of equations, and its morphisms are equivalence
classes of tuples of terms. Now the dual $FL(GS)^{op}$ of $FL(GS)$ is equivalent to
the subcategory of the finitely generated GS–algebras, i.e., those that are isomorphic to quotients of term algebras with finitely many variables, factorized
by a finite set of equations [GU71]. If GS is hierarchic the finitely generated
algebras are exactly the finite ones. More concretely this observation means that
each finite graph can be constructed as a finite colimit of instances of the atomic
graphs • (one node, no edges) and • → • (two nodes, one edge). To construct
a graph with n nodes and m edges first an n–fold coproduct of • and m-fold
coproduct of • → • is taken, then the edges are connected appropriately by a
coequalizer. The graph with four nodes and two edges as depicted on the right
below for example is the coequalizer of the graph with four isolated nodes and
two isolated edges (in the middle), glued at four points via the two morphisms
indicated by the dashed and the dotted arrows respectively on the left.

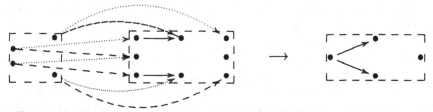

To consider finite colimits, or more specifically binary coproducts, coequalizers, pushouts, and initial objects, as operations distinguishes the algebraic from
the categorical approach. Categorically colimits are determined only up to isomorphism. That means, an object, together with a family of morphisms, may
have the *property* of being a colimit, but each isomorphic object then has the
same property. Thus being a colimit object does not define an operation. On
the other hand each category with finite colimits can be made an algebra by
defining appropriate operations that choose *designated* colimits. Let $FCCAT$
be a partial equational specification with conditional existence equations, introducing operations for binary coproducts, coequalizers, pushouts, and initial
objects. (A partial equational specification of categories with finite limits can be
found in [CGW95].) Partial $FCCAT$–algebras are then (small) categories with
designated finite colimits, and there is clearly an embedding from the category
PAlg($FCCAT$) of partial $FCCAT$–algebras to the category **FCCat** of small
categories with finite colimits. However, these categories are not equivalent, due
to the morphisms. In **FCCat** it is required that *functors preserve finite colimits*,
i.e., $F(A+B) \cong F(A)+F(B)$ etc. In **PAlg**($FCCAT$) homomorphisms must preserve *the designated colimits*; i.e., $h(A + B) = h(A) + h(B)$ etc. Thus there are
fewer $FCCAT$–homomorphisms than **FCCat** functors. Nevertheless, universal

properties of free algebras can be carried over to weakened universal properties of pseudo free categories, where the uniqueness of the mediating homomorphism is replaced by uniqueness up to isomorphism of the mediating functor. Correspondingly, free categories are only defined up to equivalence. Roughly speaking, this possibility of carrying over the universal property is due to the fact that all possible choices of colimits yield isomorphic objects, thus the different mediating functors induced by the different choices are all isomorphic.

As a consequence for our model construction we must distinguish between an *algebraic* and a *categorical* definition of the state space. In the first case we consider the *algebra of finite graphs* as state space, with composition/construction operations given by designated finite colimits. The advantage is that we can use the partial equational specification $FCCAT$ to obtain an inductive definition of the state space via the construction of the finite limit theory $FL(GS)$ as free partial $FCCAT$-algebra generated by GS. In the second case we consider the *category of finite graphs* as state space. Here the operations are given — via finite colimits — only up to isomorphism. This conception is technically easier to deal with, because it does not require concrete, fixed colimit constructions.

In any case the state space is given by the category of finite graphs, be it considered as an algebra or not. In the sequel we call this category the *horizontal category* (of states). The model of computations that is to be constructed is also given by a category, called the *vertical category* (of computations). Combining these two we end up with a *double category with finite horizontal colimits* as structure representing the algebra of graph derivations. We will denote this categorical structure as DFHC–categories for short. So we could summarize the construction by the slogan:

The algebra of graph derivations of a given graph transformation system **G** *is the double category with finite horizontal colimits freely generated by* **G** *.*

However, there are some problems with this "definition".

1. What, exactly, is an DFHC–category? This is, first of all, of course a question of understanding and getting an intuition of this categorical definition. However, also going into details, there are different possibilities to extend the definition of colimits from ordinary categories to double categories. Thus it has to be clarified which definition of horizontal colimit is the right one in this case.
2. One major advantage of the structured transition system approach is that there is a free construction relating programs and their models of computations. Passing from categories with algebraic structure to DFHC–categories we have to make sure that the corresponding free constructions still exist. Moreover, we have to make precise what "generated by" means, i.e., the embedding of the graph transformation system into the DFHC–category.
3. Beyond the categorical (external) description of the model we need a concrete algebra of graph derivations in order to compare it with the original definitions and constructions in the DPO–approach. Since the definition of

a DFHC–category is rather complex the question arises, how to practically check whether the algebra of graph derivations is indeed a DFHC–category.

As mentioned in the beginning we used algebraic specification techniques to tackle these problems. To obtain a (compositional) definition of DFHC–categories *tensor products* of specifications can be used ([Gra89,Cor90]). These are presentations of products of theories, and reflect the definition of double categories by internalization. We will explain this technique briefly below. The solution to the second problem is given for free if parameterized algebraic specifications are used for all construction steps, since they yield free functors on their model categories that induce the pseudo free categorical constructions. Due to the stepwise definition and the compositionality properties of algebraic specifications also concrete models can be constructed and checked stepwise. Moreover, this structure of the model realizes the separation of concerns principle mentioned in the introduction.

Before coming to the concrete model construction a few words on double categories and internalization are in order. A double category can be defined as *a category in* **Cat**, the category of categories. That means, a double category is given by a category of objects, a category of arrows, functors *src* and *tar* that assign source and target objects to arrows, and identity and composition functors. The category of objects is often called the *horizontal category*, and the objects of the category of arrows, with the composition induced by the composition functor, form the *vertical category*. The arrows of the category of arrows can then be naturally represented as *squares*.

$$
\begin{array}{ccc}
A & \xrightarrow{\ f\ } & B \\
u\downarrow & m & \downarrow v \\
C & \xrightarrow[\ g\ ]{} & D
\end{array}
$$

Here $f : A \to B$ and $g : C \to D$ are arrows of the horizontal category of objects, the vertical arrows $u : A \to C$ and $v : B \to D$ are objects in the category of arrows, with $src(u) = A$, $tar(u) = C$, $src(v) = B$, $tar(v) = D$, and the square m is an arrow $m : u \to v$ in the category of arrows. Using a geographical metaphor u and v are called the west and the east border, and f and g the north and south border of m respectively.

The theory of double categories is thus given by the product of the theory of categories with itself, and a specification $DCAT$ of double categories can be obtained by the tensor product of a specification CAT with itself. Given partial equational specifications $SP_i = (S_i, OP_1, CE_i)$, $(i = 1, 2)$ their tensor product $SP_1 \otimes SP_2$ is given as follows. Its sorts are the cartesian product $S_1 \times S_2$, its operations are given by the union of $OP_1 \times S_2$ and $S_1 \times OP_2$. If ob and mor are the sorts of objects and arrows in CAT this yields the sorts (ob, ob) , (mor, ob) , (ob, mor) , and (mor, mor) corresponding to objects, horizontal arrows, vertical arrows and squares of a double category respectively. Among the operations are $(comp, ob)$, $(comp, mor)$, $(ob, comp)$, and $(mor, comp)$, where $comp$ is the composition operation of CAT, corresponding to horizontal composition of horizontal arrows, horizontal composition of squares, vertical composition of vertical arrows, and vertical composition of squares respectively. We will denote both horizontal compositions by $\circ$ and both vertical compositions by $\bullet$ in the sequel. Finally the axioms of $SP_1 \otimes SP_2$ are given by the embeddings of the axioms CE_1 and CE_2, and the *homomorphism equations*, that state the compatibility of the operations from SP_1 and SP_2. For each pair $f : s_1 \ldots s_n \to s \in OP_1$ and $g : s_1' \ldots s_k' \to s' \in OP_2$ the homomorphism property

$$(f, s')((s_1, g)(x_{s_1 s_1'}, \ldots, x_{s_1 s_k'}), \ldots, (s_n, g)(x_{s_n s_1'}, \ldots, x_{s_n s_k'})) =$$
$$= (s, g)((f, s_1')(x_{s_1 s_1'}, \ldots, x_{s_n s_1'}), \ldots, (f, s_n')(x_{s_1 s_k'}, \ldots, x_{s_n s_k'}))$$

is introduced as a conditional equation, where the (omitted) condition requires that both sides are defined. Instantiating this equation with the composition operations for double categories we obtain the well known interchange law $(\delta \circ \gamma) \bullet (\beta \circ \alpha) = (\delta \bullet \beta) \circ (\gamma \bullet \alpha)$ for all composable quadruples of squares.

The tensor product allows to construct (and understand) the definition of DFHC–categories step by step, and supports the corresponding stepwise construction of the models, with stepwise correctness proofs. Moreover, partial equational specifications of programs and structured transition systems can be obtained as fragments of this specification, which yields the desired specification morphisms (inclusion) that induce the free functors.

To summarize the discussion so far, we end up with three levels of description of the model.

1. The first level is given by the *categorical description*, i.e., the fixation of the appropriate categorical structure (DFHC–categories) and the universal property of the free construction. It could be called the *semantical interface*, because it contains very compact descriptions via the universal properties and a terse characterization of the overall structure, without showing the concrete constructions and its details.

2. The second level is given by the algebraic specification of the categorical structure. It can be considered as the *technical description*, because it is only used internally to construct and check the model and guarantee the existence of free constructions. Moreover, it yields a concrete syntax (the terms of the specification) to reason about the constructions.

3. The third level is given by the *concrete model*, i.e., the algebra of graph derivations in terms of concrete graphs, graph morphisms, derivations etc. This level is needed to establish the relation with the given notions of the DPO–approach, i.e., to be able to show that our model in fact realizes the notion of computation defined there.

5   The Algebra of Graph Derivations

In this section we now describe the development of the algebra of graph derivations within the structured transition system approach in more detail.

5.1   Programs

The entities corresponding to programs in the DPO–graph rewriting approach are graph transformation systems $\mathbf{G} = (P, \pi)$. These are now represented as transition systems with algebraic structure on the states. An important observation at this point is that graph rewriting rules as well as direct derivations are not given by pairs of graphs alone, but by *graph spans*. These spans are necessary in order to express the connections between the concerned graphs. In a derivation the output is only determined up to isomorphism. Thus the preservation of identities through the state change must be made explicit by a relation between input and output. In a rule it is necessary to define a relation between its left hand side L and its right hand side R in order to prescribe the connection of R to arbitrary input graphs to which L might be matched. Both relations are given by graph spans. Thus the transitions will not relate graphs, but the graph morphisms the spans consist of. Anticipating the double category representation of the model of computations we represent the graph morphisms, that yield the states of the transition system, as horizontal arrows, and the transitions, representing the rewrite rules, as squares.

A rule $p : (L \leftarrow K \rightarrow R)$ of a graph transformation system $\mathbf{G}$ is then represented by a square $[p]$ as follows.

$$
\begin{array}{ccc}
K & \xrightarrow{\; l \;} & L \\
{\scriptstyle K}\big\downarrow & [p] & \big\downarrow{\scriptstyle p} \\
K & \xrightarrow[\; r \;]{} & R
\end{array}
$$

The morphisms $l : K \rightarrow L$ and $r : K \rightarrow R$ of the rule yield the north and south borders respectively of the square. Its west border is given by the identity morphism $K : K \rightarrow K$. The east border is given by the rule name p, considered as a new formal arrow between the graphs L and R. The whole square is denoted here by the rule name in square brackets, just to have a notational distinction between squares and (vertical formal) arrows. There is then a functional dependency from squares to their borders: The north border of $[p]$ is the first graph morphism of the graph span $\pi(p)$ etc. The program (in the STS sense) generated by $\mathbf{G}$ is thus given by the horizontal category of finite graphs, and the set of squares representing the rules of $\mathbf{G}$.

5.2   Structured Transition Systems

The first step in the construction of the structured transition system from the program is to add idle steps for all states, that will yield the vertical identities in the double category in the next step. Thus we introduce squares as depicted on the left below for all graph morphisms $f : G \to H$. As for graphs the (vertical) identity on f is denoted by the same letter.

$$
\begin{array}{ccc}
G & \xrightarrow{f} & H \\
\downarrow{G} & f & \downarrow{H} \\
G & \xrightarrow[f]{} & H
\end{array}
\qquad\qquad
\begin{array}{ccccc}
L & \longleftarrow & K & \longrightarrow & R \\
\downarrow{m} & & \downarrow{d} & & \downarrow \\
G & \longleftarrow & D & \longrightarrow & H
\end{array}
$$

Now recall that a single step rewriting $p/m : G \Rightarrow H$ in the DPO–approach is given by the double pushout diagram given on the right above and the rule name p. In the transition system we have already the left front square $[p]$ representing the rule $p : (L \leftarrow K \to R)$, and the vertical identity on $d : K \to D$, back left.

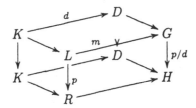

Now the horizontal category of states has pushouts. Extending these pushouts to transitions, i.e., the squares, we can construct the following completion. The graph G is the pushout object of $d : K \to D$ and $l : K \to L$ in the horizontal category of graphs, H is the pushout of $d : K \to D$ and $r : K \to R$. Thus these are the input and output of the derivation. Extending pushouts to squares this yields a pushout object of the squares $[p]$ and d, a vertical arrow that we denote by $p/d : G \to H$. The left pushout injection, denoted by $[p/d]$, given by the square $G \leftarrow D \to D \to H$ represents the whole span $G \leftarrow D \to H$.

Using coproducts of the horizontal category parallel rules are obtained, given by the coproduct of two squares representing rules. The pushout with a vertical identity d of a context morphism $d : K + K' \to D$ then represents a parallel direct derivation $p + p'/m : G \Rightarrow H$. Thus the structured transition system generated by $\mathbf{G}$ contains all parallel direct derivations of $\mathbf{G}$ as squares.

5.3   Model of Computations

Sequential composition of parallel graph derivations is obtained by the free construction of the double category with finite horizontal colimits generated by the structured transition system. Consider the sequential composition of (parallel) graph derivations $p/m : G \Rightarrow G'$ and $p'/m' : G' \Rightarrow H$. The single steps are represented in the structured transition system by the upper right and lower right squares in the following diagram.

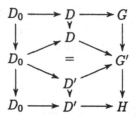

Obviously these squares are not vertically composable, because the south border of the first one does not coincide with the north border of the second one. Constructing the pullback $D_0 \to D, D_0 \to D'$ of $D \to G'$ and $D' \to G'$ the single steps can be composed horizontally with the vertical identities on $D_0 \to D$ and $D_0 \to D'$ respectively. These yield now vertically composable squares $G' \leftarrow D_0 \to D_0 \to G$ and $H \leftarrow D_0 \to D_0 \to G'$ representing the sequential composition of the steps as defined in section 3.

5.4   Interchange Laws

Consider now a derivation $p/m : G_1 \Rightarrow H_1$, represented by a square $[p/d]$. Via a pushout with the vertical identity on a morphism $g_2 : D \to G_2$ it can be embedded in a larger context, and yields a derivation $p/e : G \Rightarrow G'$. Suppose furthermore a square $[p'/d']$ representing a derivation $p'/m' : G_2 \Rightarrow H_2$ and its extension by a pushout with a vertical identity on $h_1 : D \to H_1$, represented by the vertical arrow $p'/e' : G' \to H$. These two steps overlap only in the common context D that both leave unchanged, thus they are sequentially independent (cf. section 3).

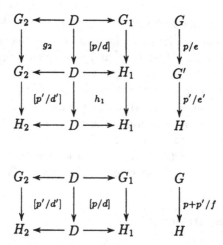

Since g_2 and h_1 are vertical identities vertical composition yields $[p'/d'] \bullet g_2 = [p'/d']$ and $h_1 \bullet [p/d] = [p/d]$. Their pushout is the vertical arrow $p+p'/f : G \to H$. Vice versa, computing first the horizontal pushouts in the upper diagram yields the vertical composition $p'/e' \bullet p/e : G \to H$. The corresponding interchange law states that the order of the operations (pushout and composition) can be exchanged, i.e., $p + p'/f = p'/e' \bullet p/e$.

The pushout decomposition of the input graph G into local graphs G_1 and G_2 in the upper diagram corresponds exactly to the decomposition that is used to prove the parallelism theorem of DPO–graph rewriting. Using this idea it can be shown that the representations of shift equivalent derivations as vertical arrows are identified by the interchange laws. Moreover, the axioms of DFHC–categories are faithful w.r.t. this representation, i.e., non–equivalent derivations are represented by distinct vertical arrows. (Concerning full details see [Hec98].)

6   Conclusion

We have presented the application of the STS–method for the definition of models of computations to DPO–graph rewriting. Its aim has been the construction of an algebra of graph derivations as a descriptive model of the semantics of graph transformation systems according to the DPO–approach. The main point in this application is to find the right algebraic structure of graphs, that model the states in this case. The model of computations is then fully determined. The criterion for the *right* structure is thereby to check, whether the so defined model of computations covers the semantics, including the notion of behavioural equivalence, that had been defined in the DPO–approach before. Since the shift equivalence classes of a graph transformation system $\mathbf{G}$ are faithfully represented by the squares of the model of computations generated by $\mathbf{G}$, and all squares have an interpretation in terms of the semantics of $\mathbf{G}$, this criterion is fulfilled.

There are several advantages of constructing the algebra of a graph derivations as a model of computations according to the STS–method. First all advantages of the STS–method are inherited (see section 2). Second we obtain in this way an inductive definition not only of graphs, but also of graph derivations and shift equivalence classes, due to the free construction of the model of computations. Finally, the free construction also yields a very compact characterization of the semantics via the universal property. Basically it is given by the slogan in section 4.

An algebra of graph derivations as semantical model has several advantages. As already discussed above, it can be used to reason about the distribution of states and computations, due to the operations of the algebra. Moreover, it can be used to define refinement or implementation relations between graph transformation systems. These would be given categorically be Kleisli–morphisms, which means that rules of one system can be mapped to derivations of the other one, i.e., the rules are refined/implemented by sequential and parallel compositions and/or instances of the rules of the more concrete system.

The application of the STS–method to DPO–graph rewriting showed moreover, that the states of a graph derivation are graphs with interfaces (i.e., graph morphisms) rather than graphs, which results in a double category with algebraic structure, induced by finite colimits, as model of computations. This yields a certain complexity of the model. For that reason the development of the algebra of graph derivations required a careful reflection on the methods we could use to reach our goal. As documented here algebraic development techniques could be applied successfully. Although the final model need not necessarily be presented in this algebraic framework, the use of algebraic techniques in the development has been necessary in order to obtain the right definitions at all. Secondly the use of double categories could be a starting point for a comparison with the tile model as general model of computations, that is also based on double categories and obviously had a great impact on the work presented here. This comparison, however, is outside the scope of this paper.

References

BC87.   M. Bauderon and B. Courcelle. Graph expressions and graph rewritings. *Mathematical Systems Theory*, 20:83–127, 1987.

CA93.   A. Corradini and A. Asperti. A categorical model for logic programs: Indexed monoidal categories. In *Proceedings REX Workshop, Beekbergen, The Netherlands, June 1992*, Springer LNCS 666, 1993.

CG97.   A. Corradini and F. Gadducci. A 2-categorical presentation of term graph rewriting. In *Proceedings CTCS'97*, Springer LNCS 1290, 1997.

CGW95.   I. Claßen, M. Große-Rhode, and U. Wolter. Categorical concepts for parameterized partial specifications. *MSCS*, 5(2):153–188, 1995.

CM92.   A. Corradini and U. Montanari. An algebraic semantics for structured transition systems and its application to logic programs. *TCS*, 103:51–106, 1992.

Cor90.   A. Corradini. *An algebraic semantics for transition systems and logic programming*. PhD thesis, Dip. Informatica, Università di Pisa, 1990.

Ehr79.   H. Ehrig. Introduction to the algebraic theory of graph grammars. In V. Claus, H. Ehrig, and G. Rozenberg, editors, *1st Graph Grammar Workshop*, Springer LNCS 73, pages 1–69, 1979.

EV97.   J. Engelfriet and J.J. Vereijken. Context-free graph grammars and concatenation of graphs. *Acta Informatica*, 34:773–803, 1997.

GH98.   F. Gadducci and R. Heckel. An inductive view of graph transformation. In *Proceedings WADT'97*, Springer LNCS 1376, 1998.

Gog91.   J.A. Goguen. A categorical manifesto. *MSCS*, 1, 1991.

Gra89.   J.W. Gray. The category of sketches as a model for algebraic semantics. *Contemporary Mathematics*, 92:109–135, 1989.

GU71.   P. Gabriel and F. Ulmer. *Lokal präsentierbare Kategorien*, Springer LNM 221, 1971.

Hec98.   R. Heckel. *Compositional Development of Reactive Systems using Graph Transformation Systems with Loose Semantics*. PhD thesis, TU Berlin, 1998.

Law63.   F. W. Lawvere. Functorial semantics of algebraic theories. In *Proc. National Academy of Science, U.S.A., 50*, pages 869–872. Columbia University, 1963.

MM90.   J. Meseguer and U. Montanari. Petri nets are monoids. *Information and Computation*, 88:105–155, 1990.

Roz97.   G. Rozenberg, editor. *Handbook of Graph Grammars and Computing by Graph Transformations, Volume 1: Foundations*. World Scientific, 1997.

Hierarchical Heterogeneous Specifications

Sophie Coudert[1], Gilles Bernot[2], and Pascale Le Gall[2] *

[1] I.R.I.N., Université de Nantes, Rue de la Houssinière, 44332 Nantes, France
`Sophie.Coudert@irin.univ-nantes.fr`
[2] L.a.M.I., Université d'Évry, Cours Monseigneur Roméro, 91025 Évry, France
`{bernot,legall}@lami.univ-evry.fr`

Abstract. We propose a definition of hierarchical heterogeneous formal specifications, where each module is specified according to its own homogeneous logic. We focus on the specification structure which we represent by a term in order to take benefit of classical knowledge on terms. For example, substitutions solve implementation sharing of modules. Then, we show how proof mechanisms can be expressed inside our framework. Our proof system involves both the homogeneous inference relations associated to the logics of modules and property inheritance relations associated to the structuring primitives. Heterogeneous primitives allow to move from one logic to another. We sketch out the specification of a travel agency given according to our particular framework of structured specifications. We demonstrate on this specification how a heterogeneous proof can be handled.

Keywords: formal specification, structured specification, proof theory, heterogeneous specification, heterogeneous proof, logical framework, inference system, modularity, algebraic specification.

Introduction

Today, a number of formal foundations and tools exist to treat specification modules independently, or hierarchical specifications: formal languages, theorem provers, test generation tools, etc. Moreover the *structure of the specifications* becomes a privileged object of study, as in the software architecture approaches [PW92]. The CoFI initiative for example [CoF96], which is defining a common language core for algebraic specifications, gives a large place to structuring issues [BST99]. Also several studies focus on the structuring primitives of algebraic specifications [Wir93,HST94,DGS93]. Bringing into operations formal methods and specifications on complete industrial projects requires reusability issues. In order to *reuse* various already implemented components, we should take them *as they are*, with their formalisms. The question addressed by this paper is precisely how to combine such heterogeneous components.

* This work was partly supported by the ESPRIT-IV Working Group 22704 ASPIRE, the ESPRIT-IV Working Group 23531 FIREworks and the French "PRC-GDR de programmation."

J.L. Fiadeiro (Ed.): WADT'98, LNCS 1589, pp. 107–121, 1999.
© Springer-Verlag Berlin Heidelberg 1999

We propose a general framework allowing to take into account both classical structuring primitives ([Wir93,HST94,DGS93]) and special translation primitives that introduce heterogeneity in specifications. We deal with structuring primitives, *uniformly* according to the syntactic, semantic and proof considerations. For this, we abstract them by the notion of *constructor* and we look for characterizing minimal requirements allowing us to combine them into a hierarchical heterogeneous specification (HHS in the sequel) in a coherent way.

From a syntactic viewpoint, we represent structured specifications as terms with specification modules as function symbols (constructors). For example, we denote the enrichment of n specifications $SP_1, \ldots, SP_n$ with a module ΔP by the term $use_{\Delta P}(SP_1, ..., SP_n)$. There are as many different *use* constructors as different enrichment modules ΔP. All other primitives, such as *forget*, *rename*, as well as the translation primitive *het*, are constructors. Moreover, each constructor is provided with an application domain giving which specification terms it may import. Then, specifications are simply terms with respect the application domains. Equal subterms of such a specification represent a unique sub-specification.

From a semantic viewpoint, the models of a specification are defined on its exported signature so that they belong to the top level constructor logic. Following previous works on modularity issues ([Bid87,NOS95]), constructor semantics are sets of functions (*implementations*) associating to the imported models a model over the exported signature. The ability to manage multiple importations from different logics, as well as the sharing aspects are solved by using semantic substitution mechanisms.

From a proof-theoretical viewpoint, we associate to each module an inference mechanism especially devoted to capture the rôle of the constructor w.r.t. to the transmitted properties from the imported specifications to the global specification. We then formalize the proof principle which consists in *delegating lemmas* along the specification structure ([HST94] uses the term *"diving"*) in such a way that pieces of homogeneous proofs can be reused.

The main contribution of our HHS framework is that the syntax, semantic and proof-theoretical parts of a specification can be systematically derived from those of the constructors (structuring primitives) occurring in it. This modelling easily admits heterogeneous components within a specification. We illustrate our purpose with a simplified HHS of a travel agency and a significant heterogeneous proof about it. The specification combines about a dozen modules and 3 formalisms, and heterogeneous components are glued together using heterogeneous bridges.

1 Homogeneous Logics

1.1 Definition

As usual, system components are specified by means of a set of sentences over their signature, according to their formalism. Homogeneous formalisms are similar to general logics [Mes89], but our requirements are weaker[1] because they are minimal with respect to our needs for HHS.

Definition 1. *A homogeneous logic l is a tuple $(Sig_l, sen_l, mod_l, \vdash_l, \models_l)$ where:*

- *Sig_l is a class whose objects are called* signatures
- *sen_l is a map from Sig_l to Set associating to each signature a set of* sentences *(Set being the class of sets)*
- *mod_l is a map from Sig_l to Class associating to each signature a class of* models *(Class being the class of classes)*
- *$\vdash_l$, called* inference relation, *is a Sig_l-indexed family such that for each signature Σ, $\vdash_{l,\Sigma}$ is a binary relation included in $\mathcal{P}(sen_l(\Sigma)) \times sen_l(\Sigma)$*
- *$\models_l$, called* satisfaction relation, *is a Sig_l-indexed family such that for each signature Σ, $\models_{l,\Sigma}$ is a binary relation included in $mod_l(\Sigma) \times sen_l(\Sigma)$*

and $\vdash_l$ is reflexive, monotonic, transitive and sound i.e., respectively[2]

- *$\forall \Sigma \in Sig_l, \forall \varphi \in sen_l(\Sigma), \{\varphi\} \vdash_{l,\Sigma} \varphi$*
- *$\forall \Sigma \in Sig_l, \forall \Gamma \subseteq sen_l(\Sigma), \forall \Gamma' \subseteq sen_l(\Sigma), \forall \varphi \in sen_l(\Sigma),$*
  $\Gamma \vdash_{l,\Sigma} \varphi$ and $\Gamma \subseteq \Gamma' \implies \Gamma' \vdash_{l,\Sigma} \varphi$
- *$\forall \Sigma \in Sig_l, \forall \Gamma \subseteq sen_l(\Sigma), \forall \Gamma' \subseteq sen_l(\Sigma), \forall \varphi \in sen_l(\Sigma),$*
  $\Gamma \vdash_{b,\Sigma} \Gamma'$ and $\Gamma \cup \Gamma' \vdash_{l,\Sigma} \varphi \implies \Gamma \vdash_{l,\Sigma} \varphi$
- *for any $\Gamma \subseteq sen_l(\Sigma)$ and any $\varphi \in sen_l(\Sigma)$, if $\Gamma \vdash_{l,\Sigma} \varphi$ then*

$$\forall M \in mod_l(\Sigma), \quad (M \models_{l,\Sigma} \Gamma) \implies (M \models_{l,\Sigma} \varphi)$$

Notation *– $\mathcal{L}$ is the class of all homogeneous logics.*
- *$Sig = \coprod_{l \in \mathcal{L}} Sig_l$ (the class of all the signatures[3])*
- *$mod : Sig \to Class$ associates $mod_l(\Sigma)$ to each signature Σ in Sig_l*
- *$sen : Sig \to Set$ associates $sen_l(\Sigma)$ to each signature Σ in Sig_l*
- *$\vdash = \coprod_{l \in \mathcal{L}} \vdash_l$ and $\models = \coprod_{l \in \mathcal{L}} \models_l$*

Our HHS example specifying a travel agency will involve three different homogeneous logics, respectively FG, OBS and ND. FG is the classical typed equational logic [EM85], finitely generated for a subset of the sorts. It allows both to use structural induction on these sorts and to import non finitely generated logics. OBS is a formalism with observational semantics [BH96] and is also a typed equational logic, not finitely generated, with set-theoretic equality for observable sorts (declared in the signature) and observational equality (based on observable contexts) for the other sorts. ND is a formalism devoted to specify non deterministic behaviours [WM95]. Non deterministic signatures are the

---

[1]   and we have actually used examples of homogeneous logics which do not satisfy the satisfaction condition [BLGA94]

[2] $\Gamma \vdash_{b,\Sigma} \Gamma'$ means $\forall \varphi \in \Gamma', \Gamma \vdash_{b,\Sigma} \varphi$ and $M \models_{b,\Sigma} \Gamma$ means $\forall \varphi \in \Gamma, M \models_{l,\Sigma} \varphi$

[3]   as usual, $\coprod$ stands for the disjoint union

same as those of typed logic. The difference is that terms evaluate to *sets* of values: all the possible values of non deterministic executions. The equality ($\doteq$) is strong: two terms are equal if evaluated to the same singleton. There are two other predicates: a strong difference ($\neq$), which requires disjoint evaluations, and an inclusion ($\prec$). Sentences are clauses and a useful remark for our purpose is that in deterministic models (where all terms are evaluated in singletons), $\doteq$ and $\prec$ have the same meaning, and Horn clauses can be seen as conditional positive sentences. While FG and OBS are nearby formalisms (see for example [Pad96]), ND is really a foreign formalism w.r.t. FG and OBS because of the possible multi-evaluations of terms.

1.2   Heterogeneous Bridges Between Logics

Our approach for formal interoperability is based on a natural idea: we use special translation modules which are new components added to the pre-existent homogeneous ones. These new components allow a module in a formalism to import a specification in another formalism. Such translations could be based on some previous works (e.g. [Mes89,AC94,Tar96]) which establish strong relationships between formalisms by means of mappings. All these mappings preserve the signature morphisms (and their semantic counterpart) which are used to model the structure. In other words these works intend to preserve the structure and all the properties through the translation so that we can retrieve them in a global flat model of the specification. Such a point of view in practice leads to translation modules which are defined from a less expressive formalism to a more expressive one (in the sense of a logical framework according to [Mes97]).

In order to define an applicable general framework, we adopt a more flexible definition of such translation modules: formalism mappings will carry models without any reference to signature morphisms, provided that the underlying translations carry some clear intuition.

Definition 2.

Let $a = (Sig_a, sen_a, mod_a, \vdash_a, \models_a)$ and $b = (Sig_b, sen_b, mod_b, \vdash_b, \models_b)$ be homogeneous logics. A heterogeneous bridge $\mu : a \to b$ consists of

- A total function $Tr_\mu : Sig_a \to Sig_b$, called signature transposition function
- A Sig_a-indexed family Ext_μ such that $Ext_{\mu,\Sigma} : mod_a(\Sigma) \to mod_b(Tr_\mu(\Sigma))$ are partial functions called model extraction functions
- A family $\Vdash_\mu$ indexed by Sig_a, such that $\Vdash_{\mu,\Sigma}$ is a binary relation included in $\mathcal{P}(sen_a(\Sigma)) \times sen_b(Tr_\mu(\Sigma))$, called heterogeneous inference bridge

satisfying the following properties:

- $\Vdash_\mu$ is monotonic
- heterogeneous soundness: *for any $\Sigma \in Sig_a$, for any $\Gamma \subseteq sen_a(\Sigma)$, for any $\varphi \in sen_b(Tr_\mu(\Sigma))$, if $\Gamma \Vdash_{\mu,\Sigma} \varphi$ then for all $M \in mod_a(\Sigma)$, if $Ext_{\mu,\Sigma}(M)$ is defined, then we have: $[M \models_a \Gamma \implies Ext_{\mu,\Sigma}(M) \models_b \varphi]$*

Homogeneous logics provided with heterogeneous bridges form a category, heterogeneous bridge composition being defined in an obvious way. Some previous works on maps between formalisms ([CM97,AC92,GB92,SS96,Mes89]) allow us to rather easily derive heterogeneous bridges (e.g. [AC94], see also [BCLG96] for a more precise discussion). Let us point out that we do not look for establishing some fine relationships between logics, but on the contrary, we look for pragmatic ones, any *ad hoc* definition of heterogeneous bridge is in fact suitable as soon as one can associate an intuitive meaning to it. For example, the partiality of $Ext_{\mu,\Sigma}$ allows translations from a more expressive formalism to a less expressive one.

Heterogeneous bridges between the logics FG, OBS and ND are defined in an obvious way. From FG to OBS, we forget in the source signature the declaration of the finitely generated sorts and all sorts in the target signature are observable. Models and sentences are preserved, by replacing the set-theoretic equal $=$ by the observational one $\approx$. So, $\Phi_{FG} \Vdash \varphi_{OBS}$ iff $\varphi_{OBS} \in \Phi_{FG} [\approx / =]$. From OBS to FG, we forget the observation part of the signature, no sort is finitely generated and we quotient the source model by the observational equivalence [BH96]. Conversely, we have $\Phi_{OBS} \Vdash \varphi_{FG}$ iff $\varphi_{FG} \in \Phi_{OBS} [= / \approx]$. From FG to ND, we forget the finitely generated sorts in the signature, values become singletons for the models, and we translate the sentences. The reverse bridge is exactly symmetric on *de facto* deterministic models: it allows to transmit the deterministic part of a specification after having forgotten the rest. We obtain a bridge from OBS to ND by combining the previous ones.

2   An Example of HSS: A Travel Agency

Our travel agency selects for its customers the operator which potentially offers the less expensive path from a city to another city. We have classical modules for booleans and positive integers (**Bool** and **Int**). A module **Map** specifies cities and direct links between them. A module **Netwk** specifies networks as sets of links. Then, a module **Path** defines paths in a network as lists of links verifying certain properties. A module **Oper** specifies two operators, each of them owning its own network. Finally, the agency is specified in the module **Agency**. Each module has its own "natural" specification language. Most of them (**Bool, Int, Map, Path, Agency**) are specified according to FG. The networks (**Netwk**) are sets, specified in OBS which is especially adequate for this. **Oper** is specified according to ND. Indeed, as in general routing problems, there can be several paths for a given travel, so that an operator proposes them in a non deterministic way.

3   HHS Theory

3.1   Syntax

We unify all the different notions of specification modules and building primitives by the notion of *specification constructor* [NOS95].

Definition 3. *A constructor universe Θ is a tuple $(\mathcal{C}, \boldsymbol{Spec})$ where*

- $\mathcal{C}$ *is a class of constructors. Each constructor is provided with a profile in Sig^+. We denote such a constructor by $f : \Sigma_1 \ldots \Sigma_n \to \Sigma$ $(n \in I\!N)$.*
- $\boldsymbol{Spec}$ *is a class of well structured specifications which is a subclass of the free term algebra on $\mathcal{C}$, $\mathcal{T}_{\mathcal{C}}$. $\boldsymbol{Spec}$ is closed by sub-terms:*
  $$\forall f : \Sigma_1 \ldots \Sigma_n \to \Sigma \in \mathcal{C}, \forall \tau_1 \in \mathcal{T}_{\mathcal{C},\Sigma_1}, \ldots, \forall \tau_n \in \mathcal{T}_{\mathcal{C},\Sigma_n},$$
  $$f(\tau_1, \ldots, \tau_n) \in \boldsymbol{Spec} \Longrightarrow \forall i = 1 \ldots n, \tau_i \in \boldsymbol{Spec}$$

Reminder: $\mathcal{C}$ *being given, the free term algebra on $\mathcal{C}$ is the least Sig-indexed family $\mathcal{T}_{\mathcal{C}} = \coprod\limits_{\Sigma \in Sig} \mathcal{T}_{\mathcal{C},\Sigma}$ such that for every $(f : \Sigma_1, \ldots, \Sigma_n \to \Sigma) \in \mathcal{C}$, if $\tau_1 \in \mathcal{T}_{\mathcal{C},\Sigma_1}$ and $\ldots$ and $\tau_n \in \mathcal{T}_{\mathcal{C},\Sigma_n}$ $(n \geq 0)$, then $f(\tau_1, \ldots, \tau_n) \in \mathcal{T}_{\mathcal{C},\Sigma}$. Notice that $\mathcal{T}_{\mathcal{C}}$ exists even if $\mathcal{C}$ is a class [DD77].*

By convention, a constructor f will be denoted by c_{text} where c indicates the nature of the constructor (e.g. *use* for an enrichment module) and *text* gives the specific informations of the module (e.g. the exported signature, the axioms, etc), possibly by means of an intermediate identifier (e.g. ΔP). A flat homogeneous presentation $P = (\Sigma, \Gamma)$ can give rise to a constructor of arity 0, $basic_P :\to \Sigma$. Also, say in the first order typed equational logic, each signature morphism $\sigma : \Sigma_1 \to \Sigma_2$ gives rise to $forget_\sigma : \Sigma_2 \to \Sigma_1$, with the obvious meaning of hiding operations as structuring operation. As a third example, we can consider heterogeneous constructors from a logic to another one based on the heterogeneous bridges presented earlier (similar to the deriving primitive introduced in [Tar96]). Each heterogeneous bridge μ allows to define a family of constructors $f = het_{\mu,\Sigma}$ provided with $\Sigma \to Tr_\mu(\Sigma)$ as profile.

Notation *If $\tau \in \mathcal{T}_{\mathcal{C},\Sigma}$, we call Σ the signature of τ. By convention, the signature of τ is denoted by Σ_τ.*
Moreover, we note $\boldsymbol{Spec}_\Sigma = \boldsymbol{Spec} \cap \mathcal{T}_{\mathcal{C},\Sigma} = \{\tau \in \boldsymbol{Spec} \mid \Sigma_\tau = \Sigma\}$

The coincidence of the signatures is a minimal requirement to connect two specification components but some specification modules are intended to be combined only with some peculiar subspecifications. For example the module $use_{\mathbf{Netwk}}$ can only import a **Map** specification such that the provided equality is reflexive, symmetric and transitive. It is the reason why $\boldsymbol{Spec}$ determines a domain for each constructor.

Definition 4. *Given a constructor universe $\Theta = (\mathcal{C}, \boldsymbol{Spec})$, the syntactical domain of a constructor $f : \Sigma_1 \ldots \Sigma_n \to \Sigma$ is the class $\mathcal{D}_f$ of tuples $(\tau_1, \ldots, \tau_n)$ such that $f(\tau_1, \ldots, \tau_n)$ belongs to $\boldsymbol{Spec}$.*

The point is that one should be able to specify a constructor without knowing the formalisms of all its subcomponents, but only the useful properties inherited from the syntactical domain and expressed on the input profile.

We can now give all the significant syntactic elements of the travel agency example: we first give its hierarchical structure by a specification term.

The structure of the specification is built on a *basic* constructor for the **Bool** presentation which does not import anything and *use* constructors for the enrichment modules (**Int, Map, Netwk, Path, Oper, Agency**). Nine heterogeneous constructors (*het*) are needed to connect these heterogeneous components. Moreover, a *forget* constructor U extracts the deterministic part of the non-deterministic specification $\overline{\textbf{Oper}}$, before applying the heterogeneous constructor numbered 9. According to our framework, this specification and its subspecifications are terms on

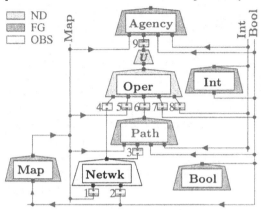

these constructors:

$$\overline{\textbf{Bool}} = basic_{\textbf{Bool}}, \ \overline{\textbf{Int}} = use_{\textbf{Int}}(\overline{\textbf{Bool}}), \ \overline{\textbf{Map}} = use_{\textbf{Map}}(\overline{\textbf{Bool}}),$$

$$\overline{\textbf{Netwk}} = use_{\textbf{Netwk}}(het_1(\overline{\textbf{Map}}), het_2(\overline{\textbf{Bool}}))$$

$$\overline{\textbf{Path}} = use_{\textbf{Path}}(\overline{\textbf{Map}}, het_3(\overline{\textbf{Netwk}}), \overline{\textbf{Bool}}, \overline{\textbf{Int}})$$

$$\overline{\textbf{Oper}} = use_{\textbf{Oper}}(het_4(\overline{\textbf{Netwk}}), het_5(\overline{\textbf{Map}}), het_6(\overline{\textbf{Path}}), het_7(\overline{\textbf{Bool}}), het_8(\overline{\textbf{Int}}))$$

$$\overline{\textbf{Agency}} = \textbf{Agency}(\overline{\textbf{Map}}, het_9(forget_U(\overline{\textbf{Oper}})), \overline{\textbf{Bool}}, \overline{\textbf{Int}})$$

We now make precise the contents of the main *use* constructors. **Map** specifies cities ($\textbf{A}, \textbf{B}, \textbf{C} :\to city$) and direct links ($\textbf{l}(\_, \_) : city \times city \to link$). Netwk specifies sets of links (sort *net*, with $\emptyset :\to net$ as empty-set and $\_ \diamond \_ : link \times net \to net$ as insertion). These sets are observable through membership ($\_ \in \_ : link \times net \to bool$): booleans are observable. Paths in a network are non-empty lists of consecutive links: $\textbf{p}(p, c, c', n)$ means that p is a path from c to c' in the network n; their cost ($\textbf{\$}()$) is their length. We only give the signature of the module **Path**. Conventionally, a star before a symbol points a generator. The **Oper** and **Agency** modules are relevant for

---

Path, FG

Inputs:
  1:Map, 2:Netwk, 3:Bool, 4:Int,
Sorts: *list*
Operations:
  $*[\_] : link \to list;$
  $*\_ :: \_ : link \times list \to list;$
  $\textbf{p}() : list \times city \times city \times net \to bool;$
  $\textbf{\$}() : list \to nat;$
Axioms: $\cdots$

Agency, FG

Inputs: 1:Map, 2:Oper, 3:Bool, 4:Int
Operations: $\textbf{sl}() : city \times city \to oper;$
Axioms:
  1: $\overbrace{\textbf{O}_2, c, c'} > \overbrace{\textbf{O}_1, c, c'} \Leftrightarrow \textbf{sl}(c, c') = \textbf{O}_1$

---

the part of the proof we consider later on. For readability, we have simplified some notations; for example, boolean functions are written like predicates (omitting the "$=\textbf{T}$"), we abbreviate by $\Leftrightarrow$ the corresponding set of conditional positive axioms between boolean values, etc.

Oper, ND

Inputs:

1:Netwk, 2:Map, 3:Path, 4:Bool, 5:Int

Sorts: oper

Operations:

$O_1 :\to oper;$ $O_2 :\to oper;$

$nw() : oper \to net;$

$pt() : oper \times city \times city \to list;$

$\widehat{-,-,-} : oper \times city \times city \to nat;$

Axioms:

1: $O_1 \doteq O_1$ 2: $O_2 \doteq O_2$

3: $nw(O_1) \doteq l(A, B) \diamond l(B, C) \diamond [l(C, A)] \diamond \emptyset$

4: $nw(O_2) \doteq l(C, B) \diamond l(B, A) \diamond [l(A, C)] \diamond \emptyset$

5: $p(pt(o, c, c'), c, c', nw(o)) \doteq T$

6: $[l(A, B)] \prec pt(O_1, A, B)$

7: $\$(pt(o, c, c')) \geq \widehat{o, c, c'}$

8: $\widehat{o, c, c'} \prec \$(pt(o, c, c'))$

The **Oper** specification defines two operators, O_1 and O_2, each of them having its own network ($nw()$). They propose paths from a city to another in a non-deterministic way ($pt()$). A function ($\widehat{-,-,-}$) gives the best cost an operator proposes for a given travel, and then, the agency selects ($sl()$) the operator with the best optimum. This is possible because the optimum function, which is *de facto* deterministic, will be preserved by the *forget* constructor and then imported by **Agency**.

In our proof example, O_1, who proposes a direct path from A to B, will be selected.

3.2 Semantics

Several previous works [Bid87,NOS95] already presented the meaning of enrichment modules as a class of functions from the models of the imported specifications to models of the global one. We consider also primitives in the same way, and the semantics of a constructor f are defined by means of partial functions, from the models of the domain signatures of f to the models of the exported signature of f:

Definition 5. *A* constructor semantics *for a constructor universe* $\Theta = (\mathcal{C}, \mathbf{Spec})$ *is a* $\mathcal{C}$-*indexed family* $\mathbf{Sem} = \coprod_{f \in \mathcal{C}} \mathbf{Sem}_f$ *such that for each* $f :$ $\Sigma_1 \ldots \Sigma_n \to \Sigma$ *in* $\mathcal{C}$, *the elements of* $\mathbf{Sem}_f$, *called* implementations *of* f, *are partial functions* ν *from* $mod(\Sigma_1) \times \ldots \times mod(\Sigma_n)$ *to* $mod(\Sigma)$. *Each definition domain* D_ν *is called the* semantic domain *of the constructor implementation* ν.

Let us give 3 examples to illustrate this idea. First, the semantics of a homogeneous presentation $basic_P$ can be seen as a set of constant functions of arity zero, one for each flat model of $Mod(P)$. Second, a natural choice for a classical constructor $forget_\sigma$ is $\mathbf{Sem}_{forget_\sigma} = \{mod(\sigma) : mod(\Sigma_2) \to mod(\Sigma_1)\}$. $mod(\sigma)$ is often called the "forgetful functor" and is usually denoted by $\mathcal{U}_\sigma$. So, the semantics of $forget_\sigma$ is reduced to $\{\mathcal{U}_\sigma\}$. The semantics of heterogeneous bridge constructors $f = het_{\mu, \Sigma} : \Sigma \to Tr_\mu(\Sigma)$ are given by the corresponding model extraction functions: $\mathbf{Sem}_{het_{\mu, \Sigma}} = \{Ext_{\mu, \Sigma}\}$.

Definition 6. *Given* $\Theta = (\mathcal{C}, \mathbf{Spec})$ *and* $\mathbf{Sem}$, *a* $(\Theta, \mathbf{Sem})$-realization *is a partial substitution* $\rho : \mathcal{C} \to \mathbf{Sem}$ *such that* $\rho(f)$, *when it is defined, belongs to* $\mathbf{Sem}_f$. *We note* $\mathbf{Sem}(\Theta)$ *the class of all* $(\Theta, \mathbf{Sem})$-realizations.

Notation *Given a (Θ, Sem)-realization $\rho : \mathcal{C} \to Sem$, we note $\bar{\rho} : Spec \to mod(Sig)$ the partial canonical extension of ρ to $Spec$.
Notice that $\bar{\rho}(f(\tau_1, \ldots, \tau_n))$ is defined if and only if: $\rho(f)$ and all the $\bar{\rho}(\tau_i)$ are defined, and $(\bar{\rho}(\tau_1), \ldots, \bar{\rho}(\tau_n))$ belongs to $D_{\rho(f)}$, the semantic domain of $\rho(f)$.*

The partiality of ρ should not confuse the reader here: it simply means that to realize a specification τ, it is not necessary to implement *all* other constructors that do not belong to τ. On the contrary, the partiality of $\bar{\rho}$ is significant. It means that incompatible implementations of the constructors of τ never result into a realization of τ. Finally, we can give the following definition:

Definition 7. *Given $\Theta = (\mathcal{C}, Spec)$, Sem, and a well structured specification τ in $Spec$, the class of all flattened models of τ is:*
$$\mathcal{M}od(\tau) = \{M \in mod(\Sigma_\tau) \mid \exists \rho \in Sem(\Theta), M = \bar{\rho}(\tau)\}.$$

Our substitution mechanism ensures that a constructor f still keeps the same implementation even for two occurrences which do not import the same subspecifications. It encompasses approaches dedicated to subspecification sharing within an homogeneous setting.

3.3   Inference Relation

We define heterogeneous inference relations similarly as [Wir93,HST94] did for homogeneous specifications. We define below a general mechanism of property transmission through a constructor. A HHS theory is then obtained by considering a sound heterogeneous inference relation for each constructor.

Definition 8. *A HHS theory is a tuple $(\Theta, Sem, \Vdash)$ where Θ is a constructor universe, Sem is a constructor semantics over Θ and $\Vdash$ is a $\mathcal{C}$-indexed family of local heterogeneous inference relations, $\Vdash = \coprod\limits_{f \in \mathcal{C}} \Vdash_f$, such that for each constructor $f : \Sigma_1 \ldots \Sigma_n \to \Sigma \in \mathcal{C}$, $\Vdash_f$ is a binary relation included in $\mathcal{P}(\coprod\limits_{i=1\ldots n} sen(\Sigma_i)) \times sen(\Sigma)$, sound with respect to Sem:*

$$\forall (\Phi, \varphi) \in \Vdash_f, \, \forall \tau = f(\tau_1, \ldots, \tau_n) \in Spec, \, \forall \bar{\rho}(\tau) \in \mathcal{M}od(\tau),$$
$$(\forall i = 1 \ldots n, \, \bar{\rho}(\tau_i) \models \Phi \cap sen(\Sigma_i)) \Longrightarrow \bar{\rho}(\tau) \models \varphi$$

4   Heterogeneous Structured Proofs

4.1   Inference System

There are two kinds of step in our heterogeneous inference system: homogeneous steps ($\vdash$) and constructor steps ($\Vdash$).

Definition 9. *$(\Theta, Sem, \Vdash)$ being given, the corresponding inference system is the least binary relation $\lVert\!\Vdash \subseteq Spec \times sen(Sig)$ such that, for any $\tau \in Spec$*

- $\lVert\!\Vdash$ is transitive via $\vdash$:
  $$\forall \Gamma \subseteq sen(\Sigma_\tau), \, \forall \varphi \in sen(\Sigma_\tau), \, (\tau \lVert\!\Vdash \Gamma) \wedge (\Gamma \vdash \varphi) \Longrightarrow (\tau \lVert\!\Vdash \varphi).$$

– ⊩ is transitive via ⊩ : *when τ is of the form $f(\tau_1, \ldots, \tau_n)$*

$$\forall \Gamma \subseteq \coprod_{i=1 \ldots n} sen(\Sigma_{\tau_i}), \ \forall \varphi \in sen(\Sigma_\tau)$$

$$[(\forall i = 1 \ldots n, \ (\tau_i \Vdash \Gamma \cap sen(\Sigma_{\tau_i}))) \wedge (\Gamma \Vdash \varphi)] \implies (\tau \Vdash \varphi)$$

With such steps, we can deduce a sentence ξ from the axioms of a heterogeneous specification SP ($SP \Vdash \xi$). The figure below illustrates how the structure of the proof follows the term structure of the specification. It also introduces our conventional proof notations. The different grey scales represent different logics. The white interstices separate the input/output sides in the structure. Properties get over it with the $\Vdash_f$-relations (doubles lines). On this shape we inherit $\delta_1(\lambda)$ from P_1 and $\delta_2(\varphi)$ from P_2 to prove ξ in the ΔP module, using its homogeneous inference $\vdash$ (simple lines). The properties inherited from P_2 are translated through the inference associated to the constructor het_{μ, Σ_2}.

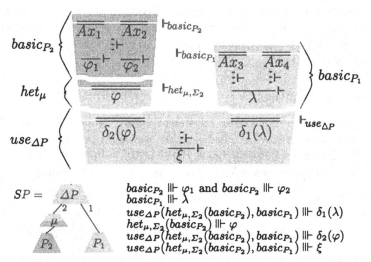

$$SP = \Delta P$$

$basic_{P_2} \Vdash \varphi_1$ and $basic_{P_2} \Vdash \varphi_2$
$basic_{P_1} \Vdash \lambda$
$use_{\Delta P}(het_{\mu, \Sigma_2}(basic_{P_2}), basic_{P_1}) \Vdash \delta_1(\lambda)$
$het_{\mu, \Sigma_2}(basic_{P_2}) \Vdash \varphi$
$use_{\Delta P}(het_{\mu, \Sigma_2}(basic_{P_2}), basic_{P_1}) \Vdash \delta_2(\varphi)$
$use_{\Delta P}(het_{\mu, \Sigma_2}(basic_{P_2}), basic_{P_1}) \Vdash \xi$

Proposition 10. *For any HHS theory , the corresponding inference system is sound. This means that for any specification τ and for any sentence φ in $sen(\Sigma_\tau)$, we have:* $\tau \Vdash \varphi \implies (\forall M \in \mathcal{M}od(\tau), \ M \models \varphi)$

The structure of a heterogeneous proof deliberately follows the structure of the specification. A direct consequence is that if a module f_1 is based on a poorly expressive logic, and if it imports a module f_2 based on a powerful logic, then f_1 will be unable to pass some properties of f_2, even to a higher level module f_0 based on the same logic as f_2. So, ⊩ is intrinsically not complete[4]. A heterogeneous proof is neither harder nor easier than a structured proof w.r.t a purely homogeneous hierarchical specification. The only specific knowledges are the constructor inferences. For *basic* and *use* constructors, it is simply the axiom introduction and/or the transmission of all the imported properties through the involved signature morphisms.

---

[4] [HST94] already pointed out that their proof search procedure was not complete for many-sorted equational logic and first-order logic with equality.

4.2   Proof Example

As illustration, let us prove that for a travel from the city A to the city B, the operator O_1 will be selected. The cost of a path being its length, O_1 is

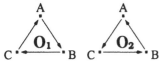

better. The general aspect of the proof is drawn in a figure given on the next page, where only the main lemmas are mentioned (rules w.r.t. ND given in Annex).

Let $x \geq 2 \wedge 1 \geq z \Rightarrow x > z$ (proved in **Int**) be denoted **@1** and $l(A, B) \in \clubsuit \approx F$ (proved in **Netwk**) be denoted **@2**, where $\clubsuit$ denotes the network of O_2: $l(C, B) \diamond l(B, A) \diamond [l(A, C)] \diamond \emptyset$. Let $p(p, A, B, \clubsuit) \Rightarrow \$(p) \geq 2$ be denoted **@8** (proved in **Path**, by induction on the length of the paths). We prove $sl(A, B) = O_1$ in **Agency**, using the inherited properties $1 \geq \widehat{O_1, A, B} \doteq T$ denoted **@5** and using $\widehat{O_2, A, B} \geq 2 \doteq T$ denoted **@11** which are proved later on in $\overline{\text{Oper}}$. (**@1**, **@2** and **@8** are formally proved in [Cou98,CLGB97])

The annotation to the right of each inference line follows the following conventions: ax means axiom introduction (resp. as when substituted); u means imported via a *use* constructor (resp. h for a heterogeneous bridge); the subscript of ax or as indicates the source module (its first character) and the superscript indicates the axiom number; the subscript of u indicates the top level module of the *use* constructor and the superscript indicates the number of the considered import slot; the subscript of h indicates the number of the bridge on the specification shape. Moreover, obvious sequences of elementary inference rules are contracted into one step. For example: the axioms are often introduced in an already instanciated form; we exploit directly any useful consequence of *modus ponens*. We also abreviate $s(s(o))$ as 2 (resp. $s(o)$ as 1).

Proof of $sl(A, B) = O_1$ in Agency:

$$\cfrac{\cfrac{\cfrac{\cfrac{@1}{x \geq 2 \wedge 1 \geq z \Rightarrow x > z} u_A^4}{\widehat{O_2, A, B} \geq 2 \wedge 1 \geq \widehat{O_1, A, B} \Rightarrow \widehat{O_2, A, B} > \widehat{O_1, A, B}} \; SUB \quad \cfrac{@5}{1 \geq \widehat{O_1, A, B} = T} h_9 u_A^2}{\widehat{O_2, A, B} \geq 2 \Rightarrow \widehat{O_2, A, B} > \widehat{O_1, A, B} \; @12} MP}{\quad}$$

$$\cfrac{\cfrac{\widehat{O_2, A, B} > \widehat{O_1, A, B} \Rightarrow sl(A, B) = O_1}{} as_A^1 \qquad \cfrac{@12 \quad \cfrac{@11}{\widehat{O_2, A, B} \geq 2 = T} h_9 u_A^2}{\widehat{O_2, A, B} > \widehat{O_1, A, B}} MP}{sl(A, B) = O_1} MP$$

Proof of @5 in Oper:

$$\cfrac{\cfrac{\cfrac{}{\$(pt(o, c, c')) \geq \widehat{o, c, c'}} ax_o^7 \quad \cfrac{\cfrac{A = A}{A \doteq A} REF}{} h_5 u_o^2 \quad \cfrac{\cfrac{B = B}{B \doteq B} REF}{} h_5 u_o^2 \quad \cfrac{}{O_1 \doteq O_1} ax_o^1}{\$(pt(O_1, A, B)) \geq \widehat{O_1, A, B} \; @4} sub}{\quad}$$

$$\cfrac{\cfrac{@4 \quad [l(A, B)] \prec pt(O_1, A, B)}{\$([l(A, B)]) \geq \widehat{O_1, A, B}} \cfrac{ax_o^6}{rg3} \qquad \cfrac{\$([l(A, B)]) = 1}{\cfrac{\$([l(A, B)]) \doteq 1}{}} \cfrac{as_P^6}{h_5 u_o^3}{rg2}}{1 \geq \widehat{O_1, A, B} \; @5}$$

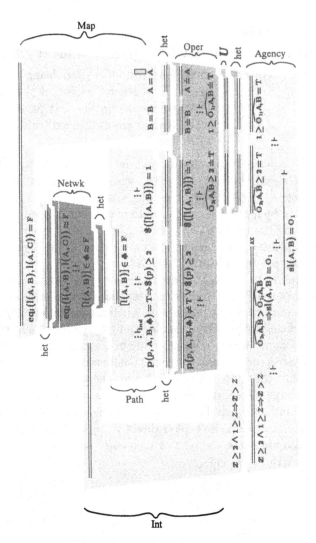

Proof of @11 in Oper, using @8:

$$\cfrac{\overline{\overline{p(pt(o,c,c'),c,c',nw(o))}}\ ax^5_O \quad \overline{\overline{A \doteq A}}\ _{REF}h_5u^2_O \quad \overline{\overline{B \doteq B}}\ _{REF}h_5u^2_O \quad \overline{\overline{O_2 \doteq O_2}}\ ax^2_O}{p(pt(O_2,A,B),A,B,nw(O_2))}\ @6\ sub$$

$$\cfrac{@6 \quad \overline{\overline{nw(O_2) \doteq \clubsuit}}\ ax^4_O}{p(pt(O_2,A,B),A,B,\clubsuit)}\ @7\ rg2$$

$$\cfrac{@7 \quad \cfrac{\cfrac{@8}{p(p,A,B,\clubsuit) \neq T \vee \$(p) \geq 2}\ h_6u^3_O \quad \overline{\overline{pt(O_2,A,B) \doteq pt(O_2,A,B)}}\ h_6u^3_O}{p(pt(O_2,A,B),A,B,\clubsuit) \neq T \vee \$(pt(O_2,A,B)) \geq 2}\ sub}{\$(pt(O_2,A,B)) \geq 2}\ cut\ @9$$

$$\cfrac{\cfrac{\overline{\widehat{o,c,c'} \prec \$(pt(o,c,c'))}}{} \; ax_o^8 \quad \overline{\overline{A \doteq A}} \; {}_{\text{\tiny REF}} h_5 u_O^2 \quad \overline{\overline{B \doteq B}} \; {}_{\text{\tiny REF}} h_5 u_O^2 \quad \overline{\overline{O_2 \doteq O_2}} \; ax_o^2}{\widehat{O_2, A, B} \prec \$(pt(O_2, A, B)) \quad @10} \; sub$$

$$\cfrac{@10 \quad @9}{\widehat{O_2, A, B} \geq 2 \quad @11} \; rg3$$

5   Conclusion

Our approach of hierarchical heterogeneous structuring is resolutely both formal and pragmatic. Our first motivation was to manage heterogeneous libraries of already implemented modules, for reuse purposes: in the French telecommunication project ECOS/CNET, hardware components specified in VHDL have to cooperate in a system with software components.

From this point of view, we do not want to look for equivalence between formalisms, or completness of proofs, but a good compromise between a sufficient power to prove what is usually needed and a reasonable simplicity in order to preserve legibility and *tractability*. For this reason, we do not require the heterogeneous bridges to be optimal in any sense.

One of the main contributions of this article is to systematically represent HHS by terms. It gives a very unified view of the hierarchical structuring mechanisms and allows us to manipulate HHS very easily, owning to the well established corpus on terms, substitutions, etc. It provides us with a well suited framework for "in the large" issues, and contributes to get a clearer view of how to heterogeneously combine formal methods in software engineering.

The agency example outlined here has been inspired by a more general routing problem in telecommunication networks. It is of course considerably simplified with respect to the original problem, however it remains representative enough to illustrate our approach. It indicates that all classical algebraic specifications approaches can be almost freely heteregeneously mixed together. This result is already very encouraging and significant. Netherless, we have tried to allow a broader scope by reducing as much as possible the hypotheses about homogeneous logics. This will hopefully allow to specialize our heterogeneous framework to model oriented specifications as well (Z,B,VDM,...). Our current researches exploit this flexibility and the term approach facilities. With our approach, it becomes possible to rigorously treat the heterogeneous refinements of a module. It amounts to replace a specification constructor by a "piece of term" which can be itself heterogeneous. A next question is possibly: "is it possible to handle object oriented structures in a similar manner?" (which is a bit out of the scope of this paper). Following the heterogeneous proof method of this article, we would also like to invent what integration testing of HHS could be [LGA96]. Details on definitions, specifications and proofs outlined in this article can be found in [Cou98,CLGB97].

References

AC92.   E. Astesiano and M. Cerioli. Relationships between logical frameworks. In *Recent Trends in Data Type Specification*, volume 655, pages 101–126, Dourdan, 1992. LNCS.

AC94.   E. Astesiano and M. Cerioli. Multiparadigm specification languages: a first attempt at foundations. *Semantics of Specification Languages*, Workshops in Computing, pages 168–185. Springer Verlag, 1994.

BCLG96. G. Bernot, S. Coudert, and P. Le Gall. Towards heterogeneous formal specifications. In *AMAST'96, Munich*, volume 1101, pages 458–472. Springer, LNCS, 1996.

BH96.   M. Bidoit and R. Hennicker. Behavioural theories and the proof of behavioural properties. *Theoretical Computer Science*, 165 (1):3–55, 1996.

Bid87.   M. Bidoit. The stratified loose approach : a generalization of initial and loose semantics. In *Recent Trends in Data Type Specification, Gullane, Scotland*, pages 1–22. Springer-Verlag LNCS 332, July 1987.

BLGA94. G. Bernot, P. Le Gall, and M. Aiguier. Label algebras and exceptions handling. *Journal of Science of Computer Programming*, 23:227–286, 1994.

BST99.   M. Bidoit, D. Sannella, and A. Tarlecki. Architectural specification in casl. In *AMAST'98, Amazonia-Manaus*, volume to appear. Springer, LNCS, 1999.

CLGB97. S. Coudert, P. Le Gall, and G. Bernot. An example of heterogeneous structured specification. Université d'Evry, Report 28-1997, 1997.

CM97.   M. Cerioli and J. Meseguer. May I borrow your logic? *Theoritical Computer Sciences*, 173(2):311–347, 1997.

CoF96.   CoFI. Common framework initiative. EATCS Bulletin, 1996.

Cou98.   S. Coudert. Hiérarchie et hétérogénéité dans les spécifications formelles. Forthcoming Thesis, Université d'Évry, France, 1998.

DD77.   R. Douady and A. Douady. *Algèbre et théories galoisiennes, Tome 1 (Algèbre)*. CEDIC, Nathan, Paris, 1977.

DGS93.   R. Diaconescu, J. Goguen, and P. Stefaneas. Logical support for modularisation. In G. Huet and G. Plotkin, editors, *Proc. Workshop on Types and Logical Frameworks*, pages 83–130, 1993.

EM85.   H. Ehrig and B. Mahr. *Fundamentals of Algebraic Specification 1. Equations and initial semantics*, volume 6. Springer-Verlag,EATCS Monographs on Theoretical Computer Science, 1985.

GB92.   J. A. Goguen and R. M. Burstall. Institutions: Abstract model theory for specification and programming. *Journal of the Association for Computing Machinery*, 39:95–146, 1992.

HST94.   R. Harper, D. Sannella, and A. Tarlecki. Structured theory presentations and logic representations. *Annals of Pure and Applied Logic*, 67, 1994.

LGA96.   P. Le Gall and A. Arnould. Formal specifications and test: Correctness and oracle. In *Recent Trends in Data Type Specification, Oslo, Norway, September 1995*, pages 342–358. Springer-Verlag LNCS 1130, 1996.

Mes89.   J. Meseguer. General logics. In *Proc. Logic. Colloquium '87*, Amsterdam, 1989. North-Holland.

Mes97.   J. Meseguer. Membership algebra as a logical framework for equational specification. In *Recent Trends in Data Type Specification*, volume 1376, pages 18–61, Tarquinia, LNCS, 1997.

NOS95.   M. Navarro, F. Orejas, and A. Sanchez. On the correctness of modular systems. *Theoretical Computer Science*, 140:139–177, 1995.

Pad96.   P. Padawitz. Swinging data types: Syntax, semantics, and theory. In *Recent Trends in Data Type Specifications, Oslo, Norway, September 1995*, pages 409–435. Springer-Verlag LNCS 1130, 1996.

PW92.   D.E. Perry and A.L. Wolf. Foundations for the study of software architectures. *ACM SIGSOFT, Software Engineering Notes*, pages 40–52, 1992.

SS96.   A. Salibra and G. Scollo. Interpolation and compactness in categories of pre-institutions. *Mathematical Structures in Computer Science*, 6:261–286, 1996.

Tar96.   A. Tarlecki. Moving between logical systems. In *Recent Trends in Data Type Specifications, Oslo*, pages 478–502. Springer-Verlag LNCS 1130, 1996.

Wir93.   M. Wirsing. Structured specifications: syntax, semantics and proof calculus. In Brauer W. Bauer F. and Schwichtenberg H., editors, *Logic and Algebra of Specification*, pages 411–442. Springer, 1993.

WM95.   M. Walicki and S. Meldal. A complete calculus for the multialgebraic and functional semantics of nondeterminism. ACM Transactions on Programming Langages and Systems, 17: 2, p. 366-393, 1995-03, 1995.

Annex

Inference system for ND ([WM95]):

R1:   a- $\dfrac{}{x \neq y, x \doteq y}\ rg1$ b- $\dfrac{}{x \neq t, x \prec t}\ rg1$ $x, y \in \mathcal{V}$

R2: $\dfrac{C_t^x \quad D, s \doteq t}{C_s^x, D}\ rg2$

R3: $\dfrac{C_t^x \quad D, s \prec t}{C_s^x, D}\ rg3$ x not in a right-hand side of $\prec$ in C.

R4: $\dfrac{C, s \preceq t \quad D, s \neq t}{C, D}\ cut$ ($\preceq$ being either $\doteq$ or $\prec$)

R5: $\dfrac{C}{C, e}\ wea$

R6: $\dfrac{C, x \neq t}{\vdash C_t^x}\ eli$ $x \in \mathcal{V} - \mathcal{V}[t]$, at most one x in C

Derived rules:

PER: a- $\dfrac{}{x \doteq x}\ per$ b- $\dfrac{}{t \prec t}\ per$

REN: $\dfrac{C}{C_y^x}\ ner$

SUB: $\dfrac{C \quad D, t \doteq t}{C_t^x, D}\ sub$

INTR: $\dfrac{C_t^y}{C_x^y, x \neq t}\ inc$ y not in a right-hand side of $\prec$

Parallel Admissible Graph Rewriting

Rachid Echahed and Jean-Christophe Janodet

Laboratoire LEIBNIZ – Institut IMAG, CNRS
46, Av. Felix Viallet, F-38031 Grenoble – France
Tel: (+33) 4 76 57 48 91,
Fax: (+33) 4 76 57 46 02
{Rachid.Echahed,Jean-Christophe.Janodet}@imag.fr

Abstract. We investigate the rewrite relation over graphs induced by constructor-based weakly orthogonal graph rewriting systems. It is well known that this relation is not confluent in general whereas it is confluent in the case of weakly orthogonal term rewriting systems. We show, however, that the considered relation is always confluent, as well as confluent modulo bisimilarity, for a large class of graphs called admissible graphs. Afterwards, we define a parallel graph rewriting relation and propose an efficient parallel graph rewriting strategy.

1 Introduction

Graph rewriting is being considered in many different areas ; see for instance [9, 15]. The contributions of this paper are theoretical results which concern graph rewriting as operational semantics of functional or algebraic programming languages [13, 5]. There are many straightforward reasons which motivate the use of graphs in the setting of declarative languages. For instance, graphs allow to represent expressions in a compact way thanks to the sharing of sub-expressions; they also permit to handle efficiently cyclic graphs which represent complex data structures as in imperative languages.

In practice, many functional programming languages are constructor-based, i.e., operators called *constructors*, which are intended to construct data structures, are distinguished from operators called *defined operators*, which are defined by means of rewrite rules. In this paper, we follow this discipline and investigate new graph rewriting systems which could be seen as a natural extension to graphs of the well known weakly orthogonal constructor-based term rewriting systems. Below, we give a sample of the considered graph rewriting systems.

```
ones    -> n:cons(1,n)         B(T,F,x) -> ones
f(x,1) -> cons(x,n:cons(1,n))  B(F,x,T) -> ones
f(1,x) -> n:cons(1,n)          B(x,T,F) -> ones
```

J.L. Fiadeiro (Ed.): WADT'98, LNCS 1589, pp. 122–137, 1999.

It is well known that weakly orthogonal term rewriting systems are confluent. However, this property does not hold for graphs even if the considered
graph rewriting system is orthogonal [10]. Indeed, the orthogonal system
which consists of the rules (R1) $A(x) \rightarrow x$ and (R2) $B(x) \rightarrow x$ induces a confluent rewrite relation on terms and a non confluent rewrite
relation on graphs as it is shown by the following counter-example [10] :
the graph n:A(B(n)) may be rewritten into two different normal forms,
namely, u:A(u) and v:B(v). The source of the non confluence of the
graph rewriting system above comes from the use of the so-called collapsing rules. A rule is collapsing if its right-hand side is a variable. However,
collapsing rules cannot be prohibited in any programming discipline since
most of access functions (e.g., car, cdr) are defined by means of collapsing
rules.

In this paper, we investigate first the confluence of the graph rewrite
relation in the framework of weakly orthogonal constructor-based graph
rewriting systems. We show that the rewrite relation is confluent, even in
the presence of collapsing rules, for a wide class of graphs called admissible
graphs. A graph is admissible if its cycles do not include defined operators
(see Definition 1).

Efficient implementation of functional languages encodes terms as
dags. The soundness of such an encoding can be easily obtained when the
considered graph rewriting system is confluent modulo bisimilarity. Two
graphs are bisimilar if they represent the same rational term. We show
that the considered graph rewriting systems are also confluent modulo
bisimilarity.

The property of confluence allows to evaluate admissible graphs in
a deterministic way by using rewriting strategies. For constructor-based
weakly orthogonal term rewriting systems, efficient strategies have been
proposed in the literature. For example, O'Donnell has shown that
parallel-outermost strategy is normalizing [12], Sekar and Ramakrishnan [16] as well as Antoy [1] improved O'Donnell's strategy by proposing
strategies which rewrite in parallel a necessary set of redexes. Their extension to graphs is not such an easy task. Indeed, the notion of outermost
redexes in a cyclic graph is not always meaningful and parallel reductions of graphs that share some subgraphs need some care. We propose
a graph rewriting strategy which reduces admissible graphs in parallel at
some necessary set of outermost redexes. This strategy is a conservative
extension of the one presented for terms in [1].

The rest of the paper is organized as follows : The next section lists
some definitions and notations used later in the paper. Section 3 defines

the graph rewriting systems we consider and establishes some confluence results. In Section 4, a parallel graph rewriting relation is proposed as well as an efficient parallel graph rewriting strategy. Section 5 concludes the paper. Due to lack of space, all the proofs have been omitted. They can be consulted in [7, 6].

2   Definitions and notations

Many different notations are used in the literature to investigate graph rewriting [9, 17, 14]. The aim of this section is to recall briefly some key definitions in order to make easier the understanding of the paper. We are mostly consistent with [5]. Some precise definitions which are omitted can be found in [6].

A *many-sorted signature* $\Sigma = \langle S, \Omega \rangle$ consists of a set S of sorts and an S-indexed family of sets of operation symbols $\Omega = \uplus_{s \in S} \Omega_s$ with $\Omega_s = \uplus_{(w,s) \in S^* \times S} \Omega_{w,s}$. We shall write $f : s_1 \ldots s_n \to s$ whenever $f \in \Omega_{s_1 \ldots s_n, s}$ and say that f is of *sort s* and *rank* $s_1 \ldots s_n$. We consider a graph as a set of nodes and edges between the nodes. Each node is labeled with an operation symbol or a variable. Let $\mathcal{X} = \uplus_{s \in S} \mathcal{X}_s$ be an S-indexed family of countable sets of *variables* and $\mathcal{N} = \uplus_{s \in S} \mathcal{N}_s$ an S-indexed family of countable sets of *nodes*. We assume that $\mathcal{X}$ and $\mathcal{N}$ are fixed throughout the rest of the paper.

A *graph g* over $\langle \Sigma, \mathcal{N}, \mathcal{X} \rangle$ is a tuple $g = \langle \mathcal{N}_g, \mathcal{L}_g, \mathcal{S}_g, \mathcal{R}oots_g \rangle$ such that $\mathcal{N}_g$ is a set of nodes, $\mathcal{L}_g : \mathcal{N}_g \to \Omega \cup \mathcal{X}$ is a *labeling function* which maps to every node of g an operation symbol or a variable, $\mathcal{S}_g$ is a *successor function* which maps to every node of g a (possibly empty) string of nodes and $\mathcal{R}oots_g$ is a set of distinguished nodes of g, called its *roots*. We also assume three conditions of well definedness. (1) Graphs are well typed : a node n is of the same sort as its label $\mathcal{L}_g(n)$, and its successors $\mathcal{S}_g(n)$ are compatible with the rank of $\mathcal{L}_g(n)$. (2) Graphs are connected : for all nodes $n \in \mathcal{N}_g$, there exist a root $r \in \mathcal{R}oots_g$ and a path from r to n. A *path* from a node n_0 to a node n_k is a sequence $[n_0, i_0, n_1, \ldots, i_{k-1}, n_k]$ of alternating nodes and integers such that $k \geq 1$ and n_{p+1} is the $i_p{}^{th}$ successor of n_p for all $p \in 0..k-1$. (3) Let $\mathcal{V}(g)$ be the set of variables of g. For all $x \in \mathcal{V}(g)$, there exists one and only one node $n \in \mathcal{N}_g$ such that $\mathcal{L}_g(n) = x$.

A *term graph* is a (possibly cyclic) graph with one root denoted $\mathcal{R}oot_g$. Two term graphs g_1 and g_2 are *bisimilar*, denoted $g_1 \doteq g_2$, iff they represent the same (infinite) tree when one unravels them [3]. We write $g_1 \sim g_2$ when the term graphs g_1 and g_2 are equal up to renaming of nodes.

As the formal definition of graphs is not useful to give examples, we introduce a linear notation [5]. In the following grammar, the variable A (resp. n) ranges over the set $\Omega \cup \mathcal{X}$ (resp. $\mathcal{N}$) :

GRAPH ::= NODE | NODE + GRAPH
NODE ::= $n{:}A$(NODE,...,NODE) | n

The set of roots of a graph defined with a linear expression contains the first node of the expression and all the nodes appearing just after a +.

Example 1. In Fig. 1, we give two examples of graphs denoted G and T. The term graph G is given by (1) $\mathcal{N}_G = \{n1, \ldots, n5\}$, (2) $\mathcal{R}oot_G = n1$, (3) $\mathcal{L}_G$ is defined by $\mathcal{L}_G(n1) = \mathcal{L}_G(n5) = c$, $\mathcal{L}_G(n2) = g$, $\mathcal{L}_G(n3) = s$ and $\mathcal{L}_G(n4) = a$ and (4) $\mathcal{S}_G$ is defined by $\mathcal{S}_G(n1) = n2.n5$, $\mathcal{S}_G(n2) = n3.n3$, $\mathcal{S}_G(n3) = n4$, $\mathcal{S}_G(n4) = \varepsilon$ and $\mathcal{S}_G(n5) = n3.n1$. An equivalent description of G is n1:c(n2:g(n3:s(n4:a),n3),n5:c(n3,n1)). On the other hand, T is a graph with two roots $\{$l1,r1$\}$ representing a rewrite rule (see Def. 2) : $T =$ l1:g(l2:s(l3:x),l4:s(l5:y)) + r1:s(r2:g(l3,l4)).

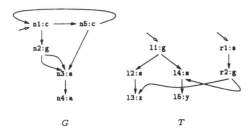

Fig. 1.

A *subgraph* of a graph g rooted by a node p, denoted $g_{|p}$, is built by considering p as a root and deleting all the nodes which are not accessible from p in g (e.g., $G_{|n2} =$ n2:g(n3:s(n4:a),n3) in Fig. 1). The *sum* of two graphs g_1 and g_2, denoted $g_1 \oplus g_2$, is the graph whose nodes and roots are those of g_1 and g_2 and whose labeling and successor functions coincide with those of g_1 and g_2.

A *pointer redirection* from a node p to a node q is a function $\rho : \mathcal{N} \rightarrow \mathcal{N}$ such that $\rho(p) = q$ and $\rho(n) = n$ for all nodes $n \neq p$. More generally, if $p_1, \ldots, p_n, q_1, \ldots, q_n$ are some nodes, we define the *(multiple) pointer redirection* ρ from p_1 to q_1, $\ldots$, p_n to q_n as the function $\rho : \mathcal{N} \rightarrow \mathcal{N}$ such that $\rho(p_i) = q_i$ for all $i \in 1..n$ and $\rho(p) = p$ for all nodes p such that $p \neq p_1$, $p \neq p_2$, $\ldots$ and $p \neq p_n$.

Given a graph g and a pointer redirection $\rho = \{p_1 \mapsto q_1, \ldots, p_n \mapsto q_n\}$, we define $\rho(g)$ as the graph whose nodes and labeling function are those of g, whose successor function satisfies $\mathcal{S}_{\rho(g)}(n) = \rho(n_1) \ldots \rho(n_k)$ if $\mathcal{S}_g(n) = n_1 \ldots n_k$ for some $k \geq 0$ and whose roots are $\mathcal{R}oots_{\rho(g)} = \{\rho(n_1), \ldots, \rho(n_k), p_1, p_2, \ldots, p_n\}$ if $\mathcal{R}oots_g = \{n_1, \ldots, n_k\}$.

Given two term graphs g and u and a node p of the same sort as $\mathcal{R}oot_u$, we define the *replacement by u of the subgraph rooted by p in g*, denoted $g[p \leftarrow u]$, in three stages : (i) Let $H = g \oplus u$. (ii) Let ρ be the pointer redirection from p to $\mathcal{R}oot_u$, $H' = \rho(H)$ and $r = \rho(\mathcal{R}oot_g)$. (iii) $g[p \leftarrow u] = H'|_r$.

Example 2. Let G be the term graph of Example 1 and $D = $ r1:s(r2:g(n4:a,n3:s(n4))). The sum $G \oplus D$ is given by n1:c(n2:g(n3:s(n4:a),n3),n5:c(n3,n1)) + r1:s(r2:g(n4,n3)) (see Fig. 2). Let ρ be the pointer redirection such that $\rho(\text{n2}) = $ r1 and $\rho(p) = p$ for all nodes $p \neq$ n2. The graph $\rho(G \oplus D)$ is defined by n1:c(r1:s(r2:g(n4:a,n3:s(n4))),n5:c(n3,n1)) + n2:g(n3,n3). Thus the replacement by D of the subgraph rooted by n2 in G is defined by $G[\text{n2} \leftarrow D] = $ n1:c(r1:s(r2:g(n4:a,n3:s(n4)),n5:c(n3,n1)). An

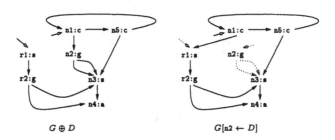

$$G \oplus D \qquad\qquad G[\text{n2} \leftarrow D]$$

Fig. 2.

example of multiple pointer redirection is shown in Fig. 3 where the graph H' is obtained from H by applying $\rho = \{p2 \mapsto r1, p4 \mapsto r1\}$.

A *(rooted) homomorphism h* from a graph g_1 to a graph g_2, denoted $h : g_1 \rightarrow g_2$, is a mapping from $\mathcal{N}_{g_1}$ to $\mathcal{N}_{g_2}$ such that $\mathcal{R}oots_{g_2} = h(\mathcal{R}oots_{g_1})$ and for all nodes $n \in \mathcal{N}_{g_1}$, if $\mathcal{L}_{g_1}(n) \notin \mathcal{X}$ then $\mathcal{L}_{g_2}(h(n)) = \mathcal{L}_{g_1}(n)$ and $\mathcal{S}_{g_2}(h(n)) = h(\mathcal{S}_{g_1}(n))$ and if $\mathcal{L}_{g_1}(n) \in \mathcal{X}$ then $h(n) \in \mathcal{N}_{g_2}$. If $h : g_1 \rightarrow g_2$ is a homomorphism and g is a subgraph of g_1 rooted by p, then we write $h(g)$ for the subgraph $g_{2|h(p)}$. If $h : g_1 \rightarrow g_2$ is a homomorphism and g is a graph, $h[g]$ is the graph obtained from g by replacing all the subgraphs shared between g and g_1 by their corresponding subgraphs in g_2. A term graph l *matches* a graph g at node n if there exists a homomorphism $h : l \to g_{|n}$. h is called *the matcher* of l on g at node n. Two term graphs g_1 and g_2 are *unifiable* if there exist a term graph g and a homomorphism $h : (g_1 \oplus g_2) \to g$ such that $h(g_1) = h(g_2) = g$. Such an h is called a *unifier* of g_1 and g_2.

Example 3. Consider the subgraph $G_{|n2}$ of Example 1, let $L =$ `11:g(12:s(13:x),14:s(15:y))` and μ the mapping from $\mathcal{N}_L$ to $\mathcal{N}_{(G_{|n2})}$ such that $\mu(11) = $ n2, $\mu(12) = \mu(14) = $ n3 and $\mu(13) = \mu(15) = $ n4. μ is a homomorphism from L to $G_{|n2}$, thus L matches G at node n2. On the other hand, let $R = $ `r1:s(r2:g(13:x,14:s(15:y)))`. R and L share the subgraphs `13:x` and `14:s(15:y)` whose images by μ are respectively `n4:a` and `n3:s(n4:a)`. Hence $\mu[R] = $ `r1:s(r2:g(n4:a,n3:s(n4)))`, i.e., $\mu[R]$ is the graph D of Example 2. Finally, consider the term graphs $L1 = $ `n1:f(n2:a,n3:x)` and $L2 = $ `m1:f(m2:y,m3:s(m4:a))`. $L1$ and $L2$ are unifiable since there exist a term graph $L3 = $ `p1:f(p2:a,p3:s(p4:a))` and a homomorphism $v : (L1 \oplus L2) \to L3$ such that $v(L1) = v(L2) = L3$.

3   Admissible graph rewriting

This section introduces the different classes of graph rewriting systems we consider and establishes new confluence results. For practical reasons, many declarative languages use constructor-based signatures. A *constructor-based signature* Σ is a triple $\Sigma = \langle S, C, D \rangle$ where S is a set of sorts, C is an S-indexed family of sets of *constructor symbols* whose rôle consists in building data structures and D is an S-indexed family of sets of *defined operations* such that $C \cap D = \emptyset$ and $\langle S, C \cup D \rangle$ is a signature. For instance, in Example 1, we suppose that c, s and a are constructors and g is a defined operation.

In the rest of the paper, we investigate graph rewriting for the class of *admissible* term graphs (atg). Roughly speaking, an atg corresponds, according to the imperative point of view, to nested procedure (function) calls whose parameters are complex constructor cyclic graphs (i.e., classical data structures).

Definition 1. *Let g be a term graph over a constructor-based signature $\Sigma = \langle S, C, D \rangle$. A node $n \in \mathcal{N}_g$ is called a* defined node *if $\mathcal{L}_g(n)$ is a defined operation ($\in D$). g is an* admissible term graph (atg) *if there exists no path from a defined node of g to itself. An atg g is a* pattern *if g has a tree structure (i.e., linear first-order term) which has one and only* *one defined operation at its root. A* constructor graph *is a graph with no defined node. An atg is* operation-rooted *if its root is a defined node.*

Example 4. The term graph G of Example 1 is admissible but $z:g(z,z)$ and $z:g(n:s(z),n)$ are not (since g is a defined operation which belongs to a cycle). $11:g(12:a,13:a)$ is a pattern whereas $11:g(12:a,12)$ is not.

The next definition introduces the notion of admissible rewrite rule. Such rules are tailored so that the set of atgs is closed by the rewrite relation induced by admissible rules (see Remark 1).

Definition 2. *A* rewrite rule *is a graph with two roots, denoted* $l \to r$. *l (resp. r) is a term graph called the* left-hand side *(resp. right-hand side) of the rule. A rule $l \to r$ is an* admissible rule *iff (1) l is a pattern (thus an atg), (2) r is an atg, (3) l is not a subgraph of r and (4) $\mathcal{V}(r) \subseteq \mathcal{V}(l)$. A rule e' is a* variant *of another rule e if e and e' are equal up to renaming of nodes and variables and all the nodes and the variables of e' are new. We say that two admissible rules $l_1 \to r_1$ and $l_2 \to r_2$* overlap *iff their left-hand sides are unifiable.*

Example 5. The graph T of Example 1 is an admissible rule. An example of a non admissible rule is given in Remark 1.

Definition 3. *A* constructor-based graph rewriting system (cGRS) *is a pair $SP = \langle \Sigma, \mathcal{R} \rangle$ where $\Sigma = \langle S, C, D \rangle$ is a constructor-based signature and $\mathcal{R}$ is a set of admissible rules.*
We say that SP is an admissible graph rewriting system (AGRS) *iff every two distinct rules in $\mathcal{R}$ do not overlap.*
We say that SP is a weakly admissible graph rewriting system (WAGRS) *iff $\mathcal{R}$ is a set of admissible rules such that if two rules $l_1 \to r_1$ and $l_2 \to r_2$ overlap, then their instantiated right-hand sides are equal up to renaming of nodes, i.e., if there exist a term graph g and a homomorphism $h : (l_1 \oplus l_2) \to g$ such that $h(l_1) = h(l_2) = g$, then $h[r_1] \sim h[r_2]$.*

Example 6. Consider the following cGRS :

```
(R1)  11:f(12:a,13:x) -> r1:d(r1,13:x)
(R2)  11:f(12:x,13:s(14:y)) -> r1:d(r1,r2:s(14:y))
(R3)  11:g(12:a,13:x) -> r1:s(r2:a)
(R4)  11:g(12:x,13:a) -> r1:s(12:x)
```

(R5) `l1:g(l2:s(l3:x),l4:s(l5:y)) ->`

$$\text{r1:s(r2:g(l3:x,l4:s(l5:y)))}$$

(R6) `l1:h(l2:x,l3:y) -> r1:h(l2:x,l3:y)`

R1 and R2 (resp. R3 and R4) overlap and their instantiated right-hand sides are equal up to renaming of nodes. Thus this cGRS is a WAGRS.

Below, we recall the definition of a graph rewriting step [5].

Definition 4. *Let* $SP = \langle \Sigma, \mathcal{R} \rangle$ *be a cGRS,* g_1 *an atg,* g_2 *a graph,* $l \to r$ *a variant of a rewrite rule of* $\mathcal{R}$ *and* p *a node of* g_1. *We say that* g_1 *rewrites to* g_2 *at node* p *using the rule* $l \to r$ *and write* $g_1 \to_{[p,l \to r]} g_2$ *if there exists a homomorphism* $h : l \to g_{1|p}$ *(i.e.,* l *matches* g_1 *at node* p*) and* $g_2 = g_1[p \leftarrow h[r]]$. *In this case, we say that* $g_{1|p}$ *is a redex of* g_1 *rooted by* p. $\xrightarrow{*}$ *denotes the reflexive and transitive closure of* $\to$.

Example 7. According to Example 3, L matches G at node n2 with homomorphism μ and $\mu[R] = $ `r1:s(r2:g(n4:a,n3:s(n4)))`. As $\mu[R]$ is equal to the graph D of Example 2, we infer that $G[\text{n2} \leftarrow \mu[R]] = $ `n1:c(r1:s(r2:g(n4:a,n3:s(n4))),n5:c(n3,n1))`. Let G' be this last graph. By Definition 4, $G \to_{[\text{n2}, L \to R]} G'$.

We can prove that the set of atgs is stable w.r.t. rewriting with admissible rules [6], i.e., if g_1 is an atg and $g_1 \to_{[p,l \to r]} g_2$ is a rewriting step, then g_2 is an atg. In the following example, we show that the set of atgs is not stable w.r.t. non admissible rewrite rules :

Remark 1. The rule `l1:g(l2:a,l3:x)` $\to$ `r1:g(l1,r2:a)` is not admissible since the root of its left-hand side is a node of its right-hand side, thus its left-hand side is a subgraph of its right-hand side, i.e., Condition 3 of Def. 2 is not fulfilled. By using this rule, the reader may check that the atg `n1:g(n2:a,n3:a)` is rewritten into `r1:g(r1,r2:a)`. This last graph is not an atg, since the defined operation g belongs to a cycle.

The property of confluence is one of the main properties of rewrite relations. We consider here the classical notion of confluence as well as confluence modulo bisimilarity. The reader may find in [4] a survey of confluence properties over acyclic term graphs.

Definition 5. *Let* $SP = \langle \Sigma, \mathcal{R} \rangle$ *be a cGRS. We say that the rewriting relation* $\to$ *is confluent modulo renaming of nodes* $\sim$ *(resp. bisimilarity* $\doteq$*) w.r.t. atgs iff for all atgs* g_1, g_2, g_1' *and* g_2' *such that* $g_1 \sim g_2$ *(resp.* $g_1 \doteq g_2$*),* $g_1 \xrightarrow{*} g_1'$ *and* $g_2 \xrightarrow{*} g_2'$, *there exist two atgs* g_1'' *and* g_2'' *such that* $g_1' \xrightarrow{*} g_1''$, $g_2' \xrightarrow{*} g_2''$ *and* $g_1'' \sim g_2''$ *(resp.* $g_1'' \doteq g_2''$*).*

We have seen in Section 1 that confluence (modulo bisimilarity) of AGRSs is not a straightforward extension of that of orthogonal term rewriting systems. In [11], it is proved that orthogonal graph rewriting systems (and thus AGRSs) are confluent modulo the equivalence of the so-called hypercollapsing graphs. A graph g is hypercollapsing if $g \to g$. We are not interested in confluence modulo the equivalence of hypercollapsing graphs in the present paper.

Theorem 1. *Let SP be a WAGRS. $\to$ is confluent modulo $\sim$ and $\doteq$ w.r.t. atgs.*

Since bisimilar graphs are naturally handled in the setting of graphs, one may wonder whether the class of weakly orthogonal graph rewriting systems, such that the instantiated right-hand sides of overlapping rules are bisimilar (and not necessarily equal up to renaming of nodes), still defines a rewrite relation which is confluent modulo bisimilarity or not.

Definition 6. *Let $SP = \langle \Sigma, \mathcal{R} \rangle$ be a cGRS. We say that SP is a bisimilar weakly admissible graph rewriting system (bWAGRS) iff $\mathcal{R}$ is a set of admissible rules such that if two rules $l_1 \to r_1$ and $l_2 \to r_2$ overlap, then their instantiated right-hand sides are bisimilar, i.e., if there exist a term graph g and a homomorphism $h : (l_1 \oplus l_2) \to g$ such that $h(l_1) = h(l_2) = g$, then $h[r_1] \doteq h[r_2]$.*

Example 8. Consider the following rules :

```
(S1)  11:f(12:a,13:x) -> r1:d(r2:d(r1,13:x),13)
(S2)  11:f(12:x,13:s(14:a)) -> r1:d(r1,r2:s(r3:a))
```

As the rules S1 and S2 overlap and their instantiated right-hand sides are bisimilar, this cGRS is a bWAGRS.

It is clear that a bWAGRS cannot be confluent modulo renaming of nodes, in general. Nevertheless, a bWAGRS may be confluent modulo bisimilarity. We can prove this property in the case where a bWAGRS is Noetherian w.r.t. atgs (i.e., for all atgs g, there is no infinite derivation $g \to g_1 \to g_2 \to \ldots$).

Theorem 2. *Let SP be a bWAGRS which is Noetherian w.r.t. atgs. Then $\to$ is confluent modulo $\doteq$ w.r.t. atgs.*

When a bWAGRS is not Noetherian w.r.t. atgs, we conjecture that the rewrite relation $\to$ is still confluent modulo $\doteq$ w.r.t. atgs.

4   Parallel admissible graph rewriting

In this section we propose a definition of parallel graph rewriting relation and define an efficient strategy for it. If parallel rewriting can be easily conceived in the framework of first-order terms, this is unfortunately not the case when one has to deal with graph structures. The main difficulty comes essentially from the sharing of subgraphs. In [13, Chap. 14], parallel graph rewriting has been investigated w.r.t. implementation point of view. That is to say, some annotations are proposed to be added to right-hand sides in order to indicate which redexes can be evaluated in parallel. In the following definition, we are rather interested in the general notion of *parallel* graph rewriting which allows to reduce several arbitrary redexes of an atg in one shot.

Definition 7. *Let* $SP = \langle \Sigma, \mathcal{R} \rangle$ *be a cGRS,* g_1 *an atg,* g_2 *a graph,* $l_1 \to r_1, \ldots, l_n \to r_n$ *n variants of rewrite rules of* $\mathcal{R}$ *and* $p_1, \ldots, p_n$ *n distinct nodes of* g_1. *We say that* g_1 *rewrites in parallel to* g_2 *at nodes* $p_1, \ldots, p_n$ *using the rules* $l_1 \to r_1, \ldots, l_n \to r_n$ *and write*

$$g_1 \xrightarrow{\ \ \ } _{[p_1, l_1 \to r_1]\ldots[p_n, l_n \to r_n]} g_2 \ \textit{iff} :$$

1. *There exists n homomorphisms* $h_i : l_i \to g_{1|p_i}$ *for all* $i \in 1..n$.
2. *Let* $H = g \oplus h_1[r_1] \oplus \ldots \oplus h_n[r_n]$.
3. *Let* $\rho_1, \ldots, \rho_n$ *be the pointer redirections such that for all* $i \in 1..k$, $\rho_i(p_i) = \mathcal{R}oot_{h_i[r_i]}$ *and* $\rho_i(p) = p$ *for all nodes* p *such that* $p \neq p_i$.
4. *Let* $\rho = \rho_{\mu(1)} \circ \ldots \circ \rho_{\mu(n)}$ *where* $\mu : 1..n \to 1..n$ *is a permutation such that if* $i < j$, *then there exists no path from* $p_{\mu(i)}$ *to* $p_{\mu(j)}$.
5. *Let* $H' = \rho(H)$ *and* $r = \rho(\mathcal{R}oot_g)$.
6. $g_2 = H'_{|r}$.

Condition (4) in the previous definition can always be fulfilled. Its rôle is to take into account the relative positions of the different redexes to be transformed so that the parallel rewrite relation $\xrightarrow{\ \ \ }$ can be simulated by sequential rewriting $\to$. Indeed, consider for example the pointer redirection ρ' such that $\rho'(p_i) = \mathcal{R}oot_{h_i[r_i]}$ for all $i \in 1..n$ and $\rho'(p) = p$ for all nodes p such that $p \neq p_1, \ldots, p \neq p_n$. ρ', which seems to be the natural candidate as a pointer redirection to define a parallel rewrite relation, does not always satisfy Condition (4). The reader may verify (see also [7]) that the parallel rewrite relation induced by ρ', say $\xrightarrow{\ \ \ }$, cannot be simulated by sequential rewriting $\to$, i.e., $\xrightarrow{\ \ \ }$ is not included in $\xrightarrow{*}$.

Example 9. Let $g = \mathtt{p1:d(p2:u(p3:a),p4:v(p2))}$ be an atg and $l_1 \to r_1$ and $l_2 \to r_2$ two admissible rules such that $l_1 = \mathtt{11:u(12:x)}$, $r_1 =$

r1:s(12:x), $l_2 = 13$:v(14:y) and $r_2 = 14$:y. l_1 matches g at node
p2 using the homomorphism $h_1 : l_1 \to g_{|p2}$ and $h_1[r_1] = $ r1:s(p3:a).
On the other hand, l_2 matches g at node p4 using the homomorphism
$h_2 : l_2 \to g_{|p4}$ and $h_2[r_2] = $ p2:u(p3:a). Let $H = g \oplus h_1[r_1] \oplus h_2[r_2] = $
p1:d(p2:u(p3:a),p4:v(p2)) + r1:s(p3) + p2 (see Fig. 3). Let $\rho_1 = $

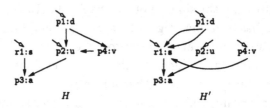

Fig. 3.

{p2 $\mapsto$ r1} and $\rho_2 = $ {p4 $\mapsto$ p2}. There exists a path from p4 to p2 in g
but none from p2 to p4. So we define $\rho = \rho_1 \circ \rho_2 = $ {p2 $\mapsto$ r1, p4 $\mapsto$ r1}.
The reader may check that $\rho(H) = H' = $ p1:d(r1:s(p3:a),r1) + r1
+ p2:u(p3) + p4:v(r1) and $\rho(\mathcal{R}oot_g) = $ p1. Hence, by Definition 7,
$g \overset{}{\longmapsto}_{[p2,l_1\to r_1][p4,l_2\to r_2]} g_2$ where $g_2 = $ p1:d(r1:s(p3:a),r1).

Proposition 1. *Let SP be a cGRS. If $g_1 \overset{}{\longmapsto} g_2$, then $g_1 \overset{*}{\to} g_2$. If $g_1 \to g_2$, then $g_1 \overset{}{\longmapsto} g_2$.*

Theorem 3. *Let $SP = \langle \Sigma, \mathcal{R} \rangle$ be an WAGRS. $\overset{}{\longmapsto}$ is confluent modulo $\sim$ and $\doteq$ w.r.t. atgs.*

In the rest of this section we describe a parallel graph rewriting strategy for WAGRSs which is c-hyper-normalyzing and computes necessary sets of redexes. We need first some preliminary definitions.

Definition 8. *Let $SP = \langle \Sigma, \mathcal{R} \rangle$ be a cGRS. A parallel graph rewriting strategy is a partial function $\bar{S}$ which takes an atg g and returns a set of pairs (p, R) such that p is a node of g, R is a rewrite rule of $\mathcal{R}$ and g can be rewritten at node p using the rule R. We write $g \to_{\bar{S}} g'$ to denote the parallel $\bar{S}$-step from g to g' such that $g \overset{}{\longmapsto}_{\bar{S}(g)} g'$. A strategy $\bar{S}$ is c-normalizing iff for all atgs g and constructor graphs c such that $g \overset{*}{\to} c$, there exists a graph c' such that $g \overset{}{\longmapsto}^*_{\bar{S}} c'$ and $c' \doteq c$. A strategy $\bar{S}$ is c-hyper-normalizing iff for all atgs g and constructor graphs c such that $g \overset{*}{\to} c$, every derivation D starting with g which alternates $\bar{S}$-steps with other reduction steps ends with a constructor graph c' such that $c' \doteq c$.*

Definition 9. *Let $SP = \langle \Sigma, \mathcal{R} \rangle$ be a cGRS, g and g' two atgs and $B = g \overset{*}{\to} g'$ a rewriting derivation. A defined node q in g is a residual node by B if q remains a node of g'. We call* descendant *of $g_{|q}$ the subgraph $(g')_{|q}$. A redex u rooted by q in g is a* needed *redex iff in every rewriting derivation from g to a constructor graph, a descendant of $g_{|q}$ is rewritten at its root q. A set of redexes $S = \{u_1, \ldots, u_n\}$ of g is a* necessary *set of redexes iff in every rewriting derivation from g to a constructor graph, a descendant of at least one redex $u \in S$ is rewritten at its root. A redex u rooted by q in g is an* outermost *redex iff $q = \mathcal{R}oot_g$ when g is a redex or else $S_g(\mathcal{R}oot_g) = r_1 \ldots r_k$ and u is an outermost redex of $g_{|r_i}$ for some $i \in 1..k$. A node q is the* leftmost-outermost *defined node of g iff $q = \mathcal{R}oot_g$ when $\mathcal{R}oot_g$ is a defined node or else $S_g(\mathcal{R}oot_g) = r_1 \ldots r_k$ and there exists $i \in 1..k$ such that q is the leftmost-outermost defined node of $g_{|r_i}$ and the subgraphs $g_{|r_j}$ are constructor graphs for all $j < i$.*

Example 10. Let $g = \texttt{n1:f(n2:f(n3:a,n3),n4:f(n2,n3))}$ where $\texttt{f}$ is defined with the rules (T1) $\texttt{l1:f(l2:x,l3:a)} \to \texttt{l2:x}$ and
(T2) $\texttt{l1:f(l2:a,l3:y)} \to \texttt{l3:y}$. The subgraphs $g_{|n2}$ and $g_{|n4}$ are outermost redexes (though there exists a path from $\texttt{n4}$ to $\texttt{n2}$). The leftmost-outermost defined node of g is $\texttt{n2}$. The set $S = \{g_{|n2}, g_{|n4}\}$ is a necessary set of redexes of g. None of them is a needed redex of g. Actually, the notion of needed redex is irrelevant in the framework of WAGRSs.

Our strategy is based on an extension of definitional trees [1] to the context of WAGRSs. A definitional tree is a hierarchical structure whose leaves are the rules of a WAGRS used to define some operation. In the following definition, *branch* and *rule* are uninterpreted symbols, used to construct the nodes of a definitional tree.

Definition 10. *Let $SP = \langle \Sigma, \mathcal{R} \rangle$ be a WAGRS. A tree $\mathcal{T}$ is a* partial definitional tree*, or* pdt*, with pattern π iff one of the following cases holds :*

- *$\mathcal{T} = rule(\pi \to r)$, where $\pi \to r$ is a variant of a rule of $\mathcal{R}$.*
- *$\mathcal{T} = branch(\pi, o, \mathcal{T}_1, \ldots, \mathcal{T}_k)$, where o is a node of π, o is labelled with a variable, o is of sort s, $c_1, \ldots, c_k$ $(k > 0)$ are different constructors of the sort s and for all $j \in 1..k$, $\mathcal{T}_j$ is a pdt with pattern $\pi[o \leftarrow p : c_j(o_1 : X_1, \ldots, o_n : X_n)]$, such that n is the number of arguments of c_j, $X_1, \ldots, X_n$ are new variables and $p, o_1, \ldots, o_n$ are new nodes.*

We write *pattern*$(\mathcal{T})$ to denote the pattern argument of $\mathcal{T}$. A definitional tree $\mathcal{T}$ of a defined operation f is a finite pdt with a pattern of the form

$p:f(o_1:X_1,\ldots,o_n:X_n)$ where n is the number of arguments of f, $X_1,\ldots,$ X_n are new variables and $p,o_1,\ldots,o_n$ are new nodes. A forest of definitional trees (fdt) $\mathcal{F}$ of an operation f is a set of definitional trees such that every rule defining f appears in one and only one tree in $\mathcal{F}$.

Example 11. Consider the WAGRS defined in Example 6. A definitional tree $\mathcal{T}_g^1$ of the operation g is represented in Fig. 4 and formally defined by

$$\mathcal{T}_g^1 = branch(\text{k1:g}(\underline{\text{k2:X1}},\text{k3:X2}),\text{k2},$$
$$rule(\text{k4:g}(\text{k5:a},\text{k6:X3}) \to \text{k7:s}(\text{k8:a})),$$
$$branch(\text{k9:g}(\text{k10:s}(\text{k11:X4}),\underline{\text{k12:X5}}),\text{k12},$$
$$rule(\text{k13:g}(\text{k14:s}(\text{k15:X6}),\text{k16:s}(\text{k17:X7})) \to$$
$$\text{k18:s}(\text{k15},\text{k16}))))$$

Notice that the rule R4 of Example 6 is not represented by a leaf of $\mathcal{T}_g^1$. Actually, it is impossible to build only one definitional tree which contains all the rules defining g. This is why we introduced the notion of fdts. In Fig. 4, we represent possible fdts $\mathcal{F}_f = \{\mathcal{T}_f^1,\mathcal{T}_f^2\}$, $\mathcal{F}_g = \{\mathcal{T}_g^1,\mathcal{T}_g^2\}$ and $\mathcal{F}_h = \{\mathcal{T}_h\}$ corresponding to the operations f, g and h of Example 6.

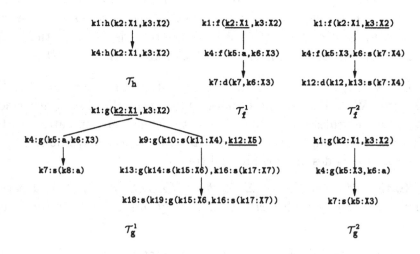

Fig. 4.

We are now ready to define our parallel graph rewriting strategy $\bar{\Phi}$. The strategy $\bar{\Phi}$ is a partial function that operates on atgs in the presence of a WAGRS. $\bar{\Phi}(g)$ returns, when it is possible, a set of pairs (p, R) where p is a node of g and R is a rewrite rule such that g can be rewritten at node p using the rule R. $\bar{\Phi}$ uses two auxiliary functions $\bar{\varphi}$ and $Outer$. $\bar{\varphi}$ takes two arguments : an operation-rooted atg and a pdt of this operation.

Definition 11. *Let $SP = \langle \Sigma, \mathcal{R} \rangle$ be a WAGRS, g an operation-rooted atg and $\mathcal{T}$ a pdt such that $pattern(\mathcal{T})$ matches g at the root. We define the partial function $\bar{\varphi}$ by :*

$$\bar{\varphi}(g,\mathcal{T}) = \begin{cases} \{(p,R)\} & \text{if } \mathcal{T} = rule(\pi \to r),\ p = \mathcal{R}oot_g \text{ and} \\ & R \text{ is a variant of } \pi \to r ; \\ \bar{\varphi}(g,\mathcal{T}_i) & \text{if } \mathcal{T} = branch(\pi, o, \mathcal{T}_1, \ldots, \mathcal{T}_k) \text{ and} \\ & pattern(\mathcal{T}_i) \text{ matches } g \text{ for some } i \in 1..k ; \\ S & \text{if } \mathcal{T} = branch(\pi, o, \mathcal{T}_1, \ldots, \mathcal{T}_k), \\ & \pi \text{ matches } g \text{ using the homomorphism } h, \\ & h(o) \text{ is labeled with a defined operation } f \text{ in } g, \\ & \mathcal{F} = \{\mathcal{T}_1', \ldots, \mathcal{T}_k'\} \text{ is an fdt of } f \text{ and} \\ & S = \bar{\varphi}(g_{|h(o)}, \mathcal{T}_1') \cup \ldots \cup \bar{\varphi}(g_{|h(o)}, \mathcal{T}_k'). \end{cases}$$

In the definition above, $\bar{\varphi}(g, \mathcal{T})$ computes a set S of pairs (p, R) where p is a node of g and R is a rule whose left-hand side matches g at node p. Some pairs (p, R) in S may be useless. Therefore, we define the function $Outer(g, S)$ which chooses a maximal set consisting of outermost defined nodes of S w.r.t. g. If an outermost defined node p occurs several times in S, only one pair (p, R) will appear in $Outer(g, S)$. $Outer(g, S)$ can be defined in a deterministic way by using some ordering on the rewrite rules.

Definition 12. *Let $SP = \langle \Sigma, \mathcal{R} \rangle$ be a WAGRS, g an atg and $S = \{(p_1, R_1), \ldots, (p_n, R_n)\}$ a set of pairs such that p_i is a node of g and R_i is an admissible rule. We define $Outer(g, S)$ as a maximal subset $\{(q_1, S_1), \ldots, (q_k, S_k)\}$ of S such that :*

1. *For all $i, j \in 1..k$, $i \neq j \Longrightarrow q_i \neq q_j$.*
2. *For all $i \in 1..k$, there exists a path $[\mathcal{R}oot_g, i_0, u_1, i_1, \ldots, i_{k-1}, q_i]$ such that for all $j \in 0..k-1$, for all rewrite rules R, $(u_j, R) \notin S$.*

Definition 13. *Let $SP = \langle \Sigma, \mathcal{R} \rangle$ be a WAGRS, g an atg, p the leftmost-outermost defined node of g, f the label of the node p in g and $\mathcal{F} = \{\mathcal{T}_1, \ldots, \mathcal{T}_k\}$ a forest of definitional trees of f. $\bar{\Phi}$ is the partial function defined by $\bar{\Phi}(g) = Outer(g, S)$ where $S = \bar{\varphi}(g_{|p}, \mathcal{T}_1) \cup \ldots \cup \bar{\varphi}(g_{|p}, \mathcal{T}_k)$.*

Example 12. Consider the fdts of Example 11. Let $g =$
`n1:c(n2:f(n3:h(n4:g(n5:a,n5),n6:g(n4,n5)),n6),n7:c(n6,n1))`.

By Definition 13, $\bar{\Phi}(g) = Outer(g, S)$ where

$$
\begin{aligned}
S &= \bar{\varphi}(g_{|n2}, \mathcal{T}_f^1) \cup \bar{\varphi}(g_{|n2}, \mathcal{T}_f^2) \\
&= \bar{\varphi}(g_{|n3}, \mathcal{T}_h) \cup \bar{\varphi}(g_{|n6}, \mathcal{T}_g^1) \cup \bar{\varphi}(g_{|n6}, \mathcal{T}_g^2) \\
&= \{(n3, k1:h(k2:X1,k3:X2) \rightarrow k4:h(k2,k3))\} \cup \\
&\quad \bar{\varphi}(g_{|n4}, \mathcal{T}_g^1) \cup \bar{\varphi}(g_{|n4}, \mathcal{T}_g^2) \cup \\
&\quad \{(n6, k4:g(k5:X3,k6:a) \rightarrow k7:s(k5))\} \\
&= \{(n3, k1:h(k2:X1,k3:X2) \rightarrow k4:h(k2,k3)), \\
&\quad (n4, k4:g(k5:a,k6:X3) \rightarrow k7:s(k8:a)), \\
&\quad (n4, k4:g(k5:X3,k6:a) \rightarrow k7:s(k5)), \\
&\quad (n6, k4:g(k5:X3,k6:a) \rightarrow k7:s(k5))\}
\end{aligned}
$$

By Condition (2) in Def. 12, $Outer(g, S)$ selects the outermost redexes of S in g, thus $\bar{\Phi}(g) = \{(n3, R6), (n6, R4)\}$. Notice that S contains two pairs with the node n4, namely (n4, R3) and (n4, R4). If $g_{|n4}$ was also an outermost redex of g, then Condition (1) of Def. 12 requires to choose one pair among (n4, R3) and (n4, R4) in order to compute $\bar{\Phi}(g)$. This choice is irrelevant since rewriting g using R3 or R4 leads to the same graph (by the definition of a WAGRS).

Theorem 4. *The redexes computed by $\bar{\Phi}(g)$ constitute a necessary set of redexes.*

As a particular case of the theorem above, it is easy to see that if SP is an AGRS such that for all defined operations f, there exists one definitional tree which contains all the rules defining f, then $\bar{\Phi}(g)$ computes a singleton $\{(p, R)\}$ such that $g_{|p}$ is a needed redex in g [6].

From the previous theorem, we deduce that if an atg g can be rewritten to a constructor graph c, then every derivation from g to c must contain a step which rewrites a node p using a rule R for some $(p, R) \in \bar{\Phi}(g)$.

Theorem 5. $\bar{\Phi}$ *is c-hyper-normalizing (thus c-normalizing).*

5 Conclusion

We gave new confluence results for a wide class of programs described by means of constructor-based graph rewriting systems and conjecture that the bisimilar weakly orthogonal admissible graph rewriting systems are confluent modulo bisimilarity. We also proposed a c-hypernormalizing parallel graph rewriting strategy, $\bar{\Phi}$, which computes necessary sets of redexes in the presence of weakly orthogonal admissible graph rewriting systems. In fact, this set is optimal with respect to strategies that do not consider the right-hand sides of the rules. The proof of this claim needs for example the machinery of so-called arbitrary reductions. The reader may find in [16, 2] good hints for it. Our strategy, which computes redexes that can be reduced in parallel, departs from the parallel graph rewriting proposed in [13] where emphasis is made on the way parallelism could be implemented on parallel machines. However, $\bar{\Phi}$ can be efficiently implemented by using the annotations proposed in [13]. $\bar{\Phi}$ can also be lifted to a complete narrowing strategy by extending the results in [8].

References

[1] S. Antoy. Definitional trees. In *Proc. of ALP'92*, pages 143–157. LNCS 632, 1992.

[2] S. Antoy, R. Echahed, and M. Hanus. Parallel evaluation strategies for functional logic languages. In *Proc. of ICLP'97*, pages 138–152, Portland, 1997. MIT Press.

[3] Z.M. Ariola and J.W. Klop. Equational term graph rewriting. *Fundamenta Informaticae*, 26(3-4), 1996.

[4] Z.M. Ariola, J.W. Klop, and D. Plump. Confluent rewriting of bisimilar term graphs. *Electronic Notes in Theoretical Computer Science*, 7, 1997.

[5] H. Barendregt, M. van Eekelen, J. Glauert, R. Kenneway, M. J. Plasmeijer, and M. Sleep. Term graph rewriting. In *PARLE'87*, pages 141–158. LNCS 259, 1987.

[6] R. Echahed and J. C. Janodet. On constructor-based graph rewriting systems. Technical report, IMAG, 1997. Available via URL : ftp://ftp.imag.fr/pub/LEIBNIZ/ATINF/c-graph-rewriting.ps.gz.

[7] R. Echahed and J. C. Janodet. On weakly orthogonal constructor-based graph rewriting. Technical report, 1998. Available via URL : ftp://ftp.imag.fr/pub/LEIBNIZ/ATINF/wa-c-graph-rewriting.ps.gz.

[8] R. Echahed and J.C. Janodet. Admissible graph rewriting and narrowing. In *Proc. of JICSLP'98*, pages 325–340. MIT Press, June 1998.

[9] H. Ehrig and G. Taentzer. Computing by graph transformation : A survey and annotated bibliography. *Bulletin of the EATCS*, 59:182–226, June 1996.

[10] J. R. Kennaway, J. K. Klop, M. R. Sleep, and F. J. De Vries. On the adequacy of graph rewriting for simulating term rewriting. *ACM Transactions on Programming Languages and Systems*, 16(3):493–523, 1994.

[11] J. R. Kennaway, J. K. Klop, M. R. Sleep, and F. J. De Vries. Transfinite reduction in orthogonal term rewriting systems. *Information and Computation*, 119(1):18–38, 1995.

[12] M. J. O'Donnell. *Computing in Systems Described by Equations*. LNCS 58, 1977.

[13] R. Plasmeijer and M. van Eekelen. *Functional Programming and Parallel Graph Rewriting*. Addison-Wesley, 1993.

[14] D. Plump. Term graph rewriting. In H. Ehrig, G. Engels, H.-J. Kreowski, and G. Rozenberg, editors, *Handbook of Graph Grammars and Computing by Graph Transformation*, volume 2. World Scientific, to appear.

[15] Grzegorz Rozenberg. *Handbook of Graph Grammars and Computing by Graph Transformations*, volume 1. World Scientific, 1997.

[16] R. C. Sekar and I. V. Ramakrishnan. Programming in equational logic: Beyond strong sequentiality. *Information and Computation*, 104(1):78–109, May 1993.

[17] M. R. Sleep, M. J. Plasmeijer, and M. C. J. D. van Eekelen, editors. *Term Graph Rewriting. Theory and Practice*. J. Wiley & Sons, Chichester, UK, 1993.

Refinements and Modules for Typed Graph Transformation Systems *

Martin Große-Rhode[1], Francesco Parisi Presicce[2], and Marta Simeoni[2]

[1] TU Berlin, FB Informatik, Germany
[2] Università di Roma *La Sapienza*, Dip. Scienze dell'Informazione, Italy

Abstract. Spatial and temporal refinement relations between typed graph transformation systems have been introduced in [6,7]. In a spatial refinement a transformation rule is refined by an amalgamation of rules while in a temporal refinement it is refined by a sequence of rules: in both cases, the refinement relation supports the modeling of implementation. In the first part of this paper, we further investigate the properties of spatial and temporal refinements while, in the second part, we employ them for the development of a module concept for typed graph transformation systems. Finally, as a first step towards an algebra of modules, we introduce the operations of union and composition of modules.

1 Introduction

Modules have been initially introduced in the programming languages framework (Ada packages and Modula–2 modules, for example) and then defined also for algebraic specifications (see [3]). In this paper we present a new module concept for Typed Graph Transformation Systems (TGTS), which are a widely known formal specification framework for dynamically evolving systems, where states are modeled by typed graphs and state transitions by typed graph transformations.

There are many definitions of a module for various kinds of formalisms but, changing the perspective, we can think to all of them as implementations of the *abstract* notion of module: a module is a syntactical unit that implements some features and offers (eventually part of) them to the outside environment. Their implementation may be realized using some other features offered by other modules and imported from the outside environment.

Following the definition of algebraic specification modules [3], our modules for TGTSs (TGTS–modules) are composed by three TGTSs playing, respectively, the role of an import interface, an export interface and a body that implements the services offered by the export interface. The import interface and the body are related by a simple inclusion morphism so that the body can use the imported features. The export interface and the body are related by a spatial or temporal

* This research is partially supported by the EC under TMR Network GETGRATS (GEneral Theory of GRAph Transformation Systems) and Esprit Working Group APPLIGRAPH.

refinement morphism, so that the exported services can be implemented by the body. By defining the sematics of a TGTS–module as the semantics of the export interface, we hide the information about the services implementation.

The paper is organized as follows: in the next section we recall the basic definitions and facts about typed graphs and TGTSs and, in section 3, we present definitions and properties of the temporal and spatial refinement morphisms. TGTS–modules are introduced in section 4, and the composition and union operations of TGTS–modules are presented in section 5. Full proofs can be found in the technical report [8].

2 Preliminaries

In this section we recall the basic definitions and properties of typed graphs and typed graph transformation systems. A *graph* $G = (N, E, src, tar)$ is given by a set N of nodes, a set E of edges and functions $src, tar : E \to N$ that assign source and target nodes to edges. A *graph morphism* $f = (f_N, f_E) : G \to G'$ is given by functions $f_N : N \to N'$ and $f_E : E \to E'$ such that $src' \circ f_E = f_N \circ src$ and $tar' \circ f_E = f_N \circ tar$. With identities and composition being defined componentwise, this defines the category **Graph**.

As in [2,6,7], we use type graphs as structuring means: let $TG \in$ **Graph** be a fixed graph, called *typed graph*. A *TG–typed graph* (G, t_G) is given by a graph G and a graph morphism $t_G : G \to TG$. A *morphism of TG–typed graphs* $f : (G, t_G) \to (G', t_{G'})$ is a graph morphism $f : G \to G'$ that satisfies $t_{G'} \circ f = t_G$. With composition and identities this yields the category **Graph**$_{TG}$. Note that **Graph**$_{TG}$ is the comma category **Graph** over TG, thus it is complete and cocomplete. Wherever the type graph TG is clear from the context, we denote a TG–typed graph G with the pair (G, t_G) and a TG–typed morphism $f : G \to G'$ with $f : (G, t_G) \to (G', t_{G'})$.

A *TG–typed graph rule* is a span $((L, t_L) \xleftarrow{l} (K, t_K) \xrightarrow{r} (R, t_R))$ where (L, t_L), (K, t_K), (R, t_R) are typed over the same type graph TG and l, r are injective TG–typed graph morphisms. The left graph (L, t_L) is matched to the actual graph when the rule is applied and the right graph (R, t_R) is substituted for the occurrence of (L, t_L). The span expresses which items of (L, t_L) are related to which items of (R, t_R) via the interface graph (K, t_K), that contains the items preserved by the rule application.

Given TG–typed rules p and p', a *typed rule morphism* $f : p \to p'$ is a triple $f = (f_L, f_K, f_R)$ of TG-typed graph morphisms that commute with the rule morphisms.

With the componentwise identities and composition this defines the category **Rule**$_{TG}$ as the comma category **Rule** over TG, where **Rule** is the category of untyped rules and rule morphisms. Since **Rule** is complete and cocomplete, so is **Rule**$_{TG}$.

Definition 1 (Retyping, Forgetful Functor and Free Functor). *Let* $f :$ $TG \to TG'$ *be a graph morphism.* f *induces a forgetful functor (backward retyping)* $f^< :$ **Graph**$_{TG'}$ $\to$ **Graph**$_{TG}$, $f^<((G', t_{G'})) = (G^*, t_{G^*})$ *and*

$f^<(k' : (G', t_{G'}) \to (H', t_{H'})) = k^* : (G^*, t_{G^*}) \to (H^*, t_{H^*})$ *by pullbacks and mediating morphisms as in the following diagram,*

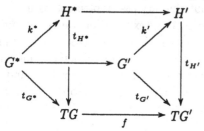

and a free functor (forward retyping) $f^> : \mathbf{Graph}_{TG} \to \mathbf{Graph}_{TG'}$, $f^>((G, t_G))$ $= (G, f \circ t_G)$ *and* $f^>(k : (G, t_G) \to (H, t_H)) = k$ *by composition.*

As shown in [6] (lemma 5.3), backward and forward retyping functors are left and right adjoints.

Definition 2 (Typed Graph Transformation Systems). *A typed graph transformation system* $\mathbf{G} = (TG, P, \pi)$ *consists of a type graph* TG, *a set of rule names* P *and a mapping* $\pi : P \to |\mathbf{Rule}_{TG}|$, *associating to each rule name a TG–typed rule.*

A morphism of typed graph transformation systems (TGTS–morphism), $f = (f_{TG}, f_P) : \mathbf{G} \to \mathbf{G}'$ *is given by an injective type graph morphism* $f_{TG} : TG \to TG'$ *and a mapping* $f_P : P \to P'$ *between the sets of rule names, such that* $f_{TG}^>(\pi(p)) = \pi'(f_P(p))$ *for all* $p \in P$.

Note that we use the free functor generated by f_{TG} to compare the rules of the source and the target systems. A more general definition of TGTS–morphism, which allows the use of a generic functor to translate types, can be found in [6]. Typed graph transformation systems and morphisms form a category, called **TGTS**, which has colimits (see [6]).

Given a typed graph transformation system $\mathbf{G} = (TG, P, \pi)$, a *direct derivation* $p/m : (G, t_G) \Rightarrow (H, t_H)$ over $\mathbf{G}$ from a graph (G, t_G) via a rule p and a matching morphism $m : (L, t_L) \to (G, t_G)$ is a pair (p, S), where $p \in P$, S is a double pushout diagram

$$
\begin{array}{ccccc}
(L, t_L) & \xleftarrow{\ l\ } & (K, t_K) & \xrightarrow{\ r\ } & (R, t_R) \\
\downarrow{\scriptstyle m} & & \downarrow{\scriptstyle k} & & \downarrow{\scriptstyle h} \\
(G, t_G) & \xleftarrow{\ l'\ } & (D, t_D) & \xrightarrow{\ r'\ } & (H, t_H)
\end{array}
$$

in $\mathbf{Graph}_{TG}$, and $\pi(p) = ((L, t_L) \xleftarrow{l} (K, t_K) \xrightarrow{r} (R, t_R))$. (G, t_G) is called the *input*, and (H, t_H) the *output* of $p/m : (G, t_G) \Rightarrow (H, t_H)$. A *derivation* $p_1/m_1, \ldots, p_n/m_n : (G, t_G) \Rightarrow (H, t_H)$ over $\mathbf{G}$ from a graph (G, t_G) via rules $p_1, \ldots, p_n$ and matching morphisms $m_1, \ldots, m_n$ is a sequence of direct derivations over $\mathbf{G}$, such that the output of the i'th direct derivation is the input of the $(i+1)$'st direct derivation. The set of all derivations over $\mathbf{G}$ is denoted $Der(\mathbf{G})$ and, considering $Der(\mathbf{G})$ as the behaviour of $\mathbf{G}$, the following property holds:

Proposition 1 (Preservation of Behaviour). *[6] Let $f = (f_{TG}, f_P) : \mathbf{G} \to$
$\mathbf{G}'$ be a TGTS–morphism. For each derivation $d : (G, t_G) \Rightarrow (H, t_H)$ with
$d = (p_1/m_1; \ldots ; p_n/m_n)$ in $Der(\mathbf{G})$ there is a derivation $f(d) : f_{TG}^{>}(G, t_G) \Rightarrow$
$f_{TG}^{>}(H, t_H)$ in $Der(\mathbf{G}')$, where $f(d) = (f_P(p_1)/f_{TG}^{>}(m_1); \ldots ; f_P(p_n)/f_{TG}^{>}(m_n))$.
Moreover, $f_{TG}^{<}(f(d) : f_{TG}^{>}(G, t_G) \Rightarrow f_{TG}^{>}(H, t_H)) = (d : (G, t_G) \Rightarrow (H, t_H))$.*

3   Refinements

A refinement of typed graph transformation systems is given by a graph homomorphism to relate the type graphs and a mapping that associates to each
rule name an instruction how to implement the associated rule as a composition
of rules of the refining system. In a spatial refinement this composition is an
amalgamation, in a temporal refinement a sequence.

Definition 3 (Refinement Instructions). *Let $\mathbf{G} = (TG, P, \pi)$ be a typed
graph transformation system. A spatial refinement instruction si on $\mathbf{G}$ is defined
by $si = (p_1 \ldots p_k, (\pi(p_i) \overset{m_{ij}}{\leftarrow} r_{ij} \overset{m'_{i,j}}{\to} \pi(p_j))_{1 \le i < j \le k})$ where $p_1, \ldots, p_k \in P$, $r_{ij} \in$
$|\mathbf{Rule}_{TG}|$ and $\pi(p_i) \overset{m_{ij}}{\leftarrow} r_{ij} \overset{m'_{i,j}}{\to} \pi(p_j)$ for $1 \le i < j \le k$ is a span of morphisms
in $\mathbf{Rule}_{TG}$.*
   *A temporal refinement instruction $ti = p_1 \ldots p_k$ on $\mathbf{G}$ is a string of rule
names $p_1, \ldots, p_k \in P$, such that $(R_i, t_{R_i}) = (L_{i+1}, t_{L_{i+1}})$ for $i \in \{1, \ldots, k-1\}$
if $\pi(p_j) = ((L_j, t_{L_j}) \leftarrow (K_j, t_{K_j}) \to (R_j, t_{R_j}))$.*

   A spatial refinement $si = (p, \emptyset)$ of length $k = 1$ will be shortly denoted by
$si = p$ in the sequel.
   The sets of typed spatial refinement instructions and typed temporal refinement instructions on $\mathbf{G}$ are denoted $TSRI(\mathbf{G})$ and $TTRI(\mathbf{G})$, respectively.
   The rule *result(si)* of a spatial refinement instruction si is given by $\pi(p_1)$ if
$k = 1$, while, for $k > 1$, it is defined as the colimit in $\mathbf{Rule}_{TG}$ of the diagram given
by all spans of si with their adjacent rules. The result of a temporal refinement in-
struction $t_i = p_1 \ldots p_k$ is given by *result(ti)=* $((L_1, t_{L_1}) \overset{l}{\leftarrow} (K, t_K) \overset{r}{\to} (R_k, t_{R_k}))$
where (K, t_K) is the limit of the diagram given by all the rules.

Definition 4 (Typed Refinements). *Let $\mathbf{G} = (TG, P, \pi)$, $\mathbf{G}' = (TG', P', \pi')$
be typed graph transformation systems. A typed spatial (resp. temporal) re-
finement morphism $tsref = (f_{TG}, sref) : \mathbf{G} \to \mathbf{G}'$ (resp. $ttref = (f_{TG}, tref) :$
$\mathbf{G} \to \mathbf{G}'$) is given by a type graph morphism $f_{TG} : TG \to TG'$ and a mapping
$sref : P \to TSRI(\mathbf{G}')$ (resp. $tref : P \to TTRI(\mathbf{G}')$) such that result($sref(p)$) $\cong$
$f_{TG}^{>}(\pi(p))$ (resp. result($tref(p)$) $\cong f_{TG}^{>}(\pi(p))$) for all $p \in P$.*
   *Two typed spatial (resp. temporal) refinement morphisms $tref : \mathbf{G} \to \mathbf{G}'$ and
$tref' : \mathbf{G} \to \mathbf{G}'$ are equivalent if $f_{TG}^{>}(result(tref(p))) \cong f_{TG}'^{>}(result(tref'(p)))$
in $\mathbf{Rule}_{TG'}$, for all $p \in P$.*

   From this definition, it follows immediately that any two spatial (temporal)
refinement morphisms $tref : \mathbf{G} \to \mathbf{G}'$ and $tref' : \mathbf{G} \to \mathbf{G}'$ are equivalent.

As shown in [6] for the untyped case, the spatial and temporal refinement relations are transitive. Those proofs can be adapted to the typed case simply by replacing all rules with typed rules and by taking the composition of the graph homomorphisms between the type graphs.

Definition 5 (Categories of Typed Refinements). *The typed spatial (temporal) refinement category* $\mathbf{TSRef}_{\equiv}$ *($\mathbf{TTRef}_{\equiv}$) has typed graph transformation systems as objects and equivalence classes of typed spatial (temporal) refinements as morphisms. Identities are given by the equivalence classes of idtref =* $(id_{TG}, id_P) : \mathbf{G} \to \mathbf{G}$.

The above defined identities are obviously typed spatial (temporal) refinements. Well definedness of the composition and the category axioms follow from the fact that any two typed spatial (temporal) refinements $tref, tref' : \mathbf{G} \to \mathbf{G}'$ are equivalent, thus denote the same morphism in $\mathbf{TSRef}_{\equiv}$ ($\mathbf{TTRef}_{\equiv}$).

Since $\mathbf{TSRef}_{\equiv}$ and $\mathbf{TTRef}_{\equiv}$ are preorders, and the category of sets is cocomplete, all colimits in both categories exist.

Proposition 2 (Colimits of Typed Refinements). $\mathbf{TSRef}_{\equiv}$ *and* $\mathbf{TTRef}_{\equiv}$ *have colimits.*

An important feature needed for the next sections is the possibility to consider plain TGTS–morphisms as refinement morphisms, both spatial and temporal ones. In fact, it is easy to see that the category $\mathbf{TGTS}$ is included in both categories $\mathbf{TSRef}_{\equiv}$ and $\mathbf{TTRef}_{\equiv}$, via spatial or temporal refinements of length one. The corresponding inclusion functors are denoted by $Emb : \mathbf{TGTS} \to \mathbf{TSRef}_{\equiv}$ and $Emb : \mathbf{TGTS} \to \mathbf{TTRef}_{\equiv}$, respectively.

The embedding mechanism allows to introduce a different way to construct a pushout of (the embedding of) an injective TGTS-morphism f and a spatial or temporal refinement morphism. It is given by the pushout of the type graphs, the names and rules of $\mathbf{G}_2$, retyped along the injection into the new type graph, and the names and rules of $\mathbf{G}_1$ that are not in the image of f, also retyped along the injection. In other words, the pushout is given by $\mathbf{G}_1$ with the image $f(\mathbf{G}_0)$ being replaced by $\mathbf{G}_2$.

Proposition 3. *Any pair* $(Emb(f) : \mathbf{G}_0 \to \mathbf{G}_1, tref : \mathbf{G}_0 \to \mathbf{G}_2)$ *of (the embedding of) an injective TGTS-morphism and a spatial (or temporal) refinement morphism has a pushout in* $\mathbf{TSref}_{\equiv}$ *($\mathbf{TTref}_{\equiv}$). The morphism induced by* $Emb(f)$ *is (the embedding of) a TGTS-morphism.*

Theorem 1 (Preservation of Behaviour). *[6] Let* $tref = (f_{TG}, ref_P) : \mathbf{G} \to \mathbf{G}'$ *be a spatial or temporal refinement morphism of typed graph transformation systems. For each derivation* $d : (G, t_G) \Rightarrow (H, t_H)$ *with* $d = (p_1/g_1; \ldots; p_n/g_n)$ *in* $Der(\mathbf{G})$ *there is a derivation* $tref(d) : f_{TG}^{>}(G, t_G) \Rightarrow f_{TG}^{>}(H, t_H)$ *with an amalgamation (or a sequential composition) of rules of* G' *according to tref. Moreover,* $f_{TG}^{<}(tref(d) : f_{TG}^{>}(G, t_G) \Rightarrow f_{TG}^{>}(H, t_H)) = (d : (G, t_G) \Rightarrow (H, t_H))$.

4   Modules for Typed Graph Transformation Systems

A module for TGTSs is composed by three TGTSs: an import interface, an export interface, and a body that implements the services offered by the export interface, eventually using the features required by the import interface. A simple inclusion morphism is used for relating the import interface and the body while a spatial or temporal refinement morphism is employed to relate the export interface and the body. In this way the body can use the rules imported from other modules and the rules at the export interface are implemented (refined) by rules of the body. Under this point of view, the rules of the export interface specify pre and post conditions of their implementations in the body.

As for programming language modules, the import interface of a TGTS–module plays an effective role only when the body needs to use external features offered by other modules. Hence, modules with empty import interface are the basic tools for the development of a module system (library) in a bottom–up way. Unlike the case of programming language modules however, the top–down approach is supported too because the import interface is used simply to describe the required resources, rather than naming specific modules to provide them (as in most imperative programming languages).

The semantics of a TGTS–module is given by the semantics of the export interface, which becomes the only visible part of the whole module from the outside environment (hence hiding of information is supported). The local components, import and body together with the export interface, are needed to define a structuring means which supports both the notions of implementation (via refinement morphisms) and information hiding.

Definition 6 (Module). *A module* $MOD = (IMP \xrightarrow{m} BOD \xleftarrow{r} EXP)$ *with spatial/temporal implementation is given by typed graph transformation systems IMP, BOD, and EXP, an injective TGTS–morphism $m : IMP \to BOD$, and a spatial/temporal refinement morphism $r : EXP \to BOD$. It can be visualized by:*

$$
\begin{array}{ccc}
 & & EXP \\
 & & \downarrow r \\
IMP & \xrightarrow{\ m\ } & BOD
\end{array}
$$

Note that, since the preservation of behaviour property holds both for TGTS–morphisms and for refinement morphisms, any derivation of the export (import) interface can be translated into a derivation of the body and this target derivation can be also reflected back to the original one.

Example 1. Consider the module $SEND = (IMP \xrightarrow{m} BOD \xleftarrow{r} EXP)$ where the three components EXP, BOD, IMP are defined as follows.

The type graph TG_{EXP} of the export interface EXP = $(TG_{EXP}, P_{EXP}, \pi_{EXP})$ is the graph where the circle node denotes a process, the dashed node denotes a message and the dashed arrow denotes that the process holds the message. The set P_{EXP} contains a single rule name *send* with underlying rule

$\pi_{EXP}(send)$:

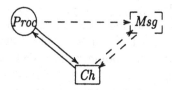

It models the action of sending a message a from the process P to the process Q. Note that $\pi_{EXP}(send)$ describes the overall effect (the pre and post conditions) of the communication between P and Q without giving any detail on how that communication is realized.

The type graph TG_{BOD} of the body $BOD = (TG_{BOD}, P_{BOD}, \pi_{BOD})$ is the following extension of the type graph TG_{EXP} of the export interface:

The square node denotes a channel, the arrows between a process and a channel denote the writing and reading accesses of the process to the channel, and the dashed arrows between a message and a channel denote that the message is on the input side or on the output side of the channel. The set P_{BOD} contains five rule names whose underlying rules are:

$\pi_{BOD}(connect)$:

$\pi_{BOD}(submit)$:

$\pi_{BOD}(transmit)$:

$\pi_{BOD}(deliver)$:

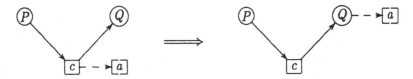

$\pi_{BOD}(disconnect)$:

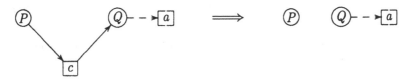

The previous rules describe all the steps needed to send the message a from P to Q: $\pi_{BOD}(connect)$ introduces the information about the channel c shared by P and Q, $\pi_{BOD}(submit)$ submits the message a to the input side of channel c, $\pi_{BOD}(transmit)$ transmits a to the output of c, $\pi_{BOD}(deliver)$ delivers a to Q and finally, $\pi_{BOD}(disconnect)$ removes the information about the channel c. It is easy to see that the sequential composition of these rules gives as result exactly the rule $\pi_{EXP}(send)$, considered as typed over TG_{BOD} along the inclusion $TG_{EXP} \to TG_{BOD}$, of the export interface. This means that the morphism $r = (r_{TG}, r_P)$ defined by $r_{TG} : TG_{EXP} \to TG_{BOD}$ being the inclusion and $r_P : P_{EXP} \to TTRI(BOD)$ defined by $r_P(send) = connect\ submit\ transmit\ deliver\ disconnect$, is a temporal refinement.

The import interface $IMP = (TG_{IMP}, P_{IMP}, \pi_{IMP})$ is defined by $TG_{IMP} = TG_{BOD}$, $P_{IMP} = \{transmit\}$ and $\pi_{IMP}(transmit) = \pi_{BOD}(transmit)$. We use IMP to import from another module the implementation of $\pi_{BOD}(transmit)$. Since in MOD there is no information about the structure of the channel c (for example, if c is a buffer the message a has to perform some intermediate steps between the input and the output sides of c), we suppose that another module offers (or will offer) an implementation of $\pi_{BOD}(transmit)$.

This example illustrates that the hiding of information is realized both by defining the semantics of the whole module as the semantics of the export interface (so the implementation details are not visible from the outside world), and by using in the body a larger type graph than in the export interface.

The following definition of *module morphism* relates modules having the same kind of refinement morphism (spatial or temporal).

Definition 7 (Module Morphism). *Let* $MOD = (IMP \overset{m}{\to} BOD \overset{r}{\leftarrow} EXP)$ *and* $MOD' = (IMP' \overset{m'}{\to} BOD' \overset{r'}{\leftarrow} EXP')$ *be two modules with the same kind of implementation. A module morphism mod : MOD $\to$ MOD' is a triple (imp : IMP $\to$ IMP', bod : BOD $\to$ BOD', exp : EXP $\to$ EXP') of TGTS-morphisms such that* $m' \circ imp = bod \circ m$ *in* **TGTS** *and* $Emb(bod) \circ r = r' \circ Emb(exp)$ *in* **TSRef**$_\equiv$ *or* **TTRef**$_\equiv$.

Since the module morphism components are TGTS–morphisms, it follows from proposition 1 that module morphisms preserve derivations.

A module morphism is injective if its three components are injective TGTS–morphisms. A module MOD is a *submodule* of MOD' if there is an injective module morphism $mod : MOD \to MOD'$. The submodule relation is transitive.

Proposition 4. *Modules and module morphisms form two categories called* **MOD-TSRef$_\cong$** *and* **MOD-TTRef$_\cong$**.

The relevance of the following closure property becomes clear in the next section where different interconnection mechanisms for TGTS–modules are defined and analyzed.

Proposition 5. **MOD-SRef$_\cong$** *and* **MOD-TRef$_\cong$** *have finite colimits.*

5   Towards an Algebra of Modules

After the introduction of a module for TGTSs, our main interest now is the development of an algebra of TGTS–modules. Thus, analogously to the algebraic specification modules [3], we introduce in this section the operations of union and composition of TGTS–modules. Both these operations take as arguments two modules having the same kind of refinement morphism between the export interface and the body.

5.1   Union of Modules

The union of two modules MOD_1 and MOD_2 w.r.t. a common submodule MOD_0 is the module MOD_3 where each component is obtained by taking first the disjoint union of the corresponding components of MOD_1 and MOD_2 and then identifying the parts in common contained in MOD_0. Formally:

Definition 8. *Let MOD_1 and MOD_2 be two modules in* **MOD-TSRef$_\cong$** *(or* **MOD-TTRef$_\cong$**) *and let MOD_0 be a submodule of both MOD_1 and MOD_2 via $mod_1 : MOD_0 \to MOD_1$ and $mod_2 : MOD_0 \to MOD_2$. The union $MOD_3 = MOD_1 \oplus_{MOD_0} MOD_2$ of MOD_1 and MOD_2 w.r.t. MOD_0, mod_1 and mod_2, is given by the pushout of MOD_0, mod_1 and mod_2.*

The union operation is based on the existence of pushouts for **MOD-TSRef$_\cong$** (or **MOD-TTRef$_\cong$**) stated in proposition 5. Since the resulting module is a pushout object, the operation is defined up to isomorphisms.

Note 1. The following facts can be proved using only standard properties of the involved categories. Hence, for their complete proofs, we refer to [11] where they are proved for algebraic specification modules.

1. MOD_1 and MOD_2 are submodules of $MOD_1 \oplus_{MOD_0} MOD_2$ (it follows from proposition 5 and standard properties of pushouts);
2. Associativity of the union: if MOD_0 is a submodule of MOD_1 and MOD_2, and MOD_3 is a submodule of MOD_2 and MOD_4, then
$$(MOD_1 \oplus_{MOD_0} MOD_2) \oplus_{MOD_3} MOD_4 \cong$$
$$MOD_1 \oplus_{MOD_0} (MOD_2 \oplus_{MOD_3} MOD_4).$$

5.2 Composition of Modules

Let $MOD = (IMP \overset{m}{\to} BOD \overset{r}{\leftarrow} EXP)$ and $MOD' = (IMP' \overset{m'}{\to} BOD' \overset{r'}{\leftarrow} EXP')$ be two modules: the idea for the composition operation is to relate them using a TGTS–morphism called *interface morphism* between the import interface of MOD and the export interface of MOD', $h : IMP \to EXP'$, and to create a new module having the import interface of MOD', the export interface of MOD and a body implementing the features of both MOD and MOD'.

Definition 9. *Let* $MOD = (IMP \overset{m}{\to} BOD \overset{r}{\leftarrow} EXP)$ *and* $MOD' = (IMP' \overset{m'}{\to} BOD' \overset{r'}{\leftarrow} EXP')$ *be two modules in* **MOD-TSRef$_\equiv$** *(or* **MOD-TTRef$_\equiv$)** *and let* $h : IMP \to EXP'$ *be an interface morphism. The composition* $MOD'' = MOD' \circ_h MOD$ *is defined by* $MOD'' = (IMP'' \overset{m^* \circ m'}{\longrightarrow} BOD'' \overset{r^* \circ r}{\longleftarrow} EXP'')$ *where:* $IMP'' = IMP'$, $EXP'' = EXP$ *and* BOD'' *is the pushout object (and* m^* *and* r^* *are the induced morphisms) of the following diagram in* **TSRef$_\equiv$** *(or* **TTRef$_\equiv$)**

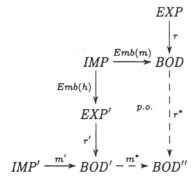

Note 2. 1. Associativity of composition: due to standard properties of composition of pushouts, $(MOD'' \circ_{h_1} MOD') \circ_{h_2} MOD \cong MOD'' \circ_{h_1} (MOD' \circ_{h_2} MOD)$;
2. Symmetric Distributivity of union and composition (see [11] for its proof): let MOD_0 be a submodule of MOD_1, MOD_2 and MOD'_0 be a submodule of MOD'_1, MOD'_2. Let $h_i : MOD_i \to MOD'_i$, $i = 0, 1, 2$ be interface morphisms such that h_0 is the restriction of h_1 and h_2. Then
$(MOD_1 \oplus_{MOD_0} MOD_2) \circ_{h_1 \oplus_{h_0} h_2} (MOD'_1 \oplus_{MOD'_0} MOD'_2) \cong$
$(MOD_1 \circ_{h_1} MOD'_1) \oplus_{MOD_0 \circ_{h_0} MOD'_0} (MOD_2 \circ_{h_2} MOD'_2)$;
3. For the composition, it is sufficient to consider the special case of $h = id$: we can recover the $h \neq id$ case by introducing $(EXP' \overset{id}{\longrightarrow} EXP' \overset{Emb(h)}{\longleftarrow} IMP)$ as intermediate module, and composing it with the given modules.

6 Conclusions

In the first part of this paper we have proven important basic properties of temporal and spatial refinement morphisms (existence of colimits in the respective categories of TGTSs and refinements, embedding of plain TGTS–morphisms into refinement morphisms, pushout closure for any pair of morphisms consisting of an injective TGTS–morphism and a refinement). In the second part of the paper, these properties have been used for introducing a module concept for TGTSs that supports the notions of implementation and information hiding.

The implementation notion is realized by the refinement morphisms (temporal or spatial): each rule of the export interface of the module is implemented (refined) by spatially or temporally composing some rules of the body. The hiding of information is achieved both by defining the semantics of the whole module as the semantics of the export interface and by the use of types to hide the implementation details of the body.

Union and composition of modules of the same kind have been presented, together with their properties: with these operations, an algebra of modules can be considered.

The next step of our investigation will be the development of a general notion of refinement as a sequence of spatial and temporal refinements. The idea is that a TGTS G is refined by another system G' via a chain of refinements $r = r_1, \ldots, r_n$, $n \geq 1$, where each $r_i : G_i \to G_{i+1}$ is either a spatial or a temporal refinement, such that $G = G_1$ and $G' = G_{n+1}$. These sequences of refinements can be assumed to be alternating, i.e., if r_i is a temporal refinement then r_{i+1} is a spatial refinement, and vice versa. Composition is then defined by juxtaposition of sequences and yields a general category of refinements, with corresponding general definition of module and module composition.

Having defined a new module concept for typed graph transformation systems, it becomes mandatory both a discussion about their relationships with the algebraic specification modules and a presentation of the other modularization approaches to graph transformation systems. To discuss the relationships and differences w.r.t the algebraic specifications modules we distinguish three different levels: *structural*, *syntax* and *semantics*.

From the *structural* point of view, we want to point out that the TGTSs are used for formally specifying dynamically evolving systems where graphs are states and graph transformations are states transitions. Hence, it is very important to preserve the dynamical behaviours of the systems. This dynamical aspect is not present in algebraic specifications since each of them specifies an algebra (initial semantics) or a class of algebras (loose semantics), that model only the static functional view of the components.

The *syntax* of a TGTS–module is quite similar to the one of an algebraic specification module: the only difference is that the TGTS–modules do not have a parameter part (up to now, we do not have a practical example where it is needed). On the other side, the *semantics* of an algebraic module is a functor from the algebras of the import interface to the algebras of the export interface, $SEM : Alg(IMP) \to Alg(EXP)$, while the semantics of the TGTS–modules is simply the semantics of the export interface and it has only an initial semantics (i.e each TGTS–module has a single model). This doesn't mean that the body and the import interface have no meaning, because the main task of a module is to implement some features (eventually using external functionalities), and all three components of a TGTS–module and the two relations between them are needed to support the notion of implementation.

We proceed now with a presentation of the other existing approaches to modularization of graph transformation systems: relationships with our TGTS–modules are pointed out case by case.

6.1   The PROGRES Approach to Modularization

The PROGRES modules (described in [12]) are inspired by Modula–2 modules: each module is composed by an *interface module* and a *body module* (corresponding to the Modula–2 definition and implementation modules, respectively). The interface module allows to specify (via a programming language like syntax) the *signature* (names and parameters) of the imported and exported features, i.e the node and edge types, and the graph transformations rules. The imported features have to be referenced through the module which provide them. The exported features are implemented by the body module and the resulting rule is obtained by selecting or composing (via imperative languages statements) simple rules explicitly given. The relation between the interface and body modules is realized by using the same names.

It is not easy to compare our approach to modularization with the one of PROGRES: first of all, our approach is completely graph–oriented while the PROGRES approach is more programming languages–like and only the lower level specifications are graph–oriented (thus the graph transformation idea is not really supported). Furthermore, in our approach the refinement relation between the export interface and the body gives all the necessary instructions on how to implement each rule of the export interface with rules in the body while, in the PROGRES approach, the implementation task is completely carried out by the body module.

6.2   Graph Transformation Units: The GRACE Approach

The GRACE approach (described in [9]) uses the transformation unit concept as structuring means. It is defined independently of a particular graph transformation approach: a transformation unit is specified by two graph class expressions that describe the allowed classes of initial and terminal graphs, a finite set of local rules, a finite set of used (imported) transformation units and a control condition which expresses a constraint on the input/output relation.

The semantics of a transformation unit is a graph transformation, i.e a binary relation on graphs containing a pair (G, G') of graphs if, first, G is an initial graph and G' is a terminal graph, second, G' can be obtained from G by interleaving direct derivations with the graph transformations specified by the used transformation units (interleaving semantics), and third, the pair is allowed by the control condition. Since the definition is recursive, the set of imported units must be initially empty, and the semantics is given in a bottom–up way.

Information hiding is supported on the semantics level: only pairs of initial and terminal graphs (not the intermediate derivation steps) are specified.

With respect to the programming languages, the transformation unit concept corresponds to the procedure abstraction: the initial graph expression can be seen as a (limited) form of parameters passing, the imported transformation units as external visible procedures, the local rules as local instructions and the control condition as a constraint on the possible derivations (executions of the procedure call). Such derivations are composed by a sequence of local instructions application interleaved with external derivations (execution of external procedure calls).

This correspondence between transformation units and programming languages procedures makes the comparison with our approach possible only in terms of procedures (the modeling of a module concept as sets of transformation units is a matter of ongoing work). In our approach each rule of the export interface can be seen as a procedure which is implemented by using statements and external procedures present in the body (all the used external procedures are required at the import interface and included into the body). More precisely, each rule of the export interface can be seen as the effect of a procedure call because its pre and post conditions are specified. The role of the control conditions is played, in a sense, by the refinement morphism which gives the instructions (the algorithm) to implement the procedure. But, while the control conditions are used for successively selecting the correct derivations, the refinement morphisms are used for building up only correct derivations.

6.3   The View–Oriented Approaches

The view–oriented approaches are inspired by Database Theory and, in particular, by the database integration of views. Their goal is to achieve the system modeling problem for graph transformation systems through the integration of (eventually partial) models (views): every situation of the real world can be formally modeled in different ways, but these different models have to be consistently integrated to form the complete formal model of the given real situation. Note that the modularization idea here is interpreted as the possibility to independently formalize different (possibly overlapping) aspects of a complex problem.

There are two distinct view–oriented approaches: the *declarative* approach (see [12]) and the *constructive* approach (see [4]). The main difference between them consists in the adopted solution for the views integration problem.

In the declarative approach, (inspired by the active database Event–Condition–Action rules), the views integration problem is solved by associating active constraints with each rule (so, the complete model is not effectively built up). In the constructive model, each view is a TGTS in the sense of definition 2, and different views are related with a common reference model (a common TGTS) by a so called view relation. Such a relation allows the *renaming* (through a TGTS isomorphism) and the *extension* (through a subrule relation) of the reference model. More precisely, a TGTS G is a view of another

TGTS **G'** if, after the renaming of **G**, each rule of the resulting system is a subrule (in the same sense of [10,7]) of a rule in **G'**. Thus, given two views, first a *model manager* is employed to build up (in a non automatic way) their common reference model and their view relations, and then the corresponding integrated model is automatically constructed as the parallel composition of the two views w.r.t their reference model. Up to now, this integration technique has not been formally generalized for more than two views.

It is clear that our approach and the views–oriented approaches are too different to make a constructive comparison. We would only point out that the subrule concept employed in the view–oriented constructive approach to relate different views to their common reference model, can be simulated by the type systems of the involved TGTSs (see [7] for the details) and thus a view is just a TGTS–morphism in our framework.

References

1. E.K. Blum, H. Ehrig, F. Parisi Presicce "Algebraic Specification of Modules and Their Basic Interconnections" *Journal of Computer and System Sciences* Vol. 34 pp. 293–339 (1987)
2. A. Corradini, R. Heckel "A Compositional Approach to Structuring and Refinement of Typed Graph Grammars" *Proc. of SEGRAGRA '95 "Graph Rewriting and Computation", ENTCS* vol. 2, Elsevier (1995)
3. H. Ehrig, B. Mahr "Fundamentals of Algebraic Specifications 2: Module Specifications and Constraints" *EATCS Monographs on Theoretical Computer Science* Vol. 21 Springer Verlag, Berlin (1990)
4. G. Engels, R. Heckel, G. Taentzer, H. Ehrig "A View-Oriented Approach to System Modelling based on Graph Transformation" *Proc. ESEC, LNCS n.1301* pp. 327–343 (1997)
5. G. Engels, A. Shürr "Encapsulated Hierarchical Graphs, Graph Types, and Meta Types" *LNCS n.1073* pp. 137–154 (1996)
6. M. Große–Rhode, F. Parisi Presicce, M. Simeoni "Spatial and Temporal Refinement of Typed Graph Transformation Systems" *Proc. of MFCS'98, LNCS n.1450* pp. 553–561 (1998)
7. M. Große–Rhode, F. Parisi Presicce, M. Simeoni "Concrete Spatial Refinement Construction for Graph Transformation Systems" Università di Roma *La Sapienza*, Dip. Scienze dell'Informazione *Technical Report* SI 97/10 (1997)
8. M. Große–Rhode, F. Parisi Presicce, M. Simeoni "Refinements and Modules for Typed Graph Transformation Systems" Università di Roma *La Sapienza*, Dip. Scienze dell'Informazione *Technical Report* SI 98/05 (1998)
9. H-J. Kreowski, S. Kuske "On the Interleaving Semantics of Transformation Units – A Step into GRACE" *LNCS n.1073* pp. 89–106 (1996)
10. F. Parisi Presicce "Transformation of Graph Grammars" *LNCS n.1073* pp. 428–442 (1996)
11. F. Parisi Presicce "Inner and Mutual Compatibility of operations on module specifications" *Technical Report 86-06 TU Berlin* (1986)
12. A. Winter, A. Schürr "Modules and Updatable Graph Views for PROgrammed Graph REwriting Systems" Aachener Informatik-Berichte 97-03

Complete Strategies for Term Graph Narrowing[*]

Annegret Habel[1] and Detlef Plump[2][**]

[1] Universität Oldenburg, Fachbereich Informatik
Postfach 2503, 26111 Oldenburg, Germany
Annegret.Habel@informatik.uni-oldenburg.de
[2] Universität Bremen, Fachbereich Mathematik und Informatik
Postfach 330440, 28334 Bremen, Germany
det@informatik.uni-bremen.de

Abstract. Narrowing is a method for solving equations in the equational theories of term rewriting systems. Unification and rewriting, the central operations in narrowing, are often implemented on graph-like data structures to exploit sharing of common subexpressions. In this paper, we study the completeness of narrowing in graph-based implementations. We show that the well-known condition for the completeness of tree-based narrowing, viz. a normalizing and confluent term rewrite relation, does not suffice. Completeness is restored, however, if the implementing graph rewrite relation is normalizing and confluent. We address basic narrowing and show its completeness for innermost normalizing and confluent graph rewriting. Then we consider the combination of basic narrowing with two strategies for controlling sharing, obtaining minimally collapsing and maximally collapsing basic narrowing. The former is shown to be complete in the presence of innermost normalization and confluence, the latter in the presence of termination and confluence. Maximally collapsing narrowing sometimes speeds up narrowing derivations drastically. Our results on minimally collapsing basic narrowing correct analogous claims by Krishna Rao [Proc. JICSLP'96] which are based on an incomplete version of term graph narrowing.

1 Introduction

Narrowing is a method for solving equations in the equational theories defined by term rewriting systems. To ensure the completeness of this method, the term rewrite relation has to be normalizing and confluent. A huge number of narrowing strategies has been proposed to reduce the search space of narrowing while maintaining completeness (see the survey of Hanus [9]). Almost all of this work considers narrowing as a relation on terms, i.e. trees, although rewriting and unification—the central operations in narrowing—are often implemented on graph-like data structures to allow sharing of common subexpressions.

[*] This work was partially supported by the ESPRIT Working Group APPLIGRAPH.
[**] Work of this author was done while he was visiting CWI, Amsterdam, and the University of Nijmegen, supported by the HCM network EXPRESS and by Deutsche Forschungsgemeinschaft, respectively.

J.L. Fiadeiro (Ed.): WADT'98, LNCS 1589, pp. 152–167, 1999.

Sharing saves space and also time, as repeated evaluations of expressions are avoided. Consider, for instance, the rule $\text{fib}(\text{s}(\text{s}(\text{x}))) \to \text{fib}(\text{s}(\text{x})) + \text{fib}(\text{x})$ from a specification of the Fibonacci function. Applying this rule to an expression of the form $\text{fib}(\text{s}(\text{s}(t)))$ requires copying the subterm t in order to obtain the result $\text{fib}(\text{s}(t)) + \text{fib}(t)$. But this copying duplicates work as the subterm t now has to be evaluated twice. The obvious solution to this problem is to use a graph-like representation of expressions in which subexpressions like t are *shared* rather than copied. Similarly, it is well-known that an efficient implementation of the unification operation requires sharing certain subexpressions (see [12,3]).

In a graph-based implementation, however, narrowing is incomplete for certain rewrite systems over which tree-based narrowing is complete. We demonstrate this by the following rules[1]:

$$\mathcal{R} \begin{cases} \text{f}(\text{x}) \to \text{g}(\text{x}, \text{x}) \\ \text{a} \to \text{b} \\ \text{g}(\text{a}, \text{b}) \to \text{c} \\ \text{g}(\text{b}, \text{b}) \to \text{f}(\text{a}) \end{cases}$$

The term rewrite relation of this system is normalizing and confluent, a sufficient condition for the completeness of (unrestricted) tree-based narrowing [20]. But the goal $\text{f}(\text{a}) =^? \text{c}$ cannot be solved in an implementation with sharing, although $\text{f}(\text{a})$ and c are equivalent terms. The reason is that sharing prevents a rewriting of $\text{f}(\text{a})$ into c, as shown in the picture below. (Notice that there is no step corresponding to the term rewrite step $\text{g}(\text{a}, \text{a}) \to \text{g}(\text{a}, \text{b})$.) For the same reason, the graph rewrite relation of the above system is neither normalizing nor confluent.

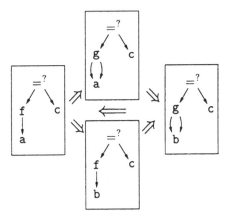

In this paper, we provide completeness results for narrowing in graph-based implementations (where completeness means that for every solution to a goal, a solution can be computed that is at least as general). More precisely, we use the

---

[1] This system was used in [17] as a counterexample to confluence of term graph rewriting. Independently, Middeldorp and Hamoen invented the same system as a counterexample to completeness of basic narrowing [15].

setting of *term graph narrowing* [7] and show completeness (and incompleteness) of various strategies.

Basic term graph narrowing is shown to be complete for innermost normalizing and confluent term graph rewriting, where innermost normalization can be relaxed to normalization if all rewrite rules are right-linear. A counterexample reveals that normalization and confluence are not sufficient in general for this strategy. We then introduce minimally collapsing and maximally collapsing narrowing. While the former introduces only as much sharing as necessary, the latter creates a full sharing prior to every rewrite step. We present an example where maximally collapsing narrowing reduces an exponential number of necessary narrowing steps to a linear number. The combination of minimally collapsing and basic narrowing remains complete for innermost normalizing and confluent graph rewriting. A counterexample shows that this condition is not sufficient for maximally collapsing narrowing. Here termination and confluence ensure completeness, even under the combination with basic narrowing.

Our results on minimally collapsing basic narrowing correct analogous claims of Krishna Rao [14] which are based on an incomplete version of term graph narrowing. The problem with that version is that it does not allow a collapsing between the application of the unifier and the rewrite step. As a consequence, narrowing is incomplete for a non-left-linear system like $\{f(x, x) \to a\}$ (belonging to all three classes of rewrite systems addressed by the main results of [14]). The goal $f(x, y) =^? a$, for instance, is not solvable with such a kind of narrowing.

2 Term Graphs and Substitutions

Let Σ be a set of *function symbols*. Each function symbol f comes with a natural number $\mathrm{arity}(f) \geq 0$. Function symbols of arity 0 are called *constants*. We further assume that there is an infinite set Var of *variables* such that $\mathrm{Var} \cap \Sigma = \emptyset$. For each variable x, we set $\mathrm{arity}(x) = 0$.

A *hypergraph* over $\Sigma \cup \mathrm{Var}$ is a system $G = \langle V_G, E_G, \mathrm{lab}_G, \mathrm{att}_G \rangle$ consisting of two finite sets V_G and E_G of *nodes* and *hyperedges*, a labelling function $\mathrm{lab}_G \colon E_G \to \Sigma \cup \mathrm{Var}$, and an attachment function $\mathrm{att}_G \colon E_G \to V_G^*$ which assigns a string of nodes to a hyperedge e such that the length of $\mathrm{att}_G(e)$ is $1 + \mathrm{arity}(\mathrm{lab}_G(e))$. Given an edge e with $\mathrm{att}_G(e) = v\,v_1 \ldots v_n$, node v is the *result node* of e while $v_1, \ldots, v_n$ are the *argument nodes*. The result node is denoted by $\mathrm{res}(e)$. The set of variables occurring in G is denoted by $\mathrm{Var}(G)$, that is, $\mathrm{Var}(G) = \mathrm{lab}_G(E_G) \cap \mathrm{Var}$. In the following, hypergraphs and hyperedges are simply called graphs and edges.

Definition 1 (term graph). *A graph G is a* term graph *if*

(1) there is a node root_G from which each node is reachable,
(2) G is acyclic, and
(3) each node is the result node of a unique edge.

The picture in the introduction shows four term graphs with function symbols $=^?$, g, f, a, b and c, where $=^?$ and g are binary, f is unary, and a, b and c are constants. We represent edges by their labels and omit nodes (as there is a one-to-one correspondence between edges and nodes). Arrows point to the arguments of a function symbol, where the order among the arguments is given by the left-to-right order of the arrows leaving the symbol.

Definition 2 (term representation). *A node v in a term graph G represents the term* $\text{term}_G(v) = \text{lab}_G(e)(\text{term}_G(v_1), \ldots, \text{term}_G(v_n))$, *where e is the unique edge with* $\text{res}(e) = v$, *and where* $\text{att}_G(e) = v\, v_1 \ldots v_n$.

By Definition 1, $\text{term}_G(v)$ is a well-defined term over $\Sigma \cup \text{Var}$. In the following we abbreviate $\text{term}_G(\text{root}_G)$ by $\text{term}(G)$.

A *graph morphism* $f : G \to H$ between two graphs G and H consists of two functions $f_V : V_G \to V_H$ and $f_E : E_G \to E_H$ satisfying $\text{lab}_H \circ f_E = \text{lab}_G$ and $\text{att}_H \circ f_E = f_V^* \circ \text{att}_G$ (where $f_V^* : V_G^* \to V_H^*$ maps a string $v_1 \ldots v_n$ to $f_V(v_1) \ldots f_V(v_n)$). The morphism f is an *isomorphism* if f_V and f_E are bijective. In this case G and H are *isomorphic*, which is denoted by $G \cong H$.

Definition 3 (collapsing). *Given two term graphs G and H, G collapses to H if there is a graph morphism $c : G \to H$ mapping root_G to root_H. This is denoted by $G \succeq_c H$ or simply by $G \succeq H$. We write $G \succ_c H$ or $G \succ H$ if c is non-injective. The latter kind of collapsing is said to be* proper. *A term graph G is* fully collapsed *if there is no H with $G \succ H$.*

It is easy to see that the collapse morphisms are the surjective morphisms between term graphs and that $G \succeq H$ implies $\text{term}(G) = \text{term}(H)$.

A *substitution pair* x/G consists of a variable x and a term graph G. Given a term graph H and an edge e in H labelled with x, the application of x/G to e proceeds in two steps: (1) Remove e from H, yielding the graph $H - \{e\}$, and (2) construct the disjoint union $(H - \{e\}) + G$ and fuse the result node of e with root_G.

Definition 4 (term graph substitution). *A term graph substitution (or substitution for short) is a finite set $\alpha = \{x_1/G_1, \ldots, x_n/G_n\}$ of substitution pairs such that $x_1, \ldots, x_n$ are pairwise distinct and $x_i \neq \text{term}(G_i)$ for $i = 1, \ldots, n$. The domain of α is the set $\text{Dom}(\alpha) = \{x_1, \ldots, x_n\}$. The application of α to a term graph H yields the term graph $H\alpha$ which is obtained by applying all substitution pairs in α simultaneously to all edges with label in $\text{Dom}(\alpha)$.*

We assume that the reader is familiar with substitutions on terms. Given a term graph substitution α, we denote by α^{term} the associated term substitution $\{x/\text{term}(G) \mid x/G \in \alpha\}$. The restriction of a term or term graph substitution σ to a subset V of Var is denoted by $\sigma|_V$.

3 Term Graph Narrowing

In this section we briefly review term graph rewriting and narrowing. We first recall some properties of relations and basic concepts of term rewriting systems (for an introduction one may consult [2] or [5,13]). Let A be a set and $\to$ be a binary relation on A. Then $\to^*$ and $\leftrightarrow^*$ denote the transitive-reflexive and symmetric-transitive-reflexive closures of $\to$. The relation $\to$ is *confluent* if for all a, b, c with $b \leftarrow^* a \to^* c$ there is some d such that $b \to^* d \leftarrow^* c$. The relation $\to$ is *terminating* if there is no infinite sequence $a_1 \to a_2 \to a_3 \to \ldots$ An element a is a *normal form* if there is no b such that $a \to b$. The relation $\to$ is *normalizing* if for each a there is a normal form b such that $a \to^* b$.

A *term rewrite rule* $l \to r$ consists of two terms l and r such that l is not a variable and all variables in r occur also in l. A set $\mathcal{R}$ of term rewrite rules is a *term rewriting system*. The term rewrite relation associated with $\mathcal{R}$ is denoted by $\to_\mathcal{R}$.

For every term t, let Δt be a tree representing t and $\Diamond t$ be a term graph representing t such that only variables are shared.[2] Given a graph G, we write $\underline{G}$ for the graph that results from removing all edges labelled with variables. For each node v, we denote by $G|_v$ the subgraph consisting of all nodes reachable from v and all edges having these nodes as result nodes.

Definition 5 (redex and preredex). *Let G be a term graph, v be a node in G, and $l \to r$ be a rule in $\mathcal{R}$. The pair $\langle v, l \to r \rangle$ is a redex if there is a graph morphism* red: $\underline{\Diamond l} \to \underline{G}$, *called the* redex morphism, *such that* red(root$_{\Diamond l}$) = v. *The pair $\langle v, l \to r \rangle$ is a preredex if there is a term substitution σ such that* term$_G(v) = l\sigma$.

While every redex is a preredex, the converse need not hold if there are repeated variables in the left-hand side l of $l \to r$. In this case a suitable collapsing of G can turn the preredex $\langle v, l \to r \rangle$ into a redex.

Definition 6 (term graph rewriting). *Let G, H be term graphs and $\langle v, l \to r \rangle$ be a redex in G with redex morphism* red: $\underline{\Diamond l} \to \underline{G}$. *Then there is a proper rewrite step $G \Rightarrow_{v,l \to r} H$ if H is isomorphic to the term graph G_3 constructed as follows:*

(1) $G_1 = G - \{e\}$ is the graph obtained from G by removing the unique edge e having result node v.

(2) G_2 is the graph obtained from the disjoint union $G_1 + \underline{\Diamond r}$ by
   - *identifying v with root$_{\Diamond r}$,*
   - *identifying red(v_1) with v_2, for each pair $\langle v_1, v_2 \rangle \in V_{\Diamond l} \times V_{\Diamond r}$ with* term$_{\Diamond l}(v_1) =$ term$_{\Diamond r}(v_2) \in$ Var.

(3) $G_3 = G_2|_{\text{root}_G}$ is the term graph obtained from G_2 by removing all nodes and edges not reachable from root$_G$ ("garbage collection").

We define the term graph rewrite relation $\Rightarrow_\mathcal{R}$ by adding proper collapse steps: $G \Rightarrow_\mathcal{R} H$ if $G \succ H$ or $G \Rightarrow_{v,l \to r} H$ for some redex $\langle v, l \to r \rangle$. A sequence $G \cong G_1 \Rightarrow_\mathcal{R} G_2 \Rightarrow_\mathcal{R} \ldots \Rightarrow_\mathcal{R} G_n = H$ is a term graph rewrite derivation and is denoted by $G \Rightarrow^*_\mathcal{R} H$.

---

[2] In other words, $\Diamond t$ is a term graph such that there exists a surjective graph morphism $\Delta t \to \Diamond t$ that identifies two edges e_1 and e_2 iff lab$_{\Delta t}(e_1) =$ lab$_{\Delta t}(e_2) \in$ Var.

The purpose of collapse steps is twofold: they are sometimes necessary to enable the application of a rule with repeated variables in its left-hand side (see the remark below Definition 5), and in certain cases they can speed up rewriting and narrowing drastically (see Example 1).

Now we turn to term graph narrowing which, like conventional term narrowing, aims at solving equations modulo the equational theory defined by a term rewriting system.

Recall that a set of terms $\{t_1, \ldots, t_n\}$ is *unifiable* if there is a term substitution σ such that $t_1\sigma = t_2\sigma = \ldots = t_n\sigma$, and that in this case there exists a *most general unifier* σ with this property.

Definition 7 (term graph narrowing). *Let G and H be term graphs, U be a set of non-variable nodes in G, $l \to r$ be a rule[3] in $\mathcal{R}$, and α be a term graph substitution. Then there is a narrowing step $G \leadsto_{U, l \to r, \alpha} H$ if α^{term} is a most general unifier of $\{\text{term}_G(u) \mid u \in U\} \cup \{l\}$, and*

$$G\alpha \succeq_{c} G' \underset{v, l \to r}{\Longrightarrow} H$$

for some collapsing $G\alpha \succeq_{c} G'$ such that $U = c^{-1}(v)$.[4] We denote such a step also by $G \leadsto_{\alpha} H$. A sequence of narrowing steps $G \cong G_1 \leadsto_{\alpha_1} G_2 \leadsto_{\alpha_2} \cdots \leadsto_{\alpha_{n-1}} G_n = H$ is a term graph narrowing derivation *and is denoted by $G \leadsto_{\alpha}^{*} H$, where $\alpha = \alpha_1\alpha_2 \ldots \alpha_{n-1}$.[5]*

The present definition of term graph narrowing extends the definition in [7] in that the latter corresponds to the special case where all nodes in the set U represent the same term.

From now on we assume that $\mathcal{R}$ contains the rule $x =^? x \to \textbf{true}$, where the binary function symbol $=^?$ and the constant $\textbf{true}$ do not occur in any other rule. A *goal* is a term of the form $s =^? t$ such that s and t do not contain $=^?$ and $\textbf{true}$. A *solution* of this goal is a term substitution σ satisfying $s\sigma \leftrightarrow_{\mathcal{R}}^{*} t\sigma$.

Example 1. The system

$$\mathcal{R} \begin{cases} \textbf{exp}(0) \to \textbf{s}(0) \\ \textbf{exp}(\textbf{s}(x)) \to \textbf{exp}(x) + \textbf{exp}(x) \\ x =^? x \to \textbf{true} \end{cases}$$

specifies the function $\textbf{exp}: n \mapsto 2^n$ on natural numbers, where the result is represented as a term over $\{0, \textbf{s}, +\}$. Figure 1 demonstrates that goals of the form

$$\textbf{exp}(x) =^? \underbrace{\textbf{s}(0) + \ldots + \textbf{s}(0)}_{2^n\text{-times}}$$

can be solved in $n + 2$ steps if narrowing steps merge two occurrences of an **exp**-call into one call. In contrast, tree-based narrowing (and also the "minimally

---

[3] We assume that this rule has no common variables with G. If this is not the case, then the variables in $l \to r$ are renamed into variables from $\text{Var} - \text{Var}(G)$.

[4] Given a graph morphism $f: G \to H$ and a node v in H, $f^{-1}(v)$ denotes the set $\{\bar{v} \in V_G \mid f(\bar{v}) = v\}$.

[5] The composition of term graph substitutions is defined analogously to the term case.

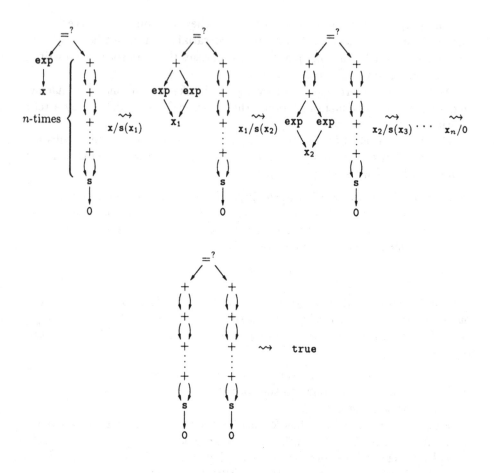

Fig. 1. A term graph narrowing derivation

collapsing narrowing" of Section 6) needs a number of steps exponential in n to solve these goals.

In [7] it is shown that term graph narrowing is sound for arbitrary term rewriting systems and complete for systems $\mathcal{R}$ with a normalizing and confluent graph rewrite relation $\Rightarrow_{\mathcal{R}}$.

Theorem 1 (soundness and completeness of narrowing). *Let G be a term graph such that $\mathrm{term}(G)$ is a goal $s =^{?} t$.*

1. *If $G \rightsquigarrow_{\alpha}^{*} \triangle\mathrm{true}$, then α^{term} is a solution of $s =^{?} t$.*
2. *If $\Rightarrow_{\mathcal{R}}$ is normalizing and confluent, then for every solution σ of $s =^{?} t$ there exists a narrowing derivation $G \rightsquigarrow_{\beta}^{*} \triangle\mathrm{true}$ such that $\beta^{\mathrm{term}} \leq_{\mathcal{R}} \sigma \, [\mathrm{Var}(G)]$.[6]*

---

[6] Given term substitutions σ and τ, and $V \subseteq Var$, we write $\sigma =_{\mathcal{R}} \tau \, [V]$ if $x\sigma \leftrightarrow_{\mathcal{R}}^{*} x\tau$ for each $x \in V$, and $\sigma \leq_{\mathcal{R}} \tau \, [V]$ if there is a substitution ρ such that $\sigma\rho =_{\mathcal{R}} \tau \, [V]$.

Sufficient conditions for confluence and termination of $\Rightarrow_{\mathcal{R}}$ can be found in [18]. We just mention that if $\Rightarrow_{\mathcal{R}}$ is normalizing, then $\Rightarrow_{\mathcal{R}}$ is confluent if and only if $\rightarrow_{\mathcal{R}}$ is confluent.

4   The Lifting Lemma

Now we show how to transform a term graph rewrite derivation $G \Rightarrow_{\mathcal{R}}^{*} H$, where $G = G'\alpha$ for some substitution α, into a narrowing derivation $G' \leadsto_{\beta}^{*} H'$ such that $H'\gamma \succeq H$ for some substitution γ. This Lifting Lemma is essential for proving the completeness of the different narrowing strategies considered in the following sections.

In [7] completeness is proved by a two-stage lifting of rewrite derivations: derivations are transformed into "minimally collapsing" rewrite derivations which in turn can be lifted to minimally collapsing narrowing derivations (being often longer than the given rewrite derivations). This lifting mechanism cannot be used to show, for example, the completeness of maximally collapsing narrowing. Therefore we establish a new Lifting Lemma which lifts rewrite derivations directly to narrowing derivations and, consequently, is more flexible to use.

Before stating the Lifting Lemma at the end of this section, we provide the lemmata used in its proof. A key construction will be the suitable lifting of collapsings "over" substitutions which is described in Lemma 3.

Lemma 1 (factorization of substitutions). *Let $G'\alpha = G$ for some normalized term graph substitution α,[7] and U be a set of nodes in G'. Suppose that there is a term l and a term substitution σ such that $\text{term}_G(u) = l\sigma$ for all $u \in U$. Moreover, let V be a finite subset of Var such that $\text{Var}(G') \cup \text{Dom}(\alpha) \subseteq V$. Then there exist term graph substitutions β and γ such that (1) β^{term} is a most general unifier of $\{\text{term}_{G'}(u) \mid u \in U\} \cup \{l\}$, (2) $(\beta\gamma)|_V = \alpha$, and (3) γ is normalized.*

Proof. Similar to the proof of the corresponding lemma in [7].   □

Lemma 2 (induced collapsing). *For every collapsing $G \succeq_c H$ and substitution α there is a collapsing $G\alpha \succeq_{\hat{c}} H\alpha$.*

The collapsing $\hat{c}$ of Lemma 2 is said to be *induced* by c and α. Below we lift a collapsing $G'\gamma \succeq H$ over the substitution γ to a collapsing $G' \succeq H'$ such that $H'\gamma \succeq H$. The collapsing $G' \succeq H'$ is constructed in such a way that it "approximates" $G'\gamma \succeq H$ as far as possible.

Lemma 3 (collapse lifting). *Let $G \succeq_c H$ be a collapsing and G' be a term graph such that $G'\alpha = G$ for some substitution α. Then there is a collapsing $G' \succeq_d H'$ such that for all nodes v and w in G', $d(v) = d(w)$ if and only if $c(v) = c(w)$ and $\text{term}_{G'}(v) = \text{term}_{G'}(w)$. Moreover, there is a collapsing $H'\alpha \succeq H$.*

---

[7] A term graph substitution $\alpha = \{x_1/G_1, \ldots, x_n/G_n\}$ is *normalized* if $G_1, \ldots, G_n$ are normal forms with respect to $\Rightarrow_{\mathcal{R}}$.

Proof. Let $\sim$ be the equivalence relation on $V_{G'}$ defined by: $v \sim w$ if $c(v) = c(w)$ and $\text{term}_{G'}(v) = \text{term}_{G'}(w)$. Let $V_{H'}$ be the set of equivalence classes of $\sim$, and let $d_V: V_{G'} \to V_{H'}$ map each node to its equivalence class. An analogous construction yields the edge set $E_{H'}$ and the mapping $d_E: E_{G'} \to E_{H'}$, where two edges in G' are equivalent if there source nodes are. Given an edge equivalence class $[e]$, define $\text{lab}_{H'}([e]) = \text{lab}_{G'}(e)$ and $\text{att}_{H'}([e]) = [v][v_1] \ldots [v_n]$ if $\text{att}_{G'}(e) = v v_1 \ldots v_n$ It is easy to see that H' is well-defined and that $d = \langle d_V, d_E \rangle$ is a graph morphism. Now the collapsing $H'\alpha \succeq_e H$ is defined by considering the collapsing $G'\alpha \succeq_{\hat{d}} H'\alpha$ induced by d and α. Given any node v in H', select some $u \in \hat{d}^{-1}(v)$ and define $e(v) = c(u)$. It is not difficult to verify that e is well-defined.

If a collapsing is followed by a rewrite step such that the redex node has only one preimage, the collapsing can be "shifted" behind the rewrite step.

Lemma 4 (collapse shifting [7]). *Let $G \succeq_c G' \Rightarrow_{v,l \to r} H$ be a collapsing followed by a proper rewrite step such that $c^{-1}(v)$ contains a single node $\overline{v}$. If $\langle \overline{v}, l \to r \rangle$ is a redex, then there is a term graph H' such that $G \Rightarrow_{\overline{v}, l \to r} H' \succeq H$.*

Now we are ready to show that a collapsing together with a subsequent rewrite step can be lifted to a narrowing step.

Lemma 5. *Let $G \succeq M \Rightarrow_{v,l \to r} H$ be a rewrite derivation with one proper rewrite step, and G' be a term graph such that $G'\alpha = G$ for some normalized substitution α. Moreover, let $V \subseteq \text{Var}$ be a finite set of variables such that $\text{Var}(G') \cup \text{Dom}(\alpha) \subseteq V$. Then there is a narrowing step $G' \leadsto_{U,l \to r, \beta} H'$ and a normalized substitution γ such that $H'\gamma \succeq H$ and $(\beta\gamma)|_V = \alpha$.*

Proof. Without loss of generality, we may assume $\text{Var}(l) \cap V = \emptyset$ (otherwise the variables of l are renamed). Let $U = c^{-1}(v)$. Since $\langle v, l \to r \rangle$ is a redex, there is a term substitution σ such that $\text{term}_G(u) = \text{term}_M(v) = l\sigma$ for each u in U. Since α is normalized, all nodes in U are non-variable nodes in G'. By Lemma 1, there exist term graph substitutions β and γ such that (1) β^{term} is a most general unifier of $\{\text{term}_{G'}(u) \mid u \in U\} \cup \{l\}$, (2) $(\beta\gamma)|_V = \alpha$, and (3) γ is normalized. Let $G'\beta \succeq_d M'$ be the lifting of the collapsing $G \succeq M$ over γ, as specified in Lemma 3. By definition of d, there is a node $\overline{v}$ in M' such that $U = d^{-1}(\overline{v})$. Moreover, for each $u \in U$ and each (repeated) variable x in l, d identifies the nodes in $G'\beta|_u$ corresponding to the occurrences of x in l. This is because c identifies these nodes, too (otherwise $\langle v, l \to r \rangle$ were not a redex). Hence $\langle \overline{v}, l \to r \rangle$ is a redex in M'.

Now, by Lemma 3, there is a collapsing $M'\gamma \succeq_e M$. The construction of e in the proof of Lemma 3 and the fact that c identifies all nodes in U imply $e^{-1}(v) = \{\overline{v}\}$. Hence, by Lemma 4, there is a term graph $\overline{H}$ such that $M'\gamma \Rightarrow_{\overline{v}, l \to r} \overline{H} \succeq H$. Since $\langle \overline{v}, l \to r \rangle$ is a redex in M', there is a restricted rewrite step $M' \Rightarrow_{\overline{v}, l \to r} H'$ such that $H'\gamma \succeq H$. This completes the proof of the lemma. $\square$

Lemma 6 (Lifting Lemma). *Let $G \Rightarrow_{\mathcal{R}}^* H$ be a rewrite derivation and G' be a term graph such that $G'\alpha = G$ for some normalized substitution α. Moreover, let V be a finite subset of* Var *such that* $\mathrm{Var}(G') \cup \mathrm{Dom}(\alpha) \subseteq V$. *Then there is a narrowing derivation $G' \leadsto_{\beta}^* H'$ and a normalized substitution γ such that $H'\gamma \succeq H$ and $(\beta\gamma)|_V = \alpha$.*

Proof. By induction on the number of proper rewrite steps in $G \Rightarrow_{\mathcal{R}}^* H$, using Lemma 5. $\qquad\square$

5 Basic Term Graph Narrowing

In order to reduce the search space of narrowing, Hullot [11] introduced *basic narrowing* as a restricted form of narrowing and showed its completeness over terminating and confluent term rewriting systems. In this section, we define basic term graph narrowing and show that it is complete whenever term graph rewriting is innermost normalizing and confluent. We also present a counterexample showing that innermost normalization cannot be relaxed to normalization.

Given two nodes v and v' in a term graph G, we write $v \geq_G v'$ if v' is reachable from v, and by $v >_G v'$ we mean $v \geq_G v'$ and $v \neq v'$.

Definition 8 (basic narrowing derivation). *Let $G_1 \leadsto_{\alpha_1} \cdots \leadsto_{\alpha_{n-1}} G_n$ be a narrowing derivation where each step has the form $G_i \mapsto G_i\alpha_i \succeq_{c_i} G_i' \Rightarrow_{v_i, l_i \to r_i} G_{i+1}$. Define sets of nodes $A_1, \ldots, A_n$ as follows: (i) $A_1 = \mathrm{Nonvar}(G_1)$[8] and (ii) for $1 \leq i < n$, $A_{i+1} = \mathrm{track}(A_i^{*\prime}) + \mathrm{Nonvar}(\Diamond r_i)$[9] where $A_i^* = \{v \in c_i(A_i) \mid c_i^{-1}(v) \subseteq A_i\}$ and $A_i^{*\prime} = A_i^* - \{v \mid v_i \geq_{G_i'} v\}$. Nodes in A_i are basic nodes and nodes in $V_{G_i} - A_i$ are non-basic for $1 \leq i \leq n$. We say that the above narrowing derivation is basic if $c_i^{-1}(v_i) \subseteq A_i$ for $1 \leq i < n$.*

Definition 9 (basic rewrite derivation). *Let $G_1 \Rightarrow_{\mathcal{R}} \cdots \Rightarrow_{\mathcal{R}} G_n$ be a rewrite derivation and $B \subseteq \mathrm{Nonvar}(G_1)$. Define sets of nodes $B_1, \ldots, B_n$ as follows: (i) $B_1 = B$ and (ii) for $1 \leq i < n$, $B_{i+1} = \mathrm{track}(B_i') + \mathrm{Nonvar}(\Diamond r_i)$, where $B_i' = B_i - \{v \mid v_i \geq_{G_i} v\}$, if $G_i \Rightarrow_{v_i, l_i \to r_i} G_{i+1}$, and $B_{i+1} = \{v \in c_i(B_i) \mid c_i^{-1}(v) \subseteq B_i\}$ if $G_i \succ_{c_i} G_{i+1}$. The above rewrite derivation is basic with respect to B if $v_i \in B_i$ for each proper rewrite step $G_i \Rightarrow_{v_i, l_i \to r_i} G_{i+1}$.*

While original narrowing considers any non-variable nodes in the goal, basic narrowing discards all nodes that have been introduced by the substitution of a previous narrowing step.

Definition 10. (innermost derivation) *A proper rewrite step $G \Rightarrow_{v, l \to r} H$ is an innermost step if $\mathrm{term}_G(v')$ is a normal form for all nodes v' with $v >_G v'$. A rewrite derivation $G \Rightarrow_{\mathcal{R}}^* H$ is an innermost derivation if all its proper rewrite*

---

[8] For a term graph G, Nonvar(G) is the set of non-variable nodes in G.

[9] For every rewrite step $G' \Rightarrow H$ there is a partial function track: $V_{G'} \to V_H$ which sends each node in G' to its descendant in H (see [7] for a formal definition).

steps are innermost steps. The term graph rewrite relation $\Rightarrow_\mathcal{R}$ *is* innermost normalizing *if every term graph has a normal form which can be reached by an innermost derivation.*

Lemma 7 (innermost derivations are basic). *Let* G' *be a term graph and* α *a normalized substitution. Every innermost term graph rewrite derivation starting from* $G'\alpha$ *is basic with respect to* Nonvar(G').

Lemma 8 (lifting of basic derivations). *Let* α *be a normalized substitution. Lemma 6 transforms every term graph rewrite derivation* $G'\alpha \Rightarrow_\mathcal{R}^* H$ *that is basic with respect to* Nonvar(G') *into a basic narrowing derivation* $G' \rightsquigarrow_\beta^* H'$.

The following property is proved in [7].

Lemma 9 (from solutions to term graph derivations). *Let* $\Rightarrow_\mathcal{R}$ *be normalizing and confluent, and* G *be a term graph such that* term(G) *is a goal* $s =^? t$. *Then for every solution* σ *of* $s =^? t$, *there exists a normalized term graph substitution* α *such that* $G\alpha \Rightarrow_\mathcal{R}^* \Delta$true *and* $\alpha^{\text{term}} =_\mathcal{R} \sigma$ [Var(G)].

Combining Lemmata 9, 7 and 8, we obtain the completeness of basic term graph narrowing.

Theorem 2 (completeness of basic term graph narrowing). *Basic term graph narrowing is complete[10] whenever term graph rewriting is innermost normalizing and confluent.*

The following counterexample demonstrates that "innermost normalizing" cannot be relaxed to "normalizing" (contrary to our claim in [8]).

Example 2. The following term rewriting system results from adding the rule $g(a, x) \rightarrow g(a, x)$ (and $x =^? x \rightarrow$ true) to the system shown in the introduction:

$$\mathcal{R} \begin{cases} f(x) \rightarrow g(x, x) \\ \qquad a \rightarrow b \\ g(a, b) \rightarrow c \\ g(b, b) \rightarrow f(a) \\ g(a, x) \rightarrow g(a, x) \\ x =^? x \rightarrow \text{true} \end{cases}$$

The new rule allows to copy a shared constant a. Now every term graph has a unique normal form, which can be shown by induction on the size of term graphs. Hence $\Rightarrow_\mathcal{R}$ is normalizing and confluent. However, the goal $f(a) =^? c$ cannot be solved by basic term graph narrowing. This can be seen from Figure 2, where we underline function symbols at non-basic positions. Note that in every application of $g(a, x) \rightarrow g(a, x)$, the second argument of g becomes non-basic.

---

[10] If not stated otherwise, completeness is always understood in the sense of the second part of Theorem 1.

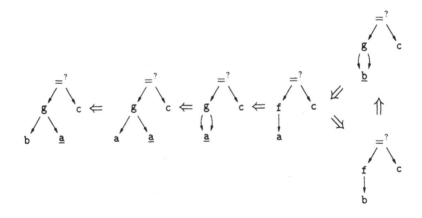

Fig. 2. Incompleteness of basic term graph narrowing

6 Minimally Collapsing Narrowing

Term graph narrowing steps as introduced in Definition 7 are non-deterministic not only with respect to the choice of the node set U and the rewrite rule $l \to r$, but also with respect to the collapsing $G\alpha \succeq_c G'$. In this and the next section we consider the two extreme choices for this collapsing, obtaining *minimally collapsing* and *maximally collapsing* narrowing.

Minimally collapsing rewrite derivations contain only collapse steps that are necessary to apply non-left-linear rewrite rules. That is, each collapse step in such a derivation turns a preredex of a non-left-linear rule into a redex.

Definition 11 (minimal collapsing). *A collapsing $G \succeq M$ is minimal with respect to a redex $\langle v, l \to r \rangle$ in M if for each term graph M' with $G \succeq M' \succ_c M$ and each preimage $v' \in c^{-1}(v)$ of v in M', the preredex $\langle v', l \to r \rangle$ is not a redex.*

In particular, if G and M are isomorphic, then $G \succeq M$ is minimal since no M' with $G \succeq M' \succ M$ exists. A proper collapsing $G \succ M$ is minimal only if $l \to r$ is non-left-linear and cannot be applied at any preimage of v in G.

Definition 12 (minimally collapsing derivation). *A rewrite derivation is minimally collapsing if each collapse step $G \succ M$ in the derivation is followed by a proper rewrite step $M \Rightarrow_{v, l \to r} N$ such that $G \succ M$ is minimal with respect to $\langle v, l \to r \rangle$. A narrowing derivation is minimally collapsing if for each narrowing step $G \mapsto G\alpha \succeq_c G' \Rightarrow_{v, l \to r} H$ in the derivation, the collapsing $G\alpha \succeq_c G'$ is minimal with respect to $\langle v, l \to r \rangle$.*

Note that in a minimally collapsing narrowing step $G \leadsto_{U, l \to r, \alpha} H$, the set U must be a singleton due to the definition of a minimal collapsing.

Theorem 3 (completeness of minimally collapsing narrowing).
Minimally collapsing narrowing is complete whenever term graph rewriting is normalizing and confluent.

Proof. By Theorem 4.8 of [7], for every rewrite derivation $G \Rightarrow^*_{\mathcal{R}} H$ there is a minimally collapsing derivation $G \Rightarrow^*_{\mathcal{R}} H'$ such that $H' \succeq H$. By the construction of lifted collapsings in Lemma 3 and the proof of Lemma 5, every minimally collapsing rewrite derivation is lifted by Lemma 6 to a minimally collapsing narrowing derivation. Combining this with Lemma 9 yields the desired result. $\square$

We now consider the combination of minimally collapsing and basic narrowing. By Example 2 we already know that this strategy is not complete in general for normalizing and confluent term graph rewriting. To ensure completeness, normalization has to be strengthened to innermost normalization or the given rewrite system has to be right-linear.

Theorem 4 (completeness of minimally collapsing basic narrowing).
Minimally collapsing basic narrowing is complete whenever term graph rewriting is innermost normalizing and confluent.

Proof. It is not difficult to check that Theorem 4.8 of [7] transforms every innermost rewrite derivation into a minimally collapsing innermost derivation. Hence, the proposition is obtained by combining Lemmata 9, 7 and 8, and by using the fact that lifting transforms minimally collapsing rewrite derivations into minimally collapsing narrowing derivations. $\square$

Innermost normalization can be relaxed to normalization if the given rewrite system is right-linear. This can be proved by using the corresponding result for term narrowing [15], exploiting the fact that for right-linear systems, every (basic) narrowing derivation on terms can be simulated by a minimally collapsing (basic) narrowing derivation on term graphs.

Theorem 5 (completeness for right-linear systems).
Minimally collapsing basic narrowing is complete for right-linear term rewriting systems over which term graph rewriting is normalizing and confluent.

Here we mean by "complete" that for every goal $s =^? t$ and every solution σ of this goal, there exists a narrowing derivation $\Delta(s =^? t) \leadsto^*_\beta \Delta\mathbf{true}$ such that $\beta^{\mathrm{term}} \leq_{\mathcal{R}} \sigma \ [\mathrm{Var}(\Delta(s =^? t))]$. That is, we consider only narrowing derivations starting from the tree representation of the goal.

7   Maximally Collapsing Narrowing

We now consider maximally collapsing narrowing, that is, narrowing derivations in which all involved collapse steps are maximal. While minimally collapsing narrowing is complete when term graph rewriting is normalizing and confluent, we show by a counterexample that this is not the case for maximally collapsing narrowing. Completeness can be restored, however, by strengthening normalization to termination.

Definition 13. (maximally collapsing derivations) *A rewrite derivation is maximally collapsing if all its collapse steps yield fully collapsed term graphs and if all proper rewrite steps start from fully collapsed term graphs. A narrowing derivation is maximally collapsing if for each narrowing step $G \mapsto G\alpha \succeq_c G' \Rightarrow_{v, l \to r} H$ in the derivation, G' is fully collapsed.*

In Example 1, for instance, the goal is solved by a maximally collapsing narrowing derivation. The following counterexample demonstrates that maximally collapsing narrowing, even when not restricted to basic narrowing, is not complete in general for normalizing and confluent term graph rewriting.

Example 3. Consider the following term rewriting system:

$$\mathcal{R} \begin{cases} g(x, y) \to g(a, a) \\ \quad\quad a \to b \\ g(a, b) \to b \\ x =^? x \to \texttt{true} \end{cases}$$

Here $\Rightarrow_{\mathcal{R}}$ is normalizing and confluent since every term graph representing a term of the form $g(\ldots)$ can be reduced to Δb. However, the tree $\Delta g(a, a)$ representing $g(a, a)$ cannot be reduced to this normal form by a maximally collapsing derivation: the picture below shows all maximally collapsing derivations starting from $\Delta g(a, a)$. As a consequence, maximally collapsing term graph narrowing cannot solve the goal $g(a, a) =^? b$, although $g(a, a) \leftrightarrow_{\mathcal{R}}^* b$.

Now we show that maximally collapsing narrowing—even in combination with basic narrowing—becomes complete when normalization is strengthened to termination.

Theorem 6 (completeness of maximally collapsing basic narrowing). *Maximally collapsing basic narrowing is complete whenever term graph rewriting is terminating and confluent.*

Proof. If $\Rightarrow_{\mathcal{R}}$ is terminating and confluent, then every term graph can be reduced to its normal form by applying as long as possible in an alternating way maximal collapse steps and (arbitrary) rewrite rules. Combining this with Lemmata 9, 7, 8 and the observation that the Lifting Lemma transforms maximally collapsing rewrite derivations into maximally collapsing narrowing derivations, we obtain the desired result. □

As a corollary of Theorem 6, maximally collapsing basic narrowing is complete for all terminating and confluent term rewriting systems. For, the latter are properly included in the class $\{\mathcal{R} \mid \Rightarrow_{\mathcal{R}}$ is terminating and confluent$\}$ (see [17,18]).

8   Conclusion

We summarize our results about the completeness of term graph narrowing strategies in the following table. Here the normalization and confluence properties refer to term graph rewriting, a "yes" indicates completeness and "no" means that there exists a counterexample.

	normalizing & confluent	rightlinear, normalizing & confluent	innermost normalizing & confluent	terminating & confluent
basic	no	yes	yes	yes
min. coll.	yes	yes	yes	yes
min. coll. basic	no	yes	yes	yes
max. coll.	no	no	?	yes
max. coll. basic	no	no	?	yes

We conjecture that innermost normalization and confluence are sufficient to make maximally collapsing basic narrowing complete.

A topic for future work is to investigate combinations of minimally and maximally collapsing narrowing with known refinements of basic (term) narrowing such as LSE narrowing [4,19].

By employing stronger restrictions on rewrite rules, like non-ambiguity, left-linearity etc., one may also adopt strategies like needed and lazy narrowing [1,16,10] and consider their completeness when combined with various sharing strategies. A first step into this direction is done in [6], where term graph narrowing over orthogonal constructor systems is considered.

References

1. Sergio Antoy, Rachid Echahed, and Michael Hanus. A needed narrowing strategy. In *Proc. Symposium on Principles of Programming Languages*, pages 268–279. ACM Press, 1994.
2. Franz Baader and Tobias Nipkow. *Term Rewriting and All That*. Cambridge University Press, 1998.
3. Franz Baader and Jörg H. Siekmann. Unification theory. In D.M. Gabbay, C.J. Hogger, and J.A. Robinson, editors, *Handbook of Logic in Artificial Intelligence and Logic Programming*, pages 41–125. Clarendon Press, 1994.
4. Alexander Bockmayr, Stefan Krischer, and Andreas Werner. Narrowing strategies for arbitrary canonical rewrite systems. *Fundamenta Informaticae*, 24:125–155, 1995.

5. Nachum Dershowitz and Jean-Pierre Jouannaud. Rewrite systems. In Jan van Leeuwen, editor, *Handbook of Theoretical Computer Science,* volume B, chapter 6, pages 244–320. Elsevier, 1990.

6. Rachid Echahed and Jean-Christophe Janodet. Admissible graph rewriting and narrowing. In *Proc. Joint International Conference and Symposium on Logic Programming 1998.* MIT Press, 1998.

7. Annegret Habel and Detlef Plump. Term graph narrowing. *Mathematical Structures in Computer Science,* 6:649–676, 1996.

8. Annegret Habel and Detlef Plump. Completeness of narrowing in non-copying implementations. Informatik-Bericht 19/97, Universität Hildesheim, Institut für Informatik, 1997.

9. Michael Hanus. The integration of functions into logic programming: From theory to practice. *The Journal of Logic Programming,* 19 & 20:583–628, 1994.

10. Michael Hanus. Lazy narrowing with simplification. *Journal of Computer Languages,* 23(2–4):61–85, 1997.

11. Jean-Marie Hullot. Canonical forms and unification. In *Proc. 5th International Conference on Automated Deduction,* volume 87 of *Lecture Notes in Computer Science,* pages 318–334. Springer-Verlag, 1980.

12. Jean-Pierre Jouannaud and Claude Kirchner. Solving equations in abstract algebras: A rule-based survey of unification. In Jean-Louis Lassez and Gordon Plotkin, editors, *Computational Logic: Essays in Honor of Alan Robinson,* pages 257–321. MIT Press, 1991.

13. Jan Willem Klop. Term rewriting systems. In S. Abramsky, Dov M. Gabbay, and T.S.E. Maibaum, editors, *Handbook of Logic in Computer Science,* volume 2, pages 1–116. Oxford University Press, 1992.

14. Madala R.K. Krishna Rao. Completeness results for basic narrowing in non-copying implementations. In *Proc. Int. Joint Conference and Symposium on Logic Programming.* MIT Press, 1996.

15. Aart Middeldorp and Erik Hamoen. Completeness results for basic narrowing. *Applicable Algebra in Engineering, Communication and Computing,* 5:213–253, 1994.

16. Aart Middeldorp, Satoshi Okui, and Tetsuo Ida. Lazy narrowing: Strong completeness and eager variable elimination. *Theoretical Computer Science,* 167(1,2):95–130, 1996.

17. Detlef Plump. Collapsed tree rewriting: Completeness, confluence, and modularity. In *Proc. Conditional Term Rewriting Systems,* volume 656 of *Lecture Notes in Computer Science,* pages 97–112. Springer-Verlag, 1993.

18. Detlef Plump. Term graph rewriting. In H. Ehrig, G. Engels, H.-J. Kreowski, and G. Rozenberg, editors, *Handbook of Graph Grammars and Computing by Graph Transformation,* volume 2. World Scientific, 1998. To appear.

19. Andreas Werner. Normalizing narrowing for weakly terminating and confluent systems. In *Proc. Principles and Practice of Constraint Programming,* volume 976 of *Lecture Notes in Computer Science,* pages 415–430. Springer-Verlag, 1995.

20. Akihiro Yamamoto. Completeness of extended unification based on basic narrowing. In *Proc. Logic Programming '88,* volume 383 of *Lecture Notes in Artificial Intelligence,* pages 1–10. Springer-Verlag, 1989.

Non-deterministic Computations in **ELAN**

Hélène Kirchner and Pierre-Etienne Moreau

LORIA-CNRS & INRIA
BP 239
54506 Vandœuvre-lès-Nancy Cedex, France

Abstract. The ELAN system is an environment for specifying and prototyping constraint solvers, theorem provers and deduction systems in
general. It also provides a framework for experimenting their combination. The ELAN language is based on rewriting logic and evaluation of
labelled conditional rewrite rules. ELAN has two originalities with respect
to several other algebraic languages, namely to handle non-deterministic
computations and to provide a user-defined strategy language for controlling rule application. We focus in this paper on these two related
aspects and explain how non-determinism is used in ELAN programs
and handled in the ELAN compiler.

1 Introduction

The ELAN system [KKV95] provides an environment for specifying and prototyping deduction systems in a language based on rules controlled by strategies.
Its purpose is to support the design of theorem provers, logic programming languages, constraints solvers and decision procedures and to offer a framework for
studying their combination.

ELAN takes from functional programming the concept of abstract data types
and the function evaluation principle based on rewriting. In ELAN a rewrite
rule may be labelled, may have conditions and may introduce local variables.
But rewriting is inherently non-deterministic since several rules can be applied
simultaneously on a same term. So in ELAN, a computation may have several
results. This aspect is taken into account through choice operations and a backtracking capability. One of the main originality of the language is to provide
strategy constructors to specify whether a function call returns several, at-least
one or only one result. Non-determinism is handled with two operators: dc standing for dont-care-choose and dk standing for dont-know-choose. Determinism is
enforced by the operator dc one standing for dont-care-choose one result. This
declarative handling of non-determinism is part of a strategy language allowing
the programmer to specify the control on rules application. This is in contrast
to many existing rewriting-based languages where the term reduction strategy is
hard-wired and not accessible to the designer of an application. The strategy language offers primitives for sequential composition, iteration, deterministic and
non-deterministic choices of elementary strategies that are labelled rules. From
these primitives, more complex strategies can be expressed. In addition the user

J.L. Fiadeiro (Ed.): WADT'98, LNCS 1589, pp. 168–182, 1999.
© Springer-Verlag Berlin Heidelberg 1999

can introduce new strategy operators and define them by rewrite rules. Evaluation of strategy application is itself based on rewriting. Moreover it should be emphasised that ELAN has logical foundations based on rewriting logic [Mes92] and detailed in [BKK96,BKK98]. So the simple and well-known paradigm of rewriting provides both the logical framework in which deduction systems can be expressed and combined, and the evaluation mechanism of the language. The current version of ELAN includes an interpreter and a compiler written in C++ and Java, a library of standard ELAN modules, a user manual and examples of applications. Among those, let us mention for instance the design of rules and strategies for constraint satisfaction problems [Cas98], theorem proving tools in first-order logic with equality [KM95,CK97], the combination of unification algorithms and of decision procedures in various equational theories [Rin97,KR98]. More information on the system can be found on the WEB site[1].

A first ELAN compiler was designed and presented in [Vit96]. Experimentations made clear that a higher-level of programming is achieved when some functions may be declared as associative and commutative (AC for short). However rewriting in such theories is computationally difficult and the challenge is then to provide an efficient compiler for the language. The difficulty is both at the level of AC-matching and rewriting, addressed in [MK98], and at the level of non-deterministic computations, addressed in this paper. After a short presentation in Section 2 of ELAN programs and of the evaluation mechanism in ELAN, we explain in Section 3 the expressive power of non-deterministic features of the language and the related constructions of the strategy language. Then in Section 4, we detail how an analysis of non-determinism is performed and exploited in the ELAN compiler. We conclude in Section 5. We assume the reader familiar with basic definitions of term rewriting given for instance in [JK86].

2   Programs and evaluation mechanism of ELAN

An ELAN program is composed of a signature describing operators with their types, a list of rules and a list of strategies. A strategy provides a way to describe which computations the user is interested in, and specifies where a given rule should be applied in the term to be reduced. We describe informally here the evaluation mechanism and how it deals with rewrite rules and strategies.

In ELAN, rules are labelled rewrite rules with an optional sequence of conditions and/or local variable assignments:

$$[\text{lab}] \quad l \Rightarrow r \quad \{ \text{ if } v \quad | \quad \textbf{where } y := (S)u \ \}^*$$

where lab is the label, l and r are terms respectively called left and right-hand sides, v is a boolean term called condition, and $y := (S)u$ is a local assignment, giving to the local variable y the results of the strategy S applied to the term u. Any sequence of **where** and **if** is allowed and their order is relevant for the evaluation. For applying such a rule on a term t at top position, first l is matched

---
[1] http://www.loria.fr/ELAN.

against t, the expressions introduced by **where** and **if** are instantiated with the matching substitution and evaluated in order. Instantiations of local variables (such as y) after **where** extend the matching substitution. When every condition is satisfied, the replacement by the instantiated right-hand side is performed.

The local assignment mechanism has been extended from variables to patterns. Rules of the following form are allowed too:

$$[\mathsf{lab}] \quad l \Rightarrow r \quad \{ \text{ if } v \quad | \quad \text{ where } p := (S)u \ \}^{*}$$

where p is a term with variables. If p matches the result of the strategy S applied to the term u, its variables are instantiated and extend the main matching substitution, as before.

Unlabelled rules are applied with a leftmost-innermost strategy which is the default strategy built in the system. On the contrary, labelled rules are used in user-defined strategies and always applied at top position in the term to be reduced. Note that instantiations of local variables after **where** also invoke ELAN strategies.

A strategy is a function which, when applied to an initial term, returns a set of possible results. The strategy fails if the set is empty. A strategy is applied to a term, thanks to an application operator with the following type:

$$[\_]\_ : Strategy \times Term \to SetOfTerms$$

whose interpretation is given by labelled rewrite rules. The strategy interpreter is fully specified in ELAN. The strategy language and its semantics are described in [BKK98]. Let us explain now how to express a strategy, analyse when it fails and how is built its set of results.

- A labelled rule is a primal strategy. The result of applying a rule labelled lab on a term t returns a set of terms. This primal strategy fails if the set of resulting terms is empty.
- Two strategies can be concatenated by the symbol ";", i.e. the second strategy is applied on all results of the first one. $S_1; S_2$ denotes the sequential composition of the two strategies. It fails if either S_1 fails or S_2 fails. Its results are all results of S_1 on which S_2 is applied and gives some results.
- $dc(S_1, \ldots, S_n)$ chooses one strategy S_i in the list that does not fail, i.e. whose application gives a non-empty set of results, and returns all its results. This strategy may return more than one result, or fails if all sub-strategies S_i fail.
- dc one$(S_1, \ldots, S_n)$ chooses one strategy S_i in the list that does not fail, and returns its first result. This strategy returns at most one result or fails if all sub-strategies fail.
- $dk(S_1, \ldots, S_n)$ chooses all strategies given in the list of arguments and for each of them returns all its results. This set of results may be empty, in which case the strategy fails.
- The strategy id is the identity that does nothing but never fails.
- fail is the strategy that always fails and never gives any result.

- repeat*(*S*) applies repeatedly the strategy *S* until it fails and returns the results of the last unfailing application. This strategy can never fail (zero application of *S* is possible) and may return more than one result.
- The strategy iterate*(*S*) is similar to repeat*(*S*) but returns intermediate results of repeated applications.

Example 1. The following small program illustrates the syntax of ELAN. It designs a function enum that takes two integer arguments i and j and enumerates all numbers between them.

```
module example
 import global int ; end
 operators global
   next(@): (int) int ;
   enum(@,@): (int int) int ;
 end
 stratop global
   enumStrat : <int> ;
 end
 rules for int
   i,j,k,l: int ;
   global
   [] next(i) => i+1 end
   [r1] enum(i,j) => i end
   [r2] enum(i,j) => l
                 if i<j
                 where k:= () next(i)
                 where l:= (enumStrat) enum(k,j)
                 end
 end
 strategies for int
   [] enumStrat => dk(r1,r2) end
 end
```

This program is for instance executed via a request enum(20,40) and then counts from 20 to 40.

ELAN also gives the possibility to the user to define recursive and parameterised strategies with rewrite rules [BKK96,BKK98]. Given a set of strategy symbols, rewrite rules on user-defined strategies are of the form [lab] $S_1 \Rightarrow S_2$ where lab is a label, S_1 and S_2 are strategy terms built from all previously introduced strategy symbols. Such strategy rewrite rules are called *implicit* since they do not involve explicitly the application operator [-]-. However, it is sometimes useful to express a strategy rule depending on the argument on which it is applied. Such rules are also allowed and are called *explicit* strategy rules. They are of the form: [lab] $[S_1]$ $t \Rightarrow t'$, where S_1 is a strategy term as before, t is a term and t' is built on function and strategy symbols and possibly the strategy application operator. From the evaluation point of view, these rules are just added to the strategy interpreter. An example of recursive strategies is given in Example 2 of Section 4.3.

3   Non-determinism in **ELAN**

Let us first explain on a simple example the expressive power of the non-deterministic features provided in ELAN. Consider the modelisation of a game: a pawn on a chessboard can move in several directions (see figure 1), each of them corresponding to one labelled rule d_i. Exploring all possibilities of moves for this pawn in one step can be expressed by a strategy symbol move and a rule move $\Rightarrow$ dk$(d_1, \ldots, d_n)$. Once a move has been performed, in some situation, it may be considered as a definitive choice and the search space related to all other moves is forgotten. This is performed via a strategy dc one(move). In order to iterate this process, ELAN provides the constructor repeat* and the strategy repeat*(dc one(move)) repeatedly moves a given pawn up to a failure: in this example, a pawn cannot move when an external square is reached.

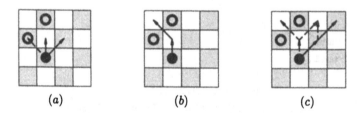

(a)   (b)   (c)

Fig. 1. Move a pawn on a chessboard. (a) – By applying dk(move) the pawn can move in three possible directions. (b) – An external square can be reached if the strategy repeat*(dc one(move)) is applied. (c) – Suppose that a final position should not be near a white pawn: backtracking is needed when applying repeat*(dk(move)); the explored search tree is illustrated by dashed arrows.

Assume now that one looks for moves that lead the pawn in a specific final position characterised by some predicate P. In this situation, when a move has been performed, it is not a definitive choice since the final position is not yet known. To be able to explore the search space, one can then replace repeat*(dc one(move)) by repeat*(dk(move)) and check if the predicate P is satisfied by the last found position. This can be expressed in ELAN by the following rule, where the current state of the game is represented by a two component structure <position, chessboard> whose first argument in the pawn's position and the second is the chessboard.

```
[win] <initPos,chessboard> => <finalPos,chessboard'>
      where <finalPos,chessboard'>:=
                  (repeat*(dk(move)))  <initPos,chessboard>
      if P(finalPos)
```

This sketch of a simple game can be instantiated by several other situations in the areas of constraint solving, rewriting and theorem proving. Let us take two more examples.

To simulate exploration of a derivation tree for instance, instead of defining move, one can define the strategy rewrite $\Rightarrow$ dk$(r_1,\ldots,r_n)$ that non-deterministically applies the n rules $r_1,\ldots,r_n$. The strategy dc one(rewrite) consists in a deterministic rewrite step by one of the rule that applies on top of the term to be reduced. The strategy repeat*(dc one(rewrite)) leads to a normal form, if the rewrite relation induced by the n rules terminates, while repeat*(dk(rewrite)) computes all normal forms. It can be specified that normal forms satisfy a given property, such as a size less than 20, for instance.

Another example is constraint solving which is now often formalised as a rewriting process that transforms a constraint into a set of solved forms providing the solutions. So computing one solution is reducing to a normal form, and finding all solutions is computing all normal forms. More specifically, for constraints on finite domains, constraint satisfaction techniques involve "generate and test" strategies which enumerate the finite set of possible values in the domain of each variable. More sophisticated strategies are developed for constraint satisfaction using the ELAN language in [Cas98].

The main difficulty when dealing with such real applications is first an efficiency problem. Thanks to new compilation techniques for matching and rewriting, as presented for instance in [MK98], rewrite rule systems can now lead to very efficient first-order functional programs, whose evaluation involves several millions of rewrite steps per second. The bottleneck is rather at the level of memory and backtracking management, related to handling non-determinism.

For implementation of backtracking, two functions are usually required: the first one, to create a choice point and save the execution environment; the second one, to backtrack to the last created choice point and restore the saved environment. Many languages that offer non-deterministic capabilities provide similar functions: for instance world+ and world- in Claire [CL96], try and retry in WAM [War83,AK90], onfail, fail, createlog and replaylog in the Alma-0 Abstract Machine [Par97,AS97]. Following [Vit96], two flow control functions, setChoicePoint and fail, have been implemented in assembly language. setChoicePoint sets a choice point, and the computation goes on. The fail function performs a jump into the last call of setChoicePoint. These functions can remind the pair of standard C functions setjmp and longjmp. However, the longjmp can be used only in a function called from the function setting setjmp. The two functions setChoicePoint and fail do not have such a limitation. Their implementation is described in [Mor98a,Mor98b]. Such functions may be useful in other contexts, for instance to implement backtracking in an imperative language, along the lines of Alma-0 [AS97].

Let us consider again the game example and suppose that several successive moves are performed by the repeat*(dc one(move)) strategy. In principle, when repeatedly applying a strategy S, the environment has to be saved between each application of the strategy, in order to be able to explore another branch in case of backtracking. In some situations, the strategy S can be known to return at most one result as it is the case in our example for dc one(move). One can then deduce that no backtracking is possible when applying such strategy and, consequently that it is no longer needed to save the environment before applying S. This informal reasoning is formalised in the next section and is made fully automatic in the ELAN environment.

4   Determinism analysis

The determinism analysis phase of the ELAN compiler annotates every rule and strategy in the program with its determinism mode for use in later phases of the compiler: matching phase, various optimisations on the generated code and detection of non termination.

4.1   Determinism modes

For each strategy, a mode is inferred according to the maximum number of results it can produce (one or more than one) and whether or not it can fail before producing its first result. We adopt the same terminology for determinism modes as in Mercury [HCS96,HSC96]:
- if the strategy cannot fail and has at most one result its mode is *deterministic* (det).
- if the strategy can fail and has at most one result, its mode is *semi-deterministic* (semi).
- if the strategy cannot fail and has more than one results, its mode is *multi-result* (multi).
- if the strategy can fail and may have more than one results, its mode is *non-deterministic* (nondet).
- if the strategy always fail, i.e. has no result, its mode is *failure* (fail).
A partial ordering on these modes is defined as follows:

$$\text{fail, det} < \text{semi, multi} < \text{nondet}$$

and intuitively corresponds to an ordering on the intervals which the number of results belongs to.

   The algorithm for inferring the determinism mode of strategies uses two operators *And* and *Or* that intuitively correspond to the composition and the union of two strategies (the union of two strategies is defined by the union of their results). Their values given in the following tables should be clear from the semantics given to the different modes. For instance, a conjunction of two strategies is semi-deterministic if any one can fail and none of them can return more than one result $(And(\mathsf{det}, \mathsf{semi}) = And(\mathsf{semi}, \mathsf{det}) = And(\mathsf{semi}, \mathsf{semi}) = \mathsf{semi})$. But they can be also computed with operations on boolean variables as for instance in [HSC96].

And	det	semi	multi	nondet	fail
det	det	semi	multi	nondet	fail
semi	semi	semi	nondet	nondet	fail
multi	multi	nondet	multi	nondet	fail
nondet	nondet	nondet	nondet	nondet	fail
fail	fail	fail	fail	fail	fail

Or	det	semi	multi	nondet	fail
det	multi	multi	multi	multi	det
semi	multi	nondet	multi	nondet	semi
multi	multi	multi	multi	multi	multi
nondet	multi	nondet	multi	nondet	nondet
fail	det	semi	multi	nondet	fail

4.2   dc one, dc, dk constructors

The non-determinism of ELAN is handled by three operators: dc one, dc and dk. These operators are heavily overloaded: they can be applied on a single rewrite rule or a single strategy, on a list of rules or a list of strategies, or a list of both strategies and rules. To describe all those combinations, we introduce four primitive operators, not accessible to the programmer, that allow us to classify the cases according to two different levels of control.

Controlling the number of results: given a rewrite rule or a strategy,
- the one operator builds a strategy that returns at most one result;
- the all operator builds a strategy that returns all possible results of the strategy or the rule.

Controlling the choice mechanism: given a list of strategies (possibly reduced to a singleton),
- the select one operator chooses and returns a non-failing strategy among the list of strategies;
- the select all operator returns all unfailing strategies.
If the list contains only failing strategies, the current operation fails.

Using these four primitives, the three ELAN strategy constructors dc one, dc, dk can be defined by the following axioms, where S_i stands for a rule or a strategy:

$$
\begin{aligned}
\mathsf{dc\ one}(S_1, \ldots, S_n) &= \mathsf{select\ one}(\mathsf{one}(S_1), \ldots, \mathsf{one}(S_n)) \\
\mathsf{dc}(S_1, \ldots, S_n) &= \mathsf{select\ one}(\mathsf{all}(S_1), \ldots, \mathsf{all}(S_n)) \\
\mathsf{dk}(S_1, \ldots, S_n) &= \mathsf{select\ all}(\mathsf{all}(S_1), \ldots, \mathsf{all}(S_n))
\end{aligned}
$$

Note that dc and dk operators are equivalent if they are applied on a unique argument : $dc(S) = dk(S) = S$.

4.3   Determinism mode inference

The algorithm for inferring the determinism mode is presented here in three steps: for a strategy, it uses the decomposed form of ELAN strategy operators into their primitives representation. For a rule, it analyses the modes of the conditions and local assignments. Finally it deals with the recursivity problem due to the fact that strategies are built from rules and that rules call strategies in their local assignments.

Strategy d-mode inference – The d-mode of a strategy is inferred from its expression using one, all, select one and select all.

- d-mode(one(S)) = semi if S is a rewrite rule, since application of a rewrite rule may fail; otherwise,

$$d\text{-mode}(one(S)) = \begin{cases} det & \text{if d-mode(S) is det or multi} \\ semi & \text{if d-mode(S) is semi or nondet} \end{cases}$$

- $$d\text{-mode}(all(S)) = \begin{cases} And(semi, d\text{-mode}(S)) & \text{if S is a rewrite rule} \\ d\text{-mode}(S) & \text{otherwise} \end{cases}$$

- $$d\text{-mode}(repeat^*(S)) = \begin{cases} det & \text{if d-mode(S) is det or semi} \\ multi & \text{if d-mode(S) is multi or nondet} \end{cases}$$

  The repeat* operator cannot fail because zero application of the strategy is allowed. Note that if S cannot fail, the repeat* construction cannot terminate.

- d-mode(iterate*(S)) = multi. The iterate* operator cannot fail either. In general, it returns more than one result because all intermediate steps are considered as results. If S cannot fail, the iterate* construction cannot terminate, but this is quite useful to represent infinite data structures, like infinite lists.
- d-mode($S_1; S_2$) = $And(\text{d-mode}(S_1), \text{d-mode}(S_2))$.
- d-mode(select one($S_1, \ldots, S_n$)) = $And(\text{d-mode}(S_1), \ldots, \text{d-mode}(S_n))$
- d-mode(select all($S_1, \ldots, S_n$)) = $Or(\text{d-mode}(S_1), \ldots, \text{d-mode}(S_n))$

Rule d-mode inference – Inferring the mode of a rewrite rule R consists in analysing the determinism mode of its conditions and local assignments.

- Evaluating a *condition* consists in normalising (with unlabelled rules) a boolean term and comparing its normal form with the builtin boolean term *true*. So evaluating a condition can never fail. If the reduced term is not *true*, the current rule cannot be applied, but this does not modify the d-mode of the rule. This is why a condition is usually said to be deterministic (det is a neutral element for the *And* operator).

The only different situation is when a variable of the boolean term occurs in the left-hand side of the rule with AC function symbols: if this variable is involved in an AC matching problem, it may have several possible instances, thus, an application of the rule may return more than one result. The condition is said to be multi.

- A *local assignment* has the determinism mode of the strategy used to compute its value. If no strategy occurs in the local assignment, it is said to be deterministic.

The mode of the rewrite rule R is the conjunction (*And* operation) of the inferred determinism modes of all conditions and local assignments.

Recursivity problem – In ELAN, strategy definitions may be (mutually) recursive. So the d-mode of a strategy may depend on itself. This is similar to the problem well-known in logic programming of finding the mode of a predicate [ST85]. To avoid non-termination of the determinism analysis algorithm, when the d-mode of a strategy depends on itself, a default mode is given. On the strategy constructors, this default corresponds to the maximum of the modes in the ordering $<$ that the strategy can have and is given in the next table.

constructor	one	all	repeat*	iterate*	;
default d-mode	semi	nondet	multi	multi	nondet

The default mode for the strategy selectors is computed as before from the default modes of the components.

Example 2. The following rule is used to implement the "N-horse problem" which consists in finding N consecutive moves for a horse on a chessboard, so that it does not visit the same square twice. The horse_strat searches all solutions for N consecutive moves.

```
rules for listOfPair
   [horse_n] horse(n) => position . listOfPositions
               if n>0
               where listOfPositions:=(horse_strat) horse(n-1)
               where position:=(move) head(listOfPositions)
               if not( position occurs in listOfPositions )
   end
strategies for listOfPair
   [] horse_strat     => dk(horse_n)       end
   [] det_horse_strat => dc_one(horse_n)   end
```

The horse_strat strategy is recursive, because it uses the rule horse_n in which a call to horse_strat is done. Its default d-mode is computed. Since dk(horse_n) = select all(all(horse_n)) = all(horse_n), the default d-mode is nondet. The second strategy det_horse_strat searches for only one solution of the horse problem.

Since dc one(horse_n) = one(horse_n), d-mode(det_horse_strat)=semi.

4.4 Impact of determinism analysis

The determinism analysis enables us to design better compilation schemes for det or semi strategies. With this approach, the search space size, the memory usage, the number of necessary choice points, and the time spent in backtracking and memory management can be considerably reduced. We can also take benefit from the determinism analysis to improve the efficiency of AC matching and detect some non-terminating strategies.

Several optimisations have been done to improve the backtracking management:

- When compiling a set of rules whose local assignments are deterministic, no choice point is needed because no backtracking can occur between local assignments.
- When compiling a set of rules with non-deterministic local assignments, some choice points are needed to handle the backtracking. But these choice points can be removed when the rule is applied with a strategy that requires at most one result. For instance, when searching only one solution to the horse problem (see Example 2), several choice points are needed for the rule horse_n, but they can be deleted when this rule is applied with the strategy dc one(horse_n).
- When dealing with non-deterministic strategies and the repeat* constructor, a lot of choice points have to be set, because the strategy is recursively called in all branches of the computation space. The situation can be depicted as follows, where the bullet represents a set choice point.

$$t \bullet \underset{\searrow_S^S}{\overset{\nearrow^S}{\lessgtr}}^S t_1 \bullet \underset{\searrow_S}{\overset{\nearrow^S}{\lessgtr}}^S s \cdots \bullet \underset{\searrow_S}{\overset{\nearrow^S}{\lessgtr}}^S t_n \bullet \underset{\searrow_S}{\overset{\nearrow^S}{\lessgtr}}^S \text{fail}$$

One choice point per step is needed, and when a failure occurs, one choice point only is deleted and the process goes on.

But this is no more the case when compiling a strategy repeat*(S) where S is det or semi. The compilation scheme then consists in setting a single choice point and trying to apply the strategy S as many times as possible. Each time the strategy S is applied, the resulting term is saved in a special variable $lastTerm$. When a failure occurs, the choice point is deleted and the saved term $lastTerm$ is returned. The situation is depicted as follows:

$$\bullet t \longrightarrow^S t_1 \longrightarrow^S \cdots \longrightarrow^S t_n \longrightarrow \text{fail}$$

Other advantages of determinism analysis are related to the rewriting process. To improve efficiency of rewriting, a well-known idea is to reuse parts of left-hand sides of rules to construct the right-hand sides [DFG+94,Vit96]. This technique avoids memory cell copies and reduces the number of allocations. Unfortunately, the presence of non-deterministic strategies and rules limits its applicability, because backtracking requires access to structures that would otherwise be reused. The determinism mode information is then used to detect cases where reusing is possible.

The determinism analysis is also important to design more efficient AC matching algorithms: when a rule is deterministic, only the first found match is needed to apply a rewrite step. This remark leads to the design of an *eager AC matching* algorithm which optimizes the construction of the dynamic data structure used in [MK98] for matching the patterns to the subject subterms. Experiments show a reduction of the number of matching attempts up to 50%, which significantly improves the overall performance of the system.

Finally the determinism analysis is also useful to detect some non-terminating strategies, such as a strategy **repeat***(S), where S never fails. Detecting this non-termination problem at compile time allows the system to give a warning to the programmer and can help him to improve his strategy design.

Any ELAN program execution can benefit from the determinism analysis techniques described in this paper. However, in order to give a more concrete estimation of the practical impact of determinism analysis, let us consider experimental results obtained on a selection of programs in different areas of programming styles.

- p5 and p8 correspond to the Knuth-Bendix completion of modified versions of the Group theory, with 5 (resp. 8) identity elements and 5 (resp. 8) inverse elements, together with the corresponding axioms. These theories are often benchmarks for theorem provers.
- minela is a small ELAN interpreter written in ELAN itself; it executes an ELAN program composed of pure conditional rules on an input term, and outputs the result together with a proof term that represents the derivation from the input term.
- queens is an implementation of the n-queens problem that searches for a solution with a chessboard of size $n = 14$. This is also a typical benchmark problem in logic programming.
- fib is a functional program that computes the 33th Fibonacci number. Again, this is a typical benchmark problem in functional programming.

Figure 2 gives for each program the number of generated setChoicePoint instructions for creating a choice point (Static CP), the number of choice points created at runtime (Dynamic CP), the memory needed to save local environments (Memory usage) and the number of applied rewrite rules per second (rwr/sec) on a Dec Alpha Station.

These results show clearly that the deterministic analysis significantly decreases the number of set choice points and improves the overall performance. But it also considerably decreases the amount of needed memory to save local environments. Let us consider the completion process for instance. Without any optimisation, the needed memory depends on the input term to reduce (p5 or p8). In practice, this memory area is fixed (1000 Kb for example) and for some other queries or programs, it is possible to get a "memory overflow" error message that stops the computation. When applying the deterministic analysis, the needed memory is usually reduced to a constant independent from the query. This constant corresponds to the number of choice points that are simultaneously

	Static CP	Dynamic CP	Memory usage	rwr/sec
p5 without DA	504	844,393	119 Kb	270,000
p5 with DA	63	528,976	**1 Kb**	751,389
p8 without DA	579	3,852,361	405 Kb	275,000
p8 with DA	66	2,464,491	**1 Kb**	844,034
minela without DA	611	1,219,960	5 Kb	66,313
minela with DA	282	1,175,180	3 Kb	72,292
queens without DA	29	28,366	2 Kb	431,861
queens with DA	3	26,481	2 Kb	**2,677,792**
fib without DA	3	11,405,773	1 Kb	584,911
fib with DA	0	0	0 Kb	**17,766,001**

Fig. 2. Impact of the deterministic analysis

set during the computation. It happened that programs running out of memory without deterministic analysis, eventually gave answers once this improvement was activated.

5   Conclusion

From the point of view of matching and rewriting, ELAN can be compared to other systems such as OBJ [GW88], ASF+SDF [Kli93], Maude [CELM96] or Cafe-OBJ [FN97]. But these languages do not involve non-deterministic strategy constructors. With respect to this feature, ELAN is closer to logic programming languages such as Alma-0 [AS97] or Mercury [HCS96]. In our case, the determinism analysis simply makes possible to run programs that could not be executed before due to memory explosion. This was the case in particular for constraint satisfaction problems. In other examples like completion processes, or the queens problem, this analysis significantly decreased the number of set choice points and improved the performance.

It seems now that further improvements of the compiler rely on the backtracking management. The setChoicePoint and fail functions implemented in assembly language turned out to be very useful for designing complex compilation schemas. But a deeper analysis reveals that useless informations are also stored in local environments. So it should be possible to improve the low-level management of non-determinism and to combine this with an efficient garbage collector. Together with this re-design of the memory management, we think of using a shared terms library, as in ASF+SDF, that would reduce the memory space needed for performing the computations.

Acknowledgements: We sincerely thank Peter Borovanský, Claude Kirchner, Christophe Ringeissen and Laurent Vigneron for helpful discussions, and the anonymous referees for their valuable comments.

References

AK90.   H. Aït-Kaci. The WAM: a (real) tutorial. Technical report 5, Digital Systems Research Center, Paris (France), January 1990.

AS97.   K. R. Apt and A. Schaerf. Search and imperative programming. In *24th POPL*, pages 67–79, 1997.

BKK96.   P. Borovanský, C. Kirchner, and H. Kirchner. Controlling rewriting by rewriting. In J. Meseguer, editor, *Proceedings of the first international workshop on rewriting logic*, volume 4 of *Electronic Notes in Theoretical Computer Science*, Asilomar (California), September 1996.

BKK98.   P. Borovanský, C. Kirchner, and H. Kirchner. A functional view of rewriting and strategies for a semantics of ELAN. In M. Sato and Y. Toyama, editors, *The Third Fuji International Symposium on Functional and Logic Programming*, pages 143–167, Kyoto, April 1998. World Scientific. Also report LORIA 98-R-165.

Cas98.   C. Castro. Building Constraint Satisfaction Problem Solvers Using Rewrite Rules and Strategies. *Fundamenta Informaticae*, 34:263–293, September 1998.

CELM96.   M. Clavel, S. Eker, P. Lincoln, and J. Meseguer. Principles of Maude. In J. Meseguer, editor, *Proceedings of the first international workshop on rewriting logic*, volume 4, Asilomar (California), September 1996. Electronic Notes in Theoretical Computer Science.

CK97.   H. Cirstea and C. Kirchner. Theorem proving Using Computational Systems: The case of the B Predicate Prover. Available at http://www.loria.fr/ ~cirstea/Papers/TheoremProver.ps, 1997.

CL96.   Y. Caseau and F. Laburthe. Introduction to the CLAIRE programming language. Technical report 96-15, LIENS Technical, September 1996.

DFG+94.   K. Didrich, A. Fett, C. Gerke, W. Grieskamp, and P. Pepper. OPAL: Design and implementation of an algebraic programming language. In J. Gutknecht, editor, *Programming Languages and System Architectures PLSA'94*, volume 782 of *Lecture Notes in Computer Science*, pages 228–244. Springer-Verlag, March 1994.

FN97.   K. Futatsugi and A. Nakagawa. An overview of CAFE specification environment – an algebraic approach for creating, verifying, and maintaining formal specifications over networks. In *Proceedings of the 1st IEEE Int. Conference on Formal Engineering Methods*, 1997.

GW88.   J. A. Goguen and T. Winkler. Introducing OBJ3. Technical Report SRI-CSL-88-9, SRI International, 333, Ravenswood Ave., Menlo Park, CA 94025, August 1988.

HCS96.   F. Henderson, T. Conway, and Z. Somogyi. The execution algorithm of Mercury, an efficient purely declarative logic programming language. *Journal of Logic Programming*, 29:17–54, October-December 1996.

HSC96. F. Henderson, Z. Somogyi, and T. Conway. Determinism analysis in the Mercury compiler. In *Proceedings of the Nineteenth Australian Computer Science Conference*, pages 337–346, Melbourne, Australia, January 1996.

JK86.   J.-P. Jouannaud and H. Kirchner. Completion of a set of rules modulo a set of equations. *SIAM Journal of Computing*, 15(4):1155–1194, 1986. Preliminary version in Proceedings 11th ACM Symposium on Principles of Programming Languages, Salt Lake City (USA), 1984.

KKV95. C. Kirchner, H. Kirchner, and M. Vittek. Designing constraint logic programming languages using computational systems. In P. Van Hentenryck and V. Saraswat, editors, *Principles and Practice of Constraint Programming. The Newport Papers.*, chapter 8, pages 131–158. The MIT press, 1995.

Kli93. P. Klint. A meta-environment for generating programming environments. *ACM Transactions on Software Engineering and Methodology*, 2:176–201, 1993.

KM95.   H. Kirchner and P.-E. Moreau. Prototyping completion with constraints using computational systems. In J. Hsiang, editor, *Proceedings 6th Conference on Rewriting Techniques and Applications, Kaiserslautern (Germany)*, volume 914 of *Lecture Notes in Computer Science*, pages 438–443. Springer-Verlag, 1995.

KR98.   C. Kirchner and C. Ringeissen. Rule-Based Constraint Programming. *Fundamenta Informaticae*, 34(3):225–262, September 1998.

Mes92. J. Meseguer. Conditional rewriting logic as a unified model of concurrency. *Theoretical Computer Science*, 96(1):73–155, 1992.

MK98.   P.-E. Moreau and H. Kirchner. A compiler for rewrite programs in associative-commutative theories. In *"Principles of Declarative Programming"*, number 1490 in Lecture Notes in Computer Science, pages 230–249. Springer-Verlag, September 1998. Report LORIA 98-R-226.

Mor98a. P.-E. Moreau. A choice-point library for backtrack programming. JICSLP'98 Post-Conference Workshop on Implementation Technologies for Programming Languages based on Logic, 1998.

Mor98b. P.-E. Moreau. Compiling nondeterministic computations. Technical Report 98-R-005, CRIN, 1998.

Par97. V. Partington. Implementation of an Imperative Programming Language with Backtracking. Technical Report P9714, University of Amsterdam, Programming Research Group, 1997. Available by anonymous ftp from ftp.wins.uva.nl, file pub/programming-research/reports/1997/P9712.ps.Z.

Rin97. C. Ringeissen. Prototyping Combination of Unification Algorithms with the ELAN Rule-Based Programming Language. In *Proceedings 8th Conference on Rewriting Techniques and Applications, Sitges (Spain)*, volume 1232 of *Lecture Notes in Computer Science*, pages 323–326. Springer-Verlag, 1997.

ST85.   H. Sawamura and T. Takeshima. Recursive unsolvability of determinacy, solvable cases of determinacy and their applications to Prolog optimization. In *Proceedings of the Second International Logic Programming Conference*, pages 200–207, Boston, Massachusetts, 1985.

Vit96. M. Vittek. A compiler for nondeterministic term rewriting systems. In H. Ganzinger, editor, *Proceedings of RTA'96*, volume 1103 of *Lecture Notes in Computer Science*, pages 154–168, New Brunswick (New Jersey), July 1996. Springer-Verlag.

War83. D. H. D. Warren. An abstract Prolog instruction set. Technical Report 309, SRI International, Artificial Intelligence Center, 1983.

Rasiowa-Sikorski Deduction Systems: A Handy Tool for Computer Science Logics

Beata Konikowska

Institute of Computer Science, Polish Academy of Sciences,
Ordona 21, 01–237 Warsaw,
fax (48+) (22) 37 65 64
beatak@ipipan.waw.pl

Abstract. A Rasiowa-Sikorski system is a sequence-type formalization of logics based on building decomposition trees of formulae labelled with sequences of formulae. Proofs are finite decomposition trees with leaves having "fundamental", valid labels. The system is dual to the tableau system. The author gives examples of applying the R-S formalism to various C.S and A.I. logic, including a logic for reasoning about relative similarity, a three-valued software specification logic with McCarthy's connectives, and a logic for nondeterministic specifications. As a new result, an R-S system for many-sorted first order logic with possibly empty carriers of some sorts is developed.

1 Introduction

An issue in computer science logics that has gained much popularity lately are the so-called labelled deductive systems [5]. The predecessors of this type of deductive systems were Beth's tableau systems [1] and Rasiowa-Sikorski (R-S) deduction systems [12], both developed over thirty years ago. Their important feature is that they give the proof a structure of a finitely-branching (usually binary) tree with vertices labelled by formulae (tableau), or sequences of formulae (R-S decomposition tree). Moreover, they are both in a sense dual. First, in a tableau system we prove the validity of a formula φ by showing that $\neg\varphi$ has a closed tableau, whereas in an R-S system we prove directly that φ has a closed, "correct" decomposition tree. Second, splitting of branches corresponds to disjunction in a tableau, and to conjunction in an R-S decomposition tree.

In spite of this duality, there is a large disparity in popularity of both these types of systems: the tableau systems have gained much popularity due to their widespread use in proof automation, whereas R-S systems have remained relatively unknown. However, in the author's experience Rasiowa-Sikorski systems have proved to be a very convenient and powerful tool for developing proof mechanisms of various kinds of logics related to software specification and knowledge representation. They have three indisputable advantages:

- A clearcut method of generating proof rules: for all the formula constructors, we give the condition for the resulting formula to be satisfied, and the condition for it to be not satisfied.

J.L. Fiadeiro (Ed.): WADT'98, LNCS 1589, pp. 183–197, 1999.

- A standard way of proving completeness by constructing a counter-model for a non-provable formula out of its "wrong" decomposition tree.
- An almost automatic way of transforming a complete R-S system into a complete cut-free Gentzen calculus system (see [3,7]).
- Proof trees very suitable for automated deduction: fairness of decomposition sewn into the system, each node contains all the historical information needed to continue the decomposition.

The aim of this paper is to describe the mechanism of the Rasiowa-Sikorski deduction system — which unfortunately is far from being generally known — and to show how it can be applied in various types of formal systems. The discussion is based on concrete examples coming from the author's experience connected with many-valued logics, nondeterminism, indiscerniblity and similarity. Finally, a new result concerning a simple formalization of many-sorted first order logic with possibly empty carriers of some sorts is given.

2   Presentation of the formalism

The Rasiowa-Sikorski deduction system belongs to the broad class of so-called "natural deduction" systems. It consists of *decomposition rules* for sequences of formulae ("inference rules" of the system and *fundamental sequences* ("axioms" of the system).

The system is used for constructing a *decomposition tree* of a formula (or finite sequence of formulae); if the tree is finite and all its leaves are labelled by fundamental sequences, then the formula (sequence) is said to be *provable*.

Below we assume the context of an arbitrary formal language with well-defined syntax and semantics. Satisfaction of a formula φ in a model M is denoted by $M \models \varphi$, and the set of all formulae - by $\mathcal{F}$.

Definition 1 *A sequence $\Omega = \varphi_1, \varphi_2, \ldots, \varphi_n$ of formulae is satisfied in a model M ($M \models \Omega$) iff $M \models \varphi_i$ for some i, and valid ($\models \Omega$) iff $M \models \Omega$ for each M.*

Fundamental sequences form a subclass of valid sequences, and are defined separately for each concrete logic. In classical first-order logic, a fundamental sequence contains both a formula and its negation.

Each *decomposition rule* is an expression of the form either

$$\frac{\Omega_1}{\Omega_2} \quad \text{or} \quad \frac{\Omega_1}{\Omega_2 \mid \Omega_3},$$

where all the Ω_i's are sequences of formulae. Ω_1 is called the *conclusion* of the rule, and Ω_2 (Ω_2, Ω_3) — its *premise(s)*. A rule is *sound* if its conclusion provided valid iff all its premises are valid.

Thus **sound decomposition rules** are equivalent rules **leading from valid sequences to valid sequences in both directions**.

An *indecomposable formula* is, intuitively, a simple formula not subject to decomposition. Its definition is tailored to a concrete logic; in classical first-order logic it is just any literal. A sequence of formulae is *indecomposable* if it contains only indecomposable formulae.

Any rule is of the form either $\dfrac{\Omega', \Sigma, \Omega''}{\Omega', \Sigma', \Omega''}$ or $\dfrac{\Omega', \Sigma, \Omega''}{\Omega', \Sigma', \Omega'' \mid \Omega', \Sigma'', \Omega''}$, where Ω' is indecomposable. Ω', Ω'' serve only as context, and the actually decomposed subsequence (formula) is Σ. Hence any decomposition rule is applied to the leftmost decomposable formula or subsequence Σ. Moreover, all indecomposable formulae are inherited by the next node in the decomposition tree.

As an example, below we give the full set of decomposition rules for first-order classical logic (quoted from [12]).

DECOMPOSITION RULES FOR CLASSICAL LOGIC:

$$\frac{\Omega', \neg\neg\alpha, \Omega''}{\Omega', \alpha, \Omega''} \qquad \frac{\Omega', \alpha \vee \beta, \Omega''}{\Omega', \alpha, \beta, \Omega''} \qquad \frac{\Omega', \neg(\alpha \vee \beta), \Omega''}{\Omega', \neg\alpha, \Omega'' \mid \Omega', \neg\beta, \Omega''}$$

$$\frac{\Omega', \alpha \wedge \beta, \Omega''}{\Omega', \alpha, \Omega'' \mid \Omega', \beta, \Omega''} \qquad \frac{\Omega', \neg(\alpha \wedge \beta), \Omega''}{\Omega', \neg\alpha, \neg\beta, \Omega''} \qquad \frac{\Omega', \forall x.\alpha, \Omega''}{\Omega', \alpha(z), \Omega''},$$

$$\frac{\Omega', \neg\forall x.\alpha, \Omega''}{\Omega', \neg\alpha(t/x), \Omega'', \neg\forall x.\alpha} \qquad \frac{\Omega', \exists x.\alpha, \Omega''}{\Omega', \alpha(t/x), \Omega'', \exists x.\alpha} \qquad \frac{\Omega', \neg\exists x.\alpha, \Omega''}{\Omega', \neg\alpha(z), \Omega''},$$

where z is a variable which does not appear above the double line, and t is any term free for x in α.

Note the mechanism of dealing with quantification in R-S systems: substitution of a new variable in case of universal quantification, and subsequent substitutions of arbitrary terms while copying the original formula in case of existential quantification. Shifting the existential quantifier to the end of the decomposed sequence assures fairness of decomposition.

Decomposition rules of any R-S system divide in **replacement rules** "breaking down" each formula into some simpler formulae, and **expansion rules** adding some formulae to the sequence, to closing it under e.g. symmetry or transitivity principle. An exemplary expansion rule is $\dfrac{\Omega', t = u, \Omega''}{\Omega', t = u, u = t, \Omega''}$.

The general idea of the R-S deduction system is to decompose the original formula with help of replacement rules into elementary, indecomposable formulae. In some logics, sequences of indecomposable formulae are "closed" by means of expansion rules. Proofs in R-S systems consist in constructing decomposition trees for formulae (sequences of formulae) using decomposition rules.

Definition 2 *A decomposition tree for a formula φ (a sequence Ω) is a maximal binary tree with nodes labelled by sequences of formulae, defined inductively as follows:*

(i) *The root of the tree is labeled by* φ (Ω).

(ii) *If a node v labelled by Σ is the leaf of a branch B of the tree constructed up to now, then*

 (a) **we terminate the branch B at node v** *if either:*

  (a1) Σ *is a fundamental sequence, or*

  (a2) Σ *is indecomposable, and no expansion rule is applicable to* Σ;

 (b) **otherwise we expand the branch B by attaching to** v:

  (b1) *a single son labelled by Σ_1, if* $\dfrac{\Sigma}{\Sigma_1}$ *is a rule applicable to Σ,*

  (b2) *two sons labelled by Σ_1, Σ_2 if* $\dfrac{\Sigma}{\Sigma_1 \mid \Sigma_2}$ *is a rule applicable to* Σ.

By refining this definition (see [8]), we can assure existence of a unique decomposition tree $DT(\Omega)$ $(DT(\varphi))$ for every sequence Ω (formula φ). Hence from now on we assume the decomposition tree is unique, and denote it as above.

Definition 3 *A decomposition tree is called a proof if it is finite and all its leaves are labelled by fundamental sequences. A formula φ (sequence Ω) is said to be provable, $(\vdash \varphi, \vdash \Omega)$ iff $DT(\varphi)$ $(DT(\Omega))$ is a proof.*

As an illustration of the R-S proof method, below give a proof of the formula $\neg a \vee (a \vee b) \wedge (a \vee c)$ in that system. Fundamental sequences — i.e. those containing both some formula and its negation — are underlined with a double line.

$$\neg \alpha \vee (\alpha \vee \beta) \wedge (\alpha \vee \gamma)$$

$$\neg \alpha, \alpha \vee \beta \qquad \neg \alpha, \alpha \vee \gamma$$

$$\underline{\underline{\neg \alpha, \alpha, \beta}} \qquad \underline{\underline{\neg \alpha, \alpha, \gamma}}$$

If the decomposition rules correctly represent semantics of a concrete language, then it is a straightforward thing to prove that the system is sound. It is more difficult to prove completeness, but there is a general strategy of the proof:

Theorem 1 *(Completeness) Any provable sequence Ω of formulae is valid.*

Proof (strategy): We argue by contradiction, showing that $\nvdash \Omega$ implies $\nvDash \Omega$.

There are two cases when $DT(\Omega)$ is not a proof. First, certain leaf might be not labelled by a fundamental sequence (Case 1), or the tree may be infinite. By König's lemma, the latter implies existence of an infinite branch B (Case 2).

In Case 1, the label Δ of the leaf must be an indecomposable sequence; in Case 2, the set Δ of all indecomposable formulae appearing in the labels on branch B cannot contain a fundamental sequence. In both cases Δ must be closed under all expansion rules due to maximality of the tree.

We construct a counter-model $CM = < C, v >$ for Δ with the universe consisting of either expressions of the language, or their equivalence classes. In Case

1, Ω cannot be true in CM. Indeed: as the rules are two-way ones, the label of a node of $DT(\Omega)$ is valid iff the labels of all its sons are valid. Since the sequence labelling a leaf of $DT(\Omega)$ is not valid and the tree is finite in Case 1, this proves Ω cannot be valid. In case 2, we prove by induction on the rank of a formula (defined as the maximal nesting of operators) that no formula on the infinite branch B can be true in CM. As the top node of this branch is the root labelled by Ω itself, then $CM \not\models \Omega$, i.e. Ω is not valid, QED.

3 Signed formulae

In many cases, the language we are interested in does not exhibit the dichotomous property characteristic for classical logic, where, given a model incorporating valuation, either a formula or its negation must be satisfied. This is the case e.g. when the logical calculus is many-valued, the negation is a non-standard one, or there is no negation at all. Such a situation is a drawback in developing the R-S deduction system. To overcome it, we can employ the mechanism of so-called signed formulae ([1]) that express satisfaction and non-satisfaction of the original formulae:

Definition 4 *A signed formula over $\mathcal{F}$ is any element of the set*

$$\mathcal{SF} = \{\mathbf{T}(\alpha) : \alpha \in \mathcal{F}\} \cup \{\mathbf{NT}(\alpha) : \alpha \in \mathcal{F}\}.$$

The notion of satisfaction of a signed formula in a model M is given by $M \models \mathbf{T}(\alpha)$ iff $M \models \alpha, M \models \mathbf{NT}(\alpha)$ iff $M \not\models \alpha$.

The $\mathbf{NT}$ operator introduces a two-valued meta-negation into the language, which helps us develop an R-S system much as in classical logic. Some examples of rules involving signed formulae will be given in the subsequent sections.

The extension of the language with signed formulae need not be permanent. Namely, the $\mathbf{T}$-$\mathbf{NT}$ operators are not nested, and can be dropped by passing from a complete R-S system for signed formulae to an equivalent Gentzen calculus for "ordinary" formulae as shown in [3,7].

The interest of such a transformation is threefold. First, it allows us to pass from a complete deduction system for a richer language of signed formulae to an equally complete deduction system for the original language in a quite automatic way. Second, in almost all cases the resulting Gentzen system is cut-free, which eliminates the clasical laborious task of proving the cut elimination theorem. Last - but not least - the Gentzen formalism is much more widely known than the Rasiowa-Sikorski one, so such a translation could generate a more widespread use of the deduction system obtained primarily using Rasiowa-Sikorski method.

4 Three-valued logics

The first example of an R-S system application we consider is McCarthy's three-valued logic with non-commutative disjunction and conjunction, which is of interest for software specification as it supports lazy, sequential computation. If we denote its three logical values by **tt** (truth), **ff** (falsity), and **ee** (undefinedness or error), then the truth tables of McCarthy's connectives are as follows:

NOT	**tt**	**ff**	**ee**
	ff	**tt**	**ee**

OR	**tt**	**ff**	**ee**
tt	**tt**	**tt**	**tt**
ff	**tt**	**ff**	**ee**
ee	**ee**	**ee**	**ee**

AND	**tt**	**ff**	**ee**
tt	**tt**	**ff**	**ee**
ff	**ff**	**ff**	**ff**
ee	**ee**	**ee**	**ee**

The R-S deduction system for this logic is developed using signed formulae (or, alternately, an "is-true" superpredicate $\mathbf{T}$ mapping three-valued predicates into two valued ones, and its classical negation $\neg\mathbf{T} = \mathbf{NT}$ — see [9]). If we accept **tt** as the only designated value, then the semantics of signed formulae is:

$$|\mathbf{T}(\alpha)| = \begin{cases} \mathbf{tt} \text{ iff } ||\alpha|| = \mathbf{tt} \\ \mathbf{ff} \text{ iff } ||\alpha|| \in \{\mathbf{ff}, \mathbf{ee}\}, \end{cases} \qquad |\mathbf{NT}(\alpha)| = \begin{cases} \mathbf{tt} \text{ iff } ||\alpha|| \in \{\mathbf{ff}, \mathbf{ee}\} \\ \mathbf{ff} \text{ iff } ||\alpha|| = \mathbf{tt} \end{cases}$$

where $||\cdot||, |\cdot|$ are interpretations of three-valued formulae and signed formulae, respectively. Hence we can "encode" all the possible values of a three-valued formula in a two-valued world by remarking that

$$||\alpha|| = \mathbf{tt} \text{ iff } ||\mathbf{T}(\alpha)|| = \mathbf{tt} \qquad\qquad ||\alpha|| = \mathbf{ff} \text{ iff } ||\mathbf{T}(\text{NOT } \alpha)|| = \mathbf{tt}$$
$$||\alpha|| = \mathbf{ee} \text{ iff } ||\mathbf{NT}(\alpha)|| = \mathbf{tt} \text{ and } ||\mathbf{NT}(\text{NOT } \alpha)|| = \mathbf{tt}$$

This allows us to develop an R-S deduction system for the language featuring McCarthy's connectives. Unlike classical logic, here we need four decomposition rules for each formula constructor ω except NOT : two of them express the conditions for $\omega(\cdot)$, NOT $\omega(\cdot)$ to be satisfied, and two — for the above formulae to be not satisfied. This follows from the fact that in a three-valued, and in general many-valued logic, "not true" does not coincide with "false".

As an example, let us give the four rules describing McCarthy's disjunction. The complete set of decomposition rules for the logic is given in [9].

$$\frac{\Omega', \mathbf{T}(\alpha \text{ OR } \beta), \Omega''}{\Omega', \mathbf{T}\alpha, \mathbf{T}\text{ NOT } \alpha, \Omega'' \mid \Omega', \mathbf{T}\alpha, \mathbf{T}\beta, \Omega''} \qquad \frac{\Omega', \mathbf{T}\text{ NOT }(\alpha \text{ OR } \beta), \Omega''}{\Omega', \mathbf{T}\text{ NOT } \alpha, \Omega'' \mid \Omega', \mathbf{T}\text{ NOT } \beta, \Omega''}$$

$$\frac{\Omega', \mathbf{NT}(\alpha \text{ OR } \beta), \Omega''}{\Omega', \mathbf{NT}\alpha, \Omega'' \mid \Omega', \mathbf{NT}\text{ NOT } \alpha, \mathbf{NT}\beta, \Omega''} \qquad \frac{\Omega', \mathbf{NT}\text{ NOT }(\alpha \text{ OR } \beta), \Omega''}{\Omega', \mathbf{NT}\text{ NOT } \alpha, \mathbf{NT}\text{ NOT } \beta, \Omega''}$$

5 Similarity logic

By a similarity relation we mean a reflexive and symmetric binary relation on a set of entities (see [6,7]). Given a set of entities and a set of properties for classifying them, we have a whole family of similarity relations: one for each subset of the set of properties. The semantic framework we work with is a *universe*

$$U = < \text{ENT}, \text{PROP}, \{sim(P)\}_{P \subseteq \text{PROP}} > \tag{1}$$

where ENT is a set of *entities*, PROP — a non-empty set of *properties*, and $\{sim(P)\}_{P \subseteq \text{PROP}}$ is a family of *similarity relations* on ENT such that:

(C1) Each $sim(P)$ is a reflexive and symmetric binary relation on ENT;
(C2) $sim(\emptyset) = \text{ENT} \times \text{ENT}$;
(C3) $sim(P \cup Q) = sim(P) \cap sim(Q)$ for any $P, Q \subseteq$ PROP.

We consider the operations of the *upper* and *lower approximations* of a set of entities E under the similarity relation $sim(P)$, defined as follows:

$$\overline{\text{sim}}(P)E = \{e \in \text{ENT} : (\exists e')((e, e') \in sim(P) \text{ and } e' \in E)\},$$
$$\underline{\text{sim}}(P)E = \{e \in \text{ENT} : (\forall e')((e, e') \in sim(P) \text{ implies } e' \in E)\} \tag{2}$$

The language is built over a fixed set PROP of properties. Its terms represent subsets of PROP, and formulae in FORM — subsets of ENT. The set TERM contains CONP $= \{\mathbf{p} : p \in \text{PROP}\}$, a constant $\mathbf{0}$, and VARSP — variables representing subsets of PROP; it is closed under $-, \cup, \cap$ representing set-theoretic operations. FORM contains VARE and VARSE — sets of variables representing individual entities and sets of entities, resp., and is closed under $\neg, \vee, \wedge$, denoting set-theoretic operations. Finally, if $A \in$ TERM and $F \in$ FORM, then $\underline{sim}(A)F, \overline{sim}(A)F \in$ FORM. We also use a derived constructor $\rightarrow$ defined by $F \rightarrow G \overset{df}{=} \neg F \vee G$,

A model $M = < U, v >$ consists of a universe U and a valuation v of variables. A formula F is satisfied in a model iff it evaluates to the whole set ENT.

The above logic is a polymodal logic, with relative modalities represented by $\underline{sim}(A)$ and $\overline{sim}(A)$. The Rasiowa-Sikorski system presented here was the first complete axiomatization of this logic, after the problem had been open for several years.

The logic is not dichotomic, since neither F nor $\neg F$ generally holds. We base deduction on formulae of the type $x \rightarrow F$, where $x \in$ VARE and F is any formula. They model set-theoretic membership relation, since $x \rightarrow F$ is satisfied in $M = < U, v >$ iff $v(x) \in ||F||_M$, and have the desired dichotomic property: for any model M, either $M \models x \rightarrow F$ or $M \models x \rightarrow \neg F$. A special kind of such formulae of the form $x \rightarrow \overline{sim}(A) \, y$, denoted shortly by $x \, sim(A) \, y$, express the similarity relation itself, since $M \models x \, sim(A) \, y$ iff $(v(x), v(y)) \in sim(|A|_M)$.

We use the signed formulae to represent "top-level" negation. It suffices to consider signed formulae over the $x \rightarrow F$ type formulae only, since we can reduce all other formulae to them with the following decomposition rules:

$$\frac{\Omega', \mathbf{T}(F), \Omega''}{\Omega', \mathbf{T}(y \in F), \Omega''} \qquad\qquad \frac{\Omega', \mathbf{NT}(F), \Omega''}{\Omega', \mathbf{NT}(x \in F), \Omega'', \mathbf{NT}(F)}$$

where $x, y \in$ VARE, y is a new variable, and, F is not of the form $z \in G$.

The relative modalities $\underline{sim}(A), \overline{sim}(A)$ are dealt with by the following rules:

$$\frac{\Omega', \mathbf{T}(x \in \overline{sim}(A)F), \Omega''}{\Omega', \mathbf{T}(y \in F), \Omega'', * \mid \Omega', \mathbf{T}(x \, s(A)y), \Omega'', *} \qquad \frac{\Omega', \mathbf{T}(x \in \underline{sim}(A)F), \Omega''}{\Omega', \mathbf{NT}(x \, s(A) \, z), \mathbf{T}(z \in F), \Omega''}$$

where $s(\cdot)$ stands for $sim(\cdot)$, $y \in$ VARE is arbitrary, * denotes the formula $\mathbf{T}(x \in \overline{sim}(A)F)$, and $z \in$ VARE is a new variable. The omitted $\mathbf{NT}$-rules reflect the duality of $\underline{sim}$ and $\overline{sim}$.

To cope with the set parameters A in modalities, before applying our deduction system we replace each A by a union of atomic "components" that evaluate to a disjoint cover of PROP in every model. In case of elementary formulas of the form $T(x\ sim(A)\ y), NT(x\ sim(A)\ y)$, we can break down a term A being the union of some components into individual components using the rules

$$\frac{\varOmega', \mathbf{T}(x\ sim(A \cup B)\ y), \varOmega''}{\varOmega', \mathbf{T}(x\ s(A)\ y), \varOmega'' \mid \varOmega', \mathbf{T}(x\ s(B)\ y), \varOmega''} \qquad \frac{\varOmega', \mathbf{NT}(x\ sim(A \cup B)\ y), \varOmega''}{\varOmega', \mathbf{NT}(x\ s(A)\ y), \mathbf{NT}(x\ s(B)\ y), \varOmega''}$$

All the above mechanisms allow us to get a complete R-S system for the polymodal similarity logic (see [8]).

6 A logic for nondeterministic specifications

The next example is a logic for nondeterministic specifications presented in [2,3]. Such specifications are needed both for specifying nondeterministic operations like *choose* and for modeling the concept of under-specifying. The logic is interpreted in multialgebras, i.e. algebras with set-valued functions. Its language has only two constructs: "let" and a "rewrite" operator $\rightarrow$ interpreted as set inclusion. In spite of such limited means (no logical connectives at all!), there is a concise R-S deduction system for the logic. This shows a decided advantage of the R-S formalism in this case, since the only two other complete deduction systems for similar kind of logics presented in [6, 13] assumed rather unnatural restrictions on the model level.

Let $\varSigma = [S, F]$ be an algebraic signature, where S is the set of sorts, and F — the set of function symbols, and let X be an S-sorted set of variables.

- A multialgebra over $\varSigma$ is a tuple $A = [S^A, F^A]$, where $S^A = \{A_s\}_{s \in S}$ is a family of carrier sets and $F^A = \{f^A\}_{f \in F}$ is a family of set-valued functions such that $f^A : A_{s_1} \times \ldots \times A_{s_n} \rightarrow P(A_s)$ with $[f : s_1 \times \ldots \times s_n \rightarrow s] \in F$.
- An n-term over $\varSigma$ is any term built over variables in X with help of the function symbols $f \in F$ and the [let $x := t'$ in t ni] construct.
- A formula is any expression of the form $t \rightarrow t'$, where t, t' are n-terms.

The set of all n-terms over $\varSigma$ and X is denoted by $NT_\varSigma(X)$, and the set of all formulae — by $F_\varSigma(X)$.

The language is interpreted in models of the form $M =< A, v >$, where A is a multialgebra and $v : X \rightarrow |A|$ is a (multi-sorted) valuation of variables. For any $x \in X$, $a \in |A|$, define $v[a/y](x) = a$ iff $x = y$, and $v(x)$ otherwise. The interpretation of n-terms in $M =< A, v >$ is a function $\bar{v} : NT_\varSigma(X) \rightarrow P(|A|)$ defined by:

- $\bar{v}(x) = \{v(x)\}$, $\qquad \bar{v}(f(t_1, \ldots, t_n)) = \bigcup_{a_i \in \bar{v}(t_i)} f^A(a_1, \ldots, a_n)$
- $\bar{v}([\text{let } x := t' \text{ in } t \text{ ni}]) = \bigcup_{a \in \bar{v}(t')} \overline{v[a/x]}(t)$ $\qquad\qquad\qquad\qquad\qquad\quad \square$

Thus the usual substitution of functions is interpreted by taking a set-theoretic union over all possible combinations of values, whereas the [let x := t' in t ni] construct limits nondeterminism and allows us to substitute the same value of t' for every occurrence of x in t.

Since $\rightarrow$ is interpreted as inclusion, with the arrow pointing to the smaller set, then satisfaction of a formula $t \rightarrow t'$ in $M = \langle A, v \rangle$ is defined by

$$M \models t \rightarrow t' \text{ iff } \overline{v}(t) \supseteq \overline{v}(t')$$

To develop an R-S system for this logic, we proceed analogously as for similarity logic. Thus we base deduction on the $t \rightarrow x$ formulae, where $x \in X$, and introduce top-level negation via signed formulae.

The two basic rules for the $\rightarrow$ operator are:

$$\frac{\Omega', \mathbf{T}(t_1 \rightarrow t_2), \Omega''}{\Omega', \mathbf{NT}(t_2 \rightarrow x), \mathbf{T}(t_1 \rightarrow x), \Omega''} \qquad \frac{\Omega', \mathbf{NT}(t_1 \rightarrow t_2), \Omega''}{\Omega', \mathbf{T}(t_2 \rightarrow y), \Omega'', * \mid \Omega', \mathbf{NT}(t_1 \rightarrow y), \Omega'', *}$$

where t_2 is not a variable in X, $x \in X$ does not appear in the conclusion, y is an arbitrary variable in X, and * denotes the formula $\mathbf{NT}(t_1 \rightarrow t_2)$.

The **T**-rules corresponding to normal substitution and to the **let** construct clearly demonstrate the difference between the two:

$$\frac{\Omega', \mathbf{T}(f(..., t_i, ...) \rightarrow x), \Omega''}{\Omega', \mathbf{T}(t_i \rightarrow y), \Omega'', * \mid \Omega', \mathbf{T}(f(..., y, ...) \rightarrow x), \Omega'', *}$$

$$\frac{\Omega', \mathbf{T}([\text{let } x := l \text{ in } t \text{ ni}] \rightarrow x'), \Omega''}{\Omega', \mathbf{T}(l \rightarrow y), \Omega'', * \mid \Omega', \mathbf{T}(t[y/x] \rightarrow x'), \Omega'', *}$$

where y is an arbitrary variable in X, and * denotes $\mathbf{T}(f(..., t_i, ...) \rightarrow x)$.

The complete set of decomposition rules for the logic is given in [2].

7   Many-sorted first order logic with possibly empty carriers of some sorts

Now we shall give a new result illustrating one more application of R-S systems.

It is a known fact that classical deduction rules for first-order logic become unsound in presence of empty carriers of some sorts. Indeed: if we interpret universal quantification over an empty set of values as trivially true, and existential quantification over such a set - as trivially false, then $\forall x. \varphi$ implies neither $\varphi(z)$ nor $\exists x. \varphi$, which contradicts classical entailment. The problem is certainly important, since empty carriers do appear as an useful tool in software specifications. The only approaches to dealing with it known in the literature (see [4, 10, 14]) are based on rather rich languages, involving concepts like dynamic sorts, and in general diverge rather far from the simplicity of classical first-order logic.

We shall provide a simple formalization of many-sorted first-order logic allowing for empty carriers of some sorts based on an R-S system. Our logic will diverge from the classical one only in introducing a context of a formula consisting of the sorts that should be nonempty in order that the formula could be interpreted.

7.1   Syntax of the language

Consider an arbitrary finite and nonempty set S of sorts, to be fixed for the sequel. We also assume the existence of a fixed sort b of logical values.

For any $s \in S$, let X_s be a countable set of individual variables of sort S such that $X_s \cap X_{s'} = \emptyset$ for $s \neq s'$, and let $X = \bigcup_{s \in S} X_s$. The unique sort of a variable $x \in X$ will be denoted by $s.x$. Each formula of the language $\mathcal{L}_S$ we shall define will be equipped with a context $C \subseteq S$.

Assume we are given sets $F_{w,s}$ ($w \in S^*, s \in S$) of function symbols of arity $f : w \to s$, and sets P_w ($w \in S^*$) of predicate symbols of arity $w \to b$.

The set $\mathcal{T} = \bigcup_{s \in S} \mathcal{T}_s$ of terms of $\mathcal{L}_S$, where $\mathcal{T}_s$ is the set of terms of sort s, is defined in the standard way over the sets of variables and function symbols given above. A term t of sort s will be sometimes denoted by t^s.

Definition 5 *The minimal context of a term t of the language L_S is*
$C_{min}(t) = \{s.x : x \in X \text{ and } x \text{ occurs in } t\}$
The minimal context of a pre-formula φ is $C_{min}(\varphi) = \{s.x : x \in Free(\varphi)\}$, where $Free(\varphi)$ is the set of all variables occurring free in φ.

Intuitively, a minimal context of a term t or a formula φ contains all the sorts whose nonemptiness guarantees definedness of t or φ, respectively. Sufficiency of the minimal context for determining the value of t or φ follows from the fact that we consider models with total functions only (see below).

Definition 6 *By a formula of $\mathcal{L}_S$ we mean every expression of the form $C.\varphi$, where $C \subseteq S$ is a context, $\varphi \in \mathcal{PF}$ is a pre-formula, and $C \supseteq C_{min}(\varphi)$.*
The set of all formulae of $\mathcal{L}_S$ is denoted by $\mathcal{F}_S$.

7.2   Semantics of the language

The language will be interpreted in models based on S-sorted structures defined below. We assume that our fixed sort b of Boolean values has a carrier $B = \{tt, ff\}$, where **tt** denotes truth, and **ff** - falsity.

Definition 7 *An S-structure is any triple $\mathcal{A} = <\{A_s\}_{s \in S}, \mathbf{F}, \mathbf{P}>$, where:*

1. *for any $s \in S$, A_s is a set (possibly empty), called the carrier of sort s;*
2. *$\mathbf{F}$ is an interpretation of function symbols such that, for any $w = s_1 s_2 \cdots s_n \in S^*, s \in S$, we have $\mathbf{F}(f) : A_{s_1} \times A_{s_2} \times \cdots \times A_{s_n} \to A_s$ for any $f \in F_{w,s}$;*
3. *$\mathbf{P}$ is an interpretation of predicate symbols such that, for any $w = s_1 s_2 \ldots s_n \in S^*$, we have $\mathbf{P}(p) : A_{s_1} \times A_{s_2} \times \cdots \times A_{s_n} \to b$ for any $p \in P_w$.*

We assume that all the function and predicate symbols are interpreted as total functions and predicates, which has important consequences for the issue of emptiness of carriers. Namely, if L_S contains a constant $f : 0 \to s$, then the carrier A_s of sort s must be nonempty in each model M. Moreover, if L_S contains a function symbol $f : s \to s'$ and the carrier $A_{s'}$ is empty in a model M, then the carrier A_s must also be empty in the model M ("propagation of emptiness") - for otherwise f could not be interpreted as a total function on A_s.

Definition 8 *By an S-sorted valuation, shortly: a valuation, of variables in a structure $\mathcal{A}$ we mean a partial mapping $v : X \to \bigcup_{s \in S} A_s$ such that $Dom(v) = \bigcup\{X_s : A_s \neq \emptyset\}$ and $v(x^s) \in A_s$ for any $x^s \in Dom(v)$.*
By a model we mean an ordered pair $M =< \mathcal{A}, v >$, where $\mathcal{A}$ is an S-sorted structure, and v is an S-sorted valuation of variables in $\mathcal{A}$.

Due to possible emptiness of carriers and introduction of contexts, both the interpretation of terms and interpretation of formulae will be partial functions.

Definition 9 *The interpretation of terms in a model $M =< \mathcal{A}, v >$ is a partial function $\mathbf{T}_M : \mathcal{T}_S \to \bigcup_s A_s$ such that: $Dom(\mathbf{T}_M) = \{t \in \mathcal{T} : (\forall s \in C_{min}(t))A_s \neq \emptyset\}$, and $\mathbf{T}_M(\mathcal{T}_s) \subset A_s$ for every $s \in S$, defined in the standard way basing on the valuation v and interpretation of the function symbols in the structure $\mathcal{A}$.*

For any model $M =< \mathcal{A}, v >$, $x \in X_s$ and $a \in A_S$, by $M[a/x]$ we denote the model $M[a/x] =< \mathcal{A}, v[a/x] >$ with $v[a/x]$ defined as in Section 6.

Definition 10 *The interpretation of formulae in a model $M =< \mathcal{A}, v >$ is a partial function $\mathbf{F}_M : \mathcal{F}_S \to \{\mathbf{tt}, \mathbf{ff}\}$ such that $Dom(\mathbf{F}_M) = \{C.\varphi \in \mathcal{F} : (\forall s \in C)A_s \neq \emptyset\}$ defined inductively as follows:*

1. *for formulae without quantifiers, $\mathbf{F}_M(C.p)$ is defined on the basis of $\mathbf{T}_M$ using the standard interpretation of logical connectives;*

2. $\mathbf{F}_M(C.(\forall x.\varphi)) = \begin{cases} \mathbf{tt} \text{ if either } A_{s.x} = \emptyset \text{ or } A_{s.x} \neq \emptyset \text{ and} \\ \quad \mathbf{F}_M[a/x].(C \cup \{s.x\}).\varphi = \mathbf{tt} \text{ for every } a \in A_{s.x} \\ \mathbf{ff} \text{ otherwise.} \end{cases}$

3. $\mathbf{F}_M(C.(\exists x.\varphi)) = \begin{cases} \mathbf{tt} \text{ if } A_{s.x} \neq \emptyset \text{ and } \mathbf{F}_M[a/x].(C \cup \{s.x\}).\varphi = \mathbf{tt} \\ \quad \text{ for some } a \in A_{s.x} \\ \mathbf{ff} \text{ otherwise.} \end{cases}$

4. *$\mathbf{F}_M$ is extended to other formulae by standard interpretation of connectives.*

7.3 Rasiowa-Sikorski deduction system

We assume that our language contains a logical constant $c : 0 \to b$, and define special 'emptiness' and 'non-emptiness' formulae' E_s, N_s for each sort $s \in S$ by

$$E_s \stackrel{df}{=} \emptyset.\forall \xi^s.c \wedge \neg c, \qquad N_s \stackrel{df}{=} \emptyset.\exists \xi^s.c \vee \neg c$$

where ξ^s is a fixed variable in X_s for any $s \in S$, and $\emptyset$ denotes the empty context.

Fact 1 *For every model* $M =< A, v >$, *we have* $M \models E_s$ *iff* $A_s = \emptyset$, *and* $M \models N_s$ *iff* $A_s \neq \emptyset$, *where* A_s *is the carrier of sort* s *in structure* A.

The above formulae play a key role in the deduction system, allowing us to deal with quantification in presence of empty carriers.

Definition 11 *A sequence* $\Omega = \alpha_1, \alpha_2, \ldots, \alpha_n$ *is* fundamental *if it contains*

1. *either both the formulae* E_s, N_s *for some* $s \in S$, *or*
2. *each of* $E_{s_1}, \ldots, E_{s_n}, C.\varphi, C.\neg\varphi$, *where* $C = \{s_1, s_2, \ldots, s_n\}$ *and* $\varphi \in \mathcal{PF}$,

Obviously, every fundamental sequence is valid. Indeed: as the carrier of sort s is either empty or nonempty, then sequence 1. is valid. In sequence 2. either one of the carries A_{s_i} is empty, or they are all nonempty and the formulae $C.\varphi, C.\neg\varphi$ are both in the domain of interpretation, whence one of them has to be true in the model, which implies such a sequence is also valid.

Definition 12 *A formula* $\alpha \in \mathcal{F}$ *is said to be* indecomposable *if it has one of the following forms:*

1. *either* E_s *or* N_s *for some* $s \in S$;
2. $C_{min}(\varphi).\varphi$, *where* φ *is a literal of the form either* $p(t_1, \ldots, t_n)$ *or* $\neg p(t_1, \ldots, t_n)$ *with* $p \in P_w, w = s_1 \ldots s_n, t_i \in \mathcal{T}_{s_i}, i = 1, 2, \ldots, n$.

A sequence of formulae is said to be indecomposable *if each element of this sequence is an indecomposable formula.*

In the decomposition rules of our R-S system for $\mathcal{L}_S$ given blow, each Ω' is indecomposable.

DR_S — an R-S deduction system for $\mathcal{L}_S$.

$$(\neg\neg) \frac{\Omega', C.\neg\neg\varphi, \Omega''}{\Omega', C.\varphi, \Omega''}$$

$$(\vee) \frac{\Omega', C.\varphi \vee \psi, \Omega''}{\Omega', C.\varphi, C.\psi, \Omega''} \qquad (\neg\vee) \frac{\Omega', C.\neg(\varphi \vee \psi), \Omega''}{\Omega', C.\neg\varphi, \Omega'' \mid \Omega', C.\neg\psi, \Omega''}$$

$$(\wedge) \ \frac{\Omega', C.\varphi \wedge \psi, \Omega''}{\Omega', C.\varphi, \Omega'' \mid \Omega', C.\psi, \Omega''} \qquad (\neg\wedge) \ \frac{\Omega', C.\neg(\varphi \wedge \psi), \Omega''}{\Omega', C.\neg\varphi, C.\neg\psi, \Omega''}$$

$$(\forall 1) \ \frac{\Omega', C.\forall x.\varphi, \Omega''}{\Omega', C.\varphi(z), \Omega''} \qquad (\forall 2) \ \frac{\Omega', C.\forall x.\varphi, \Omega''}{\Omega', E_s, (C \cup \{s.x\}).\varphi(z), \Omega''}$$

where $s.x \in C$ where $s.x \notin C$
and z is a variable which does not appear above the double line,

$$(\exists 1) \ \frac{\Omega', C.\exists x.\varphi, \Omega''}{\Omega', C.\varphi(t/x), \Omega'', C.\exists x.\varphi} \qquad (\exists 2) \ \frac{\Omega', C.\exists x.\varphi, \Omega''}{\Omega', N_s, \Omega'' \mid \Omega', (C \cup \{s.x\}).\varphi(t/x), \Omega'', *}$$

where $s.x \in C$,   where $s.x \notin C$
the symbol * stands for $C.\exists x.\varphi$, and t is any term free for x in φ

$$(\neg\forall) \ \frac{\Omega', C.\neg\forall x.\varphi, \Omega''}{\Omega', C.\exists x.\neg\varphi, \Omega''} \qquad (\neg\exists) \ \frac{\Omega', C.\neg\exists x.\varphi, \Omega''}{\Omega', C.\forall x.\neg\varphi, \Omega''}$$

$$(Cr) \ \frac{\Omega', (C \cup \{s\}).\varphi, \Omega''}{\Omega', N_s, \Omega'' \mid \Omega', C.\varphi, \Omega''} \qquad (Etr) \ \frac{\Omega', E_{s_1}, \ldots, E_{s_k}, \Omega''}{\Omega', E_{s_1}, \ldots, E_{s_k}, E_s, \Omega''}$$

where $C \supset C_{min}(\varphi)$, φ is a literal; where $s_i, s \in S$ and $F_{s_1 \cdots, s_k, s} \neq \emptyset$.

In comparison with the R-S system for classical logic given in Section 2, DR_S has additional nonclassical quantifier rules dealing with the case when the sort of the quantification variable is not in the context - i.e. its carrier might be empty. It also has rule (Cr) for reducing non-minimal contexts. Finally, rule (Etr) expresses the "propagation of emptiness" principle discussed earlier. It can be easily checked that all the rules are sound.

7.4 Soundness and completeness of the system

The following is based on the concepts of the decomposition tree, proof and provability given in Section 2.

Validity of the fundamental sequences and soundness of the decomposition rules imply soundness of the deduction system DR_S. Now we will prove that the system is also complete.

Theorem 2 *The system DR_S is complete, i.e. each valid sequence Ω of formulae is provable.*

PROOF. Following the general proof schema from Thm. 1, Sect. 2, we prove that $\nvdash \Omega$ implies $\nvDash \Omega$. The main task is to construct a counter-model for an arbitrary set Δ of indecomposable formulae that does not contain a fundamental sequence and is closed under the single expansion rule (Etr).

We build a Herbrand-style model $M_H = \langle \mathcal{H}, v \rangle$, where the carrier H_s of any sort s is defined by $H_s = \mathcal{T}_s$ if $E_s \in \Delta$, and $\emptyset$ otherwise.

Consider any $[f : w \to s]$, $w = s_1 \ldots s_n$. Since Δ is closed under (Etr), then either $E_{s_i} \notin \Delta$ for some i, or $E_s \in \Delta$. Thus either $H_{s_i} = \emptyset$ for some i, or $H_{s_i} = \mathcal{T}_{s_i}$ for each i and $H_s = \mathcal{T}_s$. In the first case we take as $\mathbf{F}_{w,s}.f$ the empty function, and in the second we put $\mathbf{F}.f.('t'_1, 't'_2, \ldots, 't'_n) =' f(t_1, t_2, \ldots, t_n)'$. Clearly, this implies that the model M_H is total.

Now let $[p : s_1 \cdots s_k \to b]$, $k \geq 0$. If $H_{s_i} = \emptyset$ for some i, then we take as $\mathbf{P}_H.p$ the empty predicate. In the opposite case, we put $\mathbf{P}_H.p('t'_1, \ldots, 't'_k) = \mathbf{ff}$ if $C_{min}.p(t_1, \ldots, t_k) \in \Delta$, and $\mathbf{tt}$ otherwise.

As the valuation v we take a partial identity valuation with $Dom(v) = \bigcup \{X_s : H_s \neq \emptyset\}$, and $v(x) =' x'$ for $x \in Dom(v)$.

It is easy to check that H is indeed a counter-model for Δ.

To end the proof, it remains to show that M_H is a counter-model for Ω too. This is done in a standard way (see again the proof of Thm. 1 and [13]) by induction on the rank of a formula. Q.E.D.

8   Conclusions

From the examples presented above it clearly follows that Rasiowa-Sikorski deduction mechanism is indeed well suited to many applications in software sepcification and AI logics, allowing us to develop complete systems for various logics in an intuitively clear way, according to an almost standard procedure. To support the above thesis, in addition to the examples given here we could also quote the extensive work of E. Orlowska (see e.g. [11]), who applied this kind of formalism e.g. to relational logic, and then to various kinds of modal logics, which she translated into relational logic.

Moreover, it can be seen that Rasiowa-Sikorski formalism could lend itself very well to automation. This follows from their duality to the tableau systems, which are widely employed in automatic deduction systems.

What is more, a Rasiowa-Sikorski system is even better suited to automation than a tableau system. Indeed: in a tableau in order to continue constructing a tableau from a given node we have to look back at the preceding nodes. This is because e.g. the conjunction $\varphi \wedge \psi$ occurring anywhere on the branch causes adittion of two nodes labelled with φ, ψ, respectively, whereas a universal quantifiers $\forall x.\varphi$ causes addition of n nodes labelled with $\varphi(t/x)$, where t is any term. However, in an R-S decomposition tree all the information needed to continue decomposition from a given node is contained in the sequence of formulae labelling that node, so instead of storing the whole tree we are constructing we need only to store the leaves of that tree.

In view of all these advantages, Rasiowa-Sikorski formalism certainly merits a greater popularity and interest as a very useful tool in many applications.

References

1. Beth, E.W. *The Foundations of Mathematics*, North-Holland, 1959.
2. Bialasik, M., Konikowska, B. *Reasoning with first-order nondeterministic specifications*, to appear in Acta Informatica.
3. Bialasik, M., Konikowska, B. *A logic for non-deterministic specifications*, to appear in: *E. Orlowska, ed., Logic at work: essays dedicated to the memory of H. Rasiowa*, Kluwer, Holland.
4. Cohn, A.G. *A many sorted logic with possibly empty sorts*, in Proceedings CADE-11, LNAI 607, pp 633-647, 1992.
5. Gabbay, D. *Labelled deductive systems*, Oxford University Press, Oxford 1991.
6. Hussmann, H. *Nondeterministic algebraic specifications and non-confluent term rewriting*, Journal of Logic Programming 12, 1992, pp. 237-255.
7. Konikowska, B. *A logic for reasoning about similarity*, E. Orlowska, ed., *Incomplete information: Rough Set Analysis*, Physica-Verlag, New York 1997.
8. Konikowska, B. *A logic for reasoning about relative similarity*, in: *H. Rasiowa, E. Orlowska, ed., Special Issue of Studia Logica, Reasoning with incomplete information*, No 1, 1997, pp. 185-226.
9. Konikowska, B. *Two over three: a two-valued logic for software specification and validation over a three-valued predicate calculus*, Journal for Applied Nonclassical Logic, Vol. **3** (1), 1993, pp. 39–71.
10. Ohlbach, H.J., Weidenbach, C. *A resolution calculus with dynamic sort structures and partial functions*, in Proceedings ECAI, ed. L.C. Aiello, Pitman, London 1990.
11. Orlowska, E. *Relational proof systems for modal logics*. In: *H. Wansing (ed) Proof Theory of Modal Logics*. Kluwer, Dordrecht, 55-77, 1996.
12. Rasiowa, H., Sikorski, R. *The mathematics of metamathematics*, Warsaw, PWN 1963.
13. Walicki, M., Meldal, S., *A complete calculus for multialgebraic and functional semantics of nondeterminism*, ACM TOPLAS, 17(2), 1995.
14. Weidenbach, C. *Unification in sort theories and its applications*, Annals of Mathematics and Artificial Intelligence, vol. 18, pp. 261-293, 1996n.

Translating OBJ3 into CASL: The Institution Level

Till Mossakowski

Department of Computer Science and Bremen Institute for Safe Systems,
Universität Bremen, P.O. Box 330440, D-28334 Bremen.
till@informatik.uni-bremen.de

Abstract. We translate OBJ3 to CASL. At the level of basic specifications, we set up several institution representations between the underlying institutions. They correspond to different methodological views of OBJ3. The translations can be the basis for automated tools translating OBJ3 to CASL.

1 Introduction

The goal of CoFI, the Common Framework Initiative [20], is to design a family of algebraic specification languages that lead to a uniform standard in the area of algebraic specification. The Common Algebraic Specification Language (CASL) [5] is the central CoFI language. From CASL, simpler sublanguages are obtained by restriction, and CASL is to be incorporated in more advanced languages (e.g. higher-order, concurrency).

The definition of CASL and some of its sublanguages has been finished. Now one step towards CASL as a uniform standard is to establish translations from existing specification languages to CASL.

In this work, we consider the translation of the specification language OBJ3 [8] into CASL. When setting up the translation, we follow the structure of the CASL language summary, which distinguishes concepts underlying the language and constructs of the language whose meaning is defined in terms of the concepts.

At the level of basic concepts, we set up several institution representations between the institutions underlying OBJ3 and the institution underlying CASL. Actually, it turns out that there are two different institutions underlying OBJ3, corresponding to different methodological views of OBJ3.

Since the semantics of the constructs is defined in terms of the concepts, the translations straightforwardly lift from the level of concepts to the level of constructs. Nevertheless, in some cases, there are more direct translations of constructs.

2 Preliminaries

At the level of basic concepts, the translation of OBJ3 into CASL will be formalized as a simple map of institutions [14], also called simple institution representation [22]. We therefore first introduce the notions of institution and institution

J.L. Fiadeiro (Ed.): WADT'98, LNCS 1589, pp. 198–215, 1999.
© Springer-Verlag Berlin Heidelberg 1999

representation, and then the institution underlying CASL, and finally some pre-
liminaries for the institutions underlying OBJ3 that will be introduced in the
next section.

2.1   Institutions and representations

Any specification formalism is usually based on some notion of signature, model,
sentence and satisfaction. These are the ingredients of Goguen and Burstall's
notion of institution [10].

Definition 1. *An* institution $I = (\mathbf{Sign}^I, \mathbf{Sen}^I, \mathbf{Mod}^I, \models^I)$ *consists of*

- *a category* $\mathbf{Sign}^I$ *of signatures,*
- *a functor* $\mathbf{Sen}^I: \mathbf{Sign} \longrightarrow \mathbf{Set}$ *giving the set of* sentences $\mathbf{Sen}^I(\Sigma)$ *over each
  signature* Σ, *and for each signature morphism* $\sigma: \Sigma \longrightarrow \Sigma'$, *the sentence
  translation map* $\mathbf{Sen}^I(\sigma): \mathbf{Sen}^I(\Sigma) \longrightarrow \mathbf{Sen}^I(\Sigma')$,
- *a functor* $\mathbf{Mod}^I: \mathbf{Sign}^{op} \longrightarrow \mathcal{CAT}$ *giving the category of* models *over a given
  signature, and for each signature morphism* $\sigma: \Sigma \longrightarrow \Sigma'$, *the reduct functor*
  $\mathbf{Mod}^I(\sigma): \mathbf{Mod}^I(\Sigma') \longrightarrow \mathbf{Mod}^I(\Sigma)$ *(* $\mathbf{Mod}^I(\sigma)(M')$ *is written as* $M'|_\sigma$*),*
- *a satisfaction relation* $\models^I_\Sigma \subseteq \mathbf{Mod}^I(\Sigma) \times \mathbf{Sen}^I(\Sigma)$ *for each* $\Sigma \in \mathbf{Sign}^I$

such that for each $\sigma: \Sigma \longrightarrow \Sigma'$ *in* $\mathbf{Sign}^I$ *the following* satisfaction condition *holds:*

$$M' \models^I_{\Sigma'} \mathbf{Sen}^I(\sigma)(\varphi) \Leftrightarrow \mathbf{Mod}^I(\sigma)(M') \models^I_\Sigma \varphi$$

for each $M' \in \mathbf{Mod}^I(\Sigma')$ *and* $\varphi \in \mathbf{Sen}^I(\Sigma)$.

An institution $I = (\mathbf{Sign}^I, \mathbf{Sen}^I, \mathbf{Mod}^I, \models^I)$ induces the category of *theories*
with *axiom-preserving theory morphisms* $\mathbf{Th}_0^I$. Objects are theories $T = (\Sigma, \Gamma)$,
where $\Sigma \in \mathbf{Sign}$ and $\Gamma \subseteq \mathbf{Sen}^I(\Sigma)$. We set $sign(T) = \Sigma$ and $ax(T) = \Gamma$.
Morphisms $\sigma: (\Sigma, \Gamma) \longrightarrow (\Sigma', \Gamma')$ in $\mathbf{Th}_0^I$ are signature morphisms $\sigma: \Sigma \longrightarrow \Sigma'$
such that $\sigma(\Gamma) \subseteq \Gamma'$, that is, axioms are mapped to axioms. It is easy to extend
$\mathbf{Sen}^I$ and $\mathbf{Mod}^I$ to start from $\mathbf{Th}_0^I$ by putting $\mathbf{Sen}^I(\Sigma, \Gamma) = \mathbf{Sen}(\Sigma)$ and letting
$\mathbf{Mod}^I(\Sigma, \Gamma)$ be the full subcategory of $\mathbf{Mod}^I(\Sigma)$ induced by the class of those
models M satisfying Γ.

Given institutions I and J, a *simple map of institutions* [14] (also called
simple institution representation [22,16]) $\mu = (\Phi, \alpha, \beta): I \longrightarrow J$ consists of

- *a functor* $\Phi: \mathbf{Sign}^I \longrightarrow \mathbf{Th}_0^J$[1],
- *a natural transformation* $\alpha: \mathbf{Sen}^I \longrightarrow \mathbf{Sen}^J \circ \Phi$, *and*
- *a natural transformation* $\beta: \mathbf{Mod}^J \circ \Phi^{op} \longrightarrow \mathbf{Mod}^I$

such that the following *representation condition* is satisfied for all $\Sigma \in \mathbf{Sign}^I$,
$M' \in \mathbf{Mod}^J(\Phi(\Sigma))$ and $\varphi \in \mathbf{Sen}^I(\Sigma)$:

$$M' \models^J_{sign(\Phi(\Sigma))} \alpha_\Sigma(\varphi) \Leftrightarrow \beta_\Sigma(M') \models^I_\Sigma \varphi$$

---

[1] Meseguer [14] requires $\Phi: \mathbf{Th}_0^I \longrightarrow \mathbf{Th}_0^J$, but since μ is simple, both formulations are
equivalent using Meseguer's α-extension.

2.2 The institution underlying CASL

The institution underlying CASL is introduced in two steps [6,2]: first, we introduce many-sorted partial first-order logic with equality ($PFOL^=$), and then, subsorted partial first-order logic with equality ($SubPFOL^=$) is described in terms of $PFOL^{=2}$.

Definition 2. *The institution* $PFOL^=$.

Signatures *A many-sorted signature* $\Sigma = (S, TF, PF, P)$ *in* $PFOL^=$ *consists of a set* S *of sorts, two* $S^* \times S$-*sorted families* $TF = (TF_{w,s})_{w \in S^*, s \in S}$ *and* $PF = (PF_{w,s})_{w \in S^*, s \in S}$ *of total function symbols and partial function symbols, respectively, such that* $TF_{w,s} \cap PF_{w,s} = \{\}$, *for each* $(w, s) \in S^* \times S$ *(constants are treated as functions with no arguments), and a family* $P = (P_w)_{w \in S^*}$ *of predicate symbols. We write* $f \colon w \longrightarrow s$ *for* $f \in TF_{w,s}$ *and* $f \colon w \to ? \, s$ *for* $f \in PF_{w,s}$.
Given signatures $\Sigma = (S, TF, PF, P)$ *and* $\Sigma' = (S', TF', PF', P')$, *a signature morphism* $\sigma \colon \Sigma \longrightarrow \Sigma'$ *consists of*
- *a map* $\sigma^S \colon S \longrightarrow S'$,
- *a map* $\sigma^{TF}_{w,s} \colon TF_{w,s} \longrightarrow TF'_{\sigma^{s^*}(w), \sigma^S(s)}$[3] *for each* $w \in S^*, s \in S$,
- *a map* $\sigma^{PF}_{w,s} \colon PF_{w,s} \longrightarrow PF'_{\sigma^{s^*}(w), \sigma^S(s)} \cup TF'_{\sigma^{s^*}(w), \sigma^S(s)}$, *and*
- *a map* $\sigma^P_w \colon P_w \longrightarrow P'_{\sigma^{s^*}(w)}$ *for each* $w \in S^*$.

Models *Given a many-sorted signature* $\Sigma = (S, TF, PF, P)$, *a many-sorted* Σ-*model* M *consists of:*
- *a non-empty carrier set* M_s *for each sort* $s \in S$,
- *a partial function* f_M *from* M_w[4] *to* M_s *for each function symbol* $f \in TF_{w,s} \cup PF_{w,s}$, *the function being total if* $f \in TF_{w,s}$, *and*
- *a predicate* $p_M \subseteq M_w$ *for each predicate symbol* $p \in P_w$.

A many-sorted Σ-*homomorphism* $h : M \to N$ *consists of a family of functions* $(h_s : M_s \to N_s)_{s \in S}$ *with the property that for all* $f \in TF_{w,s} \cup PF_{w,s}$ *and* $(a_1, \ldots, a_n) \in M_w$ *with* $f_M(a_1, \ldots, a_n)$ *defined, we have*

$$h_s(f_M(a_1, \ldots, a_n)) = f_N(h_{s_1}(a_1), \ldots, h_{s_n}(a_n)),$$

and for all $p \in P_w$ *and* $(a_1, \ldots, a_n) \in M_w$, $(a_1, \ldots, a_n) \in p_M$ *implies* $(h_{s_1}(a_1), \ldots, h_{s_n}(a_n)) \in p_N$. *Reducts are defined as usual.*

Sentences *Let a many-sorted signature* $\Sigma = (S, TF, PF, P)$ *and an* S-*sorted, pairwise disjoint family of variables* $X = (X_s)_{s \in S}$ *be given.*
The sets $T_\Sigma(X)_s$ *of many-sorted* Σ-*terms of sort* s, $s \in S$, *with variables in* X *are the least sets satisfying the following rules:*
1. $x \in T_\Sigma(X)_s$, *if* $x \in X_s$
2. $f_{w,s}(t_1, \ldots, t_n) \in T_\Sigma(X)_s$, *if* $t_i \in T_\Sigma(X)_{s_i}, f \in TF_{w,s}, w = s_1 \ldots s_n$
3. $f_{w,s}(t_1, \ldots, t_n) \in T_\Sigma(X)_s$, *if* $t_i \in T_\Sigma(X)_{s_i}, f \in PF_{w,s}, w = s_1 \ldots s_n$

---

[2] We leave out sort generation constraints [5,6] since they are not needed here.

[3] σ^{S^*} is the extension of σ^S to finite strings

[4] We write M_w for the Cartesian product $M_{s_1} \times \ldots \times M_{s_n}$, when $w = s_1 \ldots s_n$.

Note that each term has a unique sort.
We can inductively extend valuations from variables to all terms (see [3]):

Lemma 3. *Each valuation $\nu: X \longrightarrow M$ has an extension to a S-indexed family of partial maps $\nu^{\#} : T_\Sigma(X) \longrightarrow\!\!\!\!\circ\, M$, where $\mathrm{dom}\ \nu^{\#} \subseteq T_\Sigma(X)$ is the S-indexed set of ν-interpretable terms.* □

The set $AF_\Sigma(X)$ of many-sorted atomic Σ-formulae *with variables in X is the least set satisfying the following rules:*

1. *$p_w(t_1,\ldots,t_n) \in AF_\Sigma(X)$, if $t_i \in T_\Sigma(X)_{s_i}, p \in P_w, w = s_1 \ldots s_n \in S^*$*
2. *$t \stackrel{e}{=} t' \in AF_\Sigma(X)$, if $t,t' \in T_\Sigma(X)_s, s \in S$ (existential equations)*
3. *$t = t' \in AF_\Sigma(X)$, if $t,t' \in T_\Sigma(X)_s, s \in S$ (strong equations)*
4. *$\mathrm{def}\ t \in AF_\Sigma(X)$, if $t \in T_\Sigma(X)_s, s \in S$ (definedness assertions)*

Many-sorted Σ-sentences are the usual closed many-sorted first-order logic formulae, built using quantification (over sorted variables), logical connectives and atomic Σ-formulae.

Satisfaction Relation *The satisfaction of a Σ-sentence by a Σ-model M is defined as usual in terms of the satisfaction of its constituent atomic formulae w.r.t. assignments of values to all the variables that occur in them.*

The application of a predicate symbol p to a sequence of argument terms holds w.r.t. a valuation $\nu: X \longrightarrow M$ iff the values of all the terms are defined under $\nu^{\#}$ and give a tuple belonging to p_M. A definedness assertion concerning a term holds iff the value of the term is defined. An existential equation holds iff the values of both terms are defined and identical, whereas a strong equation holds also when the values of both terms are undefined; thus both notions of equation coincide for defined terms.

A detailed description of the satisfaction relation and a proof of the satisfaction condition can be found in [6], see also [1]. □

Now subsorted partial first-order logic is defined in terms of partial first-order logic:

Definition 4. *The institution $SubPFOL^=$.*

Signatures *The notion of subsorted signatures extends the notion of order-sorted signatures as given by Goguen and Meseguer [12], by allowing not only total function symbols, but also partial function symbols and predicate symbols:*

A subsorted signature $\Sigma = (S, TF, PF, P, \leq_S)$ *consists of a many-sorted signature (S, TF, PF, P) together with a reflexive transitive subsort relation $\leq_S$ on the set S of sorts.[5]*

For a subsorted signature, $\Sigma = (S, TF, PF, P, \leq_S)$, we define overloading *relations $\sim_F$ and $\sim_P$, for function and predicate symbols, respectively:*

Let $f : w_1 \to s_1, f : w_2 \to s_2 \in TF \cup PF$, then $f : w_1 \to s_1 \sim_F f : w_2 \to s_2$ iff there exist $w \in S^*$ with $w \leq w_1$ and $w \leq w_2$ and a common supersort s of s_1 and s_2.

---

[5] Note that $\leq_S$ is not required to be antisymmetric; this allows to declare isomorphic sorts, where the injections correspond to change of representations.

Let $p : w_1$, $p : w_2 \in P$, then $p : w_1 \sim_P p : w_2$ iff there exists $w \in S^*$ with $w \leq w_1$ and $w \leq w_2$.

A signature morphism $\sigma : \Sigma \to \Sigma'$ is a many-sorted signature morphism that preserves the subsort relation and the overloading relations. Note that, due to preservation of subsorting, the preservation of the overloading relations can be simplified to: $f : w_1 \to s_1 \sim_F f : w_2 \to s_2$ implies $\sigma^{TF}_{w_1, s_1}(f) = \sigma^{TF}_{w_2, s_2}(f)$ (and analogously for partial operation and predicate symbols).

With each subsorted signature $\Sigma = (S, TF, PF, P, \leq_S)$ we associate a many-sorted signature $\hat{\Sigma}$, which is the extension of the underlying many-sorted signature (S, TF, PF, P) with

- a total injection function symbol $inj : s \to s'$, for each pair of sorts $s \leq_S s'$,
- a partial projection function symbol $pr : s' \to ? \ s$, for each pair of sorts $s \leq_S s'$, and
- a unary membership predicate symbol $\in^s_{s'}$, for each pair of sorts $s \leq_S s'$.

We assume that the symbols used for injection, projection and membership are not used otherwise in Σ.

Models Subsorted Σ-models are ordinary many-sorted $\hat{\Sigma}$-models satisfying the following set of axioms $\hat{J}(\Sigma)$ (where the variables are all universally quantified):

$inj_{(s,s)}(x) \stackrel{e}{=} x$ (identity)

$inj_{(s,s')}(x) \stackrel{e}{=} inj_{(s,s')}(y) \Rightarrow x \stackrel{e}{=} y$ for $s \leq_S s'$ (embedding-injectivity)

$inj_{(s',s'')}(inj_{(s,s')}(x)) \stackrel{e}{=} inj_{(s,s'')}(x)$ for $s \leq_S s' \leq_S s''$ (transitivity)

$pr_{(s',s)}(inj_{(s,s')}(x)) \stackrel{e}{=} x$ for $s \leq_S s'$ (projection)

$pr_{(s',s)}(x) \stackrel{e}{=} pr_{(s',s)}(y) \Rightarrow x \stackrel{e}{=} y$ for $s \leq_S s'$ (projection-injectivity)

$\in^s_{s'}(x) \Leftrightarrow def\, pr_{(s',s)}(x)$ for $s \leq_S s'$ (membership)

$inj_{(s',s)}(f_{w',s'}(inj_{(s_1,s'_1)}(x_1), \ldots, inj_{(s_n,s'_n)}(x_n)))$ =
$= inj_{(s'',s)}(f_{w'',s''}(inj_{(s_1,s''_1)}(x_1), \ldots, inj_{(s_n,s''_n)}(x_n)))$

for $f_{w',s'} \sim_F f_{w'',s''}$, where $w \leq w', w''$, $w = s_1 \ldots s_n$, $w' = s'_1 \ldots s'_n$, $w'' = s''_1 \ldots s''_n$ and and $s', s'' \leq s$ (function-monotonicity)

$p_{w'}(inj_{(s_1,s'_1)}(x_1), .., inj_{(s_n,s'_n)}(x_n)) \Leftrightarrow p_{w''}(inj_{(s_1,s''_1)}(x_1), .., inj_{(s_n,s''_n)}(x_n))$

for $p_{w'} \sim_P p_{w''}$, where $w \leq w', w''$, $w = s_1 \ldots s_n$, $w' = s'_1 \ldots s'_n$, and $w'' = s''_1 \ldots s''_n$ (predicate-monotonicity)

Σ-homomorphisms are $\hat{\Sigma}$-homomorphisms.

The reduct of a Σ'-model along a subsorted signature morphism σ from Σ into Σ' is the many-sorted reduct along the obvious extension $\hat{\sigma} : \hat{\Sigma} \longrightarrow \hat{\Sigma}'$ of σ.

For later use, let $\Sigma^\#$ be the subsignature of $\hat{\Sigma}$ without projection and membership symbols, and let $J(\Sigma)$ be the subset of $\hat{J}(\Sigma)$ consisting of the identity, injectivity, transitivity axioms and those function monotonicity axioms for which $w = w' \leq w''$ in the condition. Further, let $\mu_\Sigma : \Sigma^\# \longrightarrow \hat{\Sigma}$ be the inclusion. We will write J for $J(\Sigma)$ and $\hat{J}$ for $\hat{J}(\Sigma)$ if Σ is clear from the context.

Sentences Subsorted Σ-sentences *are ordinary many-sorted $\hat{\Sigma}$-sentences.*
Note that in the sentences, injections from subsorts to supersorts must be explicit. In the CASL language considered in section 5 these are left implicit and must unambiguously be determined by the context.
Satisfaction *Satisfaction, as well as the satisfaction condition, is inherited from PFOL$^=$.*   □

We will also need some subinstitutions of $SubPFOL^=$, which are formally defined in [17]. The institution $SubPCondEq^=$ is the restriction of $SubPFOL^=$ to signatures without predicate symbols and sentences that are universally quantified conditional equations. $SubCondEq^=$ is $SubPCondEq^=$ without partial function symbols, and $CondEq^=$ is the restriction of $SubCondEq^=$ to signatures with empty subsort relation.

2.3   The institution of order-sorted algebra

The OBJ3 manual [8] claims that OBJ3 is based on order-sorted algebra as developed in [12]. We here describe the institution $COSASC$ of coherent order-sorted algebra enriched with sort constraints, as introduced by Goguen and Meseguer [12,15,7], in some detail, since it appears that there is no complete detailed description of it in the literature[6].

Definition 5. *The institution $COSASC$.*

Signatures *Order signatures are triples $\Sigma = (S, TF, \leq)$, where $\leq$ is a partial order on S and (S, TF) is a many-sorted signature, such that the following conditions are satisfied:*
  - *$f \in TF_{w,s} \cap TF_{w',s'}$ and $w \leq w'$ imply $s \leq s'$ (signature monotonicity)*
  - *for each $f \in TF_{w,s}$ and $w_0 \leq w \in S^n$, there is a least arity for f that is greater than or equal to w_0 (regularity). This condition implies that there also is a least rank (i. e. arity and coarity) for f with arity greater than or equal to w_0, see [12].*
  - *each connected component of $(S, \leq)$ is filtered, i. e. any two elements (of the connected component) have a common upper bound (local filtration). (The conjunction of regularity and local filtration is called coherence.)*
  We further assume that each signature is strongly locally filtered [18], which means that any two elements of a connected component have a least upper bound. This assumption is needed for setting up the institution representations, but it might be omitted when translating the language constructs.
  Given two signatures $\Sigma = (S, TF, \leq)$ and $\Sigma' = (S', TF', \leq')$, an OSA-signature morphism $\sigma: \Sigma \longrightarrow \Sigma'$ consists of
  - *a map $\sigma^S: S \longrightarrow S'$,*
  - *a family of maps $\sigma^{TF}_{w,s}: TF_{w,s} \longrightarrow TF'_{\sigma^S(w), \sigma^S(s)}$ for each $w \in S^*$, $s \in S$*
  such that

---

[6] Han Yan [23] comes closest to describing such an institution, but [23] is not publicly available.

- $\sigma^S(s) \leq' \sigma^S(s')$ whenever $s \leq s'$ (monotonicity),
- for $w \leq w'$, $f \in TF_{w,s} \cap TF_{w',s'}$, we have $\sigma_{w,s}^{TF}(f) = \sigma_{w',s'}^{TF}(f)$ (preservation of overloading)[7],
- for each $f \in TF_{w,s}$ and $w_0 \leq w$, $(\sigma^S)^n$ applied to the least arity for f which is $\geq w_0$ yields the least arity for $\sigma_{w,s}^{TF}(f)$ which is $\geq (\sigma^S)^n(w_0)$ (preservation of regularity).[8]

We further assume that least upper bounds of connected sorts are preserved by signature morphisms.

Models Given $\Sigma = (S, TF, \leq)$, an order-sorted Σ-algebra is a many sorted (S, TF)-algebra M such that

1. $s \leq s'$ implies $M_s \subseteq M_{s'}$ (subsort inclusion),
2. $f \in TF_{w,s} \cap TF_{w',s'}$ and $w \leq w'$ imply $f_M: M_w \longrightarrow M_s$ equals $f_M: M_{w'} \longrightarrow M_{s'}$ on M_w (algebra monotonicity).

Homomorphisms $h: M \longrightarrow N$ are many-sorted homomorphisms $h: M \longrightarrow N$ such that $s \leq s'$ and $a \in M_s$ imply $h_s(a) = h_{s'}(a)$. Reducts are defined as for many-sorted algebras. Since many-sorted reducts preserve inclusions and signature morphisms preserve overloading, the resulting many-sorted algebra is again an order-sorted algebra.

Sentences An S-sorted variable system X is a family of sets $X = (X_s)_{s \in S}$ with the X_s pairwise disjoint. Given such a variable system, the set $T_\Sigma(X)_s$ of $\Sigma(X)$-terms of sort s is inductively defined:

1. $x \in T_\Sigma(X)_s$ for $x \in X_s$
2. $f(t_1, \ldots, t_n) \in T_\Sigma(X)_s$ for $f: s_1, \ldots, s_n \longrightarrow s \in TF$ and $t_i \in T_\Sigma(X)_{s_i}$, $i = 1, \ldots, n$.
3. $T_\Sigma(X)_s \subseteq T_\Sigma(X)_{s'}$ for $s \leq s'$.

It is straightforward to make $T_\Sigma(X)$ into an order-sorted Σ-algebra. Moreover we have the following Lemma from [12], holding for regular signatures.

Lemma 6. Each valuation $\nu: X \longrightarrow M$ has a unique homomorphic extension $\nu^\#: T_\Sigma(X) \longrightarrow M$.

A Σ-sentence in OSA is a conditional formula

$$\forall X. e_1 \wedge \ldots \wedge e_n \Rightarrow e$$

where X is an S-sorted variable system and the atomic formulas e and e_i are of two kinds: Either equations

$$t_1 = t_2$$

where $t_1 \in T_\Sigma(X)_{s_1}$, $t_2 \in T_\Sigma(X)_{s_2}$ and s_1, s_2 are in the same connected component of $(S, \leq)$, or sort constraints

$$t : s$$

---

[7] This condition is needed to ensure that reduct functors preserve monotonicity of models (cf. [13]). In [23], this condition is missing, while the condition of [9] is too weak.

[8] This condition is needed to ensure that the least sort parse algorithm described below is compatible with signature morphisms.

where $t \in T_\Sigma(X)_{s'}$ and s is a sort in the same connected component as s'. Given a signature morphism $\sigma \colon \Sigma \longrightarrow \Sigma'$ and an S-sorted variable system X, we can get an S'-sorted variable system $\sigma(X)$ by putting

$$\sigma(X)_{s'} = \bigcup_{\sigma^S(s)=s'} X_s$$

The inclusion $\zeta_{\sigma,X} \colon X \longrightarrow T_{\Sigma'}(\sigma(X))|_\sigma$ has a unique homomorphic extension $\zeta^{\#}_{\sigma,X} \colon T_\Sigma(X) \longrightarrow T_{\Sigma'}(\sigma(X))|_\sigma$. Now a Σ-atomic formula $t_1 = t_2$ is translated to $\zeta^{\#}_{\sigma,X}(t_1) = \zeta^{\#}_{\sigma,X}(t_2)$, and a Σ-atomic formula $t : s$ is translated to $\zeta^{\#}_{\sigma,X}(t_1) : \sigma^S(s)$. This easily extends to conditional formulae.

Satisfaction *A Σ-algebra M satisfies a conditional axiom, if all valuations which satisfy the premises also satisfy the conclusion. A valuation $\nu \colon X \longrightarrow M$ satisfies an equation $t_1 = t_2$ if $\nu^{\#}(t_1) = \nu^{\#}(t_2)$, and it satisfies a sort constraint $t : s$ if $\nu^{\#}(t) \in M_s$. The satisfaction condition can be proved by noting that valuations $\nu \colon X \longrightarrow M|_\sigma$ are in a trivial one-one-correspondence to valuations $\nu' \colon \sigma(X) \longrightarrow M$ with the property that $\zeta^{\#}_{\sigma,X} \circ \nu'^{\#}|_\sigma = \nu^{\#}$. The satisfaction condition for sort constraints is proved in [23].*

We will also need the *reduction theorem* from [12], which translates order-sorted to many-sorted algebra.

Theorem 7. *A reduction from order-sorted to many-sorted algebra, can be formalized as a simple institution representation from COSA (coherent order-sorted algebra as introduced above, but without sort constraints) to $CondEq^=$ (many-sorted algebra), as follows.*

Signatures *A COSA-signature Σ is mapped to the $(CondEq^=)$-theory $(\Sigma^{\#}, J)$. A signature morphism $\sigma \colon \Sigma \longrightarrow \Sigma'$ in COSA is mapped to its obvious extension $\sigma^{\#} \colon \Sigma^{\#} \longrightarrow \Sigma'^{\#}$.*

Models *By Theorem 4.2 of [12], there is an equivalence of categories $(\_)^\bullet$ between $\mathbf{Mod}^{CondEq^=}(\Sigma^{\#}, J)$ and $\mathbf{Mod}^{COSA}(\Sigma)$. Basically, given a $(\Sigma^{\#}, J)$-model N, the subsort injections are replaced by set inclusions in $N^\bullet$ using colimits of filtered diagrams built up by the injections. Vice versa, any Σ-algebra M can be mapped to a $(\Sigma^{\#}, J)$-algebra $M^{\#}$ by just taking the inclusions as injections.*

Sentences *Each COSA-term $t \in T_\Sigma(X)$ has a least sort $LS_\Sigma(t)$ [12, 2.10] and a least sort parse $LP_\Sigma(t) \in T_{\Sigma^{\#}}(X)$ [12, p. 252]. They are defined inductively as follows: If $t = x$ is a variable, it has a unique sort $LS_\Sigma(x)$ due to the disjointness condition for variable systems, and $LP_\Sigma(x) = x$. If $t = f(t_1, \ldots, t_s) \in T_\Sigma(X)_s$, then by induction hypothesis, t_i has least sort s_i. Take $w_0 = s_1 \ldots s_n$. Then by the term formation rules, $f \in TF_{w',s'}$ for some w', s' with $s' \leq s$ and $w_0 \leq w'$. By regularity, there is a least rank w', s' for f such that $w' \geq w_0$. This least s' is the desired least sort of t, while $inj_{(s',s)}(f_{w',s'}(inj_{(s_1,s'_1)}(LP_\Sigma(t_1)), \ldots, inj_{(s_n,s'_n)}(LP_\Sigma(t_n))))$ is the least sort parse of t.*

Given an equation $t_1 = t_2$, let $s_1 = LS(t_1)$, $s_2 = LS(t_2)$ and $s = lub(s_1, s_2)$, the least upper bound of s_1 and s_2 which exists by strong local filtration. Then $LP_\Sigma(t_1 = t_2)$ is

$$inj_{(s_1,s)}(LP_\Sigma(t_1)) = inj_{(s_2,s)}(LP_\Sigma(t_2))$$

This can easily be extended to conditional equations, giving translations $LP_\Sigma \colon \mathbf{Sen}^{COSA}(\Sigma) \longrightarrow \mathbf{Sen}^{CondEq^=}(\Sigma^\#)$. Since signature morphisms preserve regularity and least upper bounds, the construction is natural in Σ.
Satisfaction *The representation condition follows from Theorem 4.4 of [12].*

□

The institution $COSASC$ is not yet the right institution to give a precise meaning to all the constructs of OBJ3. Most importantly, retracts are missing. The OBJ3 system automatically extends an OSA-theory (Σ, Γ) with $\Sigma = (S, TF, \leq)$ to an OSA-theory $(\Sigma^\otimes, \Gamma^\otimes)$ which is (Σ, Γ) extended by operations

$$(r : s' > s) \colon s' \longrightarrow s$$

and axioms

$$\forall \{x : s\}.r : s' > s(x) = x$$

for s, s' in the same connected component of $(S, \leq)$. Let $\kappa_{\Sigma,\Gamma} \colon (\Sigma, \Gamma) \longrightarrow (\Sigma^\otimes, \Gamma^\otimes)$ be the inclusion, and $\kappa_\Sigma = \kappa_{\Sigma,\emptyset}$. Signature morphisms $\sigma \colon \Sigma \longrightarrow \Sigma$ can also be extended to signature morphisms $\sigma^\otimes \colon \Sigma^\otimes \longrightarrow \Sigma'^\otimes$. The following lemma is important for the semantics of retracts:

Lemma 8. *Let $F_{\kappa_{\Sigma,\Gamma}} \colon \mathbf{Mod}(\Sigma, \Gamma) \longrightarrow \mathbf{Mod}(\Sigma^\otimes, \Gamma^\otimes)$ be the free construction (left adjoint) w.r.t. $\mathbf{Mod}(\kappa_{\Sigma,\Gamma})$. Then the unit $\iota_M \colon M \longrightarrow F_{\kappa_{\Sigma,\Gamma}}(M)|_{\kappa_{\Sigma,\Gamma}}$ is injective.*

Proof. The lemma follows from Theorem 3.5 of [12][9] by using the diagram method for free extensions [21]. □

3   The institutions underlying OBJ3

Joseph Goguen claims in [9] that the semantics of a theory (Σ, Γ) is neither $\mathbf{Mod}(\Sigma, \Gamma)$ nor $\mathbf{Mod}(\Sigma^\otimes, \Gamma^\otimes)$, but rather $\iota \colon Id_{\mathbf{Mod}(\Sigma,\Gamma)} \longrightarrow \mathbf{Mod}(\kappa_{\Sigma,\Gamma}) \circ F_{\kappa_{\Sigma,\Gamma}}$ (actually, he considers initial semantics only, and the above is the straightforward generalization to loose semantics). But there is no explicit description of an institution that uses ι as a semantics in the literature. Perhaps, the OBJ3 community does not feel a need of such an institution. But when translating OBJ3 to other languages, we need a precise semantics of all the underlying concepts. Therefore, in this section, we introduce two institutions that can serve as underlying institutions of OBJ3.

---

[9] Notice that here we need the assumption that all carriers are non-empty, which implies faithfulness of (Σ, Γ) in the sense of [12]. This will be further discussed in Sect. 4.3.

The following institution captures OBJ3's retracts and also allows to deal with error recovery by treating error values as first-class citizens.

Definition 9. *The institution $COSASC^{\otimes}$.*

Signatures *A $COSASC^{\otimes}$-signature (resp. signature morphism) is just a signature (resp. signature morphism) in $COSASC$.*
Models *A Σ-algebra in $COSASC^{\otimes}$ is a $(\Sigma^{\otimes}, \emptyset^{\otimes})$-algebra in $COSASC$. Reducts are inherited in the same way.*
Sentences *A Σ-sentence in $COSASC^{\otimes}$ is a $\Sigma^{\otimes}$-sentence in $COSASC$. Sentence translation is inherited in the same way.*
Satisfaction *A Σ-algebra M satisfies a Σ-sentence φ in $COSASC^{\otimes}$ if we have in $COSASC$ that the $\Sigma^{\otimes}$-algebra M satisfies the $\Sigma^{\otimes}$-sentence φ. Thus the satisfaction condition for $COSASC^{\otimes}$ follows from that for $COSASC$.* $\square$

Treating error values as first-class citizens in $COSASC^{\otimes}$ has one main disadvantage: equations involving retracts may lead to confusion among ordinary values, which generally is undesirable. So one has to prove that retract equations do not interfere with ordinary values. More importantly, in $COSASC^{\otimes}$ we entirely lose the distinction between ordinary and error values, since ordinary functions and retracts can both map ordinary values to error values and vice versa.[10]

This justifies the introduction of a more complex institution that keeps error values and ordinary values distinct. It also comes more close to Joseph Goguen's claim that the injection ι *is* the semantics, meaning that "the 'new error elements' reside in a shadowy penumbra, distinctly set off from the bright central region of pure elements by the injection, as well as from the dark outer region of error terms by a subsort relation" [9]. The best approximation of this "shadowy penumbra" seems to be the following:

Definition 10. *The institution $COSASC_{\otimes}$.*

Signatures *A $COSASC_{\otimes}$-signature (resp. signature morphism) is just a signature (resp. signature morphism) in $COSASC$.*
Models *A Σ-algebra in $COSASC_{\otimes}$ is a Σ-algebra in $COSASC$.*
Sentences *A Σ-sentence in $COSASC_{\otimes}$ is a $\Sigma^{\otimes}$-sentence in $COSASC$.*
Satisfaction *A valuation $\nu: X \longrightarrow M$ satisfies a Σ-equation $t_1 = t_2$ with $s = lub(LS(t_1), LS(t_2))$ if*

$$(\iota_M \circ \nu)^{\#}(t_1) = (\iota_M \circ \nu)^{\#}(t_2) \in \iota_M(M_s)$$

where $\iota_M \circ \nu$ is considered to be a valuation from X to $F_{\kappa_\Sigma}(M)$. A valuation $\nu: X \longrightarrow M$ satisfies a Σ-sort constraint $t : s$ if,

$$(\iota_M \circ \nu)^{\#}(t) \in \iota_M(M_s)$$

---

[10] The introduction of error supersorts, as in CafeOBJ, does not help for separating retract-generated error values from ordinary values. This is because retract functions have to go to ordinary sorts, since they serve for the purpose of coercing a value to an (ordinary) subsort of a sort.

This is extended to sentences in the same way as for COSASC.

Note that this notion of satisfaction is closely related to existential super sat-isfaction in [9], with the difference that we do not deal with error supersorts here.

In order to prove the satisfaction condition, consider a signature morphism $\sigma: \Sigma \longrightarrow \Sigma'$ and a Σ'-algebra M'. By the universal property of the free ex-tension $F_{\kappa_\Sigma}(M'|_\sigma)$, the homomorphism $(\iota_{M'})|_\sigma$ has a unique extension

$$(\iota_{M'})|_\sigma{}^\#: F_{\kappa_\Sigma}(M'|_\sigma) \longrightarrow F_{\kappa_{\Sigma'}}(M')|_{\sigma\otimes}$$

making the right triangle in the diagram below commutative. Now we again use the fact that valuations $\nu: X \longrightarrow M'|_\sigma$ are in a trivial one-one-correspon-dence to valuations $\nu': \sigma(X) \longrightarrow M'$ with the property that $\zeta^\#_{\sigma,X} \circ \nu'^\#|_\sigma = \nu^\#$. The remaining subdiagrams in the following diagram commute by freeness of the respective term algebras; thus, the outer square commutes as well.

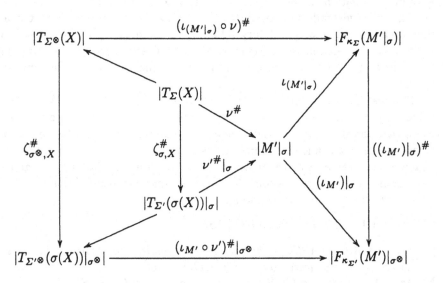

Since $((\iota_{M'})|_\sigma)^\#|_{\kappa_\sigma} \circ \iota_{(M'|_\sigma)} = (\iota_{M'})|_\sigma$, $((\iota_{M'})|_\sigma)^\#$ takes the image of $\iota_{(M'|_\sigma)}$ exactly to the image of $(\iota_{M'})|_\sigma$. Moreover, on the former image, $((\iota_{M'})|_\sigma)^\#$ is injective, since $((\iota_{M'})|_\sigma)^\#|_{\kappa_\sigma} \circ \iota_{(M'|_\sigma)} = (\iota_{M'})|_\sigma$ is injective by Lemma 8. Therefore, there exists some $a \in (M'|_\sigma)_s$ with

$$(\iota_{(M'|_\sigma)} \circ \nu)^\#(t_1) = \iota_{(M'|_\sigma)}(a) = (\iota_{(M'|_\sigma)} \circ \nu)^\#(t_2)$$

if and only if there exists some $a \in M'_{\sigma s(s)}$ with

$$(\iota_{M'} \circ \nu')^\#(\zeta^\#_{\sigma\otimes,X}(t_1)) = \iota_{M'}(a) = (\iota_{M'} \circ \nu')^\#(\zeta^\#_{\sigma\otimes,X}(t_2))$$

Since $\zeta^\#_{\sigma\otimes,X}$ is used for sentence translation, the satisfaction condition fol-lows easily.   □

In $COSASC_\otimes$, error values generated by retracts only have a virtual existence, since retracts are always interpreted freely. This means that equations involving retracts are false in all models if they do not follow already from the built-in retract equations in $\Gamma^\otimes$. In the case that all user-defined retract equations involve only one retract, and this retract occurs at the outmost position of a term, this works fine, and $COSASC_\otimes$ corresponds to the operational semantics of OBJ3.

However, $COSASC_\otimes$ does not work for error recovery, where error values should be treated as first-class values (such that functions can compute with them). In this case, we have to use $COSASC^\otimes$, though we then loose the distinction between ordinary and error values.

4   Translating the OBJ3 institutions to the CASL institution

In this section, we describe two translations of institutions underlying OBJ3 to (fragments of) the CASL institution, serving different methodological purposes.

4.1   Translating $COSASC^\otimes$ to $SubCondEq^=$

The translation from $COSASC^\otimes$ to $SubPFOL^=$ has as target the conditional fragment of $SubPFOL$ without predicates and partiality, namely subsorted conditional equational logic ($SubCondEq^=$, for a formal definition, see [17]).

Theorem 11. *The following describes a simple institution representation from* $COSASC^\otimes$ *to* $SubCondEq^=$.

Signatures *A $COSASC^\otimes$-signature Σ is mapped to $(\Sigma^\otimes, \emptyset^\otimes)$ considered as an $SubCondEq^=$-theory (which means that the retracts in the retract equations have to be explicitly qualified with their profiles). A signature morphism $\sigma \colon \Sigma \longrightarrow \Sigma'$ is mapped to the signature morphism $\sigma^\otimes \colon \Sigma^\otimes \longrightarrow \Sigma'^\otimes$. Now $\sigma^\otimes$ is monotone because σ is. It remains to show that $\sigma^\otimes$ preserves the overloading relation $\sim_F$. Let $f : w_1 \to s_1 \sim_F f : w_2 \to s_2$ in Σ, i.e. there exist $w_0 \in S^*$ with $w_0 \leq w_1$ and $w_0 \leq w_2$ and a common supersort s_0 of s_1 and s_2. By regularity of Σ, there is some $w \in S^*$, $s \in S$ with $f : w \to s$ and $w_0 \leq w \leq w_1, w_2$. Since σ preserves overloading, $\sigma^{TF}_{w_1, s_1}(f) = \sigma^{TF}_{w, s}(f) = \sigma^{TF}_{w_2, s_2}(f)$.*

Models *Given a $COSASC^\otimes$-signature Σ, the model translation is the following composite $((\_)^\bullet$ has been introduced in Theorem 7):*[11]

$$\mathbf{Mod}^{COSA^\otimes}(\Sigma) \qquad\qquad\qquad \mathbf{Mod}^{CondEq^=}(\Sigma^\otimes, \emptyset^\otimes)$$

$$\mathbf{Mod}^{COSA}(\Sigma^\otimes, \emptyset^\otimes) \xleftarrow{\;(\_)^\bullet\;} \mathbf{Mod}^{CondEq^=}(\Sigma^{\otimes\,\#}, J^\otimes) \xleftarrow{\mathbf{Mod}(\mu_{\Sigma^\otimes})} \mathbf{Mod}^{CondEq^=}(\widehat{\Sigma^\otimes}, \hat{J}^\otimes)$$

---

[11] Since $CondEq^=$ is a total framework, we have to leave out the partial projections from $\hat{\Sigma}$. Otherwise, the target of the translation would be $PCondEq^=$.

Sentences *Given a $COSASC^{\otimes}$-signature Σ, for sentences without sort constraints, the sentence translation is the following composite (LP has been introduced in Theorem 7):*

$$\mathbf{Sen}^{COSA^{\otimes}}(\Sigma)$$

$$\mathbf{Sen}^{SubCondEq^{=}}(\Sigma^{\otimes})$$

$$\mathbf{Sen}^{COSA}(\Sigma^{\otimes}) \xrightarrow{LP_{\Sigma^{\otimes}}} \mathbf{Sen}^{CondEq^{=}}(\Sigma^{\otimes\#}) \xrightarrow{\mathbf{Sen}(\mu_{\Sigma^{\otimes}})} \mathbf{Sen}^{CondEq^{=}}(\widehat{\Sigma^{\otimes}})$$

Sort constraints within sentences are translated as follows: Given $t : s$ as an atomic constituent of a sentence in $\mathbf{Sen}^{COSASC^{\otimes}}(\Sigma)$, let $s' = lub(s, LS(t))$ and translate it to $\in^{=}_{s'} (inj_{(LS(t),s')}(\mathbf{Sen}(\mu_{\Sigma^{\otimes}})(LP_{\Sigma^{\otimes}}(t))))$ as an atomic constituent in $\mathbf{Sen}^{SubCondEq^{=}}(\Sigma^{\otimes})$.

Satisfaction *The representation condition follows from that of the representation in Theorem 7. For sort constraints, we also need the axioms for membership in $\hat{J}$.*   □

4.2   Translating $COSASC_{\otimes}$ to $SubPCondEq^{=}$

When translating $COSASC_{\otimes}$ to $SubPFOL^{=}$, we need as target institution a fragment of $SubPFOL^{=}$ that also includes partiality, because we want to map retracts to partial projections. Thus, we take subsorted partial conditional equational logic ($SubPCondEq^{=}$) as target institution, which is the conditional fragment of $SubPFOL^{=}$ without predicates.

Theorem 12. *The following describes a simple institution representation from $COSASC_{\otimes}$ to $SubPCondEq^{=}$.*

Signatures *Any $COSASC_{\otimes}$-signature is a $SubPCondEq^{=}$-signature by letting the set of partial function symbols be empty.*

Models *Given a $COSASC_{\otimes}$-signature Σ, the model translation is the following composite:*

$$\mathbf{Mod}^{COSASC_{\otimes}}(\Sigma)$$

$$\mathbf{Mod}^{SubPCondEq^{=}}(\Sigma)$$

$$\mathbf{Mod}^{COSASC}(\Sigma) \xleftarrow{(\_)^{\bullet}} \mathbf{Mod}^{COSASC}(\Sigma^{\#}, J) \xleftarrow{\mathbf{Mod}(\mu_{\Sigma})} \mathbf{Mod}^{PCondEq^{=}}(\hat{\Sigma}, \hat{J})$$

Sentences *Given a $COSASC_{\otimes}$-signature Σ, sentences without sort constraints are translated with the following composite:*

$$\mathbf{Sen}^{COSA_{\otimes}}(\Sigma)$$

$$\mathbf{Sen}^{SubPCondEq^{=}}(\Sigma)$$

$$\mathbf{Sen}^{COSA}(\Sigma^{\otimes}) \xrightarrow{LP_{\Sigma^{\otimes}}} \mathbf{Sen}^{CondEq^{=}}(\Sigma^{\otimes\#}) \xrightarrow{[\_]} \mathbf{Sen}^{PCondEq^{=}}(\hat{\Sigma})$$

Here, $[\![\_]\!]$ is defined inductively as follows:

- $[\![x]\!] = x$
- $[\![inj_{(s,s')}(t)]\!] = inj_{(s,s')}([\![t]\!])$
- $[\![r : s' > s(t)]\!] = pr_{(s',s)}([\![t]\!])$
- $[\![f_{w,s}(t_1,\ldots,t_n)]\!] = f_{w,s}([\![t_1]\!],\ldots,[\![t_n]\!])$
- $[\![t_1 = t_2]\!] = [\![t_1]\!] \stackrel{e}{=} [\![t_1]\!]$
- $[\![\forall X.e_1 \wedge \ldots \wedge e_n \Rightarrow e]\!] = \forall X.[\![e_1]\!] \wedge \ldots \wedge [\![e_n]\!] \Rightarrow [\![e]\!]$

A sort constraint $t : s$ occurring in a sentence is translated to

$$\in_{s'}^{s} (inj_{(LS(t),s')}([\![LP_{\Sigma\otimes}(t)]\!])),$$

where $s' = lub(s, LS(t))$.

Satisfaction *Given a $M \in \mathbf{Mod}^{PCondEq^=}(\hat{\Sigma})$, by Theorem 7 without loss of generality we can assume that M consists of inclusions as injections already, and $(M|_{\mu_\Sigma})^\bullet = M|_{\mu_\Sigma}$ (note that also $(M|_{\mu_\Sigma})_s = M_s$). The key to prove the representation condition is the following lemma:*

Lemma 13. *Given $M \in \mathbf{Mod}^{PCondEq^=}(\hat{\Sigma})$ with $(M|_{\mu_\Sigma})^\bullet = M|_{\mu_\Sigma}$, valuations $\nu: X \longrightarrow M$ are the same as valuations $\tilde{\nu}: X \longrightarrow (M|_{\mu_\Sigma})$. For $t \in T_{\Sigma\otimes}(X)$, the following properties hold:*

1. *$\nu^\#([\![LP_{\Sigma\otimes}(t)]\!])$ is defined iff $(\iota_{(M|_{\mu_\Sigma})} \circ \tilde{\nu})^\#(t) \in \iota_{(M|_{\mu_\Sigma})}(M|_{\mu_\Sigma})$*
2. *In case of 1., $\iota_{(M|_{\mu_\Sigma})}(\nu^\#([\![LP_{\Sigma\otimes}(t)]\!])) = (\iota_{(M|_{\mu_\Sigma})} \circ \tilde{\nu})^\#(t)$*

Proof. The proof proceeds by induction over the structure of t. The only critical case is that of retracts. We have $\nu^\#([\![LP_{\Sigma\otimes}(r : s' > s(t))]\!])$ is defined iff $\nu^\#(pr_{(s',s)}([\![LP_{\Sigma\otimes}(t)]\!]))$ is defined iff $\nu^\#([\![LP_{\Sigma\otimes}(t)]\!])$ is defined and $\in M_s$ iff $(\iota_{M|_{\mu_\Sigma}} \circ \tilde{\nu})^\#(t) \in \iota_{M|_{\mu_\Sigma}}((M|_{\mu_\Sigma})_s)$ iff (since retracts are interpreted freely outside M_s) $(\iota_{M|_{\mu_\Sigma}} \circ \tilde{\nu})^\#(r : s' > s(t)) \in \iota_{M|_{\mu_\Sigma}}((M|_{\mu_\Sigma})_s)$. □

Proposition 14. *The model translation in the representation from $COSASC_\otimes$ to $SubPCondEq^=$ is a natural equivalence.*

Proof. $(\_)^\bullet$ is shown to be a natural equivalence in [12], and $\mathbf{Mod}(\mu_\Sigma)$ is a natural equivalence since $(\hat{\Sigma}, \hat{J})$ is a definitional extension of $(\Sigma^\#, J)$. □

A signature Σ is called *strict*, if for each sort, there is a ground Σ-term of that sort. (A theory is called strict if its signature is.)

A theory morphism $\sigma: T \longrightarrow T'$ is called *liberal* if the induced forgetful functor $\mathbf{Mod}(\sigma): \mathbf{Mod}(T') \longrightarrow \mathbf{Mod}(T)$ has a left adjoint.

Corollary 15. *Each theory morphism $\sigma: (\Sigma, \Gamma) \longrightarrow (\Sigma', \Gamma')$ in $COSASC_\otimes$ with Σ' strict is liberal.*

Proof. The model translation in the institution representation from $COSASC_\otimes$ to $SubPCondEq^=$, being a natural equivalence, is both left and right adjoint. Thus the result follows from the corresponding result for $SubPCondEq^=$ [2,17], noting that strictness of Σ' ensures that the restriction to non-empty carriers does not matter. □

4.3 The empty carrier problem

All institutions of order-sorted and partial algebras which we have defined in this paper do not admit empty carriers. The reader may be surprised by this, since the order-sorted algebras usually are defined in a way allowing empty carriers [12]. However, Lemma 8, which is crucial for proving the satisfaction condition of $COSASC_\otimes$, does only hold if we forbid models that mix empty and non-empty carriers.[12] We here additionally forbid models consisting only of empty carriers, but this additional restriction is not essential in any respect.

It has been argued [11] that allowing empty carriers is necessary to get initial models and free extensions. However, Corollary 15 shows that initial models and free extensions exist if we restrict ourselves to strict signatures. Now in [11] it is argued that there are useful theories that are not strict (like the theory of pre-ordered sets). However, such theories can still be used as *parameter* theory for free extensions, since Corollary 15 only requires the *target* theory to be strict. It will hardly be the case that one wants to have initial or free semantics for non-strict theories.

For those who still insist in having empty carriers, we also have set up a representation from $SubPFOL^=$ with empty carriers to $SubPFOL^=$ without empty carriers [17]. However, this representation does not have all the nice properties that one would like to have.

5 Translating OBJ3 constructs into CASL constructs

We now briefly describe how any of the institution representations defined in the previous section can be lifted to a translation of language constructs.

The first point concerns sort disambiguation of terms. Sort disambiguation in OBJ3 inserts subsort inclusions and retracts, while in CASL, only subsort injections are inserted. Note that CASL's disambiguation [19] corresponds to the least sort parse for regular signatures. Thus, at the construct level, the translation from OBJ3 to CASL has just to insert retracts. (It does not matter here that at the concepts level, CASL terms are disambiguated while OBJ3 terms are not.)

Mixfix declaration facilities are essentially the same for OBJ and CASL, and this probably will also hold for precedence annotations (for CASL, these are not fixed yet). Explicit sort disambiguation (written $t.s$ in OBJ3) is also available in CASL (written $t : s$).

Associativity, commutativity, identity and idempotence attributes are slightly more general in OBJ3 than in CASL, since in CASL, argument and result sorts of the operations with attributes have to be the same. In the case that this condition does not hold, the attribute has to be translated to an axiom.

OBJ3's subsort declarations allow chains of subsorts to be declared. This has to be split up into several declarations in CASL. Finally, OBJ3's let definitions have to be translated to CASL's operation definitions.

---

[12] It also holds if we restrict ourselves to confluent sets of axioms [12], but this does not help for defining an *institution*.

6 Conclusion

When attempting to translate OBJ3 to CASL, we first had to clarify what the institution underlying OBJ3 is. Actually, we have found two institutions for OBJ3, serving different methodological purposes. One institution ($COSASC^\otimes$) treats error values generated by retracts as first-class citizens, allowing error recovery, while the other one ($COSASC_\otimes$) treats error values as virtual values, allowing a clean separation of ordinary and error values.

We translate both $COSASC^\otimes$ and $COSASC_\otimes$ into fragments of the CASL institution. Retracts for virtual error values can be mapped to CASL's partial projections, while retracts for first-class-citizen error values have to be mapped to ordinary operations in CASL. Both translations can be modified by mapping OBJ3's Bool-valued functions to CASL's predicates (the target then being first-order logic).

Each of these translations can be lifted to a translation of the language constructs. This can be the basis for an automated tool doing the translations and allowing to use the rich pool of OBJ3 modules also for CASL.

Future work also has to consider the translation of OBJ3's module systems to CASL's one. Here, again we have the difficulty that there is no full formal semantics for OBJ3. Another direction of future work is to extend the translation to CafeOBJ, the successor of OBJ3, and to translate other specification languages like Larch, ACT and ASF into CASL.

Acknowledgements

I would like to thank Maura Cerioli, Joseph A. Goguen, Peter D. Mosses and Grigore Rosu for intensive and sometimes controversial, but always productive discussions, and further, all the participants of CoFI.

References

1. P. Burmeister. Partial algebras — survey of a unifying approach towards a two-valued model theory for partial algebras. *Algebra Universalis*, 15:306–358, 1982.
2. M. Cerioli, A. Haxthausen, B. Krieg-Brückner, and T. Mossakowski. Permissive subsorted partial logic in CASL. In M. Johnson, editor, *Algebraic methodology and software technology: 6th international conference, AMAST 97*, volume 1349 of *Lecture Notes in Computer Science*, pages 91–107. Springer-Verlag, 1997.
3. M. Cerioli, T. Mossakowski, and H. Reichel. From total equational to partial first order logic. In E. Astesiano, H.-J. Kreowski, and B. Krieg-Brückner, editors, *Algebraic Foundations of Systems Specifications*. Chapman and Hall, 1999. To appear.

4. CoFI. The Common Framework Initiative for algebraic specification and development, electronic archives. Notes and Documents accessible by WWW[13] and FTP[14], 1998.

5. CoFI Language Design Task Group. CASL – The CoFI Algebraic Specification Language – Summary 1.0. In *CoFI Archives* [4]. Documents/CASLSummary.

6. CoFI Semantics Task Group. CASL – The CoFI Algebraic Specification Language (version 1.0) – Semantics. In *CoFI Archives* [4]. Note S9.

7. J. Goguen, J.-P. Jouannaud, and J. Meseguer. Operational semantics of order-sorted algebra. In W. Brauer, editor, *Proceedings, 1985 International Conference on Automata, Languages and Programming*, volume 194 of *Lecture Notes in Computer Science*, pages 221–231. Springer, 1985.

8. J. Goguen, J. Meseguer, T. Winkler, K. Futatsugi, P. Lincoln, and J.-P. Jouannaud. Introducing OBJ. Technical Report SRI-CSL-88-8, Computer Science Lab, SRI International, August 1988; revised version from 24th October 1993.

9. J. A. Goguen. Stretching first order equational logic: Proofs about partiality using subsorts and retracts. Journal of Symbolic Computation, submitted for publication, 1998.

10. J. A. Goguen and R. M. Burstall. Institutions: Abstract model theory for specification and programming. *Journal of the Association for Computing Machinery*, 39:95–146, 1992. Predecessor in: LNCS 164, 221–256, 1984.

11. J. A. Goguen and J. Meseguer. Remarks on remarks on many-sorted equational logic. *EATCS Bulletin*, 30:66–73, 1986.

12. J. A. Goguen and J. Meseguer. Order-sorted algebra I: equational deduction for multiple inheritance, overloading, exceptions and partial operations. *Theoretical Computer Science*, 105:217–273, 1992.

13. A. Haxthausen and F. Nickl. Pushouts of order-sorted algebraic specifications. In *Proceedings of AMAST'96*, volume 1101 of *Lecture Notes in Computer Science*, pages 132–147. Springer-Verlag, 1996.

14. J. Meseguer. General logics. In *Logic Colloquium 87*, pages 275–329. North Holland, 1989.

15. J. Meseguer and J. Goguen. Order-sorted algebra solves the constructor, selector, multiple representation and coercion problems. *Information and Computation*, 103(1):114–158, March 1993.

16. T. Mossakowski. *Representations, hierarchies and graphs of institutions*. PhD thesis, Bremen University, 1996.

17. T. Mossakowski. Sublanguages of CASL. In *CoFI Archives* [4]. Note L7.

18. T. Mossakowski. Colimits of order-sorted specifications revisited. In F. Parisi Presicce, editor, *Recent trends in algebraic development techniques. Proc. 12th International Workshop*, volume 1376 of *Lecture Notes in Computer Science*, pages 316–332. Springer, 1998.

19. T. Mossakowski, Kolyang, and B. Krieg-Brückner. Static semantic analysis and theorem proving for CASL. In F. Parisi Presicce, editor, *Recent trends in algebraic development techniques. Proc. 12th International Workshop*, volume 1376 of *Lecture Notes in Computer Science*, pages 333–348. Springer, 1998.

20. P. D. Mosses. CoFI: The Common Framework Initiative for Algebraic Specification and Development. In *TAPSOFT '97: Theory and Practice of Software Development*, volume 1214 of *LNCS*, pages 115–137. Springer-Verlag, 1997. Also in *CoFI Archives* [4]. Documents/Tentative/Mosses97TAPSOFT.

---

[13] http://www.brics.dk/Projects/CoFI

[14] ftp://ftp.brics.dk/Projects/CoFI

21. A. Tarlecki. On the existence of free models in abstract algebraic institutions. *Theoretical Computer Science*, 37:269–304, 1985.
22. A. Tarlecki. Moving between logical systems. In M. Haveraaen, O. Owe, and O.-J. Dahl, editors, *Recent Trends in Data Type Specifications. 11th Workshop on Specification of Abstract Data Types*, volume 1130 of *Lecture Notes in Computer Science*, pages 478–502. Springer Verlag, 1996.
23. H. Yan. *Theory and Implementation of Sort Constraints for Order Sorted Algebra*. PhD thesis, Oxford University, 1993.

CASL: A Guided Tour of Its Design

Peter D. Mosses[1,2]

[1] BRICS and Department of Computer Science,
University of Aarhus, Denmark
[2] CoFI:The Common Framework Initiative
for algebraic specification and development

Abstract. CASL is an expressive language for the specification of functional requirements and modular design of software. It has been designed by CoFI, the international Common Framework Initiative for algebraic specification and development. It is based on a critical selection of features that have already been explored in various contexts, including subsorts, partial functions, first-order logic, and structured and architectural specifications. CASL should facilitate interoperability of many existing algebraic prototyping and verification tools.

This guided tour of the CASL design is based closely on a 1/2-day tutorial held at ETAPS'98 (corresponding slides are available from the CoFI archives). The major issues that had to be resolved in the design process are indicated, and all the main concepts and constructs of CASL are briefly explained and illustrated—the reader is referred to the CASL Language Summary for further details. Some familiarity with the fundamental concepts of algebraic specification would be advantageous.

1 Background

The algebraic approach to software specification originated in the early 1970's. Since then, dozens of algebraic specification languages have been developed—all of them supporting the basic idea of using axioms to specify algebras, but differing in design choices concerning syntax (concrete and abstract) and semantics. The lack of a *common* framework for algebraic specification and development has discouraged industrial acceptance of the algebraic method, hindered its dissemination, and limited tool applicability.

Why not agree on a common framework? This was the provocative question asked at a WADT meeting in Santa Margherita, 1994. At least the main concepts to be incorporated were thought to be clear—although it was realized that it might not be so easy to agree on a common language to express these concepts.

The following aims and scope were formulated at the start of the Common Framework Initiative, CoFI, in September 1995 [13]:

The aims of CoFI are to provide a common framework:

- by a collaborative effort
- for algebraic specification and development
- attractive to researchers as well as for use in industry

J.L. Fiadeiro (Ed.): WADT'98, LNCS 1589, pp. 216–240, 1999.
© Springer-Verlag Berlin Heidelberg 1999

- providing a common specification language with uniform, user-friendly syntax and straightforward semantics
- able to subsume many previous frameworks
- with good documentation and tool support
- free—but protected (cf. GNU)

The scope of CoFI is:

- specification of functional requirements
- formal development and verification of software
- relation of specifications to informal requirements and implemented code
- prototyping, theorem-proving
- libraries, reuse, evolution
- tool interoperability

The specification language developed by CoFI is called CASL: the Common Algebraic Specification Language. Its main features are:

- a critical selection of known constructs
- expressive, simple, pragmatic
- for specifying requirements and design for conventional software packages
- restrictions to sublanguages
- extensions to higher-order, state-based, concurrent, ...

The CASL design effort started in September 1995. An initial design was proposed in May 1997 (with a language summary, abstract syntax, formal semantics, but no agreed concrete syntax) and tentatively approved by IFIP WG1.3. Apart from a few details, the design was finalized in April 1998, with a complete draft language summary available, including concrete syntax. CASL version 1.0 was released in October 1998; the formal semantics given for the proposed design has now been updated to reflect the changes.

2   Guide

CASL consists of several major *parts*, which are quite independent and may be understood (and used) separately:

- basic specifications: declarations, definitions, axioms
- structured specifications: translations, reductions, unions, extensions, freeness, named specifications, generic specifications, views
- architectural specifications: implementation units, composition
- specification libraries: local, distributed

The above division of CASL into parts is orthogonal to taking sublanguages of CASL.

The CASL language design integrates several different *aspects*, which are here explained separately:

- pragmatic issues: methodology, tools, aesthetics
- semantic concepts: formal (institutions, environments), informal (expansions, scopes)
- language constructs: abstract syntax (structure, annotations); concrete syntax (input format, display format)

In this guided tour, each part of CASL is presented in turn, considering all the aspects listed above before proceeding to the next part. Of course the reader is free to ignore the guide, and wander through the various sections in a different order (but then the author cannot accept responsibility for any resulting disorientation...).

3   Basic Specifications

Basic specifications consist of declarations, definitions, and axioms. Section 3.1 considers various pragmatic issues affecting the CASL design. Section 3.2 presents the main concepts that underly the semantics of basic specifications. Finally, Section 3.3 provides examples that illustrate the CASL language constructs for use in basic specifications.

3.1   Pragmatic Issues

Partial and Total Functions: CASL supports both partial and total algebraic specification. Partiality is a particularly natural and simple way of treating errors such as division by zero, and error propagation is implicit, so that whenever any argument of an operation is undefined, the result is undefined too. CASL also includes subsorts and error supersorts, to allow specification of exception handling when this is relevant. Totality is of course an important property, and CASL allows it to be declared along with the types of functions, rather than relegating it to the axioms. The domain of definition of a partial function may be made explicit by introducing it as a subsort of the argument sort and declaring the function to be total on it.

For instance, consider the familiar operations on (possibly-empty) lists: the list constructor *cons* would be declared as total, whereas the list head and tail selectors would be partial, being undefined on the empty list. The domain of definition of the selectors may be made explicit by introducing the subsort of non-empty lists, and declaring them to be total functions on that subsort. (This and further examples are specified in CASL in Section 3.3.)

In the presence of partiality, equations may require definedness: so-called 'existential' equations require it, 'strong' equations do not. In general, it is appropriate to use existential equations in conditions (since properties do not usually follow from undefinedness) but strong equations when defining partial functions inductively. So CASL allows both kinds of equations.

Definedness assertions can also be expressed directly. In fact definedness of a term is equivalent to its existential equality to itself—it could also be regarded as a unary predicate. Existential equality is equivalent to the conjunction of a strong equality and two definedness assertions; strong equality is equivalent to the conjunction of two conditionals involving only existential equality.

Logic and Predicates: CASL is based on classical 2-valued first-order logic, with the standard interpretation of connectives. It supports user-declared predicates, which have some advantages over the (total) Boolean functions that were used instead of predicates in most previous languages.[1] When an argument of a predicate is undefined, the predicate application cannot hold.

CASL provides the standard universal and existential quantification and logical connectives, i.e., ordinary first-order predicate logic. The motivation for this is expressiveness: restricting to conditional equations sometimes requires quite contrived specifications. For instance, it is a straightforward exercise to specify when a string is a permutation of another using quantifiers, and negation provides the complementary property; but the latter is quite awkward to specify using (positive) conditional equations.

The usual equational and conditional specification frameworks are provided as sublanguages of CASL, simply by restricting the use of quantifiers and logical connectives.

Classes of Models: Most previous frameworks allow only one kind of model class to be specified. The default in CASL is to take all models of a specification, i.e., so-called loose semantics; but it is also possible to specify the restriction of models to the class of generated models (only expressible values are included, and properties may be proved by induction) or to the class of initial (and freely-generated) models (providing minimal satisfaction of atomic formulae). Of course initial models may not exist when disjunction, negation, etc., are used.

Overloading: In a CASL specification the same symbol may be declared with various profiles (i.e., list of argument and result sorts), e.g. '+' may be declared as an operation on integers, reals, and strings. When such an overloaded symbol is used, the intended profile is to be determined by the context. Explicit disambiguation can be used when needed, by specifying the profile (or result sort) in an application.

Subsorts: It is appropriate to declare a sort as a subsort of another when the values of the subsort are regarded a special case of those in the other sort. For instance, the positive integers and the positive odd integers are best regarded as subsorts of the sort of natural numbers, which is itself a subsort of the integers. In contrast to most previous frameworks, CASL interprets subsorts as *embeddings* between carriers—not necessarily inclusions. This allows, e.g., models where values of sort integer are represented differently from values of sort real (as in most computers). CASL still allows the models where the subsort happens to be a subset. The extra generality of embeddings seems to be useful, and does not complicate the foundations at all.

---

[1] For example, predicates hold minimally in initial models.

Subsort embeddings commute with overloaded functions, so the values are independent of which profiles are used: 2+2=4, regardless of whether the '+' is that declared for natural numbers or integers.

CASL does not impose any conditions of 'regularity', 'coherence', or 'sensibleness' on the relationship between overloading and subsorts. This is partly for simplicity (no such conditions are required for the semantics of CASL), partly because most such conditions lack modularity (which is a disadvantage in connection with structured specifications). Note that overloaded constants are allowed in CASL.

Datatype Constructors/Selectors: Specifications of 'datatypes' with constructor and (possibly also) selector operations are frequently needed: they correspond to (unions of) record types and enumeration types in programming languages. CASL provides special constructs for datatype declarations to abbreviate the rather tedious declarations and axioms for constructors and selectors. Datatypes may be loose, generated, or free.

3.2 Semantic Concepts

The essential semantic concepts for basic specifications are well-known: signatures (of declared symbols), models (interpreting the declared symbols), and sentences (asserting properties of the interpretation), with a satisfaction relation between models and sets of sentences. Defining these (together with some categorical structure, and such that translation of symbols preserves satisfaction) provides a so-called *institution* for basic specifications.

A well-formed basic specification in CASL determines a signature and a set of sentences, and hence the class of all models over that signature which satisfy all the sentences.

Signatures $\Sigma = (S, TF, PF, P, \leq)$: A signature Σ for a CASL specification consists of a set of sorts S, disjoint sets TF, PF of total and partial operation symbols (for each profile of argument and result sorts), a set of predicate symbols P (for each profile of argument sorts), and a partial order of subsort embeddings $\leq$. The same symbol may be overloaded, with more than one profile; there are no conditions on the relationship between overloading and subsorts, and both so-called ad-hoc overloading and subsort overloading are allowed.

Models $M \in \mathbf{Mod}(\Sigma)$: A model M provides a non-empty carrier set for each sort in S, a partial function for each operation symbol in $PF \cup TF$ (for each of its profiles), a relation for each predicate symbol in P (for each of its profiles), and an embedding for each pair of sorts related by $\leq$. The interpretation of an operation symbol in TF has to be a total function. Moreover, embedding and overloading have to be compatible: embeddings commute with overloaded operations.

Sentences $\Phi \in \mathbf{Sen}(\Sigma)$: A sentence Φ is generally a closed, many-sorted first-order formula. The atomic formulae in it may be equations (strong or existential), definedness and (subsort) membership assertions, and fully-qualified predicate applications. The terms in atomic formulae may be fully-qualified operation applications, variables, explicitly-sorted terms (interpreted as subsort embeddings) or casts (interpreted as projection onto subsorts).

Satisfaction $M \vdash \Phi$: The satisfaction of a closed first-order formula Φ in a model M is as usual regarding quantifiers and logical connectives; it involves the holding of open formulae, and the values of terms, relative to assignments of values to variables.

The value of a term may be undefined when it involves the application of a partial operation symbol (or a cast). When the value of any argument term is undefined, the application of a predicate never holds, and the application of an operation is always undefined (as usual in partial algebra). Definedness of terms also affects the holding of atomic formulae: an existential equation holds when both terms are defined and equal, whereas a strong equation holds when they are both undefined, or defined and equal.

Sort Generation Constraints $(S', F') \subseteq (S, F)$, where $F = TF \cup PF$: A sort generation constraint is treated as a further kind of sentence. It is satisfied in a model when the carriers of sorts in S' are generated by functions in F' (possibly from sorts in $S \setminus S'$).

Institution: The institution for basic specifications in CASL is given by equipping signatures with morphisms, and models with homomorphisms. A signature morphism σ from Σ to Σ' preserves overloading, embeddings, and totality of operation symbols. A homomorphism $h : M_1 \to M_2$ ($M_1, M_2 \in \mathbf{Mod}(\Sigma)$) preserves operation values (including definedness), and the holding predicates.

A signature morphism σ from Σ to Σ' determines a translation of sentences from $\mathbf{Sen}(\Sigma)$ to $\mathbf{Sen}(\Sigma')$, and a reduct functor $\mathbf{Mod}(\sigma) : \mathbf{Mod}(\Sigma') \to \mathbf{Mod}(\Sigma)$. Translation preserves satisfaction: $M' \vdash \sigma(\Phi)$ iff $\mathbf{Mod}(\sigma)(M') \vdash \Phi$.

Semantic Functions: Whereas applications of predicates and operations in the atomic formulae and terms of the CASL *institution* are fully qualified by their profiles, basic specifications in the CASL *language* allow the profiles to be omitted (since they are usually evident from the context). In general, there may be many ways—but possibly none at all—of expanding an atomic formula in CASL by inserting profiles to give a well-sorted fully-qualified atom for constructing a sentence of the underlying institution. The atomic formula is deemed to be well-formed when its expansion is unique (up to the commuting of embeddings with overloaded operations); the axioms of a well-formed basic specification determine a set of sentences of the CASL institution.

In fact the subsorted CASL institution outlined above may be reduced to an ordinary many-sorted CASL institution, by replacing subsort inclusion by explicit embeddings: $\Sigma = (S, TF, PF, P, \leq)$ reduces to $\Sigma^{\#} = (S, TF \cup Emb, PF \cup Proj, P \cup Memb)$ where $Emb = \{emb_{s,s'} \mid s \leq s'\}$ is a set of total operation symbols for subsort embeddings, and the sets $Proj$ (of projections onto subsorts) and $Memb$ (of subsort membership predicates) are defined similarly.

The semantics of a well-formed basic specification in CASL is given by a signature Σ together with the class of those models $M \in \mathbf{Mod}(\Sigma)$ that satisfy all the sentences determined by the specification.

3.3   Language Constructs

This section provides examples that illustrate the CASL language constructs for use in basic specifications: declarations and definitions (of sorts, operations, predicates, and datatypes), sort generation constraints, and axioms (involving variable declarations, quantifiers, connectives, atomic formulae, and terms). The examples are shown in *display format*; for input, a suggestive (ASCII or ISO Latin-1) plain text approximation is used, e.g., '$\to$' is input as '->', and '$\forall$' is input as 'forall'.

Note that CASL allows declarations to be interspersed with definitions and axioms (as illustrated in Section 3.4). Visibility is linear: symbols have to be declared before they can be used (except within datatype declarations, where non-linear visibility allows mutually-recursive datatypes—e.g., *List* and *NeList* on page 223).

Sorts: Several sorts may be declared at once, possibly as subsorts of some other sort:[2]

> **sorts** *Elem, List*
> **sorts** *Nat, Neg < Int*

The values of a subsort may also be defined by a formula, e.g.:

> **sort**   *Pos* $= \{n : Nat \bullet n > 0\}$

This corresponds to declaring *Pos < Nat* and asserting that a value n in *Nat* is the embedding of some value from *Pos* iff the formula $n > 0$ holds.

Operations: Operations may be declared as total (using '$\to$') or partial (using '$\to$?') and given familiar attributes:

> **ops** $0 : Nat$;
> $suc : Nat \to Nat$;
> $pre : Nat \to? Nat$;
> $\_ + \_ : Nat \times Nat \to Nat, \mathbf{assoc}, \mathbf{comm}, \mathbf{unit}\ 0$

So-called *mixfix notation* is allowed: place-holders for arguments are written as *pairs* of underscores (single underscores are treated as letters in identifiers). All

---

[2] CASL also allows sorts to be declared as isomorphic, with mutual subsort embeddings.

symbols should be input in the ISO Latin-1 character set, but *annotations*[3] may cause them to be displayed differently, e.g., as mathematical symbols.

In simple cases, operations may also be defined at the same time they are declared:

> **ops** $1 : Nat = suc(0)$;
> $dbl(n : Nat) : Nat = n + n$

Predicates: Predicate declarations resemble operation declarations, but there is no result sort:

> **preds** $odd : Nat$;
> $\_\_ < \_\_ : Nat \times Nat$

They too may also be defined at the same time they are declared:

> **preds** $even(n : Nat) \Leftrightarrow \neg odd(n)$;
> $\_\_ \leq \_\_(m, n : Nat) \Leftrightarrow m < n \lor m = n$

Datatypes: A datatype declaration looks like a context-free grammar in a variant of BNF. It declares the symbols on the left of '::=' as sorts, and for each alternative on the right it declares a constructor—possibly with some selectors. When datatypes are declared as 'free', the specified models are as for a free extension in a structured specification: distinct constructor terms of the same sort are interpreted as distinct values, and each declared sort is freely-generated by its constructors.

> **type** $Collection ::= empty \mid just(Elem) \mid join(Collection; Collection)$
> **free type** $Bit ::= 0 \mid 1$
> **free type** $Pair ::= pair(left, right : Elem)$

When there is more than one alternative in a datatype declaration, any selectors are generally *partial* and have to be declared as such, by inserting '?':[4]

> **free type** $List ::= nil \mid cons(hd :? Elem; tl :? List)$

Partial selectors can generally be avoided by use of subsort embeddings as constructors:

> **free types** $List \quad ::= nil \mid \textbf{sort } NeList$;
> $NeList ::= cons(hd : Elem; tl : List)$

The last declaration above illustrates non-linear visibility within a list of datatype declarations: *NeList* is used before it has been declared.

---

[3] An annotation is an auxiliary part of a specification, for use by tools, and not affecting the semantics of the specification.

[4] Constructors can also be partial.

Sort Generation Constraints: The CASL syntax allows datatypes to be declared as 'generated', so that the sorts are constrained to be generated by their constructors (and embedded subsorts):

> **generated type** *Bag ::= empty | add(Elem; Bag)*
> **generated types** *Nat ::= 0 |* **sort** *Pos;*
> *Pos ::= suc(pre : Nat)*

More generally, any group of signature declarations can be subject to a sort generation constraint, e.g.:

> **generated**
> **{ sorts** *Pos < Nat;*
> **ops** *0 : Nat;   suc : Nat → Pos* **}**

Axioms: Variables for use in axioms may be declared 'globally', in advance:

> **vars** *m, n : Nat; p : Pos*
> **axioms** $n < m \Rightarrow \ldots; suc(n) = p \Rightarrow \ldots; \ldots$

Variables may also be declared locally to an 'itemized' list of formulae:

> **vars** *x, y, z : Elem*
> • $x \leq x$
> • $x \leq y \land y \leq z \Rightarrow x \leq z$

or within a formula using explicit quantification:

> $\forall n : Nat \bullet \exists m : Nat \bullet n < m$
> $\forall p : Pos \bullet \exists! n : Nat \bullet suc(n) = p$

The logical connectives have their usual interpretation:

> $even(n) \Leftrightarrow \neg\, odd(n)$
> $m \leq n \Leftrightarrow m < n \lor m = n$
> $m < n \Rightarrow \neg\, n = 0$
> $even(m + n) \text{ if } odd(m) \land odd(n)$

Atomic Formulae: Definedness assertions can be explicit:

> $def\,pre(suc(n)) \land \neg def\,pre(0)$

or implicit in existential equations, which are distinguished from strong equations by writing '$\stackrel{e}{=}$' (input as '=e=') instead of '=':

> $def\,pre(n) \Rightarrow suc(pre(n)) \stackrel{e}{=} pre(suc(n))$
> $\neg ok(x, e) \Rightarrow find(x, cons(e, l)) = find(x, l)$

Subsort membership assertions are written suggestively using '$\in$' (input as 'in'):

> $n \in Pos \Leftrightarrow def\,pre(n)$

Applications of predicates are written the same way as those of operations, possibly using mixfix notation.

Terms: Constants and variables may be written as sequences of words (optionally separated by *single* underscores—pairs of underscores are reserved for indicating place-holders in mixfix symbols—and decorated with primes) or mathematical signs: *nil, empty_set, n, n′, CURRENT_STATE*.

Applications may be written using standard functional or mixfix notation: *cons(e, l), {|e|} ∪ s*; they may also be written with explicit qualification, e.g., *pre(n)* may be written as *(op pre : Nat →? Nat)(n)*. Sorted terms (interpreted as applications of identity or subsort embeddings) are written straightforwardly, e.g.: *dbl(suc(n)) : Nat)*. Casts (interpreted as applications of projections onto subsorts, the result of which may be undefined) are written using the reserved word 'as', e.g.: *pre(n as Pos)*.

3.4 Example

The following example illustrates a complete basic specification:

free types *Nat ::= 0 |* **sort** *Pos;*
          Pos ::= suc(pre : Nat)
op   *pre : Nat →? Nat*
axioms
        ¬def pre(0);
        ∀n : Nat • pre(suc(n)) = n

pred *even__ : Nat*
var *n : Nat*
•   *even 0*
•   *even suc(n) ⇔ ¬even n*

Notice that the second line above declares *suc : Nat → Pos* and *pre : Pos → Nat*. The subsequent declaration of *pre : Nat →? Nat* allows terms where *pre* is applied to an argument that is of sort *Nat* but not of sort *Pos*—such terms can be perfectly meaningful, e.g., *pre(pre(suc(suc(0))))*.

Further examples may be found in later sections, and in the appendices of the CASL Summary [4].

4 Structured Specifications

Structured specifications in CASL are formed in various familiar ways (union, extension, translation, reduction, etc.) starting from basic specifications; they may also be named, to facilitate reuse. Section 4.1 considers various pragmatic issues affecting the CASL design. Section 4.2 presents the main concepts that underly the semantics of structured specifications. Finally, Section 4.3 provides examples that illustrate the CASL language constructs for use in structured specifications.

4.1   Pragmatic Issues

No Model Structure: The crucial point is that structuring a specification does *not* specify any structure in models! In fact the models of structured specifications are of exactly the same kind as for basic specifications, i.e., algebras interpreting the declared symbols and satisfying all the asserted properties.

For example, consider a specification of the integers. One might choose to structure it as an extension of a specification of natural numbers, rather than giving it as a single basic specification. This choice does not affect the semantics of the specification: neither the signature nor the models reflect the structure of the extension.

Section 5 explains the 'architectural' specifications of CASL, which do allow the structure of models to be specified.

Names of Symbols: A general principle underlying the CASL design is '*same name, same thing*'. Thus when one sees two occurrences of the same sort in the same basic specification, one may be sure that they are always interpreted as the same carrier set. For operations and predicates, the situation is a little more subtle: the 'name' of an operation (or predicate) includes its profile of argument and result sorts, so there need be no relationship at all between say, '+' on integers and '+' on lists or sets, at least in the absence of subsort inclusions.

The 'same name, same thing' principle applies also in unions and extensions— but *not* between named specifications in libraries: the same sort may be used in different named specifications in the same library, with entirely different interpretations; similarly for operations or predicates with the same profiles.

When named specifications are *combined* in the same *structured* specification (by references to their names—perhaps indirectly via other named specifications), any unintended clashes can be eliminated by translating the symbols used in them to new ones. From a methodological point of view, it seems indeed appropriate for the writer of a specification to avoid *accidental* use of the same sort or (qualified) symbol for different purposes, since it could confuse readers. (The same argument does *not* apply to overloading: for example, use of the '$\leq$' predicate for partial orders on different sorts is conventional and nicely emphasises their common properties).

Another point is that in CASL, it is easy to *hide* auxiliary symbols, i.e., symbols that are not inherent to what is to be specified. For example, to specify addition and subtraction on the integers it is common practice to introduce successor and predecessor operations, but they may be regarded as auxiliary and hidden afterwards—they can in any case be recovered using addition and subtraction of 1.

Finally, tools may warn users about multiple declarations of the same name in the same specification, in case they are accidental.

Generic Extension: A specification definition *names* a specification, allowing reuse by reference to the name. For example, INT might refer to a specification of the integers. In CASL, a named specification may also have parameters, intended to vary between references; the specification body is an extension of what is specified in the parameters. Each reference to the specification requires instantiation of all its parameters. For example, LIST might refer to a specification that extends a parameter specification named ELEM; any reference to LIST has to provide an argument specification that 'fits' ELEM.

Note that generic extensions in CASL are *not* intended for defining arbitrary functions on specifications, unlike in some other frameworks such as ASL—the CASL user is expected to express the structure of specifications directly using the CASL language constructs that are provided for that purpose.

4.2   Semantic Concepts

The notions of signature and class of models are the same as for basic specifications. In fact the structuring part of CASL is (essentially) independent of the details of basic specification: the same structuring may be used regardless of whether basic specifications are restricted (e.g., by eliminating partial functions, subsorts, predicates, or explicit quantifiers) or extended (e.g., to higher-order functions). The reduct homomorphisms induced by signature morphisms in the institution for basic specifications are especially significant in the semantics of structured specifications.

In a specification, the so-called *local environment* records the symbol declarations that are currently visible. For basic specifications, visibility is linear (except within lists of datatype declarations) so the local environment merely grows as one proceeds through the declarations. For structured specifications, however, the local environments at different places may be completely unrelated.

Semantic Functions: Structured specifications can have arbitrarily deep structure, and a compositional semantics is appropriate: the denotation of a construct is determined entirely by the denotations of its components. The denotation of a self-contained specification is a signature and class of models for that signature. The denotation of a part that extends a self-contained specification is a (partial) function from signatures to extended signatures, and from corresponding model classes to extended-model classes.

4.3   Language Constructs

This section provides examples that illustrate the CASL language constructs for use in structured specifications: translation, reduction, union, extension, free extension, local specifications, specification definitions, generic parameters, instantiation, views, and compound identifiers.

Translation and Reduction: Translation of declared symbols to new symbols is specified straightforwardly by giving a list of 'maplets' of the form *old* ↦ *new*. Identity maplets *old* ↦ *old* may be abbreviated to *old*, or simply omitted altogether. Optionally, the nature of the symbols concerned (sorts, operations, predicates) may be indicated by inserting the corresponding keywords.

> NAT **with** *Nat* ↦ *Natural*, *suc* ↦ *succ__*

> NAT **with op** _ + _ ↦ *plus*, **pred** _ < _ ↦ *lt*

Reduction means removing symbols from the signature of a specification, and removing the corresponding items from models. When a sort is removed, so are all operations and predicates whose profiles include that sort. CASL provides two ways of specifying a reduction: by listing the symbols to be hidden, or by listing those to be left visible, i.e., revealed. In the latter case, (some of) the revealed symbols may also be translated to new symbols.

> NAT **hide** *Pos, suc*

> NAT **reveal** *Nat, 0, _ + _ , _ < _* ↦ *lt*

Unions and Extensions: The signature of a union of two (or more) specifications is the union of their signatures. The models of a union are those whose reducts to the component signatures are models of the component specifications. There are two extremes: when the specifications have disjoint signatures, their union provides *amalgamation* of their models; when they have the same signature, it provides the *intersection* of the model classes, giving models that satisfy both the specifications at once. For example, the signatures of NAT and STRING might be disjoint, so models of

> NAT **and** STRING

would be amalgamations of models of NAT and of STRING, whereas the signatures of MONOID and COMMUTATIVE might be the same, so models of

> MONOID **and** COMMUTATIVE

would be those that are simultaneously models of MONOID and of COMMUTATIVE (i.e., commutative monoids).

Extensions may specify new symbols (known as *enrichment*):

> NAT **then**
> **sort** *Nat* < *Int*;
> **ops** _ + _ : *Int* × *Int* → *Int*;
> . . .

or merely require further properties of old ones:

> COLLECTION **then**
> **axiom** ∀*c* : *Collection* • *join*(*c, c*) = *c*

An extension is called *conservative* when no models are lost: every model of the specification being extended is a reduct of some model of the extended specification. Whether an extension is conservative or not may be indicated by an annotation (not illustrated here).[5]

---

[5] If conservative extension were to be a construct of the language, its semantics would be the same as for ordinary extension whenever the specified extension happened to be conservative, and otherwise undefined.

Free Specifications: The simplest case of a free specification is when the component specification is self-contained. The signature of the specification is unchanged, but the models are restricted to (the isomorphism class of) its initial models. E.g., the only models of the following specification are the standard models of Peano's axioms:

free
{ **sort** *Nat*; **ops** *0* : *Nat*;   *suc* : *Nat* → *Nat* }

The conciseness and perspicuity of such specifications may account for the popularity of frameworks that support initiality. When axioms are restricted to positive conditional existential equations, initial models always exist.

More generally, a free specification may be a free extension, e.g.:

sort *Elem* **then**
free
{ **type** *Set* ::= ∅ | {|_|}(*Elem*) | _ ∪ _(*Set*; *Set*)
  op _ ∪ _ : *Set* × *Set* → *Set*, **assoc, comm, idem, unit** ∅ }

Note that free specifications are especially useful for inductively-defined predicates, since only the cases where the predicates hold need be given: all other cases are automatically false. Similarly for partial operations in a free specification, which are as undefined as possible in all its models.

Local Specifications: CASL facilitates the hiding of auxiliary symbols by allowing the local scope of their declarations to be indicated. E.g., *suc* below is an auxiliary symbol for use in specifying addition:

sort *Nat*
op *0* : *Nat*
then local
   op *suc* : *Nat* → *Nat*
within
   op _ + _ : *Nat* × *Nat* → *Nat*
   vars *m, n* : *Nat*
   • *m* + *0* = *m*
   • *m* + *suc*(*n*) = *suc*(*m* + *n*)

Ideally, the operations and predicates of interest are specified directly by their properties, without the introduction of auxiliary symbols that have to be hidden. However, there are classes of models that cannot be specified (finitely) without the use of auxiliary symbols; in other cases the introduction of auxiliary symbols may lead 'merely' to increased conciseness and perspicuity.

Named Specifications: Only self-contained specifications can be named—the local environment for a named specification is always empty. Named specifications are intended for inclusion in libraries, see Section 6. Subsequent specifications in the library (or in other libraries) may include a copy of the named specification simply by referring to its name, e.g.:

    spec NAT = **free** { ... }

    spec INT = NAT **then free** { ... }

Generic Parameters: A parameter is a closed subspecification—typically a reference to a rather simple named specification such as ELEM:

    spec ELEM = **sort** *Elem*

    spec LIST [ELEM] =
        free type *List* ::= *nil* | *cons(Elem; List)*

A named specification is essentially an extension of all its parameters. A reference to a named specification with parameters is called an *instantiation*, and has to provide an argument specification for each parameter, indicating how it 'fits' by giving a map from the parameter signature to the argument signature, e.g.:

    LIST [NAT **fit** *Elem* ↦ *Nat*]

Since there is only one possible signature morphism from ELEM to NAT, the fitting may be left implicit, and the instantiation written may be written simply as LIST [NAT]. As with translation maps, identity fittings may always be omitted. Of course the map is required to induce not just a signature morphism but also a specification morphism: all models of the argument specification must also be models of the parameter specification.

    Sharing between parameter symbols is preserved by fitting, so it may be necessary to rename symbols when separate instantiation of similar parameters is required, e.g.:

    spec PAIR [**sort** *Elem1*] [**sort** *Elem2*] =
        free type *Pair* ::= *pair(Elem1; Elem2)*

Note that the 'same name, same thing' principle is maintained here. Moreover, to use the same sort name (say *Elem*) in both parameters would require some way of disambiguating the different uses of the name in the body, similar to an explicit renaming.

    Sharing of symbols between the body of a generic specification and its arguments in an instantiation is restricted to explicit *imports*, indicated as '**given**':

    spec LIST_LENGTH [ELEM] **given** NAT =
        free type *List* ::= *nil* | *cons(Elem; List)*
        op *length* : *List* → *Nat*

Well-formed instantiations always have a 'push-out' semantics. Had NAT been merely referenced in the body of LIST_LENGTH, an instantiation such as LIST_LENGTH [NAT] would be ill-formed.

Compound Identifiers: Suppose that two different instantiations of LIST are combined, e.g.,

LIST [NAT **fit** *Elem* $\mapsto$ *Nat*] **and** LIST [CHAR **fit** *Elem* $\mapsto$ *Char*]

With the previous definition of LIST, an unintentional name clash arises: the sort *List* is declared by both instantiations, but clearly should have different interpretations. To avoid the need for explicit renaming in such circumstances, compound identifiers such as *List*[*Elem*] may be used:

spec LIST [ELEM] =
    free type *List*[*Elem*] ::= *nil* | *cons*(*Elem*; *List*[*Elem*])

Now when this LIST is instantiated, the translation induced by the fitting morphism is applied to the component *Elem* also where it occurs in *List*[*Elem*], so the sorts in the above instantiations are now distinct: *List*[*Nat*] and *List*[*Char*].

Views: To allow reuse of fitting 'views', specification morphisms (from parameters to arguments) may be themselves named, e.g.:

spec PO2NAT : PARTIAL_ORDER **to** NAT =
    Elem $\mapsto$ *Nat*, $\_ \leq \_ \mapsto \_ \leq \_$

The syntax for referencing a named specification morphism, e.g.:

LIST_WITH_ORDER [**view** PO2NAT]

makes it clear that the argument is not merely some named specification with an implicit fitting map, which would be written simply LIST_WITH_ORDER [NAT]

The rules regarding omission of 'evident' maps in explicit fittings apply to named specification morphisms too.

4.4 Example

The following example illustrates a complete structured specification definition (referencing a specification named PARTIAL_ORDER, which is assumed to declare the sort *Elem* and the predicate $\_ \leq \_$):

spec LIST_WITH_ORDER [PARTIAL_ORDER] =
  free type $List[Elem] ::= nil \mid cons(hd :? Elem; tl :? List[Elem])$
then
  local
      op $insert : Elem \times List[Elem] \rightarrow List[Elem]$;
      vars $x, y : Elem; l : List[Elem]$
      axioms $insert(x, nil) = cons(x, nil)$;
             $x \leq y \Rightarrow insert(x, cons(y, l)) = cons(x, insert(y, l))$;
             $\neg(x \leq y) \Rightarrow insert(x, cons(y, l)) = cons(y, insert(x, l))$
  within
      pred $order[\_ \leq \_] : List[Elem] \times List[Elem]$
      vars $x : Elem; l : List[Elem]$
      axioms $order[\_ \leq \_](nil) = nil$;
           $order[\_ \leq \_](cons(x, l)) = insert(x, order[\_ \leq \_](l))$
end

5   Architectural Specifications

Architectural specifications in CASL are formed by declaring the *units* that are to be implemented separately, also indicating how they are to be linked together to give the desired result. Section 5.1 considers various pragmatic issues affecting the CASL design. Section 5.2 presents the main concepts that underly the semantics of architectural specifications. Finally, Section 5.3 provides examples that illustrate the CASL language constructs for use in architectural specifications.

5.1   Pragmatic Issues

Reusability: Whereas the *structuring of specifications* into unions and extensions encourages the reuse of (self-contained) parts of specifications, it does *not* affect the models at all, and the monolithic result of implementing a structured specification is unlikely to be reusable. To allow implementation units to be reusable, CASL provides further constructs for the *specification of structure*.

For a simple example, suppose that one wishes to structure the implementation of LIST [NAT] to include:

- an implementation N of NAT,
- a function F extending *any* such N to an implementation of LIST [NAT], and
- the obvious way of obtaining the desired result: applying F to N

The models of the corresponding architectural specification in CASL are required to provide the units N and F, as well as their composition. If the implementation N of NAT is subsequently changed, F may be reused, and does not have to be re-implemented. (F may also be changed without changing N, of course.)

Interfaces: These are the explicit assumptions that parts of an implementation make about other parts. In CASL, interfaces are expressed as ordinary (structured) specifications, asserting that the symbols declared by the specification not only have to be implemented, but also have to satisfy all the asserted properties. A specification of a functional unit involves the specifications of all its arguments and of its result. It is guaranteed that the results of applying functional units to argument units will meet their target specifications, provided that the argument units meet their given specifications.

Decomposition/Composition: A crucial aspect of architectural specifications is that they provide decompositions of (possibly large) implementation development tasks into smaller sub-tasks—as well as indicating how to compose (or link together) the results of sub-tasks. A unit specification expresses all that those who are implementing it need to know.

It is clearly desirable to distinguish between structure of specifications and specification of structure, so that specifying (e.g.) INT as an extension of NAT does *not* require separate implementations of these two specifications. What may not be quite so obvious is that the distinction is actually *essential*—at least if one is using the familiar specification structuring constructs provided by CASL. Consider the union of two specifications with some declared common symbols but different axioms: if each specification is implemented separately, without taking account of the properties required by the other specification, it may well happen that the common symbols have different, incompatible implementations which cannot be combined.

5.2   Semantic Concepts

A model of an architectural specification consists of:

- a collection of named unit constructors, together with
- the unit (constructor) resulting from a particular composition of those units.

Unit constructors are either constants, or functions from units to units. In the latter case, the functions are always persistent, extending their arguments (the function F considered above should clearly not be allowed to ignore the argument implementation N and incorporate a different implementation of NAT). When functions have more than one argument, the arguments must be compatible, implementing any common symbols in exactly the same way (this follows immediately from the requirement that a function should extend each argument separately).

5.3   Language Constructs

This section provides examples that illustrate the CASL language constructs for use in architectural specifications: architectural specification definitions, unit declarations, unit definitions, unit specifications, and unit expressions.

Architectural Specifications: A definition of an architectural specification specifies some units and how to compose them, e.g.:

> **arch spec** IMP_NAT_LIST =
>   **units** N : NAT ;
> F : NAT $\rightarrow$ LIST [NAT]
>   **result** $F[N]$

A model of the above architectural specification consists of a unit N, a unit function F, and the unit $F[N]$, which is itself a model of the structured specification LIST [NAT].

Unit Declarations and Definitions: A unit declaration names a unit that is to be developed, and gives its type. When the type is an ordinary specification, the unit is to be an ordinary model of it; when the type is a function type, the unit is to be a function from (compatible) ordinary models to ordinary models that extend the arguments. Some examples of unit declarations:

> N : NAT
> L : LIST [NAT] **given** N
> F : NAT $\rightarrow$ LIST [NAT]

The form of unit declaration using '**given**' provides an implicit declaration of a unit function that gets applied just once. If the declaration of F were to be replaced by that of L in the architectural specification example given above (letting the result be simply L as well) then an implementation of the architectural specification would still involve providing a function that could give an implementation of LIST [NAT] extending any implementation N of NAT.

A unit definition names a unit that can be obtained from previous units (in the same architectural specification), possibly involving fitting, hiding, translation, etc.:

> $L = F[N]$
> $L = F[N$ **fit**...$]$ **hide**...

The unit expressions in the right-hand sides of unit definitions are of the same form as used for specifying the result unit of an architectural specification (as explained below).

Unit Specifications: A unit specification definition names a unit type, allowing it to be reused. E.g.:

> **unit spec** GEN_LIST = NAT $\rightarrow$ LIST [NAT]

A unit declaration may then refer to it, as in F : GEN_LIST.

Architectural specifications themselves may also be used as unit specifications.

Unit Expressions: The various forms of unit expression mostly resemble those of structured specifications:

- application (to compatible arguments): $F[N]$, $F[N$ **fit**...$]$
- abstraction: $\lambda N : \text{NAT} \bullet \ldots N \ldots$
- translation, reduction: U **with** ..., U **hide** ..., ...
- amalgamation (of compatible units): N **and** C

However, the semantics of unit expressions involves operations on individual models, rather than on entire model classes. In particular, amalgamation of models requires that any common symbols are interpreted the same way. Note that abstraction is needed to allow architectural specifications whose results are unit functions.

5.4 Example

The following simple example illustrates an architectural specification definition (referencing ordinary specifications named LIST, CHAR, and NAT, assumed to declare the sorts *Elem* and *List[Elem]*, *Char*, and *Nat*, respectively):

> **arch spec** CN_LIST =
> **units**
> C : CHAR ;
> N : NAT ;
> F : ELEM → LIST[ELEM]
> **result** $F[C$ **fit** *Elem* ↦ *Char*$]$ **and** $F[N$ **fit** *Elem* ↦ *Nat*$]$

Further examples of architectural specifications are given in the CASL Summary [4] and in a recent paper [1].

6 Libraries of Specifications

Libraries in CASL are formed by collecting definitions of structured specifications, views, architectural specifications, and unit specifications. Moreover, libraries can refer to specifications defined in other libraries.

Section 6.1 mentions some pragmatic issues affecting the CASL design. Section 6.1 presents the concepts that underly the semantics of libraries. Finally, Section 6.1 briefly illustrates the CASL language constructs for use in libraries.

6.1 Pragmatic Issues

When specifications are collected into libraries, the question of visibility of symbols between specifications arises. In CASL, the symbols available in a specification are only those that it declares itself, together with those declared (and not hidden) in named specifications that it explicitly references. Thus when a specification in a library is changed, it is straightforward to locate other specifications that might be affected by the changes.

Another issue concerns visibility of specification names. In CASL, it is linear: a specification may only refer to names of specifications (and views) that precede it in the library. The motivation for this restriction is partly methodological (the library is presented in a bottom-up fashion), partly from implementation considerations (a library can be processed sequentially), and partly from the difficulty of giving a satisfactory formal semantics to mutually-dependent specifications.

CASL provides direct support for establishing distributed libraries on the Internet. A registered library is given a unique name, which is used to refer to it from other libraries when 'downloading' particular specifications. Name servers provide the current locations of registered libraries (before a library is registered, it is referred to by its current URL). Version control is an important pragmatic concern, and the names of CASL libraries incorporate version numbers; however, it is possible to refer to a library without specifying a version (corresponding to using the largest version number that has so far been registered for the library concerned).

It may happen that the same name is used for specifications in different libraries. To avoid confusion between the names of local and downloaded specifications in libraries, a specification that is downloaded from a remote library may be given a different local name. In fact downloading bears a strong resemblance to the FTP command 'get', which provides similar possibilities.

6.2   Semantic Concepts

The semantics of a specification in a library is a function of a global environment that maps names of specifications (previously declared or downloaded in the same library) to their denotations. The global environment at the end of the library gives the semantics of the entire library.

A directory of registered libraries maps library names to their registered URLs. Since the names include version numbers, this directory also gives access to previous versions of libraries.

Finally, the semantics of the whole collection of CASL libraries depends on the current state of the Internet, associating URLs to the contents of particular libraries.

6.3   Language Constructs

This section outlines some examples that illustrate the CASL language constructs for use in libraries.

Local Libraries: The specifications and views in a self-contained library are simply listed in a bottom-up order: a name has to be defined before it is referenced.

library CoFI_BEANS

spec NAT = ...

view ... = ...

arch spec ... = ... NAT...

unit spec ... = ...

Distributed Libraries: Other libraries may refer to specifications in registered libraries at other Internet sites by including explicit downloadings, optionally providing a different local name for the remote specification:

from CoFI_BEANS **get** LIST, NAT ↦ NATURAL

Libraries may have different versions, indicated by their names, both when defining libraries and downloading specifications from them:

library CoFI_BEANS **version** 1.2
from CoFI_PLANT **version** 1.0.1 **get**...

If the version number is omitted in a library definition, it is implicitly 0. The default version when referring to a library is the one that has been registered with the greatest version number.

7 Foreground

Having completed the guided tour, let us review the current status of the Common Framework Initiative. Various task groups have been created, concerning language design, semantics, tools, methodology, and reactive systems. There is a substantial amount of interaction between the task groups, which is supported by many of the CoFI participants being active in more than one task group.

The overall coordination of these task groups was managed by the present author from the start of CoFI in September 1995 until August 1998, and subsequently by Don Sannella (Edinburgh). In October 1998, an ESPRIT CoFI Working Group started (CoFI had previously relied on unfunded efforts by its participants, also with initial support from the ESPRIT COMPASS Working Group until that terminated in March 1996).

Language Design Task Group: (Coordination: Bernd Krieg-Brückner, Bremen)
Until October 1998, the main language design task was finalization of the CASL design. The documentation of the final design is given by the CASL Language Summary [4]; a (by now slightly outdated) rationale for the language design was published in 1997 [16]. The semantics, tools, and methodology task groups have all provided essential feedback regarding language design proposals.

The current work in this task group involves the definition of various interesting sublanguages of CASL, e.g., total, many-sorted, equational—mostly corresponding closely to embeddings of the specification languages of other frameworks into CASL [10,11]. Some extensions are also being investigated, in particular higher-order [7] and state-based specifications (possible extensions for specification of reactive systems is a separate task group).

Semantics Task Group: (Coordination: Andrzej Tarlecki, Warsaw)

The major semantics task has of course been defining the formal semantics of CASL, which was produced for earlier versions of the CASL design (in fact CASL had a formal semantics even before its concrete syntax was designed [5]) and which has recently been updated to CASL v1.0 [6].

Apart from consideration of the semantics of sublanguages and extensions of CASL, the main work remaining for the semantics task group is the choice of proof system for CASL.

Methodology Task Group: (Coordination: Michel Bidoit, Cachan)

The major task here is the production of a user's guide for CASL. Moreover, various case studies are to be coordinated within this task group. Further topics include the relation of specifications to requirements and code, and a study of software development processes.

Tools Task Group: (Coordination: Hélène Kirchner, Nancy)

The concrete syntax for CASL has been designed in joint work between the language design and tools task groups, and its implementation by prototype parsers has provided essential feedback. The various parsers are currently being validated. A LATEX package for formatting CASL specifications has been developed [17], and can also be used for displaying CASL specifications in HTML.

A major aim of CASL is to support interoperability of existing tools [8,15,19]. Collaboration with the developers of tools for other languages will usually be needed to enable the use of CASL specifications in those tools. Other work concerns static analysis and proof tools for CASL, with a prototype (currently for CASL basic specifications only) already implemented using HOL/Isabelle [12].

Reactive System Task Group: (Coordination: Egidio Astesiano, Genova)

This task group is mainly concerned with extensions of CASL for reactive system specification, and the combination of CASL with concurrency.

External Relations Task Group: (Coordination: the present author)

The design of CASL is based on a (critical) selection of constructs from existing languages, and it should be possible to translate specifications from other languages into (sublanguages or extensions) of CASL. Preliminary investigations have considered ASF+SDF [14] and OBJ3 [9]; moreover, CASL is in many respects close to the KIV language [18]. CoFI does not currently have adequate resources to study and implement translations of other languages into CASL, and must depend on attracting the interest and collaboration of those who have the necessary expertise.

The design of CASL has been sponsored by IFIP WG1.3 (on Foundations of System Specification), which also provided expert referees to review the proposed design in June 1997 [3]. The ongoing work in CoFI is of great interest to WG1.3, and the author (who was appointed chairman of WG1.3 in 1998) is responsible for liason between CoFI WG and WG1.3.

A major pending task for external relations is to provide an attractive web presentation of CASL. This guided tour of the CASL design, which was presented in half a day as a tutorial at ETAPS'98, should also be improved—suggestions are welcome!—and supplemented by a tutorial with the emphasis on methodology and realistic examples.

Join now! All CoFI task groups welcome new participants. Please contact the coordinators via the CoFI web pages [2]. There is a moderated mailing list for each task group, with open subscription, administered by the Majordomo program (majordomo@brics.dk). All CoFI participants are requested to subscribe to a further mailing list, cofi-list@brics.dk (very low-volume, for major announcements only). All CoFI documents are available via the CoFI web pages [2].

Acknowledgements: The author is supported by BRICS (Centre for Basic Research in Computer Science), established by the Danish National Research Foundation in collaboration with the Universities of Aarhus and Aalborg, Denmark; by an International Fellowship from SRI International; and by DARPA-ITO through NASA-Ames contract NAS2-98073.

References

1. Michel Bidoit, Donald Sannella, and Andrzej Tarlecki. Architectural specifications in CASL. In *Proc. 7th Intl. Conference on Algebraic Methodology and Software Technology (AMAST'98)*, volume 1548 of *LNCS*, pages 341–357. Springer, 1998.
2. CoFI. The Common Framework Initiative for algebraic specification and development, electronic archives. Notes and Documents accessible by WWW[6] and FTP[7].
3. CoFI Language Design Task Group. Response to the Referee Report on CASL. Documents/CASL/RefereeResponse, in [2], August 1997.
4. CoFI Language Design Task Group. CASL – The CoFI Algebraic Specification Language – Summary. Documents/CASL/Summary, in [2], October 1998.
5. CoFI Semantics Task Group. CASL – The CoFI Algebraic Specification Language (version 0.97) – Semantics. Note S-6, in [2], July 1997.
6. CoFI Semantics Task Group. CASL – The CoFI Algebraic Specification Language – Semantics (Preliminary Version). Note S-9, in [2], November 1998.
7. Anne Haxthausen, Bernd Krieg-Brückner, and Till Mossakowski. Subsorted partial higher-order logic as an extension of CASL. Note L-10, in [2], October 1998.

---

[6] http://www.brics.dk/Projects/CoFI
[7] ftp://ftp.brics.dk/Projects/CoFI

8. Einar W. Karlsen. Interoperability of CASL tools using CORBA. Note T-5, in [2], October 1997.

9. Till Mossakowski. Translating other specification languages into CASL. Presented at WADT'98.

10. Till Mossakowski. Sublanguages of CASL. Note L-7, in [2], December 1997.

11. Till Mossakowski. Two "functional programming" sublanguages of CASL. Note L-9, in [2], March 1998.

12. Till Mossakowski, Kolyang, and Bernd Krieg-Brückner. Static semantic analysis and theorem proving for CASL. In *12th Workshop on Algebraic Development Techniques, Tarquinia*, volume 1376 of *LNCS*, pages 333–348. Springer-Verlag, 1998.

13. Peter D. Mosses. CoFI: The Common Framework Initiative for algebraic specification. *Bull. EATCS*, (59):127–132, June 1996.

14. Peter D. Mosses. CASL for ASF+SDF users. In *ASF+SDF'97, 2nd Intl. Workshop on the Theory and Practice of Algebraic Specifications*, volume http://www.springer.co.uk/ewic/workshops/ASFSDF97 of *Electronic Workshops in Computing*. Springer-Verlag, 1997. Invited lecture.

15. Peter D. Mosses. Potential use of SGML for the CASL interchange format. Note T-4, in [2], October 1997.

16. Peter D. Mosses. CoFI: The Common Framework Initiative for Algebraic Specification and Development. In *TAPSOFT '97: Theory and Practice of Software Development*, volume 1214 of *LNCS*, pages 115–137. Springer-Verlag, 1997. Documents/Tentative/Mosses97TAPSOFT, in [2].

17. Peter D. Mosses. Formatting CASL specifications using LaTeX. Note C-2, in [2], June 1998.

18. W. Reif. The KIV-approach to Software Verification. In *KORSO: Methods, Languages, and Tools for the Construction of Correct Software – Final Report*, volume 1009 of *LNCS*, pages 339–368. Springer-Verlag, 1995.

19. Mark van den Brand, Paul Klint, and Pieter Olivier. Aterms: Exchanging data between heterogeneous tools for CASL. Note T-3 (revised draft), in [2], March 1998.

Abstract Petri Nets as a Uniform Approach to High-Level Petri Nets

J. Padberg
e-mail: padberg@cs.tu-berlin.de

Technical University of Berlin**

Abstract. In the area of Petri nets, many different developments have taken place within the last 30 years, in academia as well as in practice. For an adequate use in practice, a coherent and application oriented combination of various types and techniques for Petri nets is necessary. In order to attain a formal basis for different classes of Petri nets we introduce the concept of abstract Petri nets. The essential point of abstract Petri nets is to allow different kinds of net structures as well as the combination of various kinds of data types. This means that in abstract Petri nets the data type and the net structure part can be considered as abstract parameters which can be instantiated to different concrete net classes. We show that several net classes, like place/transition nets, elementary nets, S-graphs, algebraic high-level nets, and predicate/transitions nets are instantiations of abstract Petri nets. Moreover, we discuss coloured Petri nets in this context.

1 Introduction

Petri nets have been used successfully for more than three decades to model concurrent processes and distributed systems. Various kinds of Petri net classes with numerous features and analysis methods have been proposed in literature for different purposes and application areas. The fact that Petri nets are one of the most relevant specification techniques used in industrial applications [DG94, DG98, JFV95, Sch96, Jen92, Jen94, Jen95] and are still considered to be an important topic in research [JR91, Roz92, Roz93, BR96, AB97], shows the usefulness and the power of this formalism. Nevertheless the situation in the field of Petri nets is far from satisfactory, partly due to the enormous interest in Petri nets, that has been leading to a vast accumulation of dissimilar approaches. The different notions, definitions and techniques, both in literature and practice, make it hard to find a common understanding and the unstructured variety of Petri net approaches causes the new formulation and examination of similar concepts. Most of the different concepts for Petri nets are defined explicitly for a single net class, although many of these notions are essentially the same for

** This work is part of the joint research project "DFG-Forschergruppe PETRINETZ-TECHNOLOGIE" between H. Weber (Coordinator), H. Ehrig (both from the Technical University Berlin) and W. Reisig (Humboldt-Universität zu Berlin), supported by the German Research Council (DFG).

J.L. Fiadeiro (Ed.): WADT'98, LNCS 1589, pp. 241-260, 1999.

different kinds of net classes. Unfortunately, however, there is no abstract notion of Petri nets up to now, that permits the abstract formulation of such notions for a large variety of different net classes.

In order to tackle this problem in [EP97] parameterized net classes have been suggested as a uniform frame for the classification and systematization of Petri nets. Abstract Petri nets, as introduced in [Pad96], constitute the formal basis of such a uniform frame and correspond to the outline of universal parameterized net classes in [EP97]. They provide an abstract description of Petri nets together with a substantial body of theoretical results, concerning operational behavior, horizontal and vertical structuring (see [Pad96]). In [KW98] another, closely related approach to a uniform description of Petri nets is given, which nevertheless lacks the explicit treatment of the data type specification. This approach is based on a more semantical notion of high-level Petri nets an only uses algebras, but no explicit syntactical description, hence colored Petri nets in the version of [Jen81] can expressed in this approach.

The idea of an abstract description using category theory is already formulated in other areas of computer science, such as graph grammars [EHKP91, EL93], algebraic specifications [GB84, EBO91, EG94], and automata [EKKK74]. The notion of abstract Petri nets captures the common components of different kinds of Petri nets like places, transitions, net structure, and a data type part. General notions, like firing behavior, that are essential for all kinds of Petri nets are formulated within the frame of abstract Petri nets independently of their specific definition within a fixed net class. Hence, the concept of abstract Petri nets provides a uniform approach that captures many known and several new net classes as special cases and allows their comparison with each other (see Table 1 in Section 5). Moreover, universal description of concepts and structures permits the general treatment of classification of structures within a uniform framework, the integration and transformation of different classes of structures, horizontal and vertical structuring. These problems are the central issues for a general frame for Petri nets and thus imply the use of universal descriptions.

Treatment of the data type is essential for high-level nets. The right abstraction of the data type has to be valid for several kinds of algebraic specifications, predicate logics, functional programming languages as ML, indexed sets, and others. In order to achieve independence of the net structure, this part should be treated separately. We achieve this aim by using the categorical notions of institutions [GB84, GB92, SS92, ST84] and specification frames [Mah89, EBO91, EG94]. The step from algebraic specifications to institutions or specification frames is based on the idea of using category theory to reformulate the classical theory of algebraic specifications for different kinds of specification formalisms. Institutions and specification frames can be used to cover classical algebraic specifications [EM85], order sorted algebraic specifications [GB84], behavioral specifications [EBO91, ST87], projection specification [EG94], predicate logic [Mah89] and model theory [Tar87].

The contents of this paper is closely related to [Pad96] and is organized in the following way. We describe how to present the data type part of abstract

Petri nets using institutions as well as specification frames in Section 2. Next we introduce abstract Petri nets and give several examples of instantiations in Section 3. In Section 4 we present results concerning the operational behavior and categorical properties. The conclusion in Section 5 summarizes the results.

2   The Data Type Part for Abstract Petri Nets

First we need some signature part for abstract Petri nets in order to obtain terms for the decoration of the net structure. The subsequent definitions are closely related to the concepts of specification frames [EBO91, EG94] and institutions [GB84]. The main idea is to give the signature formalism in an abstract way, that only relates signatures to models. The following definitions lead to the data type part for high-level abstract Petri nets, presented in Definition 2.11. As examples we consider algebraic specifications, predicate logic, and the functional programming language ML.

Definition 2.1 (Signature Part for Abstract Petri Nets) The signature part for high-level abstract Petri nets is given by a specification frame, that is a category **ASIG** of (abstract) signatures Σ and a contravariant functor $Cat : \mathbf{ASIG}^{op} \to \mathbf{CATCAT}$, where **CATCAT** is the category of all categories. This means, that for each $f_\Sigma \in MOR_{\mathbf{ASIG}}$ with $\Sigma 1 \overset{f_\Sigma}{\to} \Sigma 2$ there is the forgetful functor $V_{f_\Sigma} : \mathbf{Cat}(\Sigma 2) \to \mathbf{Cat}(\Sigma 1)$ with $V_{f_\Sigma} := Cat(f_\Sigma)$.   □

Due to the fact, that Petri nets are based on sets of transitions and places we have to provide the compatibility of specification frames with sets. This means we have to relate the models of the data type with the underlying sets.

Definition 2.2 (Set-Based Specification Frames) A set-based specification frame (Cat, U) is given by a specification frame $Cat : \mathbf{ASIG}^{op} \to \mathbf{CATCAT}$ and a family of functors $U = (U_\Sigma)_{\Sigma \in |\mathbf{ASIG}|}$ with $U_\Sigma : \mathbf{Cat}(\Sigma) \to \mathbf{Sets}$ and for each $f_\Sigma \in MOR_{\mathbf{ASIG}}$ with $\Sigma 1 \overset{f_\Sigma}{\to} \Sigma 2$ and $U_{\Sigma i} : \mathbf{Cat}(\Sigma_i) \to \mathbf{Sets}$ for $i = 1, 2$ there is a natural transformation $\pi_{f_\Sigma} : U_{\Sigma 1} \circ V_{f_\Sigma} \to U_{\Sigma 2}$, so that: π is compatible with the identity of signatures, that is for each $\Sigma \in \mathbf{ASIG}$ we have $\pi_{id_\Sigma} = id_{U_\Sigma}$ the natural identity. And π is compatible with the composition of signature morphisms, that is for $\Sigma 1 \overset{f_\Sigma}{\to} \Sigma 2$ and $\Sigma 2 \overset{g_\Sigma}{\to} \Sigma 3$ we have $\pi_{g_\Sigma \circ f_\Sigma} = \pi_{g_\Sigma} \circ \pi_{f_\Sigma}$.   □

Next we define the specification of the data type part. For this purpose we introduce sentences for signatures in the sense of institutions [GB84]. We want the possibility of restricting the data type without restricting the signature for the arc inscriptions. Due to the aim of developing the data type part for Petri nets we have to define sentences for the data type as well as for the firing conditions.

Definition 2.3 (Specifications for Abstract Petri Nets) Let the signature part $Cat : \mathbf{ASIG}^{op} \to \mathbf{CATCAT}$, a functor $Sen : \mathbf{ASIG} \to \mathbf{Sets}$ and a family of sentence satisfaction relations $\models_\Sigma^{Sen} \subseteq |Cat(\Sigma)| \times Sen(\Sigma)$ be given.

Let the following sentence satisfaction condition $V_{f_\Sigma}(M2) \models^{Sen}_{\Sigma 1} \varphi \Leftrightarrow M2 \models^{Sen}_{\Sigma 2}$ $Sen(f_\Sigma)(\varphi)$ be satisfied for $f_\Sigma : \Sigma 1 \to \Sigma 2$, $M2 \in |\mathbf{Cat}(\Sigma 2)|$ and $\varphi \in Sen(\Sigma 1)$. Then we have specifications $SPEC = (\Sigma, AXIOMS)$ where $AXIOMS \subseteq Sen(\Sigma)$. Specifications $SPEC$ together with specification morphisms (that are signature morphisms $f_\Sigma : \Sigma 1 \to \Sigma 2$, such that $Sen(f_\Sigma)(AXIOMS1) \subseteq AXIOMS2$) yield **ASPEC**, called the category of (abstract) specifications. □

Note, we have a model functor for specifications $SPEC = (\Sigma, AXIOMS)$, that yields the category of models satisfying the axioms. This category $\mathbf{Mod}(\mathbf{SPEC})$ is a subcategory of $\mathbf{Cat}(\Sigma)$. These constructions, including the following facts, are well-known for institutions [GB84]. The relationship between institutions and specification logics and frames is discussed in [EBO91] and [EG94].

Fact 2.4 (Model Functor for Specification [EBO91]) Given **ASIG**, Cat, Sen, and $\models^{Sen}$ as in Definition 2.3 the specification part for abstract Petri nets is given by the category **ASPEC** of abstract specifications $SPEC$ and a contravariant model functor Mod : $\mathbf{ASPEC}^{op} \to \mathbf{CATCAT}$, where Mod is a restriction of the functor Cat. This means for each $f_\Sigma \in MOR_{\mathbf{ASPEC}}$ with $SPEC1 \xrightarrow{f_\Sigma} SPEC2$ there is the forgetful functor $V_{f_\Sigma} : Mod(SPEC2) \to Mod(SPEC1)$ with $V_{f_\Sigma} := Mod(f_\Sigma)$. □

Fact 2.5 (Cocompleteness of ASPEC [GB84]) The category **ASPEC** is cocomplete if the category of signatures **ASIG** is cocomplete. □

Definition 2.6 (Amalgamation [EG94]) A specification frame has amalgamations, if for every pushout $SPEC1 \xrightarrow{g1} SPEC3 \xleftarrow{g2} SPEC2$ of $SPEC2 \xleftarrow{f2} SPEC0 \xrightarrow{f1} SPEC1$ in **ASPEC** we have for every $Ai \in |Mod(SPECi)|$ for $i = 0, 1, 2$ such that $V_{f1}(A1) = A0 = V_{f2}(A2)$ there is a unique $A3 \in |Mod(SPEC3)|$, called the amalgamation of $A1$ and $A2$ via $A0$, written $A1 +_{A0} A2$, such that we have: $V_{g1}(A3) = A1$ and $V_{g2}(A3) = A2$. Conversely, every $A3 \in |Mod(SPEC3)|$ has a unique decomposition: $A3 = V_{g1}(A3) +_{V_{g1 \circ f1}(A3)} V_{g2}(A3)$ Similar properties are required if we replace the objects Ai by morphisms hi in $\mathbf{Cat}(SPECi)$ for $i = 0, 1, 2, 3$ leading to a unique amalgamated sum of morphisms: $h3 = h1 +_{h0} h2$ with $V_{g1}(h3) = h1$ and $V_{g2}(h3) = h2$. □

As the variables are essential for nets, we have to express them at this abstract level. The usual treatment of variables as indexed sets assumes a certain knowledge about the sorts available in the signature. Such an approach restricts the possibility of instantiation. To avoid this conflict we treat variables in the context of specification frames as additional constants (see also [ST84]). Thus we introduce a class of morphisms $\mathcal{V}$ in **ASIG** that expresses variables as an inclusion of signatures.

Definition 2.7 (Signatures with Variables) Variables are given by a class $\mathcal{V}$ of morphisms, that are preserved by pushouts (meaning: given a pushout $\Sigma 1 \xrightarrow{g1} \Sigma 3 \xleftarrow{f2} \Sigma 2$ of $\Sigma 2 \xleftarrow{f2} \Sigma 0 \xrightarrow{f1} \Sigma 1$ in **ASIG** then we have $f1 \in \mathcal{V}$ implies

$g2 \in V$). A signature with variables (Σ', ϕ) is given by $\phi : \Sigma \to \Sigma'$ and $\phi \in V$. The expansion $Exp_{\Sigma'}(M)$ of a model $M \in |\mathbf{Cat}(\Sigma)|$ denotes all models $M' \in |\mathbf{Cat}(\Sigma')|$ such that $V_\phi(M') = M$. Each of the models of this expansion denotes an assignment. Furthermore, we demand, that the class V is compatible with the given set-based specification frame, that means for each $\phi \in V$ we have $\pi_\phi = id_{U_\Sigma}$ the natural identity. $\qquad\square$

We also have to express firing conditions. Note, there is no reason that sentences for the description of the data type and for the firing conditions are of the same kind. These two kinds of sentences are not necessarily related, although they are similar in most kinds of nets. We choose for the sake of generality two kinds and thus have two kinds of satisfaction relations, the sentence satisfaction defined above and the condition satisfaction defined below.

Definition 2.8 (Conditions for the Firing of Transitions)
Conditions are given by a functor $Cond : \mathbf{ASIG} \to \mathbf{Sets}$ and the following condition satisfaction relation $\models_\Sigma^{Cond} \subseteq |Cat(\Sigma)| \times Cond(\Sigma)$, such that the satisfaction condition $V_{f_\Sigma}(M2) \models_{\Sigma1}^{Cond} \varphi \Leftrightarrow M2 \models_{\Sigma2}^{Cond} Cond(f_\Sigma)(\varphi)$ is satisfied for $f_\Sigma : \Sigma1 \to \Sigma2$, $M2 \in |Cat(\Sigma2|$ and $\varphi \in Cond(\Sigma1)$. Conditions with free variables for a signature Σ are given by conditions of the signature with variables (Σ', ϕ) with $\phi : \Sigma \to \Sigma'$, that is by $Cond(\Sigma')$. $\qquad\square$

Fact 2.9 (Translation of Signature with Variables) The translation of the signature with variables $(\Sigma1', \phi1)$ with $\phi1 : \Sigma1 \to \Sigma1'$ along the morphism $f_\Sigma : \Sigma1 \to \Sigma2$ is given by the pushout construction in **ASIG** and leads to the translated signature with variables $(\Sigma2', \phi2)$. $\qquad\square$

Proof. The translation is given by the pushout $\Sigma2 \overset{\phi2}{\to} \Sigma2' \overset{f'_\Sigma}{\leftarrow} \Sigma1'$ of $\Sigma2 \overset{f_\Sigma}{\leftarrow} \Sigma1 \overset{\phi1}{\to} \Sigma1'$ in **ASIG**, where f_Σ is the signature morphism and $\phi1 \in V$ denotes the variables. Because V is preserved by pushouts, we have $\phi2 \in V$. Thus $(\Sigma2', \phi2)$ is a signature with variables.

Fact 2.10 (Translation of Expansions) Given a specification frame with amalgamation as in Definition 2.6, then for each signature with variables $(\Sigma1', \phi1)$, each signature morphism $f_\Sigma : \Sigma1 \to \Sigma2$, the translated signature with variables $(\Sigma2', \phi2)$, and models $M1 \in \mathbf{Cat}(\Sigma1)$, $M2 \in \mathbf{Cat}(\Sigma2)$ each expansion $Exp_{\Sigma1'}(M1) \in \mathbf{Cat}(\Sigma1')$ of $M1$ can be translated to an expansion $Exp_{\Sigma2'}(M2) \in \mathbf{Cat}(\Sigma2')$ of $M2$. $\qquad\square$

Proof. Given a model $M1 \in \mathbf{Cat}(\Sigma1)$, an expansion $Exp_{\Sigma1'}(M1) \in \mathbf{Cat}(\Sigma1')$, and a model $M2 \in \mathbf{Cat}(\Sigma2)$ with $V_{f_\Sigma}(M2) = M1$, then we obtain the translated expansion $Exp_{\Sigma2'}(M2) \in \mathbf{Cat}(\Sigma2')$ by amalgamation $Exp(M2)_{\Sigma2'} = Exp_{\Sigma1'}(M1) +_{M1} M2$. Furthermore, due to the condition satisfaction, we have for each expansion $Exp_{\Sigma1'}(M1) \in \mathbf{Cat}(\Sigma1')$:
$$Exp_{\Sigma1'}(M1) \models^{Cond} \varphi \Leftrightarrow Exp_{\Sigma2'}(M2) \models^{Cond} Cond(f'_\Sigma)(\varphi)$$

This translation of expansions provides the possibility to define as many variables as wanted and to give arbitrary names. Due to the pushout construction and amalgamation the translation inhibits the identification of variables. But it permits the definition of new variables and renaming of variables. Renaming is possible, because pushouts are unique only up to isomorphism, that is unique up to renaming. Identification of variables has to be avoided, because then morphisms cannot preserve firing behavior. Summarizing, a data specification technique, called data type part for abstract Petri nets, consists of a set-based specification frame, sentences, variables, and conditions.

Definition 2.11 (Data Type Part for Abstract Petri Nets)
The data type part for abstract Petri nets $DT = (Cat, U, Sen, V, Cond)$ consists of
1. a set-based specification frame (Cat, U) with amalgamations, where we have: $Cat : \mathbf{ASIG}^{op} \to \mathbf{CATCAT}$ (see Definition 2.1) and $U = (U_\Sigma)_{\Sigma \in |\mathbf{ASIG}|}$
2. Sentences $Sen : \mathbf{ASIG} \to \mathbf{Sets}$ (see Definition 2.3) that allow the description of data type specifications, leading to the category **ASPEC**.
3. Variables denoted by a class of morphisms V, as defined in Definition 2.7.
4. Conditions for the firing of transitions $Cond : \mathbf{ASIG} \to \mathbf{Sets}$.

Furthermore, we demand that:

5. **ASIG** is cocomplete.
6. $Cat(\Sigma)$ has an initial object T_Σ for all $\Sigma \in \mathbf{ASIG}$.   □

Note, that (5) implies cocompleteness of **ASPEC**.
In the remaining part of this section we provide different examples of specification techniques, which can be used as data type parts for abstract Petri nets.

Example 2.12 (Algebraic Specifications) Algebraic specifications are a data type part for abstract Petri nets.
The set-based specification frame $Cat : \mathbf{ASIG}^{op} \to \mathbf{CATCAT}$ is given by the category of algebraic signatures **SIG** in the sense of [EM85] and by the model functor $Alg : \mathbf{SIG} \to \mathbf{CATCAT}$.
Algebraic signatures are set-based, as $U_\Sigma : \mathbf{Alg}(\Sigma) \to \mathbf{Sets}$ is given by $U_\Sigma(A) = \biguplus_{s \in S} A_s$ the disjoint union of the carrier sets. For each signature morphism $f = (f_S, f_{OP}) : \Sigma1 \to \Sigma2$ the natural transformation $\pi : U_{\Sigma 1} \circ V_f \to U_{\Sigma 2}$ is given for all $A2 \in |\mathbf{Alg}(\Sigma 2)|$ by inclusion of data elements: $\pi_f^{A2} : \biguplus_{s \in S1}(V_f(A2))_s \to \biguplus_{s \in S2} A2_s$. π_f^{A2} is well-defined due to the definition of the forgetful functor, that is for each $s \in S1$ we have $(V_f(A2))_s = A2_{f_S(s)}$. Amalgamation is given in [EM85] (see Definition 8.10).
The sentence functor $Sen : \mathbf{SIG} \to \mathbf{Sets}$ yields for each signature the set of all equations over some set X, that is $Sen(\Sigma) = \{(X, L, R)|L, R \in T_{OP}(X)\}$. The satisfaction relation is defined by the extended assignment with respect to an assignment of variables $asg : X \to A$ onto the same data element, that is $A \models^{Sen} (X, L, R) \iff \overline{asg}_A(L) = \overline{asg}_A(R)$. $\overline{asg}$ is the usual unique extension of asg. Satisfaction is preserved due to $V_f(A) \models^{Sen} (X, L, R) \iff A \models^{Sen} (X^\#, f^\#(L), f^\#(R))$ see Fact 8.3 in [EM85]. This yields the category of algebraic

specifications **SPEC** in the sense of [EM85] with $SPEC = (\Sigma, AXIOMS)$. Mod is given by the model functor Alg.

$\mathcal{V}$, the class of morphisms denoting variables is given by inclusions into a signature with additional constants. Given $\Sigma = (S, OP)$, $\Sigma' = (S, OP')$, and $\phi : \Sigma \to \Sigma'$ with $\phi \in \mathcal{V}$ then $\phi = (id_S, \phi_{OP})$ is given by the identity on the sorts id_S and an inclusion on operations $\phi_{OP} : OP \to OP'$, such that all operations not included in the image of ϕ_{OP} are constants:
$$\forall N \in OP' : N \notin \phi_{OP}(OP) \Longrightarrow N \in OP'_{\lambda, s}$$
$\mathcal{V}$ is preserved under pushouts: Given $\Sigma i = (Si, OPi)$ and $\Sigma i' = (Si', OPi')$ for $i = 1, 2$ and the pushout $\Sigma 2 \overset{\phi 2}{\to} \Sigma 2' \overset{f'_\Sigma}{\leftarrow} \Sigma 1'$ of $\Sigma 2 \overset{f_\Sigma}{\leftarrow} \Sigma 1 \overset{\phi 1}{\to} \Sigma 1'$ in **SIG**, then $S1' = S1$ due to the componentwise construction of pushouts and due to $\phi 1 = (id_{S1}, \phi_{OP})$.

Let $N \in OP2'$ but $N \notin \phi 2_{OP}(OP2)$ then there is $N' \in OP1'$ so that $f'_{\Sigma OP}(N') = N$ and $N' \notin \phi 1_{OP}(OP1)$ due to the pushout construction in **Sets**. Thus N' is constant, that is $N' \in OP1'_{\lambda, s}$ and as signature morphisms preserve the arity of operations we conclude N is constant as well, that is $N \in OP2'_{\lambda, f_S(s)}$. The condition functor $Cond : \mathbf{SIG} \to \mathbf{Sets}$ yields for each signature the set of all ground terms, that is $Cond(\Sigma) = \{(L, R) | L, R \in T_{OP}\}$.

The satisfaction relation is defined by the evaluation onto the same data element, that is $A \models^{Cond} (L, R) \iff eval_A(L) = eval_A(R)$ and satisfaction is preserved due to $V_f(A) \models^{Cond} (L, R) \iff A \models^{Cond} (f\#(L), f\#(R))$ see fact 8.3 in [EM85]. **SIG** is cocomplete [GB84].

For each signature Σ there is the initial object, that is the term algebra T_Σ in **Alg**(Σ) ([EM85] Theorem 3.7). $\Diamond$

Example 2.13 (Predicate Logic) The predicate logic data type part for abstract Petri nets is based on the formulation of first order predicate logic in the frame of institutions [GB84] and is corresponds to the predicate logic used in [GL81, Gen91].

The set-based specification frame is given by one-sorted first order signatures $\Sigma = (\Omega, \Pi)$ where $\Omega = (\Omega^n)_{n \in \mathbf{N}}$ denotes the set of n-ary operations and $\Pi = (\Pi^n)_{n \in \mathbf{N}}$ the set of n-ary predicates. Together with morphisms preserving the arity, we have the category **FOSIG**. A model for $\Sigma = (\Omega, \Pi)$ consists of a **possibly empty** domain R and functions and predicates (R, Ω_R, Π_R) with respect to the signature. Thus we have the contravariant functor $Fosig : \mathbf{FOSIG}^{op} \to \mathbf{CATCAT}$ where **Fosig**(Σ) denotes the category of models. First order signatures are set-based: For each signature Σ there is a functor $U_\Sigma : \mathbf{Fosig}(\Sigma) \to \mathbf{Sets}$ that is given by the domain, $U_\Sigma(R, \Omega_R, \Pi_R) = R$. Thus π is the identity. Due to the fact that there is only one sort, amalgamation is given by identity. Hence, it is a special case of amalgamation of algebraic specifications. Sentences are given by closed formulas. Abstract specifications are given by abstract signatures and closed formulas. Their models are models of the signature that satisfy these formulas.

Given a set of variables X we use the usual definition of terms and formulas. The functor $FoSen : \mathbf{FOSIG} \to \mathbf{Sets}$ yields for each abstract signature $FoSen(\Omega, \Pi)$ the set of all closed formulas. First order signatures together with a set of closed formulas $AXIOMS \subseteq FoSen(\Omega, \Pi)$ denote the first order specifications $FOSPEC = (\Omega, \Pi, AXIOMS)$. The model functor $FoMod : \textbf{FOSPEC}^{op} \rightarrow \textbf{CATCAT}$ yields for each specification $FOSPEC = (\Omega, \Pi, AXIOMS)$ the category $\textbf{Fomod}(\Omega, \Pi, AXIOMS)$ with the **nonempty** models that satisfy the formulas in $AXIOMS$. The satisfaction relation $\models^{FoSen}$ is the usual one for predicate logic.

$\mathcal{V}$, the class of morphisms denoting variables is given by those inclusions, that given $\phi : \Sigma \rightarrow \Sigma'$ with $\phi \in \mathcal{V}$ the signature Σ' only has additional constants similar to algebraic specifications (see Example 2.12). Variables are given by:
$\Sigma \overset{\phi}{\rightarrow} \Sigma' \in \mathcal{V}$ if $\phi = (\phi_\Omega, id_\Pi)$ and ϕ_Ω is the inclusion so that:
$$\forall N \in \Omega' : N \notin \phi_\Omega(\Omega) \Longrightarrow N \in \Omega'^0$$
The class of morphisms $\mathcal{V}$ is preserved under pushouts due to the same argumentation as in Example 2.12.

The firing conditions are defined in the same way as the sentences. Note, we have closed formulas over some signature (Σ', ϕ) with $\Sigma \overset{\phi}{\rightarrow} \Sigma' \in \mathcal{V}$. This means, the formulas in $FoCond(\Sigma')$ with $FoCond : \textbf{FOSIG} \rightarrow \textbf{Sets}$ are closed with respect to the signature Σ', but in view of the arc inscriptions of the net we have free variables as they are given by $\phi \in \mathcal{V}$ using additional constants. These are assigned by the models of the expansion.

Due to this construction there is no confusion between variables bound by some quantifier and variables that belong to the net.

FOSIG is cocomplete ([GB84]).

Fosig(Σ) has an initial object, that is T_Σ for all $\Sigma \in \textbf{FOSIG}$ ([GB84]). $\diamond$

The empty carrier set problem is based on the subsequent facts: **Nonempty** carrier sets may yield model categories without initial object. **Empty** carrier sets may yield an unsound logic. This has some impact on abstract Petri nets. In the first case we could not necessarily use the term algebra T_Σ and would loose the cocompleteness of the category of abstract Petri nets. The second case has to be prevented anyhow. We have avoided the problem by allowing empty carrier sets for the model of the first order signature (thus we can assume the initial object) and by demanding nonempty carrier sets for the models of the specification (thus we obtain a sound logic).

Example 2.14 (ML) Including ML into this frame yields a variant of colored nets in the sense of [Jen92]. The presupposition is to express ML and its semantics within institutions [ST86, ST91]. According to D. Sannella this task has been solved in principle, but the details are not yet finished [San95]. Hence, we claim that also ML is a suitable data type part for abstract Petri nets. $\diamond$

3   Abstract Petri Nets

We now introduce abstract nets, based on a data type part as defined above and a net structure functor. The net structure functor describes the structure of the underlying net and the markings using adjoint functors. This characterization together with the definition of behavior (see Definition 3.6) describes different varieties of Petri nets.

Definition 3.1 (Net Structure Functor) We assume to have two categories **Sets** and **Struct**, called category of structure, and functors $F \dashv G : \textbf{Struct} \rightarrow \textbf{Sets}$, where F is left adjoint to G with universal morphisms $\gamma^S : S \rightarrow G \circ F(S)$ for all sets S in **Sets**. The composition $Net = G \circ F : \textbf{Sets} \rightarrow \textbf{Sets}$ is called net structure functor. Furthermore, the objects of **Struct** have to be at least commutative semigroups. □

The basis for (low-level) abstract Petri nets are sets, which are used to generate some structure. This structure, given by the category **Struct** defines the structure of the places and hence the markings (see Examples 3.2, 3.3, and 3.4). The second condition provides the addition that is needed for the definition of firing and has not been included in [EPR94b]. This condition ensures that each object in **Struct** is supplied with an associative operation +. This operation together with the splitting condition in Definition 3.6 ensures the correct behavior.

Example 3.2 (Place/Transition Nets) In this example we introduce place/transition nets in the algebraic sense, introduced by Meseguer and Montanari [MM90]. The concept of place/transition nets and free monoid graphs is a special case of abstract Petri nets. Let **Struct** = **CMON** where **CMON** is the category of commutative monoids, $G : \textbf{CMON} \rightarrow \textbf{Sets}$ the forgetful functor and $F : \textbf{Sets} \rightarrow \textbf{CMON}$ the free commutative monoid construction. Then $Net(P) = P^*$ is the underlying set of the free commutative monoid over P. Thus we have place/transition nets, where T (transition) and P (places) are sets, P^* is the free commutative monoid over P and $pre, post : T \rightarrow P^*$ give the pre- and postconditions for each transition. ◇

Example 3.3 (Elementary Nets) Elementary Nets consist of a set of places, and a set of transitions, but the arc weight always equals one and the marking consists of at most one token on each place. A transition is enabled if there are enough tokens in the predomain and no tokens in the postdomain of that transition. The marking of elementary nets is a subset of the set of places, as there is only one token allowed on each place. The arc weight of elementary nets can also be expressed by a subset of the set of places. In the algebraic version of elementary nets transitions are mapped to the powerset $\mathcal{P}(P)$ of P by a pre- and a postdomain function. Thus each transition is mapped to a subset of places for its pre- and postdomain. Let **Struct** = **PSet** and the adjunction $F \dashv G$ is given by $\mathcal{P} \dashv I$ where $\mathcal{P}$ is the usual powerset functor. Then $Net(P) = \mathcal{P}(P)$, so that elementary nets are given by $E = (T, P, pre, post)$ with $pre, post : T \rightarrow \mathcal{P}(P)$. ◇

Example 3.4 (S-Graphs) The construction of S-graph as a special case of low-level abstract Petri nets where the structure of the net and the structure of the marking do not coincide [1]. Here we exploit the dependency of categories

---

[1] Because net and marking structure can differ in [Pad98b] we have introduced different parameters for these. But this extension goes beyond the scope of this paper.

from morphisms. We use the same free commutative monoids as in Example 3.2, but use generated morphisms, that is monoid homomorphisms $f^* : A^* \to B^*$ which are generated by functions $f : A \to B$. This allows another right adjoint functor and yields another net structure. We use the following equivalence of categories:

Let **Struct** $=$ **FCMON** the category of free commutative monoids with generated homomorphisms. Then we have the equivalence, **Sets** $\cong$ **FCMON** and $F :$ **Sets** $\to$ **FCMON** is given for each set S by $F(S) = S^*$, but in contrast to place/transition nets (see Example 3.2) we have $G :$ **FCMON** $\to$ **Sets** with $G(S^*) = S$. Thus we have $Net = Id :$ **Sets** $\to$ **Sets**. Moreover, every equivalence of categories is an adjunction (see [AHS90] 18.A). Thus we obtain S-graphs with $T \rightrightarrows P$ in the category **SGraph**, markings $m \in P^*$.   ◇

Next we define pre- and postfunctions, that map each transition to a linear sum consisting of pairs of terms and places, where terms are data elements of the term algebra T_Σ and places are elements of P. These terms represent the arc inscriptions. These inscriptions and the firing conditions have to include variables, which are given as a family of variables for each transition.

Definition 3.5 (Abstract Petri Nets) Given a data type part $DT = (Cat, U, Sen, V, Cond)$ for nets (Definition 2.11) with a category **ASPEC** of abstract specifications (Definition 2.3) and a net structure functor $Net = G \circ F$ (Definition 3.1) then an abstract Petri net is given by $N = (P, T, SPEC, Var, pre, post, cond)$ with
- P : the set of places,
- T : the set of transitions,
- $SPEC \in |\mathbf{ASPEC}|$: some specification with $SPEC = (\Sigma, AXIOMS)$
- $Var = (Var(t))_{t \in T} = (\Sigma^t, \phi_t)_{t \in T}$ the signature with variables with $\phi_t : \Sigma \to \Sigma^t \in V$ for each transition $t \in T$
- $pre, post : T \to Net(U_{\Sigma^t}(T_{\Sigma^t}) \times P)$ the pre- and postcondition functions of T, defining for each transition with adjacent arcs the arc inscriptions and the weight, such that $pre(t), post(t) \in Net(U_{\Sigma^t}(T_{\Sigma^t}) \times P)$.
- $cond : T \to \mathcal{P}_{fin}(Cond(\Sigma^t))$ the function that maps each transition to a finite set of conditions over the signature with variables representing the firing conditions such that $cond(t) \in \mathcal{P}_{fin}(Cond(\Sigma^t))$.   □

The pre- and postdomain of each transition $t \in T$ consists of all places $p \in P$ occurring in $pre(t)$ and $post(t)$. Note, that we have dependent type functions $pre, post, cond$, because variables are given locally for each transition instead of being defined globally. This matches the intuitive meaning of transition inscriptions. The next step is to define the operational behavior given by the firing of transitions. A transition is enabled if the assignment of the variables yields valid firing conditions. The tokens are then removed from the predomain and added to the postdomain.

Definition 3.6 (Marking, AAS^t-Enabling, Firing) Given an abstract Petri net $N = (P, T, SPEC, Var, pre, post, cond)$ with the net structure functor Net

and the model functor Mod (see Definition 2.4) then we have for each data type model $M \in Mod(SPEC)$:

- A marking of N is given by $m \in F(U_\Sigma(M) \times P)$, where F is the left adjoint functor of G with the net structure functor $Net = G \circ F$ (see Definition 3.1).
- An abstract assignment for a transition $t \in T$ is given by $AAS^t \in Exp_{\Sigma^t}(M)$, where $Exp_{\Sigma^t}(M)$ is the expansion of M (see Definition 2.7) with respect to the signature with variables (Σ^t, ϕ^t) for $t \in T$.
  The abstract assignment AAS^t defines an abstract assignment function
  $$aas^t : F(U_{\Sigma^t}(T_{\Sigma^t}) \times P) \to F(U_\Sigma(M) \times P)$$
  with $aas^t = F(U_{\Sigma^t}(eval^t) \times id_P)$, where $eval^t$ is the unique morphism $T_{\Sigma^t} \overset{eval^t}{\longrightarrow} AAS^t$ due to initiality of T_{Σ^t}.
  aas^t is well-defined due to the fact that
  $U_\Sigma(M) = U_\Sigma \circ V_{\phi^t}(AAS^t) = U_{\Sigma^t}(AAS^t)$ and
  $U_{\Sigma^t}(eval^t) : U_{\Sigma^t}(T_{\Sigma^t}) \to U_{\Sigma^t}(AAS^t)$
- A transition vector is defined by $v \in F(\{t\})$.
- AAS^t satisfies the firing condition $cond(t)$ if and only if $AAS^t \models^{Cond} \varphi$ for all $\varphi \in cond(t)$.
- A transition vector $v \in F(\{t\})$ is AAS^t-enabled under $m \in F(U_\Sigma(M) \times P)$ and fires from the marking m to the follower marking m' if there exists $\overline{m} \in F(U_\Sigma(M) \times P)$ so that:
  - $m = \overline{m} + aas^t(\overline{pre}(v))$
  - $m' = \overline{m} + aas^t(\overline{post}(v))$
  - the following splitting condition:
    for all $r, r' \in F(U_\Sigma(M) \times P)$ with $r \neq \overline{m}$ we have:
    $\overline{m} = r + r'$ implies $m \neq aas^t(\overline{pre}(v)) + r$ and $m' \neq aas^t(\overline{post}(v)) + r$
    holds.
  where $\overline{pre} : F(T) \to F(U_{\Sigma^t}(T_{\Sigma^t}) \times P)$ is the unique extension of pre and analogously $\overline{post}$ is the unique extension of $post$.   □

In contrast to [Pad96] we have added the splitting condition in order to obtain a generic firing rule. This condition has been first formulated slightly different in [KW98] and ensures correctness of the follower marking.

We present some interesting instantiations of abstract Petri nets in this section. These instantiations do not correspond exactly to the definitions found in the literature, they are closely related and the remaining differences will be discussed in the subsequent examples. Take, e. g. the typing of places. Typing of places means, that only token of a certain type are allowed being on a place. This is usually expressed by a function from the set of places to the set of types. Algebraic high-level nets [PER95] and predicate/transition nets are given without typing, whereas colored Petri nets are typed. As untyped nets are more general we have chosen this variant, nevertheless it is obviously feasible to include a function $type : P \to S$ if we assume types S.

Example 3.7 (Algebraic High-Level Nets) There are different variants of algebraic high-level nets in literature (see [Rei91, EPR94a, PER95, Hum89, Lil94, PER95]). Here we have chosen the definition given in [PER95]. An algebraic high-level net is given by $AHL = (SPEC, P, T, pre, post, cond, A)$, where

$SPEC = (S, OP, E)$ is an algebraic specification and A is a $SPEC$-algebra in the sense of [EM85], $pre, post : T \to (T_{OP}(X) \times P)^*$ with the free commutative monoid $(\_)^*$ and $cond : T \to \mathcal{P}_{fin}((T_{OP}(X) \times (T_{OP}(X)))$. The set of variables is given by $X \cong X_{fix} \times S$ with $(x, s), (x, s') \in Var(t) \implies s = s'$ and $Var(t)$ is the set of all variables occurring in $pre(t)$, $post(t)$ or $cond(t)$.

The instantiation of abstract Petri nets with algebraic specifications as the data type part (see Example 2.12) and the net structure functor of place/transition nets (see Example 3.2) yields algebraic high-level nets without algebras, that is $N = (P, T, SPEC, Var, pre, post, cond)$ with $pre, post : T \to (T_{OP_t} \times P)^*$. The differences to the above defined algebraic high-level nets are: The instantiation lacks a $SPEC$-algebra A, which however, is available in the corresponding instantiation of abstract Petri nets with models. The variables of the instantiation are defined depending on the transitions. This dependency is given in algebraic-high level nets implicitly, by the additional condition for the set of variables X. Nevertheless both formulations denote the same net.

Other variants of algebraic high-level nets can be obtained by slight changes of the data type part. Let the condition functor $Cond : \mathbf{ASIG} \to \mathbf{Sets}$ be the constant functor, that yields for each signature the empty set $Cond(\Sigma) = \emptyset$, then the corresponding instantiation of abstract Petri nets is closer to the definition of algebraic high-level nets as defined in [Rei91]. Another example, if we choose order sorted algebraic specifications, which are shown to be an institution in [GB84], we obtain an instantiation that is closely related to the order sorted algebraic high-level nets in [Lil94]. Other extensions as flexible arcs [KV98] still have to be considered. $\diamond$

Example 3.8 (Predicate Transition Nets) The corresponding instantiation of abstract Petri nets consist of the net structure functor similar to elementary nets (see Example 3.3) and the data type part of predicate logic (see Example 2.13). This means that the instantiation of abstract Petri nets in this case is given by $PRT = (P, T, \Sigma, var, pre, post, cond)$. The differences to predicate/transition nets as defined in [Gen91] are that our instantiation is not supplied with a first order structure, but this is the case for the corresponding instantiation of abstract Petri nets with models. Moreover we have no annotation for the places. And we allow a set of firing conditions, where in [Gen91] there is only one formula, the transition selector. $\diamond$

Example 3.9 (Colored Petri Nets) An instantiation of abstract Petri nets similar to colored Petri nets (CPN), in the sense of [Jen92] requires a data type part considering ML as an institution (see Example 2.14). The corresponding instantiation of abstract Petri nets will be a close variant of colored Petri nets. Flexibility of arcs can be achieved by the corresponding data type as well. $\diamond$

Example 3.10 (Low-Level Petri Nets) Using the trivial data type description consisting of an empty specification and a model with one element only, we obtain the usual (low-level) Petri nets as well. We obtain instantiations isomorphic to those given above in the Examples 3.2, 3.3, and 3.4. $\diamond$

4   Results for Abstract Petri Nets

Morphisms for abstract Petri nets are composed using functions between the sets of transitions, between the sets of places and between the specifications. Abstract Petri nets together with the morphisms yield the category **APN**. The detailed proofs can be found in [Pad96].

Definition 4.1 (Abstract Petri Net Morphisms) Given abstract Petri nets $Ni = (Pi, Ti, SPECi, Vari, prei, posti, condi)$ for $i = 1, 2$ then an abstract Petri net morphism $f : N1 \to N2$ is given by $f = (f_P, f_T, f_\Sigma)$ and $f_P : P1 \to P2$ maps places to places $f_T : T1 \to T2$ transitions to transitions in **Sets**, $f_\Sigma : SPEC1 \to SPEC2$ maps specifications to specifications in **ASPEC**, s.t. for all $t1 \in T1$ and $f_T(t1) = t2 \in T2$ the following holds:

1. **Preservation of variables:** The translation of the signature with variables $(\Sigma 1^{t1}, \phi 1^{t1})$ with $\phi 1^{t1} : \Sigma 1 \to \Sigma 1^{t1}$ along the morphism $f_\Sigma : \Sigma 1 \to \Sigma 2$ to the signature with variables $(\Sigma 2^{t2}, \phi 2^{t2})$ is given by the pushout $\Sigma 2 \overset{\phi 2^{t2}}{\to} \Sigma 2^{t2} \overset{f_\phi}{\Leftarrow} \Sigma 1^{t1}$ of $\Sigma 2 \overset{f_\Sigma}{\Leftarrow} \Sigma 1 \overset{\phi 1^{t1}}{\to} \Sigma 1^{t1}$ in **ASIG** (see Fact 2.9).

2. **Compatibility of pre- and postcondition function:** The following diagram commutes componentwise, with the natural transformation $\pi_{f_\phi} : U_{\Sigma 1^{t1}} \circ V_{f_\phi}(T_{\Sigma 2^{t2}}) \to U_{\Sigma 2^{t2}}(T_{\Sigma 2^{t2}})$, where $eval : T_{\Sigma 1^t} \to V_{f_\phi}(T_{\Sigma 2^{t2}})$ is the unique morphism defined by $AAS1^{t1}$ due to initiality of $T_{\Sigma 1^{t1}}$ with the function $f_{ins} = (\pi_{f_\phi} \circ U_{\Sigma 1^{t1}}(eval)) \times f_P : U_{\Sigma 1^{t1}}(T_{\Sigma 1^{t1}}) \times P1 \to U_{\Sigma 2^{t2}}(T_{\Sigma 2^{t2}}) \times P2$

$$
\begin{array}{ccc}
T1 & \xrightarrow[\text{post1}]{\text{pre1}} & Net(U_{\Sigma 1^{t1}}(T_{\Sigma 1^{t1}}) \times P1) \\
f_T \downarrow & & \downarrow Net(f_{ins}) \\
T2 & \xrightarrow[\text{post2}]{\text{pre2}} & Net(U_{\Sigma 2^{t2}}(T_{\Sigma 2^{t2}}) \times P2)
\end{array}
$$

3. **Compatibility of firing conditions:** The following diagram commutes, with $f_{cond} = \mathcal{P}_{fin}(Cond(f_\phi)) : \mathcal{P}_{fin}(Cond(\Sigma 1^{t1})) \to \mathcal{P}_{fin}(Cond(\Sigma 2^{t2}))$

$$
\begin{array}{ccc}
T1 & \xrightarrow{cond1} & \mathcal{P}_{fin}(Cond(\Sigma 1^{t1})) \\
f_T \downarrow & & \downarrow f_{cond} \\
T2 & \xrightarrow{cond2} & \mathcal{P}_{fin}(Cond(\Sigma 2^{t2}))
\end{array}
$$

□

The compatibility conditions are required to obtain the preservation of firing (see Theorem 4.3) and finite cocompleteness (see Theorem 4.4).

Fact 4.2 (Category APN) Abstract Petri nets (definition 3.5) and abstract Petri net morphisms (Definition 4.1) are defining a category **APN**, called category of abstract Petri nets.   □

Proof. Due to the componentwise definition of morphisms we obtain composition, identities, and associativity of composition.

Next we show that morphisms preserve the operational behavior, if the models of the specification are compatible. We allow new sorts and operations in the specification, thus new data elements may occur in the model. But the reduct of the model in the target net has to be identical to the model of the source net. Clearly, more changes of the data elements would change the firing behavior.

Theorem 4.3 (APN-Morphism Preserve Firing)
Given an **APN**-morphism $f : N1 \to N2$ (as in Definition 4.1) and compatible data type models (that is $M1 \in Mod(SPEC1)$ and $M2 \in Mod(SPEC2)$ with $V_{f_\Sigma}(M2) = M1$) and let $v \in F(\{t\})$ with $t \in T1$ be AAS1-enabled under m, (that is $\exists \overline{m} \in F(U_{\Sigma 1}(M1) \times P1) : m = \overline{m} + aas1(\overline{pre1}(v)))$ then there is an abstract assignment $AAS2$ so that for $f_m = \pi_{f_\Sigma} \times f_P$:

1. $F(f_T)(v)$ is AAS2-enabled : $F(f_m)(m) = F(f_m)(\overline{m}) + aas2(\overline{pre2}(F(f_T)(v)))$
2. the follower marking after firing $F(f_T)(v)$ is preserved :
$$F(f_m)(m') = F(f_m)(\overline{m}) + aas2(\overline{post2}(F(f_T)(v)))$$

□

Proof. First, we have to define the abstract assignment using amalgamation:
$AAS2 = AAS1 +_{M1} M2$ which is well-defined due to $V_{f_\Sigma}(M2) = M1 = V_\phi(AAS1)$. Because of the compatibility of firing conditions we have for each $\varphi_2 \in cond2(f_T(t))$ there is $\varphi_1 \in cond1(t)$ with $Cond(f_\Sigma)(\varphi_1) = \varphi_2$ and due to the satisfaction condition we can conclude: $AAS1 \models \varphi_1 \Leftrightarrow AAS2 \models \varphi_2$

Next, note that for each $t1 \in T1$ and $f_T(t1) = t2 \in T2$ the following diagram commutes:

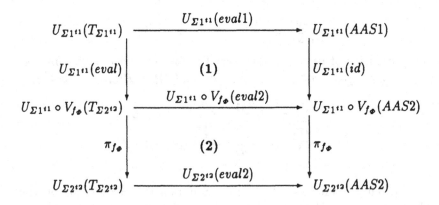

(1) commutes due to initiality of $T_{\Sigma 1^{t1}}$ in $Cat(\Sigma 1^{t1})$
(2) commutes due to natural transformation π_{f_ϕ}

Because $aas1 = F(U_{\Sigma 1^{t1}}(eval1) \times id_{P1})$, $aas2 = F(U_{\Sigma 2^{t2}}(eval2) \times id_{P2})$, and functors preserve commutativity, **(3)** commutes in **Sets** with f_{ins} as defined in Definition 4.1.2.

$$F(U_{\Sigma 1^{t1}}(T_{\Sigma 1^{t1}}) \times P1) \xrightarrow{\quad aas1 \quad} F(U_{\Sigma 1}(M1) \times P1)$$

$$F(f_{ins}) \Big\downarrow \qquad (3) \qquad \Big\downarrow F(\pi_{f_\Sigma} \times f_P)$$

$$F(U_{\Sigma 2^{t2}}(T_{\Sigma 2^{t2}}) \times P2) \xrightarrow[\quad aas2 \quad]{} F(U_{\Sigma 2}(M2) \times P2)$$

This leads to the desired propositions. First $F(f_T)(v_t)$ is $aas2$-enabled:

$F(f_m)(m)$
$$\begin{aligned}
&= F(f_m)(\overline{m} + aas1(\overline{pre1}(v_t))) && m \text{ is } AAS1\text{-enabled}\\
&= F(f_m)(\overline{m}) + F(f_m)(aas1(\overline{pre1}(v_t))) && \text{due to homomorphisms in } \textbf{Struct}\\
&= F(f_m)(\overline{m}) + aas2(F(f_{ins})(\overline{pre1}(v_t))) && \text{as (3) commutes}\\
&= F(f_m)(\overline{m}) + aas2(\overline{pre2}(F(f_T)(v_t))) && \text{due to } \textbf{APN}\text{-morphisms}\\
& && \qquad\text{(Definition 4.1)}
\end{aligned}$$

and second the follower marking after firing $F(f_T)(v_t)$ is preserved

$F(f_m)(m')$
$$\begin{aligned}
&= F(f_m)(\overline{m} + aas1(\overline{post1}(v_t))) && m' \text{ is follower marking}\\
&= F(f_m)(\overline{m}) + F(f_m)(aas1(\overline{post1}(v_t))) && \text{due to homomorphisms in } \textbf{Struct}\\
&= F(f_m)(\overline{m}) + aas2(F(f_{ins})(\overline{post1}(v_t))) && \text{as (3) commutes}\\
&= F(f_m)(\overline{m}) + aas2(\overline{post2}(F(f_T)(v_t))) && \text{due to } \textbf{APN}\text{-morphisms}\\
& && \qquad\text{(Definition 4.1)}
\end{aligned}$$

The subsequent result states that the category $\textbf{APN}$ has finite colimits. It is likely, that the category $\textbf{APN}$ of abstract Petri nets has also arbitrary coproducts, that means it is even infinitely cocomplete. But we have not treated this proposition, because this result is not relevant for practical issues, it would only imply some kind of infinite composition.

Theorem 4.4 (APN is finitely cocomplete) APN has finite colimits. $\square$

Proof. The proof is based on the fact that arbitrary finite colimits can be constructed if the category has initial objects and pushouts.

The initial object $N_\emptyset$ is given by: $N_\emptyset = (P_\emptyset, T_\emptyset, \Sigma_\emptyset, pre_\emptyset, post_\emptyset, cond_\emptyset)$ with $P_\emptyset = T_\emptyset = COND_\emptyset = \emptyset$ the initial object in **Sets**

and $SPEC_\emptyset$ is the initial object in **ASPEC**. Given a abstract Petri net $N = (P, T, SPEC, Var, pre, post, cond)$ the unique **APN**-morphism $f = (f_P^\emptyset, f_T^\emptyset, f_\Sigma^\emptyset) : N_\emptyset \to N$ is given by $f_P^\emptyset = f_T^\emptyset = f_{COND}^\emptyset$ is the empty function $f_\Sigma^\emptyset$ is given by initiality of $SPEC_\emptyset$. The conditions 1 to 3 for **APN**-morphisms (see Definition 4.1) hold, due to emptyness of $T_\emptyset$.

Given $N1 \xleftarrow{f} N0 \xrightarrow{g} N2$ with $Ni = (Pi, Ti, SPECi, Vari, prei, posti, condi)$ for $0 \le i \le 2$ and $f = (f_P, f_T, f_\Sigma)$ and $g = (g_P, g_T, g_\Sigma)$. Then the pushout $N3 = (P3, T3, SPEC3, Var3, pre3, post3, cond3)$ with $N1 \xrightarrow{g'} N3 \xleftarrow{f'} N2$ and $g' = (g'_P, g'_T, g'_\Sigma)$ and $f' = (f'_P, f'_T, f'_\Sigma)$ is constructed by $P1 \xrightarrow{g'_P} P3 \xleftarrow{f'_P} P2$ is pushout of $P1 \xleftarrow{f_P} P0 \xrightarrow{g_P} P2$ in **Sets** $T1 \xrightarrow{g'_T} T3 \xleftarrow{f'_T} T2$ is pushout of $T1 \xleftarrow{f_T} T0 \xrightarrow{g_T} T2$ in **Sets** $SPEC1 \xrightarrow{g'_\Sigma} SPEC3 \xleftarrow{f'_\Sigma} SPEC2$ is pushout of $SPEC1 \xleftarrow{f_\Sigma}$

$SPEC0 \overset{g_\Sigma}{\twoheadrightarrow} SPEC2$ in **ASPEC**. Signatures with variables are given for each transition, so we have to construct them with respect to the pushout $T3$ of transitions. For each $t3 \in T3$ we construct $\Sigma3 \overset{\phi3_{t3}}{\twoheadrightarrow} \Sigma3^t$ using pushouts in **ASIG**. $\phi3^{t3}$ is well-defined due to the pushout properties of $T3$. Pushout properties of $T3$ yield $pre3, post3 : T3 \to Net(U_{\Sigma3^{t3}}(T_{\Sigma3^{t3}}) \times P3)$ and $cond3 : T3 \to \mathcal{P}_{fin}(Cond(\Sigma3^{t3}))$. $f' = (f'_P, f'_T, f'_\Sigma)$ and $g' = (g'_P, g'_T, g'_\Sigma)$ are well-defined, that is they satisfy the conditions 1 to 3 for **APN**-morphisms in Definition 4.1. Next we check the pushout properties: Given an abstract Petri net $N4$ and two morphisms $f^* = (f^*_P, f^*_T, f^*_\Sigma)$ and $g^* = (g^*_P, g^*_T, g^*_\Sigma)$, such that $f^* \circ g = g^* \circ f$, then the induced pushout morphism $k = (k_P, k_T, k_\Sigma)$, where k_P, k_T and k_Σ are the induced morphisms of the components $P3$, $T3$ and $SPEC3$. k is well-defined with respect to the conditions 1 to 3 for **APN**-morphisms in Definition 4.1. Uniqueness of k is obtained by uniqueness of k_P, k_T and k_Σ.

5   Conclusion

In this paper we have given a uniform approach to different types of Petri nets, including low-level nets, like elementary and place/transition nets, as well as high-level nets, like algebraic high-level or predicate/transition nets. Abstract Petri nets are considered as universal parameterized net classes based on a net structure parameter for low-level nets and in addition a data type parameter for high-level nets. By instantiation of these parameters we obtain many well-known net classes studied in the literature but also several new interesting net classes in a uniform way. Moreover, results concerning the compatibility of morphisms with the operational behavior as well as results concerning categorical properties can be achieved on this abstract level. These results then also hold in all instantiations. The introduced frame of universal parameterized net classes in terms of abstract Petri nets allows presenting most important Petri net classes as instantiations. The table below shows the well-known net classes as explicit entries in the table while each blank entry corresponds to a new or less known net class.

Net ^{DT}	Triv	Alg. Spec.	Pred. Logic	ML
powerset	Elem. Nets		PrT-Nets	
monoid	P/T-Nets	AHL-Nets		CPN '92
monoid identity	S-Graphs			

Table 1: Instantiations of Abstract Petri Nets

The results for abstract Petri nets we have introduced this paper are morphisms of abstract Petri nets, that preserve the operational behavior and yield cocompleteness of the category of abstract Petri nets. These results hold as well in all instantiations. Other results that have been or will be obtained within the frame of abstract Petri nets are:

- In high-level replacement systems [EHKP91] a categorical generalization of graph transformations we have rules for replacing objects. The left hand side denotes the part which is to be deleted and the right hand side the part which is to be added. The application of a rule to an object yields a transformation, where the image of the left hand side is deleted and the image of the right hand side is added. The conditions that have to be satisfied in order establish transformations of nets analogously to graph transformations are proven in [Pad96]. Thus we have for abstract Petri nets (and thus for all instantiations) transformations based on rules with a left hand side replaced by a right hand side. These conditions ensure moreover the compatibility between horizontal structuring in terms of colimits with these transformations (see [PER95]).

- In [Pad98b] we have extended the net structure to describe different net and marking structure (see also Example 3.4). For quite many Petri net types the structure of the marking differs from the structure of the flow given by the underlying net structure (see also [KW98]). Thus [Pad98b] uses one description for the flow structure and one for the marking structure. These descriptions are given by two different adjunctions, relating the underlying sets of transitions and places to the corresponding flow structure and to the corresponding marking structure.

- Flattening is the transformation of high-level Petri nets to the underlying low-level net. This transformation is achieved by flattening the data type, that is by expressing the possible markings as places. In [Pad96] we have shown the generalized flattening for abstract Petri nets. Unfortunately the corresponding functor is not cocontinous.

- Based on the theory of high-level replacement systems and its integration with refinement morphisms [Pad98a] we have developed a rule-based refinement for algebraic high-level nets, that preserves safety properties [PGE98]. This approach can be easily extended to abstract Petri nets and will be considered in forthcoming publications.

- Invariants of place/transition nets can be characterized by equalizers of monoids (see [MM90]). This approach doubtlessly can be generalized to low-level abstract Petri nets as the underlying net structure is invariant to the computation of the equalizer. Future work comprises the examination of invariants of high-level abstract Petri nets using equalizers.

References

[AB97]   P. Azéma and G. Balbo (eds.), *Application and Theory of Petri Nets*, Springer-Verlag, LNCS 1248, 1997.

[AHS90]   J. Adamek, H. Herrlich, and G. Strecker, *Abstract and concrete categories*, Series in Pure and Applied Mathematics, John Wiley and Sons, 1990.

[BR96]   J. Billington and W. Reisig (eds.), *Proc. 17th international conference in application and theory of petri nets (ICATPN'96)*, Osaka, Japan., Springer-Verlag Lecture Notes in Computer Science, 1996.

[DG94]   W. Deiters and V. Gruhn, *The funsoft net approach to software process management*, International Journal on Software Engineering and Knowledge Engineering **4** (1994), no. 2.

[DG98]   Wolfgang Deiters and Volker Gruhn, *Process management in practice - applying the funsoft net approach to large-scale processes*, Automated Software Engineering **5** (1998), 7 – 25.

[EBO91]   H. Ehrig, M. Baldamus, and F. Orejas, *New concepts for amalgamation and extension in the framework of specification logics*, Tech. Report 91/05, 1991.

[EG94]   H. Ehrig and M. Große-Rhode, *Functorial Theory of Parameterized Specifications in a General Specification Framework*, Theoretical Computer Science (1994), no. 135, 221 – 266.

[EHKP91] H. Ehrig, A. Habel, H.-J. Kreowski, and F. Parisi-Presicce, *From graph grammars to High Level Replacement Systems*, (H. Ehrig, H.-J. Kreowski, and G. Rozenberg, eds.), 1991, Lecture Notes in Computer Science 532, pp. 269–291.

[EKKK74] H. Ehrig, K.D. Kiermeier, H.J. Kreowski, and W. Kühnel, *Universal Theory of Automata*, Teubner, Stuttgart, 1974.

[EL93]   H. Ehrig and M. Löwe, *Categorical principles, techniques and results for high-level replacement systems in computer science*, Applied Categorical Structures 1 (1993), no. 1, 21–50.

[EM85]   H. Ehrig and B. Mahr, *Fundamentals of algebraic specification 1: Equations and initial semantics*, EATCS Monographs on Theoretical Computer Science, vol. 6, Springer, Berlin, 1985.

[EP97]   H. Ehrig and J. Padberg, *A Uniform Approach to Petri Nets*, Foundations of Computer Science: Potential - Theory - Cognition (Ch. Freksa, M. Jantzen, and R. Valk, eds.), Springer, LNCS 1337, 1997.

[EPR94a] H. Ehrig, J. Padberg, and L. Ribeiro, *Algebraic high-level nets: Petri nets revisited*, Recent Trends in Data Type Specification, Springer, LNCS 785, 1994, pp. 188–206.

[EPR94b] H. Ehrig, J. Padberg, and G. Rozenberg, *Behaviour and realization construction for Petri nets based on free monoid and power set graphs*, Workshop on Concurrency, Specification & Programming, Humboldt University, 1994, Extended version as Technical Report of University of Leiden.

[GB84]   J.A. Goguen and R.M. Burstall, *Introducing institutions*, Proc. Logics of Programming Workshop, Carnegie-Mellon **Springer LNCS 164** (1984), 221 – 256.

[GB92]   J. A. Goguen and R. M. Burstall, *Institutions: Abstract Model Theory for Specification and Programming*, Journals of the ACM **39** (1992), no. 1, 95–146.

[Gen91]   H.J. Genrich, *Predicate/Transition Nets*, High-Level Petri Nets: Theory and Application, Springer, 1991, pp. 3–43.

[GL81]   H.J. Genrich and K. Lautenbach, *System modelling with high-level Petri nets*, 109–136.

[Hum89]   U. Hummert, *Algebraische High-Level Netze*, Ph.D. thesis, Technische Universität Berlin, 1989.

[Jen81]   K. Jensen, *Coloured petri nets and the invariant method*, Theorecical Computer Science **14** (1981), 317–336.

[Jen92]   K. Jensen, *Coloured Petri nets. basic concepts, analysis methods and practical use*, vol. 1, Springer, 1992.

[Jen94]   K. Jensen, *Coloured petri nets: Analysis methods*, Monographs in Theoretical Computer Science (Salomaa Brauer, Rozenberg, ed.), EATCS, Springer Verlag, 1994.

[Jen95]   K. Jensen, *Coloured Petri nets. basic concepts, analysis methods and practical use*, vol. 2, Springer, 1995.

[JFV95]   Rüdiger Jegelka, Wolfgang Ferber, and Niko Vlachantonis, *Anwendungsentwicklung in der LION Entwicklungsumgebung (LEU)*, Unpublished guideline for quality QRL-ANW-001, LION, 1995.

[JR91]   K. Jensen and G. Rozenberg (eds.), *High-Level Petri-Nets: Theory and Application*, Springer-Verlag, 1991.

[KV98]   Ekkart Kindler and Hagen Völzer, *Flexibility in algebraic nets*, Application and Theory of Petri Nets 1998, 19th International Conference (J. Desel and M. Silva, eds.), Springer-Verlag, June 1998, pp. 345–364.

[KW98]   Ekkart Kindler and Michael Weber, *The dimensions of Petri nets: The Petri net cube*, Informatik-Bericht, Humboldt-Universität zu Berlin, 1998, To appear.

[Lil94]   J. Lilius, *On the structure of high-level nets*, Ph.D. thesis, Helsinki University of Technology, 1994.

[Mah89]   B. Mahr, *Empty carriers: the categorical burden on logic*, Categorical Methods in Computer Science – with Aspects from Topology (H. Ehrig, H. Herrlich, H.J. Kreowski, and G. Preuß, eds.), Springer LNCS 393, 1989, pp. 50–65.

[MM90]   J. Meseguer and U. Montanari, *Petri nets are monoids*, Information and Computation **88** (1990), no. 2, 105–155.

[Pad96]   J. Padberg, *Abstract Petri Nets: A Uniform Approach and Rule-Based Refinement*, Ph.D. thesis, Technical University Berlin, 1996.

[Pad98a]   Julia Padberg, *Categorical Approach to Horizontal Structuring and Refinement of High-Level Replacement Systems*, Applied Categorical Structures (1998), accepted.

[Pad98b]   Julia Padberg, *Classifiucation of Petri Nets Using Adjoint Functors*, Bulletin of EACTS (1998), to appear.

[PER95]   J. Padberg, H. Ehrig, and L. Ribeiro, *Algebraic high-level net transformation systems*, Mathematical Structures in Computer Science **5** (1995), 217–256.

[PGE98]   J. Padberg, M. Gajewsky, and C. Ermel, *Rule-Based Refinement of High-Level Nets Preserving Safety Properties*, Fundamental approaches to Software Engineering (E. Astesiano, ed.), Springer, LNCS 1382, 1998, pp. 221–238.

[Rei91]   W. Reisig, *Petri Nets and Abstract Data Types*, Thooretical Computer Science (Fundamental Studies) (1991), no. 80, 1–34.

[Roz92]   Grzegorz Rozenberg (ed.), *Advances in petri nets 1992.*, vol. 609, Springer-Verlag Lecture Notes in Computer Science, Berlin, Germany, 1992.

[Roz93]   Grzegorz Rozenberg (ed.), *Advances in petri nets 1993.*, vol. 674, Springer-Verlag Lecture Notes in Computer Science, Berlin, Germany, 1993.

[San95]   D. Sanella, *Personal communiction*, 1995.

[Sch96]   K. Schimmel, *Abstimmung der Implementierungssoftware INCOME/STAR*, Arbeitsbericht des Instituts für Produktionswirtschaft und Industrielle Informationswirtschaft der Universität Leipzig, 1996.

[SS92]   S. Salibra and G. Scollo, *A soft stairway to institutions*, Recent Trends in Data Type Specification, Springer, 1992, LNCS 655, pp. 310–329.

[ST84]   D. T. Sannella and A. Tarlecki, *Building specifications in an arbitrary institution*, Proc. Int. Symposium on Semantics of Data Types, LNCS 173, Springer, 1984, pp. 337–356.

[ST86]   D. T. Sannella and A. Tarlecki, *Extended ML: an institution–independent framework for formal program development*, Proc. Workshop on Category Theory and Computer Programming, LNCS 240, Springer, 1986, pp. 364–389.

[ST87]   D.T. Sannella and A. Tarlecki, *On observational equivalence and algebraic specification*, JCSS **34** (1987), 150–187.

[ST91]   D. T. Sannella and A. Tarlecki, *Extended ML: Past, present and future*, Tech. Report ECS-LFCS-91-138, University of Edinburgh, labroratory for Foundation of Computer Science, 1991.

[Tar87]   A. Tarlecki, *Bits and pieces of the theory of institutions*, Proc. of Summer Workshop on Category Theory and Computer Programming, Springer, LNCS 240, 1987, pp. 334–363.

Using Reflection to Specify
Transaction Sequences in Rewriting Logic

Isabel Pita* and Narciso Martí-Oliet**

Escuela Superior de Informática
Universidad Complutense de Madrid, Spain
{ipandreu,narciso}@eucmos.sim.ucm.es

Abstract. We develop an application of the reflective properties of rewriting logic to the specification of the management process of broadband telecommunications networks. The application is illustrated by a process that modifies the demand of a service between two nodes in the network. The strategy language selected for controlling the process is based on the one presented in [2] which has been enhanced with a new operation that applies a strategy over a set of objects. The specification of the system is developed in the rewriting logic language Maude, which, thanks to its reflective capabilities, can also be used for specifying internally the strategies that control the system. Several modeling approaches are compared, emphasizing the benefits obtained from using reflection to control the rewriting process as opposed to the extra effort required to control the process at the object level itself.

1 Introduction

Rewriting logic was first proposed by Meseguer as a unifying framework for concurrency in 1990 [8,9]. Since then much work has been done on the use of rewriting logic as a logical and semantic framework [11,7], and on the development of the Maude language [10,2], a specification and programming language directly based on rewriting logic. Recently new research has focused on the reflective properties of rewriting logic [3,4,5,6]. Reflection allows a system to access its own metalevel, providing a powerful mechanism for controlling the rewriting process. Some *strategy languages* have already been proposed [2,1,5] to define adequate strategies to control rewriting. The important issue is that, thanks to reflection, these languages are based on rewriting and their semantics and implementation are described in the same logic, which allows us to define the strategies by rewriting rules and to implement them in a reflective rewriting logic language like Maude. In this way, control is not an extra-logical addition to the language but remains declaratively inside the logic.

In this paper we develop an application of the reflective properties of rewriting logic to the specification of the management process of broadband telecommunications networks. The application is illustrated by a process that modifies the

---

* Partially supported by CAM 06T-033-96.
** Partially supported by CICYT, TIC 95-0433-C03-01.

J.L. Fiadeiro (Ed.): WADT'98, LNCS 1589, pp. 261–276, 1999.
© Springer-Verlag Berlin Heidelberg 1999

demand of a service between two nodes in a network. The strategy language used for controlling the process is based on the one presented in [2] which has been enhanced with a new operation that applies a strategy over a list of objects. The management of a network is done through a *mediator*, a metaobject living in the metalevel and having access to the configuration of the network. In this way, we combine ideas coming from the field of logical reflection with ideas coming from the field of object-oriented reflection [10].

Regarding the system properties that can be specified, rewriting logic and reflection are well suited for the specification of system functionality, both static and dynamic, but, for example, global safety and liveness properties should be expressed in a modal or temporal logic.

The paper is organized as follows. First we present some basic notions of rewriting logic and the Maude language that will be used in the application case. Next we introduce the strategy language, and propose a new operation needed for the application. Then we present the selected scenario and define the strategies that control the modification process. Finally, the specification using reflection is compared with the specification presented in [13] without reflection, and some improvements are proposed. This paper is heavily based on our previous paper [13], which should be read for a complete understanding of the network application.

2   Rewriting Logic and Reflection

We outline here some basic notions of rewriting logic and its implementation in the specification and programming language Maude needed for the application case. For more information on the subject see [9,10].

A *rewrite theory* $\mathcal{R}$ is defined as a 4-tuple $\mathcal{R} = (\Sigma, E, L, R)$ where (Σ, E) is an equational signature, L is a set of labels, and R is a set of *rewrite rules* of the form $l : [t]_E \longrightarrow [t']_E$, where $l \in L$, t and t' are Σ-terms possibly involving some variables, and $[t]_E$ denotes the equivalence class of term t modulo the equations E. In order to simplify the presentation, in the following we will not make explicit the equivalence class of terms.

Intuitively, the signature (Σ, E) of a rewrite theory describes a particular structure for the states of a system, and the rewrite rules describe which elementary local transitions are possible in the distributed state by concurrent local transformations.

Rewriting logic is reflective [3,4], that is, there is a universal rewrite theory $\mathcal{U}$ with a finite number of operations, equations and rules that can simulate any other finitely presentable rewrite theory $\mathcal{R}$ in the following sense: given any two terms t, t' in $\mathcal{R}$ there are corresponding terms $\langle \overline{\mathcal{R}}, \overline{t} \rangle$ and $\langle \overline{\mathcal{R}}, \overline{t'} \rangle$ in $\mathcal{U}$ such that

$$\mathcal{R} \vdash t \longrightarrow t' \iff \mathcal{U} \vdash \langle \overline{\mathcal{R}}, \overline{t} \rangle \longrightarrow \langle \overline{\mathcal{R}}, \overline{t'} \rangle.$$

We will denote the representation (reification) of an object level term ot in the metalevel by $\uparrow ot$ (see [3,6] for the details of the corresponding definition).

Conditional rewriting logic (that is, equations and rules can be conditional [9]) constitutes the foundation of the specification and programming language Maude. Systems in Maude are built out of basic elements called modules. Functional modules are used for the definition of algebraic data types; system modules specify the initial model of a rewrite theory $\mathcal{R}$; and object-oriented modules are a special case of system modules, used for the definition of object-oriented classes.

An object is represented as a term $< O : C \mid a_1 : v_1, \ldots, a_n : v_n >$, where O is the object's name belonging to a set OId of object identifiers, C is the class identifier, a_i are the names of the object attributes, and v_i are their corresponding values. Rewrite rules are used to implement the method associated to a message received by an object. In general, a rewrite rule in an object-oriented module has the form

> **rl** $[l] : M_1 \ldots M_n < O_1 : C_1 \mid atts_1 > \ldots < O_m : C_m \mid atts_m >$
> $\implies \quad < O_{i1} : C'_{i1} \mid atts'_{i1} > \ldots < O_{ik} : C'_{ik} \mid atts'_{ik} >$
> $\quad\quad < Q_1 : D_1 \mid atts''_1 > \ldots < Q_p : D_p \mid atts''_p >$
> $\quad\quad M'_1 \ldots M'_q$
> **if** C

where $k, p, q \geq 0$, M_s are message expressions, $i_1, \ldots, i_k$ are different numbers among the original $1, \ldots, m$, C is a rule condition, and l is a label. The result of applying such a rewrite rule is that the messages $M_1, \ldots, M_n$ disappear; the state and possibly the class of the objects $O_{i1}, \ldots, O_{ik}$ may change; all the other objects O_j vanish; new objects $Q_1, \ldots, Q_p$ are created; and new messages $M'_1, \ldots, M'_q$ are sent.

By convention, the only object attributes $atts_1, \ldots, atts_m$ made explicit in a rule are those relevant for that rule. In particular, the attributes mentioned only on the lefthand side of the rule are preserved unchanged, the original values of attributes mentioned only on the righthand side of the rule don't matter, and all attributes not explicitly mentioned are left unchanged.

3   The Internal Strategy Language

Strategies are used to control the rewriting process, which in principle could go in many undesired directions. In Maude strategies can be made *internal* to rewriting logic, that is, they can also be defined by means of rewrite rules. In fact there is a great freedom for defining different strategy languages inside Maude (see [2,5] for two possibilities). This can be done in a completely user-definable way, so the users are not limited by a fixed and closed strategy language.

A methodology for defining a strategy language is outlined in [2]. First a kernel is defined stating how rewriting in the object level is accomplished at the metalevel. In particular, Maude supports a strategy language kernel which defines the operation

op meta-apply : *Term Label Nat* $\rightarrow$ *Term* .

A term meta-apply(t, l, n) is evaluated by converting the metaterm t to the term it represents, and matching the resulting term against all rules with the given label l. The first n successful matches are discarded, and if there is an $(n+1)$th successful match its rule is applied, and the resulting term is converted to a metaterm and returned; otherwise, error* is returned.

The strategy language STRAT defined in [2] defines sorts *Strategy* and *StrategyExp* for strategies, and extends the kernel with operations to compose strategies. In this paper, however, we will not use their solution tree structure. In particular, the operations that will be used in our application are:

- operations defining basic strategies:
  op idle : $\rightarrow$ *Strategy* .
  op apply : *Label* $\rightarrow$ *Strategy* .
  op rew_with_ : *Term Strategy* $\rightarrow$ *StrategyExp* .
  op failure : $\rightarrow$ *StrategyExp* .
- operations that compose strategies:
  op _;_ : *Strategy Strategy* $\rightarrow$ *Strategy* .
  op _;;_orelse_ : *Strategy Strategy Strategy* $\rightarrow$ *Strategy* .
  op _andthen_ : *StrategyExp Strategy* $\rightarrow$ *StrategyExp* .

These operations satisfy the following equations:

eq rew T with $(S \; ; \; S') = ($rew T with $S)$ andthen S' .
eq (rew T with idle) andthen $S =$ rew T with S .
eq failure andthen $S =$ failure .
eq rew T with apply$(L) =$
    if meta-apply$(T,L,0) ==$ error* then failure
    else rew meta-apply$(T,L,0)$ with idle fi .
eq rew T with $(S \;;\; S''$ orelse $S') =$
    if rew T with $S ==$ failure then rew T with S'
    else (rew T with $S)$ andthen S'' fi .

A strategy expression initially has the form rew T with S, meaning that we have to apply strategy S to the metaterm T. This strategy expression is then reduced by means of the equations to an expression of the form rew T' with S', where T' is the term already calculated and S' is the remaining strategy. If the reduction process succeeds, a strategy expression of the form rew T'' with idle is reached, where T'' represents the solution term obtained; otherwise, the strategy expression failure is generated.

Controlling the order in which a transaction consisting of a sequence of rewriting steps will take place at the object level requires the use of the concatenation operation on strategies, and of the operation that applies a rule at the object level. The idea is that the strategy concatenates the rewriting rules in the order that should be used in the process by means of the operation _;_. Notice that rules are applied at the object level as they are required by the strategy, and that the strategy controls the failure situations when there is no rule to apply by means of the equation that defines the apply operation using meta-apply.

We need a new operation on strategies in order to apply a strategy over a list of objects:

op Iterate : $Strategy \rightarrow Strategy$.
eq Iterate(S) = S ;; Iterate(S) orelse idle .

Intuitively, this composed strategy Iterate(S) is very general and simply applies several times a strategy S, finishing when this strategy can no longer be applied. For our purposes of applying a given rule to a list of objects, we wish to apply the same strategy but each time to a different object, that is, we want to iterate over the given list. If the strategy cannot be applied more than once to a given object (for example, when one of its effects is the removal of the object from the list), there is nothing else to consider. However, if this is not the case, as in our application, we need to make sure that each object in the list is treated exactly once. To accomplish this, we use a list parameter in the rewriting rules at the object level, keeping track of the list of objects that have not been treated yet (see the rules LinkListLoadReq in Section 5). When all the objects have matched the rule, the strategy S will fail to apply and the _;;_orelse_ operation will finish with the idle strategy . A different possibility is to keep track of the list of objects at the level of the strategy language, instead of doing it at the object level. This can be done, for example, in the strategy language that Clavel and Meseguer describe in [5], where they use substitutions and bindings to pass information from one level to the other. We have decided not to do so in order to keep the strategy language simpler, and reuse as much as possible the rules of the nonreflective application.

4   A Network Application

This strategy language is applied to the specification of a sequence of transactions that change the demand of a given service between two nodes on a telecommunications network. The selected scenario is taken from the one presented in [13], a database model of a broadband telecommunications network. The basic objects of the network are *nodes*, *links* and *connections*. Nodes represent the network points where the communication signals are treated. Links are defined between nodes as entities for which the carried information can be accessed at its two endpoints. Connections are defined as configurable sequences of links. They are used to support the communication services between each pair of nodes.

The protocol followed by the modification process is sketched in Figure 1. The network object N receives a message ChDemand($O,N,No1,No2,\ll S; D \gg$) from an external object O asking to change the demand of the connection between nodes $No1$ and $No2$ by adding a new demand D of the service S (expressed as a tuple $\ll S; D \gg$) to the existing demand. The network N sends messages to the connection, links and nodes involved in the requested change, to verify whether the modification is possible. If the returned messages indicate that the modification can indeed be done, the modification process starts by changing the service demand on the connection, the bandwidth required on the links that support the connection, and the number of ports of the traversed nodes; otherwise, the corresponding error message is sent to the external object O through the network object. Only two error messages are considered. The first

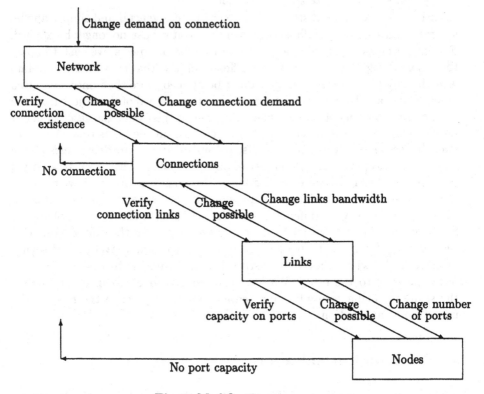

Fig. 1. Modification process

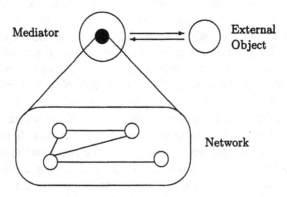

Fig. 2. Metalevel mediator for a network

one is produced by the absence of connection between the given nodes, and the second one takes place when the port capacity required by the service is not supported by one of the nodes traversed by the connection.

The system is specified using the object-oriented facilities of the Maude language. The process can be defined completely at the object level, as it is done in [13], or it can be controlled from the metalevel using the reflective properties of the logic. In the following we will illustrate the benefits obtained from using this second approach.

5   Strategies and Rules for the Modification Process

All the different objects that constitute a network (nodes, links, connections, etc.) as modelled in [13], form a configuration in the sense described in [10], that is, a distributed state of a concurrent object-oriented system at the object level. To control a network, we add at the metalevel a class of *metaobjects*

class *Mediator* | Config: *Network-Configuration* .

that play the role of the network management centers used to control ATM networks.

A *mediator* has as the value of its attribute Config a metaterm of the form $\uparrow C$ where C denotes the configuration of the network managed by the mediator. We assume that all the control of the network is done through its mediator, that is, the messages addressed to the network from an external object are processed by the mediator, that will also send back the corresponding answer. This situation is depicted in Figure 2, and constitutes a novel application of ideas from logical reflection to the description of object-oriented group reflection already sketched by Meseguer in [10].

The first approach to control the modification process through the mediator follows the protocol described in the previous section. We define two conditional rules. The first one is applied when the modification is possible, the other treats the error cases. The idea is to reduce the strategy expression that modifies the demand on the network configuration as much as possible. Depending on the resulting strategy expression, the configuration is then changed or an error message is sent to the external object.

crl [ChDemand1] : ChDemand($O, N, No1, No2, \ll S; D \gg$)
     < N : *Mediator* | Config: T >
⇒ < N : *Mediator* | Config: T' > (To O AckChDemand $No1$ and $No2$ in N)
if rew T_C with stratChDemand1 == rew T' with idle .

crl [ChDemand1] : ChDemand($O, N, No1, No2, \ll S; D \gg$)
     < N : *Mediator* | Config: T >
⇒ < N : *Mediator* > (To O NoChDemand $No1$ and $No2$ in N)
if rew T_C with stratChDemand1 == failure .

where the metaterm T represents a correct state of the network, T_C denotes the configuration $\_[T,\uparrow \text{ConnectionReq}(O, N, No1, No2, \ll S; D \gg)]$, and stratChDemand1 denotes the strategy

> apply(ConnectionReq); apply(LinkListLoadReq);
> Iterate(apply(PortNodeReq); apply(PortNodeReq); apply(LinkListLoadReq));
> apply(ChConnection); Iterate(apply(ChConnection));
> Iterate(apply(ChLinkListLoad); apply(ChPortNode); apply(ChPortNode)) .

The constants ConnectionReq, LinkListLoadReq, PortNodeReq, ChConnection, ChLinkListLoad and ChPortNode are the labels of the rules defined at the object level, which are described below for the reflective case. The rules corresponding to the nonreflective case can be found in [13].

When a ChDemand message is received by the network mediator, the condition of the rules is evaluated. This requires reducing the strategy expression

$$\text{rew } T_C \text{ with stratChDemand1 .} \tag{1}$$

using the equations of the strategy language. First it tries to apply the ConnectionReq rule at the object level, which verifies the existence of connection between nodes $No1$ and $No2$ in network N.

> **crl [ConnectionReq]** : ConnectionReq$(O, N, No1, No2, \ll S; D \gg)$
> $< C : C\text{-}Connection \mid$ Nodes: $\ll M1; M2 \gg$, LinkList: $Ll >$ (2)
> $\Rightarrow < C : C\text{-}Connection >$ LinkListLoadReq$(O, N, C, \ll S; D \gg, Ll)$
> **if** $((M1 == No1)$ **and** $(M2 == No2))$ **or**
> $((M2 == No1)$ **and** $(M1 == No2))$.

If the connection exists then the initial strategy expression (1) is reduced to

> rew meta-apply$(T_C,\text{ConnectionReq},0)$ with apply(LinkListLoadReq);
> Iterate(apply(PortNodeReq); apply(PortNodeReq); apply(LinkListLoadReq));
> apply(ChConnection); Iterate(apply(ChConnection));   (3)
> Iterate(apply(ChLinkListLoad); apply(ChPortNode); apply(ChPortNode)) .

Otherwise, the expression (1) reduces to failure because the rule ConnectionReq cannot be applied, and the failure is propagated through the rest of the expression. In this case, the condition of the second rule is fulfilled and the message (To O NoChDemand $No1$ and $No2$ in N) is sent to the external object O.

If there is no error, the strategy expression (3) reduces to:

> rew $\_[T,\uparrow$ LinkListLoadReq$(O, N, C, \ll S; D \gg, Ll)]$ with
>   apply(LinkListLoadReq);
>   Iterate(apply(PortNodeReq); apply(PortNodeReq); apply(LinkListLoadReq));
>   apply(ChConnection); Iterate(apply(ChConnection));
>   Iterate(apply(ChLinkListLoad); apply(ChPortNode); apply(ChPortNode)) .

The LinkListLoadReq rules send messages to the nodes of the link to verify whether they support the demanded capacity by means of the PortNodeReq rule. Once all the links have been verified, the connection object starts changing its service demand.

rl [LinkListLoadReq] : LinkListLoadReq($O, N, C, \ll S; D \gg, L\ Ll$)
    $< L : C\text{-}Link \mid$ Nodes: $\ll No1; No2 \gg >$
$\Rightarrow < L : C\text{-}Link >$ PortNodeReq($S, No1$)   (4)
    PortNodeReq($S, No2$) LinkListLoadReq($O, N, C, \ll S; D \gg, Ll$) .

rl [LinkListLoadReq] : LinkListLoadReq($O, N, C, \ll S; D \gg$,nil)
    $< C : C\text{-}Connection \mid$ DemandList: $Dl >$
$\Rightarrow < C : C\text{-}Connection >$ ChConnection($C, \ll S; D \gg, Dl$)

crl [PortNodeReq] : PortNodeReq(S, No)
    $< No : C\text{-}Node \mid$ Eq: $< Et : C\text{-}Eq\text{-}Trans \mid$ Capacity: $Cap > >$
    $< S : C\text{-}Service \mid$ Capacity: $Cp >$
$\Rightarrow < No : C\text{-}Node > < S : C\text{-}Service >$
if ($Cp <= Cap$) .

The application of the recursive equation Iterate continues until either some node produces an error or all the links on the connection have been treated. In the first case, the strategy expression is reduced to **failure** as the Iterate operation finishes without sending a ChConnection message in the object level and then the ChConnection rule cannot be applied. Otherwise, the modification part of the process is accomplished using the remaining strategy
    Iterate(apply(ChConnection));
    Iterate(apply(ChLinkListLoad); apply(ChPortNode); apply(ChPortNode))
which cannot fail because the verification part guarantees that the modification is possible.

The ChConnection message goes over the demand list looking for a tuple whose service identifier is the one used in the message. The Iterate operation is used until the service is found in the demand list or the demand list is nil. The Iterate operation is then reduced to idle and the ChLinkListLoad rule can be applied.

rl [ChConnection] : ChConnection($C, \ll S; D1 \gg, \ll S; D2 \gg Dl$)
    $< C : C\text{-}Connection \mid$ DemandList: $Dl1 \ll S; D2 \gg Dl2$, LinkList: $Ll >$
    $< S : C\text{-}Service \mid$ Capacity: $Cp >$
$\Rightarrow < C : C\text{-}Connection \mid$ DemandList: $Dl1 \ll S; D1 + D2 \gg Dl2 >$
    $< S : C\text{-}Service >$ ChLinkListLoad($Ll, D1 * Cp$) .

crl [ChConnection] : ChConnection($C, \ll S1; D1 \gg, \ll S2; D2 \gg Dl$)
    $< C : C\text{-}Connection >$
$\Rightarrow < C : C\text{-}Connection >$ ChConnection($C, \ll S1; D1 \gg, Dl$)
if ($S1 = / = S2$) .

rl [ChConnection] : ChConnection($C, \ll S; D1 \gg$,nil)
    $< C$: C-Connection | DemandList: Dl, LinkList: $Ll >$
    $< S$: C-Service | Capacity: $Cp >$
$\Rightarrow < C$: C-Connection | DemandList: $Dl \ll S; D1 \gg > < S$: C-Service $>$
    ChLinkListLoad($Ll, D1 * Cp$) .

The message ChLinkListLoad is applied by means of the Iterate operation until the list of links is empty and the operation finishes with idle.

crl [ChLinkListLoad] : ChLinkListLoad($L\ Ll, R$)
    $< L$: C-Physical-Link | Nodes: $\ll No1; No2 \gg$, Load: $Ld >$
$\Rightarrow < L$: C-Physical-Link | Load: $Ld + R >$ ChPortNode($No1, R$)
    ChPortNode($No2, R$) ChLinkListLoad(Ll, R)
if ($Ll = / =$ nil) .

crl [ChLinkListLoad] : ChLinkListLoad($L\ Ll, R$)
    $< L$: C-Physical-Link | Nodes: $\ll No1; No2 \gg$, Load: $Ld >$
$\Rightarrow < L$: C-Physical-Link | Load: $Ld + R >$
    ChPortNode($No1, R$) ChPortNode($No2, R$)
if ($Ll ==$ nil) .

Finally, the message ChPortNode(No,R) changes the number of ports used in node No in accordance with the new bandwidth R.

rl [ChPortNode] : ChPortNode(No, R) $< No$: C-Physical-Node |
    EqTrans: $< Et$: C-Eq-Trans | Capacity: $Cap >$, Used: $U >$
$\Rightarrow < No$: C-Physical-Node | Used: $U + R$ div $Cap > .$

Thus, the strategy expression is completely reduced, producing a metaterm T' that represents the network configuration with the changed demand. The condition of the first rule is then fulfilled and the network configuration is changed to T'.

6   Comparison of the Two Approaches

The use of reflection simplifies the rules at the object level mainly due to the metalevel control of failure situations and of the rule application order.

The ConnectionReq rule (2), used to verify the existence of connection between two nodes, replaces the following three rules defined in [13]:

crl ComMod($O, N, No1, No2, C\ Cs, \ll S; D \gg$)
    $< C$: C-Connection | Nodes: $\ll M1; M2 \gg$, LinkList: $Ll >$
$\Rightarrow < C$: C-Connection $>$ LinkListLoadReq($O, N, C, \ll S; D \gg, Ll$)
if (($M1 == No1$) **and** ($M2 == No2$)) **or**
    (($M2 == No1$) **and** ($M1 == No2$)) .

crl ComMod($O, N, No1, No2, C\,Cs, \ll S; D \gg$)
   < $C : C\text{-}Connection$ | Nodes: $\ll M1; M2 \gg$ >
$\Rightarrow$ < $C : C\text{-}Connection$ > ComMod($O, N, No1, No2, Cs, \ll S; D \gg$)
if (($M1 = / = No1$) **or** ($M2 = / = No2$)) **and**
   (($M2 = / = No1$) **or** ($M1 = / = No2$)) .

rl ComMod($O, N, No1, No2$, null, $\ll S; D \gg$)
$\Rightarrow$ (To N and O NoConnectionBetween $No1$ to $No2$) .

These rules need an extra parameter, the set of connections in the network, which is used to go over the network connections until either the one defined between the given nodes is found, or the set is empty. The first rule treats the existence of connection between the given nodes, the second rule is used to go over the set of connections passing over the connections not defined between the given nodes, and the third rule is used to send the error message once all connections have been tested and no one is defined between the given nodes.

On the other hand, using reflection only a rule to treat the existence of connection is needed. If this rule does not match, the strategy in the metalevel is in charge of sending the failure message to the external object. In this way, a lot of messages are avoided because there is no need to go over the set of all connections in the network.

The LinkListLoadReq set of rules is another example of rule simplification using reflection. The two rules (4) replace the following three rules in [13]:

rl LinkListLoadReq($O, N, C, \ll S; D \gg, L\,Ll$)
   < $L : C\text{-}Link$ | Nodes: $\ll No1; No2 \gg$ >
$\Rightarrow$ < $L : C\text{-}Link$ > PortNodeReq($O, N, C, L, \ll S; D \gg, No1$)
   PortNodeReq($O, N, C, L, \ll S; D \gg, No2$)
   LinkListLoadReq2($O, N, C, \ll S; D \gg, Ll, L, No1, No2$) .

rl LinkListLoadReq2($O, N, C, \ll S; D \gg, L\,Ll, L1, No1, No2$)
   (To $L1$ and O and N and C and $\ll S; D \gg$ PortInNode $No1$)
   (To $L1$ and O and N and C and $\ll S; D \gg$ PortInNode $No2$)
   < $L : C\text{-}Link$ | Nodes: $\ll M1; M2 \gg$ >
$\Rightarrow$ < $L : C\text{-}Link$ > PortNodeReq($O, N, C, L, \ll S; D \gg, M1$)
   PortNodeReq($O, N, C, L, \ll S; D \gg, M2$)
   LinkListLoadReq2($O, N, C, \ll S; D \gg, Ll, L, M1, M2$) .

rl LinkListLoadReq2($O, N, C, \ll S; D \gg$, nil, $L, No1, No2$)
   (To L and O and N and C and $\ll S; D \gg$ PortInNode $No1$)
   (To L and O and N and C and $\ll S; D \gg$ PortInNode $No2$)
$\Rightarrow$ (To C and O and N and $\ll S; D \gg$ LinksVerified) .

Keeping the control at the object level requires an additional message LinkListLoadReq2 used only internally for implementation purposes. The second and third rules define the behaviour of this message. It is used to go over the list of links that support the connection, sending the appropriate messages to its nodes to verify whether they can support the demanded capacity. At the same time, the rules collect the successful returning messages from the nodes of the previous link in the list. Only in the case that all the nodes of the links in the list can support the demanded capacity, a successful message is sent by the third rule to the connection object.

Using reflection, this extra message is avoided, keeping the specification free from implementation issues. The **LinkListLoadReq** rule is used to go over the list of links. If a node cannot support the demanded capacity then the **PortNodeReq** rule will not match and a failure will be automatically generated by the strategy at the metalevel, removing the need for collecting the nodes returning messages. As in the previous case this avoids the use of a lot of messages.

7   Improving Control by Changing Strategies

The strategy language allows us to simplify not only the rules but also the protocol by simultaneously carrying out the verification and the modification processes. It is also possible to differentiate the two failure situations and send different messages to the external object. Consider the following three rules:

crl [ChDemand2] : $ChDemand(O, N, No1, No2, \ll S; D \gg)$
    $< N : Mediator \mid Config: T >$
$\Rightarrow < N : Mediator \mid Config: T' > (\text{To } O \text{ AckChDemand } No1 \text{ and } No2 \text{ in } N)$
if rew T'_C with stratChDemand2 $==$ rew T' with idle .

crl [ChDemand2] : $ChDemand(O, N, No1, No2, \ll S; D \gg)$
    $< N : Mediator \mid Config: T >$
$\Rightarrow < N : Mediator > (\text{To } O \text{ NoConnectionBetween } No1 \text{ and } No2 \text{ in } N)$
if rew T'_C with stratChDemand2 $==$ rew T' with NoConnection .

crl [ChDemand2] : $ChDemand(O, N, No1, No2, \ll S; D \gg\gg)$
    $< N : Mediator \mid Config: T >$
$\Rightarrow < N : Mediator > (\text{To } O \text{ ServiceCapacityNoSupported})$
if rew T'_C with stratChDemand2 $==$ rew T' with NoPortCapacity .

where the metaterm T'_C denotes the configuration $\_[T, \uparrow MCom(O, N, No1, No2, \ll S; D \gg)]$, and stratChDemand2 denotes the strategy

```
(apply(MCom) ;; Iterate(apply(LinkListLoad);
        (apply(PortNode) ;; idle orelse NoPortCapacity);
        (apply(PortNode) ;; idle orelse NoPortCapacity))
orelse (apply(MComNS) ;; Iterate(apply(LinkListLoad);
        (apply(PortNode) ;; idle orelse NoPortCapacity);
        (apply(PortNode) ;; idle orelse NoPortCapacity))
orelse NoConnection)).
```

The main idea is to use the $\_;;\_orelse\_$ operation which allows us to verify whether the appropriate rules can be applied at the object level. In case the process succeeds the strategy ends with idle; otherwise, a special strategy (either NoConnection or NoPortCapacity) is generated, and the reduction process finishes by applying one of the following equations:

eq NoConnection andthen S = NoConnection .
eq NoPortCapacity andthen S = NoPortCapacity .

At the object level the rules MCom and MComNS integrate the rules ComMod defined in Section 6 and ComMod2 defined in [13]. They verify the existence of connection between the given nodes and change the DemandList attribute of the connection object. If the service is already defined, the rule MCom is applied and the service demand is increased; otherwise, the rule MCom cannot match and MComNS is applied, adding the new service to the demand list.

crl [MCom] : $\mathrm{MCom}(O, N, No1, No2, \ll S; D \gg)$
    $< C : C\text{-}Connection \mid \text{Nodes: } \ll M1; M2 \gg,$
    DemandList: $Dl1 \ll S; D1 \gg Dl2$, LinkList: $Ll >$
    $< S : C\text{-}Service \mid$ Capacity: $Cp >$
$\Rightarrow < C : C\text{-}Connection \mid$ DemandList: $Dl1 \ll S; D1 + D \gg Dl2 >$
    $< S : C\text{-}Service >$ LinkListLoad$(S, Ll, D * Cp)$
if $((M1 == No1)$ **and** $(M2 == No2))$ **or**
    $((M1 == No2)$ **and** $(M2 == No1))$.

crl [MComNS] : $\mathrm{MCom}(O, N, No1, No2, \ll S; D \gg)$
$< C : C\text{-}Connection \mid \text{Nodes: } \ll M1; M2 \gg,$ DemandList: $Dl1$, LinkList: $Ll >$
    $< S : C\text{-}Service \mid$ Capacity: $Cp >$
$\Rightarrow < C : C\text{-}Connection \mid$ DemandList: $Dl1 \ll S; D \gg > < S : C\text{-}Service >$
    LinkListLoad$(S, Ll, D * Cp)$
if $((M1 == No1)$ **and** $(M2 == No2))$ **or**
    $((M1 == No2)$ **and** $(M2 == No1))$.

The LinkListLoad rule modifies the bandwidth of the first link of the list and sends messages to change the number of ports of its two endnodes.

crl [LinkListLoad] : LinkListLoad$(S, L\ Ll, B)$
    $< L : C\text{-}Link \mid \text{Nodes: } \ll No1; No2 \gg,$ Load: $Ld >$
$\Rightarrow < L : C\text{-}Link \mid$ Load: $Ld + B >$ LinkListLoad(S, Ll, B)
    PortNode$(S, No1, B)$ PortNode$(S, No2, B)$
if $Ll = / =$ nil .

crl [LinkListLoad] : LinkListLoad$(S, L\ Ll, B)$
    $< L : C\text{-}Link \mid \text{Nodes: } \ll No1; No2 \gg,$ Load: $Ld >$
$\Rightarrow < L : C\text{-}Link \mid$ Load: $Ld + B >$
    PortNode$(S, No1, B)$ PortNode$(S, No2, B)$
if $Ll ==$ nil .

Finally, the rule that verifies if a node supports a given capacity, and, if possible, changes the number of ports on the node is

crl [PortNode] : PortNodes(S, No, B) $< S$: C-Service | Capacity: $Cp >$
    $< No$: C-Node | Eq: $< Et$: C-Eq-Trans | Capacity: $Cap >$, Used: $U >$
$\Rightarrow < No$: C-Node | Used: $U + B$ DIV $Cap > < S$: C-Service $>$
if $(Cp <= Cap)$.

When a ChDemand message is received by the network mediator, the condition of the rules is evaluated by reducing the strategy expression

    rew T'_C with stratChDemand2 .   (5)

If the connection between nodes $No1$ and $No2$ exists in the configuration represented by T'_C, then the rule MCom or MComNS can be applied at the object level, and the strategy expression is reduced in both cases to

    rew T''_C with Iterate(apply(LinkListLoad);
        (apply(PortNode) ;; idle orelse NoPortCapacity);
        (apply(PortNode) ;; idle orelse NoPortCapacity))

using the equations that define the operation _;;_orelse_.

Next, the recursive strategy Iterate is applied and if the nodes can treat the demanded capacity, the reduction process continues. When there are no more links in the connection the LinkListLoad rule does not match and produces a failure in the Iterate strategy, which finishes the application of the recursive strategy. The reduction process ends with the reduction of the strategy expression to the form **rew** T' with idle using the operation meta-apply. The condition of the first rule is then fulfilled and the rule is applied changing the network configuration and sending the successful message to the external object.

If the connection does not exist then the strategy expression (5) is reduced to the term **rew** T''' with NoConnection which fulfills the condition of the second rule. The case in which one node does not support a demanded capacity is treated similarly with error message NoPortCapacity.

Notice that this approach reduces even more the number of messages exchanged in the system because of the integration of the verification and the modification processes.

8 Concluding Remarks

Reflection clearly separates the object level behaviour from control and management aspects increasing the application *modularity*. In this way the object level is greatly simplified because the rewriting rules are controlled from the metalevel eliminating the necessity of extra rules at the object level. As we have explained, the internal strategies allow us to control from the metalevel

- the order in which the rewriting rules are applied,
- the management of failure situations, either in general or by distinguishing different kinds of failure,
- the successive application of one strategy, by means of the Iterate operation,
- the integration of verification and modification processes,
- the atomicity requirement of some transaction sequences that should be executed in order and without interruption of other executions.

Another advantage is *adaptability*. The same object level can be managed in several ways by changing the strategy controlling it, perhaps through the use of *metastrategies*. This would support the more flexible and runtime adaptable next generation of *active networks* currently being designed.

Of course, the price we are paying for these advantages is the need to go up to the metalevel. However, we have to point out that Maude already provides this access in general (because rewriting logic is reflective) as well as through the internal strategy language. We only need to write down the specific strategies required for our application, which is considerably simpler than complicating the rewriting rules at the object level due to control considerations.

Another important benefit is that the reflective structure facilitates a distributed environment. Different networks can be defined, which will exchange data at the metalevel, controlling each one its own object level. Then, it is easy to define a metanetwork that controls all the defined networks.

Acknowledgements. We are very grateful to José Meseguer and Manuel G. Clavel for their detailed comments on a previous version of this paper, as well as their careful explanations of their papers on reflection and internal strategies. We also thank the anonymous referees for their helpful corrections.

References

1. P. Borovanský, C. Kirchner, and H. Kirchner, Controlling rewriting by rewriting, in [12].
2. M. Clavel, S. Eker, P. Lincoln, and J. Meseguer, Principles of Maude, in [12].
3. M.Clavel and J. Meseguer, Axiomatizing reflective logics and languages, in: G. Kiczales, ed., *Proc. Reflection'96, San Francisco, CA*, April 1996, 263–288.
4. M. Clavel and J. Meseguer, Reflection and strategies in rewriting logic, in [12].
5. M. Clavel and J. Meseguer, *Internal strategies in a reflective logic*, in B. Gramlich and H. Kirchner, eds., *Proc. CADE-14 Workshop on Strategies in Automated Deduction*, Townsville, Australia, July 1997, 1–12.
6. M. Clavel, F. Durán, S. Eker, P. Lincoln, N. Martí-Oliet, and J. Meseguer, Metalevel computation in Maude, in: C. Kirchner and H. Kirchner, eds., *Proc. Second Int. Workshop on Rewriting Logic and its Applications, Pont-à-Mousson, France*, Electronic Notes in Theoretical Computer Science 15, Elsevier, Sept. 1998.
7. N. Martí-Oliet and J. Meseguer, Rewriting logic as a logical and semantic framework, Technical report SRI-CSL-93-05, SRI International, August 1993. To appear in D. M. Gabbay, ed., *Handbook of Philosophical Logic*, Kluwer Academic Pub.

8. J. Meseguer, Rewriting as a unified model of concurrency, in: J.C.M.Baeten y
    J.W.Klop, eds., *Proc. CONCUR'90*, LNCS 458, Springer-Verlag, 1990, 384–400.
9. J. Meseguer, Conditional rewriting logic as a unified model of concurrency, *Theo-retical Computer Science* **96** 1992, 73–155.
10. J. Meseguer, A logical theory of concurrent objects and its realization in the Maude
    language, in: G. Agha, P. Wegner, and A. Yonezawa, eds., *Research Directions in
    Concurrent Object-Oriented Programming*, The MIT Press, 1993, 314–390.
11. J. Meseguer, Rewriting logic as a semantic framework for concurrency: A progress
    report, in: U. Montanari and V. Sassone, eds., *Proc. CONCUR'96*, LNCS 1119,
    Springer-Verlag, 1996, 331–372.
12. J. Meseguer, editor, *Proc. First Int. Workshop on Rewriting Logic and its Applica-tions, Asilomar, CA*, Electronic Notes in Theoretical Computer Science 4, Elsevier,
    Sept. 1996.
13. I. Pita and N. Martí-Oliet, A Maude specification of an object-oriented database
    model for telecommunication networks, in [12].

Concurrency and Data Types: A Specification Method
An Example with LOTOS

Pascal Poizat[1], Christine Choppy[2*], and Jean-Claude Royer[1]

[1] IRIN, Université de Nantes & Ecole Centrale
2 rue de la Houssinière, B.P. 92208, F-44322 Nantes cedex 3, France
{Poizat, Royer}@irin.univ-nantes.fr
[2] LIPN, Institut Galilée - Université Paris XIII,
Avenue Jean-Baptiste Clément, F-93430 Villetaneuse, France
Christine.Choppy@lipn.univ-paris13.fr

Abstract. Methods are needed to help using formal specifications in a practical way. We present a specification method that takes into account both the specification of concurrent activity and the specification of the data types involved. It is applied here to LOTOS specification, but it may be used for other formalisms. Our method is both constraint oriented (for the processes decomposition into parallel subprocesses) and state oriented (for the design of the sequential components). This latter aspect is based on (i) the design of an automaton from the external behaviour description, (ii) the generation of a LOTOS specification associated with this automaton. We illustrate our method through a simple example, a hospital.

Keywords: specification, method, LOTOS, constraint oriented, state oriented, automaton

1 Introduction

While the importance of using formal specifications in software development is widely accepted, there is still a need for methods to help applying them. In this respect, we would like to quote [3]: "a formalism does not provide a method by fiat". It seems to be even more necessary to provide a method for specifications that involve both the specification of concurrent activity and the specification of the data types involved in this activity. While there is a need for describing both the dynamic (process control) and the static aspects (data type), the specification work is likely to be more complex. These two aspects are available in the LOTOS language [17,5,20] that was developed for the specification of distributed systems. The dynamic part is based on process algebra, like CCS [21] or CSP [15], and the static part is based on abstract data types, as in the algebraic specification language ACT ONE [7].

---

* This work was achieved while this author was at IRIN.

J.L. Fiadeiro (Ed.): WADT'98, LNCS 1589, pp. 277–292, 1999.
© Springer-Verlag Berlin Heidelberg 1999

Among the few methods related to LOTOS development, the main tendencies are the constraint oriented approach and the state oriented approach. In the constraint oriented approach the overall system is split into concurrent subprocesses. This approach is well suited to earlier phases of the specification process where the emphasis is put on the requirement constraints. In the state oriented approach, entities of the system are modelled as processes with internal states. The transitions between internal states express internal actions or communications between processes. This approach is well suited when links between the dynamic and static parts need to be expressed.

The method we present in this paper is applied to LOTOS specification and improves existing ones in three ways. First it is a general method that mixes the two main approaches, and produces a modular description with a dynamic behaviour and its associated data type. Secondly, the dynamic behaviour extraction is based on a guarded finite state machine. This state machine is progressively and rigorously built from the requirements. Type information and operation preconditions are used to retrieve states and transitions. The dynamic behaviour specification is computed from the automaton using some patterns. The last improvement is the assisted computation of the functional part. Our method reuses a technique which allows one to obtain an abstract data type from an automaton [1]. This technique extracts the signature and generators from the finite state machine. Furthermore, the automaton is used to generate parts of the axioms.

The paper is structured as follows. We briefly present the LOTOS language in Section 2. Section 3 discusses and compares existing methods for LOTOS specifications. Section 4 presents the general process of our method, for the dynamic part and the static part of the specification. In the conclusion we summarize the main points of our method and we mention our work on applying it to other formalisms.

2   A Short Presentation of LOTOS

LOTOS [17] (Language of Temporal Ordering Specification) is a Formal Description Technique developed within ISO (International Organization for Standardization). It is a language devoted to the specification of distributed and open systems, especially to protocols and telecommunications.

The most important characteristics of LOTOS are: complementary formalisms for data and control, the semantics based on process algebra and abstract data types, executability and modularity.

The language is usually presented in two views: basic LOTOS and full LOTOS.

2.1   Basic LOTOS

Basic LOTOS is the subset of the language where process synchronization is achieved. Following CCS [21] and CSP [15], a behaviour expression describes the process control. Synchronization and communication are possible *via rendez-vous* without sharing memory.

A system is described as a set of processes which are entities able to perform actions and to interact with other processes. The environment of a process consists of other processes. It is possible to build a hierarchy of processes.

A behaviour expression describes the behaviour of a process, it specifies which actions are possible. Actions are atomic units, and are supported by gates. A predefined set of operators is used to combine actions and behaviour expressions to form new behaviour expressions. The following operators are described to make the paper self-contained.

Notation: a lowercase name is a gate, an uppercase name represents a behaviour expression.

The prefix operator: a;A denotes a rendez-vous on gate a followed by the behaviour A. It expresses sequential composition of actions.

The choice operator: A [] B denotes a choice between two behaviours. The selective parallel operator: |[ ]| is used to specify synchronization on a list of gates between two behaviours.
A |[$g_1, ..., g_n$]| B denotes that A and B synchronize on common gates g_i. To the contrary, actions non equal to a or b are interleaved (executed asynchronously) in A and B. This operator is one of the most important. It has two variants:

- || full synchronization on all gates of A and B
- ||| interleaving, no synchronization at all (but for termination).

The **hide** operator hides a gate in a behaviour to disallow environment synchronization on that gate. For instance, **hide a in** (A |[a,b]| B) may be synchronized on b but not on a.

A special operator **stop** represents inaction. It cannot offer synchronization and it does nothing, it is a blocked process.

2.2 Full LOTOS

Full LOTOS copes with data specifications, data transfer during synchronizations and process parameterization over specified data domains. Data structures and values are described algebraically as in ACT ONE [7]. Variables are typed (X:NAT, Y:BOOL, ...), and the language is typed. Types are predefined and imported from a library or defined by a specification:
    type ... endtype.
In full LOTOS, communications on gates are enriched by value passing. For example, in the following expression: **exchange !Put ?Get:NAT**, the Put value is sent during the rendez-vous on the **exchange** gate while a natural value is received in the Get variable. A process may accept arguments:

```
process STACK[push,pop] (S : Stack) : noexit :=
...
endproc
```

This process may be called or instantiated as in STACK[push,pop](aStack).
LOTOS allows the instantiation of processes in behaviours (e.g. in recursive
processes). The noexit qualifier specifies that the process is non terminating
(respectively exit denotes a process which may terminate). A behaviour expression can be preceded by a guard, this allows one to write some kind of
conditional expression:

```
    [X >= 0] -> get; stop
[]
    [X < 0] -> put; stop
```

In the following specification example, the processes P, Q and R are composed
in parallel:

```
specification FOO[...] : noexit
    behavior
        (P[a,b] ||| Q[b,c]) || R[c]
    where
        process P[...]
        ...
        endproc
    ...
endspec
```

A LOTOS specification contains processes and data type definitions and a behaviour expression.

3   Existing Methods for LOTOS Specification

LOTOS is expressive enough to allow a wide range of specification styles, and it is
possible to specify a given problem in various ways. Guidelines for specifications
are therefore needed, but there are few papers that refer to methods for LOTOS
specification. Among the mentioned methods, there are two main approaches,
the constraint oriented approach and the state oriented one, and in both the
emphasis is put on the dynamic part of the specification.

3.1   Dynamic Part

The *constraint oriented approach* is a "divide and conquer" type method. In
general, the specifier uses the following steps: (i) structure the specification into
several subprocesses (possibly recursive), (ii) specify each subprocess, and (iii)
apply parallel composition of the subprocesses. The resulting process satisfies
a constraint set that is equal to the union of the subprocesses constraint sets
plus some synchronization constraints between them [5,20]. Figure 1 shows how
this approach is applied to the MIN3 example where two MIN2 subprocesses are
composed in parallel (with a hidden communication on gate inter).

The *state oriented approach* is a hybrid approach where objects are processes
managing data types [19]. For each state, different sets of communications may

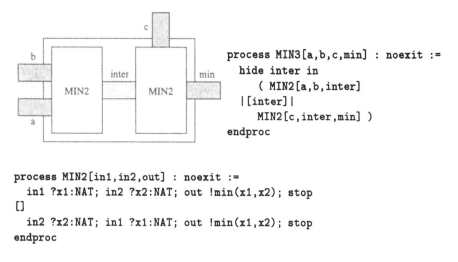

```
process MIN3[a,b,c,min] : noexit :=
  hide inter in
    ( MIN2[a,b,inter]
    |[inter]|
      MIN2[c,inter,min] )
  endproc
```

```
process MIN2[in1,in2,out] : noexit :=
  in1 ?x1:NAT; in2 ?x2:NAT; out !min(x1,x2); stop
[]
  in2 ?x2:NAT; in1 ?x1:NAT; out !min(x1,x2); stop
endproc
```

Fig. 1. An example using the constraint oriented approach

happen depending on the process internal state. The transitions represent either communications between processes or internal transitions, and generally have an effect on their data types. See Figure 2 for an example of this approach applied to an unbounded buffer.

A related method dealing with embedded systems is presented in [6]. It is based on communicating concurrent objects, every object being a process with a parameter that stands for its internal (private) state. These processes use cycles: their behaviours achieve a given service followed by a recursive call.

These approaches are compared in Section 3.4.

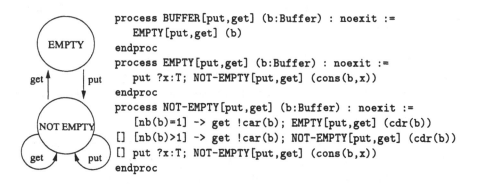

```
process BUFFER[put,get] (b:Buffer) : noexit :=
    EMPTY[put,get] (b)
endproc
process EMPTY[put,get] (b:Buffer) : noexit :=
    put ?x:T; NOT-EMPTY[put,get] (cons(b,x))
endproc
process NOT-EMPTY[put,get] (b:Buffer) : noexit :=
    [nb(b)=1] -> get !car(b); EMPTY[put,get] (cdr(b))
[] [nb(b)>1] -> get !car(b); NOT-EMPTY[put,get] (cdr(b))
[] put ?x:T; NOT-EMPTY[put,get] (cons(b,x))
endproc
```

Fig. 2. An example using the state oriented approach

3.2 Static Part

Concerning the static part, [26,11] propose to use a *constructive approach* and [11] explains it is better to deal with the data part after the dynamic part; but there is no method really for the creation of the static part (algebraic data types), and in any case it is not related to the dynamic part.

3.3 A Mixed Method

We studied the approach followed by [11] to specify a matrix switch problem. In the following, we describe our understanding of their approach. This will be a starting point for our method that adds and modifies some points of this approach.

Informal description. The system that is to be specified is described in natural language.

Parallel architecture. Let us first remark that we prefer "concurrent activity" since parallel and architecture are, usually, hardware referring terms. Here the components executed in parallel are described. Each one is modelized by a LOTOS process. The interactions between components are modeled by formal gates. The communications between the components are then determined and the processes are linked together using LOTOS parallel composition operators. If needed, the operations that are not relevant at this level of abstraction are hidden (using the **hide** operator). This step can be recursively applied to the subsystems in order to obtain purely sequential components.

Sequential components. Each sequential component can be described using a finite state automaton. This automaton is then translated into a LOTOS behaviour expression.

Data types. The sorts and operations that appeared in earlier phases are put together. The corresponding axioms are then obtained using a constructive approach. In [11], it is mentioned that this can lead to over-specification and loss of generality.

Let us note that [11] does not suggest methods for the automaton construction, and for the data type specification (apart from the recommended constructive approach). In Section 4 we extend this approach to provide these features.

3.4 Approaches Comparison

The constraint oriented approaches are well suited to service specification and make the decomposition of processes into sub-components easier.

The authors of [11] think the state oriented approach can lead to unstructured specifications. We think it allows to easily understand the internal behaviour of the processes and agree with [26] that it helps producing more efficient implementations (in purely sequential languages).

As noted by [5,9,10], there are many specification styles in LOTOS and not yet a way to give a quality measure for LOTOS specifications.

It seems to be roughly accepted [26,27] that mixed methods are of great interest and are likely to yield distributed systems specifications that enjoy the three important properties stressed by [27]: *orthogonality* (independent architectural requirements should be specified by independent definitions), *generality* (generic, parameterized definitions should be preferred over collections of special purpose definitions), and *open-endedness* (designs should be maintainable, i.e. easy to extend and modify).

4   A New Method for LOTOS Specification

4.1   Introduction

In this section we describe our method (Figure 3) for LOTOS specification and we illustrate it with the example of a hospital. As explained in the previous section it is based on our study of the approach followed by [11]. Our method brings some novel features such as the semi-automatic retrieval of the sequential components automatons and the use of the Ω-derivation principles [4] to obtain axioms from the automaton (a complete description may be found in [23]).

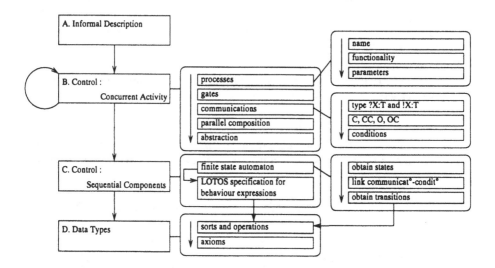

Fig. 3. Our method for LOTOS specification

4.2 Dynamic Part

This part of our method refers to the dynamic part of LOTOS specifications.

A. Informal Description. The system is described in natural language with a clear statement on its components and their interactions.

The case study is a hospital informally described as follows. There are usual admissions (patients) in a limited number and emergency admissions in an unlimited number. The admissions are processed in a first-in first-out way but the emergencies have priority. Externally, the following services (functionalities) are available: PRESENT (is a patient present in the hospital ?), ADMIT (non emergency admission), EMERGENCY (emergency admission) and EXIT (exit of the latter healed patient). Let us note that in this case study, the communication conditions will depend on the processes data.

B. Concurrent Activity. This phase consists of several activities (Figure 3) which are described below: (1) identify the different *processes* corresponding to parallel components, and provide for each process its name, functionality and parameters, (2) determine the communication *gates* between these processes, (3) study the *communications* (typing, conditions, etc.), (4) express *parallel composition* of the processes, and (5) possibly use *abstraction* to hide some communications.

B.1. Processes. Processes are used to model components that run in parallel. The processes "functionalities" (e.g. noexit when recursive) are defined. Each process has its own internal private data (static part) together with a behaviour (dynamic part). A data type is created for each process type and an object of that type is used as the process formal parameter. This decomposition is constraint-oriented.

B.2. Gates. Interactions between components (from the informal description) are modeled with formal gates representing the services (interface) of the component.

At this point, we obtain a single nonterminating process, the hospital, parameterized by an object of type Hospital, with the services PRESENT, ADMIT, EMERGENCY and EXIT:

```
process HOSPITAL[PRESENT,ADMIT,EMERGENCY,EXIT] (h:Hospital) : noexit :=
...
endproc
```

B.3. Communications. In this phase, the communications (on the gates) between the components are typed. Note that we require an explicit typing also for outputs (this symmetry is useful at the data type specification level). All data types used here have an algebraic specification. Generic types can be used but have to be instantiated later. For each process, four sets of (typed) gates are determined: C (constructors without conditions), CC (constructors with conditions), O (observers without conditions) and OC (observers with conditions). Constructors refer to operations that modify the internal data of the process and observers to operations that do not modify it. Conditions are preconditions (stating when an operation is possible or not) or "behaviour conditions" (i.e. the resulting state depends on their value). This partition helps creating the automatons in a semi-automatic way. $\sigma = C \cup CC \cup O \cup OC$ is the set of all the gates of the process. This partition is not global on the gates names but rather local to each process.

Considering the hospital process, we have:

- OC is empty
- O: PRESENT : ?p:Patient, !x:Bool
- C: EMERGENCY : ?p:Patient
- CC:
  - EXIT : !p:Patient, with conditions `c-notEmpty` (a precondition used to state that EXIT is only possible when the hospital is not empty) and `c-emergency` (a behaviour condition needed to express that the result of the EXIT action depends on whether or not there is an emergency patient)
  - ADMIT : ?p:Patient, with condition `c-notFull` (a precondition used to state that ADMIT is only possible when the hospital is not full).

We can obtain signatures from this typing ([23] for details). Note that all data types introduced in this step should be later specified.

B.4. Parallel composition. The components are composed using LOTOS parallel operators. We propose to use composition patterns when possible. See [19,10,18,14] for examples. The pattern instantiation has to be simulated (see [25] for example) since LOTOS has no way to parameterize behaviours (apart from the gate names and data parameters).

B.5. Abstraction. When necessary, communications between components can be hidden using the **hide** operator.

C. Sequential Components. As noted by [26], the use of automata is appropriate since representing whole behaviours by means of trees is practical only when the node number is limited (which is not the case for recursive processes). In this phase the LOTOS behaviour expression is obtained from a finite state automaton.

C.1. Finite State Automaton. A process has a finite number of abstract states in which it can react to finite sets of communications. The composition of the communication conditions obtained above is used (Table 1) to determine the different states of the automaton. Relationships (expressed by formulas) between the conditions eliminate the incoherent states (here: c-emergency $\Rightarrow$ c-notEmpty, and: c-notEmpty $\lor$ c-notFull). Boolean tuples characterize the states.

Table 1. Conditions composition

c-notEmpty	c-emergency	c-notFull	interpretation	reference
true	true	true	intermediate with emergency	InterEmer[1]
true	true	false	full with emergency	FullEmer
true	false	true	intermediate without emergency	InterNoEmer[1]
true	false	false	full without emergency	FullNoEmer
false	true	true	impossible	
false	true	false	impossible	
false	false	true	empty hospital	Empty
false	false	false	impossible	

The transitions of the automaton correspond to communications leading from an abstract state to another one (or possibly the same). To obtain the transitions, we will use their preconditions and postconditions (Table 2 where $\forall$ states that the condition value is not relevant). Expressing the postconditions may require the use of new conditions[2] (e.g. c-onlyOnePatient below). These new conditions will be used to guard the transitions. Relationships between these conditions ("old" and new ones) will limit the number of transitions and prevent creating transitions leading to incoherent states.

Table 2. Preconditions and postconditions

gate	preconditions		
	c-notEmpty	c-emergency	c-notFull
EMERGENCY	$\forall$	$\forall$	$\forall$
ADMIT	$\forall$	$\forall$	true
EXIT	true	$\forall$	$\forall$

gate	postconditions		
	c-notEmpty'	c-emergency'	c-notFull'
EMERGENCY	true	true	c-notFull
ADMIT	true	c-emergency	¬ c-nextFull
EXIT	¬ c-onlyOnePatient	¬ c-onlyOneEmergency	¬ c-emergency $\lor$ c-notFull

O operations (observers without conditions) are always enabled and do not modify the process data, so they are represented by transitions from a state to

---

[1] An "intermediate" state corresponds to a hospital that is neither empty nor full.
[2] See [23] for a discussion on the new conditions appearing in the postconditions.

itself (transition labelled by o in Figure 4). *OC* operations are only possible in some states and are represented by transitions from the states satisfying the conditions and leading to the same state.

For the constructors (*C* and *CC* operations) we use the following scheme: for each abstract state e identified by a tuple t_e, if t_e satisfies the preconditions of the constructor, we compute the tuple t_f corresponding to the postconditions and there is a transition from e to f.

For example, let us consider the emergency admission of a patient, EMERGENCY, and the state Empty. Its corresponding tuple is <false,false,true>. It matches the EMERGENCY precondition ($<$ $\forall,\forall,\forall$ $>$) with {c-notEmpty=false, c-emergency=false, c-notFull=true}. Applying this substitution to the EMERGENCY postcondition we obtain <true,true,true>, that characterizes the InterEmer state; therefore there is a transition labelled by EMERGENCY from Empty to InterEmer.

We now need to determine the initial state (which should be unique for data coherence sake). It is obtained from the conjunction of the preconditions of the operations that should be possible or not in this state. Here we want ADMIT and EMERGENCY to be possible, and EXIT not to be possible. Therefore the initial state should satisfy $\neg$ c-empty $\wedge$ c-notFull which corresponds to <false,$\forall$,true>, that is the (Empty) state.

The complete automaton is given in Figure 4 and the conditions associated to the numbers are given in Table 3. Let us note that our method leads us automatically to take into consideration "special cases" as one-place hospitals (see the guarded transitions [1*] and [7*] in Figure 4).

Table 3. Transitions conditions

number	condition
1, 1*	c-onlyOnePatient
2	$\neg$ c-onlyOneEmergency
3	$\neg$ c-onlyOnePatient
4	$\neg$ c-onlyOnePatient $\wedge$ c-onlyOneEmergency
5	c-onlyOneEmergency
6	$\neg$ c-nextFull
7, 7*	c-nextFull

C.2. LOTOS Behaviour Expressions. We herein summarize the retrieval of the LOTOS behaviour expressions from the automatons. This can be done using two different patterns: a single process is associated with each automaton, and (1) for each state a conditional branch is created and some simplifications are achieved to get readable behaviour expressions, or (2) a subprocess is created for each state of an automaton (this last approach requires/allows much less simplifications). Depending on the goal to be achieved, the user may then choose between both approaches. This issue is further discussed in [23].

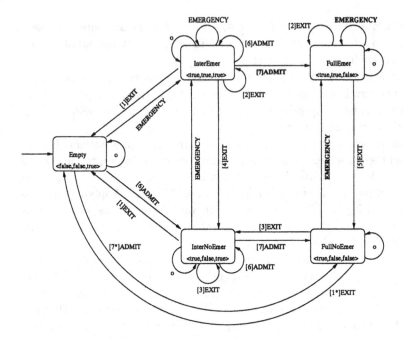

Fig. 4. Hospital automaton

We herein chose the first approach (Fig. 5). Process 1 is obtained after grouping all conditional branches corresponding to the same operation (see next page). Then Process 2 is obtained after simplification of the guards (which may be achieved using some proof tool).

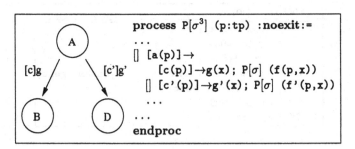

Fig. 5. Transformation pattern (1)

4.3   Static Part: D. Data Types

The last step is to build the specification of the data types associated with each process. For each data type, the work done in the preceding steps provides most

---

[3] σ denotes the process gates.

Process 1

```
process HOSPITAL[PRESENT,EMERGENCY,EXIT,ADMIT] (h: Hospital) : noexit :=
   PRESENT ?p:Patient !(present(h,p)); HOSPITAL[σ⁴] (h)
[] EMERGENCY ?p:Patient; HOSPITAL[σ] (emergency(h,p))
[] [(empty(h) ∧ ([6] ∨ [7*]))
   ∨ (interEmer(h) ∧ ([6] ∨ [7]))
   ∨ (interNoEmer(h) ∧ ([6] ∨ [7]))]→
      ADMIT ?p:Patient; HOSPITAL[σ] (admit(h,p))
[] [(interEmer(h) ∧ ([1] ∨ [2] ∨ [4]))
   ∨ (interNoEmer(h) ∧ ([1] ∨ [3]))]
   ∨ (fullEmer(h) ∧ ([2] ∨ [5]))]
   ∨ (fullNoEmer(h) ∧ ([1*] ∨ [3]))]→
      EXIT !first(h); HOSPITAL[σ] (cure(h))
endproc
```

Process 2

```
process HOSPITAL[PRESENT,EMERGENCY,EXIT,ADMIT] (h: Hospital) : noexit :=
   PRESENT ?p:Patient !(present(h,p)); HOSPITAL[σ] (h)
[] EMERGENCY ?p:Patient; HOSPITAL[σ] (emergency(h,p))
[] [c-notFull(h)]→ADMIT ?p:Patient; HOSPITAL[σ] (admit(h,p))
[] [c-notEmpty(h)]→EXIT !first(h); HOSPITAL[σ] (cure(h))
endproc
```

of the signature (cf. [23] for the automatic processing description). Indeed, the operation names and profile are retrieved from the communications typing, and from the different conditions found while building the automaton. A few additional operations may be needed to express some axioms. Most of the axioms[5] are written in a "constructive style" which requires to identify the generators. [1] develops a method for retrieving a data type associated to an automaton and to compute a minimal set of operations needed to reach all its states. In our example this set is {init, admit, emergency}. The GAT method developed in [1] uses the Ω-derivation [4] to write the axioms (conditional equations). To extract the axioms describing the properties of an operation op(h:Hospital), the states where op is possible are searched together with the generators reaching these states which leads to the left hand sides of the equations. The premises of the axioms are built from the features of the generators associated edges: (i) the edges source state characteristic function, and (ii) the edges condition. Then, an axiom is generated for each transition associated to the operation op in a given state. An additional premise may be generated whenever there is a guard on this transition. The specifier has to provide the right hand side terms when the premises are proved to be satisfiable.

---

[4] σ denotes the process gates, here: PRESENT,EMERGENCY,EXIT,ADMIT.
[5] except the formulas expressing the relationships between the conditions

We show here a part of the extraction process for the axioms of the `cure` operation that is associated with EXIT. This operation is possible in the states: `InterEmer`, `FullEmer`, `InterNoEmer`, `FullNoEmer`. Let us consider the state `FullEmer`. There are two EXIT edges in this state with respectively guards [2] and [5] and three generator edges (**ADMIT** and **EMERGENCY** in Fig. 4). We should get 3×2 axioms but some premises are not satisfiable, hence we get the following 4 axioms:

```
% AXIOM 1:  "InterEmer" + [7] admit + [2]
(interEmer(h) /\ cNextFull(h) /\ ~cOnlyOneEmergency(admit(h, p))) =>
          cure(admit(h, p)) = admit(cure(h), p);
% AXIOM 2: "InterEmer" + [7] admit + [5]
(interEmer(h) /\ cNextFull(h) /\ cOnlyOneEmergency(admit(h, p))) =>
          cure(admit(h, p)) = admit(cure(h), p);
% AXIOM 3: "FullEmer" + loop emergency + [2]
(fullEmer(h) /\ ~cOnlyOneEmergency(emergency(h, p))) =>
          cure(emergency(h, p)) = emergency(cure(h), p);
% NO AXIOM: "FullEmer" + loop emergency + [5] : not possible
% (fullEmer(h) /\ cOnlyOneEmergency(emergency(h, p)))
% NO AXIOM: "FullNoEmer" + vertical emergency + [2] : not possible
% (fullNoEmer(h) /\ ~cOnlyOneEmergency(emergency(h, p)))
% AXIOM 4: "FullNoEmer" + vertical emergency + [5]
(fullNoEmer(h) /\ cOnlyOneEmergency(emergency(h, p))) =>
          cure(emergency(h, p)) = h;
```

Once the algebraic specification is written, it may be used to prove properties that are useful to validate and verify the specification (e.g. we processed our example using LP [12] which could compute a canonical rewriting system from our axioms).

5   Conclusion

While there are good motivations for the use of formal specifications in software development, the lack of methods may restrict it to few "experts". In this paper, we address a specification method for systems where both concurrency and data types issues have to be addressed. Our method takes advantage of both the constraint and state oriented approaches that are used for LOTOS specification. The first step is the informal description of the problem to be solved with a focus on the expected services. The system is then described in terms of parallel components with well defined external interfaces (the gates and communications typing). The behaviour of the components is described by sequential processes that are associated with data types. The study of the communications and their effect on the associated data type allows one to build, in a semi-automatic way, an automaton describing the process internal behaviour. This approach is particularly appropriate for systems where communication conditions depend on the processes data. The automaton is then translated into the specification language LOTOS, for both the dynamic and the static part. So our method permits one to split processes in an easy way and to have data types that are consistent with the sequential processes at once. Note this allows the specifier to use both tools to check properties on the automaton (model checking or bisimulations e.g. [2]) and theorem provers available for algebraic specifications (e.g. LP [12]).

As in the "agendas" described by [13], our method clearly establishes for each step what is to be achieved, and what are the pieces of information to be provided and then how they can be automatically used to save part of the work the specifier has to do.

While we present our method in detail when applied to LOTOS specification, it is clear that it may be applied to other formalisms. Work on SDL [8], Estelle [16] and Object-Z [24] has been done [22] or is under study.

Our method as been used on small size examples (as a transit node [22]) but still has to be tested on industrial size case-studies.

Acknowledgements: We would like to thank our referees for their careful reading and interesting remarks.

References

1. Pascal Andr and Jean-Claude Royer.   How To Easily Extract an Abstract Data Type From a Dynamic Description.   Research Report 159, Institut de Recherche en Informatique de Nantes, September 1997. http://www.sciences.univ-nantes.fr/info/perso/permanents/andre/PUBLI/rr159.ps.gz.

2. Andr Arnold. *Systmes de transitions finis et smantique des processus communicants*. Etudes et recherches en informatique. Masson, 1992.

3. E. Astesiano and G. Reggio. Formalism and method. In M. Bidoit and M. Dauchet, editors, *TAPSOFT'97*, volume 1214 of *Lecture Notes in Computer Science*, pages 93–114. Springer-Verlag, 1997.

4. Michel Bidoit. Types abstraits algbriques : spcifications structures et prsentations gracieuses. In *Colloque AFCET, Les mathmatiques de l'informatique*, pages 347–357, Mars 1982.

5. Tommaso Bolognesi and Ed Brinksma. Introduction to the ISO Specification Language LOTOS. *Computer Networks and ISDN Systems*, 14(1):25–29, January 1988.

6. R.G. Clark. Using LOTOS in the Object-Based Development of Embedded Systems. In C.M.I. Rattray and R.G. Clark, editors, *The Unified Computation Laboratory*, pages 307–319, Department of Computing Science and Mathematics, University of Stirling, Scotland, 1992. Oxford University Press.

7. H. Ehrig and B. Mahr. *Fundamentals of Algebraic Specification*, volume 1. Springer-Verlag, Berlin, 1985.

8. Jan Ellsberger, Dieter Hogrefe, and Amardeo Sarma. *SDL : Formal Object-oriented Language for Communicating Systems*. Prentice-Hall, 1997.

9. Hubert Garavel. *Compilation et vrification de programmes LOTOS*. Thse de doctorat (PhD Thesis), Universit Joseph Fourier, Grenoble, Novembre 1989.

10. Hubert Garavel. Introduction au langage LOTOS. Technical report, VERILOG, Centre d'Etudes Rhne-Alpes, Forum du Pr Milliet, Montbonnot, 38330 Saint-Ismier, 1990.

11. Hubert Garavel and Carlos Rodriguez. An example of LOTOS Specification : The Matrix Switch Problem. Rapport SPECTRE C22, Laboratoire de Gnie Informatique — Institut IMAG, Grenoble, June 1990. http://www.inrialpes.fr/vasy/Publications/Garavel-Rodriguez-90.html.

12. Stephan Garland and John Guttag. An overview of LP, the Larch Prover. In *Proc. of the Third International Conference on Rewriting Techniques and Applications*, volume 355 of *Lecture Notes in Computer Science*, pages 137–151. Springer-Verlag, 1989.

13. Wolfgang Grieskamp, Maritta Heisel, and Heiko Dörr. Specifying Embedded Systems with Statecharts and Z: An Agenda for Cyclic Software Components. In Egidio Astesiano, editor, *FASE'98*, volume 1382 of *Lecture Notes in Computer Science*, pages 88–106. Springer-Verlag, 1998.

14. Maritta Heisel and Nicole Lvy. Using LOTOS Patterns to Characterize Architectural Styles. In Michel Bidoit and Max Dauchet, editors, *TAPSOFT'97 (FASE'97)*, volume 1214 of *Lecture Notes in Computer Science*, pages 818–832, 1997.

15. C.A.R. Hoare. Communicating Sequential Processes. *Communications of the ACM*, 21(8):666–677, August 1978.

16. ISO/IEC. ESTELLE: A Formal Description Technique based on an Extended State Transition Model. ISO/IEC 9074, International Organization for Standardization, 1989.

17. ISO/IEC. LOTOS: A Formal Description Technique based on the Temporal Ordering of Observational Behaviour. ISO/IEC 8807, International Organization for Standardization, 1989.

18. Thomas Lambolais, Nicole Lvy, and Jeanine Souquires. Assistance au dveloppement de spcifications de protocoles de communication. In *AFADL'97 Approches Formelles dans l'Assistance au Dveloppement de Logiciel*, pages 73–84, 1997.

19. G. J. Leduc. LOTOS, un outil utile ou un autre langage acadmique ? In *Actes des Neuvimes Journes Francophones sur l'Informatique — Les rseaux de communication — Nouveaux outils et tendances actuelles (Lige)*, Janvier 1987.

20. L. Logrippo, M. Faci, and M. Haj-Hussein. An Introduction to LOTOS: Learning by Examples. *Computer Networks and ISDN Systems*, 23:325–342, 1992. improved version available by ftp at lotos.csi.uottawa.ca.

21. Robin Milner. *A Calculus of Communicating Systems*, volume 92 of *Lecture Notes in Computer Science*. Springer-Verlag, Berlin, 1980.

22. Pascal Poizat, Christine Choppy, and Jean-Claude Royer. Un support mthodologique pour la spcification de systmes "mixtes". Rapport de Recherche 180, Institut de Recherche en Informatique de Nantes, Novembre 1998. http://www.sciences.univ-nantes.fr/info/perso/permanents/poizat/papers/rr180.ps.gz.

23. Pascal Poizat, Christine Choppy, and Jean-Claude Royer. Une nouvelle mthode pour la spcification en LOTOS. Rapport de Recherche 170, Institut de Recherche en Informatique de Nantes, Fvrier 1998. http://www.sciences.univ-nantes.fr/info/perso/permanents/poizat/papers/rr170.ps.gz.

24. Graeme Smith. A Fully-Abstract Semantics of Classes for Object-Z. *Formal Aspects of Computing*, 3(1), 1993.

25. K. Turner. Relating architecture and specification. *Computer Networks and ISDN Systems*, 29(4):437–456, 1997.

26. Kenneth J. Turner, editor. *Using Formal Description Techniques, an introduction to Estelle, Lotos and SDL*. Wiley, 1993.

27. C.A. Vissers, G. Scollo, M. Van Sinderen, and E. Brinksma. Specification styles in distributed systems design and verification. *Theoretical Computer Science*, (89):179–206, 1991.

The Situation and State Calculus versus Branching Temporal Logic [*]

Jaime Ramos and Amílcar Sernadas

Department of Mathematics, IST, Lisbon, Portugal

Abstract. The situation calculus (SC) is a formalism for reasoning about action. Within SC, the notion of state of a given situation is usually characterized by the set of fluents that hold in that situation. However, this concept is insufficient for system specification. To overcome this limitation, an extension of SC is proposed, the situation and state calculus (SSC), where the concept of state is primitive, just like actions, situations and fluents. SSC is then compared with a branching temporal logic (BTL). A representation of BTL in SSC is defined and shown to establish a sound and complete encoding.

1 Introduction

The situation calculus (SC) is a specialization of many-sorted first order logic with equality (MFOL). It was first proposed in [8] as "a formalism for specifying dynamic systems". Through the years several refinements and extensions have been proposed to allow SC to cope with problems like temporal reasoning, concurrency, actions with duration *inter alia* [6,4,13,10,11].

The main concepts of SC are situations, actions and fluents. A situation represents the "state" of the system that we are specifying. The system changes from one situation to another when an action is performed. The properties of the system are characterized by fluents, that may or may not hold at a given situation. Hence, there are three basic sorts in the language: *sit* for situations, *act* for actions, and *flt* for fluents (there might be other sorts, depending on the system we are specifying). There is a constant symbol of sort *sit*, S_0, denoting the initial situation. There is a function symbol, *do*, from actions and situations to situations. There are also two predicate symbols *holds* and *poss*. The predicate symbol *holds* is used to relate fluents and situations, i.e., to define when a fluent is true (or false) at a given situation. The predicate symbol *poss* relates actions and situations, i.e., defines when an action is *enabled* at a given situation. So,

[*] We would like to thank our colleagues in the ASPIRE project, and also to Alberto Zanardo, Cristina Sernadas and Javier Pinto their valuable comments and suggestions at some stages of this work. This work was partially supported by FCT, the PRAXIS XXI Projects 2/2.1/MAT/262/94 SitCalc, PCEX/P/MAT/46/96 ACL, 2/2.1/TIT/1658/95 LogComp, the ProbLog initiative of CMA, as well as the ESPRIT IV Working Groups 22704 ASPIRE and 23531 FIREworks.

J.L. Fiadeiro (Ed.): WADT'98, LNCS 1589, pp. 293–309, 1999.
© Springer-Verlag Berlin Heidelberg 1999

we may write the following sentences:

$$\forall x, s \; poss(drop(x), s) \rightarrow holds(onFloor(x), do(drop(x), s)) \tag{1}$$

$$\forall x, s \; poss(drop(x), s) \leftrightarrow holds(onHand(x), s) \tag{2}$$

In the previous sentences, *drop* is an action symbol (with one parameter), while *onHand* and *onFloor* are fluent symbols (with one parameter). The term *do(drop(x),s)* (of sort situation) denotes the situation resulting from doing action *drop(x)* in situation *s*. The sentence (1) can be understood as "if it is possible to drop an object x then, after dropping x, x will be on the floor". Sentence (2) can be regarded as meaning "an object may only be dropped when it is being held".

In [13,14] the situation calculus is axiomatized in a style similar to the Peano foundational axioms for number theory. The initial situation S_0 plays the role of the number 0. And instead of a single successor function, there is a family of successor functions $do(a, \_)$, one for each action term a. There is also a binary relation on situations, $\prec$, where $s \prec s'$ stands for s' can be obtained from s by a sequence of possible actions. The axioms, called *foundational axioms*, are:

$$\forall a, s \; S_0 \neq do(a, s) \tag{3}$$

$$\forall a_1, a_2, s_1, s_2 \; (do(a_1, s_1) = do(a_2, s_2) \rightarrow (a_1 = a_2 \wedge s_1 = s_2)) \tag{4}$$

$$\forall s \; (\neg s \prec S_0) \tag{5}$$

$$\forall a, s_1, s_2 \; ((s_1 \prec do(a, s_2)) \leftrightarrow (s_1 \preceq s_2 \wedge poss(a, s_2))) \tag{6}$$

$$\varphi_{S_0}^s \rightarrow ((\forall a, s \; (\varphi \rightarrow \varphi_{do(a,s)}^s)) \rightarrow (\forall s \; \varphi)) \tag{7}$$

where $s \preceq s'$ stands for $s \prec s' \vee s = s'$. These axioms establish an order on situations with a tree structure rooted at S_0. For a detailed discussion see [13,14]. When this axiomatization was first proposed, the main goal was to find a monotonic solution to problems like the frame problem, the ramification problem, etc. It is not our intention to study these problems here. Instead, we are going to use this axiomatization with a different purpose. It is interesting to observe that we can interpret $s \prec s'$ as "the system reached s' *after* s", i.e., we can recognize a *temporal component* in the situations. This fact was already used in [11] to compare SC with linear temporal logic. Here, we propose a comparison of the SC with a branching temporal logic.

However, using this axiomatization bears a price. In section 2, we discuss some problems that arise with this axiomatization of SC. Still in this section, we propose a solution to overcome these problems, the situation and state calculus (SSC). In section 3, SSC is compared with a branching temporal logic (BTL). This comparison is achieved via a map between the underlying *logical structures* [9] (see the appendix for a definition of logical structure and of map). In order to define this map, we have to extend SSC with the ability to refer to the lines of the branching structure of situations. We end with a completeness result for this comparison.

2   The situation and state calculus

In this section we discuss a problem that arises when we consider SC axiomatized with the foundational axioms. We propose a solution to overcome this problem, by extending SC with a new concept: the *state*. We call this extension *the situation and state calculus* (SSC). A preliminary version of SSC was presented in [12].

It is usual to define the state of a system at a given situation as the set of fluents that hold in that given situation. Thus, two situations have the same state when the set of fluents that hold is the same for both situations, i.e.,

$$samesState(s, s') \leftrightarrow (\forall f\, holds(f, s) \leftrightarrow holds(f, s')) \tag{8}$$

If we adopt this notion of state we face one major problem: *the non-determinacy of actions*. Consider for instance a *stack* of natural numbers, with only one fluent *top* of sort *nat*, one action *push* with one parameter of sort *nat*, and one action *pop* with no parameters. Let s be a (term of sort) situation, and let $s_1 = do(push(5), s)$ and $s_2 = do(push(4), s)$. Clearly, these situations do not have the same state, since the only fluent that holds in s_1 is $top(5)$ and in s_2 is $top(4)$. Consider now the situations $s_3 = do(push(3), s_1)$ and $s_4 = do(push(3), s_2)$. In this case, according to (8), s_3 and s_4 have the same state since $top(3)$ is the only (term of sort) fluent that holds in both these situations. Finally, consider the situations $s_5 = do(pop, s_3)$ and $s_6 = do(pop, s_4)$. If the stack behaves as expected, we would have $samesState(s_1, s_5)$ and $samesState(s_2, s_6)$. But this means that we had two situations with the same state (s_3 and s_4), performed the same action (pop) on these two situations and got two situations (s_5 and s_6) that do not have the same state!

Furthermore, we are unable to specify the stack, without using some auxiliary fluents. For instance, we are unable to express that "*after a push and a pop we are back at the same state*". One attempt would be to write

$$\forall n, s\ do(pop, do(push(n), s)) = s. \tag{9}$$

However, this formula clearly contradicts the foundational axioms. Obviously, we could drop some of the foundational axioms, thus making (9) a legal sentence. But as we said before, we want situations to have a temporal flavor. So, the solution is to introduce the concept of state in the language, like situations, actions and fluents.

2.1   Syntax

We define the syntax of SSC as a specialization of the syntax of MFOL. We start by defining the *set of basic sorts*, G_{bs}, composed of the sorts *sit* for situations, *act* for actions, *flt* for fluents and *stt* for states. There might be other sorts (e.g. data-types).

Definition 1. *An* SSC *signature is an MFOL signature* $\Sigma = \langle G, F, P, X \rangle$ *such that: (i)* $G_{bs} \subseteq G$; *(ii)* F *is such that* $F_{\epsilon, sit} = \{S_0\}$; $F_{act\ sit, sit} = \{do\}$; $F_{sit, stt} = \{[\_]\}$; $F_{w,s} = \emptyset$ *if* s *is* sit *or* stt, *or if* w *contains an element of* G_{bs}; *(iii)* P *is such that* $P_{flt\ stt} = \{holds\}$; $P_{act\ stt} = \{poss\}$; $P_{sit\ sit} = \{\prec\}$; $P_w = \emptyset$ *if* w *contains an element of* G_{bs}; *(iv)* X *is a* G-*indexed family of disjoint sets.*

Given an SSC signature $\langle G, F, P, X \rangle$, each element $a \in F_{w,act}$ is said to be an *action symbol* with parameters sort w, and each element $f \in F_{w,flt}$ is said to a *fluent symbol* with parameters sort w. In comparison with SC, there is a new function symbol $[\_]$. This function symbol associates a state to each situation. There is also a fixed action symbol *nil* that is present for technical reasons, that will become clear later. Each element of X_g is said to be a variable of sort g. We denote variables of sort *sit* by $s, s', s_1, \ldots$, variables of sort *act* by $a, a', a_1, \ldots$, variables of sort *flt* by $f, f', f_1, \ldots$, and variables of sort *stt* by $u, u', u_1, \ldots$. Note that now the predicate symbols *holds* and *poss* depend on the states and not on the situations.

Example 1 (Stack). We can define the following signature for a stack of natural number: $\Sigma = \langle G, F, P, X \rangle$ where $nat \in G$, $F_{\epsilon, flt} = \{top\}$, $F_{\epsilon, act} = \{nil, pop, reset\}$, $F_{nat, act} = \{push\}$.

We define signature morphisms in the usual way with the proviso that they must preserve the basic sorts. Signatures and signature morphisms constitute a category, Sig^{ssc}, which is a subcategory of Sig^{mfol}. Let $\mathcal{I} : Sig^{ssc} \hookrightarrow Sig^{mfol}$ be the inclusion functor. The functor $Sen^{ssc} : Sig^{ssc} \to Set$ is defined by $Sen^{mfol} \circ \mathcal{I}$. As in first order logic, we call each element of $Sen^{ssc}(\Sigma)$ a Σ-formula. We denote by $T_{\Sigma,g}$ the set of terms of sort g defined over Σ. From now on we assume given an SSC signature Σ.

2.2 Derivation relation

In this section we introduce the derivation relation for SSC. We start by presenting the foundational axioms. The formula (6) has to be slightly changed because in SSC the predicate symbol *poss* depends on states and not on situations.

Definition 2. *The* set of foundational axioms *for* Σ, $Ax(\mathcal{F})_\Sigma$, *contains the formulas:*

1. $\forall a, s\ S_0 \neq do(a, s)$;
2. $\forall a_1, a_2, s_1, s_2\ (do(a_1, s_1) = do(a_2, s_2) \to (a_1 = a_2 \wedge s_1 = s_2))$;
3. $\forall s\ (\neg s \prec S_0)$;
4. $\forall a, s, s'\ (s \prec do(a, s') \leftrightarrow (poss(a, [s']) \wedge s \preceq s'))$;
5. $\varphi_{S_0}^s \to ((\forall a, s\ (\varphi \to \varphi_{do(a,s)}^s)) \to (\forall s\ \varphi))$ *for every* Σ-*formula* φ.

Now we have to introduce axioms for the new objects in the language. We want to ensure that there are no *junk* states, i.e., a state is always the state of some situation. We also want to guarantee that we have *determinacy of actions*.

Definition 3. *The set of state axioms for Σ, $Ax(\mathcal{S})_\Sigma$, contains the formulas:*

1. $\forall a, s_1, s_2\ ([s_1] = [s_2] \rightarrow [do(a, s_1)] = [do(a, s_2)])$;
2. $\forall u\ \exists s\ u = [s]$.

These axioms characterize the states as "*equivalence classes*" of situations, i.e., a state is the (equivalence) class of all situations that have the same *properties*. These properties are more than just the set of fluents that hold in those situations.

Definition 4. *The set of axioms about nil for Σ, $Ax(\mathcal{N})_\Sigma$, contains the formulas:*

- $\forall u\ poss(nil, u)$
- $\forall s\ [do(nil, s)] = [s]$

Having introduced these axioms, we can define the derivation relation for SSC. For each signature Σ, the derivation relation $\vdash_\Sigma^{ssc}$ will be defined based on the derivation relation for the same signature in MFOL, $\vdash_\Sigma^{mfol}$, adding the foundational axioms, the axioms about *nil* and the state axioms as axioms of the deductive system.

Definition 5. *Let Γ be a set of Σ-formulas. We define the set of derived formulas from Γ as follows:*

$$\Gamma^{\vdash_\Sigma^{ssc}} = (\Gamma \cup Ax(\mathcal{F})_\Sigma \cup Ax(\mathcal{S})_\Sigma \cup Ax(\mathcal{N})_\Sigma)^{\vdash_\Sigma^{fol}}.$$

For each Σ, we define $\vdash_\Sigma^{ssc} \subseteq 2^{Sen^{ssc}(\Sigma)} \times Sen^{ssc}(\Sigma)$ as follows: $\Gamma \vdash_\Sigma^{ssc} \varphi$ iff $\varphi \in \Gamma^{\vdash_\Sigma^{ssc}}$.

With this notion of state, we are now in a position to write some formulas about a stack, like for instance (9).

Example 2 (Stack). Consider the signature for the stack. We can write the following Σ-formulas:

1. $\forall s\ [do(reset, s)] = [S_0]$
2. $\forall s, n\ [do(pop, do(push(n), s))] = [s]$
3. $\forall s, n, m\ holds(top(n), [do(push(m), s)]) \rightarrow n = m$
4. $\forall u\ poss(pop, u) \leftrightarrow u \neq [S_0]$
5. $\forall u, n, m\ (holds(top(n), u) \wedge holds(top(m), u)) \rightarrow n = m$

If we look at an equational specification of stack (e.g. [2]), we can observe some similarities, although here we are specifying the *behavior* of the stack and not the stack as a *data type*.

Within the *stack* example, consider two situations s_1 and s_2 such that $[s_1] \neq [s_2]$. And let $s_3 = do(push(3), s_1)$, $s_4 = do(push(3), s_2)$, $s_5 = do(pop, s_3)$ and $s_6 = do(pop, s_4)$, like before. Using axiom (2) of the stack, we derive $[s_1] = [s_5]$ and $[s_2] = [s_6]$. Hence, since $[s_1] \neq [s_2]$, then $[s_5] \neq [s_6]$. Using state axiom (1), we derive $[s_3] \neq [s_4]$. However, the only fluent that holds in both states $[s_3]$ and $[s_4]$ is $top(3)$.

2.3   Semantics

In this section we introduce the semantics of SSC. In this case however, we cannot define the SSC interpretation structures as we did for the sentences, i.e., we cannot define $Int^{ssc} : Sig^{ssc^{op}} \to Cls$ as $Int^{mfol} \circ \mathcal{I}^{op}$. From these interpretation structures, for each signature Σ, we choose the ones that satisfy all the foundational axioms for Σ, $Ax(\mathcal{F})_{\Sigma}$, all the state axioms for Σ, $Ax(\mathcal{S})_{\Sigma}$, and all the axioms about nil, $Ax(\mathcal{N})_{\Sigma}$.

Definition 6. *We define $Int^{ssc}(\Sigma)$ as the class of all interpretation structures $I \in Int^{mfol} \circ \mathcal{I}^{op}(\Sigma)$ such that:*

- *I satisfies all the foundational axioms for Σ, $Ax(\mathcal{F})_{\Sigma}$;*
- *I satisfies all the state axioms for Σ, $Ax(\mathcal{S})_{\Sigma}$;*
- *I satisfies all the axioms about nil for Σ, $Ax(\mathcal{N})_{\Sigma}$.*

For each signature morphism $\sigma : \Sigma \to \Sigma'$, $Int^{ssc}(\sigma)$ is the restriction of $Int^{mfol}(\sigma)$ to $Int^{ssc}(\Sigma')$.

Given an SSC interpretation structure for Σ, $I = \langle D, \_^F, \_^P \rangle$, we denote by o^F the interpretation of the operation symbol o in I, and by p^P the interpretation of the predicate symbol p in I (omitting any explicit reference to the arity of the symbols).

It is easy to check that Int^{ssc} is still a functor. In what follows, we are going to need the notion of *standard interpretation structure*. This concept is closely related with the notion of standard interpretation structure in number theory.

Definition 7. *An SSC interpretation structure $I = \langle D, \_^F, \_^P \rangle$ is called a standard interpretation structure when:*

- *D_{sit} is inductively defined as follows:*
    - *$S_0 \in D_{sit}$*
    - *$do(a, s) \in D_{sit}$, provided that $s \in D_{sit}$ and $a \in D_{act}$;*
- *$S_0^F = S_0$*
- *$do^F = \lambda a s. do(a, s)$*
- *$\prec^P$ is the transitive closure of $\{(s, do^F(a, s)) : s \in D_{sit}, a \in D_{act}, poss^P(a, [s]^F)\}$*

Any interpretation structure isomorphic to a standard interpretation structure will also be called standard.

2.4   Satisfaction relation

Like for the derivation relation, for each SSC signature, we define the satisfaction relation for SSC based on the satisfaction relation for MFOL.

Definition 8. *We define the satisfaction relation $\models_{\Sigma}^{ssc} \subseteq Int^{ssc}(\Sigma) \times Sen^{ssc}(\Sigma)$ as $I \models_{\Sigma}^{ssc} \varphi$ iff $I \models_{\Sigma}^{mfol} \varphi$*

2.5 Logical structure

Based on the previous definitions we can put together the logical structure for SSC.

Proposition 1. *The tuple* $\mathcal{L}_{ssc} = \langle Sig^{ssc}, Sen^{ssc}, Int^{ssc}, \models^{ssc}, \vdash^{ssc} \rangle$ *is a logical structure.*

This logical structure is obviously *sound*, i.e., if $\Gamma \vdash^{ssc}_{\Sigma} \varphi$ then $\Gamma \models^{ssc}_{\Sigma} \varphi$, and is also *complete*, i.e., if $\Gamma \models^{ssc}_{\Sigma} \varphi$ then $\Gamma \vdash^{ssc}_{\Sigma} \varphi$. The proof of this results as well as the fact that $\mathcal{L}_{ssc}$ is indeed a logical structure is straightforward.

3 SSC versus BTL

In this section we compare the situation and state calculus with a branching temporal logic (BTL). This comparison will be established via a map between the underlying logical structures [9]. In order to define this map we have to establish a relation between the two logical structures at the syntactical level (signatures and formulas), and at the semantic level (interpretation structures). This is closely related to van Benthem's *Correspondence Theory*, which studies connections between modal and classical logics [18].

We start by presenting the logical structure for the intended branching temporal logic. Then we extended SSC with the ability to refer to the *lines* of the tree of situations as objects of the language. And finally we define a map between the two logical structures and study some of its properties.

3.1 Branching temporal logic

In this section we present a logical structure for BTL. All the definitions and results are taken from [17].

A BTL signature is just a set of propositional symbols. Hence, Sig^{btl} is *Set*. For each BTL signature the set of Σ-formulas, L_{Σ}, is inductively defined as follows:

- $p \in L_{\Sigma}$ provided that $p \in \Sigma$;
- $(\neg\varphi) \in L_{\Sigma}$ provided that $\varphi \in L_{\Sigma}$;
- $(\varphi \rightarrow \psi) \in L_{\Sigma}$ provided that $\varphi, \psi \in L_{\Sigma}$;
- $(\varphi \cup \psi) \in L_{\Sigma}$ provided that $\varphi, \psi \in L_{\Sigma}$;
- $(A\varphi) \in L_{\Sigma}$ provided that $\varphi \in L_{\Sigma}$;

Then, the functor Sen^{btl} can be defined in the usual way, i.e., for each signature Σ, $Sen^{btl}(\Sigma) = L_{\Sigma}$, and for each signature morphism $\sigma : \Sigma \rightarrow \Sigma'$, $Sen^{btl}(\sigma)$ is defined by $Sen^{btl}(\sigma)(p) = \sigma(p)$ for all $p \in \Sigma$, and is structural for all the other formulas. We assume as given the usual abbreviations: the logic connectives $\vee$, $\wedge$, $\leftrightarrow$, the temporal operators X (*next*), F (*sometime in the future*), G (*always in the future*), and the path operator E (*exists a path*). [1]

---

[1] The operators A and E are sometimes represented by $\forall$ and $\exists$. However, we adopted A and E to avoid confusion with the first order quantifiers.

An interpretation structure for a given a signature Σ is a tuple $M = \langle\langle T, P\rangle, V\rangle$ where:

- $T = \langle W, R\rangle$ is a *total* transition system, i.e., for every $w \in W$ there is $w' \in W$ such that $(w, w') \in R$;
- P is a non-empty set of *infinite paths* (also called *runs*) over T such that every $w \in W$ occurs in some path $\pi \in P$ (where a path is a map $\pi : \mathbb{N}_o \to W$ such that $(\pi(n), \pi(n+1)) \in R$);
- $V : \Sigma \to 2^W$.

We denote by $\pi(n)$ the n-th position of the path π. The functor $Int^{btl} : Sig^{btl^{op}} \to Cls$ is such that, for each signature Σ, $Int^{btl}(\Sigma)$ is the class of all interpretation structures for Σ, and for each signature morphism $\sigma : \Sigma \to \Sigma'$, $Int^{btl}(\sigma) : Int^{btl}(\Sigma') \to Int^{btl}(\Sigma)$ is defined by $Int^{btl}(\sigma)(\langle\langle T', P'\rangle, V'\rangle) = \langle\langle T', P'\rangle, V\rangle$ where $V(p) = V'(\sigma(p))$ for every $p \in \Sigma$.

The satisfaction of a formula by a given interpretation structure $M = \langle\langle T, P\rangle, V\rangle$ at index $n \in \mathbb{N}_o$ of path $\pi \in P$ is inductively defined as follows:

- $M, \pi, n \models^{btl}_\Sigma p$ iff $\pi(n) \in V(p)$
- $M, \pi, n \models^{btl}_\Sigma (\neg\varphi)$ iff $M, \pi, n \not\models^{btl}_\Sigma \varphi$
- $M, \pi, n \models^{btl}_\Sigma (\varphi \to \psi)$ iff $M, \pi, n \not\models^{btl}_\Sigma \varphi$ or $M, \pi, n \models^{btl}_\Sigma \psi$
- $M, \pi, n \models^{btl}_\Sigma (\varphi \cup \psi)$ iff there is $m > n$ such that $M, \pi, m \models^{btl}_\Sigma \psi$ and for all k such that $n < k < m$, $M, \pi, k \models^{btl}_\Sigma \varphi$
- $M, \pi, n \models^{btl}_\Sigma (A\varphi)$ iff for all $\pi' \in P$ such that $\pi(n) = \pi'(n)$, $M, \pi', n \models^{btl}_\Sigma \varphi$

A formula φ is *M-true*, $M \models^{btl}_\Sigma \varphi$, if for all π and i we have $M, \pi, i \models^{btl}_\Sigma \varphi$.

An axiomatization for this logic is proposed in [17]. We are not going to detail it here, but rather use the fact that such an axiomatization exists and denote by $\Gamma \vdash^{btl}_\Sigma \varphi$ the fact that the formula φ can be derived from Γ using the proposed consequence relation.

So, we can define a logical structure for BTL:

$$\mathcal{L}_{btl} = \langle Sig^{btl}, Sen^{btl}, Int^{btl}, \models^{btl}, \vdash^{btl}\rangle$$

This logical structure is *sound* and *(weakly) complete* [17].

In what follows we are going to need some notation and technical results. Let π be a path over a transition system and $n \in \mathbb{N}_o$. We denote by π^n the suffix of π starting at n, i.e., satisfying the condition $\pi^n(k) = \pi(n+k)$, for every $k \in \mathbb{N}_o$. Let $M = \langle\langle W, R, P\rangle, V\rangle$ be a BTL interpretation structure (for a given signature Σ), and consider $\pi \in P$ and $n \in \mathbb{N}_o$. Define the set $P^{\pi,n} = \{\eta^n : \eta \in P \text{ and } \pi(n) = \eta(n)\}$, and using this set, define the BTL interpretation structure $M^{\pi,n} = \langle\langle W^{\pi,n}, R^{\pi,n}, P^{\pi,n}\rangle, V^{\pi,n}\rangle$ such that:

- $W^{\pi,n} = \{w \in W : w \text{ occurs in some } \eta \in P^{\pi,n}\}$
- $R^{\pi,n} = R \cap (W^{\pi,n} \times W^{\pi,n})$
- $V^{\pi,n}(p) = V(p) \cap W^{\pi,n}$.

Then, $M, \pi, n \models^{btl}_\Sigma \varphi$ iff $M^{\pi,n}, \pi^n, 0 \models^{btl}_\Sigma \varphi$. This result is a particular case of the *Generation Theorem* [18].

3.2 Branching situation and state calculus

Like BTL, SSC has an underlying branching structure. The main idea when comparing these two logics is to use the *temporal component* of situations as time instants, and the *lines* over the tree of situations as the paths of BTL. However, to do this we need to be able to refer to lines as objects of the language. So, we need to extend SSC with the ability to refer to lines. We call this extension, *branching situation and state calculus* (BSSC).

The first step is to put the lines in the language. So we introduce a new sort, *lin*, for lines. Furthermore, we need to be able to relate lines with situations, i.e., we need to be able to express which situations occur in a line. For this, we introduce a new predicate symbol *in*, with two arguments, a situation and a line.

Definition 9. *A BSSC signature is an SSC signature* $\Sigma = \langle G, F, P, X \rangle$ *such that (i) lin $\in G$; (ii) $P_{sit\ lin} = \{in\}$; (iii) $F_{w,s} = \emptyset$, $P_w = \emptyset$ if w contains lin or $s = lin$. A BSSC signature morphism σ is an SSC signature morphism such that $\sigma_G(lin) = lin$. BSSC signatures and morphisms constitute a category Sig^{bssc}.*

Again, there is an inclusion functor from Sig^{bssc} into Sig^{ssc}, $\mathcal{J} : Sig^{bssc} \hookrightarrow Sig^{ssc}$, and so the functor $Sen^{bssc} : Sig^{bssc} \to Set$ is defined by $Sen^{ssc} \circ \mathcal{J}$. From now on we assume that Σ denotes a BSSC signature.

Having defined the language, we need to characterize lines in terms of situations. A similar idea was proposed in [11] to compare SC with linear temporal logic, where a predicate, *actual*, is defined to select a single line from the tree of situations.

Definition 10. *The set of line axioms for Σ, $Ax(\mathcal{L})_\Sigma$, contains the formulas:*

1. $\forall l\ in(S_0, l)$;
2. $\forall l, a, s\ in(do(a, s), l) \to (in(s, l) \wedge poss(a, [s]))$;
3. $\forall l, a_1, a_2, s\ (in(do(a_1, s), l) \wedge in(do(a_2, s), l)) \to a_1 = a_2$;
4. $\forall l, s\ in(s, l) \to (\exists a\ in(do(a, s), l))$;
5. $\forall s\ S_0 \prec s \to (\exists l\ in(s, l))$

The first axiom expresses the fact that every line passes through the initial situation. The second axiom expresses the fact that there are no *gaps* in a line. The third and fourth axioms impose that at each point of the line there is exactly one successor. The last axiom expresses that there are *enough* lines, i.e., there is at least one line passing through each (*reachable*) situation. These axioms are true in every interpretation structure whose domain for sort *lin* (D_{lin}) is a set of paths (over the tree of situations) fulfilling suitable closure conditions; in the literature on branching temporal logic these sets of paths are called *bundles* [1]. In [19,20] it is shown that there is no first order formula that is true in (exactly) all the interpretation structures in which D_{lin} is the set of *all* paths.

We define the derivation relation for BSSC, by adding the line axioms to the derivation relation of SSC.

Definition 11. *Let Γ be a set of Σ-formulas. We define the set of derived formulas from Γ as follows:*

$$\Gamma^{\vdash^{bssc}_{\Sigma}} = (\Gamma \cup Ax(\mathcal{L})_{\Sigma})^{\vdash^{ssc}_{\Sigma}}.$$

We define $\vdash^{bssc}_{\Sigma} \subseteq 2^{Sen^{bssc}(\Sigma)} \times Sen^{bssc}(\Sigma)$ as follows: $\Gamma \vdash^{bssc}_{\Sigma} \varphi$ iff $\varphi \in \Gamma^{\vdash^{bssc}_{\Sigma}}$

Definition 12. *We define $Int^{bssc}(\Sigma)$ as the class of all SSC interpretation structures $I \in Int^{ssc} \circ \mathcal{J}$ that satisfy all the line axioms for Σ, $Ax(\mathcal{L})_{\Sigma}$. For each signature morphism $\sigma : \Sigma \to \Sigma'$, $Int^{bssc}(\sigma)$ is the restriction of $Int^{ssc}(\sigma)$ to $Int^{bssc}(\Sigma')$.*

The (family of) satisfaction relation(s), $\models^{bssc}$, is defined as for SSC.

Proposition 2. *The tuple $\mathcal{L}_{bssc} = \langle Sig^{bssc}, Sen^{bssc}, Int^{bssc}, \vdash^{bssc}, \models^{bssc}\rangle$ is a logical structure.*

In what follows we consider only standard interpretation structures, i.e., from now on, $Int^{bssc}(\Sigma)$ denotes the class of all standard interpretation structures. These are defined as for SSC.

3.3   A map between BTL and BSSC

We are now going to define a map between $\mathcal{L}_{btl}$ and $\mathcal{L}_{bssc}$. The first step is to translate signatures. For this, we define a functor Ω between Sig^{btl} and Sig^{bssc}. We translate each propositional symbol to a fluent (with no parameters).

Definition 13. *We define the functor $\Omega : Sig^{btl} \to Sig^{bssc}$ as follows:*

- *for each $\Sigma \in |Sig^{btl}|$, $\Omega(\Sigma) = \langle G, F, P, X\rangle$ is such that $F^{bssc}_{\epsilon, flt} = \Sigma$;*
- *for each $\sigma : \Sigma \to \Sigma'$ in Sig^{btl}, $\Omega(\sigma)$ is such that $\Omega(\sigma)(p) = \sigma(p)$, for every $p \in \Sigma$.*

The next step is to translate formulas. For this we have to define a natural transformation α from Sen^{btl} to Sen^{bssc}. But first we need to define an auxiliary function $\overline{\alpha}_{\Sigma}$, for each signature Σ. The motivation for this function, is that it translates each BTL formula to a BSSC formula at a given line and a given situation, following the semantics of BTL formulas.

Definition 14. *The function $\overline{\alpha}_{\Sigma} : Sen^{btl}(\Sigma) \times T_{\Omega(\Sigma), lin} \times T_{\Omega(\Sigma), sit} \to Sen^{bssc}(\Omega(\Sigma))$ is inductively defined by:*

- $\overline{\alpha}_{\Sigma}(p, l, s) = holds(p, [s])$
- $\overline{\alpha}_{\Sigma}(\neg\varphi, l, s) = \neg\overline{\alpha}_{\Sigma}(\varphi, l, s)$
- $\overline{\alpha}_{\Sigma}(\varphi \to \psi, l, s) = \overline{\alpha}_{\Sigma}(\varphi, l, s) \to \overline{\alpha}_{\Sigma}(\psi, l, s)$
- $\overline{\alpha}_{\Sigma}(\varphi \cup \psi, l, s) = \exists s'\ s \prec s' \wedge in(s', l) \wedge \overline{\alpha}_{\Sigma}(\psi, l, s') \wedge \forall s''\ s \prec s'' \prec s' \to \overline{\alpha}_{\Sigma}(\varphi, l, s'')$
- $\overline{\alpha}_{\Sigma}((A\varphi), l, s) = \forall l'\ in(s, l') \to \overline{\alpha}_{\Sigma}(\varphi, l', s)$.

Having defined this function, we can now define the natural transformation α. Again, following the semantics of BTL, a formula is satisfied by an interpretation structure iff it is satisfied at all points of all lines.

Proposition 3. *We define the natural transformation* $\alpha : Sen^{btl} \to Sen^{bssc} \circ \Omega$ *as follows:*

$$\alpha_\Sigma(\varphi) = \forall l, s \ (in(s, l) \to \overline{\alpha}_\Sigma(\varphi, l, s))$$

Proof. To prove that α is indeed a natural transformation from Sen^{btl} to $Sen^{bssc} \circ \Omega$ it is sufficient to show that, for every signature morphism $\sigma : \Sigma \to \Sigma'$, Σ-formula φ, $l \in T_{\Sigma,lin}$, and $s \in T_{\Sigma,sit}$ the following condition holds:

$$(Sen^{bssc} \circ \Omega)(\sigma)(\overline{\alpha}_\Sigma(\varphi, l, s)) = \overline{\alpha}_{\Sigma'}(Sen^{btl}(\sigma)(\varphi), l, s).$$

This can be easily proven by induction on the structure of φ.   □

To prove that we are defining a map we need to show that α preserves theorems.

Lemma 1. *Let* $\{\varphi\} \cup \Gamma \subseteq Sen^{btl}(\Sigma)$. *Then* $\Gamma \vdash^{btl}_\Sigma \varphi$ *implies* $\alpha_\Sigma(\Gamma) \vdash^{bssc}_\Sigma \alpha_\Sigma(\varphi)$.

Proof. It is enough to show that the α translation of each of the BTL axioms is a BSSC theorem and that the rules are preserved by α. This is straightforward.   □

Finally, we define the natural transformation β, for translating BSSC interpretation structures into BTL interpretation structures. For each signature Σ, β_Σ assigns to each BSSC interpretation structure a BTL interpretation structure over the corresponding signature. We define the transition system taking as states the set of *reachable* situations and as transition relation the *immediate transition relation* induced by the *do* over these situations. The set of paths is defined in the usual way, choosing only the ones that correspond to lines.

Proposition 4. *We define the natural transformation* $\beta : Int^{bssc} \circ \Omega^{op} \to Int^{btl}$ *as follows: for each* $I \in Int^{bssc}(\Omega(\Sigma))$, $\beta_\Sigma(I) = \langle\langle W, R, P \rangle, V \rangle$ *where*

- $W = \{s \in D_{sit} : S_0^F \prec^P s\}$
- $R = \{(s, s') : s' = do^F(a, s), \text{ for some } a \in D_{act} \text{ such that } poss^P(a, [s]^F)\}$
- $P = \left\{ \pi : \mathbb{N}_o \to W \ \middle| \begin{array}{l} \pi(0) = S_0^F, (\pi(i), \pi(i+1)) \in R, \text{ and there is } d_l \in \\ D_{lin} \text{ such that } in^P(\pi(i), d_l), \text{ for every } i \in \mathbb{N}_o \end{array} \right\}$
- $V(p) = \{s \in W : holds^P(p, [s]^F)\}$

Proof. We have to show that for each Σ and I, $\beta_\Sigma(I)$ is in fact a BTL interpretation structure for Σ. But this an immediate consequence of I being a BSSC interpretation structure which ensures that the transition system is total (due to the axioms about *nil*) and P is in fact a set of paths over T satisfying the condition on paths (due to the line axioms). We also have to show that β is a natural transformation from $Int^{bssc} \circ \Omega^{op}$ to Int^{btl}. It is enough to show that, for each morphism $\sigma : \Sigma \to \Sigma'$ and BSSC interpretation structure, I', (for $\Omega(\Sigma')$) the following condition holds:

$$\beta_\Sigma(Int^{bssc} \circ \Omega^{op}(\sigma)(I')) = Int^{btl}(\sigma)(\beta_{\Sigma'}(I')).$$

$\square$

Having established this result, we now prove the second condition in the definition of map between logical structures. But before we have to prove some technical results. Let us start by introducing some notation. Given a BSSC interpretation structure I (and with $\beta_\Sigma(I) = \langle\langle T, P\rangle, V\rangle$), we define the relation $\doteq\,\subseteq P \times D_{lin}$ by $\pi \doteq d_l$ iff $in^P(\pi(n), d_l)$, for every $n \in N_o$.

Lemma 2. *Let I be a BSSC interpretation structure and $d_s \in D_{sit}$. Then, there are $n \in N_o$ and $d_{a_1}, \dots, d_{a_n} \in D_{act}$ such that $d_s = do^F(d_{a_1} \dots d_{a_n}, S_0^F)$.*

Proof. A simple induction on the structure of d_s, taking into account that I is a standard interpretation structure, and satisfies the line axiom (4). $\square$

Lemma 3. *Let I be a BSSC interpretation structure (with $\beta_\Sigma(I) = \langle\langle T, P\rangle, V\rangle$) and $d_l \in D_{lin}$. Then, there is $\pi \in P$ such that $\pi \doteq d_l$.*

Proof. Take π to be the following path:

- $\pi(0) = S_0^F$
- $\pi(n+1) = do^F(d_a, \pi(n))$, for every $n \in N_o$, where $d_a \in D_{act}$ results from I satisfying line axiom (4) (take the assignment v such that $v(s) = \pi(n)$ and $v(l) = d_l$).

Then, prove by induction on the length of π that $\pi \doteq d_l$. $\square$

Lemma 4. *Let φ be a Σ-formula, I a BSSC interpretation structure for $\Omega(\Sigma)$, $\pi \in P$, $n \in N_o$, and v an assignment such that $\pi \doteq v(l)$ and $v(s) = \pi(n)$. Then, the following condition holds:*

$$\beta_\Sigma(I), \pi, n \models_\Sigma^{btl} \varphi \text{ iff } I, v \models_{\Omega(\Sigma)}^{bssc} \overline{\alpha}_\Sigma(\varphi, l, s)$$

Proof. We prove this by induction on the structure of φ. We just sketch the proof for the base. Let $p \in \Sigma$. Then $\beta_\Sigma(I), \pi, n \models_\Sigma^{btl} p$ iff $\pi(n) \in V(p)$ iff $holds^P(p, [\pi(n)]^F)$ iff $I, v \models_{\Omega(\Sigma)}^{bssc} holds(p, [s])$ iff $I, v \models_{\Omega(\Sigma)}^{bssc} \overline{\alpha}_\Sigma(p, l, s)$. The cases of the logical connectives are an immediate consequence of the induction hypothesis. The proof for the temporal operator and for the path operator are a consequence of the induction hypothesis and lemmas 2 and 3, respectively. $\square$

Having all these results, we can now prove the second condition in the definition of map between logical structures.

Lemma 5. *Let $\varphi \in Sen^{btl}(\Sigma)$ and $I \in Int^{bssc}(\Omega(\Sigma))$. Then, $\beta_\Sigma(I) \models^{btl}_\Sigma \varphi$ iff $I \models^{bssc}_{\Omega(\Sigma)} \alpha_\Sigma(\varphi)$.*

Proof. It follows from the previous lemmas.   □

Proposition 5. *The tuple $\langle \Omega, \alpha, \beta \rangle$ is a map between $\mathcal{L}_{btl}$ and $\mathcal{L}_{bssc}$.*

Proof. Lemmas 3 and 4 prove that α and β are natural transformations. Lemmas 1 and 5 prove that these natural transformations satisfy the two conditions in the definition of map.   □

With this result we can represent the considered BTL in BSSC. So, we can adopt BSSC as a semantics for BTL, knowing that the consequence relation is sound w.r.t. this semantics, i.e., all the temporal theorems can be proved in BSSC. Then, the natural question of completeness arises: is BTL complete w.r.t. to BSSC semantics? The answer to this question is given below. But, first we need some auxiliary results.

Lemma 6. *Let φ be a Σ-formula. Then, $\models^{bssc}_{\Omega(\Sigma)} \alpha_\Sigma(\varphi)$ implies $\models^{btl}_\Sigma \varphi$.*

Proof. Assume that $\not\models^{btl}_\Sigma \varphi$. Then, there is a BTL interpretation structure for Σ, $M = \langle \langle W, R, P \rangle, V \rangle$, such that $M \not\models^{btl}_\Sigma \varphi$, i.e., there are $\pi \in P$ and $n \in \mathbb{N}_o$ such that $M, \pi, n \not\models^{btl}_\Sigma \varphi$. Consider $M^{\pi,n}$ as defined above. Let us define the BSSC interpretation structure $I^M = \langle D, \_^F, \_^P \rangle$ satisfying the following conditions:

- $D_{act} = R^{\pi,n}$
- D_{sit} is inductively defined as follows:
    - $\pi(n) \in D_{sit}$
    - $\overline{w} \, w' \in D_{sit}$ provided that $\overline{w} \in D_{sit}$ and $(w'', w') \in R^{\pi,n}$ for some w''
- $D_{lin} = P^{\pi,n}$
- $D_{stt} = W^{\pi,n}$
- $S_0^F = \pi(n)$
- $do^F(w', w'', \overline{w}) = \overline{w} \, w''$
- $[w_0 \ldots w_k]^F = w_k$
- $poss^P((w, w'), w'')$ iff $w = w''$
- $holds^P(p, w)$ iff $w \in V(p)$
- $s \prec^P s'$ iff there are $w_1, \ldots, w_k$ such that $s' = s \, w_1 \ldots w_k$, for some $k \in \mathbb{N}$;
- $in^P(\overline{w}, \eta)$ iff $\overline{w}$ is a is a prefix of η

In I^M, situations are sequences of states, states are just the states (of $M^{\pi,n}$), actions are the pairs in $R^{\pi,n}$, and lines are the paths. The initial situation is $\pi(n)$ because all the paths in $P^{\pi,n}$ start at this state. We need to generate D_{sit} in order to have a standard interpretation structure. It is intuitive to conclude that the state of a situation is the last state of the sequence, and that an action is only enabled in a state if the first component of the action is exactly that state.

Having defined this interpretation structure, we have to prove that this is in fact a BSSC (standard) interpretation structure. It satisfies all the foundational axioms, all the state axioms and all the line axioms, due to the construction and the properties of BTL interpretation structures.

Lemma 7. *Let $\eta \in P^{\pi,n}$, $k \in \mathbb{N}_o$ and let v be an assignment such that $v(l) = \eta$ and $v(s) = \langle \eta(0) \ldots \eta(k) \rangle$. Then, the following condition holds:*

$$M^{\pi,n}, \eta, k \models^{btl}_{\Sigma} \varphi \ \text{iff} \ I^M, v \models^{bssc}_{\Omega(\Sigma)} \overline{\alpha}_{\Sigma}(\varphi, l, s).$$

Proof. The proof is similar to the proof of lemma 4.   □

Using the fact that $M^{\pi,n}, \pi^n, 0 \not\models^{btl}_{\Sigma} \varphi$, we conclude that $I^M, v \not\models^{bssc}_{\Omega(\Sigma)} \overline{\alpha}_{\Sigma}(\varphi, l, s)$, for an assignment v such that $v(s) = \pi(n)$ and $v(l) = \pi^n$. Hence, $I^M \not\models^{bssc}_{\Omega(\Sigma)} \alpha_{\Sigma}(\varphi)$. Which proves that $\not\models^{bssc}_{\Omega(\Sigma)} \alpha_{\Sigma}(\varphi)$.   □

Using this result, we can now answer the question of whether BTL is complete w.r.t. to BSSC semantics. This is equivalent to showing that the map is (weakly) conservative.

Proposition 6. *The map $\langle \Omega, \alpha, \beta \rangle$ is weakly conservative, i.e., $\vdash^{bssc}_{\Omega(\Sigma)} \alpha_{\Sigma}(\varphi)$ implies $\vdash^{btl}_{\Sigma} \varphi$.*

Proof. Assume that $\not\vdash^{btl}_{\Sigma} \varphi$. Since BTL is (weakly) complete, we have $\not\models^{btl}_{\Sigma} \varphi$. Using lemma 6 we have $\not\models^{bssc}_{\Omega(\Sigma)} \alpha_{\Sigma}(\varphi)$. And finally, using the soundness of BSSC, we may conclude that $\not\vdash^{bssc}_{\Omega(\Sigma)} \alpha_{\Sigma}(\varphi)$.   □

With this result, we may conclude that BTL is (weakly) complete w.r.t. BSSC semantics. The proof of this result depends on the existence of a complete axiomatization for BTL. So, this technique may be used for other temporal logics for which there are complete axiomatizations.

4   Concluding remarks

We started from the situation calculus with an axiomatization proposed by Reiter. The main reason for adopting this axiomatization is that it enriches situations with a temporal component. But, with this axiomatization we loose the ability to *go back* to a previous situation, i.e., we loose the notion of *situation as state* that was present in the earlier versions of SC. Some authors try to solve this problem by defining a *state as a set of fluents* that hold in a given situation. However, we showed that this notion is not enough to specify some systems. In order to solve this problem, we proposed a new extension of SC, the situation and state calculus (SSC).

We also compared SSC with a branching temporal logic (BTL). We encoded BTL in an extended version of SSC (BSSC), and showed that this coding is *sound* and *complete*, i.e., all the theorems of BTL can be translated into BSSC theorems. Furthermore, we proved that we gain no extra theorems. We have similar results for linear temporal logic, that extend [11] (we detail the translation of interpretation structures and prove similar completeness result).

The temporal logic considered here is not full CTL*, but a weaker version (where the interpretation structures are transition systems with a distinguished set of paths). However, it is important to stress out that we considered BTL instead of CTL* not because of limitations in BSSC but because the conservativeness result we wanted required a complete axiomatization, which is still an open problem for full CTL*. If such an axiomatization is found, and if it is possible to define the map between the underlying logical structures, then this map *will be* conservative.

The next step is to use these codifications of temporal logics into SSC and *import* reasoning techniques and tools that already exist for temporal logic like for instance to prove *safety properties*, *liveness properties*, etc [7]. Furthermore, we also want to extend SSC to an n-agent SSC, where it possible to specify a community of interacting agents, in the line of what is done in [15,16] for temporal logic.

References

1. J. P. Burgess. Logic and time. *Journal of Symbolic Logic*, 44:566–582, 1979.
2. H. Ehrig and B. Mahr. *Fundamentals of Algebraic Specification 1: Initial Semantics*, volume 6 of *EATCS Monographs on Theoretical Computer Science*. Springer-Verlag, New York, N.Y., 1985.
3. J. Fiadeiro and A. Sernadas. Structuring theories on consequence. In D. Sannella and A. Tarlecki, editors, *Proceedings of the 5th Workshop on Recent Trends in Data Type Specification*, volume 332 of *LNCS*, pages 44–72, Berlin, 1988. Springer.
4. M. Gelfond, V. Lifschitz, and A. Rabinov. What are the limitations of the situation calculus? In Robert Boyer, editor, *Automated Reasoning: Essays in Honor of Woody Bledsoe*, pages 167–179. Kluwer Academic, Dordrecht, 1991.
5. J. Goguen and R. M. Burstall. Introducing institutions. In E. Clarke and D. Kozen, editors, *Logics of Programs: Workshop, Carnegie Mellon University, June 1983*, volume 164 of *LNCS*, pages 221–256. Springer-Verlag, New York, N.Y., 1984.
6. V. Lifschitz and A. Rabinov. Miracles in formal theories of action. *Artificial Intelligence*, 38:225–237, 1989.
7. Z. Manna and A. Pnueli. Completing the temporal picture. *Theoretical Computer Science*, 93:97–130, 1991.
8. J. McCarthy and P. Hayes. Some philosophical problems from the standpoint of artificial intelligence. In B. Meltzer and D. Michie, editors, *Machine Intelligence 4*, pages 463–502. Edinburgh University Press, Scotland, 1969.
9. J. Meseguer. General logics. In H.-D. Ebbinghaus et al, editor, *Proc. Logic Colloquium'87*. North-Holland, 1989.
10. R. Miller and M. Shanahan. Narratives in the situation calculus. *Journal of Logic and Computation – Special Issue on Actions and Processes*, 4(5):513–530, 1994.
11. J. Pinto and R. Reiter. Reasoning about time in the situation calculus. *Annals of Mathematics and Artificial Intelligence: Papers in Honour of Jack Minker*, 14(2-4):251–268, 1995.
12. J. Ramos. The situation and state calculus. In A. Drewery, G.-J. Kruijff, and R. Zuber, editors, *Proceedings of the Second ESSLLI Student Session*, 1997.
13. R. Reiter. The frame problem in the situation calculus: a simple solution (sometimes) and a completeness result for goal regression. In V. Lifschitz, editor, *Artificial Intelligence and Mathematical Theory of Computation: Papers in Honor of John McCarthy*, pages 359–380. Academic Press, San Diego, CA, 1991.

14. R. Reiter. Proving properties of states in the situation calculus. *Articial Intelligence*, 64:337–351, 1993.
15. A. Sernadas, C. Sernadas, and J. Costa. Object specification logic. *Journal of Logic and Computation*, 1:7–25, 1995.
16. A. Sernadas, C. Sernadas, and J. Ramos. A temporal logic approach to object certification. *Data and Knowledge Engineering*, 19:267–294, 1996.
17. C. Stirling. Modal and temporal logics. In S. Abramsky, D. Gabbay, and T. Maibaum, editors, *Handbook of Logic in Computer Science. Volume 2. Background: Computational Structures*, pages 477–563. Oxford University Press, 1992.
18. J. van Benthem. Correspondence theory. In D. Gabbay and F. Guenthner, editors, *Handbook of Philosophical Logic, Volume II: Extensions of Classical Logic*, volume 165 of *Synthese Library*, chapter II.4, pages 167–247. D. Reidel Publ. Co., Dordrecht, 1984.
19. A. Zanardo. Branching-time logic with quantification over branches: The point of view of modal logic. *Journal of Symbolic Logic*, 61(1):1–39, 1996.
20. A. Zanardo, B. Barcellan, and M. Reynolds. Non-definability of the class of complete bundled trees. *The Logic Journal of IGPL*. To appear.

A   Logical structures

The concept of logical structure is proposed in [9] (where it is called logic). Other related concepts are institutions [5] and π-institutions [3].

Definition 15. *A logical structure is a tuple* $\langle Sig, Sen, Int, \models, \vdash \rangle$ *such that:*

- *Sig is a category;*
- *Sen* : *Sig* → *Set is a functor;*
- *Int* : *Sig^{op}* → *Cls is a functor;*
- $\models$ *is a* |*Sig*|*-indexed family of relations* $\{\models_\Sigma \subseteq Int(\Sigma) \times Sen(\Sigma)\}_{\Sigma \in |Sig|}$*;*
- $\vdash$ *is a* |*Sig*|*-indexed family of relations* $\{\vdash_\Sigma \subseteq 2^{Sen(\Sigma)} \times Sen(\Sigma)\}_{\Sigma \in |Sig|}$*;*

satisfying the following conditions:

- *for each* $\Sigma \in |Sig|$:
  - $\{\varphi\} \vdash_\Sigma \varphi$, *for* $\varphi \in Sen(\Sigma)$;
  - $\Gamma \vdash_\Sigma \varphi$, *provided that* $\Gamma' \vdash_\Sigma \varphi$ *and* $\Gamma' \subseteq \Gamma$, *for* $\varphi \in Sen(\Sigma)$, $\Gamma, \Gamma' \subseteq Sen(\Sigma)$;
  - $\Gamma \vdash_\Sigma \varphi$, *provided that* $\Gamma \vdash_\Sigma \psi$ *for each* $\psi \in \Gamma'$ *and* $\Gamma' \vdash_\Sigma \varphi$, *for* $\varphi \in Sen(\Sigma)$, $\Gamma, \Gamma' \subseteq Sen(\Sigma)$;
- *for each morphism* $\sigma : \Sigma \to \Sigma'$ *in Sig:*
  - *if* $\Gamma \vdash_\Sigma \varphi$ *then* $Sen(\sigma)(\Gamma) \vdash_{\Sigma'} Sen(\sigma)(\varphi)$, *for* $\varphi \in Sen(\Sigma)$ *and* $\Gamma \subseteq Sen(\Sigma)$;
  - $I' \models_{\Sigma'} Sen(\sigma)(\varphi)$ *iff* $Int(\sigma)(I') \models_\Sigma \varphi$, *for* $\varphi \in Sen(\Sigma)$ *and* $I' \in Int(\Sigma')$.

A logical structure is sound *if* $\Gamma \vdash_\Sigma \varphi$ *implies* $\Gamma \models_\Sigma \varphi$. *A logical structure is* complete *if* $\Gamma \models_\Sigma \varphi$ *implies* $\Gamma \vdash_\Sigma \varphi$.

Definition 16. *Given two logical structures* $\mathcal{L}$ *and* $\mathcal{L}'$, *a* map *between* $\mathcal{L}$ *and* $\mathcal{L}'$ *is a triple* $\langle \Omega, \alpha, \beta \rangle$ *such that:*

- $\Omega : Sig \to Sig'$ *is a functor;*
- $\alpha : Sen \to Sen' \circ \Omega$ *is a natural transformation;*
- $\beta : Int' \circ \Omega^{op} \to Int$ *is a natural transformation;*

satisfying the following conditions:

- *if* $\Gamma \vdash_\Sigma \varphi$ *then* $\alpha_\Sigma(\Gamma) \vdash'_{\Omega(\Sigma)} \alpha_\Sigma(\varphi)$;
- $\beta_\Sigma(I') \models_\Sigma \varphi$ *iff* $I' \models'_{\Omega(\Sigma)} \alpha_\Sigma(\varphi)$.

A map between logic structures is said to be conservative *iff*

$$\alpha_\Sigma(\Gamma) \vdash'_{\Omega(\Sigma)} \alpha_\Sigma(\varphi) \text{ implies } \Gamma \vdash_\Sigma \varphi.$$

Modular Specification of Concurrent Systems with Observational Logic*

Pedro Resende

Departamento de Matemática, Instituto Superior Técnico
Av. Rovisco Pais, 1096 Lisboa, Portugal

Abstract. We present a dynamic form of observational logic for specifying concurrent systems on the basis of their observable behaviour, in
particular without needing a language for describing states, which are
regarded as non-observable. The logic is based on quantales. The models
are labelled transition systems, and a weakly complete proof system is
presented. We study the logic from the point of view of modularity; vertical modularity is based on a notion of implementation of systems and
refinement of specifications, and horizontal modularity is based on parallel composition of systems and specifications. Several compositionality
results are presented. As an example we see a specification of a stack and
its implementation over an array and a pointer.

1 Introduction

This paper introduces a logic for specifying concurrent systems on the basis of
their observable behaviour, in particular without needing a language for describing states, which are regarded as non-observable and ultimately physical entities.
In this sense, the logic differs from other specification formalisms, such as the
transition system specifications of [9,8], the observational structures of [3], or algebraic specification in general. Our logic, whose models are labelled transition
systems, is a generalization of the observational logics of [1,23] that takes into
account the possibility that observations may affect the state of what is being observed. Algebraically, this generalization corresponds to the passage from frames
to quantales and their modules, as proposed in [2]. Henceforth, by observational
logic we always mean the generalized version in the present paper.

There are other specification logics that do not require description languages
for states. Typically, this is the case with modal logics such as Hennessy-Milner
logic [10] or, more recently, [13] for coalgebras. Usually, logical equivalence in such
logics coincides with a behavioural equivalence like simulation or bisimulation.
One reason for studying observational logic is its ability to handle many more
process equivalences, which is a consequence of the results in [2] and [19]; in
the former, quantales and modules were used in order to study several (strong)

---

* This work was partially supported by FCT, the PRAXIS XXI Projects 2/2.1/MAT/
262/94 SitCalc, PCEX/P/MAT/46/96 ACL and 2/2.1/TIT/1658/95 LogComp, and
the ESPRIT IV Working Groups 22704 ASPIRE and 23531 FIREworks.

J.L. Fiadeiro (Ed.): WADT'98, LNCS 1589, pp. 310–325, 1999.

equivalences ranging from trace equivalence [11] to ready-simulation [4], and in the latter strong bisimulation was addressed in a similar way, in fact showing that quantale modules subsume Hennessy-Milner logic.

The main purpose of the present paper is to further assess the applicability of observational logic to the specification of concurrent systems (in fact, labelled transition systems), namely as regards modularity, meaning both the ability to develop specifications and systems in an incremental way (vertical modularity) and in a divide-and-conquer style (horizontal modularity). In particular, we define a notion of parallel composition $\parallel$ of independent systems and a corresponding notion for specifications, and see that they match apropriately: if the system S_1 satisfies the specification Ξ_1 and the system S_2 satisfies the specification Ξ_2 then $S_1 \parallel S_2$ satisfies $\Xi_1 \parallel \Xi_2$. We also define morphisms of systems and morphisms of specifications. In particular, a system morphism from T_1 to S_1 means that T_1 is an implementation of S_1, and if also T_2 is an implementation of S_2 then $T_1 \parallel T_2$ is an implementation of $S_1 \parallel S_2$; similar remarks apply to specifications. In this way the logic provides mechanisms for structuring specifications of large systems by developing them in separate parts and then combining the results, either before or after doing the implementations. As an example we present a specification of a stack of integers and its implementation over an array and a pointer. Other specification examples can be found in [20], for instance showing how both discrete and continuous time and space properties can be handled in a uniform way.

The rest of the paper is organized as follows. In §2 we describe the basic ideas and notation. Then in §3 we introduce the logic, along with a proof system. In §4 we see the stack specification. Then §5 addresses vertical modularity, and §6 discusses horizontal modularity. Then in §7 we describe the stack implementation mentioned above, and §8 is the conclusion.

2   Systems, finite observations and quantales

We begin with some basic ideas, definitions and notation. By a *finite observation* we informally mean some communication between an observer and a system, performed in finite time and involving an exchange of a finite amount of information. This notion can be related to the semidecidable properties of [22] and to the finitely observable properties of [1] and [23], where essentially such properties are identified with open sets of topological spaces. In [23] and later in [2] it was argued that quantales [18,21] should be the right generalization of the lattices of open sets when observations can accompany changes of state of what is being observed.

Definition 1. *A quantale* $\langle Q, \leq, \cdot, 1 \rangle$ *is a complete lattice* $\langle Q, \leq \rangle$ *equipped with a monoid structure* $\langle Q, \cdot, 1 \rangle$*, satisfying*

$$a \cdot \left(\bigvee S \right) = \bigvee \{ a \cdot b \mid b \in S \} \text{ and } \left(\bigvee S \right) \cdot b = \bigvee \{ a \cdot b \mid a \in S \} ,$$

for all $a, b \in Q$ *and* $S \subseteq Q$*. A quantale homomorphism is a monoid homomorphism that preserves all joins.*

The quantales of the above definition are also known as *unital quantales* [21].

Example 2.

1. Let P be a set. The set of binary relations over P is a quantale

$$\langle 2^{P \times P}, \subseteq, \cdot, \Delta_P \rangle ,$$

   where $R \cdot S = R; S$ and $\Delta_P = \{\langle p, p \rangle \mid p \in P\}$. We call $2^{P \times P}$ the *relational quantale* (over P).
2. Let A be a set. Then $\langle 2^{A^*}, \subseteq, \cdot, \{\varepsilon\} \rangle$ is a quantale; multiplication is given by $a \cdot b = \{st \mid s \in a, \ t \in b\}$, and joins are unions: $\bigvee S = \bigcup S$. Furthermore 2^{A^*} is freely generated by A; that is, for any map f from A to a quantale Q there is a unique quantale homomorphism $f^\sharp : 2^{A^*} \to Q$ such that $f^\sharp(\{\alpha\}) = f(\alpha)$ for all $\alpha \in A$. Throughout this paper, when referring to elements of a free quantale we usually write 1 instead of $\{\varepsilon\}$ and $\perp$ instead of $\emptyset$.
3. Let Ω be a topology on a space X. Then $\langle \Omega, \subseteq, \cap, X \rangle$ is a quantale.

The connection between finite observations and quantales is established by the following slogan: *For any system, the set of finite observations that we can perform on the system has the structure of a quantale.* The idea is that a multiplication $a_1 \cdot \ldots \cdot a_n$ of finite observations is also a finite observation; the information it conveys is that of $a_1, \ldots, a_n$ together with the knowledge that a_1 preceded a_2, a_2 preceded a_3, etc. The quantale unit is the null observation, i.e., no information is exchanged. A join $\bigvee S$ corresponds to a disjunction that consists of performing one out of a set S (finite or infinite) of possible observations. Since all the observations in S are finite, so is $\bigvee S$. Distributivity corresponds to the following two almost tautological statements:

observe a and then some $b \in S$ $\iff$ for some $b \in S$, observe a and then b

observe some $a \in S$ and then b $\iff$ for some $a \in S$, observe a and then b

Notice that this has nothing to do with distributivity in process algebra, as we are dealing with the algebraic structure of observations, not processes.

In [21] several results about quantales are stated and proved, including a representation theorem which tells us that every quantale Q is isomorphic to a quotient of a quantale of languages 2^{A^*}; in other words, any quantale Q is the image of some surjective homomorphism $j : 2^{A^*} \to Q$. Hence, if Q is the quantale of finite observations that we can perform on some system, each language $a \subseteq A^*$ can be seen as a *presentation* of a finite observation $j(a)$. In the next section we will in fact *identify* finite observations with languages.

Now let S be some system, and let the (finite) observations over S form a quantale Q. Let also P be the set of possible *states* of S. The way in which the observations affect the states of S can be described by a map $T : Q \to 2^{P \times P}$. The meaning of $\langle p, q \rangle \in T(a)$ is that q can be the state of the system after we have performed an observation a initiated while the system was at state p. We use the following notation:

$$p \xrightarrow{a} q \stackrel{\text{def}}{\Longleftrightarrow} \langle p, q \rangle \in T(a),$$

$$p \xrightarrow{a} \stackrel{\text{def}}{\Longleftrightarrow} p \xrightarrow{a} q \text{ for some } q \in P.$$

In other words, we identify the map T with a relation $T \subseteq P \times Q \times P$, and thus usually refer to T as the *transition relation*. For the record we state:

Definition 3. A labelled transition system (lts) *is a structure $\langle P, A, T \rangle$ such that P is a set (of states), A is a set (of labels) and T is a map $A \to 2^{P \times P}$ (the transition relation).*

Of course, the structure $\langle P, Q, T \rangle$ is an lts, if we ignore the fact that Q is a quantale instead of just a set of labels. But the transition relation should also satisfy some conditions related to the structure of Q, namely, for all $p, q \in P$, $a, b \in Q$ and $S \subseteq Q$,

$$p \xrightarrow{1} q \iff p = q, \tag{1}$$

$$p \xrightarrow{a \cdot b} q \iff \exists_{r \in P} (p \xrightarrow{a} r \wedge r \xrightarrow{b} q), \tag{2}$$

$$p \xrightarrow{\bigvee S} q \iff \exists_{a \in S} (p \xrightarrow{a} q). \tag{3}$$

Condition (1) means that nothing happens to the system if nothing is observed. Thus the unit does not formalize hidden transitions like Milner's τ [17]. It is easy to see that these three conditions hold if and only if $T : Q \to 2^{P \times P}$ is a quantale homomorphism, which leads us to:

Definition 4. *An* elementary tropological system (ets) *is an lts $\langle P, Q, T \rangle$ whose set of labels Q is a quantale and whose transition relation is a quantale homomorphism $T : Q \to 2^{P \times P}$.*

The name "tropological" comes from the greek *trópos* (change) and was introduced in [19] because tropological systems (in particular elementary ones) generalize the topological systems of [23] (which themselves generalize topological spaces) when observations are allowed to change the state of what is being observed.

Example 5. Any topological space $\langle X, \Omega \rangle$ is an ets $\langle X, \Omega, T \rangle$, where $x \xrightarrow{a} y$ is defined to mean $x = y$ and $x \in a$. Hence, the observations (open sets) are "static", i.e., they do not change the state.

Etss can also be identified with certain *right quantale modules*, which is how they were presented in [2].

3   Observational logic

Intuitively we think of systems as black boxes equipped with buttons and lights, channels, etc., with which we can communicate, in the style of the *scenarios* of [16,5,6]. Pressing buttons, watching lights, etc., can all be seen as *elementary finite observations* on the system. Let A be a set of such elementary observations. Other finite observations can be obtained from the elementary ones by means of unions and finite concatenations (i.e., we identify finite observations with elements of the free quantale over A):

Definition 6. *A* finite observation over A *is a language* $a \subseteq A^*$.

A system (black box) can be as usual represented by an lts $\langle P, A, T \rangle$. Due to freeness of the quantale 2^{A^*} there is a unique extension $T^\sharp : 2^{A^*} \to 2^{P \times P}$ of T such that $T^\sharp$ is a homomorphism of quantales. Equivalently, there is a unique ets $\langle P, 2^{A^*}, T^\sharp \rangle$ whose transition relation $T^\sharp$ equals T on elementary observations, i.e., such that $p \xrightarrow{\{\alpha\}} q$ in the ets if and only if $p \xrightarrow{\alpha} q$ in the lts, for all $\alpha \in A$. From here on we identify ltss with their extensions as etss, e.g. writing $T(a)$ and $p \xrightarrow{a} q$ when a is a language. If $t \in A^+$ we also usually write t instead of $\{t\}$, e.g. $t \vee u$ instead of $\{t, u\}$, $t \vee a$ instead of $\{t\} \vee a$ when $a \subseteq A^*$, etc.

Definition 7. *Let A be a set.*

1. *An* observation formula *over A is a triple* $\langle a, 0, b \rangle$, *with* $a, b \subseteq A^*$, *which we write* $a = b$. *A* property formula *over A is a triple* $\langle a, 1, b \rangle$, *with* $a, b \subseteq A^*$, *which we write* $a =' b$. *As abbreviations we also write* $a \leq b$ *instead of* $a \vee b = b$, *and* $a \leq' b$ *instead of* $a \vee b =' b$.

2. *We define a* satisfaction relation $\Vdash$ *between ltss labelled over A and (observation and property) formulas over A as follows:*

   (a) $\langle P, A, T \rangle \Vdash a = b$ *if for all* $p, q \in P$, $p \xrightarrow{a} q \Leftrightarrow p \xrightarrow{b} q$
      [i.e., if $T(a) = T(b)$];

   (b) $\langle P, A, T \rangle \Vdash a =' b$ *if for all* $p \in P$, $p \xrightarrow{a} \Leftrightarrow p \xrightarrow{b}$
      [i.e., if $T(a); (P \times P) = T(b); (P \times P)$].

   When Sys $\Vdash \zeta$ holds we say that the system Sys satisfies *the formula ζ. A formula is* valid *if it is satisfied by all systems, and we write* $\models \zeta$.

3. *Let Φ be a set of formulas over A and ζ a formula over A. If every transition system that satisfies all the formulas of Φ also satisfies ζ we say Φ* entails ζ, *and write* $\Phi \models \zeta$. *We denote by $\Phi^\models$ the set of all the formulas entailed by Φ.*

4. *An* observational specification *(over A) is a pair* $\langle A, \Phi \rangle$ *where Φ is a set of formulas over A. An lts S (labelled over A)* satisfies $\langle A, \Phi \rangle$ *if it satisfies all the formulas of Φ, and we write* $S \Vdash \langle A, \Phi \rangle$.

A few comments are in order. An observation formula $a = b$ is satisfied by a system when for that system the finite observations a and b are essentially the same; that is, the transitions labelled by a are exactly the transitions labelled by b. The meaning of property formulas is different: $a =' b$ is satisfied when a and b represent the same *finitely observable property*; that is, a state has the property that a *can* be observed on it if and only if it has the property that b *can* be observed on it, regardless of whether the states reached after performing the observations are the same or not. This means we view languages over A both as finite observations and finitely observable properties, the difference being in the way they are handled by the satisfaction relation[1].

Now let us see a proof system.

Definition 8. *Let A be a set. We define the following inference rules over A $(a, b, a', \ldots \in 2^{A^*})$:*

$$\mathbf{Q} : \frac{}{a \leq b} \; (\text{if } a \subseteq b) \qquad \mathbf{QS} : \frac{a = b}{b = a} \qquad \mathbf{QT} : \frac{a = b \quad b = c}{a = c}$$

$$\mathbf{Q\bullet} : \frac{a = a' \quad b = b'}{a \cdot b = a' \cdot b'} \qquad \mathbf{QV} : \frac{\{a_i = b_i\}_{i \in I}}{\bigvee_{i \in I} a_i = \bigvee_{i \in I} b_i}$$

$$\mathbf{I} : \frac{a \leq 1}{a \cdot a = a} \qquad \mathbf{C} : \frac{a \leq 1 \quad b \leq 1}{a \cdot b = b \cdot a}$$

$$\mathbf{PP} : \frac{c \leq 1 \quad c' \leq 1 \quad c \cdot a \cdot c' = a \quad d \leq 1 \quad d' \leq 1 \quad d \cdot a \cdot d' = a}{c \cdot d \cdot a \cdot c' \cdot d' = a}$$

$$\mathbf{M} : \frac{a = b}{a =' b} \qquad \mathbf{MS} : \frac{a =' b}{b =' a} \qquad \mathbf{MT} : \frac{a =' b \quad b =' c}{a =' c}$$

$$\mathbf{M\bullet} : \frac{b =' b'}{a \cdot b =' a \cdot b'} \qquad \mathbf{MV} : \frac{\{a_i =' b_i\}_{i \in I}}{\bigvee_{i \in I} a_i =' \bigvee_{i \in I} b_i}$$

$$\mathbf{Top} : \frac{}{a \leq' 1} \qquad \mathbf{W} : \frac{c \leq 1 \quad a \leq' c}{a = c \cdot a}$$

$$\mathbf{MV\bullet} : \frac{c \leq 1 \quad a \leq' c \vee b}{a \leq' c \cdot a \vee b}$$

If Φ is a set of formulas over A we denote by $\Phi^\vdash$ the closure of Φ under all the above rules, and write $\Phi \vdash \zeta$ if $\zeta \in \Phi^\vdash$, or just $\vdash \zeta$ if $\Phi = \emptyset$.

Theorem 9 ((Soundness)). *If $\Phi \vdash \zeta$ then $\Phi \models \zeta$.*

Some of the inference rules, e.g., **QS**, **QT**, **Q•** and **QV**, are essentially rules of (infinitary) equational logic. Others are specific to observational logic. For instance, **I** (idempotence) means that any system that satisfies $a \leq 1$ also satisfies $a \cdot a = a$. The soundness of this rule follows easily from the fact that any system which satisfies $a \leq 1$ must be such that $p \xrightarrow{a} q \Rightarrow p = q$ for all states p and q.

---

[1] Algebraically, the set of all observation formulas satisfied by some system defines an equivalence relation on the quantale 2^{A^*}, and so does the set of all property formulas; but the former is a quantale congruence, whereas the latter is a congruence of *left quantale modules* (see [2] or [19]). Hence, although we view languages over A both as finite observations and as finitely observable properties, the algebraic structure in both cases is different.

Theorem 10 ((Weak completeness)). *If* $\vDash \zeta$ *then* $\vdash \zeta$.

Proof. This is essentially a corollary of the "second completeness" and "third completeness" for trace semantics in [2].   □

In fact, this completeness result only needs the "equational part" of the proof system. On the other hand, even with the whole system the logic is not strongly complete; that is, we may have $\Phi^{\vdash} \neq \Phi^{\vDash}$ for some sets Φ. This limitation is of a topological nature, being essentially a consequence of the fact that not every locale [12] is spatial, and will be expanded on elsewhere.

4   Example: Stacks

We view a stack of integers as a black box equipped with "communication channels" *push* and *top*, a "button" *pop*, and a "light" *empty*. Through the *push* channel we can send an integer number; through the *top* channel we can receive an integer number; pressing *pop* causes the top element of the stack to be discarded; finally, *empty* is on when the stack is empty. This leads to the following elementary observations on the system:

1. $push_i$: the integer i is sent through *push*.
2. top_i: the integer i was received through *top*.
3. *pop*: the *pop* button was pressed.
4. *empty*: the *empty* light is on.

We assume that each of these elementary observations can be done in finite time. Let A be the set $\{push_i \mid i \in \mathbb{N}\} \cup \{top_i \mid i \in \mathbb{N}\} \cup \{pop\} \cup \{empty\}$, and let $\mathsf{StackSpec}_0$ be the specification with elementary observations in A, with observation formulas (schemata, in fact)

Ob1 $top_i \leq 1$
Ob2 For $i \neq j$, $top_i \cdot top_j = \bot$
Ob3 $pop = \bigvee_i top_i \cdot pop$
Ob4 $push_i = push_i \cdot top_i$
Ob5 $top_i \cdot (\prod_{k=1}^n push_{j_k}) \cdot pop^n = (\prod_{k=1}^n push_{j_k}) \cdot pop^n \cdot top_i$

and with property formulas

Pr1 $push_i =' 1$
Pr2 $\bigvee_i top_i =' pop$

The meanings of these formulas are as follows. **Ob1** tells us that top_i does not change the state of the stack. **Ob2** means there are no transitions of top_i followed by top_j if $i \neq j$, because $p \xrightarrow{\perp} q$ for no p, q. **Ob3** states that *pop* may not be performed on an empty stack; that is, in order to perform it we must be able to observe a top value first, for any system that satisfies **Ob3** must be such that if $p \xrightarrow{pop}$ then $p \xrightarrow{top_i} p$ for some i. **Ob4** is similar but imposes constraints on the outcome of an action: after $push_i$ the top value must be i. **Ob5** tells us that top_i can be observed after doing $(\prod_{k=1}^{n} push_{j_k}) \cdot pop^n$ if and only if it could be observed before. Notice that instead of **Ob5** we could use the simpler $push_i \cdot pop = 1$, which implies that $push_i$ followed by pop leads back to the starting state. However, that requirement is too strong, and in particular it would cause our refinement over an array-with-pointer in Proposition 23 to fail. Now the property formulas. **Pr1** tells us that 1 can be observed on a state exactly when $push_i$ can, which amounts to saying that $push_i$ can be done at every state (for all $i \in \mathbb{N}$). Finally, **Pr2** means that pop can be done if and only if the stack is not empty.

Intuitively, the "typical stack" $\mathsf{Stack} = \langle \mathbb{N}^*, A, T \rangle$, where T is the least transition relation that satisfies, for all $s \in \mathbb{N}^*$ and $i \in \mathbb{N}$,

1. $si \xrightarrow{pop} s$,
2. $s \xrightarrow{push_i} si$,
3. $si \xrightarrow{top_i} si$,
4. $\varepsilon \xrightarrow{empty} \varepsilon$,

behaves in accordance with the above specification, and in fact we have:

Proposition 11. $\mathsf{Stack} \Vdash \mathsf{StackSpec_0}$.

Many variants of the specification are possible. For instance, we may say that an empty stack can be reached after a finite number of pop's by means of the property formula

Pr3 $1 =' \bigvee_{n \in \omega} pop^n \cdot empty$,

and in fact we should also add observation formulas such as the following, which tell us that $empty$ is the "negation" of $\bigvee_{i \in \mathbb{N}} top_i$.

Ob6 $empty \cdot top_i = \bot \ (i \in \mathbb{N})$
Ob7 $empty \vee \bigvee_{i \in \mathbb{N}} top_i = 1$

We denote by $\mathsf{StackSpec}$ the specification that results from adding these formulas to $\mathsf{StackSpec_0}$.

5 Vertical modularity

This section addresses the issue of how to *implement* systems on other systems. We mix two ideas: on one hand when doing an implementation the interface of what is being implemented remains *fixed*, and thus if a system implements another it must have both the same interface and the same observable behaviour; on the other hand we also relate systems with different interfaces by saying how observations at the abstract level are translated to observations at the implementation level.

Let $\mathcal{T} = \langle P_0, B, T_0 \rangle$ and $\mathcal{S} = \langle P, A, T \rangle$ be ltss. By freeness of the quantale 2^{A^*} we can identify a quantale homomorphism $\rho : 2^{A^*} \to 2^{B^*}$ with the map that to each elementary observation $\alpha \in A$ assigns the (no longer elementary) observation $\rho(\{\alpha\})$ over B. If $\mathcal{T}$ is a "concrete system" that we view as the *implementation level*, and $\mathcal{S}$ is an "abstract system" that we want to implement over the concrete one, a quantale homomorphism from 2^{A^*} to 2^{B^*} provides the way in which elementary observations in A are translated to "procedures" at the concrete level. Henceforth we will often abuse notation and identify such a quantale homomorphism with its restriction to elementary observations.

Let $\mathcal{T} = \langle P_0, B, T_0 \rangle$, and let $\rho : 2^{A^*} \to 2^{B^*}$ be a quantale homomorphism. By composition of homomorphisms we obtain a new lts, $\langle P_0, A, T_0 \circ \rho \rangle$, which we denote by $\mathcal{T}.\rho$:

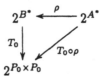

We can see $\mathcal{T}.\rho$ as the result of "hiding" $\mathcal{T}$ behind a more abstract interface. Now let $\mathcal{S} = \langle P, A, T \rangle$ be another lts (it has the same interface as $\mathcal{T}.\rho$). We can see a state $p \in P_0$ as an "implementation" of a state $q \in P$ when its observable behaviour in $\mathcal{T}.\rho$ is the same as that of q in $\mathcal{S}$; that is, when p and q satisfy the same finitely observable properties, meaning that for all $a \subseteq A^*$ we have $p \overset{a}{\to}$ if and only if $q \overset{a}{\to}$. These ideas lead to the following definition:

Definition 12. *An* implementation *of an lts $\langle P, A, T \rangle$ over an lts $\langle P_0, B, T_0 \rangle$ is a pair $\langle f, \rho \rangle$, where $\rho : 2^{A^*} \to 2^{B^*}$ is a quantale homomorphism and $f : P_0 \to P$ is a partial function, such that the following* implementation condition *holds, for all $a \subseteq A^*$ and all $p \in P_0$ where f is defined:*

$$p \overset{\rho(a)}{\to} \iff f(p) \overset{a}{\to} .$$

We make some comments about the above definition:

- The map f gives us, for each "concrete state" $p \in P_0$ where f is defined, an "abstract state" $f(p)$ that behaves like p when both are viewed through the abstract interface A.
- Those cases in which f is total mean that the implementation has no exceptions; the concrete system always behaves like some state of the abstract system.
- Those cases in which f is surjective mean that the implementation is complete, in the sense that the concrete system is able to behave like any of the states of the abstract system.

It is easy to see that implementations are closed under composition and units, which gives us a category of ltss. Composition of morphisms tells us that implementations can be constructed in a stepwise manner: if $\mathcal{S}_0$ is an implementation of $\mathcal{S}_1$ and $\mathcal{S}_1$ is an implementation of $\mathcal{S}_2$ then $\mathcal{S}_0$ is an implementation of

S_2. Associativity tells us that the order in which we do the implementations is irrelevant.

Let $\rho : 2^{A^*} \to 2^{B^*}$ be a quantale homomorphism. In what follows, if $\zeta = \langle a, n, b \rangle$ is a formula over A ($n = 0, 1$) we write $\rho.\zeta$ for the formula $\langle \rho(a), n, \rho(b) \rangle$ over B.

Theorem 13 ((Satisfaction condition)). *Let S be an lts over B, $\rho : 2^{A^*} \to 2^{B^*}$ a quantale homomorphism and ζ a formula over A. Then we have*

$$S.\rho \Vdash \zeta \iff S \Vdash \rho.\zeta .$$

Proof. Let $S = \langle P, B, T \rangle$ and $\zeta = \langle a, n, b \rangle$. Then $S.\rho = \langle P, A, T \circ \rho \rangle$ and $\rho.\zeta = \langle \rho(a), n, \rho(b) \rangle$. If ζ is an observation formula ($n = 0$) we have

$$S.\rho \Vdash \zeta \iff T \circ \rho(a) = T \circ \rho(b) \iff T(\rho(a)) = T(\rho(b)) \iff S \Vdash \rho.\zeta .$$

The case $n = 1$ is analogous:

$$S.\rho \Vdash \zeta \iff T(\rho(a)); (P \times P) = T(\rho(b)); (P \times P) \iff S \Vdash \rho.\zeta .\square$$

This condition is a satisfaction condition in the sense of the theory of institutions [7], and indeed one can show that observational logic is an institution [20]. The following notion corresponds to the morphisms of *theory presentations* of institutions.

Definition 14. *Let $\langle A, \Phi \rangle$ and $\langle B, \Gamma \rangle$ be observational specifications. A refinement of specifications from $\langle A, \Phi \rangle$ to $\langle B, \Gamma \rangle$ is a quantale homomorphism $\rho : 2^{A^*} \to 2^{B^*}$ such that $\rho.\zeta \in \Gamma^\vDash$ for all $\zeta \in \Phi$, and we write $\rho : \langle A, \Phi \rangle \to \langle B, \Gamma \rangle$.*

The following propositions are corollaries of the satisfaction condition. Their proofs are simple and similar to those for an arbitrary institution. In particular, the following proposition shows that in order to check that a system $S.\rho$ satisfies a specification $\langle A, \Phi \rangle$ it suffices to find a specification $\langle B, \Gamma \rangle$ such that $\rho : \langle A, \Phi \rangle \to \langle B, \Gamma \rangle$ and $S \Vdash \langle B, \Gamma \rangle$.

Proposition 15. *Let S be an lts over B and $\rho : \langle A, \Phi \rangle \to \langle B, \Gamma \rangle$. Then,*

$$S \Vdash \langle B, \Gamma \rangle \implies S.\rho \Vdash \langle A, \Phi \rangle .$$

Proposition 16. *Let $\rho : \langle A, \Phi \rangle \to \langle B, \Gamma \rangle$. Then $\rho.\zeta \in \Gamma^\vDash$ for all $\zeta \in \Phi^\vDash$.*

From this proposition it follows that specification refinements are closed under composition, which gives us a category of specifications. Hence, refinements of specifications are as well behaved with respect to stepwise development as implementations of systems are.

6 Horizontal modularity

In this section we address notions of parallel composition for ltss and observational specifications. We start with ltss.

Definition 17. *Let $S_1 = \langle P_1, A_1, T_1 \rangle$ and $S_2 = \langle P_2, A_2, T_2 \rangle$ be ltss, such that $A_1 \cap A_2 = \emptyset$. We define their (independent) parallel composition $S_1 \parallel S_2$ to be the lts $\langle P_1 \times P_2, A_1 \cup A_2, T \rangle$, where T is given by, for all $p_1, q_1 \in P_1$, $p_2, q_2 \in P_2$, $\alpha_1 \in A_1$ and $\alpha_2 \in A_2$,*

1. $\langle p_1, p_2 \rangle \xrightarrow{\alpha_1} \langle q_1, q_2 \rangle$ if $p_1 \xrightarrow{\alpha_1} q_1$ and $p_2 = q_2$,
2. $\langle p_1, p_2 \rangle \xrightarrow{\alpha_2} \langle q_1, q_2 \rangle$ if $p_1 = q_1$ and $p_2 \xrightarrow{\alpha_2} q_2$.

The following is a result of "diagonal compositionality" in the sense of [15]; it shows that implementations and parallel composition of ltss can be carried out in any order.

Theorem 18. *Let T_1, T_2, S_1 and S_2 be ltss, with sets of labels B_1, B_2, A_1 and A_2, respectively, such that $A_1 \cap A_2 = B_1 \cap B_2 = \emptyset$. Let also $\langle \iota_1, \rho_1 \rangle : T_1 \to S_1$ and $\langle \iota_2, \rho_2 \rangle : T_2 \to S_2$ be implementations. Then $\langle \iota_1 \times \iota_2, \rho_1 \amalg \rho_2 \rangle$ is an implementation of $S_1 \parallel S_2$ over $T_1 \parallel T_2$.*
[$\rho_1 \amalg \rho_2$ is the coproduct homomorphism $2^{(A_1 \cup A_2)^*} \to 2^{(B_1 \cup B_2)^*}$.]

Remark 19. Our category of ltss and implementations is quite different from typical categories of ltss, e.g., as in [24]. This is not surprising because usually lts morphisms express that a system is *part of* another, which is not what implementations do. In particular, $\parallel$ defines a symmetric monoidal structure on our category, but it does not give us products or coproducts.

Now specifications:

Definition 20. *Let $\langle A, \Phi \rangle$ and $\langle B, \Gamma \rangle$ be observational specifications, such that $A \cap B = \emptyset$. We define their (independent) parallel composition $\langle A, \Phi \rangle \parallel \langle B, \Gamma \rangle$ to be*

$$\langle A \cup B, \Phi \cup \Gamma \cup \{ \alpha \cdot \beta = \beta \cdot \alpha \mid \alpha \in A, \ \beta \in B \} \rangle .$$

Notice that we are expressing independence by making some observations commute, which is similar to what is done in Mazurkiewicz trace theory [14], except that we ultimately obtain partially commutative quantales instead of just monoids.

The following is diagonal compositionality for specifications.

Theorem 21. *Let $\rho : \langle A, \Phi \rangle \to \langle A', \Phi' \rangle$ and $\sigma : \langle B, \Gamma \rangle \to \langle B', \Gamma' \rangle$ be refinements, with $A' \cap B' = A \cap B = \emptyset$. Then the coproduct homomorphism $\rho \amalg \sigma$ is a refinement from $\langle A, \Phi \rangle \parallel \langle B, \Gamma \rangle$ to $\langle A', \Phi' \rangle \parallel \langle B', \Gamma' \rangle$.*

Finally, we relate the two notions of parallel composition.

Theorem 22. *Let Sys_1 and Sys_2 be ltss that satisfy $Spec_1$ and $Spec_2$, respectively, over disjoint sets of elementary observations. Then $Sys_1 \parallel Sys_2$ $\Vdash$ $Spec_1 \parallel Spec_2$.*

We can also describe the parallel composition of *interacting* systems by first composing systems independently and then restricting the resulting interface. This use of restriction is similar to what is done in [24]. In our case, restrictions can be described by quantale homomorphisms; an interacting composition of two systems S and T will in general be a system of the form $(S \parallel T).\rho$, where ρ describes the interaction. An example of interaction in the style of CCS [17] can be as follows. Let $S_1 = \langle P_1, Act, T_1 \rangle$ and $S_2 = \langle P_2, Act, T_2 \rangle$ be ltss, where $Act = \mathcal{L} \cup \{\tau\}$ and $\mathcal{L} = \{a, \bar{a}, b, \bar{b}, \dots\}$ is the set of labels, as usual in CCS ($\tau \notin \mathcal{L}$). The composition of S_1 and S_2 with communication can be obtained as $(S_1 \parallel S_2).\rho$, where first we define $S_1 \parallel S_2$ with two disjoint copies of Act, and $\rho : 2^{Act^*} \to 2^{(Act+Act)^*}$ is given by, for all labels $\ell \in \mathcal{L}$,

$$\ell \mapsto \ell^{(1)} \vee \ell^{(2)}$$
$$\tau \mapsto \tau^{(1)} \vee \tau^{(2)} \vee \bigvee \{\ell^{(1)} \cdot \bar{\ell}^{(2)} \mid \ell \in \mathcal{L}\} .$$

7   Example: Stack implementations

Now we see an implementation of a stack over an array and a pointer. First we do it for specifications and then for ltss.

Let ArraySpec be a specification for an infinite array of integers, whose elementary observations are, for all $n \in \omega$ and $i \in \mathbb{N}$,

- $write_n^i$—"write value $i \in \mathbb{N}$ at position $n \in \omega$",
- $read_n^i$—"the value stored at position $n \in \omega$ is $i \in \mathbb{N}$",

and whose formulas are

A1 $\bigvee_{i \in \mathbb{N}} read_n^i = 1$,
A2 $read_n^i \cdot read_n^j = \bot \ (i \neq j)$,
A3 $write_n^i = write_n^i \cdot read_n^i$,
A4 $read_n^i \cdot write_m^j = write_m^j \cdot read_n^i \ (n \neq m)$,
A5 $1 =' write_n^i$.

Let also PointerSpec be the specification of a pointer (i.e., a variable holding an array index) that can be read, incremented and decremented; the elementary observations are

- pos_n—"the pointer points to position $n \in \omega$",
- inc—"the pointer is incremented by one position",
- dec—"the pointer is decremented by one position".

The formulas are:

P1 $\bigvee_{n\in\omega} pos_n = 1$,
P2 $pos_n \cdot pos_m = \bot \ (m \neq n)$,
P3 $pos_n \cdot inc = inc \cdot pos_{n+1}$,
P4 $pos_{n+1} \cdot dec = dec \cdot pos_n$,
P5 $1 =' inc$,
P6 $pos_{n+1} \leq' dec$.

Now we define a refinement ρ from StackSpec to ArraySpec ‖ PointerSpec. Each of the elementary observations of StackSpec is mapped to an observation of ArraySpec ‖ PointerSpec, as follows:

$$push_i \overset{\rho}{\mapsto} \bigvee_{n\in\omega} pos_n \cdot write_n^i \cdot inc \ ,$$

$$top_i \overset{\rho}{\mapsto} \bigvee_{n\in\omega} pos_{n+1} \cdot read_n^i \ ,$$

$$pop \overset{\rho}{\mapsto} dec \ ,$$

$$empty \overset{\rho}{\mapsto} pos_0 \ .$$

For instance, we are saying that $push_i$ consists of the observation that for some $n \in \omega$ the pointer has value n, we write i at the position n of the array and then increment the pointer. Notice that the order of many of the observations in the above formulas is not relevant; for instance, it is irrelevant whether we write $pos_n \cdot write_n^i \cdot inc$ or $write_n^i \cdot pos_n \cdot inc$, for in the parallel composition we have $write_n^i \cdot pos_n = pos_n \cdot write_n^i$.

Proposition 23. ρ is a refinement.

Proof. (Sketch.) We must prove ArraySpec ‖ PointerSpec $\vDash \langle \rho(a), n, \rho(b) \rangle$ for all formulas $\langle a, n, b \rangle$ $(n = 0, 1)$ of StackSpec. The full proof is too long to be included here, but in order to see how it can be done let us for instance look at the case of **Ob2**. The translation by ρ of $top_i \cdot top_j$ is

$$\bigvee_{n\in\omega} pos_{n+1} \cdot read_n^i \cdot \bigvee_{m\in\omega} pos_{m+1} \cdot read_m^j \ .$$

By commutativity of $read_n^i$ and pos_{m+1} and by **P2** this can be rewritten as $\bigvee_{n\in\omega} pos_{n+1} \cdot pos_{n+1} \cdot read_n^i \cdot read_n^j$, which, by **A2**, equals $\bot$ if $i \neq j$. □

Now let us see an implementation of systems. Let Array be the transition system labelled over the elementary observations of ArraySpec, with $\mathbb{N}^\omega$ as set of states and with transition relation given by, for all $m, n \in \omega$ and $i \in \mathbb{N}$,

1. $a \overset{write^i_n}{\to} a'$ if
   (a) $m \neq n \implies a'_m = a_m$,
   (b) $a'_n = i$;
2. $a \overset{read^i_n}{\to} a'$ if $a = a'$ and $a_n = i$.

Hence, the states of Array represent idealized arrays whose length is infinite, and in fact we have Array ⊩ ArraySpec.

Now let Pointer be the transition system labelled over the elementary observations of PointerSpec, with ω as set of states and with transition relation given by, for all $n \in \omega$,

1. $p \overset{inc}{\to} p' \iff p' = p + 1$,
2. $p \overset{dec}{\to} p' \iff p' = p - 1$,
3. $p \overset{pos_n}{\to} p' \iff p = p' = n$.

The states of Pointer are simply integer numbers, representing positions of an infinite array, and we have Pointer ⊩ PointerSpec.

Now we define an implementation $\langle \iota, \rho \rangle$ of Stack over Array ∥ Pointer. The map of states $\iota : \mathbb{N}^\omega \times \omega \to \mathbb{N}^*$ is given by, for all $a \in \mathbb{N}^\omega$ and $p \in \omega$:

$$\langle a, p + 1 \rangle \mapsto a_0 \ldots a_p ,$$
$$\langle a, 0 \rangle \mapsto \varepsilon .$$

Proposition 24. $\langle \iota, \rho \rangle$ *is an implementation.*

Proof. (Sketch.) We must show that the implementation condition holds. It suffices to do it for observations of the form $b = \alpha_1 \cdot \ldots \cdot \alpha_n \in A^*$ $(n \in \omega)$, where A is the set of elementary observations of StackSpec, which is done by induction on n. The base case $n = 0$ (i.e., $b = 1$) is trivial, and the induction step, $b = \alpha \cdot b'$ with $\alpha \in A$ and $b' \in A^*$, splits into the four cases $\alpha = empty$, $\alpha = pop$, $\alpha = push_i$ and $\alpha = top_i$. □

8   Concluding remarks

We have introduced a dynamic form of observational logic for the specification of labelled transition systems, where these are the models and where formulas are equations that impose constraints on how systems are observed. Several compositionality results were obtained, suggesting that the logic can provide a useful way of specifying systems when large specifications are involved. Interaction was only mentioned briefly, at the end of §6; future work includes further study of parallel composition of interacting systems, namely as regards diagonal compositionality.

Observational logic is based on the idea that systems should be described in terms of the finite observations that we can perform on them, which gives us an understanding of systems at the level of operational semantics. Furthermore the notion of finite observation has roots in topology and domain theory, which contributes to keeping the framework close to the traditional denotational semantics of programming languages; a naive denotational semantics for states can consist of letting the denotation of each state p be its set of finite observations, $[\![p]\!] = \{a \mid p \xrightarrow{a}\}$. An interesting line of research would be to study such semantics from the point of view of final semantics and coalgebras.

References

1. S. Abramsky, Domain theory in logical form, *Ann. Pure Appl. Logic* **51** (1991) 1–77.
2. S. Abramsky and S. Vickers, Quantales, observational logic and process semantics, *Math. Structures Comput. Sci.* **3** (1993) 161–227.
3. E. Astesiano, A. Giovini, and G. Reggio, Observational structures and their logic. *Theoret. Comput. Sci.* **96** (1992) 249–283.
4. B. Bloom, S. Istrail, and A.R. Meyer, Bisimulation can't be traced, *J. ACM* **42** (1995) 232–268.
5. R.J. van Glabbeek, The linear time – branching time spectrum, in: J.C.M. Baeten and J.W. Klop, ed., *Proc. CONCUR'90*, LNCS 458 (Springer, Berlin, 1990) 278–297.
6. R.J. van Glabbeek, The linear time – branching time spectrum II; the semantics of sequential systems with silent moves, Tech. Report, Stanford University, 1993. Extended abstract in: E. Best, ed., *Proc. CONCUR'93*, LNCS 715 (Springer, Berlin, 1993) 66–81.
7. J. Goguen and R. Burstall, Institutions: abstract model theory for specification and programming. *J. ACM*, **39** (1992) 95–146.
8. J.F. Groote, Transition system specifications with negative premises, *Theoret. Comput. Sci.* **118** (1993) 263–299.
9. J.F. Groote and F. Vaandrager, Structured operational semantics and bisimulation as a congruence, *Inform. and Comput.* **100** (1992) 202–260.
10. M. Hennessy and R. Milner, Algebraic laws for nondeterminism and concurrency, *J. ACM* **32** (1985) 137–161.
11. C.A.R. Hoare, *Communicating Sequential Processes* (Prentice Hall, New York, 1985).
12. P. Johnstone, *Stone Spaces* (Cambridge University Press, Cambridge, 1982).
13. A. Kurz, Specifying coalgebras with modal logic. *Electronic Notes in Theoret. Comput. Sci.* **11** (1998).
14. A. Mazurkiewicz, Concurrent program schemes and their interpretations. Tech. Report DAIMI PB-78, Aarhus University, Computer Science Department, 1977.
15. P. Menezes, A. Sernadas, and J.-F. Costa, Nonsequential automata semantics for a concurrent object-based language. To appear in *Electronic Notes in Theoret. Comput. Sci.*.
16. R. Milner, A modal characterisation of observable machine behaviour, in: G. Astesiano and C. Bohm, ed., *Proc. CAAP 81*, LNCS 112 (Springer, Berlin, 1981) 25–34.
17. R. Milner, *Communication and Concurrency* (Prentice Hall, New York, 1989).
18. C. Mulvey, &, *Rend. Circ. Mat. Palermo (2) Suppl.*, No. 12 (1986) 99–104.

19. P. Resende, Quantales, finite observations and strong bisimulation. Preprint
    26/97, Dep. Math., Tech. Univ. Lisbon, 1997. Submitted. Also available by ftp
    at cs.math.ist.utl.pt/pub/ResendeP/97-R-bisim.ps.
20. P. Resende, *Tropological Systems and Observational Logic in Concurrency and
    Specification.* Ph.D. thesis, Universidade Técnica de Lisboa, 1997.
21. K. Rosenthal, *Quantales and Their Applications* (Longman Scientific & Technical,
    London, 1990).
22. M. Smyth, Powerdomains and predicate transformers: a topological view. In
    J. Diaz, ed., *Automata, Languages and Programming*, LNCS 154 (Springer, Berlin,
    1983) 662–675.
23. S. Vickers, *Topology Via Logic* (Cambridge University Press, Cambridge, 1989).
24. G. Winskel and M. Nielsen, Models for concurrency. In *Handbook of Logic in
    Computer Science*, Vol. 4. (Oxford University Press, Oxford, 1995).

Proof Normalization of Structured Algebraic Specifications Is Convergent

Martin Wirsing[1], John N. Crossley[2] , Hannes Peterreins[3]

[1] Institut für Informatik, Ludwig-Maximilians-Universität München, Oettingenstr. 67, D-80538 München, Germany, email: wirsing@informatik.uni-muenchen.de

[2] School of Computer Science and Software Engineering, Monash University, Clayton, Vic 3168, Australia, email: jnc@csse.monash.edu.au

[3] Portfolio Consulting GmbH, Bodenseestr. 4, D-81241 München

Abstract. In this paper we present a new natural deduction calculus for structured algebraic specifications and study proof transformations including cut elimination. As underlying language we choose an ASL-like kernel language which includes operators for composing specifications, renaming the signature and exporting a subsignature of a specification. To get a natural deduction calculus for structured specifications we combine a natural deduction calculus for first-order predicate logic with the proof rules for structured specifications. The main results are soundness and completeness of the calculus and convergence of the associated system of proof term reductions which extends a typed λ-calculus by appropriate structural reductions.

1. Introduction

One of the main benefits of formal specifications is the ability to perform proofs. Indeed, reasoning about specifications is an important activity in the process of formal program development where a typical task is to prove properties of a specification. In the algebraic specification area many approaches have been developed for proving properties of flat (unstructured) specifications having their origin in (conditional) equational logic and term rewriting. The situation is different if we consider large system specifications. So far few proof techniques have been investigated that support structuring aspects. For such approaches see [SB83], [HST89], [W93], [Fa92], [Ce95], [Pe96], [Hen97], [HW97].

In this paper we present a new natural deduction calculus for structured algebraic specifications and study proof transformations including cut elimination. As underlying language we choose an ASL-like kernel language which includes operators for composing specifications, renaming the signature and exporting a subsignature of a specification. To get a natural deduction calculus for structured specifications we combine a natural deduction calculus for first-order predicate logic [BS95] with the proof rules for structured specifications (see e.g. [W93, HW97]). Any sequent has the form $\Gamma \vdash_{SP} d$: A where SP denotes the current specification, Γ a set of assumptions and A a formula. The specification SP acts as an environment whose axioms and rules are used in addition to the assumptions in Γ to prove A. The proof term d gives a Curry-Howard-style representation of the proof of A.

The proof terms are also used for normalizing proofs. As in the Curry-Howard approach for first-order logic (see e.g. [CS93]), introduction rules which are followed immediately by the corresponding elimination rules lead to "superfluous" parts of the proof which can be eliminated by proof transformations. These transformations are represented by reduction rules for proof terms. For example, cut elimination, i.e. the removal of

J.L. Fiadeiro (Ed.): WADT'98, LNCS 1589, pp. 326-340, 1999.

an arrow introduction immediately followed by an arrow elimination, corresponds to β-reduction on proof terms. Here the proof rules for the specification-building operators cause other problems because structural rules may separate corresponding (logical) introduction and elimination rules. We solve these difficulties by introducing new reduction rules which, in a sense, interchange logical rules and structural rules. Thus we obtain a typed λ-calculus enhanced by additional (structural and interchange) rules. As our main new result we prove that this calculus is confluent and strongly normalizing, i.e. convergent.

The paper is organized as follows: In section 2 we review structured algebraic specifications including syntax, semantics and normal forms. In section 3 we present our natural deduction calculus for structured specifications together with soundness and completeness results. In section 4 we study proof term reductions and show the local confluence of the associated rewriting relation. In section 5 we give the essential steps of the strong normalization theorem. We conclude the paper with some remarks on possible applications in section 6.

2.   Structured algebraic specifications

We assume the reader to be familiar with the standard notions of algebraic specifications such as signature $\Sigma = (S, F)$, where S is a set of sorts and F an S-sorted family of function symbols, signature morphism $\sigma: \Sigma \to \Sigma'$, Σ-term, Σ-formula, Σ-algebra, class $Alg(\Sigma)$ of all Σ-algebras, etc.. For any Σ-formula A, sig(A) denotes the smallest subsignature of Σ which contains all sorts and function symbols of Σ.

In order to introduce proof terms the axioms of specifications will be labelled by constants $c_1, \dots$. We shall require that the labels c_i are not re-used, except that it will usually be convenient (but it is not essential) to assume that if two axioms are identical, then they have the same label. This is, of course, equivalent to treating the axioms as forming a set. (In practice it may happen that in the course of constructing a new specification, we add a new axiom which in fact was there already. Of course there are other similar possibilities such as adding a "new" axiom which in fact only differs in its choice of bound variables from a pre-existing one.) We write c:A for an axiom A with label c.

A *basic specification* consists of a signature Σ and a set $\{c_1: A_1, \dots, c_n: A_n\}$ of labelled axioms where $c_1, \dots, c_n$ are pairwise different constants and $A_1, \dots, A_n$ are Σ-formulas. A *labelled signature* is a pair (Σ, L) where Σ is a signature and L is a family of labels typed by Σ-formulas. For any labelled signature $L\Sigma = (\Sigma, L)$ there exists a canonical projection pr_{sig} computing the (traditional) signature defined by $pr_{sig}(L\Sigma) = \Sigma$. A signature morphism $\rho:(\Sigma,L) \to (\Sigma',L')$ of labelled signatures consists of a signature morphism $\rho_{sig}:\Sigma \to \Sigma'$ and a renaming $\rho_{lab}: L \to L'$ of the labels which respects ρ_{sig}; i.e. for any label $l:A \in L$ we have $\rho_{lab}(l) : \rho_{sig}(A)$.

The basic operations for constructing structured specifications from flat ones are *renaming*, *export*, and building the *sum* of two specifications. Because of the export operation we have to distinguish between the visible and the hidden symbols of a specification. For any specification SP we will define below (cf. also [Pe96])

- its *labelled signature* sigl(SP) consisting of all visible sorts, function symbols and labels, and its *signature* sig(SP) $=_{def} pr_{sig}(sigl(SP))$,

- its set of *labelled symbols* symbl(SP) consisting of all visible and hidden sorts, function symbols and labels, and its *set of symbols* symb(SP) $=_{def}$ pr$_{sig}$(symbl(SP)),
- and its set of *labelled axioms* lax(SP) consisting of all visible and hidden labelled axioms. (Thus lax(SP) consists of labelled symb(SP)-formulas.)

The symbols of SP include those of sigl(SP). The symbols in symbl(SP) - sigl(SP) are called the *hidden* symbols of SP. There is a natural injection ι_{SP} of sigl(SP) into symbl(SP).

For technical convenience, export and renaming operators are treated as in [BHK90]: For a renaming $\rho \bullet$ SP we just require that the domain $\Sigma0$ of the signature morphism ρ be a *sub*signature of the signature of SP. This is needed in the definition of substitution (Def. 4.1). Clearly there is a natural embedding which we call "in" of $\Sigma0$ into sigl(SP). Thus the morphism ρ can always be extended to a morphism ρ' with domain sigl(SP) in a canonical way by a pushout construction. In constructing the actual pushouts we follow normal practice and automatically generate new symbols. In this way we give a unique signature to any pushout. Nevertheless as we translate from one specification to another it is routine (and can be made automatic) to follow the changes we are making. In this way the semantic equivalences we give in Fact 2.4 can be automatically coded as renamings from one signature to another. For the export operation SP|$_\Sigma$ we do not require that Σ be a subsignature of sig(SP), but define the signature of SP|$_\Sigma$ to be sig(SP) $\cap \Sigma$. This facilitates the proof transformations (σ-reduction) in section 4.

In the following we define the syntax of structured specification expressions. Moreover, we define inductively the sets sigl(SP), symbl(SP), lax(SP) and the natural injection ι_{SP}. Using lax(SP) we construct the *flat normal form* of SP which consists of a basic specification <symb(SP), lax(SP)> restricted to the signature of SP.

Definition 2.1 (cf. [Pe96], [Hen97], [HW97])
1. Specification expressions. The set Spec of *specification expressions* is inductively defined as follows:
- If Σ is a signature, $A_1, ..., A_n$ are closed Σ-formulas and $c_1, ..., c_n$ are pairwise different labels, then the basic specification SP of form $<\Sigma, \{c_1: A_1, ..., c_n: A_n\}>$ is in Spec; sigl(SP) = symbl(SP) = $(\Sigma, \{c_1, ..., c_n\})$, lax(SP) = $\{c_1: A_1, ..., c_n: A_n\}$. The natural injection is the identity morphism id: ι_{SP} = id.
- If SP is in Spec and $\rho: \Sigma \to \Sigma1$ a bijective signature morphism with $\Sigma \subseteq$ sig(SP), then the renaming $\rho \bullet$ SP is in Spec;
  sigl($\rho \bullet$SP) = PO(ρ, in) = ρ'(sigl(SP)), symbl($\rho\bullet$SP) = PO(ρ',ι_{SP}) = ρ''(symbl(SP)),
  lax($\rho \bullet$ SP) = $\{\rho''(a): \rho''(A) \mid a:A \in$ lax(SP)$\}$ where ρ', ρ'', PO(ρ, in), PO(ρ', ι_{SP}),
  and $\iota_{\rho \bullet SP}$ are given by the following pushout diagram:

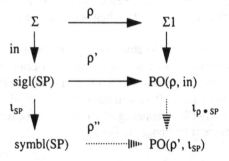

- If SP is in Spec and Σ is a signature , then the export specification $SP|_\Sigma$ is in Spec;
  $sigl(SP|_\Sigma) = (sig(SP) \cap \Sigma, L)$ where $L = \{a:A \in lax(SP) \mid sig(A) \subseteq sig(SP) \cap \Sigma\}$,
  $symbl(SP|_\Sigma) = symbl(SP)$, $lax(SP|_\Sigma) = lax(SP)$,
  $\iota_{SP|\Sigma}$ is the natural injection from $sigl(SP|_\Sigma)$ into $symbl(SP)$.
- If SP1, SP2 are in Spec, then the sum SP1+SP2 is in Spec;
  $sigl(SP1+SP2) = PO(\kappa1,\kappa2)$, $symbl(SP1+SP2) = PO(\iota_{SP1} \circ \kappa1, \iota_{SP2} \circ \kappa2)$,
  $lax(SP1+SP2) =$
  $$\{in1(a) : in1(A) \mid a:A \in lax(SP1)\} \cup \{in2(a) : in2(A) \mid a:A \in lax(SP2)\}$$
  where $\kappa1$, $\kappa2$, ι_{SP1}, ι_{SP2}, $in1$, $in2$, $PO(\kappa1,\kappa2)$, $PO(\iota_{SP1} \circ \kappa1, \iota_{SP2} \circ \kappa2)$ and $\iota_{SP1+SP2}$ are
  given by the following pushout diagram:

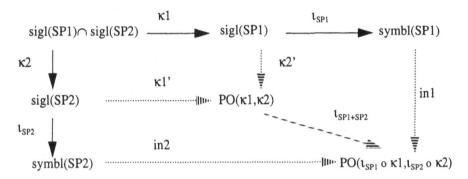

2. Flat normal form. The flat normal form nf(SP) of a specification SP is defined by
$<symb(SP), lax(SP)>|_{sig(SP)}$.   ◊

Fact 2.2 The signature of a specification expression has the following form:
$$sig(<\Sigma, Ax>) = \Sigma; \qquad\qquad sig(\rho \bullet SP) = \rho'(sig(SP));$$
$$sig(SP|_\Sigma) = sig(SP) \cap \Sigma;$$
$$sig(SP1 + SP2) \text{ is isomorphic to } sig(SP1) \cup sig(SP2).$$
Proof: Compute $pr_{sig}(sigl(SP))$ for any specification expression SP.   ◊

In the following we will use $sig(SP1) \cup sig(SP2)$ as standard representation of the
isomorphism class of $sig(SP1 + SP2)$. This simplifies the presentation of the natural deduction calculus since we do not have to write explicitly the embedding morphisms $\kappa1'$
and $\kappa2'$.

The *model class semantics* of a specification is defined as in [W90]. Two specifications are *semantically equivalent* if they have the same signatures and class of models.
SP1 is a *refinement* of SP if it contains all visible symbols of SP and all models of SP1
(suitably restricted) are models of SP.

Definition 2.3
1. Semantics. The semantics Mod(SP) of a specification SP is inductively defined as
follows:
- $Mod (<\Sigma, \{c_1: A_1, ..., c_n: A_n\}>) = \{B \in Alg(\Sigma) \mid B \models A_i \text{ for } i = 1,..., n\}$
- $Mod(\rho \bullet SP) \qquad = \{B \in Alg(\rho'(sig(SP))) \mid B|_\rho \in Mod(SP)\}$
- $Mod(SP|_\Sigma) \qquad = \{B|_{sig(SP) \cap \Sigma} \in Alg(sig(SP) \cap \Sigma) \mid B \in Mod(SP)\}$

- $\text{Mod(SP1 + SP2)} \quad =$
$$\{B \in Alg(sig(SP1+SP2)) \mid B|_{sig(SP1)} \in Mod(SP1) \wedge B|_{sig(SP2)} \in Mod(SP2)\}$$

2. Semantic equivalence. Two specifications SP1 and SP2 are semantically equivalent (written SP1 $\cong$ SP2) if sig(SP1) = sig(SP2) and Mod(SP1) = Mod(SP2).

3. Refinement. A specification SP1 is a refinement of SP (written SP ~~> SP1) if sig(SP) $\subseteq$ sig(SP1) and Mod(SP1$|_{sig(SP)}$) $\subseteq$ Mod(SP).   ◊

Fact 2.4

1) The flat normal form of any structured specification SP in Spec is semantically equivalent to SP; i.e. nf(SP) $\cong$ SP.

2) The following semantic equivalences and refinements are valid:

[I] $SP + SP \cong SP$ [C] $SP_1 + SP_2 \cong SP_2 + SP_1$

[A] $SP_1 + (SP_2 + SP_3) \cong (SP_1 + SP_2) + SP_3$

[Sig] $SP + <\Sigma, \varnothing> \cong SP$ if $\Sigma \subseteq sig(SP)$

[ρ+] $\rho \bullet (SP1+SP2) \cong \rho \bullet SP1 + \rho \bullet SP2$ [ρ<>] $\rho \bullet <\Sigma, Ax> \cong <\rho'(\Sigma), \rho'(Ax)>$

[I+] $(SP1 + SP2)|_\Sigma <\sim\sim SP1|_\Sigma + SP2|_\Sigma$

3) The structuring operators are monotonic w.r.t. refinement; i.e. for any SP, SP1, SP2, SP1', SP2', Σ, $\Sigma1$ the following hold:

- $SP \sim\sim> SP1$ implies $\rho \bullet SP \sim\sim> \rho \bullet SP1$
- $SP \sim\sim> SP1$ and $\Sigma \subseteq \Sigma1$ implies $SP|_\Sigma \sim\sim> SP1|_{\Sigma1}$
- $SP1 \sim\sim> SP1'$ and $SP2 \sim\sim> SP2'$ implies $SP1 + SP2 \sim\sim> SP1' + SP2'$

Proof: (1) by induction on the form of SP (cf. [Hen 97], (2) see e.g. [BHK90], (3) obvious.   ◊

Definition 2.5 Let $=_{ACISig}$ denote the smallest equivalence generated by [A], [C], [I], [Sig]. By $=_M$ we denote the smallest equivalence relation generated by all semantic equivalences of Fact 2.4.2.

Fact 2.6 The equivalences $=_M$ and therefore $=_{ACISig}$ is decidable.

Proof idea. Define appropriate normal forms for each equivalence relation and show that the normal form construction is recursive.   ◊

Definition 2.7 A rewriting relation is called *strongly normalizing* if all its reduction sequences are terminating. It is called *convergent* if it is confluent and strongly normalizing. This implies that any term has a unique normal form and any reduction sequence is terminating (see [BaN98]).

3. A natural deduction calculus

As deductive system we use the style of natural deduction introduced by Gentzen [Gen34]. It has sequents of the form $\Gamma \vdash d : A$ where Γ is a context, A a formula and d a proof term which gives a precise representation of the proof of A from the list of assumptions Γ. In type theory, A is considered as the type of the proof d.

To get a natural deduction calculus for structured specifications we combine a natural deduction calculus for first-order predicate logic [BS95] with the proof rules for structured specifications (see e.g. [W93, HW97]). Any sequent has the form $\Gamma \vdash_{SP} d : A$ where SP denotes the current specification. SP acts as an environment whose axioms are used in addition to the assumptions in Γ to prove the sig(SP)-formula A. W.l.o.g. we restrict ourselves to formulas built from $\bot$ ("falsum"), $\wedge$, $\rightarrow$, $\forall$. The logical rules comprise introduction and elimination rules for $\wedge$, $\rightarrow$, $\forall$, an axiom for assumption introduction and two axioms for classical logic. The structural rules reflect the proof rules of the specification operators.

A sequent $\Gamma \vdash_{SP} d : A$ is well-formed if A and the elements of Γ are sig(SP)-formulas. In the following rules we assume that any sequent is well-formed. For any formula A and context Γ, $\Gamma \overline{\cup} \{x:A\}$ in ($\rightarrow$I) denotes set-theoretic union and assumes that x:A is not element of Γ.

Logical rules
Introduction Rules

(Ass I)
$$\frac{}{\{x:A\}\vdash_{<sig(A),\,\varnothing>} ass(A,x) : A}$$

(Ax I)
$$\frac{}{\varnothing \vdash_{<\Sigma,\,Ax>} ax(<\Sigma,Ax>, x) : A}$$
if x :A$\in$ Ax

($\rightarrow$ I)
$$\frac{\Gamma \overline{\cup} \{x:A\} \vdash_{SP} d: B}{\Gamma \vdash_{SP} \lambda x:A.d: A \rightarrow B}$$

($\wedge$ I)
$$\frac{\Gamma 1 \vdash_{SP1} d: A \qquad \Gamma 2 \vdash_{SP2} e: B}{\Gamma 1 \cup \Gamma 2 \vdash_{SP1+SP2} <d, e> : A \wedge B}$$

($\forall$ I)
$$\frac{\Gamma \vdash_{SP} d: A}{\Gamma \vdash_{SP} \lambda x:s.d: \forall x:s.\, A}$$
if $x \notin$ fv(B) for every b:B $\in \Gamma$ [1]

Elimination Rules

($\rightarrow$ E)
$$\frac{\Gamma 1 \vdash_{SP1} d: A \rightarrow B \qquad \Gamma 2 \vdash_{SP2} e: A}{\Gamma 1 \cup \Gamma 2 \vdash_{SP1+SP2} de : B}$$

($\wedge$ E)
$$\frac{\Gamma \vdash_{SP} d: A_1 \wedge A_2}{\Gamma \vdash_{SP} \pi_i(d) : A_i}$$
(i=1,2)

($\forall$ E)
$$\frac{\Gamma \vdash_{SP} d: \forall x:s.\, A}{\Gamma \vdash_{SP} dt: A[t/x]}$$
if t is a sig(SP)-term of sort s

Structural rules

(ren))
$$\frac{\Gamma \vdash_{SP} d: A}{\rho'(\Gamma) \vdash_{\rho \bullet SP} \rho \bullet d: \rho'(A)}$$

(exp)
$$\frac{\Gamma \vdash_{SP} d: A}{\Gamma \vdash_{SP|\Sigma} d|_\Sigma : A}$$
if Γ is a Σ-context and A is a Σ-formula

(sum1)
$$\frac{\Gamma \vdash_{SP1} d: A}{\Gamma \vdash_{SP1+SP2} sum_1(d, SP2): A}$$

(sum2)
$$\frac{\Gamma \vdash_{SP2} d: A}{\Gamma \vdash_{SP1+SP2} sum_2(d, SP1):A}$$

Axioms for classical logic
Stability

$$\frac{}{\Gamma \vdash_{SP} stab(\Gamma,SP,A): ((A \rightarrow \bot) \rightarrow \bot) \rightarrow A)}$$
where A is atomic

ex falso quodlibet

$$\frac{}{\Gamma \vdash_{SP} ex\_falso(\Gamma,SP,A): \bot \rightarrow A}$$
where A is atomic

---

1. fv(B) denotes the set of free variables of a formula B.

The proof terms can be used to compute the following information: for any proof term d, we define

> for(d):   the derived formula,
> sp(d) :   the current specification,
> con(d) :   the current context,

such that con(d) $\vdash_{sp(d)}$ d: for(d) .The proof terms can be used to compute all these plus the free and bound assumptions, instantiated terms and abstracted sorts. We give the inductive definitions of sp(d) and for(d) and leave the definitions of the other items to the interested reader.

Definition 3.1 Let d be a well-formed proof term.

$$sp(ass(A,x)) = <sig(A), \{x{:}A\}> \quad for(ass(A, x)) = A$$
$$sp(ax(<\Sigma,Ax>, x)) = <\Sigma, Ax> \quad for(ax(<\Sigma,Ax>, x)) = A \text{ if } x{:}A \in Ax$$
$$sp(<d, e>) = sp(d) + sp(e) \quad for(<d, e>) = for(d) \wedge for(e)$$
$$sp(\pi_i(d)) = sp(d) \quad for(\pi_i(d)) = A_i \text{ if } for(d) = A_1 \wedge A_2$$
$$sp(\lambda y{:}B.d) = sp(d) \quad for(\lambda y{:}B.d) = B \rightarrow for(d)$$
$$sp(de) = sp(d) + sp(e) \quad for(de) = B, \text{ if } for(d) = A \rightarrow B \text{ and } for(e) = A$$
$$sp(\lambda y{:}s.d) = sp(d) \quad for(\lambda y{:}s.d) = \forall y{:}s.for(d)$$
$$sp(dt) = sp(d) \quad for(dt) = for(d)[t/x]$$
$$sp(ex\_falso(SP,A)) = SP \quad for(ex\_falso(SP,A)) = A$$
$$sp(stab(SP,A)) = SP \quad for(stab(SP,A)) = A$$
$$sp(\rho \bullet d) = \rho \bullet sp(d) \quad for(\rho \bullet d) = \rho'(for(d))$$
$$sp(d|_\Sigma) = sp(d)|_\Sigma \quad for(d|_\Sigma) = for(d) \text{ if } for(d) \text{ is a } \Sigma\text{-formula}$$
$$sp(sum_1(d, SP2)) = sp(d) + SP2 \quad for(sum_i(d, SP1)) = for(d), \quad i=1,2$$
$$sp(sum_2(d, SP1)) = SP1 + sp(d)$$

Note that for any proof term d the signature of for(d) is contained in the signature of sp(d). In the following we often simply write x for the proof term ass(A, x) .

Example 3.2

1) Let x:A be a new assumption which is not in Γ.

$$(\rightarrow E) \quad \frac{\Gamma \vdash_{SP} c{:} A \rightarrow B \qquad \{x{:}A\} \vdash_{<sig(A),\varnothing>} ass(A, x) : A}{\Gamma \cup \{x{:}A\} \vdash_{SP+<sig(A),\varnothing>} cx : B}$$

$$(\rightarrow I) \quad \frac{}{\Gamma \vdash_{SP+<sig(A),\varnothing>} \lambda x{:}A.cx : A \rightarrow B \qquad \Gamma1 \vdash_{SP1} d : A}$$

$$(\rightarrow E) \quad \frac{}{\Gamma \cup \Gamma1 \vdash_{SP+<sig(A),\varnothing>+ SP1} (\lambda x{:}A.cx)d : B}$$

2) Let $\Gamma = \{x{:}A, b{:}B\}$, A,B sig(SP0)-formulas.

$$(ren) \quad \frac{\{x{:}A\} \vdash_{<sig(A),\varnothing>} ass(A, x) : A}{\{\rho'(x){:}\rho'(A)\} \vdash_{\rho\bullet<sig(A),\varnothing>} \rho\bullet ass(A, x){:} \rho'(A)}$$

$$\ldots$$

$$(\rightarrow I) \quad \frac{\Gamma \cup \{\rho'(x){:}\rho'(A)\} \vdash_{SP0} d{:} C}{\Gamma \vdash_{SP0} \lambda\rho'(x){:}\rho'(A). d{:} \rho'(A) \rightarrow C \qquad \Gamma1 \vdash_{SP1} r : \rho'(A)}$$

$$(\rightarrow E) \quad \frac{}{\Gamma \cup \Gamma1 \vdash_{SP0 + SP1} (\lambda\rho'(x){:}\rho'(A). d) r : C}$$

As example 3.2.1 above shows, the use of SP1+SP2 in [→ E] and [∧ I] may lead to complicated specification expressions. Therefore we consider equivalence classes of specifications modulo $=_{ACISig}$, i.e. modulo associativity, commutativity and idempotence of "+" and the equation [Sig] (see Def. 2.5). Then we consider natural deduction sequents where the specification expression denotes an $=_{ACISig}$-equivalence class.

Example 3.3   (Use of ACISig)
1) $\Gamma \vdash_{[SP1+SP2]} d : A{\to}B$ $\qquad\qquad$ $\Gamma1 \vdash_{[SP1]} r : A$

$$\Gamma \cup \Gamma1 \vdash_{[(SP1 + SP2) + SP1]} dr : B$$
$$=_{ACISig}$$
$$\Gamma \cup \Gamma1 \vdash_{[SP1 + SP2]} dr : B$$

2) Example 3.2.1 can rewritten as follows. Let x:A be a sig(SP)-formula which is not in Γ.

$(\to E)$ $\dfrac{\Gamma \vdash_{[SP]} c: A \to B \qquad\qquad \{x{:}A\} \vdash_{[<sig(A),\varnothing>]} ass(A,x): A}{\begin{array}{l} \Gamma \cup \{x{:}A\} \vdash_{[SP+<sig(A),\varnothing>]} cx : B \qquad\qquad (\text{since sig(A)} \subseteq \text{sig(SP))} \\ =_{ACISig} \Gamma \cup \{x{:}A\} \vdash_{[SP]} cx : B \end{array}}$

$(\to I)$ $\dfrac{\Gamma \vdash_{[SP]} \lambda x{:}A.\ cx: A \to B \qquad\qquad\qquad \Gamma1 \vdash_{[SP1]} d : A}{}$

$(\to E)$ $\dfrac{}{\Gamma \cup \Gamma1 \vdash_{[SP+SP1]} (\lambda x{:}A.\ cx)\ d : B}$

Theorem 3.4 (Soundness and completeness) The natural deduction calculus for structured specifications is sound and complete.
The **Proof** uses the soundness and completeness of natural deduction, the interpolation property of first-order logic and the existence of normal forms. The completeness proof follows exactly the lines of the proof in [Ce95]; for a completeness proof of a (different) natural deduction calculus for structured specifications see [Pe96].   ◊

4.   Proof term reductions

In first-order logic a proof is normal when it does **not** contain any introduction rule immediately followed by an elimination of the same connective (we omit here Γ and SP):

[x:A]

$\ \ \ \ \ \cdot\qquad\quad\cdot$	$\ \ \ \ \cdot\qquad\qquad$
$d: A\quad e: B$	$e: B\qquad\qquad\quad\cdot$

[∧I] $\dfrac{d: A\quad e: B}{<d,e>: A \land B}$ [→I] $\dfrac{e: B}{\lambda x{:}A.e{:}A \to B \quad d: A}$

[∧E] $\dfrac{}{\pi_1<d,e>:\ A}$ [→E] $\dfrac{}{(\lambda x{:}A.e)d: B}$

since they are equivalent to the following (simpler) proofs:

d: A

$\ \ \ \ \cdot$

e[d/x]: B

$\qquad\qquad$ d: A

We will show in the following that in the case of structured specifications the same transformations can be applied. However one has to be careful with contexts Γ and specification environments SP. For example, in the case of the transformation on the left hand side above the specification environment will be simplified from $sp(\pi_1<d,e>) = sp(d)+sp(e)$ to $sp(d)$. The resulting context will be contained in the context of $\pi_1<d,e>$ (see prop. 4.5). Similarly in the case that x does not occur in d, the transformation of the right hand side above leads to simpler specification environments and contexts. The definition of *substitution* is standard except for renaming: any label of a proof term d is renamed in the proof term $\rho \bullet d$ by ρ. Thus replacing x:A by r:A in $\rho \bullet d$ means to invert the renaming and to replace $\rho^{-1'}(x)$ by $\rho^{-1} \bullet r$ in d.

Definition 4.1 (Substitution) The substitution d[r/x] is inductively defined for any labelled formula x:A and proof terms d, r with for(r) = A:

i) **Logical rules**

$$ass(A, y)\ [r/x] = \begin{cases} r & \text{if } y = x \\ ass(A, y) & \text{otherwise} \end{cases}$$

$$ax(<\Sigma, Ax>, y)\ [r/x] = ax(<\Sigma, Ax>, y)$$
$$<d, e>\ [r/x] = <d[r/x], e[r/x]>$$
$$\pi_i(d)\ [r/x] = \pi_i(d[r/x])$$

$$(\lambda y{:}B.d)\ [r/x] = \begin{cases} \lambda y{:}B.d & \text{if } y{:}B = x{:}A \\ \lambda y{:}B.d[r/x] & \text{if } y{:}B \neq x{:}A,\ y \notin fv(r),\ x \notin fv(d) \\ \lambda z{:}B.d[z/y][r/x] & \text{otherwise, where z is new} \end{cases}$$

$$(de)\ [r/x] = (d[r/x])(e[r/x])$$
$$(\lambda y{:}s.d)\ [r/x] = \lambda y{:}s.\ (d[r/x]) \qquad \text{where s is a sort}$$
$$(dt)\ [r/x] = (d[r/x])t \qquad \text{where t is a term}$$
$$ex\_falso(SP, A)\ [r/x] = ex\_falso(SP, A)$$
$$stab(SP, A)\ [r/x] = stab(SP, A)$$

ii) **Structural rules**

$$(\rho \bullet d)\ [r/x] = \rho \bullet (d[\rho^{-1} \bullet r/\rho^{-1'}(x)])$$

$$(d|_\Sigma)\ [r/x] = \begin{cases} d[r/x]|_\Sigma & \text{if A is a } \Sigma\text{-formula} \\ d & \text{otherwise} \end{cases}$$

$$sum_i(d, SP)\ [r/x] = sum_i(d[r/x], SP) \qquad\qquad \Diamond$$

Substitution preserves the derived formulae and may add contexts. If an assumption x:A is replaced by a term r which represents a proof of A in an environment SP0 then because of $sig(A) \subseteq sig(SP0)$ we have $<sig(A), \varnothing> \leadsto SP0$. More generally, $sp(d[r/x])$ is a refinement of $sp(d)$ for any proof term d. On the other hand, the sum $sp(d) + SP0$ is a refinement of $sp(d[r/x])$ since e.g. r may not occur in d.

Proposition 4.2 (Substitution properties) For any well-defined proof term d, r and labelled formula x:A, if $\Gamma \vdash_{SP} d{:}\ B$ and $\Gamma0 \vdash_{SP0} r{:}A$ then
d[r/x] is well-defined, B = for(d[r/x]) and for $\Gamma1 = con(d[r/x])$, $SP1 = sp(d[r/x])$
we have $\Gamma1 \vdash_{SP1} d[r/x]{:}\ B$, $\Gamma1 \subseteq (\Gamma \cup \Gamma0) \setminus \{x{:}A\}$ and $SP \leadsto SP1 \leadsto SP + SP0$.
Proof by structural induction on the form of d. $\qquad\qquad \Diamond$

For the structural rules we want to simplify renamings as much as possible. The injective signature morphisms with composition o and neutral element id form a group which has a convergent term rewriting system (see Def. 2.6). We can simplify two consecutive renamings $\rho_2 \bullet \rho_1 \bullet d$ of a proof term d to $(\rho_2 \circ \rho_1) \bullet d$. Moreover, the identity morphism id can be eliminated from proof terms and renamings of assumptions can be reduced to renamed assumptions. These considerations lead to the following reduction rules.

Definition 4.3 ($\beta\rho$-reduction) Let $\to_\beta$, $\to_\pi$ be the smallest relations generated by the rules:

[β]	$(\lambda x{:}A.\ d)\ r$	$\to_\beta$	$\delta[r/x]$	if for(r) = A
[π_i]	$\pi_i\,(<d_1, d_2>)\ \to_\pi$	d_i		(i=1, 2)

and let $\to_\rho$ be the smallest relation generated by a convergent rewrite system of the group of injective signature morphisms and the rules:

[ρo]	$\rho_2 \bullet \rho_1 \bullet d$	$\to_\rho$	$(\rho_2 \circ \rho_1) \bullet d$
[id]	$\text{id} \bullet d$	$\to_\rho$	d
[ρass]	$\rho \bullet \text{ass}(x, A)$	$\to_\rho$	$\text{ass}(\rho'(x), \rho'(A))$

Then let $\to_{\beta\rho} = \to_\beta \cup \to_\pi \cup \to_\rho$.   ◊

Example 4.4 (Example 3.2 continued)
1) Applying [β] reduces the proof term $(\lambda x{:}A.\ cx)d$ representing the proof in ex. 3.2.1) to cd , i.e. to the following simpler proof:

$$(\to \text{E}) \quad \frac{\Gamma \vdash_{\text{SP}} c{:}\ A \to B \qquad \Gamma1 \vdash_{\text{SP1}} d : A}{\Gamma \cup \Gamma1 \vdash_{\text{SP+ SP1}} cd : B}$$

2) The proof term $(\lambda\rho'(x){:}\rho'(A).\ d)\ r$ of ex. 3.2.2 reduces to some proof term d1 where d1 results from d by replacing ass(x, A) by $\rho^{-1} \bullet r$ and rewriting $\rho \bullet \rho^{-1} \bullet r$ to r, i.e the resulting proof has the form:
Let $\Gamma = \{x{:}A, b{:}B\}$, A,B sig(SP0)-formulas.

(ren)
$$\frac{\rho^{-1}{}'(\Gamma1) \vdash_{\rho^{-1} \bullet \text{SP1}} \rho^{-1} \bullet r : A}{\rho'(\rho^{-1}{}'(\Gamma1)) \vdash_{\rho\bullet\rho^{-1} \bullet \text{SP1}} \rho \bullet \rho^{-1} \bullet r: \rho'(A)}$$

$\to_\rho$ $\qquad \Gamma1 \quad \vdash_{\text{SP1}} r: \rho'(A)$

$\cdots$

$$\Gamma \cup \Gamma1 \vdash_{\text{SP0[SP1} / \rho\bullet<\text{sig(A)},\ \varnothing>]} d1 : C \qquad\qquad ◊$$

β-, π- and ρ-reduction preserve derived formulae. The context of the right hand side is contained in the one of the left hand side. Similarly, the left hand side is a refinement of the right hand side.

Proposition 4.5 Let $l \to_\xi r$ with $\xi \in \{\beta, \pi, \rho\}$ be an instance of a $\beta\rho$-reduction rule. Then the following holds:
$$\text{for}(r) = \text{for}(l),\ \text{con}(r) \subseteq \text{con}(l),\ \text{sp}(r) \rightsquigarrow \text{sp}(l)$$
In particular, for $\xi = \rho$ we have con(r) = con(l) and sp(r) $\cong$ sp(l).
Proof by structural induction on the structure of l.   ◊

Theorem 4.6 The relation $\to_{\beta\rho}$ is locally confluent.

Proof sketch: The relation $\to_{\beta\cup\pi} =_{def} \to_\beta \cup \to_\pi$ is locally confluent (see e.g. [Bar84]). The local confluence of $\to_{\beta\rho}$ follows from this by examining all critical pairs of $\to_\rho$ and all critical pairs where rules of $\to_\rho$ and $\to_{\beta\cup\pi}$ overlap.   ◊

But this is not the whole picture. Structural rules which separate elimination rules from introduction rules may hide possible reductions.

Example 4.7

In the following proof a renaming separates ($\to$I) from ($\to$E).

$$(\to \text{I}) \quad \frac{\Gamma \cup \{x{:}A\} \vdash_{SP} d : B}{\Gamma \vdash_{SP} \lambda x{:}A.\, d: A \to B}$$

$$(\text{ren}) \quad \frac{\Gamma \vdash_{SP} \lambda x{:}A.\, d: A \to B}{\rho'(\Gamma) \vdash_{\rho\bullet SP} \rho\bullet(\lambda x{:}A.\, d): \rho'(A) \to \rho'(B)} \qquad \Gamma 1 \ \vdash_{SP1} r : \rho'(A)$$

$$(\to \text{E}) \quad \frac{}{\rho'(\Gamma) \cup \Gamma 1 \vdash_{\rho\bullet SP+\, SP1} (\rho\bullet(\lambda x{:}A.\, d))\, r : \rho'(B)}$$

By exchanging ($\to$I) and (ren) one obtains a proof term where β-reduction can be applied:

$$(\text{ren}) \quad \frac{\Gamma \cup \{x{:}A\} \vdash_{SP} d : B}{\rho'(\Gamma) \cup \{\rho'(x){:}\rho'(A)\} \vdash_{\rho\bullet SP} \rho\bullet d : \rho'(B)}$$

$$(\to \text{I}) \quad \frac{\rho'(\Gamma) \cup \{\rho'(x){:}\rho'(A)\} \vdash_{\rho\bullet SP} \rho\bullet d : \rho'(B)}{\rho'(\Gamma) \vdash_{\rho\bullet SP} \lambda\rho'(x){:}\rho'(A).\, \rho\bullet d : \rho'(A) \to \rho'(B)} \qquad \Gamma 1 \vdash_{SP1} r : \rho'(A)$$

$$(\to \text{E}) \quad \frac{}{\rho'(\Gamma) \cup \Gamma 1 \vdash_{\rho\bullet SP+\, SP1} (\lambda\rho'(x){:}\rho'(A).\, \rho \bullet d)r : \rho'(B)} \qquad\qquad ◊$$

To solve this problem we add new reduction rules which allow to exchange systematically structural rules with introduction rules: structural rules (below introduction rules) are moved towards the root of proof. This follows an idea of [Pe96] (where structural rules are exchanged with all logical rules and not only the introduction rules.)

Definition 4.8 (σ-reduction) Let $\to_\sigma$ be the smallest relations generated by rules of the form

$$S(\lambda x{:}A.d) \to_\sigma \lambda S(x){:}S(A).S(d) \qquad\qquad \text{if } S(\lambda x{:}A.d) \text{ is wellformed}$$
$$S(\lambda x{:}s.d) \to_\sigma \lambda x{:}S(s).S(d) \qquad\qquad \text{if } S(\lambda x{:}s.d) \text{ is wellformed}$$
$$S(<d, e>) \to_\sigma <S(d), \Sigma(e)> \qquad\qquad \text{if } S(<d, e>) \text{ is wellformed}$$

where $S(.) \in \{\rho\bullet., .|_\Sigma, \text{sum}_i(., SP)\}$ denotes a structuring (proof term) operator,

$$S(x) =_{def} \rho'(x),\ S(A) =_{def} \rho'(A),\ S(A) =_{def} \rho'(A) \text{ if } S(.) = \rho\bullet., \text{ and}$$
$$S(x) =_{def} x,\ S(A) =_{def} A, \text{ otherwise.}$$

Then let $\to_{\beta\rho\sigma} = \to_\beta \cup \to_\pi \cup \to_\rho \cup \to_\sigma$.   ◊

If $S(.)$ is an export $.|_\Sigma$, then the wellformedness of $(\lambda x{:}A.d)|_\Sigma$ ($<e, f>|_\Sigma$, resp.) ensures that the context and the derived formula of $\lambda x{:}A.d$ ($<e, f>$, resp.) consist of Σ-formulas and therefore introduction and structural rule can be exchanged.

σ-reduction preserves contexts and derived formulae. Commuting structural rules with λ-abstraction also preserves the associated specification. But commutation with pairing changes the structure of the associated specification: in the case of export the left hand side is a refinement of the specification associated with the right hand side. For sum and renaming the specification environments are preserved up to semantic equivalence.

Proposition 4.9 Let $S(\lambda x:A.d)$ and $S(<e, f>)$ be wellformed proof terms.
Then $\lambda S(x):S(A).S(d)$ and $<S(e), \Sigma(f)>$ are also wellformed.
Moreover, the following holds:

$$\text{att}(S(\lambda x:A.d)) = \text{att}(\lambda S(x):S(A).S(d)) \text{ and att}(S(<e, f>)) \circledR \text{att}(<S(e), \Sigma(f)>)$$

where att $\in$ {for, con, sp} and $\circledR$ is syntactic equality for att $\in$ {for, con} and

$\circledR$ is $=_{\rho^+}$ if $S = \rho\bullet.$, $=_{ACl}$ if $S = \text{sum}_i(.,SP)$, $<\sim\sim$ if $S = .|_\Sigma$.

Proof by structural induction. The wellformedness of $<e|_\Sigma, f|_\Sigma>$ follows from the particular choice of definition of $SP|_\Sigma$ (see Def. 2.1). $\Diamond$

The well-formedness of $\lambda S(x):S(A).S(d)$ and $<S(e), \Sigma(f)>$ in the proposition above ensures that any corresponding introduction and elimination rules which are separated only by structural rules can be made immediate neighbors by applying σ-reductions. Thus "hidden" β- or π-reductions can be made "visible" by σ-reduction.

Theorem 4.10 (Peterreins) σ-reduction terminates and is confluent.
Proof: σ-reduction is obviously terminating. The rules do not have any critical pairs. Thus σ-reduction is also confluent. $\Diamond$

Lemma 4.11 $\beta\rho\sigma$-reduction is locally confluent.
Proof: The critical pairs between rules of $\to_{\beta\rho}$ and $\to_\sigma$ stem from unifying the left hand sides of $[\sigma]$ and the rules of $[\rho]$ and are easily shown to be convergent. $\to_{\beta\rho}$ and $\to_\sigma$ are locally confluent. Thus $\beta\rho\sigma$-reduction is locally confluent. $\Diamond$

5.   Strong normalization

Since $\beta\rho$-reduction and σ-reduction have function symbols in common the proof of strong normalization for $\beta\rho\sigma$-reduction is not as easy as for $\beta\rho$-reduction. In particular, the termination proof is a (non-trivial) refinement of the usual termination proof for simply typed λ-calculus. In this case we use Tait's notion of reducibility in combination with Girard's improvements [GLT90]. We only sketch some of the cases. The others are routine.

As in [GLT90] we define a set Red_A of *reducible proof terms* with derived formula ("type") A and identify three important properties (CR1-3) of reducibility which induce termination of $\beta\rho\sigma$-reduction. Reducibility is an abstract notion which should not be confused with reduction.

Definition 5.1 (Reducibility, neutrality, CR)
1. Reducibility. The set RED_A of reducible terms of type A is defined by induction on the form of A:

i)   For d with for(d) atomic, d is reducible if it is strongly normalisable.

ii)   For d with for(d) = A∧B, d is reducible if $\pi_1(d)$ and $\pi_2(d)$ are reducible.

iii)   For d with for(d) = A→B, d is reducible, if for all reducible r with for(r) = A, dr is reducible with for(dr) = B.

2. Neutrality. A term is called neutral if it is **not** of form <u, v> or λx:A.v. In other words, neutral terms are those of the form:

ass(A,x), ax(<Σ,Ax>,x), π_1(d), π_2(d), de, ex_falso(SP,A), stab(SP,A),

ρ•d, d|$_\Sigma$, sum$_i$(d, SP1)

3. CR conditions. The CR conditions are the following:

(CR 1) If d ∈ RED$_A$, then d is strongly normalisable.

(CR 2) If d ∈ RED$_A$ and d →* d', then d' ∈ RED$_A$.

(CR 3) If d is neutral, and whenever we convert a redex of d we obtain
a term d' ∈ RED$_A$, then d ∈ RED$_A$.

As a special case of the last clause:

(CR 4) If d is neutral and normal, then d ∈ RED$_A$.   ◊

Lemma 5.2 All proof terms satisfy the properties (CR1-3).

Proof by induction on the form of the derived formula, see [GLT90].   ◊

Lemma 5.3 For all proof terms d, e,

1)   if d and e are reducible, so is <d, e>;

2)   if for all reducible proof terms r with derived formula A,
d[r/x] (where x:A) is reducible, then so is λx:A.d.

Proof see [GLT90].   ◊

Lemma 5.4 For all proof terms d, e, and any S(.) ∈ {ρ•., .|$_\Sigma$, sum$_i$(., SP)}

1) if S<d,e> is wellformed and S(d) and S(e) are reducible, then S<d,e> is reducible;

2) if S(λx:A.d) is wellformed and if for all reducible proof terms r with derived
formula SA, (Sd)[r/Sx] (where x:A) is reducible, then S(λx:A.d) is reducible.

Proof by noetherian induction on the reduction sequences.   ◊

Lemma 5.5 For all proof terms d, any natural number n≥1 and structuring proof opera-
tors S_1(.), ..., S_n(.) ∈ {ρ•., .|$_\Sigma$, sum$_i$(., SP)}, if d is **not** of the form S(e) for some e then

if S_1(... S_n(d)...) is wellformed and d is reducible, then S_1(... S_n(d)...) is reducible.

Proof by natural induction on the size of n. For n=1 we use an induction on the complexity of the derived formula. For the inductive case we use side induction on the complexity of the derived formula d and (since by induction hypothesis d is reducible and
therefore strongly normalizing) noetherian induction on the reduction sequences of d.◊

Theorem 5.6 Let d be any proof term (not assumed to be reducible) with context
{x_1:A_1,...,x_n:A_n}.

1)   d[ass(A_1,x_1)/x_1,...,ass(A_n,x_n)/x_n] reduces to d.

2)   If r_1,...,r_n are reducible proof terms with derived formulas A_1,...,A_n,
then d[r_1/x_1,...,r_n/x_n] is reducible.

Proof see Appendix.   ◊

Corollary 5.7 All proof terms are reducible.

Proof: Choose r_i=ass(A,x_i). It is reducible by (CR4). Thus by Theorem 5.6.2)
d[ass(A,x_i)/x_i] is reducible. Hence by Theorem 5.6.1) and (CR2) d is reducible too.◊

Corollary 5.8 (Strong Normalization and Convergence Theorem)

βρσ-reduction is confluent and strongly normalizing; i.e. it is convergent.

The **proof** follows directly from Lemma 4.11 and Corollary 5.7 (by CR1).   ◊

Now any proof of a formula A can be transformed by βρσ-reduction of the associated proof term into a cut-free proof of the same formula such that the cut free proof has the same or smaller context and a more abstract specification.

Corollary 5.9 (Cut Elimination Theorem)
Any proof of a formula A ending with $\Gamma \vdash_{SP} d$: A can be transformed by βρσ-reduction into a cut-free proof ending with $\Gamma 1 \vdash_{SP1} d1$: A such that
        d1 is the βρσ-normal form of d and $\Gamma 1 \subseteq \Gamma$, SP1 ~~> SP.
Proof by Cor. 5.8., Prop. 4.5 and 4.9.   ◊

6.   Concluding remarks

In this paper we have presented a natural deduction calculus for structured algebraic specifications which can be seen as a suitable instantiation of a proof calculus for ASL-like specification-building operators.

The main advantage of the new calculus is that it gives Curry-Howard-like representations of proofs which encode informations about the visible and hidden symbols, the axioms and also the proof rules used in the proof. This allows us to study proof transformations. In particular, we have studied cut-elimination for proofs in structured specifications and shown that in contrast to first-order predicate calculus β-reduction is not sufficient for eliminating all cuts. Additionally we need reductions for commuting structural rules with logical rules.

This paper is just a first step for exploiting the power of Curry-Howard-like proof terms in the study of structured specifications. There are at least two other interesting topics which can profit from the use of proof terms: change of specifications and extraction of modular programs from proofs.

For the former topic we plan to use some results of Peterreins' thesis where he has shown that one can use proof terms to check, in the case of a change of the specification environment, whether a formula A remains valid in the new environment.

Another goal is to use structured proofs for extracting modular programs. To do this we have to extend the natural deduction calculus to parameterized specifications (cf. [A97]) and to calculi for refinement of specifications (see e.g. [Fa92, W93, Pe96]).

Acknowledgements We would like to thank R. Hennicker, D. Sannella and A. Tarlecki for inspiring discussions and helpful suggestions for improving a draft of this paper. We thank the unknown referees for many helpful suggestions for improving the paper.

References
[A97]   D.R. Aspinall: Type Systems for Modular Programs and Specifications. PhD thesis, Univ. of Edinburgh, 1997.
[BaN98]   F. Baader, T. Nipkow: Term Rewriting and All That, Cambridge Univ. Press, 1998.
[Bar84]   H. Barendregt: The Lambda Calculus: Its Syntax and Semantics. Studies in Logics and the Foundations of Mathematics 103, Amsterdam: Elsevier, 1984.
[BS95]   U. Berger, H. Schwichtenberg: Program development by proof transformation. In H. Schwichtenberg (ed.): Proof and Computation, Springer ASI Series 139, 1995, 1-46.
[BHK90]   J.A. Bergstra, J. Heering, P. Klint: Module algebra. J. ACM 37, 1990, 335-372.

[Ce95]   M.V. Cengarle: Formal specifications with higher-order parameterization. PhD thesis, LMU München, 1995.

[CS93]   J.N. Crossley, J.C. Sherpherdson: Extracting programs from proofs by an extension of the Curry-Howard process. In J.N. Crossley et al. (eds.): Logical Methods, Boston: Birkhäuser, 1993.

[Fa92]   J. Farres-Casals: Verification in ASL and related specification languages. PhD thesis, Univ. of Edinburgh, 1992.

[Gen34]   G. Gentzen: Untersuchungen über das logische Schließen. Math. Zeitschrift 39, 1934, 176-210, 405-431.

[GLT90]   J. Girard, Y. Lafont, P. Taylor: Proofs and Types. Cambridge Tracts in TCS 7, 1990.

[Hen97]   R. Hennicker: Structured specifications with behavioural operators: Semantics, proof methods and applications. Habilitation thesis, LMU München, 1997.

[HST89]   R. Harper, D. Sannella, A. Tarlecki: Structure and representation in LF. In: Proc. 4th LICS '89, Asilomar, California, 1989, 226-237.

[HW97]   R. Hennicker, M. Wirsing: Proof systems for structured algebraic specifications: An overview. In B. Chlebus, L.Czaja (eds.): FCT '97, LNCS 1279, Springer, 1997, 19-37.

[Pe96]   H. Peterreins: A natural-deduction-like calculus for structured specifications. PhD thesis, LMU München, 1996.

[SB83]   D. Sannella, R. M. Burstall: Structured theories in LCF. In G. Ausiello, M. Protasi (eds.): 8th CAAP, L'Aquila. LNCS 159, Springer, 1983, 377-391.

[W90]   M. Wirsing: Algebraic specification. In J. van Leeuwen (ed.), Handbook of Theoretical Computer Science, Elsevier, Amsterdam, 1990, 675-788.

[W93]   M. Wirsing: Structured specifications: syntax, semantics and proof calculus. In: F.L. Bauer et al. (eds.): Logic and Algebra of Specification,, Springer, 1993, 411-442.

Appendix: Proof of Theorem 5.6

For the **proof of (1)** we show (by a slightly stronger induction) that the term $d[ass(A_i,x_i)/x_i]$ is the same as d with the assumptions $ass(B,y)$ replaced by proof terms of the form $\rho 1 \bullet ... \bullet \rho k \bullet ass(A,x)$ such that $\rho 1'(... \rho k'(A)...) = B$ and $\rho 1'(... \rho k'(x)...) = y$. Thus using the rule [pass] one can reduce $d[ass(A,x_i)/x_i]$ to d.   ◊

Proof of (2) by induction on the form of d. We write $d[\underline{r}/\underline{x}]$ for $d[r_1/x_1,...,r_n/x_n]$. The cases (1)-(5) are as in [GLT90]:

0) d is $ax(<\Sigma,Ax>, x)$: $d[\underline{r}/\underline{x}] = d$ which is reducible.

1) d is $ass(A,x_i)$: $d[\underline{r}/\underline{x}] = r_i$ which is reducible by assumption.

2) d is $\pi_i(e)$: By I.H. for every sequence $\underline{r}$ of reducible proof terms $e[\underline{r}/\underline{x}]$ is reducible. This implies by definition the reducibility of $\pi_i(e[\underline{r}/\underline{x}])$ which is syntactically equal to $\pi_i(e)[\underline{r}/\underline{x}]$.

3) d is $<e, f>$: By I.H. both $e[\underline{r}/\underline{x}]$ and $f[\underline{r}/\underline{x}]$ are reducible. Lemma 5.3.1 says that $d[\underline{r}/\underline{x}] = <e[\underline{r}/\underline{x}],f[\underline{r}/\underline{x}]>$ is reducible.

4) d is e f : By I.H. $e[\underline{r}/\underline{x}]$ and $f[\underline{r}/\underline{x}]$ are reducible, so by definition (since for($e[\underline{r}/\underline{x}]$) has the form $A\rightarrow B$) $e[\underline{r}/\underline{x}](f[\underline{r}/\underline{x}])$ is reducible.

5) d is $\lambda y:A.e$ with for($\lambda y:A.e$) = $A\rightarrow B$: By I.H. $e[\underline{r}/\underline{x}, t/y]$ is reducible for all t with for(t) = A. Lemma 5.3.2 says that $d[\underline{r}/\underline{x}] = \lambda y:A.(e[\underline{r}/\underline{x}])$ is reducible.

6) d is $S_1(... S_m(e)...)$ with n≥1, e **not** of the form S(f) for some f and $S_1(.), ..., S_m(.) \in \{\rho\bullet., .|_\Sigma, sum_i(., SP)\}$: $d[\underline{r}/\underline{x}]$ has the form $S_1(... S_m(e[\underline{r1}/\sigma(\underline{x})])...)$ for $\underline{r1} = \rho_{j1}\bullet...\rho_{jk}\bullet\underline{r}$ and $\sigma(\underline{x}) = \rho_{j1}'(...\rho_{jk}'(x)...)$ if $S_{j1},..,S_{jk}$ are the renamings among $S_1, ..., S_m$. By Lemma 5.5 $\rho_{j1}\bullet...\rho_{jk}\bullet\underline{r}$ is reducible. By I.H. $e[\underline{r1}/\sigma(\underline{x})]$ is reducible. Lemma 5.5 again implies that $d[\underline{r}/\underline{x}] = S_1(... S_n(e[\underline{r1}/\sigma(\underline{x})])...)$ is reducible.   ◊

Author Index

Springer
and the
environment

At Springer we firmly believe that an international science publisher has a special obligation to the environment, and our corporate policies consistently reflect this conviction.

We also expect our business partners – paper mills, printers, packaging manufacturers, etc. – to commit themselves to using materials and production processes that do not harm the environment. The paper in this book is made from low- or no-chlorine pulp and is acid free, in conformance with international standards for paper permanency.

 Springer

Lecture Notes in Computer Science

For information about Vols. 1–1569
please contact your bookseller or Springer-Verlag

Vol. 1608: S. Doaitse Swierstra, P.R. Henriques, J.N. Oliveira (Eds.), Advanced Functional Programming. Proceedings, 1998. XII, 289 pages. 1999.

Vol. 1609: Z. W. Raś, A. Skowron (Eds.), Foundations of Intelligent Systems. Proceedings, 1999. XII, 676 pages. 1999. (Subseries LNAI).

Vol. 1610: G. Cornuéjols, R.E. Burkard, G.J. Woeginger (Eds.), Integer Programming and Combinatorial Optimization. Proceedings, 1999. IX, 453 pages. 1999.

Vol. 1611: I. Imam, Y. Kodratoff, A. El-Dessouki, M. Ali (Eds.), Multiple Approaches to Intelligent Systems. Proceedings, 1999. XIX, 899 pages. 1999. (Subseries LNAI).

Vol. 1612: R. Bergmann, S. Breen, M. Göker, M. Manago, S. Wess, Developing Industrial Case-Based Reasoning Applications. XX, 188 pages. 1999. (Subseries LNAI).

Vol. 1613: A. Kuba, M. Šámal, A. Todd-Pokropek (Eds.), Information Processing in Medical Imaging. Proceedings, 1999. XVII, 508 pages. 1999.

Vol. 1614: D.P. Huijsmans, A.W.M. Smeulders (Eds.), Visual Information and Information Systems. Proceedings, 1999. XVII, 827 pages. 1999.

Vol. 1615: C. Polychronopoulos, K. Joe, A. Fukuda, S. Tomita (Eds.), High Performance Computing. Proceedings, 1999. XIV, 408 pages. 1999.

Vol. 1616: P. Cointe (Ed.), Meta-Level Architectures and Reflection. Proceedings, 1999. XI, 273 pages. 1999.

Vol. 1617: N.V. Murray (Ed.), Automated Reasoning with Analytic Tableaux and Related Methods. Proceedings, 1999. X, 325 pages. 1999. (Subseries LNAI).

Vol. 1618: J. Bézivin, P.-A. Muller (Eds.), The Unified Modeling Language. Proceedings, 1998. IX, 443 pages. 1999.

Vol. 1619: M.T. Goodrich, C.C. McGeoch (Eds.), Algorithm Engineering and Experimentation. Proceedings, 1999. VIII, 349 pages. 1999.

Vol. 1620: W. Horn, Y. Shahar, G. Lindberg, S. Andreassen, J. Wyatt (Eds.), Artificial Intelligence in Medicine. Proceedings, 1999. XIII, 454 pages. 1999. (Subseries LNAI).

Vol. 1621: D. Fensel, R. Studer (Eds.), Knowledge Acquisition Modeling and Management. Proceedings, 1999. XI, 404 pages. 1999. (Subseries LNAI).

Vol. 1622: M. González Harbour, J.A. de la Puente (Eds.), Reliable Software Technologies – Ada-Europe'99. Proceedings, 1999. XIII, 451 pages. 1999.

Vol. 1625: B. Reusch (Ed.), Computational Intelligence. Proceedings, 1999. XIV, 710 pages. 1999.

Vol. 1626: M. Jarke, A. Oberweis (Eds.), Advanced Information Systems Engineering. Proceedings, 1999. XIV, 478 pages. 1999.

Vol. 1627: T. Asano, H. Imai, D.T. Lee, S.-i. Nakano, T. Tokuyama (Eds.), Computing and Combinatorics. Proceedings, 1999. XIV, 494 pages. 1999.

Col. 1628: R. Guerraoui (Ed.), ECOOP'99 - Object-Oriented Programming. Proceedings, 1999. XIII, 529 pages. 1999.

Vol. 1629: H. Leopold, N. García (Eds.), Multimedia Applications, Services and Techniques - ECMAST'99. Proceedings, 1999. XV, 574 pages. 1999.

Vol. 1631: P. Narendran, M. Rusinowitch (Eds.), Rewriting Techniques and Applications. Proceedings, 1999. XI, 397 pages. 1999.

Vol. 1632: H. Ganzinger (Ed.), Automated Deduction – Cade-16. Proceedings, 1999. XIV, 429 pages. 1999. (Subseries LNAI).

Vol. 1633: N. Halbwachs, D. Peled (Eds.), Computer Aided Verification. Proceedings, 1999. XII, 506 pages. 1999.

Vol. 1634: S. Džeroski, P. Flach (Eds.), Inductive Logic Programming. Proceedings, 1999. VIII, 303 pages. 1999. (Subseries LNAI).

Vol. 1636: L. Knudsen (Ed.), Fast Software Encryption. Proceedings, 1999. VIII, 317 pages. 1999.

Vol. 1638: A. Hunter, S. Parsons (Eds.), Symbolic and Quantitative Approaches to Reasoning and Uncertainty. Proceedings, 1999. IX, 397 pages. 1999. (Subseries LNAI).

Vol. 1639: S. Donatelli, J. Kleijn (Eds.), Application and Theory of Petri Nets 1999. Proceedings, 1999. VIII, 425 pages. 1999.

Vol. 1640: W. Tepfenhart, W. Cyre (Eds.), Conceptual Structures: Standards and Practices. Proceedings, 1999. XII, 515 pages. 1999. (Subseries LNAI).

Vol. 1642: D.J. Hand, J.N. Kok, M.R. Berthold (Eds.), Advances in Intelligent Data Analysis. Proceedings, 1999. XII, 538 pages. 1999.

Vol. 1643: J. Nešetřil (Ed.), Algorithms – ESA '99. Proceedings, 1999. XII, 552 pages. 1999.

Vol. 1644: J. Wiedermann, P. van Emde Boas, M. Nielsen (Eds.), Automata, Languages, and Programming. Proceedings, 1999. XIV, 720 pages. 1999.

Vol. 1645: M. Crochemore, M. Paterson (Eds.), Combinatorial Pattern Matching. Proceedings, 1999. VIII, 295 pages. 1999.

Vol. 1647: F.J. Garijo, M. Boman (Eds.), Multi-Agent System Engineering. Proceedings, 1999. X, 233 pages. 1999. (Subseries LNAI).

Vol. 1649: R.Y. Pinter, S. Tsur (Eds.), Next Generation Information Technologies and Systems. Proceedings, 1999. IX, 327 pages. 1999.

Vol. 1650: K.-D. Althoff, R. Bergmann, L.K. Branting (Eds.), Case-Based Reasoning Research and Development. Proceedings, 1999. XII, 598 pages. 1999. (Subseries LNAI).

Vol. 1651: R.H. Güting, D. Papadias, F. Lochovsky (Eds.), Advances in Spatial Databases. Proceedings, 1999. XI, 371 pages. 1999.

Vol. 1652: M. Klusch, O.M. Shehory, G. Weiss (Eds.), Cooperative Information Agents III. Proceedings, 1999. XI, 404 pages. 1999. (Subseries LNAI).

Vol. 1653: S. Covaci (Ed.), Active Networks. Proceedings, 1999. XIII, 346 pages. 1999.

Vol. 1654: E.R. Hancock, M. Pelillo (Eds.), Energy Minimization Methods in Computer Vision and Pattern Recognition. Proceedings, 1999. IX, 331 pages. 1999.

Vol. 1663: F. Dehne, A. Gupta. J.-R. Sack, R. Tamassia (Eds.), Algorithms and Data Structures. Proceedings, 1999. X, 367 pages. 1999.